AMERICAN EXPERIENCE

Slavery in America

Dorothy Schneider and Carl J. Schneider

Facts On File
An imprint of Infobase Publishing

Note on Photos

Many of the illustrations and photographs used in this book are old, historical images. The quality of the prints is not always up to modern standards, as in many cases the originals are from glass negatives or the originals are damaged. The content of the illustrations, however, made their inclusion important despite problems in reproduction.

For Elizabeth Knappman

Slavery in America

Copyright © 2007, 2000 by Dorothy Schneider and Carl J. Schneider
This is a revised edition of the Eyewitness History volume.

Maps © 2007, 2000 Infobase Publishing

Facts On File, Inc.
An imprint of Infobase Publishing
132 West 31st Street
New York NY 10001

Library of Congress Cataloging-in-Publication Data
Schneider, Dorothy.
Slavery in America / Dorothy Schneider and Carl J. Schneider.
p.   cm.   — (American experience)
Includes bibliographical references and index.
ISBN 0-8160-6241-2 (hardcover : alk. paper) 1. Slavery—United States—History.
I. Schneider, Carl J. II. Title.
E441.S36 2007b
973.7'1—dc22   2006024798

Text design by Joan M. McEvoy
Cover design by Cathy Rincon
Maps and graphs by Dale Williams

Printed in the United States of America

VB JM 10 9 8 7 6 5 4 3 2 1

This book is printed on acid-free paper.

Contents

Author's Preface for the Revised Edition

Slavery began in North America long before the colonies covenanted with one another to form a union, and though that union survived the horrors of the "peculiar institution" and the Civil War, slavery's scars still blemish the United States of America. We welcome the chance to extend our account from the end of the Civil War in 1865 through the Reconstruction Era, to 1877.

To this end, we have expanded some chapters of the original book. For instance, in Chapter 9 we have followed the fortunes of Native Americans and their former black slaves after the Civil War, as they struggled to develop new relationships with one another; and in Chapter 11 we have reported adventures of black "buffalo" soldiers as they fought for the United States in the West, sometimes against the very Indians who had formerly been their masters. We have added a chapter (historical context, chronicle of events, eyewitness accounts, and pictures) focused on the politics and social and economic changes of the Reconstruction Era, so that readers may learn more about that chaotic period. We have also supplied a new appendix with supplementary statistics presented in tables and graphs.

In the process, we hope, we have underlined the efforts and achievements of blacks throughout our history in protecting their identities and claiming their freedom and rights as Americans—assisted intermittently by the federal army, the Republican Party, the Freedmen's Bureau, and volunteer white reformers, and opposed by the still rampant Southern establishment of former slaveowners and their supporters. These additions, we should like to think, will also help readers to glimpse the complexities of the political and social context in which the United States dealt not only with the disaster of slavery but simultaneously with the building of a national economy and social structure, with the Industrial Revolution and its consequences, and above all with the question of whether a nation conceived in liberty and dedicated to the proposition that all men are created equal can long endure.

We repeat our thanks to the many who have contributed to the making of this book, and add to that list Ania Antoniak, editorial assistant at Facts On File; and the folks at the Bayard Taylor Memorial Library of Kennett Square, Pennsylvania, and the Chester County Library System, based in Exton, Pennsylvania.

Acknowledgments

Along the way, many people have helped us. Mary Attridge procured innumerable books for us through interlibrary loan. The staff of the Library of Congress Photographic Division steered us through their impressive collection, and we owe gratitude also to the librarians at the Schomburg Center and other sections of the New York Public Library system. We thank the libraries of Connecticut College and Wesleyan University for use of their scholarly journals and government publications. Prof. Robert Forbes of Yale, Adam Rothman of Columbia, and Pam Sessours and Dr. William L. Andrews at the Davis Library, University of North Carolina, lent us their expertise. Anne Penniman generously allowed us to quote from her family letters. Frances Cloud Taylor helped us understand the workings of the Underground Railroad in southern Pennsylvania; we are most grateful to her artist husband, Tom Taylor, for permission to use his pictures. Wanda Castner, Sam Connor, Jean Pieretti, Richard Tietjen, and Kay Tucker called our attention to materials we might otherwise have missed. We particularly thank our agent, Elizabeth Knappman, who originally conceived of the book; our editor, Nicole Bowen, who is always a joy to work with; her assistant Laura Shauger, who has efficiently dealt with many technical details; and the extraordinarily efficient and helpful copy editor Beth Ammerman.

CHAPTER ONE

The West Coast of Africa
1441–1866

Slavery in Africa

Africans knew slavery long before Europeans sailed to their shores. They enslaved their enemies and their criminals. Sometimes they enslaved debtors. Like all other peoples in the long history of slavery, Africans enslaved outsiders—members of other tribes or erring members of their own tribes.

Slavery became an integral part of Africa's economic organization. According to slave trader Theodore Canot, "The financial genius of Africa, instead of devising bank-notes or the precious metals as a circulating medium, has from time immemorial declared that a human creature—the true representative and embodiment of labour, is the most valuable article on earth."[1] The slave system was both entrenched and widespread. No one will ever know how many Africans owned how many slaves in the early days, but scholars speculate that in the late 19th century, a majority of Africans were either slaves or the descendants of slaves.[2]

For several reasons, however, most slaves in Africa did not experience anything like the horrors that beset Africans shipped to Europe and the New World as slaves. Why not? Most important, African slaves and their masters shared the same race. Their masters might consider them inferiors—but not by birth, only in that they had been outwitted or overpowered. Second, enslavement did not mean entering a completely alien world. Most slaves and captors looked much alike, spoke similar languages, practiced similar ceremonies, ate similar food, and had similar traditions and customs. Third, many slaves in Africa were criminals or prisoners of war—though sometimes a tribe raided its neighbors to take slaves, and sometimes kidnappers stole children from other tribes to enslave them. Fourth, slaves often lived and worked under conditions quite like those of their captors, though they lacked status in the tribe.

For many slavery was simply a matter of degree. African societies were organized into kinship groups headed by leaders to whom members owed respect and labor. Many slaves were simply more dependent and of lower class than other tribespeople.[3] What mattered was not freedom, but belonging, and slavery offered a new belonging, assimilation into a new group—albeit at first in a lowly position. A slave might be educated along with the free members of the tribe. When a male slave married, he might move away from his master's compound, work his own fields in exchange for fixed dues, accumulate property, and even take another wife. Eventually he could expect manumission and kinship within the tribe. Concubines were freed when they bore children, and their children along with them.

About 1755 Gustavus Vassa reminisced about slavery in his boyhood home in Guinea: "Those prisoners which were not sold or redeemed, we kept as slaves; but how different was their condition from that of the slaves in the West Indies! With us, they do no more work than other members of the same community, even their master; their food, clothing, and lodging were nearly the same as theirs (except that they were not permitted to eat with those who were free-born); and there was scarce any other difference between them, than a superior degree of importance which the head of a family possesses in our state, and that authority which, as such, he exercises over every part of his household. Some of these slaves have even slaves under them as their own property, and for their own use."[4]

Not every African-owned slave was so gently treated. Slave experiences differed from time to time, from place to place, and, of course, from master to master. Different tribes employed slaves in different ways. Some used them as human sacrifices. Tribes who forced them to work gold mines or hunt elephants for ivory inflicted hardships unknown to those of tribes who existed on agriculture. Tribes who owned just a few might assimilate them in one to three generations. Among the larger tribes, where slaves lived farther from their masters, the process might take longer.

Slavery by its very nature invited corruption. A desire for more slaves could cause a war or prompt kidnappings. The system might tempt a tribesman to enslave his unwanted wife or his enemy within the tribe.

From the 15th to the 19th centuries, as the slave trade with Europeans (and eventually Americans) burgeoned, the system of African slavery increased in scope and brutality. "Kings used imports to buy captives . . . , and the goods allowed monarchs to build up larger retinues of slave retainers, more isolated and more dependent" than slaves had formerly been.[5] As their numbers increased, the slaves were more removed from their masters. Hope for assimilation into the new tribes faded. Slaves were often sold and had to begin again and again as helpless aliens in new communities, which expected harder work. Africans sold their own slaves to white traders.[6] African slaveowners, no longer thinking in terms of assimilation into the tribe, were apt to treat slaves more severely and exploit them more.

As the African economy changed, slaveowners employed their slaves in newly developed occupations. Slaves labored not only on plantations and in mines but also as porters for merchants; as company boatmen; and as staff for administrative, military, and commercial establishments. Arabs sent them on expeditions to the African interior to obtain ivory, from which only a few returned. Reporter Henry Morton Stanley wrote about long lines of half-starved slaves, bound with chains that would have restrained an elephant, on marches that would last for months. Those who lagged behind were killed, he said, and estimated that every pound of ivory cost the life of a man, woman, or child in Africa. Missionary David Livingstone calculated that not more than one in five slaves who started to the coast reached their destination, not more than one in nine on some routes.[7]

Europeans Command the Slave Trade

By the time Europeans arrived, Africans were long accustomed to foreign invasions for slaves. As Henrietta Buckmaster writes, "The progenitors of the first American slaves were those who had fought against the battering tides of Romans, Persians, Byzantines, and at last with their empires weakened, had seen their civilization slowly collapse before the Moslems who brought religion and slave traders from the East, and the Christians who brought religion and slave traders from the West."[8]

So it came as nothing out of the ordinary when, in the mid-15th century, the Portuguese began transporting slaves out of Africa. Other European nations soon competed in the profitable enterprise, and the Dutch and the English successively dominated it. At first the Europeans raided unarmed family groups or undefended villages, until they realized that it was easier to bargain for slaves and gold with Africans in villages near the west coast. Soon they began planting small settlements, defended by forts, at intervals along that coast, usually near the mouth of a river or on an island. These *slave factories* they manned with *factors*—agents—who negotiated with the Africans, encouraging them to organize slave-hunting expeditions.

Beginning in 1636 Americans too sent ships to Africa, at first to transport slaves to the British colonies in North America but later more often on a triangular voyage. They sailed from, say, Rhode Island to Africa with a cargo of rum to trade for slaves; on the next leg, the Middle Passage, they carried slaves to the Caribbean islands and South America; finally, they returned home with molasses, with which to make more rum. American traders were never major players, even in their busiest years (from 1783 to 1807), carrying no more than a sixth of the slaves transported. Nonetheless, between 1725 and 1807 more than 900 vessels left Rhode Island ports (whence most American slaving voyages began) for the west coast of Africa, carrying away more than 105,000 slaves.[9]

In one variation of the triangle trade route, ships carried tobacco, cotton, or sugar from America to Europe, where they were traded for manufactured goods. These goods were then taken to Africa and traded for slaves. On the Middle Passage, the slaves were brought to South America, the Caribbean, and the plantation states. (© *Infobase Publishing*)

The enterprise was dangerous and economically risky but, if it succeeded, lucrative. The explorations of the 15th, 16th, and 17th centuries were opening up huge new parts of the world. To European and later American ears, these areas cried out for labor to develop and exploit their riches. Africa itself discouraged development: Its fragmentation into tiny tribes made it difficult to conquer; its terrain and climate were hazardous, a "graveyard for white men"; and it already produced in plenty what Europeans wanted—gold, ivory, and spices. But the Caribbean islands and the vast continents of South and North America could be developed only with thousands, millions, of laborers.

As slaves the Indians of the Americas ultimately proved unsatisfactory to the Europeans. Also, with their familiarity with the countryside, they were capable of frequent escapes. In contrast, Africans were adapted by birth to subtropical weather that often killed and always disheartened European laborers. Many whites thought them divinely created for just such a purpose.

Few whites thought of slavery as a moral issue. What history they knew of ancient Greece and Rome taught them that slavery had long been commonplace, ordinary, the way things were. Europeans too dwelt in societies organized into hierarchies, in which the rich and powerful exercised harsh control over the workers whose labor supported their lives of privilege and luxury. Greed, racial prejudice, and the conviction that Africans lived in ignorance and misery combined to justify—or excuse—making them slaves.

Then too, Christians were determined to convert the world to Christianity, with or without the consent of the "converted." Churchmen from the pope down gave slavery license, sometimes representing it as a crusade against pagans. God, they said, intended for some men to rule over other people, and slavery offered an opportunity to convert thousands. So church fathers approved mass baptisms of slaves just before they embarked on the ships that would take them forever from their homelands.

If anyone questioned slavery, answers lay ready to hand. What with all the slaves that Africans owned, traders could persuade themselves that they were merely moving Africans from one master to another. They argued that the slave trade disposed of Africa's criminals and that without it Africans would slay their prisoners of war. Once on the plantations of the New World, they said, slaves would live better than in Africa, for masters would take good care of their property.[10]

So the trade flourished, and nations competed for it. Portuguese, Dutch, and English rulers tried to shut out even their own subjects from the trade, bestowing rights to it on favored relatives and merchants. The Portuguese, the Dutch West India Company, and the British Royal African Company in turn maintained on the African coast the slave factories from which most slave ship captains bought their slaves.

Africans in the Slave Trade

Over the centuries, the slave trade grew increasingly sophisticated, commercializing the African economy. By 1788 slave ship's doctor Alexander Falconbridge reported, "The slaves are bought by the black traders at fairs, which are held for that purpose, at the distance of upwards of two hundred miles from the sea coast; and these fairs are said to be supplied from an interior part of the country. Many negroes . . . have asserted that they have travelled during the revolution of several moons [months] . . . before they have reached the places where they were purchased by the black traders. At these fairs, which are held at uncertain periods, but generally every six weeks, several thousands are frequently exposed to sale who had been collected from all parts of the country for a very considerable distance round."[11]

Free Africans as a group by no means objected. Enslavement did not offend their moral sense. As far as the record shows, though nobody wanted to *be* enslaved, only a few Africans protested against the slave trade. A good many Africans engaged in the commerce, especially the most powerful leaders. The shrewdest of their followers also profited in the flourishing new economy. This African participation in the New World slave trade has often been overlooked, both by historians and in the folklore developed by slaves, which "almost universally downplayed the active role of African merchants and elites in their enslavement."[12] It was hard enough for slaves to face the fact of enslavement, without painfully acknowledging betrayal by members of their own race.

European goods created new markets with eager buyers, dazzling many Africans. Slaver John Barbot in 1746 described their uses: "The broad linen serves to adorn themselves, and their dead men's sepulchers within; they also make clouts [patches] thereof. The narrow cloth to press palm-oil; in old sheets they wrap themselves at night from head to foot. The copper basins to wash and shave, the Scotch pans serve in lieu of butcher's tubs, when they kill hogs or sheep; from the iron bars the smiths forge out all their weapons and country and household tools and utensils. Of friezes and perpetuanas [cloth] they make girts [belts] four fingers broad, to wear about the waist, and hang their sword, dagger, knife, and purse of money or gold, which they commonly thrust between the girdle and their body. They break Venice coral into four or five parts, which afterwards they mould into any form, on whetstones, and make strings or necklaces, which yield a considerable profit. . . . Muskets, firelocks, and cutlaces they use in war. Brandy is most commonly spent at their feasts. . . . With tallow they anoint their bodies from head to toe, and even use it to shave their beards, instead of soap.[13]

The trade not only commercialized the economy and changed the everyday life of Africans but also corrupted them. Allegedly, African kings sold wives with whom they were angry; African parents sold children whom they could not feed; and desperate Africans sold themselves. Barbot told of a son who defeated his royal father's efforts to sell him by first selling his father—only to be met on his return home by fellow tribesmen who took his profits and sold *him*.[14]

To meet the demands of the market for more slaves, traders stirred up wars among tribes. Tribal kings began to look for excuses to attack. Kidnapping turned into a business. As Zachary Macaulay wrote in his journal in 1793, "If a child, for instance, is devoured by one of these animals [leopards], the [local African] King, glad of an opportunity, immediately brings a palaver against [accuses] the people of the town to which the child belongs. It avails them nothing to protest their innocence or to give assurance of their total ignorance of what became of the child. They are found guilty of making away with the child, on which the whole town, men, women and children are condemned to slavery."[15]

Soon enough, Africans learned the ways of sharp trading. The Europeans cheated them, and they cheated the Europeans. As John Newton wrote, "Not an article that is capable of diminution or adulteration, is delivered genuine, or entire [by the European traders to the Africans]. The spirits are lowered [diluted] by water. False heads are put into the kegs that contain the gun powder; so that, though the keg appears large there is not more powder in it, than in a much smaller one. The linen and cotton cloths are opened, and two or three yards, according to the length of the piece, cut off, not from the end, but out of the middle, where it is not readily noticed. The natives are cheated, in the number, weight, measure, or quality of what they purchase, in every possible way; and by habit and emulation, a marvellous dexterity is acquired in these practices. And thus the natives, in their turn, in proportion to their commerce with the Europeans, and (I am sorry to add) particularly with the English, become jealous, insidious, and revengeful."[16]

The Africans learned fast. African kings demanded gifts and the payment of customs—at a fee always subject to negotiation. They changed their minds about agreements that Europeans regarded as firm contracts. They plucked gray hairs from slaves' heads and beards to make them look younger and greased their bodies to make them appear healthy. They dallied in producing slaves, causing delays of weeks or even months and thereby driving up the price. Kings and courtiers traded on their own accounts, insisting that their own slaves be bought first, regardless of quality. At the factories, African employees cheated and stole from the foreign captains.

Even a tribal chieftain could see only what was happening in his own small sphere. How was he to evaluate the enormous impact of the trade on the culture and economy of the continent? Only a few highly placed Africans came to deplore the effects of slavery—the change to a market economy, the tribal wars stimulated by the demand for more slaves, and the forcible removal of so many people. Most African kings, their visions restricted to the horizons of their own small tribes, simply went with the flow, profiting as best they could from the growing commerce. European goods opened up new opportunities for upward mobility for other Africans, too.

Europeans in the Slave Trade

Far more lethal than its inhabitants, the continent of Africa itself took its revenge on the white intruders. They had undertaken to invade an alien environment. Against its hardships and diseases their guns offered no protection. Factors who had to live in Africa almost all died from one tropical illness or another, after a few years usually passed in drunkenness and disgust. They might enjoy their black mistresses, whom it cost almost nothing to maintain and whom they could dismiss at will, but in most ways their lives were miserable. They lived in factories built among stinking swamps, attacked by mosquitoes that robbed them of sleep unless they drugged themselves with opium or liquor. Their employers suspected them of cheating and trading for their own profit and charged them sky-high prices for supplies. Sometimes companies enforced an almost military discipline among their factors, fining, imprisoning, even flogging them.

For obvious reasons, competent agents were hard to find. "Lament you may [about our poor bookkeeping] without you send over people fitting to doe it," one factor wrote the Royal African Company, "for what by sickness & mortallity in this damn'd cursed country we have hardly any People that are able to put penn to paper that understand anything."[17] But William Bosman thought the rapid turnover a good thing: "[I]f men lived here as long as in Europe, 'twould be less worth while to come hither, and a man would be obliged to wait too long before he got a good post, without which nobody will easily return rich from Guinea. . . . [T]he money we get here is indeed hardly enough acquired: if you consider we stake our best pledge, that is our lives, in order to [get] it."[18]

The factories were vulnerable to attack. The Europeans had to depend heavily on the goodwill of African kings and their own abilities to persuade Africans that their presence was a good thing. As agent Thomas Thurloe wrote to the Royal African Company in 1679, "[A] factor once settled ashoare is absolutely under the command of the king of the country where he lives, and liable for the least displeasure to loose all the goods he hath in his possession with danger also of his life. Besides in case of mortallity it is very difficult to recover of the negroes any thing that was in the hands of the deceased."[19] Occasionally a European going about his business in the slave trade was seized and held for ransom or as hostage by an African king, or simply enslaved.

The slaver captains who sailed to Africa found themselves adrift in an alien world, in which only the most astute and lucky flourished. They did not know the territory, they did not know the languages, and they did not know the culture. Their job was to buy slaves and get out as cheaply and as quickly as possible. Time was of the essence, for the sake of their own health and that of the slaves, on whom their profits depended. Sometimes their ships could not sail home because so many of the crews had died.

Everyone and everything seemed to conspire to delay the slavers. When they sailed up the rivers to capture, entice, or buy slaves, tribesmen attacked, burned, and sank them. In 1759, the *Gazette and Country Journal* of South Carolina reported, "[A sloop commanded by Captain Ingledieu, while] slaving up the River *Gambia*, was attacked by a number of Natives, about the 27th of *February* last, and made a good Defence; but the Captain finding himself desperately wounded, and likely to be overcome, rather than fall into the Hands of such merciless Wretches, when about 80 Negroes had boarded his Vessel, discharged a Pistol into his Magazine, and blew her up."[20] Though some captains continued to venture inland, others decided that they might be better off to pay higher prices to the established factors on the coast.

The slaver captain had to depend on Africans at every turn. When he arrived with his trading goods, he did not dare leave them unguarded on the beach. He had to hire an African "captain of the sand" to watch over them until he could hire other Africans to transport them inside the fort. When he bought slaves, he had to employ a "captain of the slaves" to get them to the beach. Then he had to house them somewhere until he could complete his cargo. He learned that if he immediately loaded the slaves he first bought, he ran the risk of having them jump overboard. If he kept them in chains, too many of them inconveniently sickened and died. So he arranged to send his early purchases to barracoons (holding pens) in the forts, to be guarded and fed by Africans under a "captain of the trunk." If he did not find enough slaves for sale on the coast, he might have to entrust trading goods to Africans who would make excursions inland to buy slaves for him. When he finally completed his purchases of slaves and the supplies to maintain them and his crew on the way home, he had to hire canoes manned by Africans to transport them all to his ship. He had to negotiate prices and rely on local judgment as to when the tides and weather permitted loading. Even if these "canoo-men" upset their rafts and lost his goods, the captain dared not reproach them, for fear of reprisals.

Meanwhile, his employers at home were pressuring him to buy only choice slaves, from preferred areas. Some especially wanted Africans from the Gold

Coast (modern Ghana) and Whydah (modern Ouidah, in Benin), reputedly hard workers in their own countries and able to endure even the hardships of sugar plantations. Slave buyers in the Caribbean islands and South America wanted male slaves 15 to 25 years old. In North America, particularly as the 18th century progressed, purchasers also wanted women of childbearing age. The owners set their captains no easy task, for much of the time they had to take what slaves they could get.

The competition for slaves made the task so much the harder, complained a Rhode Island slaver in 1736 at a spot where seven ships carrying rum to barter for slaves lay at anchor: "We are ready to devour one another, for our case is desperate. . . . I have got on board sixty-one slaves and upwards of thirty ounces of gold, and have got thirteen or fourteen hogsheads of rum yet left on board, the trade is so very dull it is actually enough to make a man crazy."[21] The dishonest dealings of one slave captain might bring the wrath of Africans down on others, cutting off the supply of slaves altogether.

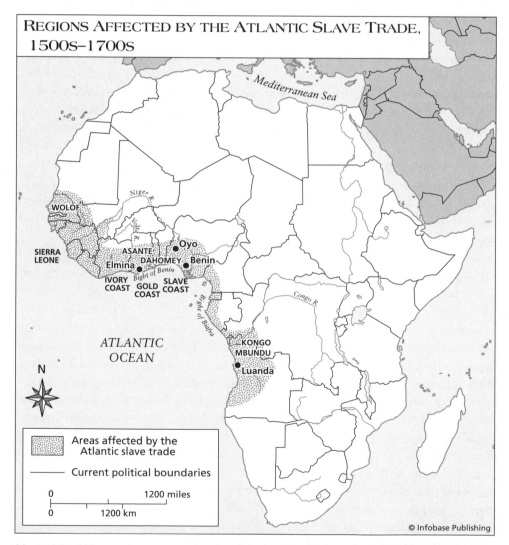

Most of the Africans who were captured and enslaved came from the West African coastal region that stretches from modern Senegal in the north to Angola in the south. (© Infobase Publishing)

The trading companies also struggled to fight off competition. The Portuguese, having established some influence with the Africans through their missionaries, tried to stop the Africans from selling slaves to the English and Dutch on the grounds that these "heretics"—Protestants—would not provide the slaves with a good Roman Catholic environment. All the nationalities involved tried to force or cajole African kings into giving them exclusive trade rights. Thus the agent recorded in the journal of Fort William in Whydah: "*Oct. 10, 1717* . . . Sent Bank and Fettera [junior factors?] to Dedoon to open a correspondence [negotiations] with that King for Trade, that I may have all his Slaves. Such as are Good for my Self and the rest to sell for him to Shipps. But withall they are to stipulate it so that he may [not] demand more for his Slaves than the common price nor ask better Goods than the Capt'ns at Town give. What Advantages I propose to him is that if I have any Goods better than another which none else shall happen to have, he may take them all unto his hands and by that means be able to command them at what price he pleases. . . . I sent him a wickered Bottle [of] Sperits."[22]

Just as the companies tried to control the source of supply, so they did with the market. For years they vied for the *asiento*, by which the king of Spain awarded the exclusive privilege of selling slaves to the Spanish-controlled islands in the New World. Once it was attained, there followed complaints from the Spanish buyers: The numbers of slaves shipped were inadequate to the needs of the plantations, and the slaves themselves were unsatisfactory, sickly, weakened by their long voyage—and overpriced. The companies countered with accusations of bad faith by the Spanish after the slaves reached their ports and complained that they were not even making a profit. Besides, they said, the Spanish had not paid the agreed-upon price.

The companies constantly sought trade advantages, as in 1686 when the British Royal African Company complained to the British government that the Dutch had bought up all the *perpetuanas*, a hard-wearing fabric then much in demand among the Africans. But they also went beyond mere complaints. In 1784 the British African Committee ordered the governor at Cape Coast Castle, "[Do not] suffer the Americans or any foreign ships to trade on that part of the coast under your command on any account whatsoever . . . and if any such attempt should be made . . . you are to fire on such ships and use every other means in your power to force them off the coast."[23]

When at the end of the 17th century the Royal African Company was finally forced to offer its facilities to other English traders, its leaders repeatedly grieved that these independent traders were not paying the company fees high enough to cover their expenses and that in their ignorance of trading they were driving up the prices of slaves. Besides, the company said, these boorish new traders misbehaved: "The [Royal African] Company further complain that the Natives grow insolent, and are encouraged by other Traders to insult the Companys Forts, and bring them out of Difficultys on purpose to obtein Bribes, to compose Differences of their own creating. . . . [T]his they say appears by Letters from their Factors, and particularly that one of the Separate Traders, having made a bargain for some Negroes carried them to Barbadoes without paying for the same, but that the Company in order to secure the Peace and a friendly correspondence with the Negroe kings, sent to Barbadoes and bought the said Negroes and returned them to the king from whome they were so taken."[24]

The path to profitability never did run smooth.

As for the Slaves . . .

Slaves brought from inland had endured not only the shock of capture but also the dreadful experience of coffles (slave processions), in which they traveled sometimes for hundreds of miles over periods of six months or more, enduring poor food, cold, and new diseases. Large numbers of the old and very young died on the trail, and all were weakened. Whether they walked or traveled downriver in canoes, they suffered and sickened. In 1789, trader William James testified before a British Privy Council committee: "Twenty or Thirty Canoes, sometimes more and sometimes less, come down at a Time. In each Canoe may be Twenty or Thirty Slaves. The Arms of some of them are tied behind their Backs with Twigs, Canes, Grass Rope, or other Ligaments of the Country; and if they happen to be stronger than common, they are pinioned above the Knee also. In this Situation they are thrown into the Bottom of the Canoe, where they lie in great Pain, and often almost covered with Water."[25] Slaves provided by the Foola tribe were invariably infested with worms, reported Dr. Thomas Winterbottom: "This probably arises from the very scanty and wretched diet which they are fed in the *path*, as they term the journey [from the place of capture to the coast], and which, from the distance they are brought inland, often lasts for many weeks, at the same time that their strength is further reduced by the heavy loads they are obliged to carry."[26]

In the barracoons on the coast, thousands more died as a result of bad food, impure water, and disregard for sanitation. "[I]t was common lore that . . . slavers simply disposed of the sick or the slow or any other sort of disabled captive whose handicap threatened to spoil the value of others. Since everyone knew that delays in the ports of embarkation would bring on epidemics among slaves penned up in cramped barracoons for long periods of time, it became the practice to kill the first slaves to show symptoms of diseases feared to be contagious. Slavers simply could not release infected slaves alive, for fear of spreading contagion even more widely and to avoid loosing freedmen capable of inciting revolts. Instead, they murdered a few in order to save the costs of mortality among the remainder."[27] The bodies

A coffle travels from the interior to the coast. *(Library of Congress)*

Slaves are branded after being purchased. *(Blake,* History of Slavery and the Slave Trade*)*

of the dead, partially burned or thrown out to be eaten by hyenas, surrounded the barracoons.

Some authorities argue that the causes of slave mortality at sea lay not so much in conditions on the Middle Passage as in the slaves' state of health when they were loaded onto the ships. Slaves coming aboard were already weakened by the natural catastrophes of drought, famine, and epidemics; by the rough treatment imposed by their captors; by the delays in loading; or by the unfavorable seasons for shipping, all of which were part of the whole haphazard system.

Dazed by capture, the coffle, and the barracoons, these men, women, and children were thrust into ugly, strange, inhumanly crowded environments, far from home. Few understood the languages of their oppressors. Worse still, they often could not understand one another, so many different tribes did they represent, and so far from home had they been driven. The branding to which the traders subjected them (to prevent the substitution of inferior slaves) further humiliated people used to signifying status by tattooing their skins. Many of them had never seen an ocean or a large ship.

What had happened to their familiar world? What was to become of them?

Outlawing the International Slave Trade

In the 18th century, new ideas about the rights of individuals inspired the American and French revolutions and lowered the level of comfort with slavery among Europeans and Americans. Throughout the slave-trade era, a few voices had been raised against it. In the early 17th century, for instance, Englishman Richard Jobson had replied to an African trader who offered him slaves, "I made answer we were a people, who did not deal in any such commodities, neither did we buy or sell one another, or any that had our owne shapes; he [the African trader] seemed to marvel much at it, and told me it was the only merchandise they carried down into the country, where they fetch all their salt, and that they were sold there to white men who earnestly desired them."[28] Now such words began to prick the consciences of the many.

In 1807 both England and the United States outlawed the international slave trade. Over the next decades other nations followed suit. England at once began to enforce the ban on the high seas. Constrained by space and its greater dependence on commerce than on agriculture, Britain had never relied much on slaves for its home labor force, although thousands had labored, suffered, and died on its New World plantations. Now the rapidly growing Industrial Revolution offered more profits than the slave trade. As British slave trader James Jones wrote to the president of the Board of Trade in 1788, "[The slave trade] is a very uncertain and precarious trade, and if there is not a probable prospect of considerable Profit no Man of Property who hath any Knowledge of it would embark or continue in it. . . . It is a lottery, in which some men have made large fortunes, chiefly by being their own insurers, while others follow the example of a few lucky adventurers and lose money by it."[29]

In the United States, the situation was more complex, with sharp divisions between northern commercial and southern agricultural interests. But it was clearly inconsistent to argue passionately for the liberties of white American men on the grounds of human equality and inalienable rights, and at the same time to enslave blacks. Moreover, the United States, unlike other slaveholding nations, had discovered the advantages of relying on natural increase for its supply of slaves. Encouraged or enforced reproduction among black women provided cheaper and better slaves than importation of slaves weakened by conditions in Africa and on the Middle Passage, who had to be taught the ways of plantation life. During the American Revolution, the North American colonies had suspended the slave trade, and all had gone well. Besides, the prohibition on the importation of new slaves increased the value of those already there. All in all, the country could get along without an international slave trade.

However, not everyone in the country agreed. Sporadic efforts to legalize the international trade again were made until 1865. Many American ships and entrepreneurs participated in an extensive illegal trade throughout that period. Certainly the insecure young nation had little interest in spending money to suppress it; for the most part, the United States made only token efforts to enforce the ban.

Slave ships of several nations—notoriously the Portuguese—continued to smuggle slaves, concocting ruses to defy England's powerful navy. Ships of other nations often flew an American flag because the United States did not allow other nations to board its vessels. Slavers frequently carried several flags, shifting them according to those of their pursuers.

Even when the British or American navy captured slave ships, their owners and captains were seldom convicted. No one knows the size of this illegal trade, but it evidently was substantial. For whatever the evidence of a pirate and smuggler is worth, slaver captain Richard Drake wrote, "Out of seventy-two thousand slaves received and transshipped from Rio Basso, in five years, we lost only eight thousand and this included deaths by accidental drowning, suicides, and a smallpox epidemic in 1811, when our barracoons were crowded and when we shipped 30,000 blacks to Brazil and the West Indies."[30] Even when a slaver was convicted, American judges often imposed light sentences. Of six captains and owners tried under the slave-trade acts in 1839, for instance, one escaped while free on bail, two forfeited bail, two were acquitted, and one's case was discontinued.

But throughout the Western world, antislavery sentiment was strengthening, and the demand for slaves was decreasing. In their homeland, Africans were confused and often dismayed by the ending of the slave trade. As Malcolm Cowley commented, "Slavery was their economic system and their justice. Their work was performed by slaves; their wealth was established by slaves; their gunpowder, rum, and cotton were purchased by slaves. At law, slavery was almost the only punishment for crime."[31] King Holiday of Bonny considered the ending of the trade a blow to African culture: "[Our] country fash [custom is to have] too much wife and too much child. God made we black and we no sabby book [can't read], and we no havy head for make ship for send we bad mans for more country [to send our rogues to another country], and we law is, 'spose some of we child go bad and we no can sell 'em [if slave-trading stops], we father must kill dem own child; and 'spose trade be done we force kill too much child the same way."[32]

All in all, scholars estimate, Africa exported some 11,698,000 people to the New World during the Atlantic slave trade. Some 7 percent of these came to what is now the United States.[33]

Chronicle of Events

1441
• For the first time, Europeans (Portuguese) carry slaves from Africa to European markets.

1448
• By this date, Portugal has established a regular trade in slaves between Africa and the Iberian Peninsula.

1452
• Pope Nicholas V gives King Alfonso of Portugal general powers to conquer and enslave pagans (non-Christians).

1481
• Portugal makes the Guinea trade a monopoly of the ruling house.

1482
• Portugal establishes the trading post El Mina (Elmina) on the Gold Coast of Africa.

1494
• The Treaty of Tordesillas, approved by the pope, gives Portugal a trading monopoly in Africa, Asia, and Brazil and gives Spain a monopoly in the rest of the New World.

1502
• Ovando's instructions as governor of Hispaniola allow him to transport black slaves born in Spain or Portugal ("slaves born in the power of Christians"). Later in the year, Ovando requests that no more slaves be sent to Hispaniola, because they encourage the Indians to revolt. Queen Isabella of Spain so orders.

1505
• The flow of slaves into Hispaniola resumes after the death of Queen Isabella of Spain.

1506
• Ovando, governor of Hispaniola, is ordered to expel all Berber and pagan slaves.

1510
• Regular slave traffic from Spain to Hispaniola begins, after King Ferdinand of Spain orders 250 "Christian" blacks sent out.

1513
• King Ferdinand of Spain begins to sell licenses to import blacks.

1518
• King Charles of Spain grants to Lorenzo de Gomenot, governor of Bresa, the right to ship 4,000 blacks to Hispaniola.

1526
• Lucas Vásquez de Ayllón, a Spanish explorer, tries to establish a settlement in the region of North America that later becomes the Carolinas; he brings in slaves who escape and live with the Indians.

1538
• Henry Eynger and William Sailler are licensed to carry 4,000 blacks to the Indies in four years, during which they will hold a monopoly. But the Council of the Indies soon annuls the contract, because they deliver "inferior" blacks.

1552
• Fernando Ochoa is granted a seven-year monopoly under which to deliver 23,000 slaves to Hispaniola, but the contract is never fulfilled and is eventually annulled.

1554
• M. Gainsh takes five Africans to England.

1562
• Englishman Sir John Hawkins begins his first slave-trading voyage to Africa.

1564
• Sir John Hawkins begins his second slave-trading voyage to Africa.

1567
• Sir John Hawkins begins his third slave-trading voyage to Africa.

1580
• The crowns of Portugal and Spain are united, with Portugal supplying slaves for the Spanish empire in the New World

1592
• The Dutch end the two-century-old Portuguese monopoly of trade in Africa.

1595

- Spaniard Gomez Reynal receives the first *asiento* (the privilege of supplying slaves to Spain's colonies) from Spain to deliver 38,250 slaves to Hispaniola in nine years, at the rate of 4,250 annually, of whom 3,500 must be landed alive; the slaves must be fresh from Africa, including no mulattoes, mestizos, Turks, or Moors.

1600

- On Reynal's death, the *asiento* is transferred to Portuguese Juan Rodrigues Coutinho and extended to 1609.

1611

- The Dutch build Fort Nassau at Mouri, on the Gold Coast.

1618

- James I of England creates the Company of Adventurers of London to trade in Africa.

1621

- The Dutch establish the Dutch West India Company, which secures a monopoly of African trade and the right to develop the Dutch possessions in the New World, thus gaining control over the source of slaves and the market for them.

1631

- The English establish their first important African settlement on the Gold Coast, at Kormantin.

1633

- The French grant a Rouen company a monopoly of trade between Cape Verde and the Gambia.

1636

- Massachusetts shipbuilders launch the slaver *Desire*—and the American slave trade begins.

1637

- The Dutch take El Mina, the strongest Portuguese fortification on the African coast.

1640

- With the revolt of Portugal, Philip IV of Spain forbids all commerce with Portugal, including the slave trade.

This diagram shows a slave factory on the West Coast of Africa. *(Library of Congress)*

- The introduction of sugarcane into English and later into French islands in the Caribbean increases the demand for black slaves.

1641–1648
- The Portuguese and the Dutch engage in war in Angola.

1642
- Louis XIII of France authorizes the entry of France into the slave trade, "for the good of their [the slaves'] souls."

1645
- Two Bostonians sail for Guinea to trade for blacks. On their return, they are arrested; the General Court directs that the blacks be returned to Africa.

1657
- England's East India Company receives a new charter.

1659
- Virginia encourages the international slave trade by reducing import duties for merchants who bring black slaves into the colony.

1663
- The Company of Royal Adventurers in England is chartered to trade with Africa.

1664–1667
- The English and the Dutch battle in West Africa.

1664
- The French become established in northwest Africa, particularly in Senegal. They form the Compagnie des Indes Occidentales to trade in Africa from Cape Verde to the Cape of Good Hope.

1666
- The French begin to grant licenses to trade in Africa to private traders.

1672–1678
- The French and the Dutch fight in West Africa.

1672
- Charles II of England charters the Royal African Company, giving it a monopoly to trade in British territories in Africa.

- The French form the Compagnie du Sénégal, abandoning the Compagnie des Indes Occidentales. The new company soon fails, as do subsequent monopolistic companies.

1688
- England's Glorious Revolution nullifies all charters, forcing the Royal African Company to struggle for legal sanction of its monopoly on African trade.

1689
- The British parliament issues a new charter to the Royal African Company, without a monopoly, and grants permission for all Englishmen, including those resident in America, to trade with Africa.
- The Royal African Company contracts to supply the Spanish West Indies with slaves.

1698
- The British throw open trade in West Africa to all subjects of the Crown.

1703
- Massachusetts imposes a duty of four pounds upon every black imported.

1713
- England gains the *asiento*, the privilege of supplying 4,800 slaves a year for 30 years to Spain's American colonies.

1752
- The British dissolve the Royal African Company.

1775–1783
- The American Revolution drastically cuts the international slave trade.

1807–1808
- England and the United States prohibit the international slave trade, but the trade continues to operate illegally, despite the vigorous efforts of the Royal Navy to stop it.

1811
- In Africa, slave trading begins to shift northward.

1844
- British commissioners in Sierra Leone inform the British foreign secretary that they "believe that the slave trade is increasing, and that it is conducted perhaps more systematically than it has ever been hitherto . . . notwithstanding

the stringent methods adopted by the British Commodore with the powerful force under his command" to stop it.

1845
• Cornelius E. Driscoll boasts in a Rio de Janeiro bar that in New York City for a thousand dollars he can get any man off a charge of slave smuggling.

1858
• Thomas Savage, U.S. vice consul in Cuba, reports that his efforts to stop the use of the American flag for slave trading have aroused hostility.

1860
• Richard Drake publishes *Revelations of a Slave Smuggler.*

Eyewitness Testimony

Enslavement: Capture

They seize numbers of our free or freed black subjects, and even nobles, sons of nobles, even the members of our own family.

Letter from Afonso, king of Congo, to João III, king of Portugal, October 18, 1526. Available online at URL: http://www.bbc.co.uk/worldservice/africa/features/storyofafrica/index_section9.shtml.

Slaves. Those sold by the Blacks are for the most part prisoners of war, taken either in fight, or pursuit, or in the incursions they make into their enemies territories; others stolen away by their own countrymen; and some there are, who will sell their own children, kindred, or neighbors. . . .

The kings are so absolute, that upon any slight pretence of offences committed by their subjects, they order them to be sold for slaves, without regard to rank, or possession. . . .

Abundance of little Blacks of both sexes are also stolen away by their neighbours, when found abroad on the roads, or in the woods; or else in the Cougans, or cornfields, at the time of the year, when their parents keep them there all day, to scare away the devouring small birds, that come to feed on the millet. . . .

In times of dearth and famine, abundance of those people will sell themselves, for a maintenance, and to prevent starving. . . .

Slave trader John Barbot's ca. 1682 description of Guinea, in Donnan, Slave Trade Documents *1:284–85.*

In February, 1730, Job's father hearing of an English ship at Gambia River, sent him with two servants to attend him, to sell two Negroes, and to buy paper, and some other necessaries; but desired him not to venture over the river, because the country of Mandingoes, who are enemies to the people of Fanta lies on the other side. . . . [Job disobeyed.] He crossed the River Gambia, and disposed of his Negroes for some cows. As he was returning home, he stopped for some refreshment at the house of an old acquaintance; and the weather being hot, he hung up his arms in the house, while he refreshed himself. . . . [A] company of the Mandingoes, who live upon plunder, passing by at that time, and observing him unarmed, rushed in . . . at a back door, and pinioned Job, before he could get to his arms, together with his interpreter, who is a slave in Maryland still. They then shaved their heads and beards, which Job and his man resented as the high-

est indignity; tho' the Mandingoes meant no more by it, than to make them appear like slaves taken in war. On the 27th of February, 1730, they carried them to Captain Pike at Gambia, who purchased them. . . .

Bluett, Life of Job, *in* Africa Remembered, *39–41.*

When a trader wants slaves, he applies to a chief for them, and tempts him with his wares. . . . Accordingly, he falls on his neighbours, and a desperate battle ensues. If he prevails, and takes prisoners, he gratifies his avarice by selling them; but, if his party be vanquished, and he falls into the hands of the enemy, he is put to death: for, as he has been known to foment their quarrels, it is thought dangerous to let him survive. . . . I was once a witness to a battle in our common. . . . There were many women as well as men on both sides; among others my mother was there, and armed with a broad sword. After fighting for a considerable time with great fury, and many had been killed, our people obtained the victory. . . . The spoils were divided according to the merit of the warriors. Those prisoners which were not sold or redeemed we kept as slaves. . . .

African Olaudah Equiano, about 1755, in Africa Remembered, *77–78.*

On the Windward Coast another mode of procuring slaves is pursued; that is, by *boating,* a mode that is very destructive to the crews of the ships. The sailors . . . go in boats up the rivers, seeking for negroes among the villages situated on the banks of these streams. But this method is very slow and not always effectual. After being absent from the ship during a fortnight or three weeks, they sometimes return with only from eight to twelve negroes. . . .

Ship's doctor Alexander Falconbridge, Account of the Slave Trade (1788), *in Dow,* Slave Ships, *136.*

[A] captain of a Liverpool ship had got, as a temporary mistress, a girl from the king of Sierra Leone, and instead of returning her on shore on leaving the coast, as is usually done, he took her away with him. Of this the king complained to Sir George Young very heavily, calling this action *panyaring* [kidnapping] by the whites.

Testimony before a committee of the British House of Commons, 1790, in Blake, Slavery and the Slave Trade, *112.*

Granny Judith said that in Africa they had very few pretty things, and that they had no red colors in cloth, in fact

European traders haggle with dealers. *(Library of Congress)*

they had no cloth at all. Some strangers with pale faces come one day and drapped [dropped] a small piece of red flannel down on the ground. All the black folks grabbed for it. Then a larger piece was drapped a little further on, and on until the river was reached. Then a large piece was drapped in the river and on the other side. They was led on, each one trying to git a piece as it was drapped. Finally, when the ship was reached, they drapped large pieces on the plank and up into the ship till they got as many blacks on board as they wanted. Then the gate was chained up, and they could not get back. That is the way Granny Judith say they got her to America.

Ex-slave Richard Jones, in Botkin, Lay My Burden Down, *57.*

I was born in Africa, several hundred miles up the Gambia river. . . .

For some years [before 1821], war had been carried on in my Eyo Country, which was always attended with much devastation and bloodshed; the women, such men

as had surrendered or were caught, with the children, were taken captives. The enemies who carried on these wars were principally the Oyo Mahomedans, with whom my country abounds—with the Foulahs, and such foreign slaves as had escaped . . . , joined together, making a formidable force of about 20,000, who annoyed the whole country. They had no other employment but selling slaves to the Spaniards and Portuguese on the coast.

. . . [A] rumour was spread in the town that the enemies had approached with intentions of hostility. It was not long after that when they had almost surrounded the town to prevent any escape of the inhabitants; the town being rudely fortified with a wooden fence, about four miles in circumference, containing about 12,000 inhabitants, which would produce 3,000 fighting men. . . . [T]he enemies entered the town, after about three or four hours' resistance. Here a most sorrowful imaginable scene was to be witnessed—women, some with three, four, or six children clinging to their arms, with the infants on their backs, and such luggage as they could carry on their heads, running as fast as they could through prickly shrubs, which, hooking their . . . loads, drew them from the heads of the bearers. . . . While they were endeavouring to disentangle themselves from the ropy shrubs, they were overtaken and caught by the enemies with a noose or loop thrown over the neck of every individual, to be led in the manner of goats tied together, under the drove of one man. In many cases a family was violently divided between three or four enemies, who each led his away, to see one another no more. Your humble servant was thus caught—with his mother, two sisters (one an infant about ten months old), and a cousin.

Samuel Crowther, Anglican bishop of West Africa, describing events of 1821, letter of February 22, 1837, in Africa Remembered, *299–301.*

Enslavement: The Path to the Coast

All those slaves the Portuguese cause to be bought, by their *Pombeiros,* a hundred and fifty or two hundred leagues up the country, whence they bring them down to the seacoasts. . . .

These slaves, called *Pombeiros,* have other slaves under them, sometimes a hundred, or a hundred and fifty, who carry the commodities [trading goods] on their heads up into the country.

Sometimes these *Pombeiros* stay out a whole year, and then bring back with them four, five and six hundred new slaves. Some of the faithfullest remain often there, sending what slaves they buy to their masters, who return them other commodities to trade with anew.

James Barbot, A Voyage to New Calabar, *1699, quoted in Rawley,* Transatlantic Slave Trade, *35.*

[S]ome slaves are also brought to these Blacks, from very remote inland countries, by way of trade, and sold for things of very inconsiderable value; but these slaves are generally poor and weak, by reason of the barbarous usage they have had in traveling so far, being continually beaten, and almost famish'd; so inhuman are the Blacks to one another. . . .

Slave trader John Barbot's description of Guinea, 1732, in Donnan, Slave Trade Documents *1:284–85.*

Here they [our kidnappers] tied our hands, and continued to carry us as far as they could, till night came on. . . .

[I traveled far and was sold several times; sometimes I had hopes of being adopted.] From the time I left my own nation, I always found somebody that understood me till I came to the sea coast. The languages of different nations did not totally differ, nor were they so copious as those of the Europeans, particularly the English. They were therefore, easily learned; and, while I was journeying thus through Africa, I acquired two or three different tongues . . . I never met with any ill treatment, or saw any offered to their slaves, except tying them, when necessary, to keep them from running away. . . .

. . . At last I came to the banks of a large river. . . . I had never before seen any water larger than a pond or a rivulet; and my surprise was mingled with no small fear when I was put into one of these canoes, and we began to paddle and move along the river. We continued going on thus till night, and when we came to land, and made fires on the banks, each family by themselves; some dragged their canoes on shore, others stayed and cooked in theirs, and laid in them all night. . . . [A]t the end of six or seven months after I had been kidnapped, I arrived at the sea coast. . . .

Gustavus Vassa, describing events of 1756, in Bontemps Great Slave Narratives, *21–26.*

In the march, a scouting party was detached from the main army. To the leader of this party I was made waiter, having to carry his gun, etc. . . . The distance they had now brought me was about four hundred miles. All the march I had very hard tasks imposed on me, which I must perform on pain of punishment. I was obliged to carry on my head a large flat stone used for grinding our corn, weighing . . . as much as twenty-five pounds; besides victuals, mat and cooking utensils. . . . Though I was pretty large and stout of my age, yet these burdens were very grievous to me, being only six years and a half old.

Venture, Life and Adventures *(1798), 8–10.*

Enslavement: The Barracoons

As the slaves come down to Fida from the inland country, they are put into a booth, or prison, built for that purpose, near the beach, all of them together; and when the Europeans are to receive them, they are brought out into a large plain, where the surgeons examine every part of every one of them, to the smallest member, men and women being all stark naked. Such as are allowed good and sound, are set on one side, and the others by themselves; which slaves so rejected are there called Mackrons, being above thirty five years of age, or defective in their limbs, eyes or teeth; or grown grey, or that have the venereal disease, or any other imperfection. These being so set aside, each of the others, which have passed as good, is marked on the breast, with a red-hot iron, imprinting the mark of the French, English, or Dutch companies, that so each nation may distinguish their own, and to prevent their being chang'd by the natives for worse, as they are apt to do. In this particular, care is taken that the women, as tenderest, be not burnt too hard.

The branded slaves, after this, are returned to their former booth. . . . There they continue sometimes ten or fifteen days, till the sea is still enough to send them aboard; for very often it continues too boisterous for so long a time. . . . Before they enter the canoes, or come out of the booth, their former Black masters strip them of every rag they have, without distinction of men or women; to supply which, in orderly ships, each of them as they come aboard is allowed a piece of canvas, to wrap around their waist. . . .

Slave trader John Barbot's description of Guinea, 1732, in Donnan, Slave Trade Documents *1:293.*

The traders frequently beat the negroes which are objected to by the captains and use them with great severity. It matters not whether they are refused on account of age, illness, deformity or for any other reason. At New Calabar, in particular, the traders have frequently been known to put them to death. Instances have happened at that place, when negroes have been objected to, that the traders have dropped their canoes under the stern of the vessel and instantly beheaded them in sight of the captain.

Ship's doctor Alexander Falconbridge, Account of the Slave Trade *(1788), in Dow,* Slave Ships, *141.*

[In the barracoon] our slaves had two meals a day, one in the morning consisting of boiled yams and the other in the afternoon of boiled horse-beans and slabber sauce poured over each. This sauce was made of chunks of old Irish beef and rotten salt fish stewed to rags and well seasoned with cayenne pepper. The negroes were so fond of it that they would pick out the little bits and share them out; but they didn't like the horse-beans.

The brandy that we brought out for trade was very good but the darkies thought it was not hot enough and didn't bite—as they called it; therefore, out of every puncheon we pumped out a third of the brandy, put in half a bucketful of cayenne pepper, then filled it up with water and in a few days it was hot enough for Old Nick, himself, and when they came to taste it, thinking that it was from another cask, they would say, "Ah, he bite."

Mariner William Richardson, ca. 1793, in Dow, Slave Ships, *13.*

The Slaving Establishment in Africa: European Factors and Factories

[1672] Account of the Limits and Trade of the Royal African Company. . . . they took Cabo-Corso Castle from the Dutch, which is now their chief port and place of trade, with 100 English, besides slaves, and the residence of their Agent-General, who furnishes thence all their under-factories with goods, and receives from them gold, elephants' teeth and slaves. Near Cabo-Corso is the great Dutch castle called the Mina; and more leewardly the company have another factory at Acra for gold. Their next factory is at Ardra for slaves only, which are there very plentiful; next follows Benin with a factory where they procure great quantities of cotton cloths to sell at Cabo-Corso and on the gold Coast; then more leewardly lies the Bite, whither many ships are sent to trade at New and Old Calabar for slaves and teeth, which are there to be had in great plenty, and also in the rivers Cameroons and Gaboons which are near, but no factories, those places being very unhealthy.

Donnan, Slave Trade Documents *1:192–93.*

[The Dutch Castle of El Mina, a fort that protects trading rights,] is justly famous for beauty and strength, having no equal on all the coasts of Guinea. . . . The general's lodgings are above in the castle, the ascent to which is up to a large white and black stone staircase, defended at the top by two small brass guns, and four pattareroes, of the same metal, bearing upon the Place of Arms; and a *corps de garde* pretty large, next to which is a great hall of small arms of several sorts, as an arsenal; through which and by a bypassage you enter a fine long gallery, all wainscotted, at each end of which are large glass windows, and through it is the way to the general's lodgings, consisting of several good chambers and offices along the ramparts.

French description of 1682, in Pope-Hennessy, Sins of the Fathers, *73.*

Our factory . . . stands low near the marshes, which renders it a very unhealthy place to live in; the white men the African Company send there, seldom returning to tell their tale; 'tis compass'd round with a mud wall, about six foot high, and on the south-side is the gate; within is a large yard, a mud thatch'd house, where the factor lives, with the white men; also a storehouse, a trunk for slaves, and a place where they bury their dead white men, call'd, very improperly, the hog-yard; there is also a good forge and some other small houses: To the east are two small flankers of mud, with a few popular-guns and harquebusses, which serve more to terrify the poor ignorant negroes than to do any execution. . . .

The factory is about 200 yards in circumference, and a most wretched place to live in, by reason of the swamps adjacent, whence proceed noisome stinks. . . . This factory, feared as 'tis, proved very beneficial to us, by housing our goods which came ashore late, and could not arrive at the king's town where I kept my warehouse, ere it was dark, when they would be very incident [vulnerable] to be pilfer'd by the negro porters which carry them, at which they are most exquisite [skilled]; for in the day-time they would steal the cowries [shells used as money], altho' our white men that attended the goods from the marine watched them, they having instruments like wedges, made on purpose to force asunder the staves of the barrels, that contain'd the cowries, whereby the shells dropt out; and when any of our seamen . . . came near . . . , they would take out their machine, and the staves would insensibly close again, so that no hole did appear, having always their wives and children running by them to carry off the plunder; which with all our threats and complaints made to the king, we could not prevent, tho' we often beat them cruelly. . . .

Capt. Thomas Phillips, journal of the 1693 voyage of the Hannibal, *in Dow,* Slave Ships, *58–60.*

We find you are sensible how much wee have suffered in our trade by Ned Barter's promoting his own private interest before our common good, his dealing with & giving encouragement to other traders, which gives us good assurance you will not only use all endeavours to seize his person & estate in order to make satisfaction for the murther he has committed and the damage he has done, but will be very carefull that none of our servants under your care shall practise the like for the future.

Royal African Company, 1702, to Cape Coast, in Davies, Royal African Company, *280–81.*

The factory consists of merchants, factors, writers, miners, artificers and soldiers; and excepting the first rank, who are the Council for managing affairs, are all of them together a company of white negroes, who are entirely resigned to the Governor's commands, according to the strictest rules of discipline and subjection; are punished (garrison fashion) on several defaults, with mulcts [fines], confinement, the dungeon, drubbing or the wooden horse; and for enduring this, they have each of them a salary sufficient to buy canky [fermented corn], palm-oil and a little fish to keep them from starving. . . . When a man is too sober to run in debt, there are arts of mismanagement or loss of goods under his care, to be charged or wanting. Thus they are all liable to be mulcted for drunkenness, swearing, neglects and lying out of the Castle, even for not going to church (such is their piety); and thus by various arbitrary methods their service is secured *durante bene placito* [at the pleasure of the company].

Ship's surgeon John Atkins, Voyage to Guinea, *1737, quoted in Pope-Hennessy,* Sins of the Fathers, *162–63.*

[We conclude] that a private trade, directly tending to Monopoly, hath been set up and established by the Governors and Chiefs of the Forts in *Africa;* and that this private Trade, so injurious to the Interests of the Public, hath been carried on by them in Conjunction with Persons at Home, some One or more of whom have at the same Time been Members of the Committee [the Company of Merchants Trading to Africa] above Mentioned.

The British Board of Trade to the House of Commons, 1777, in Coughtry, Notorious Triangle, *127.*

The Slaving Establishment in Africa: Africans and the Slave Trade

[Your merchants] are taking every day our natives, sons of the land and sons of our noblemen and vassals and our relatives . . . *it is our will that in these kingdoms there should not be any trade of slaves.* . . .

Congo chief Afonso I, 1526, letter to the king of Portugal, in Rawley, Transatlantic Slave Trade, *29.*

The [African] gold mines were seven in number. . . . The kings have slaves whom they put in the mines and to whom they gave wives, and the wives they [the slaves] take with them; and they bear and rear children in these mines. The kings, also, furnish them with food and drink.

16th-century Portuguese traveler, in Reynolds, African Slavery, *8.*

[At Whydah the] queen is about fifty years old, as black as jet, but very corpulent. . . . She received us very kindly, and made her attendants dance after their manner before us. She was very free of her kisses to Mr. Buckerige, whom she seemed much to esteem. . . . We presented her with an anchor of brandy each, and some hands of tobacco, which she received with abundance of thanks and satisfaction, and so bid her good night. She was so extremely civil before we parted, to offer each of us a bed-fellow of her young maids of honour while we continued there, but we modestly declined. . . .

Capt. Thomas Phillips, journal of the 1693 voyage of the Hannibal, in Dow, Slave Ships, 56.

. . . Pepprell, the king's brother, made us a discourse, as from the king, importing, He was sorry we would not accept of his proposals; that it was not his fault, he having a great esteem and regard for the Whites. . . . That what he so earnestly insisted on thirteen bars for male, and ten for female slaves, came from the country people holding up the price of slaves at their inland markets, seeing so many large ships resort to Bandy for them. . . .

We had again a long discourse with the king, and Pepprell his brother, concerning the rates of our goods and his customs. This Pepprell being a sharp blade, and a mighty talking black, perpetually making sly objections against something or other, and teazing us for this or that dassy, or present, as well as for drams, etc. it were to be wish'd, that such a one as he were out of the way, to facilitate trade.

We fill'd them with drams of brandy and bowls of punch till night, at such a rate, that they all, being about fourteen with the king, had such loud clamorous tattling and discourses among themselves, as were hardly to be endured.

Thus, with much patience, all our matters were adjusted indifferently, after their way, who are not very scrupulous to find excuses or objections, for not keeping literally to any verbal contract; for they have not the art of reading and writing, and therefore we are forced to stand to their agreement, which often is no longer than they think fit to hold it themselves. . . .

John Barbot, A Voyage to New Calabar, 1699, in Donnan, Slave Trade Documents 1:430–34.

The king of Almammy had, in the year 1787, . . . enacted a law, that no slave whatever should be marched through his territories. At this time, several French vessels lay at anchor in the Senegal, waiting for slaves. The route of the black traders in consequence of this edict of the king, was stopped, and the slaves carried to other parts. The French . . . remonstrated with the king. He was, however, very unpropitious to their representations, for he returned the presents that had been sent him by the Senegal company . . . , declaring, at the same time, that all the riches of that company should not divert him from his design. In this situation of affairs, the French were obliged to have recourse to . . . the Moors . . . , [who] set off in parties to surprise the unoffending negroes, and to carry among them all the calamities of War.

C. B. Waldstrom, in Donnan, Slave Trade Documents 2:600.

[A black trader at Bonny] informed me that only one ship had been there for three years during that period [the American Revolution]. . . . Upon further inquiring of my black acquaintance what was the consequence of this decay of their trade, he shrugged up his shoulders and answered, *"Only making us traders poorer and obliging us to work for our maintenance."* One of these black merchants being informed that a particular set of people, called Quakers, were for abolishing the trade, he said *it was a very bad thing, as they should then be reduced to the same state they were in during the war, when, through poverty, they were obliged to dig the ground and plant yams.* . . .

Alexander Falconbridge, Account of the Slave Trade (1788), in Dow, Slave Ships, 136.

There is a famous Smart—named Gumbu Smart. Historically, they say he was born in a northern province, the Bombali district, and lived from 1750 to 1820. He was captured when he was a young boy. The story goes that he had killed a brother of his, and he ran away from his village, where he was then caught by slave bounty hunters. He was sold to the factors at Bunce island. . . . [Because the white factors thought him intelligent,] Smart was sent out with goods to purchase slaves. And because he realized what he was doing, he bought a lot of his countrymen, the Loko people, and he kept them and he built up a formidable force. He got enough power to control an area of the country around the town of Rokon.

Smart's descendant Peter Karefa-Smart, in Ball, Slaves, 422–23.

The Slaving Establishment in Africa: Europeans and Americans in the Slave Trade

The voyage made by M. John Hawkins Esquire, and afterward knight, . . . begun in An. Dom. 1564.

. . . In this place [near Cape Verde and the mouth of the Sierra Leone River] the two shippes riding, the two Barkes, with their boates, went into an Island of the Sapies, called La Formio, to see if they could take any of them, and there landed to the number of 80 in armour, and espying certaine made to them, but they fled in such order into the woods, that it booted them not to follow: so going on their way forward till they came to a river, while they could not passe over, they espied on the other side two men, who with their bowes and arrowes shot terribly at them. Whereupon we discharged certaine harquebuzes to them againe, but the ignorant people . . . knewe not the danger thereof: but used a marveilous crying in their flight with leaping and turning their tayles, that it was most strange to see, and gave us great pleasure to beholde them. At the last, one being hurt with a harquebuz upon the thigh, looked upon his wound and wist [knew] not howe it came, because hee could not see the pellet. Here master Hawkins perceiving no good to be done amongst them, because we could not finde their townes, and also not knowing how to goe into Rio Grande, for want of a Pilote, . . . and finding so many sholes, feared with our great ships to goe in, and therefore departed. . . .

Hakluyt, Principal Navigations, *in Donnan,* Slave Trade Documents *1:47–57.*

[The slave trade is] indeed the best Traffick the Kingdom [of Great Britain] hath, as it doth occasionally give so vast an Imployment to our People both by Sea and Land. . . . [The African trade is] a Trade of the most Advantage to this kingdom of any we drive, and as it were all profit. . . . [The African and West Indian trades are] the most profitable of any we drive, and [I] do joyn them together because of their dependence on each other.

John Cary, 1695, quoted in Rawley, Transatlantic Slave Trade, *173–74.*

And first having monopolized all the Coast of Africa . . . Which vast Tract of Coast is lockt up from none but the Subjects of England, but, in a manner, free to all strangers, as French, Dutch, Portuguese, Danes, and Hamburghers. . . .

 . . . [T]he Royal Company . . . oppress their Fellow-Subjects, by taking their Ships, imprisoning and starving their Seamen, illegally condemning the said Shipps and Goods without any Jury, and converting the said Ships and Goods to their own use.

To this, add the Injuries committed upon those persons which miserably fall under their power, as the breaking open their Chests, and rifling their Writings, concealing and hiding their Books of Accompts. . . . If after such Cruelties they escape with their Lives to return home, which few do, by reason of the barbarous usage of their persons by the Agents of the Company aforesaid, who have often declared, That they will shew more mercy to a Turk, than to an Interloper, as they term those of the King's Subjects which Trade upon the Coast of Africa without their Licence. . . .

Anonymous 1690 pamphlet of complaints against the Royal African Company, in Donnan, Slave Trade Documents *1:377–380.*

It is scarce possible to conceive what a Number of English Vessels this Permission [the end of the Royal African Company's monopoly in 1698] brought to the [Gambia] and what Confusion it occasioned in the Trade. Each Captain out-bidding the other to get the sooner loaded, the Price of Negros at Jilfray rose to forty Bars a head; so that the Mercadores or Mandingo Merchants would no longer sell their Slaves either at Barakonda, or Guioches, to the French or England Company for the usual Price of fifteen or seventeen Bars, but chose to come down the River, tempted by the great Profits made, which sufficiently compensated their Trouble. By this Means the Servants of the French and English Companies were forced to sit idle, and wait patiently to see the Issue of this ruinous Commerce. Between January and June, 1698, these separate Traders exported no fewer than three thousand six hundred Slaves, by which Means they overstocked the Country with more Goods than they could consume in some Years.

Astley, Voyages and Travels, *2:78, in Donnan,* Slave Trade Documents *1:429–30, n 3.*

The Prussian general receiv'd us at his fort very civilly, but told us, he had no occasion for any of our goods; the trade being every where on that coast, at a stand, as well by reason of the vast number of interlopers and other trading ships, as for the wars among the natives, and especially that which the English and Dutch had occasion'd on account of a black king the English had murder'd. . . .

John Barbot, A Voyage to New Calabar, *1699, in Donnan,* Slave Trade Documents *1:430.*

Liverpool, 14 April, 1762.
Capn Ambrose Lace,
Sir.—You being Master of the ship *Marquis of Granby,* . . . ready to sail for Africa, America, and back to Liverpoole, the Cargoe we have shipd on Board . . . we consign you for sale, For which you are to have the usual Commission of 4 in 104 on the Gross Sales, and your Doctor, Mr. Lawson, 12d. per Head on all the slaves sold, and we give you these our orders. . . . We . . . Recommend your keeping a good Look out that you may be Prepaird against an attack, and should you be Fortunate enough to take any

Health inspections of slaves are conducted before boarding. *(Blake,* History of Slavery and the Slave Trade*)*

vessell or vessells From the enemy, we recommend your sending them Home or to Cork . . . , and on your arrival at Old Callebar if one or more ships be there you will observe to make an agreement with the Master or Masters so as not to advance the Price on each other. . . . [P]ray mind to be very Choice in your Slaves. Buy no Distemperd or old Ones, But such as will answer at the Place of Sale and stand the Passage. . . . The Privilege we allow you is as Follows: yourself ten Slaves, your first mate Two, and your Doctor Two, which is all we allow except two or three Hundred wt of screveloes amongst your Officers, but no Teeth [ivory].

> *Instructions from the ship's owners, in Dow,*
> Slave Ships, *93–95.*

[Captain Saltonstall of the Boston slaver *Commerce* in trying to persuade the Fantes to break their exclusive trade treaty with the English] used every argument to inflame the minds of the Blacks, and instill into them that spirit of Republican freedom and independence, which they [the Americans] through rebellion have established for themselves.

> *Gov. Morgue of Cape Coast Castle, 1783, in Coughtry,*
> Notorious Triangle, *115.*

On the arrival of the ships at Bonny and New Calabar, it is customary for them to . . . begin to build what they denominate a *house*. . . . The design of this house is to secure those on board from the heat of the sun . . . and from the wind and rain . . . , [but] The slight texture of the mats admits both the wind and the rain, . . . [and] increases the heat of the ship to a very pernicious degree, especially between decks. The increased warmth occasioned by this means, together with the smoke produced from the green mangrove (the usual firewood) which, for want of a current of air to carry it off, collects and infects every part of the ship, render a vessel during its stay here very unhealthy. The smoke also, by its acrimonious quality, often produces inflammations in the eyes which terminates sometime in the loss of sight.

Another purpose for which these temporary houses are erected is to prevent the purchased negroes from leaping overboard.

> *Ship's doctor Alexander Falconbridge,* Account of the Slave
> Trade *(1788), in Dow,* Slave Ships, *133–34.*

This trip we cast anchor in a small river not far from the American colony of Liberia and our captain took me ashore with his first mate and a dozen of the crew, all of us well armed and sober. We had several breakers of rum with us, as a "dash" [present] for the negro chief, King Boatswain, a half-Christian black, and spent the day feasting in his village. When night came he summoned several hundred of his warriors and we sallied out against a tribe of blacks called Queahs. We came upon them while all were asleep and burnt their bamboo huts and made a general slaughter. The men and women were massacred and the boys and girls driven to the river where they were soon transferred to the *Gloria's* bowels.

The next day Captain Ruiz invited king Boatswain to a big banquet on board the brig. The old fellow was sick but his son came with over two hundred of his principal men. We had abundance of rum and tobacco, the former, thanks to my medical skill, heavily drugged with laudanum. Before night we had every darkey under hatches and were off with a flying jib. Our entire cargo cost no more than the "dash" given to the savage chief.

Richard Drake, Revelations of a Slave Smuggler *(1860), in Dow,* Slave Ships, *242–43.*

The Slaving Establishment in Africa: Christendom in the Slave Trade

[We ask] that leave be given to them to bring over heathen negroes, of the kind of which we have already experience. . . . Your Highness may believe that if this is permitted it will be very advantageous for the future of the settlers of these islands, and for the royal revenue; as also for the Indians your vassals, who will be cared for and eased in their work, and can better cultivate their souls' welfare, and will increase in numbers.

Petition from the Jeronimite Fathers to the King of Spain, about 1518, in Donnan, Slave Trade Documents *1:15–16. They sought an exception to the king's edict that only Christian slaves could be shipped.*

Almost everybody is convinced that the conversion of these barbarians is not to be achieved through love, but only after they have been subdued by force of arms and become vassals of Our Lord the King [of Portugal].

Jesuit missionary writing from Angola, 1575, in Boxer, Portuguese Seaborne Empire, *101.*

Your Reverence writes me that you would like to know whether the negroes who are sent to your parts have been legally captured. . . . I think your Reverence should have no scruples on this point, because this is a matter which has been questioned by the Board of Conscience in Lisbon. . . . Nor did the bishops who were in Sao Thome, Cape Verde, and here in Loando—all learned and virtuous men—find fault with it. We have been here ourselves for forty years and there have been [among us] very learned Fathers; . . . never did they consider this trade as illicit. . . . [S]ince the traders who bring those negroes [to Brazil] bring them in good faith, those inhabitants can very well buy from such traders without any scruple. . . . Therefore, we here are the ones who could have greater scruple, for we buy these negroes from other negroes and from people who perhaps have stolen them. . . . [T]here are always a few who have been captured illegally because they were stolen or because the rulers of the land order them to be sold for offenses so slight that they do not deserve captivity, but . . . to lose so many souls as sail from here—out of whom many are saved—because some, impossible to recognize, have been captured illegally does not seem to be doing much service to God, for these are few and those who find salvation are many and legally captured.

Jesuit Brother Luis Brandaon, letter from Angola, March 12, 1610, in Donnan, Slave Trade Documents *1:123–24.*

At the same time the Most Reverend Cardinal Cibo writ us a letter in the name of the sacred college [of cardinals], complaining that the pernicious and abominable abuse of selling slaves was yet continued among us, and requiring us to use our power to remedy the said abuse; which, notwithstanding, we saw little hopes of accomplishing, by reason that the trade of this country lay wholly in slaves and ivory.

Italian Father Jerom Merolla da Sorrento, describing his stay in the Congo, ca. 1704, in Donnan, Slave Trade Documents *1:319–20.*

CHAPTER TWO

The Middle Passage
1500–1866

Preparations for the Middle Passage

The slaving captains who sailed to Africa from Europe or America usually set out, as we have noted, on a triangular voyage. On the first leg, they traveled from their home ports to Africa with goods to trade for slaves. On the second leg, the dreaded Middle Passage, they carried the slaves they had purchased or captured from Africa to the slave marts of the New World. On the third leg, they transported sugar, tobacco, or other agricultural products from the Caribbean islands or colonies in South or North America back to their home ports. Danger threatened throughout the voyage but especially on the Middle Passage, where other ships might attack in the hopes of capturing the cargo of slaves, the slaves might rebel, or illness might sweep the ship.

The Middle Passage would take at best six weeks, usually much longer. Before it could begin, unless the captain had managed to buy a full load of slaves and supplies at one place, the slaver would have to sail along the coast of Africa, touching at several ports, to bargain for more. For example, the log of the Dutch ship *St. Jan*, cruising along the Slave Coast in 1659, shows the captain's indecision and frustration: "*Sunday.* Again resolved to proceed on our voyage, as there also but little food was to be had for the slaves in consequence of the great rains which fell every day, and because many of the slaves were suffering from the bloody flux in consequence of the bad provisions we were supplied with at El Mina, amongst which were many barrels of groats [grain], wholly unfit for use."[1] In the end, the *St. Jan* set out on the Middle Passage with insufficient supplies, only to have its water supply drain away through leaks in its barrels—leaks that no one could fix, the ship's cooper having died.

A captain probably carried with him the instructions of the owners of his ship, spelling out how to handle the slaves, specifying his bonus for keeping mortality among them low, and stating whether he was to be allowed to ship some slaves for his own profit. One way or another he (and probably his ship's surgeon) had a personal stake in getting as many slaves as possible to market in the New World, a stake in the form either of a bonus ("head money") for each slave delivered or in profits to be anticipated from selling the slaves he carried on his own account. To increase these profits, the captain might give his own slaves the best food and accommodations and have the ship's carpenter or cooper teach them a trade, to add to their value. He might even steal a few extra slaves, by reporting that they had died on the voyage and then selling them himself. Suspecting that they might be cheated in such ways, owners instituted all sorts of regulations, like requiring death certificates signed by two or three people on the ship for each slave lost. But, thousands of miles away from their ships, how were they to enforce their rules? In this corrupt trade, the owners had to hire as honest a captain as they could and hope for the best.

At his home port, the captain picked up a crew one way or another. Service on slavers had a bad reputation among sailors, so he might have to resort to trickery or impressment to fill out his crew. In 1808, historian Thomas Clarkson described English public houses where, "the young mariner, if a stranger to the port, and unacquainted with the nature of the Slave Trade, was sure to be picked up. The novelty of the voyages, the superiority of the wages in this over any other trades, and the privileges of various kinds, were set before him. Gulled in this manner he was frequently enticed to the boat, which was waiting to carry him away. If these prospects did not attract him, he was plied with liquor till he became intoxicated, when a bargain was made over him between the landlord and the mate. . . . Seamen also were boarded in these houses, who, when the slave-ships were going out, but at no other time, were encouraged to spend more than they had money to pay for; and to these . . . but one alternative was given, namely a slave-vessel, or gaol."[2] A crew thus recruited was a sullen, angry lot, whose brutishness the experiences on a slaving ship hardened into cruelty and sadism.

The captain usually had on board a surgeon (that is, a doctor), on whom he had to depend to separate healthy slaves from weak or infected ones before embarking them in Africa and to preserve the health of the slaves loaded. At best, the captain was leaning on a broken stick. If medical knowledge in general was severely limited—and it was—knowledge of tropical diseases hardly existed. Physicians had little to guide them, beyond their own observations and what they could glean from those more experienced. To make matters worse, physicians also avoided service on slavers. The ship's surgeon had probably signed on only because he could not make a living elsewhere or because he faced personal problems. "Abundance of these poor Creatures [slaves] are lost on Board Ships to the great prejudice of the Owners and Scandal of the Surgeon, merely thro' the Surgeon's Ignorance," wrote Dr. T. Aubrey in 1729, "because he knows not what they are afflicted with, but supposing it to be a Fever, bleeds and purges, or vomits them, and so casts them into an incurable *Diarrhoea*, and in a few Days they become a Feast for some hungry Shark."[3]

Officers and crew of the ship almost certainly fell sick in the pestilential climate of Africa. Through the 17th century, perhaps as many as 60 percent of them died, and few replacements were available—certainly none for the surgeon. Then the captain, supposing he had survived, had to face the daunting dangers of the Middle Passage: storms, insufficient water and food, epidemics, misconduct and mutinies among his crew, slave revolts and suicides, and attacks from pirates and ships of other nations, to whom he might lose his crew and his cargo, if not his vessel itself. The slave ships sailed in a miasma of fear and distrust.

Boarding the Slaves

As for the slaves arriving at the coast from the interior of Africa, many had never before looked upon an ocean or a ship. Exhausted and terrified by the shock of capture; the long, forced march from inland; the trip downriver chained and crammed into canoes; and imprisonment for weeks or months in the barracoon, they were taken aboard vessels for which their languages might have no word. They were under the harsh control of white men—a phenomenon that they might be experiencing for the first time. Who could blame them if they took the Europeans for devils?

Rumors and questions flew among these frightened people—at least among those who could understand one another. Who were these creatures with white skins and long hair? Was the white man's country this hollow place, the ship? Did it move, and if so, how? The enslaved Gustavus Vassa (Olaudah Equiano) remembered his own experiences in about 1756: "I asked how the vessel could go? They told me they could not tell; but that there was cloth put upon the masts by the help of the ropes I saw, and then the vessel went on; and the white men had some spell or magic they put in the water when they liked, in order to stop the vessel. I was exceedingly amazed at this account, and really thought they [the white men] were spirits. I therefore wished much to be from amongst them, for I expected they would sacrifice me."

What did the white men want them for? Were the whites going to eat them, or grind their bones for gunpowder? Even when told that the white men wanted him only to work for them, Equiano said, "Still I feared I should be put to death, the white people looked and acted, as I thought, in so savage a manner; for I had never seen among any people such instances of brutal cruelty; and this not only shown toward us blacks, but also to some of the whites themselves. One white man in particular I saw, when we were permitted to be on deck, flogged so unmercifully with a large rope near the foremast, that he died in consequence of it."

Thrust into a series of alien environments, stunned by the loss of control over their own lives and bodies, the captive Africans had lost also all standards by which they could reasonably judge probabilities.

They knew for certain only that they were being removed farther and farther from their homes. Many of them believed that if they could die near Africa their spirits could return to the places and people they loved. So, of course, they were willing to take almost any risk while they remained in sight of land, certainly including rising against their captors or jumping overboard. Olaudah Equiano testified, "[A]lthough not being used to the water, I naturally feared that element the first time I saw it, yet, nevertheless, could I have got over the nettings [put up to prevent suicides], I would have jumped over the side, but I could not; and besides, the crew used to watch us very closely who were not chained down to the decks, lest we should leap into the water; and I have seen some of these poor African prisoners most severely cut, for attempting to do so."[4]

Boarding itself was terrifying. Taken directly from their voyage downriver in African canoes or removed from the barracoons where they had been held, the slaves were lined up on the beaches and subjected to a series of demeaning experiences. The ship's surgeon inspected them, looking in their mouths and private parts, trying to weed out the weak and old, and to permit on board no one with a venereal or other infectious disease. In the early days the slaves were baptized as Christians with holy water contained in the "hog-troughs" from which they would eat on the ship. The mass ceremony must have bewildered them. Theoretically they had all been instructed enough to understand what was going on, but the instruction was conducted in a "common" African language that they may or may not have understood. Afterward, they were flung to the ground and branded with hot irons—in the early days on the breast, later on the shoulder. Africans stripped them, claiming their clothing for their own use, leaving them nude. The heads of both men and women slaves might be shaved, and they were scrubbed down with sand. Then African "Canoo-men" loaded them into their crafts for the trip through the surf to the ships lying at anchor.

Life on Board

The slaves now faced the physical horrors of the voyage. As long as the ship was within sight of shore, they were chained or closely confined to keep them from jumping overboard. Once out of sight of land, the men were kept in chains below decks during the night but brought on deck in daytime in fair weather, at least for meals and an exercise period. The women and children, judged less likely to rebel successfully, enjoyed more freedom.

How much space was allowed each slave below decks depended partly on national practice and partly on the greed of the ship's owners and master. They were always crowded, whether they traveled standing, sitting, or lying down. Seated, one slave might have to sit between the legs of another. Lying down, he might not have space enough to turn over. The height of the space between decks often did not allow him to stand erect, perhaps not even to sit up. Slaver John Barbot reported on Portuguese practice about 1700: "[I]t is pitiful to see how they croud those poor wretches, six hundred and fifty or seven hundred in a ship, the men standing in the

This diagram shows the hold of a slaver. (*Blake,* History of Slavery and the Slave Trade*)*

hold ty'd to stakes, the women between decks, and those that are with child in the great cabin, and the children in the steeridge. . . ."[5]

Usually each man was shackled either to another man (whose language he might or might not understand) or to a group of men by a long chain that ran through rings on their arms and was attached at either end to fittings on the bulkhead. That meant that, unable to reach the tubs and buckets used as toilets, they were forced to relieve themselves where they lay, sat, or stood. Since almost everyone was seasick and had diarrhea, or "the bloody flux," these lodgings stank unbearably. Candles would not burn in the fetid air.

Experienced captains advised novices to wash these spaces down frequently. The Portuguese provided mats that at least kept the slaves off the damp decks, but these soon became soaked from the decks, the sweat of the slaves, and the rain that came in through the scuttles. The mats were changed every two or three weeks. Bad weather and high seas often forced the sailors to cover the barred portholes and gratings designed to give the slaves a bit of air; with the heat from packed bodies, the temperature soared.

In daytime, the slaves were taken up on deck to be fed and exercised—forcibly, if necessary—under the watchful eyes, guns, and whips of the crew and the African trusties brought along to guard them (about such individuals, more below). They exercised, willy-nilly, by dancing, the male slaves still in chains. On occasion a sailor played a fiddle or bagpipes for them to dance to; sometimes the captain offered rewards or liquor for the best performances. Despite fears that the slaves might in their dances construct a secret code in a step toward rebellion, the slave-runners used this dancing to demonstrate their mastery over the slaves, to entertain themselves, and to exercise the slaves. No one knows just how the slaves perceived it—possibly as a means of bonding with their fellows, possibly as a renewal of their ancient custom of dancing to honor their ancestors or their gods, or possibly as one more evidence of their subjugation.[6] But even on deck, the men might spend most of the day in irons, on a long chain locked to ringbolts fixed in the deck, 50 or 60 of them fastened to one chain.

Many slaves were too depressed to want to eat, or they might not like the food offered. Captain and crew tried to make them eat, by thrashing them—even babies—or forcing food down their throats with a specially designed *speculum orum*, holding hot coals on a shovel near their lips to make them open their mouths, pouring hot lead on them, or breaking their teeth. "I was soon put down under the decks, and there I received such a salutation in my nostrils as I had never experienced in my life; so that, with the loathsomeness of the stench, and crying together, I became so sick and low that I was not able to eat, nor had I the least desire to taste anything," Equiano remembered. "Two of the white men offered me eatables; and, on my refusing to eat, one of them held me fast by the hands, and laid me across, I think, the windlass, and tied my feet, while the other flogged me severely."[7]

But if supplies ran low, slaves might be given little to eat. "Numberless quarrels take place among them [the slaves] during their meals; more especially when they are put upon short allowance, which frequently happens if the passage . . . proves of unusual length," wrote Alexander Falconbridge. "In this case, the weak are obliged to be content with a very scanty portion. Their allowance of water is about half a pint each at every meal."[8]

Some captains tried to prevent sexual intercourse between the whites and the slaves. Others regarded seduction and rape as natural benefits for sailors and officers on slaving ships. As slave trader John Newton remarked in the 1750s, "Where resistance or refusal would be utterly in vain, even the solicitation of consent is seldom thought of."[9] So, many a sailor simply forced himself on a slave woman. Others relied on seduction, and often a slave woman would go ashore with a broken heart, and perhaps pregnant, her sailor lover having abandoned her to her fate.

On the Middle Passage, the slaves of course succumbed to seasickness, a condition inevitable in the bad air and rank smells of the holds in which they were confined at night and in storms. More dangerous were the illnesses brought on by their exposure to infection from European diseases little known in Africa. When one slave sickened, he or she inevitably infected the others. Epidemics of smallpox raged among them, as well as of unidentified fevers. Skin ailments made the slaves itch unbearably and produced terrible sores and abscesses on their bodies. Ophthalmia blinded them, temporarily or permanently. Record after record talks about the flux, a particularly violent form of diarrhea, in which the patients involuntarily discharged blood and mucus.

No wonder that even those who lived were in dreadful condition when they landed—"crippled, covered with mange, losing their hair, emaciated in frame, suffering from fevers and dysenteries, often barely alive."[10]

The better ship's surgeons tried to cope, setting up infirmaries on board or even persuading the captain to stop at some island when an epidemic threatened. But in the face of most illnesses, they were helpless. "Almost the only means by which the surgeon can render himself useful to the slaves," wrote ship's doctor Alexander Falconbridge in 1788, "is by seeing that their food is properly cooked and distributed among them. It is true, when they arrive near the markets . . . , care is taken to polish them for sale by an application of the lunar caustic to such as are afflicted with the yaws. This, however, affords but a temporary relief."[11]

Now and then a captain and crew, panicked by sickness aboard and fearful that their profits were vanishing before their eyes, would resort to murder to retrieve them. "The insurer takes upon him the risk of the loss, capture, and death of slaves, or any other unavoidable accident to them; but natural death is always understood to be expected: by natural death is meant, not only when it happens by disease or sickness, but also when the captive destroys himself through despair, which often happens: but when slaves were killed, or thrown into the sea in order to quell an insurrection on their part, then the insurers must answer."[12] So the slave traders might choose to thrust the cost on the insurance company by throwing the weak but still breathing slaves to the sharks.

The more humane or more intelligent slavers tried to ease the terrible shipboard conditions as much as they could, if only to increase their profits. Observing that "the fewer in number [the slaves on board,] the better accommodations and better feed and care they will have taken of them and the healthier they will arrive at market," Rhode Islanders designed their ships smaller to carry fewer slaves and sail faster.[13] As slavers grew more experienced, they learned the importance of better ventilation, better sanitation, vaccination against smallpox, lime juice to protect against scurvy, and food that the Africans liked.

Slave Rebellions on Board

Deep depression among the slaves led many to attempt suicide, either individually or in groups. Ships' logs tell of their pathetic wailing as they mourned for homes

Sometimes slaves were thrown overboard—for illness, rebellion, or insurance. *(Library of Congress)*

and families. Despite all efforts to force them to eat, some starved themselves. Some went mad. Thousands more in effect died of broken hearts, too weakened by all they had suffered, the hopelessness of their plight, and grief to survive the hardships of the voyage. Perhaps worst of all, they experienced loss of identity. As one scholar writes, "For how do you spell 'I am' when you are deprived of home, of place, of your sense of direction? . . . when you are branded, when you are stacked away in the claustrophobic hell below the deck of a slave ship, when you are discarded because a commodity is damaged? . . . on water without boundaries?"[14]

Desperation drove those of different temperament to rebellion. The odds against them were long. What chance had they, after all, with so many of them chained for so much of the time, closely confined and vigilantly watched by ruthless, armed seamen, being themselves without weapons and having no knowledge of navigation and little of geography, uncertain even what moved the ship? If the mutiny succeeded, how were they to sail the ship, how were they to navigate, and where was home? As English sailor William Richardson commented, with remarkable detachment, "I could not but admire the courage of a fine young black who, though his partner in irons lay dead at his feet, would not surrender but fought with his billet of wood until a pistol ball finished his existence. The others fought as well as they could, but what could they do against fire-arms?"[15]

Bewilderment about their fates compounded the slaves' desperation. John Atkins observed in 1721, "When we are slaved and out at Sea, it is commonly imagined, the Negroes Ignorance of Navigation, will always be a Safeguard; yet, as many of them think themselves bought to eat, and more, that Death will send them into their own Country, there has not been wanting Examples of rising and killing a Ship's Company."[16] Some captains hired African healers who could understand the captives' languages, both to keep them calm and to spy out budding mutinies.[17] These trusties tried to reassure the slaves by telling them where they were going and what was wanted of them—at least quelling their fears of being eaten.

Women slaves—less closely watched, less likely to be chained, and freer to move around the ship—joined the men in conspiring to mutiny. "[P]utt not too much confidence in the Women nor Children lest they happen to be Instrumental to your being surprised which might be fatall," warned Samuel Waldo, owner of the slaver *Africa,* in his 1734 instructions to the ship's captain.[18]

The slaves improvised weapons by breaking their shackles, seizing the troughs from which they ate, or stealing tools from the ship's carpenter. Occasionally an unwary crew member would give a slave a knife. One cargo of slaves, discovering an old anchor, possessed themselves of a hammer and broke it up for weapons. In another instance, the slaves "laid on him [the captain] and beat out his Brains with the little Tubs, out of which they eat their boiled Rice. . . ."[19] More observant slaves tried first to seize the ship's store of arms and ammunition.

Now and then, most likely if they were still near the shore, the slaves won and escaped. "We have an account from Guinea, by Way of Antigua," reported the *Boston News Letter* of September 25, 1729, "that the *Clare* Galley, Capt. Murrell, having completed her Number of Negroes had taken her Departure From the Coast of Guinea for South Carolina; but was not got 10 Leagues on her Way, before the Negroes rose and making themselves Masters of the Gunpowder and Fire Arms, the Captain and Ship Crew took to their Long Boat, and got shore near Cape Coast Castle. The Negroes run the Ship on Shore within a few Leagues of the said Castle, and made their Escape."[20] Most notable were the successful *Amistad* mutineers, who demanded that the surviving officers sail toward the rising sun, for they believed that they had come from the east. The officers complied by day but at night steered to the north, so as to land in Connecticut. There, with the support of abolitionists and after prolonged court suits, the slaves eventually managed to extricate themselves and return to Africa.

But most mutinies failed: The slavers' guns were almost always too powerful for the mutineers' improvised weapons. Sometimes everyone lost, as when in 1735 slaves on the British ship *Dolphin* "overpowered the crew, broke into the powder room, and finally in the course of their effort for freedom blew up both themselves and the crew."[21]

Most commonly the slavers won Pyrrhic victories, suffering losses among the crew or damage to the ship they could ill afford and almost certainly the loss of slaves, on whom their profits depended. In the 1727 mutiny aboard the English slaver *Ferrers,* "all the grown Negroes on board . . . run to the forepart of the Ship in a body, and endeavored to force the Barricadeo on the Quarter-Deck, not regarding the Musquets or Half Pikes, that were presented to their Breasts by the white Men, through the loop-Holes. So that at last the chief Mate was obliged to order one of the Quarter-deck Guns laden with Partridge-Shot, to be fired amongst them; which occasioned a terrible destruction: For there were near eighty Negroes killed and drowned, many jumping overboard when the Gun was fired. This indeed put an end to the Mutiny, but most of the Slaves that remained alive grew so sullen, that several of them were starved to death, obstinately refusing to take any Sustenance."[22]

In defending against slave uprisings captains were often handicapped by lack of manpower, because of the frequent illnesses and deaths among their sailors. In the uprising of 1704 on the *Eagle Galley*, which carried four hundred slaves, not more than ten seamen capable of service were on board, another dozen having left in the boats to find wood and water on a nearby island. Fortunately for the crew, only some 20 slaves actively participated in the rebellion.

Probably the most effective step a captain could take to prevent quarrels and rebellion was to hire Africans who understood something of what was going on to supervise the slaves. On the voyage of the *Hannibal* in 1693–94, Captain Thomas Phillips noted: "[W]e have some 30 or 40 Gold Coast negroes, which we buy, and are procur'd us there by our factors, to make guardians and overseers of the Whidaw negroes, and sleep among them to keep them from quarreling, and in order, as well as to give us notice, if they can discover any caballing or plotting among them, which trust they will discharge with great diligence; they also take care to make the negroes scrape the decks where they lodge every morning very clean, to eschew any distempers that may engender from filth and nastiness. When we constitute a guardian, we give him a cat of nine tails as a badge of his office, which he is not a little proud of, and will exercise with great authority."[23]

But often the best efforts of the captain could not prevent a mutiny. Eighteenth-century captain William Snelgrave prided himself on his humane treatment of slaves. Through an interpreter he would tell the adults among them that they had been bought to till the soil. He instructed them in how to behave on board. If any white man abused them, he said, they should complain to the interpreter, who would inform him, and he would deal justly with the offenders; if they made disturbances or attacked the white men, however, they would be severely punished. To the captain's bewilderment, the slaves would rebel anyway. Seldom did it occur to any white man to ask himself what he might have done in their circumstances.

Scholars have discovered fairly detailed accounts of 55 mutinies on slavers from 1699 to 1845, plus references to more than 100 others. Slaves may have mutinied on some 10 percent of the voyages.[24]

Slave Mortality Rates

All in all, the miracle is that so many slaves survived the voyages, which lasted from five or six weeks to several months. In their debilitated state, they could so easily have died. An accounting of the *James* in 1675 assigns all sorts of reasons for the deaths of the slaves it had carried: convulsions, fevers, consumption, worms, and refusal to eat. One woman "Miscarryed and the Child dead within her and Rotten and dyed 2 days after delivery." Another, "Being very fond of her Child Carrying her up and downe, wore her to nothing by which means fell into a feavour and dyed."[25]

Mortality rates on slavers on some disastrous early voyages ran to more than 50 percent, but they gradually fell, thanks in part to increased speed and in part to somewhat better care of the slaves. "In all, total slave mortality at sea dropped irregularly from something like 25 to 30 percent early in the eighteenth century to 10 to 15 percent by the end of the eighteenth century and finally to 5 to 10 percent by the 1820s."[26] Most modern scholars believe that conditions on a ship had less to do with mortality rates at sea than did the length of the voyage, the region of Africa from which individual slaves came, their health before embarkation, the length of the trip from the interior and of detention at the barracoons before sailing, and the demand for slaves.[27]

Still, and even under the best conditions, the Middle Passage remained hazardous for all on the ship, especially for the slaves. Only the whites' concern for profits protected the slaves, and when push came to shove, the whites simply abandoned the blacks to whatever terrible fate threatened. Take once again the *St. Jan*, which on March 4, 1659, sailed from the Gold Coast of Africa to spend months cruising along the Slave Coast trying to buy slaves and supplies. Ultimately it ran out of both bread and water; 59 male slaves, 47 women, and four children died thereby. On November 1, the *St. Jan* was lost on the Reef of Rocus, "and all hands immediately took to the boat, as there was no prospect of saving the slaves, for we must abandon the ship in consequence of the heavy surf." On November 4, the crew arrived at Curaçao, where "the Hon'ble Governor Beck ordered two sloops to take the slaves off the wreck, one of which sloops with eighty four slaves on board, was captured by a privateer."[28]

Navigation and Defense

Whatever problems he had to handle on board during the Middle Passage, the slaver captain also had to make the quickest possible passage across the Atlantic, taking into consideration distance, the likelihood of bad weather or of being becalmed, and the hazard of attacks from other ships. Every day he cut from the Middle Passage contributed to profits—not to mention that conditions aboard the slavers were so disagreeable even for the ship's officers as to encourage all possible speed.

Storms at sea frequently spelled not merely discomfort but disaster for the ships, their crews, and their human cargoes. "Suddenly the weather closes in, and the seas rise so high and so strongly that the ships must obey the waves, sailing at the mercy of the winds without true course or control," wrote Brazilian Sebastiao Xavier Botelho in 1840. "It is then that the din from the slaves, bound to one another, becomes horrible. . . . The tempo of the storm increases, and with it the danger. A portion of the food provisions is heaved overboard, and also other objects, to save the cargo and the crew. Many slaves break legs and arms; others die of suffocation. One ship or another will break apart from the fury of the storm, and sink. Another drifts on, dismasted, its rigging ruined by the will of the ocean, unable to heed the helm, on the verge of capsizing."[29]

The significant variations in the times recorded for the voyage across the Atlantic suggest how much depended on the captain's skills. John Barbot commented in 1700, "[T]he great mortality, which so often happens in slave-ships, proceeds as well from taking in too many, as from want of knowing how to manage them aboard, and how to order the course at sea so nicely [precisely], as not to overshoot their ports in America, as some bound to Cayenne with slaves, have done; attributing the tediousness of their passage, and their other mistakes, to wrong causes, as being becalm'd about the line [equator], etc.[,] which only proceeded from their not observing the regular course, or not making due observations of land when they approach'd the American continent; or of the force and strength of the current of the Amazons. Others have been faulty in not putting their ships into due order before they left the Guinea coast."[30]

The captain also had to keep an eye out for pirates and the vessels of other nations, any of which might attack his ship to steal the slaves and the ship. The records show many such attacks. Successfully maneuvering sailing ships on the high seas under battle conditions required both art and luck. Some owners insured against risks "of the Seas, Men of War, Fires, Enemies, Pirates, Rovers, Thieves, Jettisons, Letters of Mart, and Counter Mart, Surprizals, Takings at Sea, Arrests, Restraints and Detainment of all Kings, Princes, and people of what Nation, Condition or Quality soever."[31] Others took their chances.

To some degree, of course, the success of a voyage depended on the design and soundness of the ship. Capt. William Sherwood wrote in 1790, "I think the construction [of a slave ship] is more material [to the health of slaves] than the tonnage; in a long narrow ship the air circulates more freely: a short quarter deck, no top-gallant forecastle, no gangway, and a very low waist, are Circumstances of greater advantage than a mere extension of tonnage."[32] Sheathing the ship's bottom with copper increased its speed.

Recent scholarship places the total number of slaving trips to the New World between 1527 and 1866 at 27,233. Almost 12 million slaves were embarked from Africa, and about one and a half million died on the Middle Passage.[33]

Chronicle of Events

1684

• Portugal enacts a measure regulating the slave-carrying capacity of a ship and setting the quantity of provisions that must be carried.

1731

• On the ship of slave trader Capt. George Scott of Rhode Island, slaves mutiny and kill members of the crew.

1732

• Slaves in his cargo kill Capt. John Major of Portsmouth, New Hampshire, and all his crew and seize the schooner and cargo.

1747

• Slaves on board the ship of Captain Beers of Rhode Island rise and kill most of the crew.

1761

• Captain Nichols of Boston loses 40 of his slaves by insurrection but saves his ship.

1770

• Increased prices for slaves in Brazil result in somewhat better conditions on slave ships.
• The Portuguese governor's order imposes new standards of hygiene on slave ships out of Luanda (in modern Angola).

1785

• The Portuguese empire makes it more difficult for slavers to evade legal restrictions on loading and requirements for carrying a certain amount of provisions for slaves.

1788

• England imposes official restrictions on slave ships— limiting the number of slaves to be carried, outlawing insurance on cargoes of slaves except for fire and the perils of the sea, requiring the employment of trained surgeons, and offering premiums to surgeons and captains if the mortality rate of a Middle Passage is no more than 3 percent.

1790

• The use of fruits and vegetables to combat scurvy on slave ships begins to spread.

1799

• England changes the requirements for slave ships, specifying the height between decks rather than tonnage, thus further reducing capacity.

1800–1830

• The *bergantim* emerges as the main type of slaving vessel, with more hold space for provisions than other slave ships.

1802

• Denmark abolishes the slave trade.

1807

• Great Britain and the United States prohibit the international slave trade.

1808

• The British undertake to stop all maritime trading in slaves from West Africa.
• The introduction of copper-sheathed hulls marginally lowers the average sailing times of slave ships.

1810

• Increased freight charges for shippers and higher fees to agents on commission in Africa ease the economic pressures that had caused inadequate provisioning of slave ships.
• Trained physicians begin to influence policy on slaving in Africa and Brazil.

1813

• Sweden abolishes the slave trade.

1814

• The Netherlands abolishes the slave trade.

1820

• Vaccination against smallpox comes into wider use in the slave trade.
• Spain abolishes the slave trade.

1830

• The legal international slave trade ends.

Death of the *Amistad* captain *(Library of Congress)*

1835

• The British parliament authorizes the Royal Navy to capture slave ships flying the Portuguese flag as though they were British.

1839

• *July:* African captives, led by Joseph Cinqué, rebel aboard the Spanish slaver *Amistad.*

• *August 26:* Lieutenant Gedney, U.S. Navy, captures the *Amistad* and takes it to New London, Connecticut, where its African captives are imprisoned.

1841

• The British parliament authorizes British admiralty courts to adjudicate cases of slave vessels operating contrary to an Anglo-Brazilian treaty of 1826.

Eyewitness Testimony

Embarking and Provisioning

To the greater glory of God and the Virgin Mary, with the help of God, we are undertaking to go from Vannes, where we were outfitted, to the coast of Guinea in the ship The Diligent, belonging to the brothers Billy and Mr. LaCroix, and from thence to Martinique to sell our blacks and make our return to Vannes.

Lt. Robert Durand, 1731, Hartford Courant, *September 21, 1998.*

I was carried on board. I was immediately handled, and tossed up to see if I were sound, by some of the crew; and I was now persuaded that I had gotten into a world of bad spirits, and that they were going to kill me. Their [white] complexions, too, differing so much from ours, their long hair, and the language they spoke . . . united to confirm me in this belief. . . . When I looked round the ship too, and saw a large furnace of copper boiling, and a multitude of black people of every description chained together, every one of their countenances expressing dejection and sorrow, I no longer doubted of my fate; and, quite overpowered with horror and anguish, I fell motionless on the deck and fainted. When I recovered a little, I found some black people about me, who I believed were some of those who had brought me on board, and had been receiving their pay; they talked to me in order to cheer me, but all in vain. I asked them if we were not to be eaten by those white men with horrible looks, red faces, and long hair.

Gustavus Vassa (Olaudah Equiano), experiences of about 1756, in Bontemps, Great Slave Narratives, *27.*

[We desire you to go to New Calabar, and there barter your cargo] for good healthy young negroes and ivory, and . . . not to buy any old slaves or children but good healthy young men and women, . . . and when you are half-slaved don't stay too long if there is a possibility of getting off for the risk of sickness and mortality then become great. . . .

[L]et no candle be made use of in drawing spirits or to go near the powder. . . . We recommend you to treat the negroes with as much lenity as [as leniently as] safety will admit and suffer none of your officers or people to abuse them under any pretence whatever, be sure you see their victuals well dressed and given them in due season. . . . We recommend you to make fires frequently in the negroes' rooms as we think it healthy and you have

iron kettles on board for that purpose. We recommend mutton broth in fluxes [sicknesses], so that you'll endeavour to purchase as many sheep and goats to bring off the coast for that purpose as you conveniently can.

Instructions to Capt. George Merrick of the Africa, *from John Chilcott & Company, 1774, in Pope-Hennessy,* Sins of the Fathers, *109.*

The Slaves: Living Conditions at Sea—Food and Drink

Their chief diet is call'd dabbadabb, being Indian corn ground as small as oat-meal, in iron mills, which we carry for that purpose; and after mix'd with water, and boil'd well in a large copper furnace, till 'tis as thick as a pudding, about a peckful of which in vessels, call'd crews, is allow'd to 10 men, with a little salt, malagetta, and palm oil, to relish; they are divided into messes [eating groups] of ten each, for the easier and better order in serving them: Three days a week they have horse-beans boil'd for their dinner and supper, great quantities of which the African company do send aboard us for that purpose; these beans the negroes extremely love and desire, beating their breast, eating them, and crying Pram! Pram! which is Very good! they are indeed the best diet for them, having a binding quality, and consequently good to prevent the flux, which is the inveterate distemper that most affects them, and ruins our voyages by their mortality.

Capt. Thomas Phillips, journal of a voyage of the Hannibal, *1693–1694, in Donnan,* Slave Trade Documents *1:406.*

Frequently bought from the natives considerable quantities of dried shrimps to make broth; and a very excellent dish they made, when mixed with flour and palm oil and seasoned with pepper and salt. Both whites and blacks were fond of this mess [food]. In addition to yams we gave them for a change, fine shelled beans and rice cooked together, and this was served up to each individual with a plentiful proportion of the soup. On other days their soup was mixed with peeled yams, cut up thin and boiled, with a proportion of pounded biscuit. For the sick we provided strong soups and middle messes, prepared from mutton, goats' flesh, fowls, etc., to which were added sago and lilipees, the whole mixed with port wine and sugar. . . . [The slaves'] personal comfort was also carefully studied. On their coming on deck, about eight o'clock in the morning, water was provided to wash their hands and faces, a mixture of lime juice to cleanse their mouths, towels to wipe with and chew sticks to clean their teeth. These were generally pieces of young branches of the common lime or of the citron of sweet lime tree. . . . They are used about the thickness of a quill and the end being chewed, the white, fine fibre of the wood soon forms a brush with which the teeth may be effectually cleaned by rubbing them up and down. These sticks impart an agreeable flavor to the mouth and are sold in little bundles, for a mere trifle, in the public markets of the West Indies. A draw of brandy bitters was given to each of the men and clean spoons being served out, they breakfasted about nine o'clock. About eleven, if the day were fine, they washed their bodies all over, and after wiping themselves dry, were allowed to use palm oil, their favorite cosmetic. Pipes and tobacco were then supplied to the men and beads and other articles were distributed among the women to amuse them, after which they were permitted to dance and run about on deck to keep them in good spirits. A middle mess of bread and cocoa-nuts was given them about mid-day. The third meal was served out about three o'clock and after everything was cleaned out and arranged below, they were generally sent down about four or five o'clock in the evening.

Memoirs of Capt. H. Crow, 1830, in Dow, Slave Ships, 184–85.

The Slaves: Living Conditions at Sea—Lodging

If it be in large ships carrying five or six hundred slaves, the deck in such ships ought to be at least five and a half or six foot high, . . . for the greater height it has, the more airy and convenient it is for such a considerable number of human creatures; and consequently far the more healthy for them. . . . We build a sort of half-decks along the sides with deals and spars . . . ,that half-deck extending no farther than the sides of our scuttles and so the slaves lie in two rows, one above the other, and as close together as they can be crouded. . . .

We are very nice [careful] in keeping the places where the slaves lie clean and neat, appointing some of the ship's crew to do that office constantly, and several of the slaves themselves to be assistant to them in that employment; and thrice a week we perfume betwixt decks with a quantity of good vinegar in pails, and red-hot iron bullets in them, to expel the bad air, after the place has been well wash'd and scrubb'd with brooms: after which, the deck is clean'd with cold vinegar. . . .

John Barbot's voyage to the Congo, 1700, in Donnan, Slave Trade Documents 1:459, 465.

The hold of the slaver *Gloria* was packed with people. *(Library of Congress)*

The stench of the hold while we were on the coast was so intolerably loathsome, that it was dangerous to remain there for any time. . . . [N]ow that the whole ship's cargo were confined together, it became absolutely pestilential. The closeness of the place, and the heat of the climate, added to the number in the ship, which was so crowded that each had scarcely room to turn himself, almost suffocated us. This produced copious perspirations, so that the air soon became unfit for respiration, from a variety of loathsome smells, and brought on a sickness among the slaves, of which many died. . . . This wretched situation was again aggravated by the galling of the chains, now become insupportable, and the filth of the necessary tubs [toilets], into which the children often fell, and were almost suffocated. . . .

> Gustavus Vassa (Olaudah Equiano), experiences of about 1756, in Bontemps, Great Slave Narratives, 30.

In each of the apartments are placed three or four large buckets, of a conical form, nearly two feet in diameter at the bottom and only one foot at the top and in depth about twenty-eight inches, to which, when necessary, the negroes have recourse. It often happens that those . . . at a distance from the buckets, in endeavoring to get to them, tumble over their companions. . . . These accidents, although unavoidable, are productive of continual quarrels. . . . In this situation, unable to proceed and prevented from getting to the tubs, they desist from the attempt; and as the necessities of nature are not to be resisted, they ease themselves as they lie. This becomes a fresh source of broils and disturbances. . . . The nuisance . . . is not unfrequently increased by the tubs being much too small for the purpose intended and their being usually emptied but once every day.

> Ship's doctor Alexander Falconbridge, Account of the Slave Trade (1788), in Dow, Slave Ships, 142–43.

We were thrust into the hold of the vessel in a state of nudity, the males being crammed on one side and the females on the other; the hold was so low that we could not stand up, but were obliged to crouch upon the floor or sit down; day and night were the same to us, sleep being denied us from the confined position of our bodies, and we became desperate through suffering and fatigue.

> Mahommah G. Baquaqua, native of Zoogoo, describing his experiences ca. 1840, transcribed in Baquaqua and Moore, Biography of Mahommah G. Baquaqua, 42–43. Available online at URL: http://docsouth.unc.edu/ neh/baquaqua/baquaqua.html.

The Slaves: Living Conditions at Sea—Exercise

If they [the slaves] go about it [dancing for exercise] reluctantly, or do not move with agility, they are flogged; a person standing by them all the time with a cat-o'-nine-tails in his hand for that purpose. Their music, upon these occasions, consists of a drum . . . [T]he poor wretches are frequently compelled to sing also; but when they do so, their songs are generally, as may naturally be expected, melancholy lamentations of their exile from their native land.

> Ship's doctor Alexander Falconbridge, Account of the Slave Trade (1788), in Pope-Hennessy, Sins of the Fathers, 4 n.

The Slaves: Living Conditions at Sea—Sickness

But our greatest care of all is to buy none that are pox'd, lest they should infect the rest aboard; for tho' we separate the men and women aboard by partitions and bulk-heads, to prevent quarrels and wranglings among them, yet do what we can they will come together, and that distemper which they call the yaws, is very common here, and discovers itself by almost the same symptoms as the . . . clap does with us; therefore our surgeon is forced to examine the privities of both men and women with the nicest scrutiny, which is a great slavery, but what can't be omitted.

> Capt. Thomas Phillips, journal of the 1693 voyage of the Hannibal, in Dow, Slave Ships, 61.

The distemper which my men as well as the blacks mostly die of, was the white flux, which was so violent and inveterate, that no medicine would in the least check it. . . . I cannot imagine what should cause it in them so suddenly, they being free from it till about a week after we left the island of St. Thomas. And next to the malignity of the climate, I can attribute it to nothing else but the unpurg'd black sugar, and raw unwholesome rum they bought there, of which they drank in punch to great excess, and which it was not in my power to hinder. . . .

> Capt. Thomas Phillips, journal of a voyage of the Hannibal, 1693–1694, in Dow, Slave Ships, 67.

As for the sick and wounded . . . our surgeons, in their daily visits betwixt decks, finding any indisposed, caus'd them to be carried to the Lazaretto [sick bay], under the fore-castle. . . . Being out of the croud, the surgeons had more conveniency and time to administer proper remedies; which they cannot do leisurely between decks, because of the great heat . . . , which is sometimes so excessive, that the surgeons would faint away, and the candles would not burn; besides, that in such a croud of brutish people, there are always some very apt to annoy and hurt others, and all in general so greedy, that they will snatch from the sick slaves the fresh meat or liquor that is given them. . . .

John Barbot's voyage to the Congo, 1700, in Donnan, Slave Trade Documents *1:459f.*

The ship *Zong* . . . sailed from . . . the coast of Africa, the 6th September , 1781 . . . and on the 27th November following she fell in with [Jamaica]; but . . . the master, either through ignorance or a sinister intention, ran the ship to leeward, alleging that he mistook Jamaica for Hispaniola. . . .

The sickness and mortality on board the *Zong* . . . was not occasioned by the want of water . . . : yet [on November 29th] . . . before there was any present or real want of water, "the master of the ship called together a few of the officers, and told them . . . that, if the slaves died a natural death, it would be the loss of the owners of the ship; but if they were thrown alive into the sea, it would be the loss of the underwriters": and, to palliate the inhuman proposal, he . . . pretended that "it would not be so cruel to throw the poor sick wretches . . . into the sea, as to suffer them to linger out a few days under the disorders with which they were afflicted. . . ." [T]he same evening . . . [he] picked, or caused to be picked out, from the cargo of the same ship, one hundred and thirty-three slaves, all or most of whom were sick or weak, and not likely to live; and ordered the crew by turns to throw them into the sea; which most inhuman order was cruelly complied with . . . [F]ifty-four persons were actually thrown overboard alive on the 29th of November; and . . . forty-two more were also thrown overboard on the 1st December.

1783 account, in Donnan, Slave Trade Documents *2:554–56.*

The same day the Smallpox declared itself on the ship we immediately began innoculating the slaves and such of the officers and sailors as had not gone through the operation before. . . . [We then landed on an uninhabited island, where we constructed shelters for the diseased slaves and fed them turtle soup.] In twenty-nine days they were all perfectly cleansed of smallpox.

Capt. Samuel Chase to his Newport, Rhode Island, shipowners, December 1797, in Coughtry, Notorious Triangle, *149.*

The Slaves: Living Conditions at Sea—Abuse

[My officers urged me to] cut off the legs and arms of the most wilful [slaves] to terrify the rest, [but I refused] to entertain the least thought of it, much less put in practice such barbarity and cruelty to poor creatures, who, excepting their want of Christianity and true religion (their misfortune more than fault) are as much the works of God's hands, and no doubt as dear to him as ourselves; nor can I imagine why they should be despised for their colour, being what they cannot help, and the effect of the climate it has pleased God to appoint them. I can't think there is any intrinsic value in one colour more than another, nor that white is better than black, only we think so because we are so, and are prone to judge favourably in our own case, as well as the blacks, who in odium of the colour, say, the devil is white and so paint him.

Thomas Phillips, journal of the 1693–1694 voyage of the Hannibal, *in Pope-Hennessy,* Sins of the Fathers, *99.*

The Reader may be curious to know their [the mutinous slaves'] punishment: . . . Captain Harding weighing the Stoutness and Worth of the two Slaves, did as in other Countries they do by Rogues of Dignity, whip and scarify them only; while three others, Abettors, but not Actors, nor of Strength for it, he sentenced to cruel Deaths; making them first eat the Heart and Liver of one of the killed [whites]. . . . The woman he hoisted up by the Thumbs, whipp'd and slashed her with Knives, before the other Slaves till she died.

Ship's doctor's report of mutiny on the English slaver Robert, *1721, in Harding,* River, *13.*

[T]he enormities committed in an African ship, though equally flagrant, are little known *here* and are considered *there*, only as a matter of course. When the women and girls are taken on board a ship, naked, trembling, terrified, perhaps almost exhausted with cold, fatigue, and hunger, they are often exposed to the wanton rudeness of white savages. The poor creatures cannot understand the language they hear, but the looks and manner of the speakers are sufficiently intelligible. In imagination, the prey is divided, upon the spot, and only reserved till opportunity offers.

John Newton, Journal of a Slave Trader, *1750–1754, quoted in Reynolds,* African Slavery, *50–51.*

In the afternoon while we were off the deck, William Cooney seduced a woman slave down into the room and lay with her brutelike in view of the whole quarter deck, for which I put him in irons. I hope this has been the first affair of the kind on board and I am determined to keep them quiet if possible. If anything happens to the woman I shall impute it to him, for she was big with child. Her number is 83.

John Newton, Journal of a Slave Trader, *1750–1754, quoted in Pope-Hennessy,* Sins of the Fathers, *100.*

The [nine-month-old] child took sulk and would not eat. . . . [T]he captain took the child up in his hand, and flogged it with the cat [o'-nine-tails]. . . . [T]he child had swelled feet; the captain desired the cook to put on some water to heat to see if he could abate the swelling, and it was done. He then ordered the child's feet to be put into the water, and the cook putting his finger into the water, said, "Sir, it is too hot." The captain said, "Damn it, never mind it, put the feet in," and so doing the skin and nails came off, and he got some sweet oil and clothes and wrapped round the feet in order to take the fire out of them; and I myself bathed the feet with oil, and wrapped cloths around; and laying the child on the quarter deck in the afternoon at mess time, I gave the child some victuals, but it would not eat; the captain took the child up again, and flogged it, and said, "Damn you, I will make you eat," and so he continued in that way for four or five days at mess time, when the child would not eat, and flogged it, and he tied a log of mango, eighteen or twenty inches long, and about twelve or thirteen pound weight, to the child by a string round its neck. The last time he took the child up and flogged it, and let it drop out of his hands, "Damn you (says he) I will make you eat, or I will be the death of you"; and in three quarters of an hour after that the child died. He would not suffer any of the people that were on the quarter deck to heave the child overboard, but he called the mother of the child to heave it overboard. She was not willing to do so, and I think he flogged her; but I am sure that he beat her in some way for refusing to throw the child overboard; at the last he made her take the child up, and she took it in her hand, and went to the ship's side, holding her head on one side, because she would not see the child go out of her hand, and she dropped the child overboard. She seemed to be very sorry, and cried for several hours.

Isaac Parker, testimony before the Commons Select Committee, 1764, in Anstey, Atlantic Slave Trade, *33.*

The Slaves: Living Conditions at Sea—Depression and Suicides

The negroes are so wilful and loth to leave their own country, that they have often leap'd out of the canoos, boat and ship, into the sea, and kept under water till they were drowned, to avoid being taken up and saved by our boats. . . . We have likewise seen divers [several] of them eaten by the sharks, of which a prodigious number kept about the ships in this place, and I have been told will follow her hence to Barbadoes, for the dead negroes that are thrown over-board in the passage. . . . We had about 12 negroes did wilfully drown themselves, and others starv'd themselves to death, for 'tis their belief that when they die they return home to their own country and friends again. . . .

Thomas Phillips, journal of the 1693 voyage of the Hannibal, *in Dow,* Slave Ships, *62–63.*

It frequently happens that the negroes on being purchased by Europeans, become raving mad and many of them die in that state, particularly the women. One day at Bonny, I saw a middle-aged, stout woman, who had been brought down from a fair the preceding day, chained to the post of a black trader's door, in a state of furious insanity. On board the ship was a young negro woman chained to the deck, who had lost her senses soon after she was purchased and taken on board. In a former voyage we were obliged to confine a female negro of about twenty-three years of age, on her becoming a lunatic. She was afterwards sold during one of her lucid intervals.

Ship's doctor Alexander Falconbridge, Account of the Slave Trade *(1788), in Dow,* Slave Ships, *150–51.*

The slaves in the night were often heard making a howling melancholy kind of noise, sometimes expressive of extreme anguish. I repeatedly ordered the woman, who had been my interpreter in the latter part of the voyage, to inquire into the particular causes of this very melancholy noise. [She answered that it was because the slaves had dreamed they were back in their own country, only to wake to the reality of the slave ship.]

Ship's surgeon Thomas Trotter, testifying before the Select Committee of the House of Commons, 1789–1791, in Pope-Hennessy, Sins of the Fathers, *193.*

The Slaves: Living Condition at Sea—Rebellions

When our slaves are aboard we shackle the men two and two, while we lie in port, and in sight of their own country, for 'tis then they attempt to make their escape, and mutiny; to prevent which we always keep centinels [sentinels] upon the hatchways, and have a chest full of small arms, ready loaden and prim'd, constantly lying at hand upon the quarter-deck, together with some granada shells; and two of our quarter-deck guns, pointing on the deck thence, and two more out of the steerage.

Slaver captain, 1693, in Harding, River, 10.

We are sometimes sufficiently plagued with a parcel [group] of slaves, which come from a far in-land country, who very innocently persuade one another, that we buy them only to fatten and afterwards eat them as a delicacy.

When we are so unhappy as to be pestered with many of this sort, they resolve and agree together (and bring over the rest of their party) to run away from the ship, kill the Europeans, and set the vessel a-shore: by which means they design to free themselves from being our food.

Dutchman William Bosman, description of the coast of Guinea, 1701, in Donnan, Slave Trade Documents 1:443.

On the first day of January [1701], Casseneuve's journal takes notice of their sailing out of Cabinde bay, . . . in order to proceed to Jamaica, . . . himself, the super-cargo, Mr. Barbot, the captain, and the first mate, with several of their men being sick, and having buried here and at sea, six of their crew and the third mate . . . : which gave an opportunity to the slaves aboard to revolt on the fifth. . . .

About one in the afternoon, after dinner, we according to custom caused them, one by one, to go down between decks, to have each his pint of water; most of them were yet above deck, many of them provided with knives, which we had indiscreetly given them two or three days before, as not suspecting the least attempt of this nature from them; others had pieces of iron they had torn off our forecastle door. . . . [T]hey had also broken off the shackles from several of their companions feet, which served them, as well as billets they had provided themselves with, and all other things they could lay hands on, which they imagin'd might be of use for their enterprize. Thus arm'd, they fell in crouds and parcels [groups] on our men, upon the deck unawares, and stabb'd one of the stoutest of us all, who receiv'd fourteen or fifteen wounds of their knives, and so expir'd. Next they assaulted our boatswain, and cut one of his legs so round the bone, that he could not move, the nerves being cut through; others cut our cook's throat to the [wind]pipe, and others wounded three of the sailors, and threw one of them over-board in that condition, from the fore-castle into the sea; who,

however, by good providence, got hold of the bowline of the fore-sail, and sav'd himself, along the lower wale of the quarter-deck, where, (says Casseneuve;) we stood in arms, firing on the revolted slaves, of whom we kill'd some, and wounded many; which so terrify'd the rest, that they gave way, dispersing themselves some one way and some another between decks, and under the fore-castle; and many of the most mutinous, leapt over board, and drown'd themselves in the ocean with much resolution, shewing no manner of concern for life. Thus we lost twenty seven or twenty eight slaves, either kill'd by us, or drown'd. . . .

James Barbot's voyage to the Congo River, in Dow, Slave Ships, 83–84.

The story told by the Mendians [of the *Amistad* rebellion] is as follows: They belong to six different tribes living near each other in Africa, and yet can well understand each other's dialect. They are not related and met for the first time at the Slave Factory at Lomboko, near the mouth of the Gallinas river. They had been previously kidnapped singly, and hurried down to the coast, by the Spaniards or the natives who had been instigated by them. At Lomboko they were put on board the Portuguese ship Tecora, in chains, with several hundreds of other Africans, and taken to Havana. Here they were landed and kept in a Baracoon (an oblong enclosure without a roof) for ten days, when Ruiz purchased them, forty-nine in number. Montez also purchased the boy Ka-li and three girls, who were brought from Africa in another ship. The whole fifty-three were put on board the Spanish coaster Amistad, which cleared for Principe, about 300 miles distant, where Ruiz and Montez lived. On the passage the Mendians had dealt out to them a very small quantity of food and drink. When they took any water without leave, and at other times, they were severely scourged by order of their masters. The cook told them that on arriving at Principe they were to be killed and eaten. The Mendians took counsel, and resolved on attempting to recover their liberty. They contrived to rid themselves of their chains—armed themselves with case-knives—killed the cook—attacked the captain, who slew two of the Africans and wounded others—and achieved a victory. Two sailors took to the boat and escaped. Cinqué took command. Ruiz and Montez were put in irons, and had dealt out to them the same quantity of food and water that they had dealt out to the Africans. This continued for two days only, when their irons were removed, and they were treated very well. When the water became short, Cinqué refused it to himself and his comrades, supplying the children and the Spaniards with a small quantity daily!

Two were killed in the rencontre [fight], seven died on board the Amistad, eight died at New Haven, one was drowned at Farmington, and thirty-five survive.

Philanthropist, December 29, 1841, in Blassingame,
Slave Testimony, *201–02.*

Captains and Crews: Recruitment and Duties

[T]he Compa. [company] not having of late had any good satisfaction of the purchasing and disposing of our Negroes doe order that all Negroes as they are brought aboard shall be taken Notice off and Numbered by the Master, the Mates, and Boatswaine, Chirurgeon [doctor], and Carpenter, or soe many of them as shall be aboard, and dayly entered into the bookes signed by our Sub: Gov'r: or Dep'ty Gov'r: and that the said Officers doe signe the bookes as often as any Negroes come aboard, and that all said Negroes brought aboard be Expressed in bills of Lading to be signed by the Comander and witnessed by some of the said officers before they weigh anchor and one or more bills of lading to be left with our Factors ashoare if there be any, or with the next ship that is to follow to be sent to us. And that the Negroes be mustered within 14 days after setting saile and soe from 14 days to 14 days all the voyage until their arrival and that every Muster be entered into the said booke by the said Officers[.] And if any Mortality shall happen amongst

Joseph Cinqué led the successful mutiny on the *Amistad.*
(Library of Congress)

your Negroes in yo'r Voyage wee require for our satisfaction that you send or bring home a Certificate under yo'r Mates and Chirurgeons hands testefying the time of the death of such as shall happen to dye, for Wee shall allow none but what are soe certified to be dead.

Instructions from the Royal African Company to Captain Robert Barrett, October 25, 1687, in Donnan, Slave Trade Documents *1:361–62.*

[The crews for our ships] are for the most part supplied with the refuse and dregs of the nation. The prisons and glass houses furnish us with large quotas of boys impatient of their parent or masters, or already ruined by some untimely vice and for the most part devoid of all good principles.

John Newton, Journal of a Slave Trader, 1750–1754, *quoted in Reynolds,* African Slavery, *30.*

It was not until after we had done with cruising off the Azores Islands [in 1860] and had taken our departure for other parts, that our [the crew's] suspicions were aroused that the whaling business was merely a blind. The first evidence came to light after the crew had been set to work breaking out the hold, and it appeared in the shape of huge quantities of rice, hard-tack, salt beef, pork, etc., in quantities large enough to feed a regiment for a long time. . . .

For weeks the sham of whaling was carried on. . . .

The crew generally seemed to be well pleased at the new phase the voyage had taken and were anxious for the time to come when the ship would be well filled with "blackfish" oil, as they termed the negroes.

Sailor Edward Manning, Six Months on a Slaver, *in Dow,* Slave Ships, *282–83.*

Captain and Crews: Dangers and Difficulties

Thursday the 23d. From noon yesterday we had but faint small breezes of wind until three in the evening, at which time the ship that stood after us was got within random gun-shot of us, appearing a fine long snug frigate; so that now we no longer doubted but she was an enemy, therefore letting fly my colours, we fir'd a shot athwart his fore foot; upon which he shew'd an Engllish ensign; but for all his cheat we knew what he was. . . . [At] four . . . being within carbine shot of us, he run out his lower tier of guns . . . and struck his false colours, and hoisted the French white sheet. I . . . order'd all my men to their guns, . . . and expected his broad-side, which when within pistol-shot, he gave us, and his volley of small shot. We return'd his civility very heartily with ours; after which he shot ahead of us, and brought to, and fell along our larboard side, and gave us his other broadside, as we did him; then each of us loaded and fired as fast as we could, until ten o'clock at night, when his foretop mast came by the board [fell]; then he fell astern of us . . . and took his leave of us. . . . I was extremely glad that by God's assistance we defended the ship, though she was most miserably shatter'd and torn in her mast and rigging. . . .

Thomas Phillips, journal of the 1693 voyage of the Hannibal, *in Dow,* Slave Ships, *36–37.*

[The 1806 insurance policy for the slaver *Rambler,* out of Rhode Island, covered risks] of the Seas, Men of War, Fires, Enemies, Pirates, Rovers, Thieves, Jettisons, Letters of Mart, and Counter Mart [Letters of Marque, that is, license to capture the merchant shipping of an enemy nation], Surprizals, Takings at Sea, Arrests, Restraints and Detainment of all Kings, Princes, and people of what Nation, Condition or Quality soever . . . Risque of Captures at Sea by American Cruisers and insurrection of Slaves but not of Common Mortality.

Coughtry, Notorious Triangle, *98–99.*

Captains and Crews: Profit and Loss

With this praye [prey—three hundred Negroes] hee [Capt. John Hawkins] sayled over the Ocean sea unto the Island of Hispaniola, and arrived first at the port of Isabella: and there hee had reasonable utterance [disposal of goods by sale or barter] of his English commodities, as also of some part of his Negros, trusting the Spaniards no further, then that by his owne strength he was able still to master them. From the port of Isabella he went to Puerto de Plata, where he made like sale . . . ; from thence also hee sayled to Monte Christi another port on the North side of Hispaniola, and the last place of his touching, where he had peaceable traffique, and made vent of [sold] the whole number of his Negros: for which he received in those 3. places by way of exchange such quantitie of merchandise, that hee did not onely lade his owne 3. shippes with hides, ginger, sugars, and some quantities of pearles, but he fraighted also two other hulkes with hides and the like commodities, which hee sent into Spaine. . . . And so with prosperous success and much gaine . . . , he came home, and arrived in the moneth of September 1563.

Richard Hakluyt, Principal Navigations, *in Donnan,* Slave Trade Documents *1:44–47.*

It also concerns the adventurers [entrepreneurs] in Guinea voyages for slaves, not to allow the commanders, supercargo [agent in charge of cargo] or officers, the liberty of taking aboard any slaves for their own particular account, as is too often practised among European traders, thinking to save something in their salaries by the month: for experience has shown, that the captain's slaves never die, since there are not ten masters in fifty who scruple to make good their own out of the cargo; or at least such licence-slaves are sure to have the best accommodations aboard, and the greatest plenty of subsistance out of the ship's stock: and very often those who were allow'd to carry but two slaves, have had ten or twelve, and those the best of the cargo, subsisted out of the general provisions of the ship, and train'd up aboard, to be carpenters, coopers, and cooks, so as to sell for double the price of other slaves. . . .

James Bardot's voyage to the Congo, 1700, in Donnan, Slave Trade Documents *1:465.*

If any of the slaves die, the surgeon loses [on] his head money [usually one shilling for each slave sold], and the Captain [on] his commission; if the slaves are brought in bad order to market, they average low, and the officers' privilege slaves [bought for the officers' own profit], which are generally paid them on an average with the cargo, are of less value to them.

Parliamentary Accounts and Papers, 1790, in Anstey, Atlantic Slave Trade, *34.*

The Illegal International Slave Trade after 1807

[After the Spaniards had bought me from an African,] I was put on board with a great many others, until the vessel was quite full. When we got clear of the mouth of the river we saw an English man of war brig, commanded by Capt. Hagan. The Spaniards prepared to fight, but the shot of [the] man of war [was] too much for them. Three of the Spaniards were killed, and several wounded, and a shot cut the mast in two, when she was taken. Captain Hagan took the slaves out of irons, when all very glad and danced too much.

Captain Hagan took us to Sierra Leone, where we were made free.

WILLIAM THOMAS x his mark. Anti-Slavery Reporter, *February 8, 1843, in Blassingame,* Slave Testimony, *226.*

After the next shot, the topgallant yard [of the slaving vessel we were pursuing] swayed for a few minutes and fell forward. The order was given to cease firing;

A pirate slaver is captured after the ban on the international slave trade. *(Library of Congress)*

she was at our mercy. . . . From the time we first got on board we had heard moans, cries, and rumblings coming from below, and as soon as the captain and crew were removed, the hatches had been taken off, when there arose a hot blast as from a charnel house, sickening and overpowering. In the hold were three or four hundred human beings, gasping, struggling for breath, dying; their bodies, limbs, faces, all expressing terrible suffering. In their agonizing fight for life, some had torn or wounded themselves or their neighbors dreadfully; some were stiffened in the most unnatural positions. . . .

[Leaving me in command of the captured vessel,] the captain returned to the brig, giving me final orders to proceed with all possible dispatch to Monrovia, Liberia, [to] land the Negroes. . . . [In Monrovia officials told me that] I might not land the captives at Monrovia, but might land them at Grand Bassa, about a hundred and fifty miles to the eastward. . . . [Though the governor there was cooperative, King George of Grand Bassa threatened and tried to bargain for guns and slaves but settled for cloth and buttons and allowed the surviving Africans aboard to land.]

Wood, "Capture of a Slaver," describing events ca. 1850, in The Atlantic Monthly *(October 1900), 451–63. Available online at* URL: http://www.niggerati.net/node/185.

For some time the American ship *Nightingale* of Boston, Francis Bowen, master, has been watched on this coast under the suspicion of being engaged in the slave trade. . . . A few days ago observing her at anchor at Kabenda, I came in and boarded her and was induced to believe she was then preparing to receive slaves. Under this impression the ship was got under way and went some distance off but with the intention of returning under the cover of the night; which was done and at 10 P.M. we anchored and sent two boats under Lieutenant Guthrie to surprise her and it was found that she had 961 slaves on board and was expecting more. Lieut. Guthrie took possession of her as a prize. . . .

Taylor of the U.S. sloop of war Saratoga, *describing the capture of the* Nightingale, *April 21, 1861, in Dow,* Slave Ships, *275.*

CHAPTER THREE

Americans in the Slave Trade
1526–1865

The Introduction of Slavery

Rudimentary records show that even in the 16th century when the continent was still largely wilderness, black slaves were brought to North America at intervals. In 1526, a Spaniard from Hispaniola tried to set up a colony in what is now North Carolina. He failed, and the hundred-odd slaves he had brought along escaped, presumably taking refuge with Indians. Two years later, a slave survived a shipwreck in a part of New Spain now in Texas. In 1538, Estevanico de Dorante (also known as Esteban), the slave of a Spaniard, guided a party of explorers searching for gold. Zuni Indians killed him.

Africans arrived in North American British colonies almost as soon as European settlers did. In 1619, Dutch traders brought ashore near Jamestown in Virginia some 19 blacks whom they had seized from a captured Spanish slave ship. Settlers eagerly sought their labor. Probably they hired the blacks as indentured servants, bound to work for a fixed term of years, rather than as slaves for life. At that time, English law considered baptized Christians exempt from slavery, and the Spanish usually baptized slaves in Africa before embarking them. Little else is known about their lives, though at least one for a time enjoyed freedom and property. Others certainly came in the early days as indentured servants, but by 1660 the Virginia labor force included blacks in bondage for life.[1]

In all the English colonies, north and south, slavery got off to a slow start in the 17th century but increased rapidly in the 18th century, as the colonists recognized the need for a large labor force to develop the new continent. They looked first to the Indians and then to Africans, who were already laboring as slaves in vast numbers elsewhere in the New World.

The European governments of almost all of the colonies encouraged slavery. In the Dutch colony of New Netherlands, African slavery was the primary labor system. When New Netherlands fell to Britain in 1664, creating New York and New Jersey, the articles of capitulation recognized slavery as a legal institution. In prerevolutionary

South Carolina, land policies under "headright" granted families 50 acres per settler. Slaves were counted in calculating their masters' entitlement to land. By the eve of the American Revolution, slavery was legal in all of the original colonies.

Over time, slavery moved south. White immigrants, many of them indentured servants who worked for an agreed-upon time and thereby earned their freedom, provided ample labor in the North; as their numbers swelled, northern colonial governments passed laws shutting out blacks from some occupations. But the heat, the swamps, and the low wages of the South did not appeal to free laborers. Settlers of the Deep South who came from slaveholding territories looked on slavery as a way of life. So it was that slavery gradually died out on the northern Atlantic coast, with its poor, rocky soil and small farms, but flourished in the South, where planters needed many hands to clear, drain, and cultivate the fertile lands along the coast. With the invention of the cotton gin and the boom in the international demand for southern cotton, planters turned to the Southwest for new, fertile land and to slavery to supply the workers for this labor-intensive crop. Even in 1790, more than 600,000 of the 697,624 slaves in what has become the continental United States lived in southern states. By 1830 the North had only 3,568 slaves, two-thirds of them in New Jersey, while the Old South had 2,005,457.[2]

In 1725 the North American British colonies held about 75,000 slaves. In the United States, what with the international slave trade; the acquisition of territories from France, Spain, and Mexico; and natural increase by birth, this number grew to 700,000 by 1790, a million and a half in 1820, more than 3 million in 1850, and nearly 4 million in 1860.[3]

The International Slave Trade

From the earliest years of settlement, Americans, especially New Englanders, participated in the profitable international slave trade, building and outfitting ships and transporting slaves. After 1664, with the encouragement of New York's royal proprietor, the duke of York (whose wealth was invested in slaving), Americans began to import slaves solely for sale. International traders landed most of the slaves below the Mason-Dixon Line—perhaps sailing up and down the tidal rivers and exchanging slaves for tobacco at plantation wharves; perhaps delivering their cargoes to commission merchants, who sold them by auction on the York Peninsula of Virginia, at Yorktown, West Point, Hampton, and Bermuda Hundred.

As the early slaveholders became experienced, they began to look for slaves from particular African tribes. Koromantees, including the Fanti and the Ashanti, were said to be "remarkable for their extraordinary strength and symmetry, their distinguished appearance and proud bearing. They were blacker and taller and handsomer than their fellow slaves; vigorous, muscular and agile, intelligent, fierce, ruthless in war, fanatically attached to the idea of liberty, and strangers to fear."[4] On the other hand, natives of Guinea were more experienced in growing rice. Congo blacks were supposed to be placid; Ibos sensitive and despondent, apt to commit suicide.

American owners often shunned slaves imported from the Caribbean, preferring those who came directly from Africa. As William Beverly wrote to John Fairchild in 1743, "[P]eople are Cautious of buying such negroes as can talk English from yr [your] Island [Barbados] (such use they fancy are great rogues which was ye [the] Case of yr Negros wch [which] you ordd [ordered] Ford to sell for you). Yet they make no scruple to buy New Negs [Negroes from Africa]."[5]

In 1807, the U.S. Congress joined a European movement aimed at closing down the international slave trade—partly because the country was overstocked with slaves, partly because by then many people thought slavery wrong. Several colonies, such as Virginia in 1769, had long since agreed not to import slaves from Africa; several states, including Rhode Island, Massachusetts, and Connecticut, which collectively owned most of the American slave ships, had forbidden their citizens to engage in the trade. But many ignored the laws, and some experts estimate that even after the federal ban, 10,000 to 20,000 African slaves were imported illegally every year.[6] It proved next to impossible to stop ships from landing slaves in Georgia and Louisiana or to stop immigration from Mexico and Cuba. Nor did the U.S. government try very hard. In 1820, the collector of customs at Mobile, Alabama, reported, "From the Chandalier Islands to the Perdido river [a distance of more than a hundred miles] including the coast, and numerous other islands, we have only a small boat, with four men and an inspector, to oppose the whole confederacy of smugglers and pirates." In 1817 the governor of Georgia estimated that 20,000 slaves were smuggled into that state from Florida each year.[7]

From time to time, diehards tried to make the international trade legal again. In the late 1850s, for instance, some southerners argued for its restoration to encourage more people to own slaves so that they would support secession. But popular opinion, fueled by fear of insurrection and eagerness to preserve the value of the slaves already in the United States, opposed such a move. Even immediately before the Civil War, a Georgia secessionist asked, "Suppose we re-open the African slave trade, what would be the result? Why, we would soon be drowned in a black pool; we would be literally overwhelmed with a black population."[8] Scholars estimate that after 1862 some 74,200 slaves entered the United States.[9]

Breeding Supplants Importing Slaves

As in other slaveholding regions, in the early years almost all slaves brought into North America were men, being better suited to heavy labor. That the misery of the new slaves would be aggravated by the absence of women mattered little—though occasionally a few women were purchased "to keep [the male slaves] at home and to make them Regular."[10]

Gradually, however, American slaveholders realized that they could acquire slaves more easily through breeding than buying. Slaves born in North America were not weakened by the shock of capture, the hardships of the African coffle and barracoon, and the horrors of the Middle Passage. They were born into the American slave world, not abruptly introduced into an alien environment. They had to be supported during infancy and early childhood, but no purchase price had to be paid for them.

So in the first half of the 18th century, American slaveholders began buying women in numbers equal to those of men. The gender ratio of imported slaves evened out. Nowhere else did this phenomenon occur: reliance on "natural increase" for the supply of slaves was unique to the North American colonies and later the United States.

Gradually, agriculture in the Upper South faltered as the soil wore out. Slave owners recognized that they could profit by exporting slaves to regions of the country with a growing need for labor—the Deep South and the Southwest. By the 1790s, Virginia, Maryland, and Delaware were exporting more slaves than they imported. From 1820 to 1860, the interregional movement of slaves—from North to South and especially to the Southwest—averaged each year some 20,000 slaves, partly through planter migrations but mostly through trading. "For slave children living in the Upper South in 1820, the cumulative chance of being 'sold South' by 1860 might have been something like 30 percent. . . . In the exporting states it would have been quite rare [for a slave] to have survived into middle age without being sold locally or interregionally."[11]

Henry Clay remarked to the Kentucky Colonization Society in 1829, "Nowhere in the farming portion of the United States would slave labor be generally employed, if the proprietor were not tempted to raise slaves by the high price of the Southern market, which keeps it up in his own."[12] Also, as a Virginia judge noted in 1848, "The scantiness of net profit from slave labor has become proverbial, and . . . nothing is more common than actual loss, or a benefit merely in the slow increase of capital from propagation."[13]

Slave-breeding farms never existed in these states or elsewhere—if for no other reason than that it took too long to rear a baby to an age of productive and profitable labor. But slave owners North and South did all they could to encourage, entice, or force slave women to have babies early and often. Some masters even promised slave women freedom if they bore a certain number of babies. Women slaves thus did double duty, laboring in the fields and creating new capital for their masters in the form of babies. As a former slave remarked, "A white man start out wid a few womenfolk slaves, soon him have a plantation full of little niggers runnin' 'round in deir shirt tales and a kickin' up deir heels, whilst deir mammies was in de field a hoeing and geeing at the plow handles, workin' lak a man."[14]

Georgian John C. Reed's grandfather advised him, "John, get as many young breeding-women as you can. Hire them out where they will not be abused, and after a while you can collect them on a good plantation of your own. The increase of your negroes will make you rich."[15]

The Domestic Slave Trade

Thus the domestic slave trade—the trade within and among the colonies—was well developed by the end of the 18th century. For the slaves this trade meant insecurity about the future, little permanence, and all too often separation from family and friends.

In the South, slaveholders increasingly regarded their slaves as their major capital—even more so than their land. Few plantation owners or farmers worried about depleting their holdings; with so much new land available, they simply exhausted their soil and moved west. Their slaves, however, were a renewable resource, fresh supplies always available. They were also mobile, capable of moving on. What was more, they were a cash crop.

If worst came to worst, or if an owner had too many slaves, they could be sold. As Alabama attorney Henry Watson Jr. complained in 1834, "[M]ost owners sought to acquire all they could afford—sometimes more. [My neighbors] all run in debt—invariably, never pay cash, and all always one year behind hand. They wait for a sale of their crops. The roads are bad, the prices low, they cannot pay. They all wait to be sued. A suit is brought—no defense is made—an execution is taken out and is paid with all the costs and they even think it a good bargain. The rate of interest allowed is but 8 pr. cent. So much is this below the real value that a man will let his debts go unpaid, pay interest and costs and buy negroes for making cotton or land and think it even then profitable and will be much obliged to his plaintiff if he will wait for the due course of law and not personally fall out with him. [To requests for payment] his answer is "you must wait, I *can't* pay you, I *must* buy a *negro*, it is out of the question, I have the money but I *must* buy a *negro*."[16]

Slave ownership conferred not only wealth but also prestige and status. Even the two-thirds or so of white southerners who did not own slaves had a stake in the slave system, for it supported the myth of white superiority.

Though some slave owners boasted of never selling the family slaves, others became addicted to the trade. They mortgaged their land and the slaves they already owned to buy more—to the point that in 1840 Missourians hesitated to buy slaves from Mississippi or Alabama for fear that they were already mortgaged.

Slave traders and slave owners gambled on the future prices of slaves. As Frederick Olmsted pointed out, "The supply of hands [laborers] is limited. It does not increase in the ratio of the increase of the cotton demand. If cotton should double in price next year, or become worth its weight in gold, the number of negroes in the United States would not increase four per cent. unless the African slave-trade were re-established. Now step into a dealer's 'jail' in Memphis, Montgomery, Vicksburg, or New Orleans, and you will hear the mezzano [muezzin, auctioneer] of the cotton lottery crying . . . 'If you have got the right sile [soil] and the right sort of overseer, buy [this slave], and put your trust in Providence! He's just as good for [producing] ten bales [of cotton] as I am for a julep at eleven o'clock.' And this is just as true as that any named horse is sure to win the Derby. And so the price of good labourers is constantly gambled up to a point, where, if they produce ten bales to the hand, the purchaser will be as fortunate as he who draws the high prize of the lottery; where, if they produce seven bales to the hand, he will still be in luck; where, if rot, or worm, or floods, or untimely rains or frosts occur, reducing the crop to one or two bales to the hand, as is often the case, the purchaser will have drawn a blank."[17]

The gambling fever fed on itself. By 1860, however, some professional traders were backing off, in the face of mounting abolitionist feeling in the North. In 1859, trader Philip Thomas wrote to a colleague, "I am firmly of the opinion that times are growing worse and worse as fast as the moments flee and the sooner we get out of [slave trading] the better."[18] Slaves overhearing their owners' comments on the approach of war wondered why people still wanted to buy more slaves. Nonetheless on January 17, 1860, the Milledgeville, Georgia, *Federal Union* reported, "There is a perfect fever raging in Georgia now on the subject of buying negroes. Several sales which have come under our eye within a month past afford an unmistakable symptom of the prevalence of a disease in the public mind on this subject. . . . Men are borrowing money at exorbitant rates of interest to buy negroes at exorbitant prices. . . . [Slaves are 25 percent higher,] with cotton at ten and one-half cents than they were two or three years ago, when it was worth fifteen or sixteen cents. Men are demented upon the subject."[19]

From time to time and for one reason or another, slave states tried to limit the domestic traffic in slaves, forbidding their importation into the state for sale—though citizens were left free to import as many as they wished for their own use. In 1855, Judge H. L. Benning of the Georgia Supreme Court speculated on that state's motives: "The main reason . . . was, I think, a fear that this traffic, if permitted, would in the end, empty the more northerly of the slave states of their slaves, and thus convert those states from friends and allies into enemies and assailants. The chief reason was, I think, not at all to promote abolition in this State, but to prevent abolition in other States. Another reason was, no doubt, a disposition to keep the proportion of the free population to the slave from being materially changed. And avarice probably had some degree of influence—the avarice of slaveholders already in the state, the value of whose slaves would be diminished as the supply from abroad [outside the state] should be increased."[20]

In any case, slave traders continually flouted these laws. Often, they simply went across the border to a neighboring state to execute the necessary papers. If to protect itself against receiving troublemakers a state demanded certificates of good character for slaves on sale, traders soon reduced the requirement to a travesty. Thus, slave trader Bacon Tait in 1832 advised a friend to take along a certificate for slaves he was planning to sell in Mississippi: "[Y]ou can put as many negroes as you please in *one certificate*. The usual way as I understand of obtaining these certificates is to get two freeholders to go along and look at your negroes. You then tell them the name of each negro—the freeholders then say that they know the negroes and give the certificates accordingly."[21]

Domestic Slave Traders

After the end of the legal international trade in 1808, domestic slave traders grew ever more sophisticated and professional. Smelling profit, they foraged through the Upper and Deep South for slaves they could buy and resell. Traders in Maryland and Virginia often pretended to be planters buying slaves for their own use or to be agents purchasing families for some unnamed planter. Though some worked only on commission, typically they bought slaves outright. They paid cash—which appealed to the planters, who were almost always short of cash in their credit-based

The Charleston slave market shows a great deal of activity. *(Crowe,* With Thackeray in America*)*

economy.[22] Sometimes the traders protected their investments by vaccinating and insuring the slaves.

They bought roughly equal numbers of males and females—though they paid less for women (except for the light-skinned "fancy girls" destined to become concubines or prostitutes). They preferred younger slaves, concentrating most heavily on those 15 to 25. Sometimes they asked for certificates of good conduct with their purchases, but they were not above palming off persistent runaways and rebels on unsuspecting new owners. Only rarely did they buy, or have the opportunity to buy, complete nuclear families; slaves were usually on the market either for the convenience of the master or because of the demand for a particular kind of slave. "Trading . . . accounted from the 1810s or 1820s onward for at least 60 percent of the overall interregional movement; and those sales occurred, not because of crippling debt or the death of owners, but overwhelmingly for speculative reasons. In the antebellum South, the slaveowning class was generally willing, simply for reasons of financial advantage, to separate black families. The scale of those separations was such that one out of every five marriages of Upper South slaves would have been prematurely terminated by the trade; if other interventions by masters are added, the proportion rises to about one in three. Furthermore, the trade would have separated about one in three of the exporting region's slave children (under fourteen years) from their parents; again local sales and other actions by masters would have raised this proportion to about one in two. And, with very intensive rates of importation into Lower South states throughout the antebellum period, the impact on the importing states was similarly profound."[23] Occasionally an owner would specify that a slave was not to be sold out of the state or that members of a family group were not to be separated—though, of course, slave traders preferred to buy without such restrictions and did not always honor them.

Everyone professed to scorn slave traders, those dealers in human flesh. But they not only flourished financially but often enjoyed high social position and were elected to public office. In fact, they performed a necessary function in the slave-based economy, and many who professed contempt for them nonetheless bought from and sold to them or loaned them money to carry on their business. As Angelina Grimké cogently remarked, "There is no difference in *principle*, in Christian ethics, between the despised slave dealer (who makes his fortune by trading in the bodies and souls of men, women and children) and the Christian who buys slaves from, or sells slaves to him; indeed, if slaves were not wanted by the respectable, the wealthy, and the religious in a community, there would be no slaves in that community and of course no slave-dealers."[24]

The slave traders had no trouble finding willing sellers and willing buyers. As profits soared, speculation in slaves increased. Most sales were not forced: only 4 or 5 percent were occasioned by the death or debt of masters. Sales multiplied in good times, with the demand for more labor.[25] In this respect, the slave trade did not differ from any other type of business: Profit drove it.

The Coffles

The traders moved the slaves they bought south and west, shipping them down the coast, transporting them by train, or more often driving them in coffles on forced marches, sometimes in chains and irons. (Other slaves traveled in coffles with their owners to new homes.)

A slave trader's coffle sets out. *(Library of Congress)*

These sad processions usually began with a false show of gaiety, motivated either by fear of the lash wielded by the trader or his black drivers or by a little rum measured out to the slaves. The slaves knew all too well that they were leaving friends and family behind. Sometimes traders simply gave slave babies too heavy for their mothers to carry to anyone who would take them. On the journey itself most of the slaves walked the weary miles, only the toddlers riding in the wagons. They walked day after day, in good weather or bad, cold or heat. "We have got along very well," reported one Thomas Burton, who supervised a coffle that set out from North Carolina to Mississippi in December 1845. "So far all well and able to eat a good allowance, with the exception of colds. J. D. Long and myself has very severe colds. We are worse off than any of the negroes. . . . We have travelled 20 miles per day since we left you. We are now 150 miles from home. We have had a severe time for travelling today. . . . [It] has been raining and freesing all day but slow and we have drove some 22 or 3 miles. . . ."[26] At night, they bivouacked where they could. On the journey some traders abused the bodies of the younger slave women for their own pleasure or made them available to other whites. The journey ended with the slave jail, the slave auction or salesroom, and an unknown future with a new master.

Slave Auctions and Sales

The slave traders were abetted by the owners of "nigger jails," who "fixed up" the slaves to look more attractive to purchasers; by brokers or commission merchants, who took on the task of selling slaves for owners who did not wish to dirty their own hands; and by auctioneers.

The slave jails served a triple function—as places to confine and punish slaves who had angered their masters, as temporary stopping places for masters traveling with their slaves, and as holding pens for slaves waiting to be sold. Slaves held there for sale were better fed than the others, so as to fatten them in order to raise their purchase prices. Even so, former slave Sella Martin remembered, "[My mother] was sickened to the heart by the systematic falsehoods which the trader made the slaves tell to those who came to purchase them; by the vice which was inseparable from crowding men and women together, and by the terrible cruelty

This holding pen for slaves confined them in grim captivity. *(National Archives)*

which the trader practised upon those who would not give up their virtue and their honour at his bidding."[27] Some slave jails offered slaves directly for inspection and sale.

Slaves were also sold at various other places: on the wharves where ships had landed them, in courthouse yards, in marketplaces, or in the offices of brokers who purchased or received slaves for sale on commission. Slave traders schemed to get the highest possible prices, hiding defects and advanced age as much as they could. They learned that planters preferred to buy slaves in the spring, when they could immediately put them to work on the new crop, rather than having first to carry them over the winter; also, they found that it was better to offer a large lot for sale, because the big sale would attract more buyers, who might bid each other up. In all these situations, prospective buyers thought themselves entitled to inspect the slaves for defects, handling them freely and demanding that the slaves move on command to demonstrate their strength and health. Usually an auctioneer ran the sale, pushing the bidding as high as he could.

In this auction house in New Orleans would-be purchasers bid for slaves. *(Library of Congress)*

Private Sales

Some owners bypassed the traders by advertising their own slaves for sale, asking interested persons to apply to a printer, editor, or owner of the slave jail or to inspect the slaves on the owner's premises.[28] Now and then a master sent a slave around to find a purchaser, carrying a note signed by the owner attesting to his or her health, good temper, and skills. "The bearer, Mary Jane, and her two daughters, are for sale," wrote an owner in Washington, D.C. "They are sold for no earthly fault whatever. She is one of the most ladylike and trustworthy servants I ever knew. She is a first rate parlour servant; can arrange and set out a dinner or party supper with as much taste as the most of white ladies. She is a pretty good mantua maker; can cut out and make vests and pantaloons and roundabouts and joseys for little boys in a first-rate manner. Her daughters' ages are eleven and thirteen years, brought up exclusively as house servants. The eldest can sew neatly, both can knit stockings, and all are accustomed to all kinds of house work. They would not be sold to speculators or traders for any price whatever."[29]

In these private sales, it was easier for an owner to show some concern for the slave's wishes—not to leave the neighborhood or not to be parted from family. A country owner might yield to a slave's yearning to live in the city. Or, on the other hand, the owner might show the indifference to the slaves' feeling manifested in an advertisement in the *New Orleans Bee:* "NEGROES FOR SALE.—A negro woman, 24 years of age, and her two children, one eight and the other three years old. Said negroes will be sold SEPARATELY or together, *as desired.* The woman is a good seamstress. She will be sold low for cash, or EXCHANGED FOR GROCERIES."[30]

Kidnapping and Slave Stealing

Because slaves were valuable property, both owners and traders faced the hazard of slave stealing. For instance, the Murrell gang, which operated in the Southwest in the early 1830s, would conspire with a slave, promising him a reward (perhaps his freedom) if he would run off with them, let himself be sold, and then escape to rejoin them; sometimes the gang repeated the process until the slave threatened to expose them, at which point they murdered him.[31]

But if slave owners and slave traders risked losing their property, free blacks risked much worse—losing their liberty. Being kidnapped and sold into slavery was a real and present danger for free blacks in both free and slave states. It could happen to children, adults, or whole families. In 1846, the Raleigh, North Carolina, *Star* reported the "taking off of a little son of a poor blind free negro . . . under such circumstances as to justify the suspicion that he was stolen to enslave him."[32] Former slave J. W. Lindsay remarked in an 1863 interview, "There are speculators there who are all the time speculating in human flesh & blood,—buying up men, women & children and if they find out that there are any free families who are not much noticed by the inhabitants, they will go in the dead hour of the night & kidnap them, take them off 25 or 30 miles, put them into a slave pen, & that is the last of them. . . ."[33]

Since southern courts did not allow blacks to testify against whites, and since the word of a white was almost always taken against that of a black, kidnappers' victims were hard put to prove their right to freedom. In December of 1851, for instance, Marylander Thomas McCreary snatched 16-year-old Elizabeth Parker, who lived just over the Pennsylvania line, and sold her in New Orleans for $1900. Two weeks later, he stole her younger sister, Rachel, fighting off the Millers, her employers, with a knife. Mr. Miller and a rescue party pursued them to Baltimore, had Rachel transferred from a slave pen to prison, and petitioned for her freedom; on the way home Miller was poisoned. The aroused citizens of Chester County, Pennsylvania, finally succeeded in getting both Parker girls back to their homes, after an 1853 trial in Maryland in which 49 white witnesses came from Pennsylvania to testify.[34]

The records show that many alleged victims of kidnappers, mostly black but some white, served in slavery for years, making effort after vain effort to regain their freedom. Even those few who succeeded could gain no recompense for their sufferings and losses.

Slave Participation in the Slave Trade

One way and another, slaves sometimes managed to influence their own sales. The men who ran slave jails recognized this and threatened slaves who did not cooperate with them. As former slave Washington Taylor remembered, "Pussuns [being inspected in the slave pens] had ter be on dere p's an' q's an' showin' off so as to sell well when some one come ter buy 'em, an' ef yo' didn't put on dat pleasin' look, yo'd pay fer it when de pussuns went out o' de ya'd. An' ef dey sol' yo' on trial an' yo' was brought back, yo' 'd be 'mos' killed."[35] Owners also recognized that the attitude of the slave could make a difference. In 1833, one master advertised in the Cambridge, Maryland, *Chronicle:* "I will sell one or more or all of three Negro men, to persons in the county that they will consent to live with. . . ."[36] Other sellers used rewards, like North Carolinian speculator Obadiah Fields, who said, "It was understood that I should give the negroes a present if they would try to get homes and not do anything against the interest of their sales, and to Isaac I gave $3; to Dick $2; to Fan $1; to Isabel $2; Dick and Isaac a hat each at 1 = $2."[37]

At an auction a slave might hang his head and shuffle listlessly before a buyer who looked mean or put his best foot forward when a kind-looking buyer approached. Sometimes slaves on the auction block would boast of their own abilities simply out of pride in bringing a high price. Now and then a slave succeeded in blocking a sale completely—like Lucy, who was being sold away from her child. Her owner finally wrote to the auctioneer to whom he had entrusted her, "I fear you cannot sell Lucy, in her low spirited situation for more than four hundred and twenty five dollars, which sum I am not disposed to take. Therefore if you cannot get four hundred and fifty dollars twenty four hours after the receipt of this be so kind as to send her [back]."[38] Slaves even cut off their own hands to prevent their sale.

A slave might write to a former mistress asking to be brought back. Another might find possible buyers for herself and ask to be sold in order not to be parted from husband or child. Or a slave might seek out a buyer who would allow him to hire his own time and eventually buy himself. At least one slave begged a Moravian church to buy him, "for he wanted to find salvation, and feared to be lost."[39]

Buying Freedom and Manumission

Although slaves had to have extraordinary intelligence, determination, and luck to make it work, a surprising number actually bought themselves. Legally, slaves could own nothing, but in fact some earned a little money for themselves. Plantation owners often permitted their slaves to farm small plots and sell their produce or make baskets or brooms for sale; in gray-market transactions, slaves sold "moonshine" and stolen goods.

A more likely way for slaves to accumulate money, however, arose from the practice of "hiring out," by which owners who did not for a period need the services of slaves leased their labor to someone else. It occurred to some slaves that they might, with their masters' assent, hire their own time. That is, a slave would promise to support himself and pay his owner a profit out of the wages he earned by running his own business or working for another employer. Frederick Douglass, for instance, while still a slave in Baltimore, hired his own time and went to work in a shipyard, eventually saving up the funds that he used in his escape. Other slaves managed to save enough to buy their own freedom.

Buying oneself was always a risky business, because owners often failed to keep their promises. A slave and his owner might agree on a purchase price and the slave make regular payments toward it, perhaps even pay off the whole amount, but if the master denied that the payments had been made or otherwise defaulted on the agreement, the slave could do little. Courts often held to the letter of the law rather than the actualities of the slave economy, refusing to enforce the bargains on the grounds that a slave, as property, could not make a contract.

All the same, numbers of slaves not only bought themselves but went on to buy other members of their families in order to set them free. Former slave Jerry Moore told the story of his father, who had belonged to "a old bachelor named Moore, in Alabama. Moore freed all his niggers 'fore 'mancipation except three. They was to pay a debt, and my father was Moore's choice man and was one of the three. He bought hisself. He had saved up some money, and when they went to sell him he bid $800. The auctioneer cries round to git a raise, but wouldn't nobody bid on my father 'cause he was one of Moore's 'free niggers.' My father done say after the war he could have buyed hisself for $1.50."[40]

Some free blacks, both women and men, devoted their energies and earnings to buying slaves to liberate them. In 1831 in Petersburg, Virginia, John Updike manumitted a slave, whom he described as "lately purchased by me from Shadrach Brander, so that the said Rheuben Rhenlds shall be and remain free from this time henceforth forever."[41]

Here and there a master, convinced that slaveholding was wrong, decided to free his slaves. Difficulties lay in his path. His conscience might trouble him. "You know, my dear Son," wrote Henry Laurens, "I abhor Slavery. I am not the man who enslaved them. . . . [N]evertheless I am devising means for manumitting many of them and for cutting off the entail of Slavery. . . . [But] what will my Children say if I deprive them of so much Estate?"[42]

Other masters genuinely worried about what would happen to their slaves once freed. Could they manage on their own, support themselves, save up against sickness and old age? After all, free blacks faced a hostile environment, filled with racial prejudice. Even in free states they were shut out of many occupations, and their civil rights were rigorously limited. Some free states would not admit them at all. How would they survive? What kind of fresh start did their former masters owe them? In about 1816, William Sumner of Tennessee worried about just such problems; he proposed to take 40 slaves to Indiana to give them a fresh start there. "I think," he wrote, "that after a man has had the use of slaves and their ancestors, twenty or thirty years, it is unjust and inhuman to set them free, unprovided with a home, &c. &c."[43] Yet for cash-poor planters costs like these could be formidable.

Further, slave states frequently limited the power of masters to manumit. Because they feared the presence of a large free black population, some states absolutely forbade the practice. Others required the assent of the legislature to each individual manumission. If they did permit manumission, most slave states required that the freed blacks leave the state within a short time. In the 1850s, Louisiana and Tennessee ordered that freed slaves be sent out of the United States.

Out of the difficulties of manumission developed an unofficial status of semi-freedom. Especially in the 1840s and 1850s, a number of slaves attained quasi freedom. That is, they lived as independently as possible, though they remained legally enslaved—a position that some whites assured them was better than freedom, since it still brought them their masters' support. In fact, of course, it depended on the favor of the master; if he changed his mind or died, it ended.

A good many masters chose to wait until they died to free their slaves. All too often they drew their wills improperly or failed to foresee events. What if, for instance, the will freed a slave but did not provide a bond that he would never become dependent on the state for support? Was the manumission valid? Sometimes the court did rule for the slave—as in the case of Dolly Mullin, whose master in 1821 had left her a tract of land but had neglected to free her. The court nonetheless gave her both freedom and the land, on the grounds that slaves could not own land and therefore her master must have intended to free her. One master in 1801 executed a deed freeing his slave Catin, "with the qualification and condition, . . . that she shall hold and enjoy freedom, . . . immediately after my death. But during my life she is to remain in my service and power. . . ." Between 1801 and her master's death, Catin had children; when he died she was indeed freed, but her children remained slaves, because they had been born to a slave mother.[44]

Relatives of owners often contested wills that manumitted; they demanded ownership of the slaves for themselves or simply lied to the illiterate slaves and denied them their freedom. The British traveler Eyre Crowe told a pathetic story "of a lax white trader, who, besides his legitimate offspring, left a second family of dusky-coloured children. Not knowing, what was a fact, that he was insolvent, he left them free by his will. The creditors, not to be baulked, sold these little mulattoes as slaves, to be sent down South."[45] One wary master, well aware of the difficulties, in his will freed his black daughter and left her half his estate, taking the precaution of bribing his sister into cooperation by leaving the other half to her, *if she arranged for the boarding and education of his daughter as the will provided.*[46]

Despite all this, some manumissions did occur, most often freeing a master's child or a slave who had long rendered faithful service. In the year 1860, when slaves numbered almost 4 million, some 3,000 of them were manumitted.[47]

Because of the clash of the laws of free states with those of slave states, some slaves were able to claim involuntary manumission. They argued, that is, that if their master had taken them into a free state, he had by the laws of that state freed them. Since the laws of the various free states differed one from another, involuntary manumission could easily occur. In Ohio, for instance, any master who made certain purchases that could be interpreted as showing intention to settle in the state thereby freed any slaves traveling with him—but it took a knowledgeable slave or friend of a slave to prove it. How many slaves were so freed no one knows, but state supreme courts rendered decisions in only 575 such cases during the entire slaveholding era, in 57 percent of which the slave won his freedom.[48]

Chronicle of Events

1526

• Lucas Vásquez de Ayllón, a Spanish official from Hispaniola, attempts to establish a colony in North America, landing two hundred Spaniards and one hundred black slaves near what is now Cape Fear, in North Carolina.

1528

• A shipwrecked slave arrives in Texas (part of New Spain).

1538

• Estevanico de Dorantes, a black slave of a Spanish master, guides a party sent by the Conquistadores to find the golden cities of Cibola in New Spain, only to be killed by Zuni Indians.

1619

• *August:* The first African blacks in the British North American colonies are brought ashore at Jamestown, Virginia, from a "Dutch man of Warr." They apparently serve as indentured servants for a term of years.

1626

• The Dutch West India Company imports 11 black male slaves into New Netherlands.

1629

• In the charter of the New Netherlands, the Dutch West India Company promises "to supply the colonists with as many Blacks as they conveniently can."

1636

• The first American slave vessel, the *Desire,* is built and launched at Marblehead, Massachusetts.

1638

• *December 10:* At Salem, Massachusetts, Capt. W. Pierce exchanges a group of captive Pequot Indian warriors for "salt, cotton, tobacco, and Negroes."

1641

• A Virginia court in *re Negro John Punch* sentences three runaway servants, adding one year to the indentures of the two white men but sentencing the black to lifetime service.

The first blacks land at Jamestown in 1619. *(Library of Congress)*

• Massachusetts sanctions slavery for captives taken in "just" wars, strangers sold into slavery, and individuals required by the colonial authorities to be sold into servitude.

• A Virginia court allows John Graweere, a "negro servant," to purchase his child from the owner of the child's mother, in order to raise the child as a Christian.

1642

• Blacks captured by the Dutch from the Spanish try to claim their freedom in New Amsterdam but are sold into slavery.

1644

• The Dutch Bureau of Accounts suggests to the West India Company that it allow the colonists to import into New Netherlands as many blacks as they can pay cash for.

1645

• Virginian A. Vanga emancipates a number of slaves in his will.

1646

• Francis Potts sells a black woman and child to Stephen Carlton, "to the use of him forever."

1659

• A Virginia law reduces taxes on exporting tobacco whenever slaves are traded for tobacco.

1661

• A treaty between the Dutch and the English provides for the delivery of 2,000–3,000 hogsheads of tobacco annually in return for slaves and merchandise.

1662

• A Virginia law sets a tax on "all negroes, male and female being imported."

1664

• At the fall of New Netherlands to the British, creating New York and New Jersey, the articles of capitulation recognize slavery as a legal institution.

1678

• Boston merchants sell blacks in Virginia as slaves or indentured servants.

1682

• A law decrees that "all servants brought into Virginia, by sea or land, not being Christians, whether negroes, Moors, mulattoes, or Indians . . . and all Indians, which shall hereafter be sold by neighboring Indians, or any other trafficking with us, as slaves, shall be slaves to all intents and purposes."

1691

• Virginia prohibits freeing a black or mulatto without also providing for her or his transportation out of the state within six months.

1695

• Maryland levies a duty of ten shillings on imported blacks. Several other colonies soon follow suit.

1699

• Virginia sets a tax of 20 shillings for every slave imported.

1702

• Queen Anne directs that the Royal African Company take care that New York have "a constant and sufficient supply of merchantable Negroes, at moderate rates."

1703

• Massachusetts requires masters manumitting slaves to post a bond so that freed slaves will not become public charges.

1706

• Louisiana settlers send a request to France that they be allowed to trade American Indian slaves in the West Indies for black slaves, at the rate of three Indians for two blacks.

1715

• Maryland enacts a law providing that all slaves imported into the province, and their descendants, shall be slaves during their natural lives.

1719

• The first shipment of African slaves lands in Louisiana—about 500 "well-made and healthy negroes" between eight and 30 years old, including some "who know how to cultivate rice."

1723

• Virginia passes an act to limit the importation of slaves.

1730–1750

• The gender ratio of male and female slaves evens out, as more women are imported.
• Slaveholders begin to set an economic value on women slaves' child bearing.

1732

• James Oglethorpe and other officials forbid the importation of slaves into Georgia.

1734

• Virginia again sets a tax on importing slaves.
• A law is drafted, to take effect in 1735, prohibiting slavery in Georgia. It will be widely disregarded.

1735

• The first major petition for legal slavery in Georgia is sent to London.

1749

• Over the opposition of the Scots of New Inverness, Georgia, trustees permit the importation of black slaves.

1767

• Members of the Virginia House of Burgesses, meeting as a private body, boycott the British slave trade, resolving "[t]hat they will not import any Slaves or purchase any imported, after the First day of *November* next, until the said Acts of Parliament [the Townshend Acts] are repealed." Similar boycotts are soon adopted in South Carolina, Georgia, and North Carolina.

1770

• King George III instructs the governor of Virginia "upon pain of the highest displeasure, to assent to no law by which the importation of slaves should be in any respect prohibited or obstructed."

1772

• The Virginia House of Burgesses tells George III that "the importation of slaves into the colonies from the coast of Africa hath long been considered a trade of great inhumanity, and under its present encouragement, we have too much reason to fear will endanger the very existence of your Majesty's American dominions."

1774

• The First Continental Congress suspends trade with Great Britain, providing that Americans will not import slaves or buy slaves imported after December 1, "after which time, we will wholly discontinue the slave trade."
• Connecticut forbids anyone to bring slaves into the Colony "to be disposed of, left, or sold."
• The outbreak of open hostilities with England shuts down the international American slave trade until the end of the American Revolution.
• *August:* The Provincial Convention in North Carolina resolves "[t]hat we will not import any slave or slaves, or purchase any slave or slaves imported or brought into the Province by others . . . after the first day of November next."

1776

• The Second Continental Congress votes "[t]hat no slaves be imported into any of the thirteen United Colonies."

1778

• Virginia abolishes the importation of blacks into the state.

1779

• Rhode Island forbids residents to purchase slaves for removal from the state or to remove them from the state without their consent.

1782

• Virginia encourages private manumissions by removing earlier restrictions; most southern colonies soon follow suit.

1785

• New York prohibits the importation of slaves and passes manumission acts, stating that masters freeing slaves need no longer post 200 pounds' security to prevent their becoming dependent on the community.

1787

• The Northwest Ordinance provides that "there shall be neither slavery nor involuntary servitude in the said territory [the Northwest Territory] otherwise than in punishment of crimes."
• South Carolina closes its overseas and domestic slave trade.
• Delaware passes legislation to regulate slave trading to other states, especially the trade in kidnapped free blacks.
• North Carolina lays a prohibitive duty on slaves imported from Africa.
• Rhode Island prohibits its residents from participating in the slave trade—without much effect.

1788

• Connecticut and Massachusetts prohibit their residents from participating in the slave trade.
• South Carolina decides to permit the continuation of its domestic slave trade.

1789

• Maryland refuses the request of a group of Quakers to prohibit the exportation of slaves.

1791

• Massachusetts courts find the brigantine *Hope,* John Stanton, master, guilty of violating the statute against participation in the international slave trade.

1792

- Inhabitants of Beaufort, South Carolina, petition against the practice of northerners who "have for a number of years past been in the habit of shipping to these Southern States, slaves, who are scandalously infamous and incorrigible."

1794

- Congress prohibits the slave trade between the United States and any foreign place or country.

1798

- Georgia prohibits the international slave trade.

1799–1804

- The federal government prosecutes a series of cases against Rhode Island slave traders, with limited success.

1800

- Congress places restrictions on the international slave trade, forbidding citizens and residents any interest in vessels engaged in carrying slaves from one foreign place to another.

1803

- South Carolina bans the importation of slaves from the French West Indies, for fear they may instigate a rebellion.
- South Carolina opens a port for the importation of slaves from Africa.

1804

- The United States forbids the importation of blacks from foreign territory into the Louisiana Purchase after October 1.

1806

- Virginia requires that manumitted slaves leave the state within 12 months.

1807–1808

- The United States prohibits the importation of slaves, on penalty of fine, imprisonment, and loss of ships and cargoes; captured smuggled slaves are to be disposed of according to state law.

1816

- Mexican revolutionary Manuel Herrera creates a government at Galveston, which begins smuggling slaves into Louisiana.

1817

- Jean Lafitte begins capturing Spanish slave ships and selling them in Galveston, whence slaves are smuggled into the United States.
- Georgia officially bans the slave trade.

1819

- Virginia and North Carolina remove restraints on interstate slave trade.
- Congress passes an anti–slave trade act, providing that Africans illegally taken from Africa and recaptured by the U.S. government be returned to the coast of Africa, there to be looked after by U.S. agents. The act prompts President James Monroe to send out agents to selected African territories for this purpose.
- The United States sends a squadron to the coast of Africa to suppress the slave trade illegally carried on by American vessels.

1820

- The United States forces Jean Lafitte out of slave trading.

1826

- Pennsylvania passes a personal liberty or antikidnapping law, penalizing anyone who shall "take or carry away from the State any negro with the intention of selling him as a slave, or of detaining or causing to be detained such negro as a slave for life."

1827

- Tennessee officially bans the slave trade.
- *September 15:* The Texas congress decrees that state records of slaves be kept and that a tenth of the slaves belonging to any estate passed along by inheritance be freed.
- *November:* The Texas congress provides that slaves may be sold from one owner to another.

1832

- Alabama removes restraints on the interstate slave trade.

1833

- Kentucky forbids residents (except immigrants) to buy and import slaves even for their own use, unless those slaves are acquired "by will, descent, distribution, or marriage, or gift in consideration of marriage."

1834

- Louisiana removes restraints on the interstate slave trade.

1835

- The *Enterprise*, en route between Alexandria, Virginia, and Charleston, South Carolina, with about 75 slaves, is driven by a storm to Bermuda, where the slaves are freed.
- Spain and Great Britain sign a treaty giving British cruisers authority to seize Spanish vessels suspected of carrying slaves.

1836

- The provisional government of Texas makes it unlawful "for any free negro or mulatto to come within the limits of Texas"; violators are to be sold at auction.

1839

- Slaves stage a successful mutiny on the *Amistad*, which lands in an American port.

1841

- Slaves aboard the *Creole*, en route from Virginia to Louisiana, mutiny under the leadership of Madison Washington and take the ship to Nassau.
- The U.S. Supreme Court declares the Africans of the *Amistad* free men.

1842

- The Ashburton Treaty with Great Britain requires the United States to keep near the coast of Africa a naval force adequate to suppress the slave trade.

1843

- Commodore Matthew Perry is sent to the African coast with four vessels to suppress the slave trade, but slavers often evade this force.

1846

- Mississippi removes restraints on the interstate slave trade.

1848

- South Carolina removes restraints on the interstate slave trade.

1849

- Kentucky removes restraints on the interstate slave trade.

1850

- Maryland removes restraints on the interstate slave trade.

1855

- Tennessee and Georgia remove restraints on the interstate slave trade.

Young black men await auction in the Charleston open-air slave market. *(Crowe,* With Thackeray in America*)*

1858

• *December:* The slaver *Wanderer* illegally lands about 420 African slaves near Brunswick, Georgia.

1859

• The secretary of the navy reports the capture of 11 slave ships by U.S. warships.

1860

• Manumissions reportedly number some 3,000.

• *July:* The slaver *Clotilde* illegally delivers 103 slaves into Mobile Bay, whence they are transshipped up the Alabama River.

1861

• Texas, now a member of the Confederacy, absolutely prohibits manumission.

Eyewitness Testimony

Breeding for Profit

And I Shd. [should] Be obliged to Yr. Excellency, for advising those who may be concerned for me, in such Encrease of Negroes, not so much to Consult my most Immediate Profit, as to render the Negroes I now have happy and contented, wch [which] I know they cannot be without having each a Wife. . . . [T]ho the Women will not work all together so well as ye [the] Men, Yet Amends will be sufficiently made in a very few years by the Great Encrease of Children who may easily [be] traind up and become faithfully attached to the Glebe and to their Master.

The earl of Egmont, 1769, in Littlefield,
Rice and Slaves, *65.*

The exportation [of slaves from Virginia to other southern states] has averaged 8,500 for the last twenty years. . . . It is a practice, and an increasing practice in parts of Virginia, to rear slaves for market. How can an honorable mind, a patriot, and a lover of his country, bear to see this ancient dominion . . . converted into one grand menagerie where men are to be reared for market like oxen for the shambles[?]

Thomas Jefferson Randolph to the Virginia House of Delegates, January 21, 1832, in Bancroft, Slave Trading, *69–70.*

Massa, he bring some more women to see me. He wouldn't let me have jus' one woman. I have 'bout fifteen and I don't know how many children. Some over a hunerd, I's sho'.

Ex-slave Elige Davison, in Tadman, Speculators and Slaves, *123.*

Buying Oneself

[Ellen] having been found to be a remarkably steady and industrious woman . . . the extraordinary character of the said petitioner and her husband induced her master about two years ago when she was likely to be separated from her husband, in consequence of the removal of her master . . . to encourage her in her endeavouring to raise money by subscription to purchase herself and her . . . child. The master subscribed a considerable sum for this purpose and many of your petitioners also subscribed. By this means and by her own indefatigable efforts and industry she has raised money sufficient for the purchase of herself and her child Ellen.

Petition to the state of Virginia, 1815, in Johnston, Race Relations, *7.*

My uncles paid fifteen hundred dollars apiece for themselves. They bought themselves three times. They got cheated out of their freedom in the first instance, and were put in jail at one time, and were going to be sold down South, right away; but parties who were well acquainted with us, and knew we had made desperate struggles for our freedom, came forward and advanced the money, and took us out of jail, and put us on a footing so that we could go ahead and earn money to pay the debt. . . . My uncles bought me and my mother, as well as themselves. . . . I had a grandfather who had long been free, and when the boys grew up, he would take them and learn them a trade, and keep them out of the hands of the traders. . . .

Gutman, Black Family, *203–4.*

Coffles

The next morning but one we started with this negro trader upon that dreaded and despairing journey [from North Carolina] to the cotton fields of Georgia. . . . A long row of men chained two-and-two together, called the "coffle," and numbering about thirty persons, was the first to march forth from the "pen"; then came the quiet slaves—that is, those who were tame in spirit and degraded; then came the unmarried women, or those without children; after these came the children who were able to walk; and following them came mothers with their infants and young children in their arms.

This "gang" of slaves was arranged in travelling order, all being on foot except the children that were too young to walk and too old to be carried in arms. These latter were put into a waggon. But mothers with infants had to carry them in their arms; and their blood often stained the whip when, from exhaustion, they lagged behind. When the order was given to march, it was always on such occasions accompanied by the command, which the slaves were made to understand before they left the "pen," to "strike up lively," which means that they must begin a song.

[T]he negroes, who have very little hope of ever seeing those again who are dearer to them than life, and who are weeping and wailing over the separation, often turn the song thus demanded into a farewell dirge.

Sella Martin in Blassingame, Slave Testimony, *704–5.*

In the afternoon, before one of these gangs was sent off, a very dark woman was brought [in] with quite a light-colored baby. One of the traders asked the owner, likewise a trader, what he was going to do with that brat. "D—d if I know" , was the reply. "I'm bothered to know what to do with it."—"We can't take it in the wagons and have it squalling all the way!"—"Here," said the owner to an inhabitant of Platte City, who just then came in with a boy for sale, "don't you want this thing? You may have it for twenty-five dollars. D—n it," he continued, snatching the babe from its mother's arms by the shoulder and hefting it, "it weighs twenty-five pounds! Will you take it?"—"Yes."—"Take it now."—And the child was carried off amid the heart-rending shrieks and pleadings of the agonized mother.

John Doy, in Bancroft, Slave Trading, *137, n. 38.*

[The trader] has [in his coffle] about 16 fellows, seven boys, the balance women and girls, except one child. . . . He has 12 fellows in the chain all of which jumping Jinny [the trader's wife] drives before her. She carries up the rear armed and equipped in a style which reduces it to a certainty that if life lasts you will see her in Montgomery.

Letter to Isaac Jarratt, March 3, 1834, in Tadman, Speculators and Slaves, *76.*

Domestic Slave Trade

[Wanted:] One hundred Negroes, from 20 to 30 years old, for which a good price will be given. They are to be sent out of state, therefore we shall not be particular respecting the character of any of them—Hearty and well made is all that is necessary.

1787 advertisement by Moses Austin in Richmond, Virginia, in Tadman, Speculators and Slaves, *15.*

[In 1799 a shortage of $10,000 in the Georgia treasury led to the discovery that a Mr. Sims, a member of the legislature, had "borrowed" the money and commissioned one Speers to buy slaves in Virginia.] Speers accordingly went and purchased a considerable number of negroes; and on his way returning to this state the negroes rose and cut the throat of Speers and another man who accompanied him. The slaves fled, and about ten of them, I think, were killed. In consequence of this misfortune Mr. Sims was rendered unable to raise the money at the time the legislature met.

Charleston *(S.C.)* City Gazette, *December 21, 1799, in Phillips,* American Negro Slavery, *189.*

A slave woman is sold by the pound. *(Library of Congress)*

I took your Negroe George some time ago home, thinking I might be the better able to Sell him: who after beening [being] with me a night behaved himself in such an Insolent manner I immediately remanded [him] back to the Gaol [jail]. About a Week since [ago] I put him up at Public Sale at Christopher Witman's Tavern, where there was a Number of Persons who inclined to Purchase him. But he protested publicly that he would not be sold, and if Any one should purchase him he wou'd be the Death of him and Words to the like purpose which deter'd the people from biding [bidding].

Trader George Nagel, in Wax, "Negro Resistance," 14.

The enterprising and go-ahead Colonel Jennings has got a raffle under way now. . . . [The prizes are] the celebrated trotting horse "Star," buggy and harness . . . [and a] stout mulatto girl "Sarah," aged about twenty years, general house servant.

The New Orleans True Delta, *in Bancroft,* Slave Trading, *328.*

Dear Sir. The demand brisk for likely Negroes

Extra No. 1 men	$1500
No. 1 "	$14–1475
Extra No. 1 fieldgirls	$13–1350
No. 1 "	$12–1275
Likely ploughboys 17 and 18	$12–1350
" " 15 and 16	$1050–1175
" " 12 to 14	$850–1050
Likely girls 14 and 15	$1000–1150
" " 12 and 13	$850–1000
Girls 10 and 11	$700–825
No. 1 woman and child	$1250–1350

Families rather dull [not in demand] and hard to sell
Yours respectfully, Dickinson, Hill & Company

Circular, December 20, 1858, in Tadman,
Speculators and Slaves, 61.

Fancy Girls

[In 1710 a pastor denounced Louisianians for] maintain[ing] scandalous concubinages with young Indian women, driven by their proclivity for the extremes of licentiousness. They have bought them under the pretext of keeping them as servants, but actually to seduce them, as they in fact have done.

Usner, "American Indians," 107.

[In 1854 in Lexington, Kentucky, I visited] a negro jail—a very large brick building with all the conveniences of comfortable life, including hospital. 'Tis a place where negroes are kept for sale. Outer doors and windows all protected with iron grates, but inside the appointments are not only comfortable, but in many respects luxurious. Many of the rooms are well carpeted and furnished, and very neat, and the inmates whilst here are treated with great indulgence and humanity, but I confess it impressed me with the idea of decorating the ox for the sacrifice. In several of the rooms I found very handsome mulatto women, of fine persons and easy genteel manners, sitting at their needle work awaiting a purchaser. The proprietor made them get up and turn around to show to advantage their finely developed and graceful forms.

Kentuckian Orville H. Browning, describing slave women to be
sold as "fancy girls," in Bancroft, Slave Trading, 130–31.

Kidnapping

In many cases [in Delaware], whole families of free colored people have been attacked in the night, beaten *nearly* to death with clubs, gagged and bound, and dragged into distant and hopeless captivity, leaving no traces behind, except the blood from their wounds. . . .

. . . A monster in human shape, was detected in the city of Philadelphia, pursuing the occupation of courting and marrying mulatto women, and selling them as slaves. . . . They have lately invented a method of attaining their object, through the instrumentality of the laws:—Having selected a suitable free colored person, . . . the kidnapper employs a confederate, to ascertain the distinguishing marks of his body; he then claims and obtains him as a slave, before a magistrate, by describing those marks, and proving the truth of his assertions, by his well-instructed accomplice.

Philadelphian Dr. Torrey, 1817, in Child, Appeal, 34–35.

A colored man and a fugitive slave [in New Bedford, Massachusetts,] were on unfriendly terms. The former was heard to threaten the latter with informing his master of his whereabouts. Straightway a meeting was called among the colored people under the stereotyped notice, "Business of importance!" The betrayer was invited to attend. The people came at the appointed hour, and organized the meeting by appointing a very religious old gentleman as president, who, I believe, made a prayer, after which he addressed the meeting as follows: *"Friends, we have got him here, and I would recommend that you young men just take him outside the door, and kill him!"* With this, a number of them bolted at him; but they were intercepted by some more timid than themselves, and the betrayer escaped their vengeance, and has not been seen in New Bedford since.

Frederick Douglass, reminiscing about his experiences of
1835–1836, in Narrative, 117.

Whites kidnap free blacks to sell them into slavery. *(Library of Congress)*

The nigger stealers done stole me and my mammy outen the Choctaw Nation, up in the Indian Territory, when I was 'bout three years old. Brother Knox, Sis Hannah, and my mammy and her two stepchildren was down on the river washing. The nigger stealers driv up in a big carriage, and mammy just thought nothing, 'cause the ford was near there and people going on the road stopped to water the horses and rest awhile in the shade. Bimeby [by and by], a man coaxes the two biggest children to the carriage and give them some kind of candy. Other children sees this and goes, too. Two other men was walking round smoking and getting closer to mammy all the time. When he can, the man in the carriage got the two big stepchildren in with him, and me and Sis climb in too, to see how come. Then the man holler, "Git the old one and let's git from here." With that the two big men grab Mammy, and she fought and screeched and bit and cry, but they hit her on the head with something and drug her in and throwed her on the floor. The big children began to fight for Mammy, but one of the men hit 'em hard, and off they driv, with the horses under whip.

. . . Down in Louisian' us was put on what they call the block and sold to the highest bidder. My mammy and her three children brung $3,000 flat. The stepchildren was sold to somebody else.

Spence Johnson, born free about 1859, in Botkin, Lay My Burden Down, *157.*

Manumission

YANIMEROW IN THE RIVER GAMBIA Jan: 27th: [1735/6]

Sir, This is to acquaint you of my safe arrival at and return here from Bonda being conducted safe and used with great civility all the way, which was owing to the respect and regard all the natives in every part have for the Company and by being conducted by one white man only which was the Governors nephew on the Companys behalf which made no little noise and was of much service to me, one of my wives had got another husband in my room and the other gave me over, my father died soon after my misfortune of being seized and sold for a slave, but my children are all well. . . .

Job Ben Solomon, letter, in Blassingame, Slave Testimony, *5. Solomon was freed from slavery through the offices of Gov. James Oglethorpe of Georgia.*

A Negro slave named Kitt, owned by Hinchia Mabry . . . has rendered meritorious service in making the first information against several counterfeiters, and is hereby emancipated and his owner ordered paid 1,000 pounds out of the public treasury.

1779 Act of Virginia legislature, in Higginbotham, In the Matter of Color, *49.*

From a full conviction that slavery is an evil of great magnitude and no less repugnant to the Divine command of doing to others as we would they should do unto us [and] that it is inconsistent with the true interest and prosperity of my country, I did confirm freedom to all the Negroes that by law, I had property in by a Deed of Emancipation bearing date the first of the 8th month, 1782, duely acknowledged and admitted to record in the Clerk's office of Henrico County, . . . but as it is still necessary that those who are ancient and incapable of getting a living (being over forty-five years of age at the time of emancipation) should be supported, I now desire and direct it to be done and that the young ones may have learning sufficient to enable them to transact the common affairs of life for that purpose I have had a Schoolhouse put on my land called Gravely hills tract containing by estimation 350 acres the use and profits whereof I give for that purpose forever, or so long as the Monthly Meeting of Friends in this County may think it necessary for the benefit of the children and descendants of those who have been emancipated by me, or other black children whom they may think proper to admit; reserving only to my heirs hereafter named the priviledge of cutting timber occasionally for building. . . .

Will of Robert Pleasants, 1800, in Journal of Negro History 2 (1917): 329–30.

No Northern man began the world with more enthusiasm against slavery than I did. For forty years and upwards, I have felt the greatest desire to see Maryland become a free State, and the strongest conviction that she could become so. . . . No slave State adjacent to a free State can continue so. . . .

I have emancipated seven of my slaves. They have done pretty well, and six of them, now alive, are supporting themselves comfortably and creditably. Yet I cannot but see that this is all they are doing now; and, when age and infirmity come upon them, they will probably suffer. It is to be observed, also, that these were selected individuals, who were, with two exceptions, brought up with a view to their being so disposed of, and were made to undergo a probation of a few years in favorable situations, and, when emancipated, were far better fitted for the duties and trials of their new condition than the general mass of slaves. Yet I am still a slaveholder, and could not, without the greatest inhumanity, be otherwise. I own, for instance, an old slave, who has done no work for me for years. I pay his board and other expenses, and cannot believe that I sin in doing so. The laws of Maryland contain provisions of various kinds, under which slaves, in certain circumstances, are entitled to petition the courts for their freedom. As a lawyer, I always undertook these cases with peculiar zeal, and have been thus instrumental in liberating several large families and many individuals. I cannot remember more than two instances, out of this large number, in which it did not appear that the freedom I so earnestly sought for them was their ruin.

Francis Scott Key, 1838 letter to Benjamin Tappan, in Fox, American Colonization Society, *17–18.*

SAMUEL MARTIN, a man of color, and the oldest resident of Port Gibson, Mississippi, emancipated six of his slaves in 1844, bringing them to Cincinnati where he believed they would have a better opportunity to start life anew. These were two mulatto women with their four quadroon children, the color of whom well illustrated the moral condition of that State, in that each child had a different father and they retained few marks of their partial African descent. Mr. Martin was himself a slave until 1829. He purchased his freedom for a large sum most of which he earned by taking time from sleep for work. Thereafter he acquired considerable property. He was not a slave holder in the southern sense of that word. His purpose was to purchase his fellowmen in bondage that he might give them an opportunity to become free.

Cincinnati Morning Herald,
June 1, 1844, quoted in Journal of African History 3
(1918): 91.

Migrations

Mississippi is ruined. Her rich men are poor and her poor men are beggars. . . . The people are running their Negroes to Texas and Alabama and leaving their real estate and perishable property to be sold. So great is the [economic] panic and so dreadful the distress that there are a great many farms prepared to receive crops, and some of them actually planted, and yet deserted. . . .

North Carolingian, *1840, in Buckmaster,* Let My People Go, *101.*

On the Emigrant Road into Texas: . . . We overtook, several times in the course of each day, the slow emigrant trains, for which this road, though less frequented than years

ago, is still [in the 1850s] a chief thoroughfare. . . . Several families were frequently moving together, coming from the same district, or chance met and joined, for company, on the long road from Alabama, Georgia, or the Carolinas. . . . As you get by, the white mother and babies, and the tall, frequently ill-humoured master, on horseback, or walking with his gun, urging up the black driver and his oxen. As a scout ahead, is a brother, or an intelligent slave, with the best gun, on the look-out for a deer or a turkey. . . . They travel ten or fifteen miles a day, stopping wherever night overtakes them. The masters are plainly dressed, often in home-spun, keeping their eyes about them, noticing the soil, sometimes making a remark on the crops by the roadside; but generally dogged, surly, and silent. The women are silent too, frequently walking, to relieve the teams; and weary, haggard, mud be-draggled, forlorn, and disconsolate, yet hopeful and careful. The negroes, mud-incrusted, wrapped in old blankets or gunny-bags, suffering from cold, plod on, aimless, hopeless, thoughtless, more indifferent, apparently, than the oxen, to all about them.

Olmsted, Cotton Kingdom, *284–86.*

Sales of Slaves

EXECUTORS' SALE.—Agreeable to an order of the Court of Wilkinson County, will be sold on the first Tuesday of April next, before the Court-House door in the town of Irwington, ONE NEGRO GIRL, about *two years old,* named Rachel, belonging to the estate of William Chambers, deceased. Sold for the benefit of the *heirs* and CREDITORS of said estate.

Samuel Bell,
Jesse Peacock. *Executors.*
Advertisement in the Milledgeville Journal, *December 26, 1837, quoted in* Goodell, *Slave Code, 66.*

[The slaves] were dressed in every possible variety of uncouth and fantastic garb, in every style and of every imaginable color; the texture of the garments was in all cases coarse, most of the men being clothed in the rough cloth that is made expressly for the slaves. . . . The women, true to the feminine instinct, had made, in almost every case, some attempt at finery. All wore gorgeous turbans, generally manufactured in an instant out of a gay-colored handkerchief by a sudden and graceful twist of the fingers; though there was occasionally a more elaborate turban, a turban complex and mysterious, got up with care, and ornamented with a few beads or bright bits of ribbon. Their dresses were mostly coarse stuff, though there were some gaudy calicos; a few had ear-rings, and one possessed the treasure of a string of yellow and blue beads. The little children were always better and more carefully dressed than the older ones, the parental pride coming out in the shape of a yellow cap pointed like a mitre, or a jacket with a strip of red broadcloth round the bottom. The children were of all sizes, the youngest being fifteen days old. . . .

The negroes were examined with as little consideration as if they had been brutes indeed; the buyers pulling their mouths open to see their teeth, pinching their limbs to find how muscular they were, walking them up and down to detect any signs of lameness, making them stoop and bend in different ways that they might be certain there was no concealed rupture or wound; and in addition to all this treatment, asking them scores of questions relative to their qualifications and accomplishments. All these humiliations were submitted to without a murmur, and in some instances with good-natured cheerfulness—where the slave liked the appearance of the proposed buyer, and fancied that he might prove a kind "Mas'r."

The auctioneer . . . is a rollicking old boy, with an eye ever to the look-out, and that never lets a bidding nod escape him; a hearty word for every bidder who cares for it, and plenty of jokes to let off when the business gets a little slack. Mr. Walsh has a florid complexion, . . . possibly not more so than is natural in a whiskey country. Not only is his face red, but his skin has been taken off in spots by blisters of some sort, giving him a peely look; so that, taking his face all in all, the peeliness and the redness combined, he looks much as if he had been boiled in the same pot with a red cabbage.

Report by "Doesticks" (Mortimer Thompson) of a sale in Savannah, in the New York Daily Tribune, *March 9, 1859.*

Pierce Butler has gone to Georgia to be present at the sale of his Negroes. It is highly honorable to him that he did all he could to prevent the sale, offering to make any personal sacrifice to avoid it. But it cannot be avoided, and by the sale he will be able to keep Butler Place & have a fortune of 2 or 300,000 dollars, after paying his debts. . . . It is a dreadful affair, however, selling these hereditary

Slaves wait for buyers in a slave trader's shop. *(Crowe,* With Thackeray in America*)*

Negroes. There are 900 of them belonging to the estate, a little community who have lived for generations on the plantation, among whom, therefore, all sorts of relations of blood & friendship are established. Butler's half, 450, to be sold at public auction & scattered over the South. Families will not be separated, that is to say, husbands & wives, parents & young children. But brothers & sisters of mature age, parents & children of mature age, all other relations & the ties of home & long association will be violently severed. It will be a hard thing for Butler to witness and it is a monstrous thing to do.

Sidney George Fisher, diary entry for February 17, 1859, in A Philadelphia Perspective, *317.*

I saw slaves sold. I can see that old block now. My cousin Eliza was a pretty girl, really good-looking. Her master was her father. When the girls in the big house had beaus coming to see 'em, they'd ask, "Who is that pretty gal?" So they decided to git rid of her right away. The day they sold her will always be remembered. They stripped her to be bid off and looked at. I wasn't allowed to stand in the crowd. I was laying down under a big bush. The man that bought Eliza was from New York. The Negroes had made up 'nough money to buy her off theyself, but they wouldn't let that happen. There was a man bidding for her who was a Swedelander. He always bid for the good-looking colored gals and bought 'em for his own use. He ask the man from New York, 'What you gonna do with her when you git her?" The man from New York said, "None of your damn business, but you ain't got money 'nough to buy her." When the man from New York had done bought her, he said, "Eliza, you are free from now on." She left and went to New York with him. Mama and Eliza both cried when she was being showed off, and Master told 'em to shut up before he knocked their brains out.

Ex-slave Doc Daniel Dowdy, in Botkin, Lay My Burden Down, *155.*

Separation of Families

I have . . . heard you have lost some of your Small Negroes by death, do when you write inform me which of them are dead. I have to inform you that I have had one child since I last Saw you, his Name is Joshua, you will please to tell my Sister Clary not to Let my poor children Suffer & tell her she must also write & inform me how she & my children are. . . . Mr. Miller is now on the brink of death, & is about to sell 40 of his Negroes and it is likely [my husband] Joshua may be one. I wish to Stay with

Him as long as possible as you must know its very bad to part man & wife. I should be glad to no [know] what sort of a life Clary leads. . . . be pleased to inform me how my little daughter Judith is & if she is now injoying health. I have no more at present only my best wishes to all my friends & relations and Except my warmest Love & friendship for your Self. . . .

Letter of November 30, 1807, from Virginia slave Gooley to her former owner, who had moved to Kentucky, taking some of Gooley's children and other relatives with her, in Gutman, Black Family, *184.*

It would certainly have been harsh to separate these four boys, and sever ties which bind even slaves together. True, it must be done, if the executor discovers that the interest of the estate requires it; for he is not to indulge his charities at the expense of others.

Chief Justice Ruffin of North Carolina, first half of the 19th century, in Judicial Cases 2:59.

Dear Husband I write you a letter to let you know my distress my master has sold albert to a trader on Monday court day and the other child is for sale also and I want you to let [me] hear from you very soon before next cort if you can I don't know when don't want you to wait till Christmas I want you to tell dr Hamelton and your master if either will buy me they can attend to it know [now] and then I can go afterwards I don't want a trader to get me they asked me if I had got any person to buy me and I told them no they took me in the court house too they never put me up a man buy the name of brady bought albert and is gone I don't know where they say he lives in Scottesville my things is in several places some is in staunton and if I should be sold I don't know what will become of them I don't expect to meet with the luck to get that way till I am quite heartsick nothing more I am and ever will be your kind wife.

Maria Perkins of Charlottesville, 1852 letter to Richard Perkins, in Gutman, Black Family, *35.*

[The slaves] said that "when your child dies you know where it is, but when he is sold away, you never know what may happen to him."

Northern traveler, 1866, in Gutman, Black Family, *193.*

Slave Jails

I may as well describe here the order of the daily proceedings, as during the whole time I remained in the pen [in

New Orleans], they were, one day with the other, pretty much the same. . . .

As may be imagined, the slaves are bought from all parts, are of all sorts, sizes, and ages, and arrive at various states of fatigue and condition; but they soon improve in their looks, as they are regularly fed and have plenty to eat. As soon as we were roused in the morning, there was a general washing, and combing, and shaving, pulling out of grey hairs, and dying the hair of those who were too grey to be plucked without making them bald. When this was over—and it was no light business—we used to breakfast, getting bread and bacon, and coffee, of which a sufficiency was given us, that we might plump up and become sleek. Bob [a mulatto assistant of the trader] would then proceed to instruct us on how to show ourselves off, and afterwards form us into companies, according to size; those who were nearly the same height and make being put into separate lots; the men, the women, and the children of both sexes, being divided off alike. In consequence of this arrangement, the various members of a family were of necessity separated, and would often see the last of each other in that dreadful showroom. . . .

The buying commenced at about ten in the morning, and lasted till one, during which time we were obliged to be sitting about in our respective companies ready for inspection. At one we used to go to dinner, our usual food being a repetition of the morning meal, varied with vegetables, and a little fruit sometimes. After dinner we were compelled to walk, and dance, and kick about in the yard, for exercise; and Bob, who had a fiddle, used to play up jigs for us to dance to. If we did not dance to his fiddle, we used to have to do so to his whip, so no wonder we used our legs handsomely, though the music was none of the best. When our exercises were over, we used to be "sized out" again, ready for the afternoon sale, which commenced at three, and ended at six. This over, we had tea, and were then free to do what we liked in the pen, until Bob rang us off to bed at ten.

Ex-slave John Brown, in Tadman, Speculators and Slaves, *98–99.*

[At Lumpkin's Jail] I entered a large open court. Against one of the posts sat a good natured fat man, with his chair tipped back. It was Mr. Lumpkin. I duly introduced myself as from New York, remarking that I had read what the Abolitionists had to say, and that I had come to Richmond [Virginia] to see for myself. Mr. Lumpkin received me courteously and showed me over his jail. On one side of the open court was a large tank for washing, or lavato-

ry. Opposite was a long, two-story brick house, the lower part fitted up for men and the second story for women. The place, in fact, was a kind of hotel or boardinghouse for negro-traders and their slaves. I was invited to dine at a large table with perhaps twenty traders, who gave me almost no attention, and there was little conversation. They were probably strangers to one another.

Otis Bigelow, describing a visit in the 1850s, in Bancroft, Slave Trading, *102–3.*

The Sugar House of Charleston [South Carolina] is a building created for the purpose of punishing and selling slaves in. I visited it. It is simply a prison with a treadmill, a work yard, putrid privies, whipping posts and a *brine barrel* attached. There are, I think, three corridors. Many of the cells are perfectly dark. They are all very small. . . .

If a planter arrives in the city with a lot of slaves for sale, he repairs to the Sugar House and places them in custody, and there they are kept until disposed of, as usual—"by auction for cash to the highest bidder."

If any slaveholder, from any or from no cause, desires to punish his human property, but is too sensitive, or what is far more probable, too lazy to inflict the chastisement himself—he takes *it* (the man, woman, or child), to the Sugar House, and simply orders *how* he desires it to be punished; and, without any trial—without any questions asked or explanations given, the command is implicitly obeyed by the officers of the institution. A small sum is paid for the board of the incarcerated.

If any colored person is found out of doors after ten o'clock at night, without a ticket of leave from its owner, the unfortunate wanderer is taken to the Sugar House and kept there till morning; when, if the master pays one dollar fine, the slave is liberated; but, if he refuses to do so, the prisoner is tied hand and foot and lashed before he or she is set at liberty.

Redpath, Roving Editor, *60.*

Slave Traders

Mr. Whitehead [a former slave trader] is a gentleman of great intelligence, high minded and honorable. He possesses fine business qualities, an energetic character, persevering and laborious habits and great moral worth.

Memorandum from members of the Virginia legislature to President James Polk, late 1840s, in Tadman, Speculators and Slaves, *197.*

[T]he most utterly detestable of all southern Yankees is the Negro Trader—Speculator he delights to call himself in late years. . . . [He stands] pre-eminent in villainy and a greedy love of filthy lucre. . . . The natural result of their calling seems to be to corrupt; for they have usually to deal with the most refractory and brutal of the slave population, since good and honest slaves are rarely permitted to fall into the unscrupulous clutches of the speculator. . . . [Of his stock] nearly nine-tenths [are] vicious ones sold for crimes or misdemeanors, or otherwise diseased ones sold because of their worthlessness as property. These he purchases at about half what healthy and honest slaves would cost him; but he sells them as both honest and healthy, mark you.

Southerner David Hundley, 1860, quoted in Tadman, Speculators and Slaves, *183.*

[T]hey was 258 niggers out of them nigger yards in Memphis [Tennessee] what gits on that boat. They puts the niggers upstairs and goes down the river far as Vicksburg [Mississippi], that was the place, and then us gits offen the boat and gits on the train 'gain and that time we goes to New Orleans.

They has three big trader yard in New Orleans. . . . We hears some of 'em say there's gwine to throw a long war, and us all think what they buy us for if we's gwine to be sot free. . . .

They have big sandbars and planks fix round the nigger yards, and they have watchmans to keep them from running 'way in de swamp. Some of the niggers they have just picked up on the road, they steals them. They calls them "wagon boy" and "wagon gal." . . . You sees, if they could steal the niggers and sell 'em for the good money, them traders could make plenty money that way.

Ex-slave Betty Simmons, in Botkin, Lay My Burden Down, *158.*

[His master, having recaptured Louis Talbert, who had not only escaped twice but also led many other slaves to freedom, dared not put him to work among his oth-

er slaves but sold him to a trader, from whom he again escaped.] The slavetrader was much enraged when he discovered his loss and blamed the captain of the [Mississippi River] boat for having his yawl [with which Talbert made his escape] where it was so easy of access. When they arrived at Memphis, he sued the captain for the price of his slave, contending that the captain was responsible for the loss of his property. The trader lost the suit and had the costs to pay, then the captain sued him for the detention of the boat, and gained the suit, and the trader had to pay seven hundred dollars. Then the captain sued him for the value of the yawl which his slave had carried off and got judgment against him, which it is said cost him seven hundred dollars more.

Coffin, Reminiscences, *156.*

Voluntary Enslavement

Your petitioner respectfully shews unto your worships, that she is desirous of becoming a slave, and for that purpose has selected John Clark for her master, and now makes this public declaration of the same and asks the court that a record may be made of the same according to law, and that she may become the slave and property of said John Clark for life. She further states that this request is made by her of her own free will and accord without any force or compulsion from any one; and she asks that all necessary and proper orders and decrees may be made in the premises, to fully carry out the law in such cases made and provided—that she is now about twenty-eight years old—copper color—weighs about 125 pounds—stout.

Janet Wright's petition, approved August 24, 1861, by the Court of Pleas and Quarter Sessions for Guilford County, North Carolina, in Franklin, "Enslavement of Free Negroes," 423. This action may not have been legal, since Wright later applied unsuccessfully to the state legislature for voluntary enslavement.

CHAPTER FOUR

Slave Life
1619–1865

"The Southern States are an aggregate . . . of communities, not of individuals," wrote John C. Calhoun. "Every plantation is a little community, with the master at its head."[1] That master exercised absolute power over his slaves. Although the law forbade him to kill them *intentionally*, the isolation of the plantation and the legal inability of blacks to testify against whites effectively gave the master the power of life and death.

Slaves born in Africa who came to North America exchanged the temporary chaos and suffering of the Middle Passage for the confusion and hardship of life in a strange land. They did not know where they were. Few if any of the people around them understood what they said, and they understood little or none of what they heard. They were surrounded by strange objects, whose uses they could not imagine. Almost always the slave traders and slave owners who received them treated them as savages to be subdued, workers whose power had to be harnessed, and sources of profit—not as human beings. The slaves had been stripped of their status, their names, their families and friends, and their customs and culture. They were surrounded by fear, distrust, and sometimes hatred. No wonder it was commonplace for newly arrived slaves to try to run away or sink into a deep, sometimes suicidal depression. They stood naked to misery, not knowing what would happen to them.

Slaves who had been born in North America—almost all of them, that is, as time went on—still had a struggle to survive in subjection. Their families could offer them only limited protection against hunger, cold, and separation and almost none against the cruelties of whites and the ever-harsher laws constructed to control blacks.

Ninety-five percent of the slaves lived in rural places, usually raising cotton, sugar, tobacco, and rice.[2] The size of the master's farm or plantation affected every aspect of a slave's life. How closely did the slave live and work with the master and mistress? Would the slave be put to a specialized task or have to combine farm and housework? Would the slave's spouse live on the same plantation or "abroad"? Was the farm or plantation large enough to support a slave community? Would the slave be isolated from other blacks? In the 1850s, most of the 400,000 or so slaveholders owned 10 or fewer slaves—usually only one or two. But the typical slave lived in a community of some 40 slaves—only about a quarter of them in communities as large as 50.[3] The *proportion* of white families owning slaves decreased during the antebellum era, from 36 percent in 1830 to 31 percent in 1850 and 26 percent in 1860.[4]

The relatively few slaves in cities usually lived under somewhat better conditions and more independently than country slaves. "A city slave," wrote Frederick Douglass, "is almost a freeman, compared with a slave on the plantation. He is much better fed and clothed, and enjoys privileges altogether unknown to the slave

These pictures of slave children and wharf hands were drawn from life in contrast to the stereotypes frequent in abolitionist propaganda. *(Crowe,* With Thackeray in America)

on the plantation. There is a vestige of decency, a sense of shame, that does much to curb and check those outbreaks of atrocious cruelty so commonly enacted upon the plantation. He is a desperate slaveholder, who will shock the humanity of his non-slaveholding neighbors with the cries of his lacerated slave. Few are willing to incur the odium attaching to the reputation of being a cruel master; and above all things, they would not be known as not giving a slave enough to eat. There are, however, some painful exceptions to this rule."[5]

Slave Life: Food, Shelter, and Clothing

Slave owners had to regard blacks as their inferiors—how else could they go on calling themselves Christians and professing democracy? Accordingly, they felt called upon to house, clothe, and feed their slaves only sufficiently to enable them to work. An 1846 statement of Louisiana planters of the usual expenses of a sugar plantation shows an annual income of $3,650, with these expenditures:[6]

Household and family expenses $1,000
Overseer's salary 400
Food and clothing for 15 working hands [slaves] at $30 450
Food and clothing for 15 old negroes and [slave] children 250
1-1/2 per cent on capital invested . . . , to keep it in repair 600

How well or badly the slaves lived varied with the wealth or poverty of their owner, his generosity or miserliness, and his understanding of his own economic interests.

On the larger plantations, the overseer typically distributed the slaves' food to heads of families or to unmarried adults once a week, perhaps on Saturday nights—or perhaps in midweek, to prevent them from selling it for whiskey on Sunday. Every night the slaves took the next day's portion to a cookhouse, where a cook prepared two of their daily meals. The slaves ate where they could, near their work, from troughs or gourds, with spoons, shells, or their bare hands. Slave wives and mothers, after a day's hard labor in the fields, might cook their families' evening meal in their cabins: "a bit of bacon fried, often with eggs, corn-bread baked in the spider [frying pan] after the bacon, to absorb the fat, and perhaps some sweet potatoes roasted in the ashes."[7] Diets consisting mainly of rice, fatback, cornmeal, and salt pork rendered slaves vulnerable to blindness, sore eyes, skin irritations, rickets, toothaches, pellagra, beriberi, and scurvy. In 1850 in Louisiana, the life expectancy of a black male at birth was 29 years, of a black female 34 years.[8]

Industrious slaves, if the master permitted, might supplement their diets with vegetables grown on their own small plots, berries picked in the woods, or animals they hunted. Some "stole" from masters; many slaves reasoned that they were entitled to the fruits of their own labor, and others were driven by hunger. Some masters and overseers used food to control the slaves, awarding an extra pound of meat weekly to slaves who had done their work and caused no trouble, or passing out extra rice to those who had picked a given amount of cotton. House slaves could feast on scraps from their master's table—but often they were allowed no time for meals and had to eat in what spare moments they could snatch.

If they were not required to sleep in the bedroom (or just outside its door) of a member of the master's family, or left to find rest where they could, slaves lived in cabins—two families to each cabin. These varied from solid brick structures to the more common plank or log huts, the chinks stuffed perhaps with rags, moss, or red mud. The cabins were usually dark and drafty. Fanny Kemble (a British actress who had married a planter) described those on her husband's plantations as "filthy and wretched in the extreme. . . . Firewood and shavings lay littered about the floors, while the half-naked children were cowering round two or three smouldering cinders. The moss with which the chinks and crannies of their ill-protecting dwelling might have been stuffed was trailing in dirt and dust upon the ground, while the back door of the huts, opening upon a most unsightly ditch, was left wide open for the fowls and ducks, which they are allowed to raise, to travel in and out, increasing the filth of the cabin by what they brought and left in every direction."[9] Slave women were often simply too exhausted after working all day in the fields, or too heavily tasked by their mistresses with weaving in the evenings, to keep their dwellings tidy—though some owners set apart three days a year for housecleaning.

Slave owners furnished slaves every year with either clothes or the material to make them. Pierce Butler, for example, handed out to each slave two pairs of shoes and a few yards of flannel and of another material called "plains," a stiff, heavy, dark gray or blue woolen cloth, rather like carpet. Such materials were intolerable in the hot summers, so the slaves often worked nearly naked—scrambling for cover when a stranger approached. Because no replacements were available if children tore or wore out their clothes—if indeed they received any—many of them also went naked. On some plantations, slave women wove all the materials for clothing and household linens.

Slave Life: Medical Care, Child Care, Care of the Aged

What with the sanitary conditions, the slaves' poor diet, their miserable working situations (particularly on the rice plantations), and their exposure to the weather, they often fell ill. Besides the usual fevers, diseases of malnutrition, and the almost universal rheumatism, they suffered from leprosy, pleurisy, lockjaw, venereal diseases, tuberculosis, and pneumonia. Epidemics of cholera and yellow fever were frequent. Hard labor too late in pregnancy or while nursing and inadequate care during childbirth left women who survived debilitated.

Given the state of medical knowledge in the days of slavery, it probably did not make much difference whether or not a slave owner hired a doctor to look after ailing slaves. Dr. Samuel A. Cartwright of the University of Louisiana wrote of a "disease" he called "Dysaesthesia Aetheiopica, or Hebetude of Mind and obtuse Sensibility of Body," which, he said caused slaves to "break, waste, and destroy everything they handle—abuse horses and cattle—tear, burn, or rend their own clothing, and, paying no attention to the rights of property, steal others to replace what they have destroyed. They wander about at night, and keep in a half-nodding state by day. They slight their work—cut up corn, cane, cotton, and tobacco, when hoeing it, as if for pure mischief. They raise disturbances with their overseers, and among their fellow-servants, without cause or motive, and seem to be insensible to pain when subjected to punishment." He also believed he could cure the "disease" of running away, which he called *Drapetomania*.[10]

Many masters trusted more to their own medical treatments, based on experience and observation. "I never have employed Doctors to my Negroes," wrote

Pierce Butler, ". . . because they seldom feel for Negroes as they ought to, and therefore are light on their prescriptions. . . . If the complaint is a fever and in the summer, let a vomit [emetic], unless to pregnant women, be given, after that some gruel, the next day if the fever continues let 12 ounces of blood be taken and a purge given of 5 grains Calomel and ten of Jallop[;] if that should not operate in three hours, let the doce [dose] be repeated till it operates 4 or 5 times, then let them have gruel, or fowl broth. If the fever continues a second bleeding must take place and after it plenty of tea or gruel, when the fever is checked let them drink plenty of decoction of wild cherry bark. In winter bleed, purge and sweat freely with snake root for fevers."[11] At the first hint of cholera, many owners would move their entire households to the woods, correctly "supposing there might be some local cause for the diseases."[12] Other owners handed over the care of the sick to older slave women, who used folk remedies, such as fence-grass tea to avert fever and elder twigs and dogwood berries for chills.

Plantations of any size usually cared during the day for babies and toddlers, a necessary provision when all slave mothers worked throughout the daylight hours and the early deaths of slave mothers left many babies motherless. On the better-run plantations, the mistress herself would oversee the care of these children or an experienced slave mother would be given their charge. All too often, however, care was left to slave girls seven or eight years old. One advocate of putting slaves to work in the fields at age five argued that they would be better employed there than in the nursery, for they often caused severe injuries and even death among infants. His charge was probably true. One ex-slave reminisced about how she detested taking care of children: "I'd drop 'em, leave 'em, pinch 'em, quit walking 'em and rocking 'em. I got tired of 'em all the time."[13]

As they aged, slaves lost value for their owners. If they had skills, slaves too old to sell could still be hired out to other employers, at a rate that brought in more money than if they had been sold and the profits invested. But field hands without such skills eventually could no longer do field work, and they then became heavy burdens on the master, for no return. All too often, conscienceless masters simply turned them away, to survive as best they could on the charity of other slaves. Sojourner Truth told about the death of her father while she was still a slave in New York State. She was not permitted to care for him or even to visit him. After several makeshift arrangements, in his last days he was left alone. "Yet, lone, blind, and helpless as he was, James for a time lived on. One day, an aged colored woman, named Soan, called at his shanty, and James besought her, in the most moving manner, even with tears, to tarry awhile and wash and mend him up, so that he might once more be decent and comfortable; for he was suffering dreadfully with the filth and vermin that had collected upon him. Soan was herself an emancipated slave, old and weak, with no one to care for her; and she lacked the courage to undertake a job of such seeming magnitude. . . . And shortly after her visit, this faithful slave, this deserted wreck of humanity, was found on his miserable pallet, frozen and stiff in death."[14]

Marriage and Maternity

Slaves could not enter into legal marriages, for they could make no valid contracts. But could they be married in the eyes of God? Churches waffled. Some white clergymen presided at slave marriages, but they usually omitted from the ceremony the phrases "until death do us part" and "let no man put asunder," for they knew that the master might sell husband away from wife or wife from husband. In 1835 the Savannah River Baptist Association of Ministers ruled, "Such separation among persons situated as our slaves are, is civilly, a separation by death. . . . The slaves are not free agents, and a dissolution by death is not more entirely without their consent and beyond their control than by such separation."[15]

Some masters tried to regulate slave marriages and divorces, providing gifts for first-time marriages and penalizing divorces. At least one overseer arbitrarily "divorced" couples who had minor spats, whether or not they wished it. Sometimes masters simply arranged newly arrived slaves in two lines, gestured to the men to pick the wives they wanted, and unceremoniously declared, "All right, you're married." Other masters told male slaves to move in with women whom they thought ready for childbearing. Still others let the slaves initiate marriages but reserved the right to approve them. For favored slaves, masters might even provide formal marriage ceremonies in their own houses.

Some left marriages up to the slave community, which might exercise some judgment about whether or not a wedding should take place—in a way sanctioning the wedding. Caroline Johnson Harris remembered that where she lived the slaves did not have to ask the master: "Just go to Aunt Sue an' tell her you want to git mated. She tells us to think 'bout it hard fo' two days, 'cause marryin' was sacred in the eyes of Jesus. Arter two days Mose an' me went back an' says we done thought 'bout it and still want to git married. Den she called all de slaves arter tasks to pray for de union dat God was gonna make. Pray we stay together an' have lots of chillun an' none of 'em git sol' away from de parents. Den she lay a broomstick 'cross de sill of de house we gonna live in an jine our hands together. Fo' we step over it she ast us once mo' if we was sho' we wanted to git married. 'Course we say yes. Den she say, 'In de eyes of Jesus step in to de Holy land of mat-de-money.' When we step 'cross de broomstick, we was married. Was bad luck to tech de broomstick. Fo'ks always stepped high 'cause dey didn't want to have a spell cast on 'em—Aunt Sue used to say whichever one teched de stick was gonna die fust." Other slave communities arranged marriages more or less formally, with a ceremony performed by a black preacher, or with marriage "by the blanket": "We comes together in the same cabin; and she brings her blanket and lay it down beside mine; and we gets married that a-way."[16]

Slaves often married slaves on neighboring plantations. "Saturday nights," a former slave reminisced, "the roads were . . . filled with [slave] men on their way to the 'wife house' [the plantation or farm of a different owner], each pedestrian or horseman bearing in his bag his soiled clothes and all the good things he could collect during the week for the delectation of the household."[17] Of course, as another ex-slave said, "If a man married abroad it meant that he wouldn't see his wife only about once a week."[18] Some of these "abroad" marriages were bigamous. "[Hector] told me," wrote Fanny Kemble, the wife of his owner, "that a great number of the men on all the different plantations had *wives* on the neighboring estates as well as on that to which they properly belonged. 'Oh, but,' said I, 'Hector, you know that cannot be; a man has but one lawful wife.' Hector knew this, he said, and yet seemed puzzled himself, and rather puzzled me to account for the fact, that this extensive practice of bigamy was perfectly well known to the masters and overseers, and never in any way found fault with or interfered with. Perhaps this promiscuous mode of keeping up the slave population finds favor with the owners of creatures who are valued in the market at so much per head."[19]

Whatever the form of the wedding, marriages that could be ended by the whim of a master enjoyed no security. A master might order an already-married man to take another wife or surrender his wife to himself for the night. In either case, the slave could not effectively protest. Slave Molly told Fanny Kemble that Tony "was not her *real* husband. . . . [H]er real husband had been sold from the estate for repeated attempts to run away. . . . [S]he did not know whither or to whom her *real* husband had been sold; but in the meantime Mr. K . . . had provided her with . . . Tony, by whom she had had nine children, six of whom were dead; she, too, had miscarried twice."[20]

Their marriages denied slaves their traditional roles as husband and wife. The slave husband could not support his family, for he could own nothing; he could not even protect his wife and children against beatings and rape. The wife, exhausted by her labor, was hard put to cook, clean, and care for her family. Slave men were emasculated—sometimes literally, castrated by way of punishment. Women were unsexed: sexual advances from slaveholders, separation of mothers and children, physical brutality, and assignment of "men's work" all destroyed the female slave's identity as a woman.

Under such circumstances, what was a slave man or woman to think of marriage? How seriously were they to take it? Yet slaves fell in love, experiencing anguish when they were separated from their spouses, and slave communities managed to preserve a standard of monogamy—though, of course, it was not always met. Insofar as they could, these communities also held to the standard of fidelity within a marriage. Many slave couples lived together in a trial period before marriage. Some black communities did not consider it wrong for a woman to have a child before she married; others thought she ought to find a husband before the child was born.[21]

Masters obviously had an interest in slave women's bearing babies early and often. Owners were frequently ambivalent in their treatment of pregnant and nursing women—pulled one way by their desire for healthy babies and another by their eagerness to get as much work as possible out of the mothers. Some masters took pregnant women off field labor in about the fifth month of pregnancy, placing them in special work gangs with lighter tasks. James H. Hammond's manual for plantation operations required that no plowing or lifting be required of them, instructed that the plantation midwife attend deliveries, allowed the mothers to "lie up" for a confinement of one month, and gave them extra allowances of sugar, coffee, rice, and flour. Babies were to be furnished with layettes of pieces of cloth and rags. During the 12-month period of suckling, the manual said, nursing mothers should not have to leave their homes until sunrise, and their work must always lie within half a mile of the "children's house," where the babies were tended. Mothers were to go there for a forty-five-minute period three times a day until the babies were eight months old, then twice a day until the twelfth month, and once a day during the twelfth month. Only about three-fifths as much work was to be expected of nursing mothers as of other slaves.[22]

Practice did not always meet these requirements. "Mother said she knowed she could not go home [from the field] and suckle dat child and git back in 15 minutes [as the overseer ordered]," said Celia Robinson, "so she would go somewhere an' sit down an' pray de child would die."[23] Pregnancy and nursing sometimes failed to protect slave mothers against brutal beatings.

Infant mortality before 1865 ran high among whites as well as blacks, but Fanny Kemble's survey of its incidence among the slaves on her husband's plantation still horrifies: "The practice of sending women to labor in the fields in the third week after their confinement is a specific for causing . . . infirmity. . . . *Fanny* has had six children; all dead but one. . . . *Nanny* has had three children; two of them are dead. . . . *Leah,* Caesar's wife, has had six children; three are dead. *Sophy* . . . has had ten children; five of them are dead. . . . *Sally,* Scipio's wife, has had two miscarriages and three children born, one of whom is dead. . . . *Charlotte,* Renty's wife, has had two miscarriages, and was with child again. . . . [*Die*] had had sixteen children, fourteen of whom were dead; she had had four miscarriages: one had been caused with falling down with a very heavy burden on her head, and one from having her arms strained up to be lashed."[24]

All slave mothers faced the heartbreaking knowledge that their babies, whether mulatto, black, or mostly white, were born into lifelong slavery. Since the status of the baby was that of its mother, many a child who looked white—and whose father and grandfathers had been white—was treated as black and a slave.

Slave mothers could not count on watching their children grow up, even if the children survived. Masters who resided in a city might send new slave babies back to their plantations as soon as they were weaned but keep the slave mothers in the city to tend their own children, "because they do not want the time of the mother taken up with attendance upon *her own children,* it being too valuable to the mistress. As a *favor* she is sometimes permitted to go to see them once a year."[25] Frederick Douglass could remember seeing his field-hand mother only four or five times in his life, each time very briefly and at night, when after her day's work she walked the twelve miles from the plantation where she was hired out, knowing that she had to walk twelve miles back again before sunrise and another day of labor. She died when he was seven; he was not allowed to see her during her illness or attend her funeral.

Such treatment explains the bitter recollections of Jennie Hill: "How well I remember how I would sit in my room with the little ones on my lap and the tears would roll down my cheeks as I would ponder the right and wrong of bringing them into the world. What was I bringing them into the world for? To be slaves and go from morning to night. They couldn't be educated and maybe they couldn't even live with their families. They would just be slaves. All that time I wasn't even living with my husband. He belonged to another man. He had to stay on his farm and I on mine. That wasn't living—that was slavery."[26]

Sometimes emotions like these, or a desire for revenge on a white man who had impregnated her against her will, moved a slave mother to action. Rumor had it that slave women knew how to abort unwanted babies. Records exist of "barren" slave women who bore babies after emancipation, but no one knows for sure how often slave women deliberately aborted. Between 1790 and 1860, smothering was reported as responsible for the deaths of some 60,000 slave infants, but these figures are unreliable. Not only are they probably wrong in themselves, but many of these deaths may have resulted from sudden infant death syndrome or poor prenatal or postnatal care rather than infanticide.[27]

White-Black Sexual Relations

The atmosphere of the plantation was laden with sexuality, tinged with the lure of the forbidden. State and church alike banned white-black sexual relationships.[28] White wives were humiliated by them, and most black women dreaded them. The press deplored them as encouraging "insolence" from black women. Nonetheless these relationships were commonplace throughout the history of slavery—mostly between white men and black women. In many ways this was inevitable, for blacks and whites lived intimately. It was also fed by the myth of the passionate sexuality of black women, a myth propagated by white men ever since the early days of the African slave trade, and many a white man tested out this theory, raping a black woman. Under slavery black women and their husbands were helpless in such exercises of white force. Economic motives also counted. White masters peopled their plantations with slaves of mixed blood, as they and their sons fathered the babies of their slave women in casual couplings or long-term relationships. Without regard for morality some of them committed incest on their black daughters or sisters. White men bought beautiful slaves to serve as concubines, sometimes setting them up in high style. Overseers harassed and raped slave women. Some white hosts offered their male guests black women to sleep with. Perverted sexuality prompted some of the terrible beatings inflicted on black women.

As traveler William Blane commented in 1824, "Indeed in the Southern States, the ladies would be very angry, and turn anyone out of society, who kept a white woman for his mistress; but would not scruple even to marry him, if he had a colored one, and a whole family of children by her."[29] One family eager for a marriage between a young man in his twenties and a much younger girl arranged for him to maintain a black mistress until his fiancée reached marriageable age. Rumors flew. In 1828, Sarah Haysworth Gayle wrote in her diary of a neighbor: "His children and his son's children are their slaves, and probably, nay I think I heard, that his *child* and his *grand-child* have one mother."[30] Fanny Kemble observed tartly, "[I]t seems, indeed, as if marriage (and not concubinage) was the horrible enormity which cannot be tolerated, and against which, moreover, it has been deemed expedient to enact laws. Now it appears very evident that there is no law in the white man's nature which prevents him from making a colored woman the mother of his children, but there *is* a law on his statute books forbidding him to make her his wife."[31]

This social phenomenon became such a problem that fathers often sent their sons north to school. As one southern merchant told landscape architect Frederick Law Olmsted, "I tried to get my brother to send them [his sons] North with me to school. I told him he might as well have them educated in a brothel at once, as in the way they were growing up."[32]

Society felt differently about and reacted much more severely to white women's sleeping with black men. Ever since blacks were introduced into American society, of course, white women sometimes had sexual relations with black men. In colonial days indentured white women had borne children fathered by the black male slaves who served in the same household, and throughout American history white women and black men went right on being attracted to one another. In 1681 in Maryland white Eleanor Butler, known as Irish Nell, married a slave known as Negro Charles, despite the warnings of the third Lord Baltimore, of whom she was the indentured servant, that she would thereby enslave herself and her children. One Benjamin Jameson reported that when Baltimore "asked how she would like to go to bed to a Negro, she answered him that she would rather go to bed to Charles than His Lordship."[33] Court records also show outraged white husbands divorcing their white wives when they discovered such a relationship. "I believe the only cause of Lewis ------'s wife quitting him and taking up with this slave," testified a witness in an 1824 Virginia divorce case, "was that the slave was much younger and a more likely man than ------. There being a great difference in the age of Lewis ----- and his wife."[34] Some white mistresses took advantage of their powers of sexual coercion over their husbands' slaves.

White men did not want black men invading this most intimate of their bailiwicks. Moreover, because the child followed the condition of the mother, the children of free white women were white, no matter who fathered them, and the children of enslaved black women were slaves.[35] White males emphatically did not want an increase in the free black population, but they welcomed more slaves. So most affairs between white women and black men were kept secret. But even when they became known, white society did not invariably punish either man or woman violently.

Astonishingly, until the end of the Civil War, society in some degree acknowledged and even tolerated such relationships—more easily if the women involved were poor, lower-class women, who were commonly believed to share black women's passionate sexuality. Monied upper-class men were more sensitive about the stain on their honor inflicted by a white relative's involvement with a black man and by her violation of the presumption of her purity. She was disgraced, gossiped about, and sometimes disowned and even completely ostracized. White women consorting with black men might also be fined.

White woman–black man couples were prosecuted not under charges of having violated the laws against such relationships but under laws against fornication, adultery, and bastardy, all charges that could also be and were brought against white couples. However, enslaved black men were more vulnerable because they could not legally marry, and consequently any sexual relationships with white women could result in one or more of these charges. Still, black men so accused were more often whipped or castrated than killed, and sometimes they were exonerated even of charges of rape. Thus in North Carolina in 1825 when Polly Lane, a poor white, accused Jim, a black slave, of rape, the court procedure revealed that a liaison between the two was known and tolerated in the local community, which divided its sympathies between Polly and Jim after Polly bore a child determined to be of mixed blood.[36] Other black men who had sexual relations with white women went scot-free because the black fathers of white women's children were often not identified.

Significantly, until 1865 few charges of rape were brought against black men. White society, which deeply feared black insurrections, did not develop the widespread fears of black rape with anything approaching the intensity of the postbellum era. In 1739, for instance, a Maryland woman slave reported to her mistress a Maryland plot, alleging that black men were going to massacre all whites except young females, "whom they intended to keep for their wives," but her mistress dismissed this story.[37] Black leader and former slave Frederick Douglass observed that until after the war black men were "seldom or never . . . accused of the atrocious crime of feloniously assaulting white women."[38]

The *relative* toleration of white woman–black man relationships until 1865 contrasts with the attitudes that developed during Reconstruction and strengthened in the late 19th century and the first quarter of the 20th century. The change is symbolized in the 1864 invention of the word *miscegenation*—a term intended to connote an absolute taboo. Thereafter white fears of rapes committed by blacks soared. As black men became free enfranchised citizens, the white men who had previously held absolute power over them perceived them as threatening and responded with violence against both them and black women. No longer restrained by qualms about damaging property in the persons of slaves, whites in the second half of the 19th century established a reign of terror that lasted until the 1940s and later, freely employing charges of rape as a cover for economic motives or personal grievances. From the end of Reconstruction in 1877 to World War II (1939–1945), in 3,500 documented cases whites lynched or otherwise exercised mob violence against blacks.[39]

The Powers That Be: Masters and Mistresses

The slave culture twisted all it touched. It damaged the white people who lived in it as surely as it did the blacks. It allowed, even expected, whites to discipline and punish and sell away from their families black people with whom they had lived all their lives. It taught young white sons and daughters contempt for the black mammies who had raised them and for the black children with whom they had played. It shut out the slave states from the development of industry, roads, schools, and other services and conveniences proceeding so rapidly in the North.

The relative power of white men over white women and free blacks, and their absolute power over their slaves, inevitably corrupted them. Aside from his conscience and his own economic interest, the only restraint on the slave owner's conduct was community opinion—and that was weak in an agricultural economy where most slaves lived on remote plantations and farms and racism was rampant. As Frederick Law Olmsted wrote, "Suppose you are my neighbour; if you maltreat your negroes, and tell me of it, or I see it, am I going to prefer charges against you to the magistrates? I might possibly get you punished according to law; but if I did, or did not, I should have you, and your family and friends, far and near, for my mortal enemies."[40]

The white master typically based his behavior on patriarchal attitudes, by which he was the overlord of his wife, his children, and his servants, his lightest word to be obeyed by all. His ultimate means of control over his slaves—physical force—encouraged him to indulge his tempers and passions, and hardened him to cruelty. In Thomas Jefferson's words, "The whole commerce between master and slave is a perpetual exercise of the most boisterous passions; the most unrelenting despotism on the one part, and degrading submission on the other. . . . [T]he parent storms; the child looks on, catches the lineaments of wrath, puts on the same airs in the circle of smaller slaves, gives a loose tongue to the worst of passions, and, thus nursed, educated, and daily exercised in tyranny, cannot but be stamped with odious peculiarities. The man must be a prodigy who can retain his manners and morals undepraved by such circumstances."[41]

Masters varied, of course. Some lived close to their slaves and were familiar with every aspect of their lives and work. Others resided in distant cities, leaving the management of the plantation and the supervision of the slaves to overseers. Some owners were jovial and genial, others mean-spirited and vindictive. A consensus among both whites and slaves held "adopted" or "Yankee" slaveholders—those not born to the practice—to be among the worst.

The white slave owner typically thought of his wife as morally pure and mentally inferior. She shared none of the growing independence of women in the free states. Whatever property she had owned, including slaves, became her husband's when she married. If she married a small farmer, she might well have to labor in the fields alongside him and his slaves. If she married a plantation owner, she usually came to the heavy responsibilities of running a large household without much preparation. She had not been trained to it, for she had been taught to consider physical labor and household tasks beneath her. The richer her husband and the more numerous his slaves, the more time she had to devote to caring for them—planning and checking on their work, providing them with clothes, supervising the care of their children. Forbidden to travel without a chaperone (or at all), isolated on her husband's plantation, she suffered loneliness, especially for the company of other white women.

As her slaves well knew, a mistress's authority derived from her husband. Plantation mistress Mary Hamilton Campbell told how her husband's slave Eliza spoke to her of *"our master."*[42] The plantation overseer might ignore or defy the mistress's orders. Her husband might refuse to back her decisions, and she might be reduced to coaxing and wheedling to persuade him to right what she perceived as injustices inflicted on his slaves. "I had a long and painful conversation with Mr. [my husband] upon the subject of the flogging which had been inflicted on the wretched Teresa," Fanny Kemble wrote. "These discussions are terrible: they throw me into perfect agonies of distress for the slaves, whose position is utterly hopeless; for myself, whose intervention in their behalf sometimes seems to me worse than useless; for Mr., whose share in this horrible system fills me by turns with indignation and pity."[43]

Some plantation mistresses genuinely loved certain of their slaves—particularly their house servants—and did their best to make their lives a little more bearable. Others lived at sword's point with the people who served them. One slave owner's wife went into the kitchen at the end of every meal and spat in the leftovers to keep the slaves from eating them. Another put out her cook's eye with a fork for serving underdone potatoes.

Many a slave owner's wife was humiliated by the daily presence of her husband's black mistress(es); her children and theirs played together and often looked much alike. In 1824, a woman sought a divorce shortly after her wedding; her husband had just told her "that he had two mulatto children who were more comely and handsome than any she would ever have and that he would bring the [slave] mother and her children home. . . . In a few more days this negro woman and two mulatto children were brought upon the plantation. They were received by her husband with much interest and shew of affection. He now again acknowledged the children openly, and admitted the eldest to every act of familiar intercourse of which its age was capable. He would take it upon his knee, and instructed it to abuse your unhappy applicant and place her under the most positive and threatening injunction not to correct it—declaring his strong attachment for the mother and stating that the two children were his and that he meant to do more for them, upon principle, than for his lawful children."[44]

Some blacks owned slaves. Most blacks who bought slaves did so to free them, but a few, having managed to accumulate some property, used slaves to work their land or to assist them in their trades or businesses. In 1860 free blacks in the slave states numbered some 261,918, most of whom lived in the Upper South.[45] Their states imposed on them one restriction after another, such as a poll tax (a per-person tax), a law forbidding them to return to the state should they ever leave it, and a law requiring that each male over 15 must have a white guardian, on pain of enslavement. Danger lurked around every corner, constricting their social and economic lives. Because whites meant to keep them subordinate, free blacks had to guard against any act that a white might consider insolent. Fifty-five percent of free black men and 75 percent of free black women could find jobs only as laborers.[46] Craftspeople were better off, but most of them depended on white customers. Even the farmers who owned their own land had to rely on trading with whites, for free blacks were too few in number and often too poor to buy all their services or products.

Naturally, many free blacks saw finding favor with whites and at least appearing to accept white values as their best protection. The employees among them had to show themselves to be obedient and uncomplaining; the tradesmen had to maneuver tactfully to keep their customers and collect the money owed them. Some of them saw owning slaves as one way to persuade whites that they were not troublemakers, that they would not stir up black rebellions, and that in fact they did not disapprove of the institution of slavery. Others, like white masters, simply wanted the benefits of slave ownership.

There were never many black masters, and most of those owned only a few slaves. Black slave ownership probably peaked in 1830, at which time only a quarter of black masters owned more than 10 slaves.[47] Like whites, they varied from relatively kind to sadistic in their treatment of their slaves, but most people, white or black, rated black masters low, whether because of their individual characters or because of the inferior status of all blacks. Slaves could derive little status from a black master, who from the very condition of being black himself had little standing.

The Powers That Be: Punishment

The slave system was founded on and sustained by brute force—physical punishment. Both masters and mistresses themselves could beat their slaves or order them beaten by overseers, black drivers, or men employed for that purpose in slave jails. These slaves were the intimates of their owners, yet, as Elizabeth Fox-Genovese writes, "Mistresses whipped slave women with whom they might have shared beds, whose children they might have delivered or who might have delivered theirs, whose children they might have suckled and who frequently suckled theirs."[48]

The power of the state sanctioned these beatings and other even more severe punishments. Only rarely could slaves find protection in the justice system. The laws of slave states solidly backed the absolute authority of owners. Laws grew harsher as the numbers of slaves increased and white fears rose. They denied the slave freedom of movement; if he ventured off his owner's property without a written pass, any white person or patrollers hired to catch him out could stop him. He had no right of *habeas corpus*, for he did not own his own body. He could not testify against a white person. Except on the frontier, where fear of Indians sometimes outran fear of blacks, the law forbade him to carry a gun. He usually was legally forbidden to buy and sell goods without his owner's specific permission. He could not go to church or be baptized unless his master approved. Only lack of enforcement of the local slave code, the conflicting laws of the free states, or abolitionist defiance of fugitive slave laws could help him.

The punishments inflicted on slaves testify to the worst side of human nature. Slave owners inflicted not only commonplace beatings with lashes designed to hurt but also horrifyingly inventive tortures. They were often tinged with perverted sexuality and sadism. For proof of their excesses historians do not need the writings of abolitionists, who focused on them with a kind of sick fascination. The testimony of former slaves, the diaries of southern women, southern newspapers, and public records teem with accounts of these unspeakable cruelties.

African-American Culture: Status, Self-Respect, and Community

Influence goes both ways. No two groups can live together without compromises and without changing each other. Slaves resisted—sometimes directly, more often subtly. They used their skills in everything from cooking to growing cotton to making iron to protect themselves and expand their independence within the system. They asserted their freedom by finding ways to exercise choice. They reclaimed their own identities, their own cultures. They clung to remnants of their African memories and customs. "[S]laves established families, created churches, selected community leaders, and carved out a small realm of independent economic activity. An elaborate network of kinship—with its own pattern of courtship, rites of marriage, parental responsibilities, and kin obligations—linked slaves together. . . . In addition to preachers, slaves chose other leaders from their own ranks. Often these were drivers or artisans, but sometimes men and women of no special status in the owners' view."[49]

Individual slaves found ways, sometimes pathetic, of protecting their own self-respect; many of these depended on whites. Blacks bragged of having been born in North America and boasted about the status of their owners. Black drivers laying out work for other slaves, and "mammies" presiding over kitchens and nurseries proudly exercised the minor powers delegated to them by their owners. But others dominated by sheer force of personality.

Slaves invested one another with dignity, as when they taught their children to address the aged as "aunt" and "uncle"—a practice picked up by some whites. Despite the heavy odds against them, many slaves established and maintained stable families. Within the black community, slaves cared for each other, covered for each other, and supported each other in times of trouble. A runaway hiding in nearby woods could count on his friends for food from their own meager rations. By song, drums, or grapevine, slaves passed on to their friends and relations on other farms and plantations the news garnered on their masters' errands or at their masters' tables.

Some slaves gained influence by expertise—whether in reading, arithmetic, voodoo, or herbal medicine. They exercised their talents in music to earn freedom from field labor. They made themselves indispensable by their skills.

Humiliated, deprived of identity, forced to work endless hours, and tortured, slaves nonetheless somehow maintained a culture and community of their own.

African-American Culture: Literacy, Folklore, and Religion

Slave owners insisted on the inferiority of Africans and the benefits to be gained by living in a superior (white) civilization. Yet they denied their slaves access to much of that civilization by making it a crime to teach slaves to read. Some learned anyway. Henry Bibb started by tracing out the letters from his passes, though he did not know what they symbolized. Frederick Douglass bribed white children to teach

Slaves enjoy a holiday in Petersburg, Virginia. *(Crowe,* With Thackeray in America*)*

him a little at a time. Those who learned taught others. Slaves risked beatings to attend schools operated by whites like Levi Coffin—until slave owners closed down the schools. But, of course, most slaves remained illiterate: As her husband's slave Israel told Fanny Kemble when she asked him why he had never tried to learn, "Missis, what for me learn to read? me have no prospect!"[50]

Masters did not always deny Christianity to slaves. Some thought it—or the form of it they permitted—helpful in keeping blacks in line. Former slave Lunsford Lane would remember that "on Sabbath there was one sermon preached expressly for the colored people, which it was generally my privilege to hear. I became quite familiar with the texts: 'Servants be obedient to your masters'—'not with eye service as men pleasers'—'He that knoweth his master's will and doeth it not, shall be beaten with many stripes,' and others of this class: for they formed the basis of most of these public instructions to us. The first commandment impressed upon our minds was to obey our masters, and the second was like unto it, namely, to do as much work when they or the overseers were not watching us as when they were."[51]

Regardless of white perceptions, however, slaves were not children, and they had brought with them from Africa their own religious concepts, their own reverence of divinity, and their own respect for the priesthood. In America, writes W. E. B. DuBois, the African priest or medicine man became the African-American minister, who "found his function as the healer of the sick, the interpreter of the Unknown, the comforter of the sorrowing, the supernatural avenger of wrong, and the one who rudely but picturesquely expressed the longing, disappointment, and resentment of a stolen and oppressed people."[52]

From the remnants of African religion there arose a black American church based on the principles of Vodun (Voodoo) and Obeah worship. Under the influence of the white culture and Christian missionary work,[53] this religion gradually mutated over two centuries into a Calvinistic Christian denomination, spreading from plantation to plantation. But shreds of its African roots endured, both in theology and in the use of dance and song as worship. John Thompson, an early

19th-century slave, was probably accurate in observing that "most worshipped outside a church in . . . the 'invisible institution.'[54] Slaves secretly sang or prayed in their cabins, covering their heads with pots so that the sound would not be heard, or they attended their own services in the woods. "The antebellum Negro was not converted to God. He converted God unto himself."[55]

Dutch factor William Bosman commented in 1705 that Africans believed in one omnipotent and omnipresent God, but, they said, He must be approached through their idol-gods to whom He had committed the government of the world.[56] Union army chaplain W. G. Kiphant noted the slaves' emphasis on "the deliverance of the children of Israel. Moses is their *ideal* of all that is high, and noble, and perfect, in man. I think they have been accustomed to regard Christ not so much in the light of a *spiritual* Deliverer, as that of a second Moses who would eventually lead *them* out of their prisonhouse of bondage."

Blacks' spirituals, "shouts," and physical modes of worship influenced white Christians, particularly through common attendance at camp meetings. In 1819, Methodist John Watson complained that at these religious gatherings, "in the *blacks'* quarters, the coloured people get together, and sing for hours together, short scraps of disjointed affirmations, pledges, or prayers, lengthened out with long repetitious *choruses.* These are all sung in the merry chorus-manner of the southern harvest field, or husking-frolic method, of the slave blacks; and also very greatly like the Indian dances. With every word so sung, they have a sinking of one or other leg of the body alternately; producing an audible sound of the feet at every step, and as manifest as the steps of actual negro dancing in Virginia &c. [I]f some, in the meantime sit, they strike the sounds alternately on each thigh. . . . [T]he evil is only occasionally condemned and the example has already visibly affected the religious manners of some whites. From this cause, I have known in some camp meetings from 50 to 60 people crowd into one tent, after the public devotions had closed, and there continue the whole night, singing tune after tune, . . . scarce one of which were in our hymn books. Some of these from

Slaves attend a ball in Charleston, South Carolina. *(Crowe,* With Thackeray in America*)*

their nature, (having very long repetition choruses and short scraps of matter) are actually composed as sung and are almost endless."[58]

Meanwhile, remnants of African conjuring and witchcraft survived alongside Christianity. Many a slave went to the plantation magician for a powder to make his owner merciful, for a love potion, or even for a ritual to make himself invulnerable in an insurrection. As ex-slave William Adams put it, "There are lots of folks, and educated ones, too, what says we-uns believes in superstition. Well, it's 'cause they don't understand. 'Member the lord, in some of His ways, can be mysterious. The Bible says so. There am some things the Lord wants all folks to know, some things just the chosen few to know, and some things no one should know. Now, just 'cause you don't know 'bout some of the Lord's laws, 'tain't superstition if some other person understands and believes in such."[59]

African-American folklore told stories that explained natural phenomena and passed along folk wisdom: "Tain't no use o' sp'ilin de Sat'day night by countin' de time to Monday mornin.'"[60] It also portrayed slaves as outwitting their masters, often allegorically through animal stories. Former slave Cecelia Chappel told about "a partridge and a fox who killed a beef and skinned it. The fox (the master) managed to get all the beef except the liver, by saying that his wife needed it for soup. They agreed to eat the liver, so as soon as the partridge (the slave) had cooked it, he ate his portion quickly and then feigned sickness, whereupon the fox concluded that the beef was poisoned and gave it all back to the partridge."[61]

Hard physical work preempted the time and energy of the slaves. Some masters gave them Saturdays off, and almost all allowed them free Sundays—little enough time for looking after the tasks of daily life and the hunting, fishing, gardening, and berrying with which they might supplement their diets. But some of them stole time on Sundays for wrestling, running races, strumming a banjo, singing, dancing, playing marbles, telling stories, fiddling, drinking, gambling, or visiting. A planter got big tasks like cornshucking done by inviting all the slaves in the neighborhood to work in his barn in return for whiskey and a meal. The slaves' most important holidays came just before harvesting and at Christmas, when celebrations might go on for six days, with much feasting and drinking at the owner's expense and perhaps dances and athletic contests.

Chronicle of Events

1630

- A Virginia court sentences Hugh Davis to a whipping for having intercourse with a black woman.

1639

- Virginia enacts a law requiring that all men except blacks secure arms and ammunition or be subject to fine.

1640

- Virginia court sentences Robert Sweat to public penance for having gotten a "negro woman" with child; it sentences her to whipping.

1654

- By denying John Casor's suit for freedom from his black master, Anthony Johnson, a Virginia court recognizes the right of blacks to hold slaves.

1660

- The king of England orders the Council for Foreign Plantations to consider how people purchased "from other parts" as servants or slaves may be converted to Christianity.

1662

- Virginia enacts a law declaring that slave offspring inherit the status of the mother.
- Virginia and Maryland prohibit intermarriage between blacks and whites.

1667

- Virginia rules that Christian baptism "does not alter the condition of the person as to his bondage or freedom."

1674

- New York provides that "no Negro slave who becomes a Christian after he has been bought shall be set at liberty."

1680

- Virginia enacts a statute ruling that "no Negro or slave" may carry arms, on pain of 20 lashes; no black may lift up his hand against any "Christian," on pain of 30 lashes; if any black runs away and resists recapture, he may be killed.

1684

- The New York assembly prohibits slaves from selling goods.

1691

- A Virginia statute banishes any white man or woman intermarrying with a black, mulatto, or Indian and fines any English woman having a child out of wedlock by a black, the child to be bound out until age 30 (in 1765, this was reduced to 21 for males and 18 for females).

1701

- The Society for the Propagation of the Gospel in Foreign Parts is established and begins Christian missionary work among slaves.

1702

- New York passes "An Act for Regulating Slaves," prohibiting meetings of more than three slaves, trading by slaves, testimony by slaves except in cases of slave conspiracy, and self-protection by slaves against whites; authorizing masters to punish slaves at will; and creating the office of Common Whipper for slaves.

1704

- The South Carolina legislature grants ministers of the gospel the right to hold "all such negroes as shall be given and allotted to the several parishes by the Society . . . for the Propagation of the Gospel in Foreign Parts, or by any other charitably disposed persons."

1705

- The Virginia "slave code" defines the status of slaves, ruling that all non-Christian servants brought into the colony (that is, most Indians and blacks) are slaves, even if they later are converted to Christianity; that "all Negro, mulatto, and Indian slaves within this dominion shall be held to be real estate"; that any master who kills a slave while "correcting" her or him shall be acquitted of blame; that no black, mulatto, or Indian, bond or free, may ever lift his hand against any white person; and that no slave has the right to bear arms or to move about without written permission from the master.
- Virginia law provides that a minister marrying a black man and a white woman shall pay a fine of ten thousand pounds of tobacco.

1706

- New Jersey becomes the first North American colony to pass a castration law for slaves who *attempt* rape.

1708

- A New York act makes it a capital crime for a black, Indian, or slave to kill any "of her Majesties Leige People *not* being Negroes Mulattoes or Slaves within this Colony."

1710

- A New York law forbids black, Indian, and mulatto slaves to appear in the streets at night without a lantern with a lighted candle in it.

1712

- A New York statute makes it a crime for a black, Indian, or other slave "wilfully [to] murder any Negro, Indian or mulatto slave within this colony."
- A New York law forbids any freed black, Indian, or mulatto slave to own real estate.
- New York provides that "no Negro, Indian or mulatto, that shall hereafter be made free, shall enjoy, hold or possess" property within the colony.

1730

- The decision in the Virginia case *Tucker* v. *Sweney* allows executors to treat slave children born after the master's death as "Horses or Cattle."

1740

- South Carolina passes a comprehensive "Negro Act," proscribing slaves from "freedom of movement, freedom of assembly, freedom to raise food, to earn money, [and] to learn to read English," and restricting them to low-quality, inexpensive clothing.

1751

- George II repeals the Virginia act of 1705 that made slaves real estate.

1769

- A Virginia statute authorizes the castration of any slave who attempts to rape a white woman.

1773

- Slave M. Palmer of Silver Bluff, South Carolina, establishes the first black church in America with a group of slaves and free blacks.

1775

- Virginia slaveholder William Pitman beats and stomps a slave boy to death and incurs the penalties of the law.

1785

- Virginia law declares that "every person, who has one-fourth or more of Negro blood shall be deemed a mulatto, and the word negro in any section of this or any other statute, shall be construed to mean mulatto as well as negro."

1788

- The New York legislature passes the first new, comprehensive slave code since 1730, stipulating that every presently enslaved person be a slave for life.

1790

- Congress confines the privilege of naturalization to free whites.

1800

- South Carolina forbids blacks to hold religious meetings at night and subjects to fines nonresident plantation owners who have no white overseers.

This display shows some instruments of torture used on slaves. *(Library of Congress)*

1801

- Congress decrees that the laws of Virginia and Maryland will continue in force within the District of Columbia, thus establishing there a slave code enforced by federal authority.

1804

- Ohio writes its first black laws, patterned after southern slave codes, to deter slaves from escaping into Ohio from Virginia and Kentucky.

1805

- Virginia statute declares it lawful for a master to allow slaves to accompany his family to religious worship conducted by a white man.

1809

- New York recognizes black marriages, even between slaves, and makes the law retroactive to give legitimacy to all children of slaves.

1813

- New York extends jury trial to slaves.

1816

- Southern slaveholders begin settling in Texas.

1820s and 1830s

- The Christian clergy mounts efforts to see that slaves are instructed in religion, to propagandize masters on their duties, to provide catechisms for slaves, and to send missionaries to slaves.

1823

- Episcopalian priest Frederick Dalche urges religious instruction for slaves to teach respect for their masters.

1829

- The decision in the North Carolina case of *State* v. *Mann* asserts that the purpose of the legal system is to convince each slave that he has no will of his own and that "[t]he power of the master must be absolute to render the submission of the slave perfect."

1831

- Virginia passes a law by which any slave who attends a meeting where a free colored person preaches may be whipped not more than 39 lashes, and any slave who listens to any white preacher at night may receive the same punishment.

- North Carolina passes a law by which any colored person, free or slave, teaching a slave to read or write, or providing him with any book or pamphlet, may be punished by imprisonment or whipping.

1832

- Mary Prince becomes the first woman to write a slave narrative.

1836

- The Dixwell Avenue Congregational Church of New Haven, Connecticut—the first black Congregational church—calls as its pastor ex-slave Rev. James W. C. Pennington, D.D., of the University of Heidelberg.

1837

- The Connecticut Supreme Court frees a slave held "temporarily" in Connecticut for about two years.
- Texas makes insurrection, poisoning, rape of a white female, assault on a white with intent to kill, maiming a white person, arson, murder, and burglary punishable by death if committed by a slave.

1840

- Texas law criminalizes unauthorized trading (buying and selling goods) with slaves.
- Texas forbids slaves to carry deadly weapons without written permission of their owners.

1841

- Ex-slave James W. C. Pennington writes *The Origin and History of the Colored People.*
- Ex-slave Frederick Douglass begins speaking against slavery and racial prejudice.
- Texas gives all Texans the lawful right and responsibility to apprehend runaway slaves and take them before a local justice of the peace, to be returned to their owners or jailed and later sold at auction.

1846

- The Texas legislature creates a formal slave-patrol system.

1849

- Forty Alabama men compete in an essay contest, run by the Baptist State Convention, on "The Duties of Christian Masters."
- James W. C. Pennington publishes his slave narrative, *The Fugitive Blacksmith.*

1850

• *The Narrative of Sojourner Truth* is published.

1852

• Texas law permits slave owners to collect indemnities for any slave convicted and executed for committing a capital offense.

1853

• Ex-slave William Wells Brown publishes *Clotel,* the first novel written by a black.

1857

• In *Dred Scott* v. *Sanford,* the United States Supreme Court rules that a slave, an ex-slave, or a descendant of slaves cannot be a citizen of the United States and that Congress cannot prohibit slavery in the territories.

1859

• Jermain Wesley Loguen publishes his fugitive slave narrative.
• New Mexico enacts a slave code for its slaveless society.
• Arkansas passes a law enslaving all free blacks in the state by January 1, 1860.

1862

• "Refugeeing"—taking slaves to Texas to keep them away from the advancing Union forces—becomes common.

Eyewitness Testimony

Arriving from Africa

We were landed up a river a good way from the sea, about Virginia county, where we saw few or none of our native Africans, and not one soul who could talk to me. I was a few weeks weeding grass and gathering stones in a plantation. . . . [T]he gentleman, to whom I suppose the estate belonged, being unwell, I was one day sent for to his dwellinghouse to fan him. . . . I had a fan put in my hand, to fan the gentleman while he slept, and so I did indeed with great fear. While he was fast asleep I indulged myself a great deal in looking about the room, which appeared to me very fine and curious. The first object that engaged my attention was a watch which hung from the chimney, and was going. I was quite surprised at the noise it made, and was afraid it would tell the gentleman anything I might do amiss; and when I immediately after observed a picture hanging in the room, which appeared constantly to look at me, I was still more affrighted. . . .

Gustavus Vassa on his experiences about 1756, in Bontemps,
Great Slave Narratives, *34–35.*

[When receiving a new group of slaves, the owners would] arrange the men in one row and the women in another and make signs to them to choose each man a wife and would read the marriage service to them and thus save time by settling their matrimonial affairs. The young people of the family would select names from novels they had read and other sources, and sew these names into the clothes of each.

Emmaline Eve, in Fox-Genovese,
Plantation Household, *135.*

Necessities: Food

I rec'd a letter from Valley a few days ago which has made me very uneasy. He says my Negroes are starving, they have been without a grain of corn for two weeks & living entirely on Fish & Oysters. I cannot expect you to know how my mind is hurt by this information, and the inattention of Mr. Wayne [overseer] to whom I had written to purchase corn and draw on either my Factors [agents] in Charleston, or myself to pay for it, yet he has let my Negroes suffer, and my work stand.

Major Pierce Butler, 1794 letter, in Bell, Major Butler's
Legacy, *131.*

We [slave children] were not regularly allowanced. Our food was coarse corn meal boiled. . . . It was put into a large wooden tray or trough, and set down upon the ground. The children were then called, like so many pigs, and like so many pigs they would come and devour the mush; some with oyster-shells, others with pieces of shingle, some with naked hands, and none with spoons. . . . There were four slaves of us in the kitchen—my sister Eliza, my aunt Priscilla, Henny, and myself; and we were allowed less than a half of a bushel of corn-meal per week, and very little else, either in the shape of meat or vegetables. It was not enough for us to subsist upon. We were therefore reduced to the wretched necessity of living at the expense of our neighbors. This we did by begging and stealing, whichever came handy in the time of need, the one being considered as legitimate as the other.

Douglass, Narrative, *33, 44, 65–66.*

I have seen pa go out at night with a big sack and come back with it full. He'd bring sweet potatoes, watermelons, chickens and turkeys. . . . Where he went I cannot say, but he brought the booty home. The floor of our cabin was covered with planks. Pa had raised up two planks, and dug a hole. This was our storehouse.

Former slave, in Webber, Deep like the Rivers, *170.*

Necessities: Clothing

Their yearly clothing consisted of two coarse linen shirts, one pair of linen trousers, like the shirts, one jacket, one pair of trousers for winter, made of coarse negro cloth, one pair of stockings, and one pair of shoes; the whole of which could not have cost more than seven dollars. . . . The children unable to work in the field had neither shoes, stockings, jackets, nor trousers, given to them; their clothing consisted of two coarse linen shirts per year. When they [the clothing articles] failed them, they went naked until the next allowance-day. Children from seven to ten years old, of both sexes, almost naked might be seen at all seasons of the year.

Douglass, Narrative, *28.*

[For religious services and parties the slave] gals come out in the starch dresses. . . . They took their hair down outen the strings. . . . De gals charmed us wid honeysuckle and rose petals hid in dere bosoms. . . . Dey dried chennyberries and painted dem and wo' em on a string around dere necks. . . . [C]ourting gals . . . tried to do just like the young white missus would do.

Gus Feaster, in White, Ar'n't I a Woman? *143–44.*

[I]jes had two dresses. De best one was made of plain, white muslin. . . . [I] got walnut bark to color it brown. . . . [I] allus had to wash it on Saturday, 'cause we all had to go to church on Sunday. . . . [I made my walking dress] jes like old Miss taught me . . . with a cord 'round de bottom, a cord as big as my little finger, so's I couldn't tear it, cause I went over fences like a deer.

Sarah Waggoner, in Fox-Genovese, Plantation Households, *183.*

Necessities: Shelter

Among Isabella's [Sojourner Truth's] earliest recollections was the removal of her master, Charles Ardinburgh, into his new house, which he had built for a hotel, soon after the decease of his father. A cellar, under this hotel, was assigned to his slaves, as their sleeping apartment,—all the slaves he possessed, of both sexes, sleeping (as is quite common in a state of slavery) in the same room . . . its only lights consisting of a few panes of glass, through which she thinks the sun never shone, but with thrice reflected rays; and the space between the loose boards of the floor, and the uneven earth below, was often filled with mud and water, the uncomfortable splashings of which were as annoying as its noxious vapors must have been chilling and fatal to health. . . . [S]he wonders not at the rheumatisms, and fever-sores, and palsies, that distorted the limbs and racked the bodies of those fellow-slaves in after-life.

Sojourner Truth's report of her early life as a slave in New York State, in Narrative, *4–13.*

Slave quarters ranged from crude random nooks and crannies to cabins like these. *(Library of Congress)*

These cabins consist of one room, about twelve feet by fifteen, with a couple of closets smaller and closer than the staterooms of a ship, divided off from the main room and each other by rough wooden partitions, in which the inhabitants sleep. They have almost all of them a rude bedstead, with the gray moss of the forests for mattress, and filthy, pestilential-looking blankets for covering. Two families (sometimes eight and ten in number) reside in one of these huts, which are mere wooden frames pinned, as it were, to the earth by a brick chimney outside, whose enormous aperture within pours down a flood of air, but little counteracted by the miserable spark of fire, which hardly sends an attenuated thread of lingering smoke up its huge throat. A wide ditch runs immediately at the back of these dwellings, which is filled and emptied daily by the tide. Attached to each hovel is a small scrap of ground for a garden, which, however, is for the most part untended and uncultivated.

Kemble, Journal, *67–68.*

Medical Care

I am impelled by feelings of humanity to call upon you . . . in behalf of a poor sufferer. . . . She is the property of on[e] Posten in whose service she was burnt almost to death before Easter, & has ever since remained in the most shocking situation, she is now loathsome to every beholder, without a change of clothing, or one single necessary of life, or comfort. Can you not compel the savage creature who owns her to do something for her?

Concerned citizen, letter to the mayor of Alexandria, Virginia, 1813, in Owens, Property, *48.*

The infirmary is a large two-story building, terminating the broad orange-planted space between the two rows of houses which form the first settlement; it is built of whitewashed wood, and contains four large-sized rooms. . . . But [only] half the casements, of which there were six, were glazed, and these were obscured with dirt, almost as much as the other windowless ones were darkened by the dingy shutters, which the shivering inmates had fastened to in order to protect themselves from the cold. In the enormous chimney glimmered the powerless embers of a few sticks of wood, round which, however, as many of the sick women as could approach were cowering, some on wooden settles, most of them on the ground, excluding those who were too ill to rise; and these last poor wretches lay prostrate on the floor, without bed, mattress, or pillow, buried in tattered and filthy blankets, which, huddled round them as they lay strewed about, left hardly space to move upon the floor. . . . I left this refuge for Mr.'s [my husband's] sick dependents with my clothes covered with dust, and full of vermin. . . .

Kemble, Journal, *70–73.*

Yesterday morning [Sina] lost an infant. The doctor was with us all day, and when he left just before sunset he did not express any special fears about her situation. I had been with her until two o'clock, and went over after the doctor left. After tea your sister and myself were engaged giving out Negro cloth. Your father rode over at nine o'clock and said he saw no change except a profuse perspiration. She was perfectly sensible, but drowsy from the influence of opiates, and her pulse numbered 100. He returned to the house but a short time when he was summoned back; and she died at ten o'clock without a struggle. . . .

Eve left four children, and [Sina] leaves five. Nine motherless ones now to care for!

Plantation mistress Mary Jones, November 20, 1856, in Myers, Children of Pride, *265.*

[My] mother was a kind of doctor too. [She] would ride horseback all over the place an' see how they was gettin' along. She'd make a tea out o' herbs for them who had fever an' sometimes she gave them water from slippery elms.

R. S. Taylor, in Fox-Genovese, Plantation Households, *171.*

'Twa'n't no used to send fo' a docta, no'm, 'cause dey didn't have no medicine. My grandmother got out in de woods and got 'erbs. She made sage bam [balm]. One thing I remember, she would take co'n shucks—de butt end of de shucks—and boil 'em and make tea. 'Twould breck de chills and fever. De Lo'd fixed a way. We used roots for medicine too.

Goodson, "Medical-Botanical Contributions," in Hine, Black Women in American History *2:480.*

Slave Life: Care for the Aged

[M]y poor old grandmother . . . had served my old master faithfully from youth to old age. She had been the source of all his wealth; she had peopled his plantation with slaves; she had become a great grandmother in his service. She had rocked him in infancy, attended him in childhood, served him through life, and at his death wiped from his icy brow the cold death-sweat, and closed his eyes forever. She was nevertheless left a slave—a slave for life—a slave in the hands of strangers; and in their hands she saw her children, her grandchildren, and her great-grandchildren, divided, like so many sheep, without being gratified with the small privilege of a single word, as to their or her own destiny. . . . [H]er present owners finding she was of but little value . . . took her to the woods, built her a little hut, put up a little mud-chimney, and then made her welcome to the privilege of supporting herself there in perfect loneliness; thus virtually turning her out to die!

Douglass, Narrative, *61–62.*

He is a quiet orderly old Man, not able to do much Work and therefore is never drove to Labour, but suffer'd to go his own way. I observe he makes larger Crops of Rice and Corn for himself than most able Young Negroes, which I believe is greatly owing to their Aid for they all Respect and Love him. . . . I shall order proper Care to be taken of him, if his Life shall happen to surpass his Strength for Labour . . . and continue to make the same Annual Allowance during all the Time that he is able to perform any Work.

Plantation owner Henry Laurens, 1755(?), in Littlefield, Rice and Slaves, *71.*

Slave Life: Maternity

When her fourth baby was born and was about two months old, she just studied all the time about how she would have to give it up, and one day she said, "I just decided I'm not going to let Old Master sell this baby; he just ain't going to do it." She got up and give it something out of a bottle, and pretty soon it was dead."

Lou Smith in Rawick, American Slave *6:302.*

Pappy was a driver under de overseer, but mammy say dat she stay at de little nursery cabin and look after all de little babies. Dey had a cabin fixed up with homemade cradles and things where dey put all de babies. Der mammies would come in from de field about ten o'clock to nurse 'em and den later in de day, my mammy would feed de youngest on pot-likker and de older ones on greens and pot-licker. Dey had skimmed milk and mush, too, and all of 'em stayed as fat as butter balls, me among 'em.

Ex-slave Callie Williams, in Rawick, American Slave, *1:284.*

Slave Life: Marriage

One general principle prevails in all the States . . . and that is, that *a slave cannot make a contract, not even the contract of matrimony.*

Wheeler, Law of Slavery, *quoted by Goodell,* Slave Code, *93.*

After I been at he place 'bout a year, de massa come to me and say, "You gwine live with Rufus in dat cabin over yonder. Go fix it for livin'." I's 'bout sixteen year old and has no larnin', and I's jus' igno'mus chile. I's thought dat him mean for me to tend de cabin for Rufus and some other niggers. . . .

[After I had two children by Rufus, I quit him.] I never marries 'cause one 'sperience am 'nough for this nigger. After what I done for de massa, I's never wants no truck with any man. De lawd forgive dis cullud woman, but he have to 'scuse me and look for some others for to 'plenish [replenishl de earth.

Ex-slave Rose William, in Gutman, Black Family, *84–85.*

I laks Essex mighty well, an' I'll be sorry ter see him go— I'll be sorry too fer lil Robert not to have no daddy, but I can't go! . . . I knows . . . dat it's mighty easy ter git a good husband, an' mighty hard ter git a good mistis.

Fannie, explaining why she refused to be sold with her first husband, in Eppes, Negro, *56–57.*

Send me some of the children's hair in a separate paper with their names on the paper. Will you please git married, as long as I am married. My dear, you know the Lord knows both of our hearts. You know it never was our wishes to be separated from each other, and it never was our fault. Oh, I can see you so plain, at any-time. I had rather anything to had happened to me most than ever to have been parted from you and the children. As I am, I do not know which I love best, you or Anna. If I was to die, today or tomorrow, I do not think I would die satisfied till you tell me you will try and marry some good, smart man that will take care of you and the children, and do it because you love me; and not because I think more of the wife I have got than I do of you.

The woman is not born that feels as near to me as you do. You feel this day like myself. Tell them they must remember they have a good father and one that cares for them and one that thinks about them every day—My very heart did ache when reading your very kind and interesting letter. Laura I do not think I have change any at all since I saw you last.—I think of you and my children every day of my life.

Ex-slave Spicer, post–Civil War letter to his wife, Laura, who with their children had been sold away from him before the war, in Gutman, Black Family, *6–7.*

Slave Life: White-Black Sexual Relations

His [Benjamin Banneker's] maternal grandmother, Molly Welsh, a native of England, . . . came to Maryland—, with a ship load of emigrants, and, to defray the expense of the voyage was sold to a master with whom she served an apprenticeship of seven years. After her term of service had expired, she bought a small farm—, and purchased as laborers, two Negro slaves, from a ship which lay in Chesapeake Bay. They proved valuable servants. One of them, said to have been the son of an African king, a man of industry, integrity, fine disposition, and dignified manners, she liberated from slavery and afterwards married.

Martha E. Tyson, 1854, quoted in Johnston, Race Relations, *189.*

[Captain Davis'] most visible Foible, was keeping a Mulatto Servant (or Slave) who in Reality was his Mistress. . . . [H]e suffered almost every Thing to pass through her Hands, having such Confidence in her, that she had the Custody of all his Cash, as well as Books. . . . [A]ll Persons who had any Business with Captain Davis, were expected not to treat her with Contempt.

William Stephens, 1739, in Higginbotham, In the Matter of Color, *231.*

I had often heard of the beauty of quadroons. . . . They . . . have the appearance of being virtuous: but they are generally prostitutes and kept mistresses. Young men and single men of wealth have each a quadroon for his exclusive use. They are furnished with a Chamber and a sitting room and servants, and the comforts and elegancies of life. It generally costs from $1,500 to $2,000 a year to keep a quadroon. I am informed that the quadroon is faithful to a proverb in these arrangements. Married men in this City [New Orleans] are frequently in the habit of keeping quadroons.

Davidson, Diary (1836), 348, in Clinton, Plantation Mistress, *212.*

[Ephraim Christopher, now in his 80s, has been] living in the same house with the slave Maria [a woman of 37 years], and living with her as his mistress. Her 13 children were all mulattos. . . . He had been selling one [of the children] almost every year.

South Carolina court record, 1854, in Tadman, Speculators and Slaves, *127.*

A negro has been arrested for a rape on a respectable white lady. We expect he has been hung up a tree [lynched] before this.

Austin, Texas, State Gazette, *1860, in Campbell,* Empire, *105.*

My mammy was a white woman. Her daddy and mammy were poor folks, and they took sick and died and left her a little baby. Old Man Snell, back in Missouri, took her and put her on the yard with the other children. She was . . . raised as a Snell slave. When she was about fourteen, Marse Snell, he married her to a full-blood Indian that he had on the place, named Ephram Snell. He was Marse Snell's slave same as the Negroes, but I never knew how or why. Now that's the tale about my mammy that Old Man Snell told. But my black grandmother what raised my mammy, she said that my mammy belonged to [was the child of] a niece of Old Man Snell, and that she [the niece] was not married right like the white folks always did. And that Old Man Snell took Mammy and raised her up that way, and sent his niece up North to hide the disgrace.

Della Bibles, interviewed in Waco, Texas, October 1937, in Minges, Black Indian Slave Narratives, *26–27.*

Slave Culture: Folklore

I knows why that boll weevil done come. . . . Away back yonder a spider live in the country, 'specially in the bottom. He live on the cotton leaves and stalks, but he don't hurt it. These spiders kept the insects eat up. They don't plow deep then, and plants cotton in February, so it made 'fore the insects git bad.

Then they gits to plowing deep, and it am colder 'cause the trees all cut, and they plows up all the spiders and the cold kill them. They plants later, and there ain't no spiders left to eat up the boll weevil.

Ex-slave Caroline Matthews, in Botkin, Lay My Burden Down, *13.*

Every time I think of slavery and if it done the race any good, I think of the story of the coon and dog who met. The coon said to the dog, "Why is it you're so fat and I am so poor, and we is both animals?" The dog said: "I lay round Master's house and let him kick me and he gives me a piece of bread right on." Said the coon to the dog: "Better, then, that I stay poor." Them's my sentiment. I'm like the coon, I don't believe in 'buse.

Ex-slave Stephen McCray, in Botkin, Lay My Burden Down, *14.*

Slave Culture: Funerals

When a slave dies, the master gives the rest day, of their [the slaves'] own choosing, to celebrate the funeral. This, perhaps a month after the corpse is interred, is a jovial day with them; they sing and dance and drink the dead to his new home, which some believe to be in old Guinea.

Henry C. Knight, 1824 letter, in Blassingame, Slave Community, *37.*

Negro graves were always decorated with the last article used by the departed, and broken pitchers and broken bits of colored glass were considered even more appropriate than the white shells from the beach nearby. Sometimes they carved rude wooden figures like images of idols, and sometimes a patchwork quilt was laid upon the grave.

Mrs. Telfair Hodgson, reporting on her father's Georgia plantation in the 1850s, in Blassingame, Slave Community, *37.*

Slave Culture: Literacy

I was never so surprised in my whole life as when [on the Middle Passage] I saw the book talk to my master. . . . When nobody saw me, I open'd it and put my ear down close upon it, in great hope that it would say something to me.

Slave Olaudah Equiano in Lambert, "'I Saw the Book Talk,'" *191.*

"Now," said he, "if you teach that nigger (speaking of myself) how to read, there would be no keeping him. It would forever unfit him to be a slave. He would at once become unmanageable, and of no value to his master. As to himself, it could do him no good, but a great deal of harm. It would make him discontented and unhappy." These words sank deep into my heart. . . . I now understood . . . the white man's power to enslave the black man. . . . From that moment, I understood the pathway from slavery to freedom.

Douglass, Narrative, *50.*

Judge Scalaway . . . addressed her as follows: "Margaret Douglass, stand up. You are guilty of one of the vilest crimes that ever disgraced society; and the jury have found you so. You have taught a slave girl to read in the Bible. . . . The Court, in your case, do not feel for you one solitary ray of sympathy, and they will inflict on you the utmost penalty of the law. In any other civilized country you would have paid the forfeit of your crime with your life, and the Court have only to regret that such is not the law in this country. The sentence for your offence is, that you be imprisoned one month in the county jail, and that you pay the costs of this prosecution."

Ex-slaves William and Ellen Craft, Running, *in Bontemps,*
Great Slave Narratives, *288–89.*

Slave Culture: Music

My ole Mistiss promise me,
W'en she died she'd set me free.
She lived so long dat 'er head got bal'.
an' she give out 'n de notion a-dyin' at all.
Ole Massar lakwise promise me,
W'en he died, he'd set me free.
But ole Massar go an' make his will
Fer to leave me a-plowin' ole Beck still.
Yes, my ole Massar promise me;
But "his papers" didn' set me free.
A dose of pizen he'ped 'im along.
May di Devil preach 'is funer'l song.

In Webber, Deep like the Rivers, *76.*

Dey tried to make 'em [the slaves] stop singin' and prayin' durin' de war, 'case all dey'd ask for was to be sot free, but de slaves would get in de cabins and turn a big wash pot upside down and sing into dat, and de noise couldn't get out.

Ex-slave Callie Williams, in Rawick, American Slave,
1:285.

I'd jump up dar and den and holler and shout and sing and pat, and dey would all cotch de words and I'd sing it to some old shout song I'd heard 'em sing from Africa, and dey'd all take it up and keep at it, and keep a-addin' to it, and den it would be a spiritual.

Former slave, in Blassingame, Slave Community, *27–28.*

Slave Culture: Recreation

The days between Christmas and New Year's day are allowed as holidays; and, accordingly, we were not required to perform any labor, more than to feed and take care of the stock. This time we regarded as our own, by the grace of our masters; and we therefore used or abused it nearly as we pleased. Those of us who had families at a distance, were generally allowed to spend the whole six days in their society. This time, however, was spent in various ways. The staid, sober, thinking, and industrious ones of our number would employ themselves in making corn-brooms, mats, horse-collars, and baskets; and another class of us would spend the time in hunting opossums, hares, and coons. But by far the larger part engaged

in such sports and merriments as playing ball, wrestling, running foot-races, fiddling, dancing, and drinking whisky; and this latter mode of spending the time was by far the most agreeable to the feelings of our masters. . . .

[The slaveholders'] object seems to be, to disgust their slaves with freedom, by plunging them into the lowest depths of dissipation. . . . One plan is, to make bets on their slaves, as to who can drink the most whisky without getting drunk. . . .

Douglass, Narrative, *83–85.*

Before him [the banjo player] stood two athletic blacks, with open mouth and pearl white teeth, clapping "Juber" to the notes of the banjo; the fourth black man held in his right hand a jugy gourd of persimmon beer, and in his left, a dipper or water gourd, to serve the company. . . . The rest of the company, male and female, were dancers, except a little squat wench, who held the torch light.

*Visitor's report of a persimmon beer celebration in slave
quarters, in Owens,* Property, *146.*

Slave Culture: Religion

Q: Who is duty bound to give to Servants comfortable clothing, wholesome and abundant food?
A: The master.
Q: Who is duty bound to instruct Servants in a knowledge of the Holy Scriptures, and to give them every opportunity and encouragement to seek their soul's salvation?
A: The master.
Q: Who is the Master of us all in Heaven?
A: God.
Q: Does God show favour to the Master more than to the Servant, and just because he is a Master?
A: No.
Q: What are the Servants to count their Masters worthy of?
A: All honour.
Q: How are they to try to please their Masters?
A: Please them well in all things, not answering again.
Q: Is it right for a Servant when commanded to do anything to be sullen and slow, and answering his Master again?
A: No.
Q: But suppose the Master is hard to please, and threatens and punishes more than he ought, what is the Servant to do?
A: Do his best to please him.

The Rev. Charles Colcock Jones, Catechism *(1837),*
127–30.

After the praise meeting is over, there usually follows the very singular and impressive performance of the "Shout," or religious dance of the negroes. Three or four, standing still, clapping their hands and beating time with their feet, commence singing in unison one of the peculiar shout melodies, while the others walk round in a ring, in single file, joining also in the song. Soon those in the ring leave off their singing, the others keeping it up the while with increased vigor, and strike into the shout step, observing most accurate time with the music. This step is something halfway between a shuffle and a dance, as difficult for an uninitiated person to describe as to imitate. At the end of each stanza of the song the dancers stop short with a slight stamp on the last note, and then, putting the other foot forward, proceed through the next verse. . . . The shout is a simple outburst and manifestation of religious fervor—a "rejoicing in the Lord"—making a "joyful noise unto the God" of their salvation.

H. G. Spaulding, 1863, in Blassingame, Slave Community, *65–66.*

One of his [John Watson's] slaves was a preacher, and a favourite among them. He sometimes went to plantations twenty miles away—even further—on a Sunday, to preach a funeral sermon, making journeys of fifty miles a day on foot. . . . He was the most rascally negro, the worst liar, thief, and adulterer on his place. Indeed, when he was preaching, he always made a strong point of his own sinfulness, and would weep and bellow about it like a bull of Bashan, till he got a whole camp meeting into convulsions.

Olmsted, Cotton Kingdom, *375.*

[W]hile in North Carolina, I heard of two recent occasions, in which public religious services had been interrupted, and the preachers—very estimable coloured men—publicly whipped.

Olmsted, Cotton Kingdom, *175–76.*

After I had paid [the conjurer] his charge, he told me to go to the cowpen after night, and get some fresh cow manure, and mix it with red pepper and white people's hair, all to be put in a pot over the fire, and scorched until it could be ground up into snuff. I was then to sprinkle it about my master's bedroom, in his hat and boots, and it would prevent him from ever abusing me in any way. After I got it all ready prepared, the smallest pinch of it scattered over the room was enough to make a horse sneeze from the strength of it; but it did no good. . . . It was my job to make a fire in my master's chamber, night and morning. Whenever I could get a chance, I sprinkled a little of this dust about the linen of the bed. . . . This was to act upon them as what is called a kind of love powder, to change their sentiments of anger, to those of love toward me. But this all proved to be vain imagination.

Ex-slave Henry Bibb, Narrative, *71.*

"Dey didn't 'low us to go to church, neither. Sometimes us slip off an' hav a little prayer meetin' by usse'ves in a old house wid a dirt flo'. Dey' git happy an' shout an' couldn't nobody hyar 'em, caze dey didn't make no fuss on de dirt flo', an' one stan' in de do' an' watch. Some folks put dey head in de wash pot to pray [so that the sound would not be heard], an' pray easy, an' sombody be watchin' for de overseer. Us git whupped for ev'ything iffen hit was public knowed.

Ex-slave George Young, in Rawick, American Slave, *1:310.*

Slave Culture: Self-Respect and Status

In complimenting a woman called Joan upon the tidy condition of her house, she answered, with that cruel humility that is so bad an element in their [slaves'] character: "Missis no 'spect to find colored folks' house clean as white folks'." The mode in which they have learned to accept the idea of their own degradation and unalterable inferiority is the most serious impediment that I see in the way of their progress, since assuredly "self-love is not so vile a sin as self-neglecting." In the same way yesterday, Abraham the cook, in speaking of his brother's theft at the rice island, said "it was a shame even for a colored man to do such things."

Kemble, Journal *(1839), 298.*

When Colonel Lloyd's slaves met the slaves of Jacob Jepson, they seldom parted without a quarrel about their masters; Colonel Lloyd's slaves contending that he was the richest, and Mr. Jepson's slaves that he was the smartest, and most of a man. Colonel Lloyd's slaves would boast his ability to buy and sell Jacob Jepson. Mr. Jepson's slaves would boast his ability to whip Colonel Lloyd. These quarrels would almost always end in a fight between the parties, and those that whipped were supposed to have gained the point at issue. They seemed to think that the greatness of their masters was transferable to themselves. It was considered as being bad enough to be a slave; but to be a poor man's slave was deemed a disgrace indeed.

Douglass, Narrative, *36–37.*

The Powers That Be: Masters

The haughty and imperious part of a man develops rapidly on one of these lonely sugar plantations, where the owner rarely meets with any except his slaves and minions.

Rutherford B. Hayes, in Campbell, Empire, *201.*

[T]he children of slaveholders are universally inferior to themselves, mentally, morally, physically, as well as pecuniarily. . . . The young master not being able to own as many slaves as his father, usually works what he has more severely, and being more liable to embarrassment, the slaves' liability to be sold at an early day is much greater. For the same reason, slaves have a deep interest, generally, in the marriage of a young mistress. Very generally the daughters of slaveholders marry inferior men; men who seek to better their own condition by a wealthy connection. . . . Sometimes these are the sons of already broken-down slaveholders. In other cases they are adventurers

In this slave owner's vision of slave life, the caption reads: *"God bless you massa! you feed and clothe us. When we are sick you nurse us and when too old to work, you provide for us!" "These poor creatures are a sacred legacy from my ancestors and while a dollar is left me, nothing shall be spared to increase their comfort and happiness."* (Library of Congress)

from the North who remove to the South, and who readily become the most cruel masters.

Ex-slave James W. C. Pennington, Fugitive Blacksmith *(1849), in Bontemps,* Great Slave Narratives, *258–59.*

Were I to be again reduced to the chains of slavery, I should regard being the slave of a religious master the greatest calamity that could befall me. For of all slaveholders with whom I have ever met, religious slaveholders are the worst.

Former slave Frederick Douglass, 1845, in his Autobiography, *117.*

During the three hours, or more, in which I was in company with the proprietor [of a Virginia farm], I do not think ten consecutive minutes passed uninterrupted by some of the slaves requiring his personal direction or assistance. He was even obliged, three times, to leave the dinner-table.

"You see," said he, smiling, as he came in the last time, "a farmer's life, in this country, is no sinecure. . . . I only wish your philanthropists would contrive some satisfactory plan to relieve us of it; the trouble and the responsibility of properly taking care of our negroes, you may judge, from what you see yourself here, is anything but enviable."

Olmsted, Cotton Kingdom, *42.*

This exceptional condition [of the master's family living relatively well on a Virginia farm] . . . is maintained at an enormous expense, not only of money, but of nerve, time, temper, if not of humanity, or the world's judgment of humanity. There is much inherited wealth, a cotton plantation or two in Mississippi and a few slips of paper in a broker's office in Wall Street, that account for the comfort of this Virginia farmer. . . . And after all he has no road on which he can drive his fine horses; his physician supposes the use of chloric ether, as an anaesthetic agent, to be a novel and interesting subject of after-dinner eloquence; he has no church within twenty miles, but one of logs, attendance on which is sure to bring on an attack of neuralgia with his wife, and where only an ignorant ranter of a different faith from his own preaches at irregular intervals; there is no school which he is willing that his children should attend; his daily papers come weekly, and he sees no books except such as he has especially ordered from Norton or Stevens.

Olmsted, Cotton Kingdom, *86.*

[In Louisiana a slave] said . . . that there were many free negroes all about this region. Some were very rich. He pointed out to me three plantations, within twenty miles, owned by coloured men. These bought black folks, he said, and had servants of their own. They were very bad masters, very hard and cruel—hadn't any feeling. "You might think, master, dat dey would be good to dar own nation; but dey is not. I will tell you de truth, massa; I know I'se got to answer; and it's a fact, dey is very bad masters, sar. I'd rather be a servant to any man in de world, dan to a brack man. If I was sold to a brack man, I'd drown myself. I would dat—I'd drown myself! dough I shouldn't like to do dat nudder; but I wouldn't be sold to a coloured master for anyting."

Olmsted, Cotton Kingdom, *262.*

The Powers That Be: Mistresses

[W]oman . . . has but one right and that is the right to protection. The right to protection involves the obligation to obey. A husband, lord and master . . . nature designed for every woman.

George Fitzhugh, Sociology for the South, *214.*

Go inter de *house*, Miss Carrie! Yer ain't no manner er use heah only ter git yer face red wid de heat. I'll have dinner like yer wants it. Jes' read yer book an' res' easy til I sen's it ter de dining room.

Caroline Merrick's slave cook, in Fox-Genovese, Plantation Household, *142.*

The overseer has driven off many of the most valuable negroes. . . . I can no longer leave the Miserable creatures prey to the worst part of mankind without endeavouring to mitigate as far as it is in my power, the pangs of their cruel situation.

Fanny Bland Tucker, 1787 letter to her husband, in Clinton, Plantation Mistress, *191.*

I despise myself for suffering my temper to rise at the provocations offered by the servants. I would be willing to spend the rest of my life at the north, where I never should see the face of another negro. . . . Indulgence has ruined them. . . . I believe my servants are going to craze me. . . .

Sarah Haynsworth Gayle, diary, 1827, July 21, 1828, and July 6, 1835, in Fox-Genovese, Plantation Household, *22–23.*

I would be glad if you could ride down [to our plantation] and see after little matters for me before it gets too warm. When Patience gets through house-cleaning, etc., with Flora, I want her to go to Arcadia [another family plantation]

and pick all the geese carefully (also those at Montevideo) and have the feathers put into bags and sunned regularly. We want Gilbert to shear the sheep at both places now at once, and then Patience and Flora must pick and wash the wool until it is free from all grease or smell of any kind, and then have it all carded up ready to be made into mattresses. . . . And when Niger goes to the Island, they must take care of the poultry. Do charge them about the cats and Jet. . . . Tell Flora she must weed around all the flowers in the garden; I am afraid to trust the old man. . . . Cato can find employment for Miley and Kate. . . . I hope you have a *comfortable house* for your servant [slave] Lucy. You must not forget her welfare, for she is an excellent woman, and I think will be faithful to you.

Mary Jones giving instructions to her newly married daughter for care of the family plantations in her absence, May 22, 1857, in Myers, Children of Pride, *318–19.*

In this abolitionist vision, a mistress whips a slave woman. *(Library of Congress)*

I attended to my work well, and [my master] treated me well; but [my mistress] could not bear to hear me praised. *This sort of tyranny, occasioned by jealousy, is one of the most common causes of the bad treatment of the domestic servants of the South.* It is far more common than anybody knows of; for Southern gentlemen, generally, are very partial to colored girls. This makes a continual feud in families.

Slave woman, 1850s, quoted in Redpath, Roving Editor, *263.*

I wonder if it be a sin to think slavery a curse to any land. . . . God forgive us, but ours is a *monstrous* system and wrong and iniquity. Perhaps the rest of the world is as bad—this *only* I see.

Journal entry, March 18, 1861,
in Mary Chesnut's Civil War, *29.*

Miller McKim . . . told me . . . that some of the worst cases were those of concubines, mulattoes, who suffered from the jealousy of the wives of their masters. He mentioned two beautiful mulatto girls whose statements of barbarous cruelty were so shocking that he could not believe them and had their persons examined by a lady of his party, who found on their lacerated backs full confirmation of their dismal story. The parties whose names he mentioned were ladies of some of the best families.

Fisher, diary entry of August 31, 1863, A Philadelphia
Perspective, *459.*

The Powers That Be: Punishments by Civil Authority

[When slaves are executed] the Planters suffer little or nothing by it, for the Province is obliged to pay the full value they judge them worth to the Owner. . . .

John M. Brickell, Natural History of
North Carolina *(1737), quoted in Kay and Cary,*
Slavery in North Carolina, *87.*

In it [the Work House of Charleston, South Carolina] there were about forty individuals of both sexes. In the basement, there is an apparatus upon which the negroes, by order of the police, or at the request of their masters, are flogged. The latter can have nineteen lashes inflicted on them according to the existing law. The machine consists of a sort of crane, on which a cord with two nooses runs over pullies; the nooses are made fast to the hands of the slave and drawn up, while the feet are bound tight to a plank. The body is stretched out as much as possible, and thus the miserable creature receives the exact number of lashes as counted off! . . .

A tread-mill has been erected in a back building. . . . Two treadmills [are] in operation. Each employs twelve prisoners. . . . Six tread at once upon each wheel, while six rest upon a bench placed behind the wheel. Every half minute the left hand man steps off the treadwheel, while the five others move to the left to fill up the vacant place; at the same time the right hand man sitting on the bench, steps on the wheel, and begins his movement. . . . Thus, even three minutes sitting, allows the unhappy being no repose. The signal for changing is given by a small bell attached to the wheel. The prisoners are compelled to labour eight hours a day in this manner. Order is preserved by a person, who, armed with a cowhide, stands by the wheel.

Traveller Karl Bernhard, Duke of Saxe-Weimar, 1825–26,
in Ball, Slaves, *305–6.*

Heard a man at the tavern [in Middletown, Delaware] describe minutely a scene he had lately witnessed at St. Louis, the burning of a *Negro alive* for killing a sheriff. . . . Was surprised and shocked to find all present thought the punishment a just one & not too severe for a Negro!

Fisher, diary entry for April 12, 1856,
Philadelphia Perspective, *256.*

The Powers That Be: Punishments by Private Citizens

I perceived . . . something resembling a cage, suspended to the limbs of a tree, all the branches of which appeared covered with large birds of prey, fluttering about and anxiously endeavouring to perch on the cage. . . . I perceived a Negro, suspended in the cage and left there to expire! . . . [T]he birds had already picked out his eyes; his cheekbones were bare; his arms had been attacked in several places; and his body seemed covered with a multitude of wounds. From the edges of the hollow sockets and from the lacerations with which he was disfigured, the blood slowly dropped and tinged the ground beneath. No sooner were the birds flown than swarms of insects covered the whole body of this unfortunate wretch, eager to feed on his mangled flesh and to drink his blood.

Letter published 1782, in De Crèvecoeur, Letters from an
American Farmer, *178.*

The wife of Mr. Giles Hicks, living but a short distance from where I used to live, murdered my wife's cousin, a young girl between fifteen and sixteen years of age. . . . She had been set that night to mind Mrs. Hicks's baby, and during the night she fell asleep, and the baby cried. She, having lost her rest for several nights previous, did not hear the crying. They were both in the room with Mrs. Hicks. Mrs. Hicks, finding the girl slow to move, jumped from her bed, seized an oak stick of wood by the fireplace, and with it broke the girl's nose and breastbone, and thus ended her life. . . . There was a warrant issued for her arrest, but it was never served. . . . It was a common saying, even among little white boys, that it was worth a half-cent to kill a "nigger," and a half-cent to bury one.

Douglass, Narrative, *41–42.*

She then described to me that they were fastened up by their wrists to a beam or a branch of a tree, their feet barely touching the ground, so as to allow them no purchase for resistance or evasion of the lash, their clothes turned over their heads, and their backs scored with a leather thong, either by the driver himself, or, if he pleases to inflict their punishment by deputy, any of the men he may choose to summon to the office; it might be father, brother, husband, or lover, if the overseer so ordered it.

Kemble, Journal *(1839), 215.*

When they wanted to whip severely, they put the head and hands in stocks in a stooping posture.

The last two years I was in Tennessee, I saw nine persons at different times, made fast to four stakes, and whipped with a leather strap from their neck to their heels and on the bottoms of their feet, raising blisters: then the blisters broken with a platted whip, the overseer standing off and fetching hard blows.

William A. Hall, in A North-Side View *in* Four Fugitive Slave Narratives, *220–21.*

I's seen po' niggers 'mos' tore up by dogs and whupped 'tell dey bled w'en day did'n do lak de white folks say.

Ex-slave Charity Anderson, American Slave, *Alabama.*

[Forman] is a Georgian, a slaveholder and a warm advocate of slavery. . . . He admitted that . . . he had himself known instances of slaves being whipped to death, and of their being tied before a fire for the purpose of torture. But he added that persons guilty of such barbarities were always hated & despised by the community, and generally murdered by the slaves. "And what do you do with the slaves who kill such masters?" said I. "Oh, of course," he answered, "we are obliged to put them to death."

Fisher, diary entry of December 26, 1852, Philadelphia Perspective, *244.*

Finally my father let his sister take me and raise me with her children. She was good to me, but before he let her have me he willed I must wear a bell till I was twenty-one year old, strapped round my shoulders with the bell 'bout three feet from my head in a steel frame. That was for punishment for being born into the world a son of a white man and my mammy, a Negro slave. I wears this frame with the bell where I couldnt reach the clapper, day and night. I never knowed what it was to lay down in bed and get a good night's sleep till I was 'bout seventeen year old, when my father died and my missy took the bell offen me.

Ex-slave J. W. Terrill, in Botkin, Lay My Burden Down, *166.*

CHAPTER FIVE

Slave Work
1619–1865

Slaves newly arrived in the American colonies or the United States found only one familiar element—agriculture. Most came from agrarian economies in some ways similar to that of the American South. In Africa, some of them had grown rice, a major crop in the South. Until the end of the Civil War, southern agriculture, like that of Africa, depended primarily upon manual labor rather than on machines. So the slaves understood the field labor to which most of them were assigned, though probably in the small African villages they had worked more independently. The gender division of work might also have differed.

On the smaller southern farms, where the owner possessed or hired the use of only one or two slaves, they worked alongside him, and quite possibly his wife and children, in the fields. Additionally, they probably had to labor at household tasks. Ex-slave Mary Lindsay remembered how hard that kind of living was: "I have to git up at three o'clock sometimes so I have time to water the hosses and slop the hogs and feed the chickens and milk the cows, and then git back to the house and git the breakfast."[1]

House Servants

The larger the farm or plantation, the more specialized the work assigned. On the larger plantations, some slaves toiled only in their master's house. On the largest, the kitchen staff might include a presiding cook, her assistants, and numerous servers to transport the food from the kitchen—separate from the main house—and wait at table. "My job," reminisced Mammy Charity Anderson, "was lookin' atter de corner table whar nothin' but de desserts set."[2]

Several slaves might be assigned to the tasks of looking after the master's white children—though many families preferred white women as chief nurses. "Mrs. B favored me with the congratulations I have heard so many times on the subject of my having a white nurserymaid for my children," wrote Fanny Kemble. "Of course, she went into the old subject of the utter incompetency of Negro women to discharge such an office faithfully; but, in spite of her multiplied examples of their utter inefficiency, I believe the discussion ended by simply our both agreeing that ignorant Negro girls of twelve years old are not as capable or as trustworthy as well-trained white women of thirty."[3] But on many a plantation, black women did indeed raise white children, caring for them every moment of the day and night.

House servants also cleaned; did the huge washings and ironings required by 19th-century styles; spun, wove, and sewed; and acted as maids and valets. Some slaves preferred this work, partly because they escaped the hard physical labor of the fields and partly because it bestowed special privileges and status on them. They picked up information as they waited at table, overheard conversations, and went on errands off the property. Carriage drivers, trusted slaves carefully chosen for reliability and skill with equipage, got to leave the plantation frequently as they drove white men on business errands or white ladies shopping and visiting. Similarly, midwives often worked off their home plantations. Black "mammies" sometimes parleyed their authority over white children into power within the household generally, acting as surrogate mistresses and mothers.[4] The "mammy," John Cocke noted in his diary in 1863, "of course lives as well as the Mistress of the House & Mother of the children under her care. . . . She too like the foreman of the plantation, has her perquisites of office—and the privileges of bestowing small benefits upon her children & [all] the family and its visitors calling her Aunt—as Uncle is universally bestowed upon the Male House Servants."[5]

Cooks proudly carried the keys to the pantry, the symbol of household authority. Specialized skills also gave slaves a bit of leverage with their masters. One Henry Watson found himself in a dilemma about his cook Ellen, who tried his patience, but, as he remarked, "It is very difficult to get a negro who understands good cooking. If they do then ten to one they have some bad habits or bad temper & are not fit to be about. . . . Yet at times I think I can never be as well-suited—Ellen is a good *milker*, a negro rarely is. She makes *good bread*, few can do it, or do do it. She makes Excellent *coffee*. . . ."[6]

Other slaves detested household assignments because they came continually under the eye of master and mistress; they might even have to sleep in bedchambers or just outside their doors. Such intimacy might make for affection between master or mistress and slave—or, like all close living, it might rankle.

Artisans and Other Skilled Workers

Large plantations also afforded opportunities for outside slaves to specialize. W. E. B. Du Bois justly remarked, "There was one thing that the white South feared more than Negro dishonesty, ignorance, and incompetency, and that was Negro honesty, knowledge, and efficiency."[7] Yet determined as masters might be to keep slaves ignorant and dependent, their own comfort and convenience and their own economic interests argued for teaching slaves more skills. The slave who could read, write, and calculate could better secure his master's profits when he took a load of cotton to be sold or a load of corn to be milled. Owners who wished to live with a modicum of comfort and ease on their isolated plantations needed slaves with special skills.

The richest owners might send a slave lad to England to learn landscape gardening, just as they sent their cooks abroad to learn French cuisine. Slightly less affluent masters apprenticed promising slave youngsters to neighboring artisans for training as carpenters, coopers, blacksmiths, and shoemakers. Other slaves learned their crafts on their own plantations from their seniors or from skilled white workers. Blacks found their way about the forests and picked up survival skills from their fellow Indian slaves. Some of those who ran their masters' boats on the coast and the inland rivers became expert pilots. In his travels through the South, Frederick Law Olmsted ran across a slave who in his youth "had been employed, for some years, as a waiter, but, at his own request, was eventually allowed to learn the blacksmith's trade, in the plantation shop. Showing ingenuity and talent, he was afterwards employed to make and repair the plantation cotton-gins. Finally, his owner took him to a steam-engine builder, and paid $500 to have him instructed as a machinist. After he had become a skilful workman, he obtained employment as an engineer. . . ."[8]

Women slaves were usually confined to the domestic arts. Even so, some of them were prized for their deftness in dressing hair, making hats and shawls, spinning, weaving, tailoring, or cooking.

With slave artisans, a plantation could produce almost everything needed for daily consumption. When a slave acquired a reputation for expertise in, say, blacksmithing, neighbors might order their tools from him, to the profit of his owner. "Of my working Negroes," Major Pierce Butler informed a prospective buyer of his plantation in 1809, "I keep from 40 to 50 male slaves out of the field, to wit, about 14 house carpenters, 2 mechanics, 6 ship carpenters, 12 to 15 Ditchers, 4 Tanners, Curriers and Shoemakers. I turn my own leather, make my own shoes and those of my Neighbors—my own harness, etc. 4 Blacksmiths, three masons, 2 brick makers, two painters who are also sailmakers. . . ."[9]

The more adroit of these artisans sometimes progressed to inventing. Former slave John Parker told how he had invented a "clod smasher, which was a very important farm implement of that period with so much new land to break up." He made a model and showed it to the white superintendent—who stole both the model and the idea.[10] The Mississippi master of a slave who invented a "double plow" tried to get it patented, but the U.S. attorney general refused on the ground that "a machine invented by a slave, though it be new and useful, cannot, in the present state of the law, be patented," adding that even "if such a patent were issued to the master, it would not protect him in courts against persons who might infringe it."[11]

Field Hands

The great majority of slaves did field work, where day after day they dug ditches to drain the fields, patched eroded land, built fences, plowed, planted, hoed weeds, and picked and harvested. The strongest men and women were put to digging ditches, cutting trees, hauling logs with leather straps attached to their shoulders, and building and repairing roads and railroads. They began at sunrise or shortly before and labored on with a couple of breaks for meals until sundown. By common practice, slaves had part of Saturday and all Sunday off to cultivate their garden patches, maintain their cabins, amuse themselves, or rest; harsh masters, however, worked their slaves seven days a week, and far beyond the usual 12–14 hours daily that most required.

This dull, backbreaking labor sapped slaves' strength, aged them prematurely, and shortened their lives. Fanny Kemble wrote of "Engineer Ned's" plea that his wife be placed on lighter tasks: "[S]he had to work in the rice fields, and was 'most broke in two' with labor, and exposure, and hard work while with child, and hard

Slaves pick cotton. *(Library of Congress)*

work just directly after childbearing; he said she could hardly crawl, and he urged me very much to speak a kind word for her to massa. She was almost all the time in the hospital, and he thought she could not live long."[12]

On the larger farms and plantations, field workers were typically placed in gangs, depending on strength and in some cases on gender. At about six, children were set to work running errands, gathering wood, looking after babies and toddlers, or toting seed. Children just beginning field work, usually at about age 10 or 12; old women; nursing mothers; and women in the last months of pregnancy made up the trash gangs, clearing debris off roadsides, raking stubble, pulling weeds, doing light hoeing, and picking cotton.

Healthy women who were not pregnant were considered three-quarter hands, pregnant women half-hands. Some plantations put women in separate gangs—to which they occasionally assigned men as punishment, forcing them to do "women's work," like washing. Yet on other plantations women, particularly after they reached the menopause, were put to the hardest tasks. "I split rails like a man," ex-slave Sally Brown remembered. "I used a huge glut [a wedge] made out's wood, and a iron wedge drove into the wood with a maul, and this would split the wood."[13] At night, women still had cooking and housework to do, besides stints of spinning and quilting set by their mistresses.

The papers of a Louisiana plantation described its field hands' annual cycle of hard labor. In January and February, for instance, mule teams hauled manure, and the hands racked it up; other hands shelled and shucked corn, hauled fence rails, put up fences, and cleared corn stalks by plowing them under or burning them. The manager of one plantation noted that on a February day, "Four hands chopped down willows in the bottoms. Others were chopping weeds, hauling cottonseed, and cleaning out the ditch in the bottom of No. 8 field. While Allen, one of the few skilled slaves, was repairing harrows and sharpening ploughs, twenty-four hands were rolling logs, picking up chunks and brush in the deadening, stopping up washings [erosion] and making a levee in the bottoms of No. 2. Several cleaned the gutters on the gin, while five sickly hands were picking wool."[14]

On many plantations, slaves worked by the *gang* system—that is, for a specific time each day. Under such a system, with no prospect but another hard day's labor on the morrow, how were slaves to be motivated? Some, perhaps, would respond to praise; most could be moved to work by the lash. But left unsupervised, as they inevitably must be for much of the time on large plantations, what was to keep them at it? Even if an overseer was riding horseback up and down the rows, slaves might slack off when he was at the other end of their rows.

In fact, masters and the overseers and slave drivers they designated as supervisors had a lot of trouble getting work done. Out of their sight, slaves slowed down or stopped their work. Slaves broke or lost tools. Frederick Olmsted, who traveled extensively throughout the slave South, believed that slave labor on most farms and plantations was egregiously inefficient. In desperation, some slave owners and supervisors resorted to some kind of reward—perhaps extra food, or tobacco, or even money. "[T]o git mutch ditching done," wrote overseer Roswell King, "I must give them rum."[15]

Especially in South Carolina and Georgia, owners used the more efficient system of *task labor*, allotting slaves specific tasks to be accomplished on any one day, after which their time was their own. "For instance, in making drains in light, clean meadow land, each man or woman of the full hands is required to dig one thousand cubic feet; in swamp-land that is being prepared for rice culture, where there are not many stumps, the task for a ditcher is five hundred feet: while in a very strong cypress swamp, only two hundred feet is required; in hoeing rice, a certain number of rows, equal to one-half or two-thirds of an acre, according to the condition of the land; in sowing rice (strewing in drills), two acres; in reaping rice (if it stands well), three-quarters of an acre; or, sometimes a gang will be required to reap, tie in sheaves, and carry to the stack-yard the produce of a certain area. . . . Hoeing cotton, corn or potatoes; one half to one acre. Threshing: five to six hundred sheaves. In ploughing rice land (light, clean, mellow soil) with a yoke

Buyers test tobacco. The sign reads: "In General Pierce We Put Our Manly Trust." *(Crowe, With Thackeray in America)*

Slaves take cotton to market. *(Blake,* History of Slavery and the Slave Trade*)*

of oxen, one acre a day, including the ground lost in and near the drains—the oxen being changed at noon. A cooper, also, for instance, is required to make barrels at the rate of eighteen a week. . . . These are the tasks for first-class able-bodied men; they are lessened by one quarter for three-quarter hands. . . ."[16] Slaves who knew they could finish their tasks early if they hurried had a reason to work quickly.

Supervisors

Some masters lived on their plantations or moved with the seasons from one of their plantations to another. Others chose to live elsewhere: Pierce Butler avowed that "my principal object is to be saved the necessity of ever going to see my Estate."[17] In either case, they might delegate the supervision of the slaves to one among the slaves or, more rarely, to a white "overseer."[18] With an absentee landlord, the overseer bore heavy responsibilities. Ideally, he would plan the farm work, decide when to plant and when to harvest, closely superintend the slaves, clothe them, distribute their food, look after their health and well-being, and discipline them. (Masters did not want their slaves—their capital—crippled or sick, but they did want the best possible profit.) The overseer's wife assisted him. She was charged with supervising the household servants.

Overseers seldom thought their lot a happy one. "If there ever was or ever will be a calling in life as mean and contemptible as that of an overseer," one of them complained, "I would be right down glad to know what it is, and where to be found. . . . If there be . . . a favorable crop, the *master* makes a splendid crop; if any circumstances be unpropitious and an inferior crop is made, it is the overseer's fault, and if he flogs [the slaves] to keep them at home, or locked up . . . he is a brute and a tyrant. If no meat is made, the overseer *would* plant too much cotton. . . . If hogs are taken good care of the overseer is wasting corn, and 'the most careless and thriftless creature alive.' If he does not 'turn out' [waken and set to work] hands in time, he is *lazy;* if he 'rousts' them out as your dad and mine had to do, why he is a brute." Another wailed, "If I donte please every negro on the place they run away rite strate."[19]

Overseeing was not a job for an educated man. It carried little prestige. Many overseers exploited their power over the slaves, raping and torturing them cruelly. Frederick Douglass wrote of one who shot a disobedient slave in cold blood.[20] Some stole from their employers. Overseers of such a kind earned the Simon Legree* reputation often associated with the position.

To the slaves, the overseer was usually a natural enemy. On occasion they bore tales about him to the master, who, wary that the overseer might cheat him, was likely to listen to the slaves' complaints. "The negroes have great spite and hatred towards them [overseers] and frequently fight them, when the overseer pretends [dares] to whip them," complained Elijah Fletcher. "The negroes think as meanly of the poor white people, as the rich white people do themselves and think anybody that is so poor as to be an overseer mean [lowly] enough."[21]

Because he could not be everywhere on the plantation at all times, the overseer might delegate part of his authority to black slave drivers—also called variously foremen, overlookers, leading men, headmen, bosses, whipping bosses, crew leaders, overdrivers, underdrivers, and straw bosses. Masters might use such drivers as stewards in place of a white overseer. A few of them acquired astonishing power and status. Olmsted tells of one whom his owner called a "watchman": "He carried by a strap at his waist, a very large number of keys, and had charge of all the stores of provisions, tools, and materials of the plantations, as well as of all their produce, before it was shipped to market. He weighed and measured out all the rations of the slaves and the cattle; superintended the mechanics, and made and repaired, as was necessary, all the machinery, including the steamengine [that ran the rice mill]. In all these departments, his authority was superior to that of the overseer. The overseer received his private allowance of family provisions from him, as did also the head-servant at the mansion, who was his brother. His responsibility was much greater than that of the overseer; and Mr. X. said he would trust him with much more than he would any overseer he had ever known."[22]

A driver usually lived in the first house in the yard. Every morning he awakened the other slaves with a blast on a conch shell or by ringing a bell. As instructed by the overseer or owner, he assigned tasks to the workers in his charge and checked their work. In many ways slave drivers resembled army sergeants. They were, so to speak, non-commissioned officers, providing liaison between superiors and slaves, whites and blacks. They belonged to the ranks of slaves, but they had the power and responsibility of authority over the others, and they were responsible for their welfare—even to the point of distributing their food. Their powers of punishment were usually limited to a given number of strokes of the lash. They could sometimes also act as ombudsmen for the other slaves, intervening if they thought the tasks assigned too heavy. Inevitably, some of them swaggered about and abused their fellows; other drivers protected the slaves they supervised, only pretending to whip them.

Almost all slave drivers were male. Now and then, however, the records show a slave forewoman in charge of the slave women, the adolescents, and the old people on the plantation. A South Carolina planter liked to appoint women as temporary overseers to cover each hill of corn and make sure that it was properly sown.[23]

---

*An overseer who has Tom flogged to death in Harriet Beecher Stowe's novel *Uncle Tom's Cabin*.

Breeders

Of all the kinds of work that slaves performed, probably the most valuable to their owners, and the worst compensated, was reproduction. In an economy where an owner's most valuable property was his slaves, women of childbearing age were a double asset. In them the owner had a win-win investment: They could do both productive and reproductive work.

In 1858, the magazine *Southern Cultivator* published an article on the economics of breeding: "I own a woman who cost me $400 when a girl, in 1827. Admit she made me nothing—only worth her victuals and clothing. She now has three children, worth over $3000 and have been field hands say three years; in that time making enough to pay their expenses before they were half hands, and then I have the profit of all half hands. She has only three boys and a girl out of a dozen [pregnancies]: yet, with all her bad management, she has paid me ten per cent. interest, for her work was to be an average good, and I would not this night touch $700 for her. Her oldest boy is worth $1250 cash and I can get it."[24]

Slave owners read magazine articles on the best conditions for breeding and talked about the capabilities of particular women for that task. Masters were obsessed with the potential for increasing their capital. They forced male slaves to take more than one wife and to stand at stud. They pressured slave women to have babies by reminding the women whom they gave permission to marry, "Don't forget to bring me a little one or two for next year." They threatened barren women with being sold away. They assigned easier work to pregnant women and nursing mothers. They rewarded prolific women with money, dresses, occasionally even emancipation if they bore a certain number of children. One owner gave every woman with six children alive at one time every Saturday off. Pauli Murray writes of attempts to hire out her beautiful great-grandmother to breed her.[25]

Town and City and Institutional Slaves

The small minority of slaves who lived in towns or cities—less than 6 percent—frequently worked as body or household servants.[26] But the male slaves also worked in shipyards, brickyards, cotton presses, and warehouses. They assisted masters who were tailors and saddlemakers. They were employed as butchers, waiters, barbers, painters, masons, bricklayers, and glaziers. Some kept taverns. As a rule, they had better working conditions than field hands.

Institutions, such as churches, might also buy slaves, usually to hire out to other employers. Southern factories and mines relied heavily on slave labor, either from slaves they owned or from slaves hired out from other masters. The Manchester and Wilmington Railroad, running along what James Redpath called "the most desolate looking country in the Union," owned most of its hands. "The railroad hands sleep in miserable shanties along the line," Redpath reported. "Their bed is an inclined pine board—nothing better, softer, or warmer, as I can testify from my personal experience. Their covering is a blanket. The fireplaces in these cabins are often so clumsily constructed that all the heat ascends the chimney. . . . [T]he temperature of the cabin, at this season of the year (November), is bitterly cold and uncomfortable. . . . Of course, as the negroes are not released from their work until sunset, and as, after coming to their cabins, they have to cook their ash-cakes or mush, or dumplings, these huts are by no means remarkable for their cleanly appearance.

Poor fellows! In that God-forsaken section of the earth they seldom see a woman from Christmas to Christmas."[27]

In 1856, the governor of Tennessee advocated that the state buy slaves to build a canal on Muscle Shoals, picturing it as an idyllic arrangement (from the point of view of the state): "In this way the work would only cost the interest on the money invested [in the slaves], the loss sustained on the property by death or casualty, the subsistence of the hands, and the charges of superintendence—the work would be accomplished without any difficulty in its details, and with just reference to its durability and usefulness. With the effective hands, it might be convenient to purchase a suitable number of women to cook, wash, and perhaps perform the lighter parts of the work, and this would be perfectly consistent with the humanity of purchasing men with their wives, whenever such opportunities of purchase might offer. . . . At suitable places along the canal, the hands might cultivate . . . the vegetables which would be proper to promote their comfort, and the preservation of their health. . . . This corps of pioneers [construction workers] . . . might afterwards be employed on Railroads, Turnpike roads, improving the navigation of our rivers, and opening other canals where the public good might require."[28]

Hiring Out

Particularly in the later years of slavery, many urban slaves were engaged in the practice of "hiring out"—used also to a lesser extent in the countryside. Masters usually hired out slaves whose labor they did not immediately need, renting out their labor for a specific period of time in return for a fixed amount of money. But in some cases, masters bought slaves with the intent of hiring them out. A German farmer near Natchez owned four slave men, whom he hired out as porters or servants in town, while he employed a white man to work with him on his farm. "To explain the economy of this arrangement, he said that one of his men [slaves] earned in Natchez $30 a month clear of all expenses, and the others much more than he could ever make their labour worth to him. A negro of moderate intelligence would hire, as a house-servant, for $200 a year and his board, which was worth $8 a month; whereas he hired this white fellow, who was strong and able, for $10 a month."[29]

Other masters used hiring out as a means of training their slaves. They might, like Frederick Douglass's master, hire them to a farmer notorious for "breaking" defiant slaves, or they might hire them to craftsmen.[30] "The slaveholders in that state [Maryland] often hire the children of their slaves out to non-slaveholders, not only because they save themselves the expense of taking care of them, but in this way they get among their slaves useful trades," wrote James Pennington. "They put a bright slave boy with a tradesman, until he gets such a knowledge of the trade as to be able to do his own work, and then he takes him home."[31]

If a slave developed an unusual talent, like playing a musical instrument or jigging, his master might hire him out as an entertainer. One planter in 1856 advertised the services of a kind of slave combo led by "Robin," who had taught himself to play the fiddle, using bows of twigs on horses' hairs strung across pieces of wood, and had taught his three brothers to play as well. His master had then hired a teacher to polish their musical skills.[32] Another made money by betting on the ability of his slave to outdance all challengers.

Some scholars think that slaves were hired out five or six times as often as they were sold.[33] So many slaves were hired out and so diverse were the occupations for which they were hired that annual days were set aside for arrangements to be made. The practice also spun off subsidiary businesses. In some cities, agencies sprang up to hire out as servants or factory hands slaves whom their owners sent into town for that purpose.[34]

Of course hiring out had its problems. Slaves hired out acquired some degree of independence. If they were dissatisfied with their working or living conditions, they might complain to their masters; the owners, wanting their slaves kept healthy, might then threaten to end the contract, or at least not renew it the next year unless the situation improved. One ironworks superintendent reported gloomily, "Our [slave] hands are here today wanting flour, coffee & tobacco. I have for the past month been putting them off—I am afraid they will leave in a body & throw us behind. . . . We by all means should have something to satisfy them if we wish to keep them."[35] What was more, the use of task work in some industries gave slaves a degree of control over their own time and labor. In certain lumber camps, for example, slaves on the task-work system actually subcontracted with runaway slaves hiding in the forest to do their jobs for them. These hired-out slaves paid the runaways with part of the bonus they received for producing shingles over and above their stint—not to mention their profits from the sale of the fur from animals they hunted in the woods in their spare time.[36]

Employers who hired slaves were expected to return them at the end of the contract in good condition. "Whoever hired a negro gives on the spot a bond for the amount, to be paid at the end of term, even should the hired negro fall sick or run off in the meantime," wrote traveler Johann Schoepf in the early 1780s. "The hirer must also pay the negro's head tax, feed him and clothe him. Hence a negro is capital put out at a very high interest, but because of elopement and death very unstable."[37] If an employer who had hired a slave called a doctor for him, who was to pay—the master or the hirer? If a hirer shot and wounded a slave attempting to run away, was he liable for the damage to her? What if a slave were killed doing dangerous work that the hirer had set him to?

Lawsuits were brought asking that hirers recompense owners for the loss of or damage to slaves. For instance, one master won the full price of his slave, who had run away and been hired to unload a ship; its owners were held responsible for the slave's drowning.[38] Hirers ran another risk, too, as Olmsted pointed out: "But a more serious loss frequently arises, when the slave, thinking he is worked too hard, or being angered by punishment or unkind treatment, 'getting the sulks,' takes to 'the swamp,' and comes back when he has a mind to. Often this will not be till the year is up for which he is engaged, when he will return to his owner, who glad to find his property safe, and that it has not died in the swamp, or gone to Canada, forgets to punish him, and immediately sends him for another year to a new master."[39]

When a hiring-out arrangement proved satisfactory all around, it might be renewed year after year. Enterprising slaves sought out people to hire them whom they thought desirable as masters. Some persuaded their owners to let them hire out their own time, assuming financial responsibility for their own keep and, in addition, agreeing to pay their owners either a percentage of their wages or a fixed amount weekly, monthly, or annually.

Residents of the slave states argued about whether this practice was wise. "Recent events demonstrate the fact that the employment of free negroes, mulattoes, and . . . slaves who hire their own time, on board of steamboats on the western waters, is a cause of serious loss and danger to the slave states and slave owners," wrote the editor of the St. Louis *Daily Evening Gazette* on August 18, 1841. "These have the opportunity of constant communication with slaves of Missouri, Kentucky and the other southern States, and have also very frequent communication with the free negroes and abolitionists of Illinois, Indiana, Ohio, and Pennsylvania. This communication renders the slaves restless and induces them to run away, and furnishes them a means of escape. . . . The negro hands on board the steamboats can frequently conceal runaway negroes . . . without the consent of the captain."[40] Attorney Charles Colcock Jones lamented the increased freedom of the hired-out slave: "There are, you may say, hundreds of Negroes in this city [Savannah] who go about from house to house—some carpenters, some house servants, etc.—who never see their masters except at pay day, live out of their yards, hire themselves without written permit, etc."[41]

But slave owners also feared the likely reactions of white workers, who could vote. What if they opposed the slave system, seeing slaves as competitors for jobs? "Drive out negro mechanics and all sorts of operatives from our Cities, and who must take their place[?]" asked industrialist C. G. Memminger. "The same men who make the cry in the Northern Cities against the tyranny of Capital—and there as here would drive all before them . . . who interfere with them—and would soon raise hue and cry against the Negro, and be hot Abolitionists—and every one of those men would have a vote."[42]

The whole debate over slaves' hiring their own time got tangled up with the issue of whether whites or blacks were better workers. "Take I say again and again one of my most faith[ful] servants [slaves] give him some encouragement or fourth part of what you must give to a white lad [and] take my word for it you'll find him ten times better than any you can hire," wrote David Ross of the Oxford Iron Works. "[H]e will labour day by day[,] he has ten time[s] more experience and [is] a much honester man, he will receive your instructions with patience and humility & if a reprimand becomes necessary he will receive it without putting out your eyes."[43]

The hiring-out system triumphed, simply because it worked too well to be abandoned. On the frontier, the practice met the need for diversification of labor. Widows and orphans who inherited slaves could avoid the problems of managing them by hiring them out. Small farmers who could not scrape together the price of a slave might rent one. A horse owner might rent an expert jockey for a particular race. A plantation mistress in need of new dishes might briefly hire an expert potter. Most important of all, hiring out paid masters well.

After all, owners could hire out skilled slaves, even aged ones, for more than double a good rate of interest on what they would bring in a sale.[44] "While employers of hired, rented, or leased slaves paid owners annual fees ranging from $80 to $100, payments made by self-hired slaves averaged from $150 to over $200 annually, in the thirty-year period before the Civil War." Prices for renting slaves fluctuated with the prices of buying them, "but generally slave owners could expect a return of 10 to 20 percent of the local value of a male slave per year."[45] A prospective buyer might rent a slave for a year to test him. Mines and factories rented slaves as employees. During the Civil War, the Confederacy hired slaves as hospital nurses.

Slaves as Entrepreneurs

No matter how many laws forbade them to own anything, slaves could not be kept out of the money economy. In 1859, Robert F. W. Allston, noting that during a two-year absence his slaves had taken possession of his hogs, so that he had few to sell, decided to experiment with letting them raise the hogs for him, giving every slave who headed a family the privilege of keeping one hog, provided that every fall the slave should bring the overseer two young hogs fit for killing during the next winter. For the smaller of the two, the slave was to be paid at the rate of $5 per hundred pounds. The rest of the litter(s) belonged to the slave, though he could not sell them off the plantation.[46] Alabama planter William Jemmison set up his slaves as sharecroppers.[47]

Without such incentives, slaves grew expert in dodging work, feigning illness, running away to hide in the woods for a while, and goldbricking. Other owners resorted to offering prizes, sometimes including money, for the fastest cotton picking. Thrifty slaves sometimes arranged with their masters to sell off unneeded rations of cornmeal for the slaves' profit. Industrious slaves grew their own cotton and garden produce, raised poultry, collected moss, wove baskets, carved trays, and manufactured brooms for sale.

Slave entrepreneurs moved from hiring out their own time to setting up their own businesses. They turned particularly to occupations where close supervision was impractical or to occupations that southern white laborers scorned, like the food and personal services industries, but slaves also worked as carpenters, coopers, wheelwrights, painters, masons, bricklayers, teamsters, draymen, liverymen, and boatmen. Unskilled slaves became peddlers and hawkers. Others set up groceries and secondhand clothing shops and truck farms. Women did laundry, catered, and sold their services as midwives and nurses. Elizabeth Keckley, who bought her own freedom with the profits of her dressmaking business in St. Louis, went on to

A black barber plies his trade in Richmond, Virginia. (*Crowe,* With Thackeray in America)

Market women await customers. *(Crowe,* With Thackeray in America*)*

become dressmaker to Mary Todd Lincoln. A few blacks not only bought their own freedom and that of their families but also acquired land and slaves to till it.

In conducting any business, the slave entrepreneur faced enormous difficulties. The law was always on the side of the whites with whom the slave dealt. They could take advantage of the slave at will. If he deposited money in a bank, the bank might refuse to return it—after all, the law said that slaves could not own property. "I have been cheated by a rich slaveholder out of half a bushel of corn in buying half a barrel," wrote David West. "I knew it and he knew it; but he knew I would not dare say anything about it,—the law was such that he could have me whipped, if I were to contradict him."[48]

Chronicle of Events

1492
• Columbus discovers the West Indies, opening markets for slaves to work in the mines.

1643
• The introduction of sugar planting into the West Indies creates a demand for slaves.

1665
• The "Duke of York laws" promote slave labor in the British North American colonies, discourage the presence of white indentured servants, and grant port and warehouse privileges to ships in international slaving.

1694
• The introduction of rice culture into Carolina leads to the rapid importation of slaves.

1711
• A market house is established in New York City as the central location for the hiring of all slaves.

1780
• Ex-slave Dr. James Derham, born 1757, practices medicine in New Orleans.

1793
• Eli Whitney patents the cotton gin, thereby increasing the market value of slaves by making cotton

An artist depicts his conception of the first cotton gin. *(Library of Congress)*

production more profitable and swelling the demand for cheap labor.

1810
• Congress denies blacks the right to work as mail carriers.

1813
• Congress restricts employment on American ships to citizens of the United States and "persons of color, natives of the United States."

1821
• The South Carolina legislature requires that black crew members of any ship coming into port must be arrested and held in jail while their ship lies in harbor.

1829
• The poems of slave George Moses Horton are published to raise money for his freedom and transportation to Liberia; the plan fails.

1846
• Texas passes a law (widely violated) forbidding slaves to hire their own time for more than one day a week, except during Christmas holidays.

1853
• The Marshall Mechanics Association is formed in Texas to prevent "as far as possible, mechanical labor by slaves, from coming in competition with that of white men."

1856
• Congress denies blacks preemption rights on public lands.

1859
• An outcry arises in the South for renewal of the slave trade to meet labor demands and produce more cotton.

Artist Eyre Crowe ironically enthrones a Black atop a bale of cotton. (*Crowe,* With Thackeray in America*)*

• White workers in Charleston, South Carolina, petition the legislature for relief from competition with blacks, whether slave or free.

1865
• Free black Martin A. Delany is commissioned a field officer in the U.S. Army.
• Congress charters the Freedman's Bank, an interstate bank.
• Shipyard caulkers in Baltimore strike to prevent yards from hiring black caulkers.

Eyewitness Testimony

The Workers: Artisans and Other Skilled Workmen

Master Hugh . . . took me into the ship-yard of which he was foreman, in the employment of Mr. Walter Price. There I was immediately set to calking, and very soon learned the art of using my mallet and irons. In the course of one year . . . I was able to command the highest wages given to the most experienced calkers. I was now of some importance to my master. I was bringing him from six to seven dollars per week.

Ex-slave Frederick Douglass, Narrative, *103.*

You must know then that many of my servants [slaves] at Oxford have double trades, some of them treble, most of my Blacksmiths are also potters, and part of them go into the pot houses when the furnace is in blast. . . .

Ironworks owner David Ross, letter of July 25, 1813, in Lewis, Coal, Iron, and Slaves, *28.*

[On a trip to New Orleans about 1830] We were all bound to take our turn at the helm, sometimes under direction of the captain, and sometimes on our own responsibility, as he could not be always awake. . . . [A]s I was the only negro in the boat, I was compelled to stand at least three turns at the helm to any other person's one; so that . . . I learned the art of steering and managing the boat far better than the rest. I watched the manoeuvres necessary to shoot by a "sawyer" [tangle of dead trees], to land on a bank, avoid a snag, or a steamboat, in the rapid current of the Mississippi, till I could do it as well as the captain.

Henson, Autobiography, *50–51.*

My father . . . liberated all the children he had by my mother, and one other slave woman, with one exception—that was a daughter whom he had educated and put to the milliner's trade. After she had learned the trade, he went to the place where she was, with money to establish her in business. But he found she had two children by a white man. This so enraged him, that he carried her and her two children back to his farm, and put her to work in the field, and there, he said, she was to die.

Mrs. Henry Gowens, in Four Fugitive Slave Narratives, *100.*

I sought to distinguish myself in the finer branches of the business [blacksmithing] by invention and finish; I fre-

quently tried my hand at making guns and pistols, putting blades in pen knives, making fancy hammers, hatchets, sword-cases, &c., &c. . . .

James W. C. Pennington, Fugitive Blacksmith, *1850, in Owens,* Property, *180.*

Henry Fort . . . had been stoker for the engineer and Tuesday morning [after the white employees who had been running the mill went off to fight for the Confederacy] he came to the Master and asked permission to fire up—"Henry," said the Master, "it will be no use to fire up without an engineer." "No sir, I kno's dat but I ben a'studyin' an' a'studyin' on dat ingin' a long time—an I kin run her jis' as well as John Cardy—an' Marse Ned, me an' Mac an' Peter kin run dat whole cuncern if you will keep de books an' will let us pick out de helpers we wants." The Master was surprised and pleased, but also somewhat doubtful. "Do you think you boys can do it?" "Yes Marse Ned we sho' kin—jis' as I sed I kin run de ingin' same as John Cardy—Peter is run de saw fur Wheeler when you didn't know nuthin' erbout it—an' Mac is jis' as good a miller as yer wants ter see."

Reminiscences of a slaveholder's daughter, Eppes, Negro, *108.*

Rev. Emperor Williams was . . . a master mason, and from 1846 to 1858 was the trusted foreman of his owner. . . . His master had a difficult piece of cornice work on the corner of Perdido and Carondelet Streets. None of the white men could put it up. Williams said he could, and his master replied that if he did he should have his freedom. He took the plans of the difficult piece of work, laid them on the floor of his cabin, and studied them all night until he got every part perfectly in his mind. The next day he took his gang of men and accomplished his difficult work.

W. D. Goodman interview, in Blassingame, Slave Testimony, *621.*

Tom has been doing very well thus far; has made eight pair of shoes for the children, besides mending, and over a dozen lasts of various sizes, all of which display quite a genius in design and execution. I will make him for the present complete the tanning and make up some shoes for the needy ones here. He is certainly a smart boy, and learned well in Mount Vernon.

Plantation mistress Mary Jones, October 7, 1863, in Myers, Children of Pride, *1110.*

The Workers: Breeders

Planters oblige [slave women who do not bear children after a year or two of cohabitation with their husbands] to take a second, third, fourth, fifth or more Husbands or Bedfellows; a fruitful woman amongst them being very much valued by the Planters, and numerous Issue esteemed the greatest riches in the Country.

John Brickell, Natural History of North Carolina, *in Oakes*, Ruling Race, *26.*

Mr. Covey was a poor man; he was just commencing in life; he was only able to buy one slave; . . . he bought her, as he said, for a *breeder*. . . . She was a large able-bodied woman, about twenty years old. She had already given birth to one child, which proved her to be just what he wanted. After buying her, he hired a married man of Mr. Samuel Harrison, to live with him one year; and him he used to fasten up with her every night!

Ex-slave Frederick Douglass, describing events of the early 1830s, Narrative, *74–75.*

Women with six children alive at any one time are allowed all Saturday to themselves.

Bassett, Southern Plantation Overseer, *32.*

[Master was] mighty careful about raisin' healthy nigger families and used us strong, healthy young bucks to stand the healthy nigger gals. When I was young they took care not to strain me and I was as handsome as a speckled pup and was in demand for breedin'.

Ex-slave Jeptha Choice, in Tadman, Speculators and Slaves, *123.*

The Workers: Drivers

[When a pregnant woman fainted in the field], de driver said dat she was puttin' on an' dat she ort ter be beat. De master said dat she can be beat but don't ter hurt de baby. . . . [The driver put the woman into a hold in the ground] 'bout ter her arm pits, den he kivers her up an' straps her han's over her haid, [and took] de long bull whup an' he cuts long gashes all over her shoulders an' raised arms, den he walks off an' leaves her dar fer a hour in de hot sun. . . . De flies an' de gnats day worry her, an' de sun hurts too an' she cries a little, den de driver comes out wid a pan full of vinegar, salt an' red pepper an' he washes de gashes. De 'oman faints an' he digs her up, but in a few minutes she am stone dead.

Analiza Foster's mother, in Fox-Genovese, Plantation Households, *190.*

[N]early all the drivers I have seen are tall and strong men—but a great deal of judgment, requiring greater capacity of mind than the ordinary slave is often supposed to be possessed of, is certainly needed in them. A good driver is very valuable and usually holds office for life. His authority is not limited to the direction of labour in the field, but extends to the general deportment of the negroes. He is made to do the duties of policeman, and even of police magistrate. It is his duty, for instance, on Mr. X's estate [a flourishing rice plantation in Georgia], to keep order in the settlement; and, if two persons, men or women, are fighting, it is his duty to immediately separate them, and then to "whip them both". . . .

Having generally had long experience on the plantation, the advice of the drivers is commonly taken in nearly all the administration, and frequently they are, *de facto*, the managers. Orders on important points of the plantation economy, I have heard given by the proprietor directly to them, without the overseer's being consulted or informed of them; and it is often left with them to decide when and how long to flow the rice-grounds—the proprietor and overseer deferring to their more experienced judgment. Where the drivers are discreet, experienced, and trusty, the overseer is frequently employed merely as a matter of form, to comply with the laws requiring the superintendence or presence of a white man among every body of slaves; and his duty is rather to inspect and report than to govern. Mr. X . . . has sometimes left his plantation in care of one of the drivers for a considerable length of time, after having discharged an overseer. . . .

Olmsted, Cotton Kingdom, *193–94.*

The Workers: Factory Operators, Miners, and Lumbermen

[I recommend to the owner of an ironworks] as soon as he Can conveniently do it to get Young Negro Lads to put under the Smith Carpenters Founders Finers & Fillers as also to get a certain number of able Slaves to fill the Furnace Stock the Bridge Raise Ore & Cart and burn the same. Wood Cutters may for some Time be hired here. There should be Two master Colliers one at the Furnaces another at the Forge with a Suitable Number of Slaves or Serv[an]ts under Each who might Coal in the Summer and Cut wood in the winter.

Charles Carroll, 1753 "Proposals," in Lewis, Coal, Iron, and Slaves, *25.*

[People in North Carolina] make money almost from nothing. [Slaves do most of the work, and] the profit arising is so much greater because no establishment is necessary beyond the working hands themselves. [Each working hand] what with these [making tar, pitch, and turpentine] and other uses made of the forest, should bring in to his master one to two hundred pounds current a year.

Johann Schoepf, report of his travels in the early 1780s, in Kay and Cary, Slavery in North Carolina, *44.*

The employ of the plantation negroes is not by any means so fatiguing, and laborious, as those employed here; they [plantation negroes] can generally find conveniency to Skulk [shirk], more or less at their respective jobbing about a plantation; a thing intirely out of the question here where every negroe is under the eye of the superintendant.... Added to this the work is of the most fatiguing kind; digging, Shoveling & wheeling dirt, tumbling large pieces of the Rock, where every muscle of the body must be strained, boring holes, and driving wedges, & fellows [pieces in wheels to which the spokes are attached?] & Tongs with heavy Sledges; indeed the handling of the bits, sledges, crowbars, drills, Fellows & tongues &c is heavy work of itself, and requires a constant exertion of muscular power....

Robert Leckie to the commissioner of public buildings, marble quarries [near Washington, D.C.], May 16, 1817, quoted in Starobin, Industrial Slavery, *35.*

The weather here [in Mississippi] is very warm, too warm for our hands to work all the day without killing them up—the exercise of walking a little, makes the sweat roll off from any one in large drops.... All our negroes [14 male and nine female slaves who came from North Carolina] seem to be dissatisfied here. Such Shantees as they have will not do in the winter—the Mosquitoes torment them almost to death in the night time—the meat they use is very salty and a little spoiled.

Agent Joseph Hicks to railroad contractor Samuel Smith Downey, July 1836, quoted in Starobin, Industrial Slavery, *67.*

As you approach near the [Chowan River, in North Carolina,] fishery beach, the hum and song indicate business and good humor ... [You are] hearing the merry songs and pithy original jests and sayings of the workmen and attendants—seeing the two fine large boats loaded down with the sein [seine] rowing out to the middle of the river more than three miles wide to shoot it, that is, to drop it out into the river. First—the two boats row off in company and astern of each other, the leading boat, bow foremost, the hinder stern foremost, for the sein is astern.

When they have gone out far enough, they separate, one boat going down, the other up the river, as far as they design, dropping out the sein as they separate and so continue until they reach shore on their return. Then while the sein is drawn up by mules and horses, the sein hallers sleep, eat, or otherwise amuse themselves until the sein comes ashore—then all hands—if it is discovered it is a large hall [haul], the excitement, motions, and preparations are thrilling.... Now the shelters are crowded with the processors, the cutters &c.... They halled all night as they do in a big run of fish.

W. D. Valentine diary, 1840, quoted in Starobin, Industrial Slavery, *27.*

In each of them [three southern cotton factories] are employed from 80 to 100 persons, and about an equal number of white and black. In one of them, the blacks are the property of the mill-owner, but in the other two they are the slaves of planters, hired out at monthly wages to work in the factory. There is no difficulty among them on account of colour, the white girls working in the same room and at the same loom with the black girls; and boys of each colour, as well as men and women, working together without apparent repugnance or objection.

Britisher James Silk Buckingham, Slave States *(1842), quoted in Starobin,* Industrial Slavery, *141.*

The immense profits which have and still continue to reward well directed industry in the gold mines of California, exceed those which have ever flowed from mere labor, inexhaustible in extent and indefinite in duration. Had this wide field for investment been open to the slave labor of the Southern States, wages would have risen, and consequently the value of slaves at home would have been greatly enhanced.

Mississippi governor John A. Quitman, 1850, bemoaning the admission of California to the Union as a free state, in Starobin, Industrial Slavery, *218.*

I would respectfully urge on the board the propriety of purchasing a sufficient number of young men and boys ... to keep ... the canal in repair; for the following reasons: 1st because of the difficulty, trouble, and expense to the company of hiring them even at exorbitant rates[;] ... 2ndly because of the great savings to the company as an economical measure.

"James River and Kanawah Canal Report," Virginia Board of Public Works Report, 1854, quoted in Starobin, Industrial Slavery, *29.*

The great feature of success is the number and sort of hands we shall use the machinery [in the cotton mill] with. These we have already selected out, and have them training; they run thus: one old man sixty five years old at the "gin and lap"; one man (maimed, forefinger off) at "cards"; one old man sixty years old at "drawing"; one boy ten and one girl twelve years old at "speeders"; three boys seven to nine, and three girls and boys, ten years old, "spinning"; six women and girls to the reels; but one good field hand, and she a girl but fourteen years old—17 all told.

DeBow's Review (1858), quoted in Starobin,
Industrial Slavery, 167.

My owner hired me to the contractors for building the railroad between Charleston and Savannah and I was employed in the construction of the road both at my trade of blacksmithing and in getting out and laying the ties.

Interview with Solomon Bradley, 1863, American Freedmen's
Inquiry Commission, in Blassingame, Slave Testimony,
371.

The Workers: Field Hands

[Isabella, later known as Sojourner Truth], became more ambitious than ever to please [her master]; and he stimulated her ambition by . . . boasting of her to his friends, telling them that "*that* wench . . . is better to me than a *man*—for she will do a good family's washing in the night, and be ready in the morning to go into the field, where she will do as much at raking and binding as my best hands." . . .

When Isabella went to the field to work, she used to put her infant in a basket, tying a rope to each handle, and suspending the basket to a branch of a tree, set another small child to swing it. It was thus secure from reptiles and was easily administered to, and even lulled to sleep, by a child too young for other labors. . . .

Sojourner Truth's life as a slave, in Narrative,
| 20–21, 25.

[Rice-growing was] the most unhealthy work in which the slaves were employed, and in spite of every care, . . . they sank under it in great numbers. The causes of this dreadful mortality, are the constant moisture and heat of the atmosphere, together with the alternate floodings and drying of the fields, on which the negroes are perpetually at work, often ankle deep in mud, with their bare heads exposed to the fierce rays of the sun.

Captain Basil Hall, in Bell, Major Butler's Legacy, 127.

Slaves gather sugarcane. *(Blaker, History of Slavery and the Slave Trade)*

After I got to be some size, my owner hired me out to some poor people that lived in the country. I was only about six years old, but I think he got about three dollars per month for me. They hired me to nurse, but I had to nurse, cook, work in the fields, chop wood, bring water, wash, iron, and in general just do everything. . . .

Every morning I was up at five o'clock. I slept in the room with the white folks. I made a pallet in the corner every night, and in the morning I took it up. After dressing myself, I made the fires, went and milked two cows, drove them to the pastures, and came back and brought water from the spring for the house. Then I cleaned up, helped with breakfast, and got ready to go to the field to work. . . .

In the field my boss used to take two rows and give me one, and I had to be at the end with my one row when he finished his two.

Ex-slave, in Johnson, God Struck Me Dead, 116–17.

[S]ome thirty men and women were at work, repairing the road. The women were in majority, and were engaged at exactly the same labour as the men: driving the carts, loading them with dirt, and dumping them upon the road; cutting down trees, and drawing wood by hand, to lay cross the miry places; hoeing, and shovelling. They were dressed in coarse gray gowns, generally very much burned, and very dirty; which, for greater convenience of working in the mud, were reefed up with a cord drawn tightly around the body, a little above the hips—the spare amount of skirt bagging out between this and the waist-proper. On their legs were loose leggins, or pieces of blanket or bagging wrapped about, and lashed with thongs; and they wore very heavy shoes. Most of them had handkerchiefs, only, tied around their heads; some wore men's caps, or old slouched hats, and several were bareheaded.

Olmsted, Cotton Kingdom, *161–62.*

I never knowed what it was to rest. I just work all de time from mornin' till late at night. I had to do everythin' dey was to do on de outside. Work in de field, chop wood, hoe corn, till sometimes I feels like my back surely break. . . .

In de summer we had to work outdoors, in de winter in de house. I had to card and spin till ten o'clock. Never get much rest, had to get up at four de next mornin' and start again.

North Carolina ex-slave Sarah Gudger, in Hymowitz and Weissman, History of Women in America, *43.*

Slaves work in a field on a tobacco plantation. *(Library of Congress)*

The field negroes, as a class, are coarse, filthy, brutal, and lascivious; liars, parasites, hypocrites, and thieves; without self-respect, religious aspirations, or the nobler traits which characterize humanity. . . . Morally, they are on a level with the whites around them. The slaveholder steals their labor, rights and children; they steal his chickens, hogs and vegetables. . . . The laws forbidding the acquisition of knowledge, and the fact that slavery and intelligence are incompatible, keep them, as nearly as possible, as ignorant and degraded as the quadrupeds of the fields.

Redpath, Roving Editor, *222.*

The Workers: House Servants

[My mother] just raised the whole kaboodle of them together [her mistress's children and her own. I] was born about the same time as the baby Jennie. They say I nursed on one breast while that white child, Jennie, pulled away at the other!

Ex-slave Mattie Logan, in Fox-Genovese, Plantation Household, *151–52.*

I could not bring my baby [on a visit] without assistance. She is a great deal fonder of her *Mammy* than she is of me. She nurses her and it would be a great trial to go without her.

Laura S. Tibbetts, in Fox-Genovese, Plantation Household, *162.*

[I] learnt to spin, knit an' weave, [and I] helped wid de washing an' toted loads o' water . . . to de long wash troughs [hewn-out logs, set on racks]. We had to rub de clothes by hand, some beat 'em on blocks wid hickory battling sticks. . . . Deir wuz a heap o' ironing to be done. De white folks wore lots of white ruffled up, full things dat had to be starched and ironed.

Julia Stubbs, in Fox-Genovese, Plantation Households, *178.*

Betsy, recalcitrant maid of the Williamses, is sold to a telegraphy man. She is handsome as a mulatto ever gets to be. And clever in every kind of work. My [maid] Molly thinks her mistress very lucky in getting rid of her. She was a dangerous inmate. But she will be a good cook, a good chamber maid, a good dairy maid, a beautiful clear starcher (and the most thoroughly good-for-nothing woman I know) to her new owners, if she chooses.

Diary entry, May 29, 1862, Mary Chesnut's Civil War, *350.*

A driver accompanies his mistress on her shopping expedition. *(Crowe,* With Thackeray in America*)*

But, thank de Lawd, I had good white folks and dey sho' did trus' me, too. I had charge of all de keys to de house, and I waited on de Missis' and de chillun. I laid out all de clo'se on Sat'dy night, and den Sunday mawnin's I'd pick up all de dirty things. Dey did'n' have a thing to do.

Ex-slave Charity Anderson in Rawick, American Slave, *1:25.*

The Workers: Overseers, Managers, and Stewards

I have allmost constantly found Nigroes tell Truth enough of distant overseers & I am now told that Moore has sold every grain of his own Corn yet Suds [feeds?] his own horse three times a day out of mine, that he has now seven Hoggs raised in my Estate that the Nigroes can't get a drop of Milk tho' there is a plenty even to spare Old Buidine & his [Moore's] Pigs every day. . . . I remember

all the Bacon I laid in for Mill Wrights, Carpenters &c was also expended. . . .

Planter James Mercer, December 5, 1778, in Mullin, Flight and Rebellion, *31.*

As for old Betty, she is free already. She does as she pleases, and you feed and cloth her. As for Jacob he certainly is a most deserving Negro. If you liberated Jacob, what will Bram say? He has earned you more than Ten thousand Dollars. I know of no people more Jealous of their rights and privileges than Negroes—be assured if you begin you will create a great Murmur among the people. Jacob is very useful as head carpenter—his health is bad and I dont allow him to do anything but lay off work, as he has a large family of fine Children on the Estate. I think it would be better for to restrict one hundred dollars to be paid him yearly as long as he was useful would be much better for him, for freedom would force him to work hard for a living, which would soon kill him. As for Molley, you are no stranger to her long wish for freedom (when in Phila). I have no doubt she would have gone off with the British if her husband and children was with her, yet she is certainly a very deserving Woman and I wish the eve of her days comfortable, but I cannot (believe) freedom would be any blessing to her. As for Abraham, he and many more are very deserving Negroes. Abram is truly a faithful, sober honest negro I believe, and if you wish to do something for him send for him to Philada. Let him serve you seven years, he is the one that can git a good living free, and the only one in four that you mentioned. Be assured you have not 50 negroes but what it would be a curse to free them.

Overseer Roswell King objecting to his employer's proposal to free four slaves, in Bell, Major Butler's Legacy, *141.*

In the management of slaves, the temper and disposition of each negro should be particularly consulted. Some require spurring up, some coaxing, some flattering, and others nothing but good words. When an overseer first goes upon a plantation to live, he should study their dispositions well, before he exerts too much rigor. Many a noble spirit has been broken down by injudicious management, and many a lazy cunning fellow has escaped, and put his work on the shoulders of the industrious. Give me a high spirited and even a high tempered negro, full of pride, for easy and comfortable management. Your slow sulky negro although he may have an even temper, is *the devil* to manage.

The negro women are all harder to manage than the men. The only way to get along with them is by kind words and flattery. If you want to cure a sloven, give her something nice occasionally to wear, and praise her up to skies whenever she has on any thing tolerably decent.

Southern Agriculturalist (July 1834), quoted in Blassingame, Slave Community, *151–52.*

[The overseer, Mr. Austin] Gore, was proud, ambitious, and persevering. He was artful, cruel, and obdurate. He was just the man for such a place, and it was just the place for such a man. . . . He was just proud enough to demand the most debasing homage of the slave, and quite servile enough to crouch, himself, at the feet of the master. He was ambitious enough to be contented with nothing short of the highest rank of overseers, and persevering enough to reach the height of his ambition. He was cruel enough to inflict the severest punishment, artful enough to de-

scend to the lowest trickery, and obdurate enough to be insensible to the voice of a reproving conscience. . . .

Overseers will sometimes indulge in a witty word, even with the slaves; not so with Mr. Gore. He spoke but to command, and commanded but to be obeyed; he dealt sparingly with his words, and bountifully with his whip, never using the former where the latter would answer as well. . . . He was, in a word, a man of the most inflexible firmness and stone-like coolness. I was made overseer. The management was pretty much left to me. . . .

I was harder on the servants than [my master] wanted I should be.

Dan Josiah Lockhart, in Four Fugitive Slave Narratives, *38–39.*

No wonder, then, that the overseer desires to have entire control of the plantation. . . . *presses everything at the end of the lash; pays no attention to the sick, except to keep them in the field as long as possible; and drives them out again at the first moment, and forces sucklers and breeders to their utmost. He has no other interest than to make a big cotton crop.*

Southern Agriculturalist, quoted in Olmsted, Cotton Kingdom, *440.*

[The overseer tried to whip my mother and] she knocked him down and tore his face up . . . [He told the master] that he went down in the field to whip the hands and that he just thought he would hit Lucy a few licks to show the slaves that he was impartial. The master replied, "Well, if that is the best you can do with her, damned if you won't just have to take it."

Leonard Franklin, in Fox-Genovese, Plantation Households, *187–88.*

Now my heart is nearly broke. I have lost poor *Leven,* one of the most faithful black men [that] ever lived. [H]e was truth and honesty, and without a fault that I ever discovered. He has overseed the plantation nearly three years, and [has] done much better than any white man [had] ever done here. . . .

Louisiana planter, in Fogel and Engerman, Time on the Cross, *77.*

Work Practices: Hiring Out

I have formerly advertis'd all Persons not to employ my Negro Man *Lancaster* in white washing or any other kind of Work whatever, but to little purpose; since he constantly earns Money (which he loses either by *Gaming* or spends among the little *Punch-Houses*) altho' he has been *run away* for this Month past: I do therefore once more peremptorily forbid all Persons from employing the said *Lancaster* in any Manner whatever.

Notice in the South-Carolina Gazette, *October 24, 1741, in Wax, "The Great Risque," 146.*

To be Hired as a wet Nurse, A HEALTHY YOUNG NEGRO WOMAN, With a good breast of milk and no child. Enquire at No. 106, King-street.

Charleston, South Carolina, Royal Gazette, *May 1, 1782, in Bancroft,* Slave Trading, *155, n. 27.*

Decr' 3, 1837 Campbill County, Va. Mrs. Elizabeth Brown) You Sent us word that you wanted us your Servants [slaves] to come out to Kentucky this fall past and since that has wrote that we must not come untill next fall and as we all was very anxious to come we are very sorry of the disappointment.... I myself am verry sorry and is in hopes that you will send after us all next Spring if you Please and if you cant Send for all Pray be so good as to Send for me and my Son Harrison I have to work for $11 per month and as I am getting old it is rather more than I can make and clothe myself.... I have had the misfortune Since you left here to loose my wife and daughter and if you dont send for me verry quick I shall be compelled to get me another wife If you should not send for me next Spring be so good as send what is the least money you will take for me by the month.... If you please madam. Nothing more at Present but remain your good old Servant Matthew Watts

Blassingame, Slave Testimony, *27.*

Tell Howell I cannot agree for Betty to be hired to Matilda [a free negro]; her [Matilda's] character is too bad. I know her of old, she is a drunkard, and is said to be bad in every respect. I should object to her [Betty's] being hired to any colored person no matter what their character was, and if she cannot get into a respectable family I had rather she came home and if she can't work out put her to spinning and weaving. Her relatives here beg she may not be hired to Matilda. She would not be worth a cent at the end of the year.

Georgian Mrs. S. R. Cobb, letter of January 9, 1843, in Bracey, Meirer, and Rudwick, American Slavery, *12.*

The negro hiring days have come, the most woeful of the year! So housekeepers think who do not own their own servants; and even his class is but a little better off than the rest, for all darkeydom must have holiday this week, and while their masters and mistresses are making fires and cooking victuals or attending to other menial duties the negroes are promenading the streets decked out in their finest clothes....

I was rather amused at the efforts of a market gardener to hire a young woman as a domestic servant. The price her owner put upon her services was not objected to by him, but they could not agree about other terms. The grand obstacle was that she would not consent to work in the garden, even when she had nothing else to do. After taking an hour's walk in another part of town I again met the two at the old bargain. Stepping towards them, I now learned that she was pleading for other privileges—her friends and favourites must be allowed to visit her. At length she agreed to go and visit her proposed home and see how things looked.

Atlantic Intelligencer, January 5, 1859, in Phillips, American Negro Slavery, *407–8.*

A restaurant waiter *(Crowe,* With Thackeray in America*)*

Work Practices: Slave Entrepreneurship

[Their small plots provide slaves with a] sufficient quantity of Tobacco for their own use, a part of which they may sell, and likewise on Sundays, they gather Snake-root, otherwise it would be excessive dear if the Christians were to gather it; with this and the Tobacco they buy Hats, and other Necessaries for themselves, as Linen, Bracelets, Ribbons, and several other Toys for their Wives and Mistresses.

John Brickell, before 1740, in Kay and Cary, Slavery in North Carolina, *37–38.*

After toiling all day for my mistress, I used to sleep three or four hours, and then get up and work for myself the remainder of the night. I made collars for horses, out of plaited husks. I could weave one in about eight hours; and I generally took time enough from my sleep to make two collars in the course of a week. I sold them for fifty cents each. One summer, I tried to take two or three hours from my sleep every night; but I found that I grew weak, and I was obliged to sleep more. With my first money I bought a pig. The next year I earned for myself about thirteen dollars; and the next about thirty. There was a good deal of wild land in the neighborhood that belonged to Congress. I used to go out with my hoe, and dig up little patches, which I planted with corn, and got up in the night to tend it. My hogs were fattened with this corn. . . . Besides this, I used to raise small patches of tobacco, and sell it to buy more corn for my pigs. In this way I worked for five years, at the end of which time, after taking out my losses, I found that I had earned one hundred and sixty dollars. With this money I hired my own time for two years. . . . At the end of the two years, I had earned three hundred dollars, besides feeding and clothing myself. I now bought my time for eighteen months longer, and went two hundred and fifty miles west, nearly into Texas, where I could make more money.

James L. Bradley, quoted in Blassingame, Slave Testimony, *688.*

The laborers [at Graham's coal pits] are permitted to do extra work for their own gain, and . . . do earn money in that manner. I even saw afterwards where they had opened two (not very deep,) shafts to the coal, for their own private working—though their proceedings had been stopped, and certainly should not have been permitted to be commenced, on so distinct and independent a footing.

Edmund Ruffin, Farmer's Register, *August 1, 1837, in* Lewis, Coal, Iron, and Slaves, *120.*

A slave woman sells peanuts. *(Crowe,* With Thackeray in America*)*

[My grandmother] was much praised for her cooking; and her nice crackers became so famous in the neighborhood that many people were desirous of obtaining them. In consequence of numerous requests of this kind, she asked permission of her mistress to bake crackers at night, after all the household work was done; and she obtained leave to do it, provided she would clothe herself and her children from the profits. . . . She had laid up three hundred dollars, which her mistress one day begged as a loan, promising to pay her soon. . . . [N]o promise or writing given to a slave is legally binding. . . .

Jacobs, Slave Girl, *12–13.*

Work Practices: Task Labor

[The] Dayly Task for a Negro Wood Cutter is a Cord, some can cut more but I never knew more than a Cord Required, if they Cut more, it is usual to pay them for it.

James Millis, North Carolina ironworks superintendent, 1777, in Kay and Cary, Slavery in North Carolina, *37.*

The ordinary plantation task is easily accomplished, during the winter months in 8 to 9 hours and in summer my people seldom exceed 10 hours labor *per day*. Whenever the daily task is finished the balance of the day is appropriated to their own purposes. In severe freezing weather no task is exacted, and such work is selected as can be done with least exposure. During heavy rains and in thunder showers, my people are always dismissed and allowed to go home. The task is allotted to each slave in proportion to his age and physical ability. Thus they are considered 1/4, 1/2, 3/4, or full task hands. . . . Men and women are all engaged together in the planting, cultivation and harvesting of the Crop, but in the preparation [*sic*] of the Rice Lands, as ditching, embanking etc. the *men* alone are engaged with the spade. It is customary (*and never objected to*) for the more active and industrious hands to assist those who are slower and more tardy in finishing their daily task.

James R. Sparkman, March 10, 1858, in Easterby, South Carolina Rice Plantation, *346.*

Slaves prepare cotton for processing. *(Library of Congress)*

Work Laws

The negro act of South Carolina contains the following language: "Whereas many owners of slaves, and *others*, who have the care, management, and overseeing of slaves, *do confine them so closely to hard labor, that they have not sufficient time for natural rest;* be it therefore enacted, that if any owner of slaves, or others having the care, &c., shall put such slaves to labor more than *fifteen* hours in twenty-four, from the twenty-fifth of March to the twenty-fifth of September ; or more than *fourteen* hours in twenty-four hours, from the twenty-fifth of September to the twenty-fifth of March , any such person shall forfeit a sum of money. . . ."

Child, Appeal, *43.*

CHAPTER SIX

Runaways
1619–1865

Escaping

From the beginning of slavery in North America, slave owners had a hard time holding onto their slaves. If those slaves were Indians, they knew the terrain, knew how to live in the forest, and had friends nearby; they escaped successfully at a rate discouraging to their owners. Many more problems confronted African slaves, but they too fled. Their desperation may be measured by the report of one slave that he ran away so that his master would "sell me running"—that is, sell the chance of owning him to a new master if he could catch the fugitive, for, said the slave, he didn't much care whose hands he fell into as long as he could get away from his present master.

Most African runaways were short term. Slave owners came to accept as a fact of life the periodic absence in nearby woods and swamps of slaves who ran away to avoid punishment or a heavy work assignment, to join their "abroad" spouses (living on another plantation), or just to take a break from slavery's dreadful monotony. So ordinary were these departures that one mistress who knew her missing slave was about to deliver a baby went out into the woods to visit her and carried the infant back to the plantation.

Some runaways stayed out for long periods. For instance, a young house servant struck her mistress and fled to escape the beating promised when the master came home. Her husband hid her in a cave. He eventually finished the cave with pine logs, made furniture for it, and installed a stove with a pipe running out into the swamp (to hide the source of the smoke). There she lived for seven years, during which time she bore three children with only her husband to attend her. Other slaves gave them food. As another slave told the story, "It was freedom 'fore she come out of that cave for good."[1]

Fugitives were a different matter: They ran to escape bondage completely. Escape was hardest for newly imported African slaves, who did not speak English and had no idea where they were or in what direction to move. But even slaves born in this country usually knew little about geography and climate, let alone free and slave territories, beyond their own immediate area. Only gradually did word get around that for most of them the best advice was to "follow the North Star."

As various northern states abolished slavery, a trickle of fugitives headed toward them. Thus Vermont in 1779, Massachusetts and Pennsylvania in 1780, New Hampshire in 1783, Connecticut and Rhode Island in 1784, the Northwest Territory in 1787, New York in 1799, and New Jersey in 1804 successively became refuges for a few escaped slaves.[2]

Although blacks began to flee northward before 1800, information about Canada did not circulate much before the War of 1812. When it did, masters did their best to suppress and distort it: No one could long survive there, they said, with such poor soil and such a cold climate—particularly not people with African blood. But truth will out: Slaves hired out by Virginia and Kentucky masters to Ohio farmers lived near enough Canada to hear rumors, and they passed them on to slaves back in the border states. Slaves sold farther south carried the word with them. Later, escaped fugitives returning to rescue their families, the few white abolitionists who went south to encourage escapes, and sometimes even casual travelers dared to inform slaves about ways and means, as well as destinations. Of all informants, blacks were by far the most important. As W. E. B. Du Bois writes, "[T]he running away of slaves was too systematic to be accidental; without doubt there was widespread knowledge of paths and places and times for going. Constant communication between the land of freedom and the slave states must be kept up by persons going and coming,"[3] so that in time an underground telegraph was elaborated. Blacks in the free states—notably in Greenwich, New Jersey; Jackson and Brown Counties, Ohio; and Hamilton County, Indiana, stood ready to help fugitives establish themselves in their new communities. In some places, such as Oberlin, Portsmouth, and Cincinnati, Ohio; Detroit, Michigan; Philadelphia, Pennsylvania; and Boston, Massachusetts, blacks and white abolitionists cooperated to hide and pass along runaways.[4]

Even armed with such information, slaves faced long odds. Most successful escapes were second, third, even sixth tries. Henry Bibb, sold to speculators after his sixth attempt, finally won his freedom by accepting their offer to give him a percentage of the proceeds and directions to Canada if he would cooperate in getting himself sold for a high price.

Slaves pondering escape had to overcome the natural fear of leaving familiar territory and beloved family and friends. As a North Carolina slave told James Redpath, "[I don't run away because if I were caught] I might be sold away from [my family], which I won't be, if I don't try to run away—leastways till I'm old."[5]

They had also to weigh the risks of going through country where most whites and some blacks were against them, and of the terrible punishments inflicted on captured fugitives.

Almost all slave masters were both determined to defend the slave system and personally insulted by "desertion." Almost all of them thought of a captured fugitive as almost totally useless thereafter, indeed dangerous to have around, because he might encourage discontent and inspire other slaves to escape. Instead of shrugging and concluding that they were better off without such troublemakers, however, masters were determined to get vengeance, to keep slaves from getting away with escape. Commonly, they imposed a brutal whipping followed by hanging, or a beating and a sale south.

No wonder that fugitives often fought desperately to keep from being recaptured. Frederick Olmsted tells of a black man arrested on suspicion of being a runaway, whose captors put him in a skiff and told him to row them to shore. Instead, he seized a hatchet and assaulted one of them. In the scuffle they both fell overboard. The suspected fugitive was rescued and put ashore, his captors going to fetch arms and a pack of "negro dogs" with which to pursue him. Eventually they found him standing at bay on a large raft, armed with a club and a pistol, threatening death to any man who approached. They shot him, and he fell into the water. They attempted rescue, but he preferred to drown, battling against them even as he sank.

What strikes the reader now is the utter inability of most slave owners to empathize with the condition of the runaways, to wonder what misery drove slaves to such risks. Instead, even the most intelligent of masters focused on what the escape had done to themselves. "Our negroes run away, which troubles us to catch them, and our servants vex us, which troubles us to whip them," complained David Bush of Louisiana.[6] George Washington wrote, "The running off of my cook has been a most inconvenient thing to this family, and what rendered it more disagreeable is that I had resolved never to become the master of another slave by purchase. But this resolution I fear I must break."[7]

Escaping: Who Ran?

In the face of all this, slaves still fled. Which of them? Fewer escaped from the Deep South than from Maryland, Virginia, Kentucky, or Missouri, all closer to free territory. Often the most privileged slaves escaped, their expectations apparently raised by their favored positions. Most successful fugitives were robust young males. The fugitive traveled fastest who traveled alone; taking along the family multiplied the risks. Infants and young children could not walk the long distances required, could not go for long periods without food and drink, and were given to crying at inconvenient moments.

Male slaves, more apt to be sent on off-plantation errands and be hired out, more likely to visit their "abroad" wives than vice versa, knew the local territory better than the women. They were a more common sight on the roads than women slaves and so were less likely to be stopped. Whereas mothers and small children were usually sold as "families," fathers were more often sold singly and had less to keep them in their unfamiliar new homes.

When women did decamp, they more often played truant than became genuine fugitives. At the ages of most fugitives, from 16 to 35, most slave women were bearing, nursing, and caring for babies and small children, whom they could neither endure to leave nor hope to take with them. During those years, too, as pregnant and nursing mothers they received the best care of their lives, as their masters eased demands in order to protect the lives and health of the new slave babies. Slave owners of course were well aware of this obstacle. Fanny Kemble, wife of a slave owner, overheard a conversation about the dangers of taking slaves into the northern states, where they might try to claim their freedom or be set free by abolitionists—but there was a sure preventive: "Oh, stuff and nonsense; I take care, when my wife goes North with the children, to send Lucy with her; *her children are down here, and I defy all the abolitionists in creation to get her to stay North.*"[8]

Escaping: How Many?

No one knows how many slaves actually escaped, let alone how many tried, or how many more took to nearby woods for a time. Benjamin Drew, who interviewed fugitives in Canada, estimated about 30,000 there in 1855, but the figure was and is widely disputed. Estimates of how many had escaped to the North by the time of the Civil War range, almost meaninglessly, from 25,000 to 100,000.[9]

Escaping: Where?

Until 1850 and the passage of the harsh Fugitive Slave Law, fugitives made new lives for themselves in the northern free states and territories. After that year, many of them, as well as newly fleeing slaves, found more security in Canada. While the Spanish held Florida, fugitives from the Deep South accepted their invitation to freedom. Some Indian tribes, particularly in Florida, gave fugitives refuge, either in a relatively benign form of slavery or as tribal members. In the early 18th century, slaves escaping from South Carolina fled to the Creek Indians of Georgia. Mexico provided shelter and freedom to other fugitives, especially those from Texas. A few made their escape down the Mississippi River to New Orleans and its oceangoing vessels.

Escaping: When and How?

Many fugitives took advantage of free time on weekends and during the Christmas holidays to escape. They also favored the months when the corn was high enough in the fields to conceal them.

They devised all sorts of ruses. Traveling on foot, they took to water and used pepper to throw dogs off their trails. The bolder stole horses and money to help them on their way. Some stowed away on boats, where often they were helped by black sailors. Some could and did pass for white. Others waited for the trail to cool by hiding for weeks, months, even years in kitchens or attics before they took flight. They adopted disguises, women posing as men, or occasionally the other way round. Ellen Crafts escaped with her husband by posing as his white master. Some daring men had themselves packed in boxes to be shipped north—at least one foresighted fugitive bringing along a fan. Fugitives obtained passes by paying poor whites to forge them or through acquaintance with a slave who could write.

Occasionally, fugitives were able, by threatening suicide, to scare off would-be captors, who dared not make themselves liable to the master for the loss of his slave property.

Escaping: What Became of Them?

Though they were a self-selected, persistent, venturesome group, fugitives who had escaped still faced all sorts of problems. Only a small proportion of them could read and write. Few indeed had any money. Most of them had left behind all that was familiar and loved. They mourned for and worried about their still-enslaved families and friends. As one successful fugitive wrote back home, "I wish to tell All that wantes to know how I made my escape that I made it in the knight when the Moon was gon away and thar was no eyes To see but god and it was threw him that I am know gitting along and ples to say to my Farther and to my fartherinlaw that I feel happy in my ascape untill I thinkes about my Wife and I hope that you bouth will talk to her and tell Her to be not dischomfiered for I thinks that I shall see you agin. Tell him to tell her if she is not sole [sold] at Chrismous she mus let me know how she and the childrens are agatting along and dear farther ples to see her and see If thar is anney way for me to Send a man to by her. . . . [A]ll I wantes is En opportunity to send a man to by her."[10]

In the havens they sought out, either in the free states and territories or in foreign countries, the fugitives faced among most of the populace—even among abolitionists—both racial prejudice and an assumption of the inferiority of black people. Workmen resented the competition of the fugitives for jobs. In the free states, the fugitives lived in constant danger of being kidnapped or of being dragged back into slavery under the fugitive slave laws. Through no fault of their own, security eluded them.

Yet, even putting aside blacks of such extraordinary gifts as Frederick Douglass and Harriet Tubman, some of the fugitives succeeded in establishing themselves through sheer determination and wit. The highly skilled among them, of course, had a better chance than the rest, but the records occasionally show touching stories of black women who by washing clothes educated their families and bought their own homes. In the major cities of the North, some black communities protected their own members and helped new arrivals.

Helping the Fugitives: "Negro Stealing"

Although many pursued the slaves so mercilessly, fortunate fugitives found help along the way. The slave states called people who aided the fugitives "Negro stealers." Of course, slaveholders detested them. As a white Alabaman wrote, "Some time last march a white man by the name of Miller appeared in the nabourhood and abducted the above negroes, was caught at vincanes, Indi. With said negroes and was thare convicted of steling and remanded back to Ala. to Abide the penalty of the law and on his return met his Just reward by getting drowned at the mouth of cumberland River on the Ohio in attempting to make his escape."[11]

Some of the "Negro stealers" were white southerners born and bred. Most of these apparently worked for profit. Slave Aaron Sidles and one Timothy Guard, a white man, conspired for Sidles's freedom and Guard's profit. Sidles would run away, forcing the trader who owned him to "sell him running" at a reduced price. Guard would buy Sidles, permit him to go into business for himself, guarantee to collect debts owed him, and eventually let him buy himself for $1600. Guard was as good as his word, and Sidles, working as steward on a steamboat, paid him off in about seven years.[12] Deals like these presented many hazards to slaves, though. The Murrell gang, operating in the Southwest in the 1830s, specialized in "helping" blacks to escape on condition that they would then allow themselves to be sold. The gang promised then to help them in real escapes, but in actuality they continued to resell them; if the slaves threatened exposure, the gang murdered them.

But some southern "Negro stealers" worked from conscience or a liking for adventure, or

William Still, a successful runaway, aided the escapes of many others. *(Seibert,* Underground Railroad*)*

both. John Fairfax so operated for some 12 years, now and then serving jail sentences but completing one daring rescue after another until he was finally cruelly imprisoned and his health broken. He was said to have "stolen"—liberated—all the slaves of both his father and his uncle, among many others. His friends in the Underground Railroad anxiously awaited word from him as he adventured through the South, posing as a proslavery advocate. He always went armed, armed the fugitives he was helping, and wanted no slave with him who was not willing to fight for his freedom.

Of the "Negro stealers" from the North, by far the bravest were themselves successful fugitives. Ex-slaves like Harriet Tubman and Josiah Henson, who had ended their own bondage by flight, left safety to rescue not only their families but slaves whom they did not even know. With a price on their heads, they went back into deadly danger time after time. Although most northerners, even abolitionists, had too much respect for the law of property to approve of abducting slaves, a handful of whites, prominent among them Laura Haviland and the Canadian doctor Alexander Ross, ventured into the slave states to encourage and abet escapes.

Helping the Fugitives: The Underground Railroad

The Underground Railroad consisted of a chain of "stations"—hiding places—linked by routes and improvised transportation from one to another, along which fugitive slaves could make their way north. It originated among blacks, slave and free, who from pre-Revolutionary times passed from one to another the news of refuges in North America where freedom existed for all and information on how to get there. In time, black settlements in the free states, in their interiors as well as along their southern frontiers, organized to aid and protect the fugitives passing through or settling into their communities and became stations of the Underground. (These were particularly important because fugitives had little reason to trust even apparently friendly whites who offered help.) Just before the Civil War, journalist James Redpath wrote; "In the Canadian provinces there are thousands of fugitive slaves; they are the picked men of the Southern states, many of them are intelligent and rich and all of them are deadly enemies of the South; five hundred of them at least annually visit the slave states, passing from Florida to Harper's Ferry on heroic errands of mercy and deliverance. They have carried the Underground Railroad and the Underground Telegraph into nearly every Southern state. Here obviously is a power of great importance for a war of liberation."[13]

Gradually whites joined in efforts to help the escaping slaves, at first one by one—a kindly housewife who could not deny food to a starving fugitive, a compassionate farmer who allowed a desperate man to sleep in his hayloft. Over time others came into the movement, men and women of principle who truly believed that all are created equal—abolitionists and other humanitarians. The whites seldom risked their lives, but they did stand to lose their status in the community, their property, and even their freedom. They came from all walks of life, young and old, women and men; many were ministers and many Quakers. Their neighbors called them *niggerites, amalgamationists,* and *nigger-thieves* and accused them of using the labor of the fugitives they sheltered and then hurrying them off without paying them. Sometimes their churches expelled them. Their neighbors spied on them, and slave hunters and their sympathizers threatened and terrorized them. Their work demanded conviction, courage, and willingness to sacrifice property and reputation. Blacks and whites working together constituted the personnel of the Underground Railroad.

Levi Coffin, often called the president of the Underground Railroad, always insisted that the network began in the South. Arnold Cragston remembered how, when still a slave, he had gone to another plantation courting and an old woman there asked him to row a pretty girl across the river. He had refused out of fright, but then he saw the girl—a *very* pretty girl. The trip across the river terrified him: "It took me a long time to get over my scared feeling, but I finally did, and I soon found myself going back across the river, with two and three people, and sometimes a whole boatload. I got so I used to make three and four trips a month."[14]

In the free states, the Underground Railroad usually originated among free blacks, who opened their homes to the fugitives, aided them with money and clothes, and when possible passed them on to other friends. In time whites joined the network. In the 1830s and 1840s, the federal government opened up new cotton fields by driving the Indians from the Gulf states. Consequently the demand for slaves increased, more slaves fled lest they be sold south, antislavery sentiment grew, and the Underground Railroad became nationwide. It was probably busiest in the 1850s and early 1860s when the incursions of Union troops into the South drastically altered circumstances. About 1850 the Underground Railroad began to send fugitives by real railroads as well as by the wagons, buggies, sleighs, and boats it had always used.

This map shows the lines of the Underground Railroad in Chester and neighboring counties of Pennsylvania. *(Courtesy of the artist, Thomas B. Taylor)*

The Cox Home was a station on the Underground Railroad in Chester County, Pennsylvania. *(Courtesy of the artist, Thomas B. Taylor)*

Most active in states such as Ohio, which was separated only by a river from the slave state of Kentucky and was linked by Lake Erie to Canada, the Underground Railroad also had many "conductors" and "station masters" in Pennsylvania and the New England states. Only a few of its operators—Coffin, the Reverend Samuel J. May, Frederick Douglass, and Harriet Tubman—knew more than five or six other people in it.

Everyone connected with the Underground Railroad had stories of narrow escapes and hairbreadth rescues. Laura Haviland told about an abolitionist woman preparing food for the journey of the fugitive Zack when her husband came in saying that their house had been surrounded by nine slave hunters. "Wife, what shall we do?" "Let them search the two lower rooms first, and while you go with them you tell Zack to slip into my room while you are with them, and I'll see to him." Working quickly, she rolled up her feather bed, drew the straw mattress to the front of the bed frame, ordered Zack to jump in, threw back the feather bed, and herself lay down on the front side. After a thorough search of the clothespress, the wardrobe, and under the bed, the slave hunters withdrew in frustration.[15]

Coffin's *Reminiscences* is packed with one such tale after another, no doubt polished to a high gloss by frequent retelling. A stiff-backed Quaker of conscience and nerves of steel, he nevertheless injected an antic humor into the whole desperate undertaking. At one point, he concocted a plan to get a bit of his own back from certain slave hunters. He knew that they believed he and his wife were still sheltering a young fugitive—whom in fact they had already sent on and who had arrived safely in Canada. Coffin mischievously hired a free black woman who resembled the fugitive in build and general appearance and set her to work in his house. After she had been there about a week, he organized an "escape" for her, in an obvious disguise, in the hope that the marshal would give chase, the driver of the escape vehicle would manage to be captured, and ultimately Coffin could have the marshal and his posse arrested for kidnapping a free black woman.

Deterring Runaways: Laws to Restrict Mobility

As the slavery period wore on, slave owners tried to allay their fears of losing slaves by ever-harsher laws restricting their mobility, chiefly by curfews and passes. Some of these restrictions extended to free blacks, whom whites always suspected of inspiring and aiding slave escapes. North and South Carolina, Georgia, Florida, Alabama, Louisiana, and Texas all had laws requiring that free black sailors should be jailed while their vessels were in port, at the expense of their employers.

Deterring Runaways: Patrols

In the slave states, patrollers responsible for the "pursuit, capture, suppression, and punishment" of runaways watched the roads for slaves who did not have passes permitting them to leave their masters' property. Practice varied from state to state. In some places patrollers were connected with the state militia; elsewhere the county courts or city councils appointed them. Some assigned the task as a civic duty, expecting their white male residents to take turns patrolling, usually at night, for two or three weeks. But many planters disliked the job and avoided it for themselves and their sons by seeking exemptions, paying fines, or hiring replacements. Some communities hired patrollers, who were apt to be poor, uneducated, and conscienceless. Often such men looked forward to patrolling as a way to get out with the boys, a break from the dull routine of the farm, or a chance to pick up a little money—not only from wages and rewards but also from bribes exacted from their victims. The sadists among them enjoyed the legal privilege of beating up blacks who could not account for themselves, who offered resistance, or who offended simply because they were black. Free blacks who could not show freedom papers were assumed to be slaves and treated accordingly. The system invited corruption.

Patrollers fully understood that their communities expected them to maintain white supremacy at any cost. They were not only to catch runaways but also to squash incipient insurrections, of which Southern whites lived in fear. As well as hunting through slave quarters for slaves from other plantations and absent slaves, they searched for weapons and evidence of literacy—which they believed might lead to revolt. They visited plantations where owners and overseers were away, for who knew what unsupervised slaves might do? They repeatedly broke up gatherings of slaves for any purpose other than assigned labor, particularly religious services. They especially targeted night meetings, for then more slaves were away from home.

The system did not work well. In the cities patrollers were frequently called away to other tasks, like keeping order among whites. In the country, where they were expected to check the roads on Sundays and at night, when the slaves were not at work, they might be diverted to deal with depredations by runaways, suspicious fires, and unusual gatherings of slaves—or simply by dereliction of duty. Corruption went both ways, as slaves learned to bargain with patrollers for liquor and favors. Blacks also helped runaways hide, concealing them and supplying them with food. And blacks fought back, stringing grapevines and ropes across roads at heights calculated to knock unwary patrollers from their horses.[16]

In this two-panel pro-Southern cartoon, on this and the facing page, artist Edward Williams Clay satirizes Northern opposition to the Fugitive Slave Act of 1850. "What's Sauce for the Goose Is Sauce for the Gander." *(Library of Congress, Prints and Photographs Division)*

Deterring Runaways: "Negro Hunters"

Far more wide-ranging than the local patrollers were the "Negro hunters," who operated either on their own, as entrepreneurs looking to collect rewards for returning fugitives, or as agents of slave holders trying to retrieve fugitives from afar. Some of them were ne'er-do-well northerners who preferred tracking down human beings to working at regular jobs. For operations close to home, most southern "Negro hunters" had packs of dogs trained to trace, tree, and attack black fugitives. The more disreputable of these slave hunters—and as a class they did not stand high in public repute—descended to kidnapping free blacks (and, it was whispered, even whites) and selling them into slavery or to encouraging slaves to escape in order to catch them and collect the rewards for their capture.

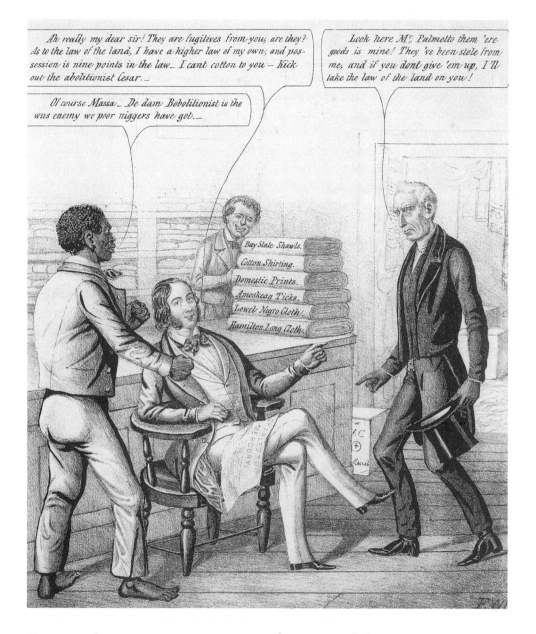

Deterring Runaways: The Fugitive Slave Laws

Of all the deterrents against running away, the most controversial and virulent were the various fugitive slave laws. From the earliest days of slavery in America, slave owners had tried to get agreements among the colonies or states for the return of fugitives. In 1643, the several colonies of the New England Confederation had made such a pact with one another. Throughout the colonial era, public sentiment continued to support such a policy.

The American Revolution forced some reevaluation; nevertheless, the 1787 ordinance for the government of the Northwest Territory provided that "any person escaping into the same, from whom labor or service is lawfully claimed in any one of the original states, such fugitive may be lawfully reclaimed and conveyed to the person claiming his or her labor or service aforesaid." Southerners forced into the Constitution a similar provision (Article 4, Section 2): "No person held to Service or Labour in one State, under the Laws thereof, escaping into another, shall, in Consequence of any Law or Regulation therein, be discharged from such Service or Labour, but shall be delivered up on Claim of the Party to whom such Service or Labour may be due." Still dissatisfied, southerners then fought through the Congress the Fugitive Slave Law of 1793, empowering slave owners and their agents to seize or arrest an alleged fugitive, take her or him before a federal judge or local magistrate, and obtain a warrant to remove the fugitive. This law's notorious omission of protections for falsely accused "fugitives" opened the way to kidnappings.

But to pass a law is not to enforce it. As antislavery sentiment grew during the early 19th century, slave escapes multiplied, and free states more often refused to obey fugitive slave laws. Some of them even passed "personal liberty laws" that obstructed their operation and tried to protect free blacks from enslavement by false allegations or mistaken identity. These states did, after all, have responsibilities to their own free black populations—and, truth to tell, sometimes they used these personal liberty laws to protect real fugitives.

Because of the contradictions among the laws of the various states and between state and federal laws, the situation of the accused fugitive in the state courts was chancy. In 1816, for instance, a Pennsylvania court ruled in *Commonwealth* v. *Halloway* that Pennsylvania birth guaranteed freedom to the daughter of a slave mother who had fled from her Maryland master before she became pregnant. "Whatever may have been our ideas of the rights of slave holders in our sister states," said the court, "we cannot deny that it was competent to the legislature to enact a law ascertaining the freedom of the issue of slaves born after the passing of the act within this state." But in 1823, a Massachusetts court held in *Commonwealth* v. *Griffith* that his Virginia owner's agent was justified in arresting the fugitive Randolph, a resident and property owner of New Bedford. Here the court decreed that the agent was protected by federal law, even though under Massachusetts law Randolph owed service to no one. For, said the court, the Constitution is "a compact by which all are bound," and "we there entered into an agreement that slaves should be considered as property."

Federal courts upheld the traditional fugitive slave policy, most famously in *Prigg* v. *Pennsylvania*. In this 1842 case, the Supreme Court of the United States ruled that "the owner of a slave is clothed with entire authority in every State in the Union, to seize and recapture his slave, whenever he can do it without any breach of the peace, or any illegal violence"; it proclaimed the responsibility of the federal government "to enforce all the rights and duties growing out of [the fugitive slave clause] in the constitution." The Court also denied that the individual states had any authority to legislate the treatment of fugitive slaves. The Court went on to declare that all state judges and officials ought to enforce the federal law but that the federal government could not force them to do so. Abolitionists immediately seized on this part of the ruling to argue that the Court had released states from any obligation to assist in the return of fugitive slaves, and they persuaded more free states to pass personal liberty laws.

In *Jones* v. *Van Zandt* in 1847, the Supreme Court again harshly enforced the Fugitive Slave Law of 1793. Van Zandt, a conductor in the Underground Railroad, was sued for damages for offering fugitives a ride in his wagon. The defense pled that he had had no means of knowing that these persons were escaped slaves; being in Ohio, where no slavery existed, he had naturally assumed all persons to be free. The defense attorneys also attacked the law itself, arguing that the federal government lacked power to support slavery, that slavery was incompatible with the Declaration of Independence and contrary to natural right, that the law violated the Bill of Rights, and that Congress was not empowered to enforce the fugitive slave clause of the Constitution. Van Zandt lost. The Court ruled that the law was constitutional and that a judge was bound to uphold it regardless of whether he agreed with it morally.

Differences continued to sharpen between the slave and free states over the treatment of fugitive slaves, heightening the emotions of both slaveholders and abolitionists. Slaveholders accused the free states of failing to honor their obligations as members of the Union and of luring away their slaves. Abolitionists accused slave states of trying to force their assistance in the operation of a system that they deemed immoral. Feelings rose higher and higher, and the struggle over slavery began to test whether the Union could endure half free and half slave.

In 1850, the South pushed through Congress an even harsher and more punitive law, more invasive of the rights claimed by free states. The Fugitive Slave Law of 1850 specifically required all marshals and deputy marshals to carry out its provisions—that is, to arrest and keep safe fugitives—under personal penalty of large fines and liability to damages in civil suits, and to assist slaveholders in removing their slaves. It "commanded" citizens to aid and assist the execution of the law. It ordered local courts to issue to slaveholders (properly attested by their home states) certificates empowering them to use force and restraint to remove fugitives. It forbade either interference with this process or any other help to fugitives, under penalty of imprisonment, heavy fines, and civil damages. It prohibited local courts from considering the testimony of alleged fugitives or affording them trial by jury. The law was a slaveholder's dream and an abolitionist's nightmare, an invitation to open confrontation. The invitation was accepted.

Confrontation

The Fugitive Slave Law of 1850 was simultaneously cause and result. Almost inevitably, given the South's strength in Congress, it was produced by the divisions in lifestyle, beliefs, and economic interests that slavery had created between the North and the South. In turn, it wrought havoc, widening differences and tripling the distrust and dislike between the two parts of the country. The free states defied the law in two ways—officially, by actions of the state and local governments, and unofficially, often illegally, by the actions of private citizens.

For some years, as noted, the free states had responded to fugitive slave laws and the kidnapping of their black people with personal liberty laws. In drafting these, the states usually maneuvered to take advantage of loopholes in the federal laws without directly contradicting their letter. Personal liberty laws barred state officers from enforcing federal fugitive slave laws and required them to defend fugitives; prohibited the use of state-owned buildings to detain fugitives; and offered alleged fugitives the protections of due process, habeas corpus, and trial by jury. After 1850, personal liberty laws multiplied.

Private citizens immediately responded to the 1850 federal fugitive slave legislation with defiant words and deeds. "To law framed of such iniquity I owe no allegiance," the Reverend Theodore Parker of Boston preached. "Humanity, Christianity, manhood revolts against it. . . . For myself I say it solemnly, I will shelter, I will help, and I will defend the fugitive with all my humble means and power. I will act with any body of decent and serious men, as the head, or the foot, or the hand, in any mode not involving the use of deadly weapons, to nullify and defeat the operation of this law."[17]

"Owen Lovejoy lives at Princeton, Illinois, three-quarters of a mile east of the village, and he aids every fugitive that comes to his door and asks it," proclaimed that congressman in 1859. "Thou invisible demon of slavery, dost thou think to cross my humble threshold, and forbid me to give bread to the hungry and shelter to the homeless! I bid you defiance in the name of my God!"[18] All over the North, attempts to rescue arrested fugitives resulted in riots.

Officials, theoretically governed by both federal and state laws, were placed in an unenviable situation. Pity those of Troy, New York, who in 1859 arrested one Charles Nalle at the request of his master (who was also Nalle's white half-brother). According to one version, Harriet Tubman, who was visiting Troy, rushed to the office of the U.S. commissioner who was holding Nalle prisoner. A crowd had already gathered there and had become so excited that the officials dared not take Nalle down to a waiting wagon. Tubman added to the disorder by sending little boys to cry "Fire!" The officers tried to clear the stairs, but there stood Tubman, the revered "Moses" of her people, in the way.

Whatever Tubman's role, efforts by the officers to take Nalle down through the crowd resulted in "pulling, hauling, mauling, and shouting"; pistols were drawn, and chisels were used as weapons. Rescuers seized Nalle and put him in a skiff, to be ferried across the river to West Troy. But there, still manacled, he was again arrested; 400 persons again rushed to the rescue, attacking the barricaded office where he was being held. According to a newspaper account, "Soon a stone flew against the door—then another—and bang, bang! went off a couple of pistols but the officers who fired them took good care to aim pretty high. The assailants were forced to retreat for a moment. 'They've got pistols,' said one. 'Who cares?' was the reply; 'they can only kill a dozen of us—come on.' More stones and more pistol-shots ensued. At last the door was pulled open by an immense negro, and in a moment he was felled by a hatchet in the hands of Deputy-Sheriff Morrison; but the body of the fallen man blocked up the door so that it could not be shut, and a friend of the prisoner pulled him out."[19] Nalle ultimately found a safe haven in Canada.

But another mob was unable to rescue from jail the fugitive slave and Baptist preacher Anthony Burns. Hired out by his owner, he had stowed away on a vessel bound from Richmond to Boston, where his owner had tracked him down and had him arrested on a false charge of theft. After the failed rescue attempt, in which a policeman was killed, federal troops, the state militia, and the Boston police were called out to restore order. They faced some 50,000 infuriated Massachusetts residents. Nonetheless, the federal government returned Burns to Virginia, at an estimated cost of $100,000.

Often during these confrontations, peaceably inclined abolitionists tried to resolve matters by offering to purchase the fugitive, only to have their offers refused. So it was with Charles Nalle, with Anthony Burns, and also with Shadrach, a fugitive arrested in Massachusetts in 1851 by federal officers and held in the federal courthouse because the state refused the use of any of its buildings. He was ultimately rescued by a crowd of blacks, who sent him to Canada. Rejections of their offers of money hardened the conviction of many abolitionists that only force could end the abuses of slavery.

Some 900 fugitive slaves were returned to their owners between 1850 and 1861, many of them without resistance, especially along the Ohio River and the Mason-Dixon Line. But according to southern estimates, they represented no more than a tenth of the slaves who escaped during those years. The fugitive slave laws did little to protect the property of slaveholders and much to propel the nation into war.

Chronicle of Events

1660

- Virginia provides that any English servant who runs away with blacks who are servants for life (and therefore cannot be punished by having the term of their servitude extended) shall himself serve extended time to compensate for the blacks' absence.

1687

- Eleven slaves flee by boat to Spanish Florida, asking for Roman Catholic baptism and claiming that their former owners will not allow them to learn Roman Catholic doctrine. The Spaniards refuse to return them but pay their former masters for them. (See 1731.)

1699

- A Spanish royal decree promises protection "to all Negro deserters from the English who [flee] to St. Augustine and [become] Catholics."

1717

- New York passes legislation prohibiting slaves from running away.

1730

- The Spanish decide that slaves who flee from Carolina to Florida will be sold and the proceeds given to their former masters. (See 1731.)

1731

- The Spanish decide that slaves who flee from Carolina to Florida will be neither returned nor paid for.

1733

- A Spanish decree welcomes English slaves to Florida, with the result that many march there in groups from South Carolina.
- The governor of South Carolina offers £20 alive and £10 dead for "Several Run away Negroes who are near the Congerees, & have robbed several of the Inhabitants thereabouts."

1738

- *March:* Spanish Florida grants freedom and land to runaway slaves and proclaims that all runaways who come in the future will be free, encouraging them to "unite themselves to our arms" in the coming war against the English.

- *June 10:* The freed runaway slaves promise that "they [will] always be the most cruel enemies of the English."
- *November 21:* When 23 runaway slaves arrive in St. Augustine, the governor announces that he will establish them at a well-fortified settlement at Mosa at the mouth of the St. Johns River.

1739

- *September:* Slaves sack and burn the armory at Stono, South Carolina, then march toward a Spanish Florida fort manned by a black militia company. On the way they enlist more fugitives, gather arms, kill whites, and stir expectations of freedom. The rebellion is crushed by the state militia.
- *December:* South Carolina militia is called out to pursue a group of fugitive slaves committing robberies around Dorchester.

1740

- *May–July:* In the "Inglorious Expedition," Georgia and Carolina troops attempt to invade Florida in retaliation for "the Protection our deserted Slaves have met with" there.

1763–1783

- Florida, under (temporary) British rule, no longer functions as a haven for fugitive slaves.

1776

- During the American Revolutionary War, the Company of Negroes, free Black Loyalists (including fugitive slaves) who have fought on the British side, are evacuated from Boston to Halifax, Nova Scotia.

1779

- The British commander in chief issues the Phillipsburg Proclamation, offering freedom to every slave who deserts to the British forces.

1783

- The British leaving New York issue General Birch certificates (so named for a British general) guaranteeing freedom and permission to go to Nova Scotia, or wherever else they choose, to slaves who claim refugee status under the Phillipsburg sanction of 1779.

1787

- The Northwest Territory Ordinance requires residents of that territory to return fugitive slaves from other American territories and states.

- The Constitution of the United States includes a fugitive slave clause.

1791

- The British parliament charters the Sierra Leone Company to establish a government of the colony of ex-slaves there and to trade with the colony and its hinterland. Black Loyalists in Nova Scotia are invited to settle in Sierra Leone.

1792

- Eleven hundred freed slaves who had migrated to Nova Scotia after the American Revolution found Freetown, Sierra Leone, in West Africa.

1793

- The Fugitive Slave Law of 1793 makes the aiding of fugitive slaves a penal offense punishable by a fine of 500 dollars.

1804

- The Underground Railroad is "incorporated" (though still not named) when General Thomas Boude of Columbia, Pennsylvania, shelters a slave and refuses the demands of her owner to carry her off; the townspeople's sympathies are further roused by the arrival of 56 slaves manumitted by their Virginia owner but claimed by his heirs.

1814

- In the War of 1812, British vice admiral Alexander Cochrane invites American slaves to take refuge with British forces.

1819

- The United States annexes East Florida, which has been a refuge for runaway slaves.

1829

- Mexico abolishes slavery and welcomes fugitives from the United States.

1830–1840

- The removal of the Indians from the Gulf states and the consequent opening of new cotton fields motivates many slaves to flee for fear of being sold south.

1831

- The Underground Railroad receives its name.

Isaac Hopper is credited with using Underground Railroad methods as early as 1787. *(Library of Congress)*

1836

- Texas slaveholders complain about slaves escaping to Mexico.
- Texas law provides punishments for harboring runaway bondsmen.
- Philadelphians organize a society called the Underground Railroad, in actuality a branch of the much larger informal network.

1837

- A group of fugitive slaves kills a Texas sheriff and escapes into Mexico.

1844

- Twenty-five mounted and armed slaves leave Bastrop, Texas, for Mexico; seven or eight apparently make good their escape.

1845

• *July:* Seventy-five Maryland slaves arm and begin to march toward Pennsylvania; some are killed, and 31 are recaptured.

1847

• Sam Houston asks Pres. James Polk to initiate action on a measure to require the extradition of runaway slaves from Mexico.

1848

• In Kentucky a white college student leads 75 slaves toward the Ohio River; after two battles all the slaves are killed or recaptured.
• Residents of a small Michigan town defy slave catchers by escorting a fugitive family out of town.
• Black women in Cincinnati, armed with washboards and rolling pins, prevent the recapture of fugitives who have just crossed the Ohio River.
• Seventy to 80 slaves attempt to escape from Washington, D.C., on the schooner *Pearl,* only to be captured.

1849–1850

• Seminole Indian chief Wild Cat immigrates to Coahila, Mexico, with 150–800 Indians and fugitive blacks.

1850

• The new fugitive slave law strengthens the property rights of slaveholders and endangers blacks living in free states. The federal government rigorously enforces it, but states react by passing personal liberty laws.
• Many blacks leave for Canada, including 200 armed Pittsburgh waiters vowing to die before being taken back into slavery.
• Several hundred blacks rout Creek Indians and escape to Mexico.
• Thirty Missouri slaves arm themselves and march toward freedom, but they surrender when surrounded by heavily armed whites.

1851

• In Boston, Shadrach, seized by slave catchers and brought into court, is rescued. Eight blacks and whites are indicted, but the jury does not convict.
• In Syracuse, New York, the fugitive Jerry is rescued from a police station. Eighteen are indicted, but the jury does not convict.
• In Christiana, Pennsylvania, armed blacks under the leadership of William Parker, in a pitched battle to pre-

In 1848 Ellen Craft escaped while disguised as a young planter, with her husband as her valet. *(Seibert,* Underground Railroad*)*

vent the recapture of four fugitive slaves, kill Maryland slave owner Edward Gorsuch.
• John Brown forms the black League of Gileadites in Springfield, Massachusetts, to resist the Fugitive Slave Law of 1850.
• Philadelphians form the General Vigilance Committee to resist the Fugitive Slave Law of 1850.

1854

• Despite strong opposition from Massachusetts citizens, the federal government returns fugitive Anthony Burns to his Virginia master, at a cost of $100,000.

1856

• In Colorado City, Texas, a large group (perhaps four hundred) of free and hired-out Negroes, assisted by

Mexicans, devise a plan for slaves to rise and fight their way to Mexico.

1857

• The Mexican government again rebuffs U.S. overtures for a treaty providing for the return of fugitive slaves.

1858

• A Texas law stipulates that anyone returning a runaway from a nonslave area will receive one-third of the value of the slave from the state treasury.

• Allegedly, black leaders George De Baptiste and William Lambert organize in Detroit a secret society (African-American Mysteries? Order of the Men of Oppression? Order of Emigration?) to assist fugitives.

• A biracial group from Oberlin, Ohio, rescues fugitive John Price and sends him to Canada.

1862

• In Corinth, Mississippi, blacks in a contraband camp organize a cohesive community for work, education, and worship. In 1863 the federal military demands that it be dismantled.

Eyewitness Testimony

Escaping

Whereas many persons of this Colony [Connecticut] doe for their necessary use purchase negroe seruants, and often times the sayd seruants run away to the great wronge, damage and disapoyntment of their masters and owners, for prevention of which for the future, as much as may be, it is ordered by this Court that Whateuer negroe or negroes shall hereafter, at any time, be fownd wandring out of the towne bownds or place to which they doe belong, without a ticket or pass from the authority, or their masters or owners, shall be stopt and secured by any of the inhabitants, or such as shall meet with them, and brought before the next authority to be examined and returned to their owners, who shall sattisfy for the charge if any be. . . .

1690, in Williams, History of the Negro Race *1:253–54.*

Whereas many times negroes, mulattoes, and other slaves unlawfully absent themselves from their masters and mistresses service, and lie hid and lurk in obscure places killing hoggs and committing other injuries to the inhabitants . . . *Be it enacted* . . . their majesties justices of the peace of the country [where such Negroes are hiding out] . . . are hereby impowered and commanded to issue out their warrants directed to the sherrife . . . to apprehend such negroes, mulattoes, and other slaves, which said sherriffe is hereby likewise required upon all such occasions to raise such and soe many forces from time to time as he shall think convenient and necessary for the effectual apprehending . . . [and] it shall and may be lawfull . . . to kill and destroy such negroes . . . slaves by gunn or any otherwise whatsoever.

Provided that where any negroe or mulattoe slave or slaves shall be killed . . . the owner . . . shall be paid . . . four thousand pounds of tobacco by the publique.

Virginia act, 1691, Finkelman, Law of Freedom, *18.*

[The fugitive is] sensible and artful, speaks quick, and sometimes stutters a little; HE MAY POSSIBLY HAVE A TICKET THAT I GAVE HIM TWO DAYS BEFORE HE WENT AWAY, DATED THE 6TH OF APRIL, MENTIONING HE WAS IN QUEST OF A RUNAWAY, AS I DID NOT MENTION WHEN HE WAS TO RETURN, HE MAY ENDEAVOUR TO PASS BY THAT.

Advertisement in South Carolina Gazette, *May 1, 1786, quoted in Blassingame,* Slave Community, *115.*

[I]n the evening of the 19th December 1815, . . . a black woman, destined for transportation to Georgia with a coffle, which was about to start, attempted to escape, by jumping out of the window of the garret of a three story brick tavern in F. street, about day-break in the morning. . . . [A doctor] was called to visit her immediately after her fall, and found, besides her arms being broken, that the lower part of the spine was badly shattered, so that it was doubtful whether she would ever be capable of walking again, if she should survive. . . .

. . . Asking her what was the cause of her doing such a frantic act as that, she replied, "They brought me away with two of my children, and wouldn't let me see my husband—they didn't sell my husband, and I didn't want to go;—I was so confused and 'istracted, that I didn't know

This abolitionist's conception shows a slave trying to escape her captors. *(Torrey,* American Slave Trade*)*

hardly what I was about—but I didn't want to go, and I jumped out of the window;—but I am sorry now that I did it;—they have carried my children off with 'em to Carolina."

Torrey, American Slave-Trade, 67–69.

The chief practical difficulty . . . was connected with the youngest two of the children. They were of three and two years respectively, and of course would have to be carried. . . . Sometime previously I had directed her [my wife] to make me a large knapsack of two-cloth, large enough to hold them both, and arranged with strong straps to go round my shoulders. . . . I resolved to start on the night of the following Saturday. Sunday was a holiday; on Monday and Tuesday I was to be away on farms distant from the house; thus several days would elapse before I should be missed. . . .

It was a dark, moonless night, when we got into the little skiff, in which I had induced a fellow-slave to set us across the river. . . . In the middle of the stream the good fellow said to me, "It will be the end of me if this is ever found out; but you won't be brought back alive, Sie, will you?" "Not if I can help it;" I replied; and I thought of the pistols and knife I had bought some time before of a poor white. . . . For a fortnight we pressed steadily on, keeping to the road during the night, hiding whenever a chance vehicle or horseman was heard, and during the day burying ourselves in the woods. Our provisions were rapidly giving out. Two days before reaching Cincinnati they were utterly exhausted. All night long the children cried with hunger, and my poor wife loaded me with re-proaches for bringing them into such misery. . . . But now something must be done; it was necessary to run the risk of exposure by daylight upon the road. . . . [At the first house] I asked if he would sell me a little bread and meat. He was a surly fellow. "No, I have nothing for niggers!" At the next, I succeeded no better, at first. The man of the house met me in the same style; but his wife, hearing our conversation, said to her husband, "How can you treat any human being so? If a dog was hungry I would give him something to eat." . . . She asked me to come in, loaded a plate with venison and bread, and, when I laid it into my handkerchief, and put a quarter of a dollar on the table, she quietly took it up and put it in my handkerchief, with an additional quantity of venison. . . .

[That night they reached Cincinnati, where members of the underground railroad provided rest and shelter and sent them thirty miles by wagon. After that they walked, traveling by night and resting by day, almost starving

when their road cut through a wilderness. But they came upon an Indian village, where the Indians fed them, gave them a wigwam in which to rest, and guided them on their way. In Sandusky, Ohio, Henson found work loading a ship, and a sympathetic captain, who agreed to take the Henson family to Buffalo.] The next evening we reached Buffalo, but it was too late to cross the river that night. "You see those trees," said the noble-hearted captain, next morning, pointing to a group in the distance; "they grow on free soil, and as soon as your feet touch that, you're a *mon.*" . . . "Here, Green," said he to a ferryman, "What will you take this man and his family over for—he's got no money?" "Three shillings." He then took a dollar out of his pocket and gave it to me. . . .

It was the 28th of October, 1830, in the morning, when my feet first touched the Canada shore.

Autobiography of the Rev. Josiah Henson, in Four Fugitive
Slave Narratives, 60–69 passim.

[In 1845 in Maryland on a road there appeared] a group of slaves numbering about seventy-five men . . . in marching order headed for the free state of Pennsylvania. One of the slaves had a gun, another a pistol, and the rest carried scythe blades, swords and clubs. They went six abreast headed by a powerful negro fellow, sword in hand.

In Harding, River, 113–14.

Early yesterday morning a negro drayman carried to the office of Adams & Company's Express, two large square boxes addressed to "Williamson, No.———, Button-wood Street, Philadelphia." On being interrogated as to whence they came, the negro showed some confusion. Still the boxes were placed on the Express wagon and transported to the cars. As the driver of the wagon turned one of the boxes over rather roughly, he heard a sort of grunt, which proceeded from it. Suspicion was aroused, the boxes opened, and each one found to contain a stout negro, carefully folded up, with a small quantity of bread and a bladder of water, and one of them with a fan—a useful article in his warm situation.

New Orleans, Daily Delta, May 7, 1849, quoted in Bracey,
Meirer, and Rudwick, American Slavery, 17.

The Dismal Swamps [in the Carolinas] are noted places of refuge for runaway negroes. They were formerly peopled in this way much more than at present. . . . [C]hildren were born, bred, lived, and died here. Joseph Church [a slave owned by a church] told me [in 1853] he had seen skeletons, and had helped to bury bodies recently dead. There were people in the swamps still, he thought, that were the children of runaways, and who had been runaways themselves "all their lives." . . .

[Nowadays] They cannot obtain the means of supporting life without coming often either to the outskirts to steal from the plantations, or to the neighbourhood of the camps of the lumbermen. They depend much upon the charity or the wages given them by the latter. The poorer white men, owning small tracts of the swamps, will sometimes employ them, and the negroes frequently. In the hands of either they are liable to be betrayed to the negro-hunters. . . .

Olmsted, Cotton Kingdom, *121.*

I have known runaways to lodge in the kitchen of a gentleman in town for months at a time, without ever being discovered and supported entirely by his own servants; there is scarcely a runaway in any neighborhood but a portion of the servants know about it and assist in supporting him.

Virginia overseer, in Cole, "Militant Black Women," in Hine,
Black Women in American History, *266.*

I lived in that dismal little hole, almost deprived of light and air, and with no space to move my limbs, for nearly seven years [after I had hidden from my master]. . . . [M]y body still suffers from the effects of that long imprisonment, to say nothing of my soul. . . . Countless were the nights that I sat late at the little loophole scarcely large enough to give me a glimpse of one twinkling star. . . . Season after season, year after year, I peeped at my children's faces, and heard their sweet voices, with a heart yearning all the while to say, "Your mother is here." Sometimes it appeared to me as if ages had rolled away since I entered upon that gloomy, monotonous existence. At times, I was stupefied and listless; at other times I became very impatient. . . .

Jacobs, Slave Girl, *224–25.*

The trader . . . sold the chance of me to [Timothy] Guard for $1,000. The conditions were, if Guard ever saw me in the United States, he was to pay the money. He saw me the next night, for I went in. I had a previous understanding with Guard, that if he bought me, I was to have a chance to buy myself. He gave me a paper signed before witnesses, that I was to be free, when I paid him $1,600. He also gave me papers stating that I was allowed to trade for myself: if I would not pay, he would, and if any one

would not pay me, he would compel them. I went to work as steward of a steamboat [on the Mississippi]. At first, I got $35 a month, which raised till I got $100 a month. I paid off Guard between six and seven years after. . . .

Aaron Sidles, A North-Side View, *in* Four Fugitive Slave Narratives, *190.*

I hope you will remember me now just the same as you did when I was there with you because my mind are with you night and day the Love that I bear for you in my breast is greater than I thought it was if I had thought I had so much Love for you I dont think I ever Left being I have escape and has fled into a land of freedom I can but stop and look over my past Life and say what a fool I was for staying in bondage as Long My dear wife I dont want you to get married before you send me some letters because I never shall get married until I see you again My mind dont deceive and it appears to me as if I shall see you again.

Samuel Washington Johnson, in Gutman, Black Family,
266–67.

Helping the Fugitives: "Negro Stealing"

Divers evil and ill-disposed persons have hitherto attempted to steal away negroes or other slaves, by specious pretence of promising them freedom in another country, against which pernicious practice no punishment suitable hath been yet provided.

South Carolina legislature, 1712, in Higginbotham,
In the Matter of Color, *187.*

[John] Fairfield, [a southern abolitionist], . . . would go South into the neighborhood where the slaves were whom he intended to conduct away and, under an assumed name and a false pretence of business, engage boarding, perhaps at the house of the master whose stock of valuable property he intended to decrease. He would proclaim himself to be a Virginian and profess to be strongly pro-slavery in his sentiments, thus lulling the suspicions of the slaveholders while he established a secret understanding with the slaves—gaining their confidence and making arrangements for their escape. Then he would suddenly disappear from the neighborhood and several slaves would be missing at the same time. . . .

Fairfield was several times betrayed and arrested in the South and put in prison, but being a Free Mason, high in the Order, he managed to get out of prison without being tried. . . .

. . . At one time I was told of one of Fairfield's adventures up the Kanawha River, near Charleston, Virginia. Several colored people in Ohio, who had relatives in slavery at and near the salt works, importuned Fairfield to bring them away. . . . Taking two free colored men with him whom he claimed as his slaves, he went to the salt works on the Kanawha and professing to be from Louisville, Kentucky, said that he had come to engage in the salt trade. He contracted for the building of two boats and for salt with which to load them when finished. These arrangements afforded time for his colored men to become acquainted with the slaves he wished to rescue, gain their confidence, and mature the plans for their escape.

Some of the slaves were good boatmen, as also were Fairfield's men, and it was planned that when the first boat was finished, one of the slaves and one of Fairfield's men should get into it on Saturday night and float down the river a short distance and to a point agreed upon and take in a company of slaves, both men and women. They were then to take advantage of the high water and swift current of the Kanawha, and make all possible speed to the Ohio River. . . .

When Fairfield learned that one of his boats and one of his men were gone, he affected to be much enraged and accused his other man of having some knowledge of the affair, and threatened him with severe punishment. The man denied having any part in the plot, but Fairfield professed to doubt him and said that he should watch him closely.

. . . Fairfield remained at the salt works to await the completion of his other boat and to watch his other negro servant, of whom he professed to be very distrustful. In a few days the boat was completed and the next Saturday night it disappeared, together with Fairfield's negro man and ten or twelve slaves. Fairfield was now ruined! both his boats and both his slaves were gone; and the loss of his property made him almost frantic. He started in hot pursuit, accompanied by several men. . . . When they reached the Ohio River they found the boat tied to the bank on the Ohio side, but the fugitives were gone.

The pursuers ferried across the river and, according to Fairfield's suggestion, divided company and took different routes, with the understanding that they were all to meet at a point designated. But Fairfield never met them and was never seen at the salt works afterward. . . .

Coffin, Reminiscences, *275–79 passim.*

To me, it [the publication of *Uncle Tom's Cabin*] was a command. A deep and settled conviction impressed me that it was my duty to help the oppressed to freedom. . . .

I was initiated into a knowledge of the relief societies, and the methods adopted to circulate information among the slaves of the South; the routes to be taken by the slaves, after reaching the so-called free states; and the relief posts, where shelter and aid for transportation could be obtained. . . .

On my arrival in Richmond [in 1857], . . . I spent a few weeks in quietly determining upon the best plans to adopt. Having finally decided upon my course, I invited a number of the most intelligent, active and reliable slaves to meet me at the house of a colored preacher, on a Sunday evening. On the night appointed for this meeting, forty-two slaves came to hear what prospect there was for an escape from bondage. . . . I explained to them my . . . purpose in visiting the slave states, the various routes from Virginia to Ohio and Pennsylvania, and the names of friends in border towns who would help them on to Canada. I requested them to circulate this information discreetly among all upon whom they could rely. . . . I requested as many as were ready to accept my offer, to come to the same house on the following Sunday evening, prepared to take the "Underground Railroad" to Canada.

On the evening appointed nine stout, intelligent young men declared their determination to gain their freedom, or die in the attempt. To each I gave a few dollars in money, a pocket compass, knife, pistol, and as much cold meat and bread as each could carry with ease. . . . I learned, many months after, that they all had arrived safely in from slavery; all of whom I had the privilege of forwarding to Canada by the Underground Railroad.

Canadian Alexander Ross, Recollections, *3, 5, 10–12.*

[John Mason, a fugitive slave] was willing to risk the forfeiture of his own freedom, that he might, peradventure, secure the liberty of some. He commenced the perilous business of going into the State from whence he had escaped and especially into his old neighborhood, decoying off his brethren to Canada. . . . This slave brought to my house in nineteen months 265 human beings whom he had been instrumental in redeeming from slavery; all of whom I had the privilege of forwarding to Canada by the Underground Railroad. . . . He kept no record as to the number he had assisted in this way. I have only been able, from conversations with him on the subject, to ascertain about 1,300, whom he delivered to abolitionists to be forwarded to Canada. Poor man! He was finally captured and sold.

Black missionary W. M. Mitchell, in Siebert,
Underground Railroad, *184.*

Helping the Fugitives: The Underground Railroad

Soon after we located at Newport [Indiana], I found that we were on a line of the U.G.R.R. [Underground Railroad]. Fugitives often passed through that place, and generally stopped among the . . . families of free colored people, mostly from North Carolina, who were the descendants of slaves who had been liberated by Friends many years before. . . . I learned that the fugitive slaves who took refuge with these people were often pursued and captured. . . . [I] inquired of some of the Friends in our village why they did not take them in and secrete them, when they were pursued, and then aid them on their way to Canada? I found that they were afraid of the penalty of the law. . . .

In the winter of 1826–27, fugitives began to come to our house. . . .

Many of my pro-slavery customers left me for a time, my sales were diminished, and for a while my business prospects were discouraging, yet my faith was not shaken, nor [did] my efforts for the slaves lessen. New customers soon came in. . . . My trade increased and I enlarged my business. I was blessed in all my efforts and succeeded beyond my expectations. The Underground Railroad business increased as time advanced, and it was attended with heavy expenses, which I could not have borne had not my affairs been prosperous. . . . We had different routes for sending the fugitives to depots, ten, fifteen, or twenty miles distant, and when we heard of slave-hunters having passed on one road, we forwarded our passengers by another. . . .

[T]hree principal lines from the South converged at my house. . . . The roads were always in running order, the connections were good, the conductors active and zealous, and there was no lack of passengers. . . . We knew not what night or what hour of the night we would be roused from slumber by a gentle rap at the door. That was the signal announcing the arrival of a train of the Underground Railroad, for the locomotive did not whistle, nor make any unnecessary noise. . . .

[Slave-hunters] often threatened to kill me and at various times offered a reward for my head. I often received anonymous letters warning me that my store, porkhouse, and dwelling would be burned to the ground, and one letter, mailed in Kentucky, informed me that a body of armed men were then on their way to Newport to destroy the town. . . .

Coffin, Reminiscences, *70, 72–73, 76.*

In the year 1831, a fugitive named Tice Davids came over the line and lived just back of Sandusky. . . .

When he was running away, his master, a Kentuckian, was in close pursuit and pressing him so hard that when the Ohio River was reached he had no alternative but to jump in and swim across. It took his master some time to secure a skiff, in which he and his aid followed the swimming fugitive, keeping him in sight until he had landed. Once on shore, however, the master could not find him. . . . [A]fter a long . . . search the disappointed slave-master went into Ripley, and when inquired of as to what had become of his slave, said . . . he thought "the nigger must have gone off on an underground road." . . . [T]his incident gave the name to the line. First the "Underground Road," afterwards "Underground Railroad."

Smedley, Underground Railroad, *34, 35.*

The abolition incendiaries are undermining, not only our domestic institutions, but the very foundations of our capital. Our citizens will recollect that the boy, Jim, who

Harriet Tubman was the "Moses" who guided escaped slaves to freedom. *(Siebert,* Underground Railroad*)*

was arrested while lurking about the Capitol in August, would disclose nothing until he was subjected to torture by screwing his fingers in a blacksmith's vice, when he acknowledged that he was to have been sent North by railroads. . . . Nothing more could be got from him until they gave the screw another turn, when he said, *"the railroad went underground all the way to Boston."*

Washington, D.C., newspaper, October 1839, in Buckmaster, Let My People Go, *108–9.*

The way was so toilsome over the rugged mountain passes, that often the *men* who followed [Harriet Tubman] would give out, and foot-sore, and bleeding, they would drop on the ground, groaning that they could not take another step. They would lie there and die, or if strength came back, they would return on their steps, and seek their old homes again. Then the revolver carried by this bold and daring pioneer, would come out, while pointing it at their heads she would say, "Dead niggers tell no tales; you go on or die!" And by this heroic treatment she compelled them to drag their weary limbs along on their northward journey. . . .

Sarah Bradford, describing Tubman's methods in leading slaves to freedom, in Harriet, *39.*

Lawrence [Kansas] *April 4th,* 1859
Mr. F. B. Sanbourn

Dear Sir . . . Lawrence has been . . . known and cursed by all slave holders in and out of Mo. for being an abolition town. . . .

. . . In the last four years . . . nearly three hundred fugitives hav[e] passed through and received assistance from the abolitionists here at Lawrence. Thus you see we have been continually strained to meet the heavy demands that were almost daily made upon us to carry on this (not very) *gradual emancipation.* . . . Many of the most zealous in the cause of humanity complained (as they had good cause to) that this heavy (and continually increasing) tax was interfering with their business to such a degree that they could not stand it longer. . . . This was about the state of affairs last Christmas when as you are aware the slaves have a few days holiday. Many of them chose this occasion to make a visit to Lawrence and during the week some twenty four came to our town, five or six of the number brought means to assist them on their journey. These were sent on, but the remainder must be kept until money could be raised to send them on. $150 was the am't necessary to send them to a place of safety. Under the circumstances it necessarily took some time to raise

that am't. . . . Lawrence like most all towns has her bad men pimps and worst of all a few democrats, all of whom will do *anything* for money. Somewhere in the ranks of the intimate friends to the cause these traitors to God and humanity found a judas who for thirty pieces of silver did betray our cause. . . . Every thing goes to prove that the capture of [Dr.] Day's party was the work of a traitor. . . . We would like . . . that you plead our cause with those of our friends who are disposed to censure us and convince them we are still worthy and in great need of their respect and cooperation. . . . [H]eavy expenses of the trial of Dr Day and son . . . has been principally borne by the society here and has amounted to near $300. . . . We have some eight or ten fugitives now on hand who cannot be sent off until we get an addition to our financial department.

Col. J. Bowles to Mr. F. B. Sanborn of Concord, Massachusetts, in Siebert, Underground Railroad, *347–50.*

LOW MOOR, May 6, 1859
Mr. C. B. C.,

Dear Sir:—By to-morrow evening's mail, you will receive two volumes of the "Irrepressible Conflict" bound in black. After perusal, please forward, and oblige,

Yours truly,
G. W. W.

Coded letter announcing the arrival of two fugitives, in Siebert, Underground Railroad, *58.*

We have been expending our sympathies, as well as congratulations, on seven newly arrived Slaves that Harriet Tubman has just pioneered safely from the Southern part of Maryland. One woman carried a baby all the way, & brot two other childn. that Harriet & the men helped along, they brot a piece of old comfort & blanket, in a basket with a little kindling, a little bread for the baby with some laudanum, to keep it from crying during the day. They walked all night, carrying the little ones, and spread the old comfort on the frozen ground, in some dense thicket, where they all hid, while Harriet went out foraging, & sometimes cd. not get back till dark, fearing she wd. be followed. Then if they had crept further in, & she couldn't find them, she wd. whistle, or sing certain hymns, & they wd. answer.

Abolitionist and woman's rights reformer Martha Pelham Wright, letter to her daughter Ellen, from Auburn, New York, December 30, 1860, in the Garrison Family Papers, Sophia Smith Collection, Smith College. Available online at URL: http://womhist.binghamton.edu.

[To hide fugitives] I built an addition to my house in which I had a room with its partition in pannels. One pannel could be raised about a half inch and then slid back, so as to permit a man to enter the room. When the pannel was in place it appeared like its fellows. . . . In the abutment of Zanesville bridge on the Putnam side there was a place of concealment prepared.

Eli F. Brown, in Siebert, Underground Railroad, *64.*

Deterring Runaways: Patrols

Sir:

According to the law I have appointed Paterrolers [patrollers] to Kech our Negroes in order & to serch all Disorderly houses after night & unlawful Meetings & where they find a large quantity of Negroes assembled at night to take them up and cary them before a justice which has been done but we have a set of disorderly People who calls themselves Methodists and are joined by some of those who call themselves Baptists, who make it a rule two or three times a week to meet after dark & call in all the Negroes they can gather & a few whites & free mulattoes who pretend under the cloak of Religion to meet at a School house where no one lives & there they pretent to preach & pray with a sett of the greatest Roges of Negroes in this County & they never break up Till about two or three o'clock in the morning & those Negroes who stays with them goes through the neighborhood and steels everything they can lay there hands on. . . . & I have ordered the Peterrolers to go to such unlawfull meetings & to take up all the Negroes that they should find at such places which they have done & the masters of the Negroes has approved of this plan very much, but these people who are determined to encorige or [our] Negroes to wrong & the other day they sent to the Capt. of the Paterrolers that on Friday night they wood have a Meeting & if they came there and offered to toch a Negro That they wood protect the Negroes & if they said a word would beat them [the patrollers]. . . .

Letter from Holt Richardson to the governor of Virginia, September 5, 1789, in Johnston, Race Relations, *97–98.*

I have known the slaves to stretch clothes lines across the street, high enough to let the horse pass, but not the rider: then the boys would run, and the patrols in full chase would be thrown off by running against the lines. The patrols are poor white men, who live by plundering and stealing, getting rewards for runaways, and setting up little shops on the public roads. They will take whatever the slaves steal, paying in money, whiskey, or whatever the slaves want. They take pigs, sheep, wheat, corn,—any thing that's raised they encourage the slaves to steal: these they take to market next day. It's all speculation—all a matter of self interest, and when the slaves run away, these same traders catch them if they can, to get the reward. If the slave threatens to expose his traffic, he does not care—for the slave's word is good for nothing—it would not be taken. There are frequent quarrels between the slaves and the poor white men.

Francis Henderson, in Drew, Refugee, *157.*

The patrols were something like our mounted police, they were men who rode around the country and if they found any colored people off the plantations where they belonged, they would lash them and turn them over to their masters. Nights they would go around to the houses where the slaves lived and go in the houses to see if there was anybody there who had no right to be there. If they found any slave in a house where they had no right to be, or where they did not have a permit to be, they would ask the reasons why and likely arrest them and whip them. My mother had a board floor to her house and underneath that . . . a hole dug out to keep potatoes and things out of the way. When she heard the patrol coming she raised up one of the boards of the floor and I jumped down in the cellar and when the men on the patrol came in they did not find me. That cellar was my hiding place and sleeping place for three years.

William Henry Singleton, Recollections, *7.*

Deterring Runaways: "Negro Hunters"

Two or three days since, a gentleman of this parish, in *hunting runaway negroes,* came upon a camp of them in the swamp, arrested two of them, but the third made fight; and upon being *shot in the shoulder,* fled to a sluice, where the *dogs succeeded in drowning him.*

St. Francisville (La.) Chronicle, *February 1, 1839, in Dumond,* Antislavery, *15.*

No particular breed of dogs is needed for hunting negroes: blood-hounds, foxhounds, bull-dogs, and curs were used. . . . They are shut up when puppies, and never allowed to see a negro except while training to catch him. A negro is made to run from them, and they are encouraged to follow him until he gets into a tree, when meat is given them. Afterwards they learn to follow any particular negro by scent, and then a shoe or a piece of clothing is taken off a negro, and they learn to find by scent who it belongs to, and to tree him, etc. . . .

When the hunters take a negro who has not a pass, or "free papers," and they don't know whose slave he is, they confine him in jail, and advertise him. If no one claims him within a year he is sold to the highest bidder, at a public sale, and this sale gives title in law against any subsequent claimant.

Olmsted, Cotton Kingdom, *122.*

Deterring Runaways: The Fugitive Slave Laws

If any servant runn away from his master into any other of these confederated Jurisdiccons, That in such case vpon the Certyficate of one Majistrate in the Jurisdiccon out of which the said servant fled, or upon other due proofs, the said servant shall be deliuered either to his Master or any other that pursues and brings such Certificate or proofe.

Articles of Confederation of the New England Confederation, 1643, in Siebert, Underground Railroad, *19.*

We have obtained a right [in the U.S. Constitution] to recover our slaves, in whatever part of America they may take refuge, which is a right we have not had before. In short, considering the circumstances, we have made the best terms for the security of this species of property it was in our power to make. We would have made better if we could; but, on the whole, I do not think them bad.

Pinckney of South Carolina, 1788, in Siebert, Underground Railroad, *294.*

There was a man came to Hartford [Connecticut] from Savannah. . . . He brought a slave girl with him to care for the smaller children. . . . All went on well for about two years. . . . One day when I was at work in the store, a gentleman came where I was; he asked if this was deacon mars. I said "Yes, sir." He said Mr. Bullock was about to send Nancy to Savannah, "and we want to make a strike for her liberty, and we want some man to sign a petition for a writ of habeas corpus to bring Mr. Bullock before Judge Williams; they tell me that you are the man to sign the petition." . . . The court said it was the first case of the kind ever tried in the State of Connecticut. . . .

At the time appointed all were in attendance to hear from Judge Williams. The judge said that slavery was tolerated in some of the States, but it was not now in this State; we all liked to be free. This girl would like to be free; he said she should be free,—the law of the State made her free, when brought here by her master. . . .

Ex-slave James Mars, describing an experience in the 1820s (?) Life, *55–56.*

[T]he master . . . a stranger, must go into a free state, seize his slave without form or process of law, and unaccompanied by a single civil officer, must carry that slave, in the face of a fanatical and infuriated population, perhaps from the centre of extremists of the state, a distance of two or three hundred miles to the place where the judge may happen to reside. . . . [Even when the master gains a favorable judgment,] there is no provision in that law [the Fugitive Slave Law of 1793] by which the judgment can be enforced. . . .

General Assembly of Virginia, 1849–1850, in Campbell, The Slave Catchers, *8.*

[In consequence of the Fugitive Slave Law of 1850] people held indignant meetings, and organized committees of vigilance whose duty was to prevent a fugitive from being arrested, if possible, or to furnish legal aid, and raise every obstacle to his rendition. The vigilance committees were also the employees of the U. G. R. R. and effectively disposed of many a *casus belli* [cause of dispute] by transferring the disputed chattel to Canada.

Abolitionist Rev. Theodore Parker of Boston, in Siebert, Underground Railroad, *71.*

And Rev. Dr. Dewey, whom we accounted one of the ablest expounders and most eloquent defenders of our Unitarian faith,—Dr. Dewey was reported to have said at two different times, in public lectures or speeches during the fall of 1850 and the winter of 1851, that "he would send his *mother* into slavery, rather than endanger the Union, by resisting this law [the Fugitive Slave Law of 1850] enacted by the constituted government of the nation." He has often denied that he spoke thus of his "maternal relative," and therefore I allow that he was misunderstood. But he has repeatedly acknowledged that he did say, "I would consent that my own brother, my own son, should go, *ten times rather* would I go myself into slavery, than that this Union should be sacrificed."

May, Recollections, *367.*

Shall we resist Oppression? Shall we defend our Liberties? Shall we be FREEMEN or SLAVES? . . . Should any one attempt to execute [the] provisions [of the

Fugitive Slave Law of 1850] on any one of us, either by invading our home or arresting us in the street, we will treat such an one as assaulting our persons with intent to kill, and, God being our helper, will use such means as will repel the aggressor and defend our lives and liberty.

New York City blacks, National Anti-Slavery Standard, *October 10, 1850, in Pease and Pease,* Fugitive Slave Law, *15.*

If any man approaches [my] house in search of a slave—I care not who he may be, whether constable, or sheriff, magistrate or even judge of the Supreme Court—nay let it be President Millard Fillmore surrounded by his cabinet and his bodyguard, with the Declaration of Independence waving above his head as his banner, and the constitution of his country upon his breast as his shield—if he crosses the threshold of my door, and I do not lay him a lifeless corpse at my feet, I hope the grave may refuse my body a resting place, a righteous heaven my spirit a home.

Black abolitionist Martin Delany, in Harding, River, *159.*

I know that . . . colored men, men of my complexion . . . cannot expect . . . any mercy from the laws, from the constitution, or from the courts of the country. . . . I stand here to say that if, for doing what I did . . . I am to go in jail six months and pay a fine of a thousand dollars, according to the Fugitive Slave law . . . I . . . say that I will do all I can for any man thus seized and held, though the inevitable penalty . . . hangs over me.

Charles Langston of Ohio, 1858, jailed for aiding a fugitive, in Harding, River, *210.*

In nineteen cases out of twenty where a fugitive slave enters Illinois, he is arrested and returned without any judicial process whatever. Those portions of the State which border on the Kentucky and Missouri lines are in harmony with their neighbors on the other side, and a fugitive slave is returned as regularly as a stolen horse.

Senator Stephen A. Douglas, in Campbell, The Slave Catchers, *112.*

Dismal Swamp [extending from Norfolk, Virginia, to the upper part of the Carolinas,] is divided into tree or four parts. . . . When we wanted fresh pork we goed to Gum Swamp, 'bout sun-down, run a wild hog down from de cane-brakes into Juniper Swamp, whar dar feet can't touch hard ground, knock dem over, and dat's de way we kill dem. De same way we ketch wild cows. We trod [threw] dar bones . . . to one side de fire. Many's de time we waked up and seed de bars skulking round our feet for de bones. Da neber interrupted us; da knowed better; coz we would gin dem cold shot. Hope I shall live long enough to see de *slaveholders* feared to interrupt us! . . .

Old man Fisher was us boys' preacher. He runned away and used to pray. . . . I b'lieve God is no inspector of persons; an he knows his childer, and kini hear dem jest as quick in de Juniper Swamp as in de great churches. . . .

Dar is families growed up in dat ar Dismal Swamp dat never seed a white man, an' would be skeered most to def to see one. Some runaways went dere wid dar wives, an' dar childers are raised dar. We never had any trouble 'mong us boys; but I tell you pretty hard tings sometimes 'cur dat makes ye shiver all over. . . . De master will offer a reward to some one in de swamp to ketch his runaway. So de colored folks got jist as much devil in dem as white folks; I sometimes tink de are jist as voracious arter money. Da 'tray de fugitives to dar masters. Sometimes de masters comes and shoots dem down dead on de spot. . . .

I feared to stay dar arter I seed such tings; so I made up my mind to leave. . . . 'Spect I better not tell de way I comed; for dar's lots more boys comin' same way I did.

Verbatim report of account of life in the Dismal Swamp, told by a Canadian runaway, at some time before 1859, in Redpath, Roving Editor, *243ff.*

CHAPTER SEVEN

Canada, Other Refuges, and the Colonization/Emigration Movement
1501–1877

Slavery in Canada

Throughout most of its history, Canada has put up with a great deal of pother from its neighbor to the south, a good bit of which sprang from that neighbor's ugly and awkward dealings with slavery.

Why did Canada itself not institutionalize slavery? After all, some form of slavery, whether among the native Indians or imported by Europeans, probably existed as early in Canada as in the rest of North America. Early on, though, climate, geography, economics, religion, and politics combined to stunt its growth and to let it die a natural and relatively painless death.

In New France, French policy fairly consistently called for an economy based on furs and fish—an economy that would not threaten the industries of the mother country. Neither trapping nor fishing required a large labor force, so neither created a demand for slaves. Now and then someone in New France, whether an official sent out from France or a local inhabitant, pled for slaves wherewith to promote shipbuilding or mining, but France regularly dismissed these pleas in short order.

The dominant Roman Catholic church condoned slavery—monks and nuns owned slaves—but also insisted on the slave's possession of an immortal soul and the virtue of pleasing God by freeing slaves. Most slaves were baptized into Christianity, often with the master as godfather. With its inheritance of Roman law, France regarded slavery as a temporary plight, not as a condition based on natural inferiority. Most slaves in New France, whether Indians (*panis*) or blacks, lived in or near Montreal, rather than in the isolated countryside. Most worked as domestics, a few in each household, living closely with their masters and mistresses. In such intimate circumstances, slaves and owners sometimes intermarried, white men usually marrying *panis* and white women usually marrying black slaves.

All these factors tended to mitigate slavery in New France. Slaves there were sold publicly, often alongside livestock. But slave trading was limited and almost entirely domestic. The number of slaves in New France probably never exceeded 4,000, and Indian slaves significantly outnumbered blacks. In 1759, of the 3,604 slaves recorded, only 1,132 were black.[1]

If slavery was seldom questioned in New France, neither was it defended. It just was, but only the slaves cared very much, nobody needed slaves very much, nobody was profiting from slaves very much, and nobody was gaining status from owning slaves. Eventually slavery dwindled, though it still existed when in 1763 the British took over the colony, and the Treaty of Paris of that date recognized it.

In the rest of what is now Canada slavery existed only incidentally among some of the Indian tribes and among settlers who brought slaves with them. The northern climate did not call for large gangs to work the land, and indentured servants met the need for laborers at least as well as slaves would have. It was expensive to maintain slaves throughout the long, cold winters. Particularly after 1787, when the American Northwest Territory was declared legally free of slavery, it was difficult to hang on to slaves: They could so easily flee south, and the Canadian courts were apt to rule against masters in favor of fugitives. The very hardships of the Canadian terrain and climate gave prestige to manual work more quickly than in the American South. Over the years, Canadians came to think of slavery as an American phenomenon, to be deplored rather than adopted.

Sadly, the early demise of slavery in Canada did not end prejudice against non-whites, which to the contrary mounted through the years with successive increases in the black population.

The First Wave: The Loyalist Blacks of the American Revolution

From the time of the American Revolution, the black population in Canada grew almost entirely because American blacks sought freedom there. Providing and sustaining a refuge for these fugitives was no easy task.

Invariably, whether slaves fled to Canada individually or were transported there in mass migrations, resettlement proved much more difficult than anyone had anticipated. On the whole, Canadian governments set an admirable record in dealing with refugees, trying persistently to help them, however slowly and inefficiently. Individually, white Canadians reacted to the blacks in much the ways of humans anywhere and at any time: some generously, some indifferently, some jealously, and some with the cruelties of racial prejudice.

When in the 1770s American colonists loyal to the king of England (known as Tories in the thirteen colonies, Loyalists elsewhere) realized that American patriots were going to defy the British government, they began moving to Canada, taking their slaves with them. The numbers of these Loyalists were significant—perhaps as many as 30,000, 10 percent of them black.[2] They usually settled in Quebec or in land east of Montreal. Over the years many of them manumitted their slaves—or simply abandoned responsibility for them. The work these slaves had formerly done did not exist in their new homes, and their owners now found it expensive to feed, shelter, and clothe them. With the Tories, though, came an increase in the domestic slave trade. Quebec's black population also increased in 1777, when Vermont outlawed slavery and many owners sold their slaves into Quebec. But in the Revolutionary period, most blacks immigrated into Nova Scotia.

Throughout the history of American slavery, wartime gave slaves opportunities to seek refuge with the enemy. So it was with wars between the Indians and the white settlers, the American Revolution, the War of 1812, and the Civil War. Sometimes, blacks fleeing to their masters' enemies found the freedom they sought, sometimes not, for some of those enemies regarded the slaves as spoils of war, to be sold for individual profit. Moreover, Englishmen who promised the slaves freedom in the heat of battle usually had no firm plan about what to do with them afterward. Sometimes, they genuinely wanted to help the slaves, but more often they were focused on depriving the Americans of labor and valuable property. During the Revolution and the War of 1812, the English might use the defecting slaves' labor to their own advantage or even enlist them to fight against their former masters—but what was to be done with them later?

Indians who took black captives in wars or raids might sell them back to white Americans or adopt them into their tribes. But for the British during the American Revolution and the War of 1812, the usual solution was to remove them to another location. Among the locations considered, Canada always featured prominently.

At the end of the American Revolution, but before the Treaty of Paris, Sir Guy Carleton, commander in chief of British troops in North America, guaranteed the freedom of all slaves who sought asylum behind British lines and formally claimed British protection. Carleton tried to handle the disposition of these blacks fairly, promising to recompense their owners and to offer the former slaves a choice of places in which to settle—the West Indies, Florida (temporarily), or Canada. On what basis were these newly freed slaves, many of them former field hands, to choose? Most opted for Jamaica or St. Augustine, but many could find no work there and later had to be transferred elsewhere. Ultimately, a good many of them landed in Nova Scotia—by about 1783 the province probably contained about 3,000 free blacks, of whom 1,336 were men, 914 women, and 750 children.[3] Carleton had not stopped to get the consent of the authorities in Nova Scotia, leaving them to cope as best they could with this influx of immigrants, most of whom through no fault of their own were indigent, unskilled, and illiterate and lacked experience in living independently.

The authorities of Nova Scotia tried to deal with the situation, conscious that the British had made promises to the blacks, some of whom, indeed, had fought for England. The Nova Scotians got their neighbors in New Brunswick to take in some; they kept some at work for a while repairing military barracks. To many they gave grants of land, seeds, and rations to sustain them until their first crops were harvested.

But everything went wrong. Most of the black immigrants had little if any experience in farming on their own, certainly not in the thin soil and endless winters of Canada. They felt, sometimes with reason, that the authorities were not dealing with them fairly. Unable to read or do accounts, they fell prey to the scams of opportunistic whites. Too many of them lived in near peonage, sharecropping for their neighbors; miserably clothed, housed, and fed; and repeatedly having to be rescued from starvation. In these circumstances, they could not rally to build a self-sustaining community. Only here and there did a black clergyman provide the leadership to stimulate the cooperation necessary to lift the community by its own efforts.

Sierra Leone, a Refuge from a Refuge

Into this misery hope came in 1791, in the form of an offer to emigrate once again, this time to Sierra Leone in West Africa. The idea originated in England, where a 1772 court decision effectively ending slavery precipitated the question of what was to become of the blacks there, now free. The answer—establish in Africa the black colony of Sierra Leone. The answer made more sense at the end of the 18th century than it would later, for many of the new freedmen had actually been born in Africa.

The colony was founded in 1791. That year, black leader Thomas Peters arrived in England with a petition from 102 Nova Scotian and 100 New Brunswick black families complaining of their wrongs and asking "to procure . . . some establishment where [they] may attain a competent settlement for themselves and be enabled by their industrious exertions to become useful subjects to His Majesty."[4] Sierra Leone seemed the obvious solution.

Peters certainly thought so. When the Sierra Leone Company, formed by a group of British abolitionists, offered to transport to the new colony free blacks with good character references, pay off their debts, and give each adult male 20 acres of land there, Peters enthusiastically began recruiting in Canada—too enthusiastically. Things got off to a bad start; both Peters and his English coworker exceeded their authority, propagandizing rather than trying to select only blacks genuinely dissatisfied with their lot in Canada, and promising that the future landholders would have to pay neither rent nor taxes, though the Sierra Leone Company had made no such guarantee.

Black clergy in Canada supported the project, and in short order the recruiters signed up nearly a thousand blacks. They gathered around Halifax, camping out in the December weather, while the representatives of the Sierra Leone Company scrambled for supplies and ships. On January 10, 1792, 15 ships carrying people and supplies set out on the six-week voyage to Sierra Leone.

It is hard to overestimate the problems confronting the Sierra Leone Company and the new settlers in the infant colony. The settlers must have spent many a despairing night asking themselves why they had ever moved. Provisions arrived late and spoiled. A fever that assailed them on the ships turned into an epidemic on shore, and about a hundred settlers died. So did many of the doctors and storekeepers sent to help them. Materials arrived in the wrong order, equipment for growing cotton before building supplies. Storms destroyed their huts. Quarrels broke out. When land was finally allotted in November, the promised 20 acres dwindled to four. Understandably, when the company tried to collect rents, the settlers rebelled.

One way and another, though, they muddled along. They had come hoping to give their children better opportunities. So most of them stuck it out, clinging together, calling themselves "the Nova Scotians," holding themselves aloof from later immigrants, and furnishing much of the energy and many of the skills on which Sierra Leone depended. This clannishness was encouraged by the strikingly different background of the next group of immigrants to the colony.

The Second Wave: The Jamaican Maroons

Meanwhile, in 1796, Nova Scotia had once again been called upon to deal with another group of black refugees—the Jamaican Maroons. They came from a colony of escaped slaves who for a century had been hiding in the Jamaican interior, con stantly reinforced by slaves newly escaped from plantations. They had raided white settlements and intermittently engaged in wars. The last of these wars, begun in 1795, had ended with a negotiated settlement by which the Maroons (possibly from a corruption of the Spanish *cimarron*, meaning "wild" or "untamed") surrendered on condition that they could stay on their own land; the British government of Jamaica had broken faith and deported 556 of them to Nova Scotia. The much-tried Nova Scotia authorities again had not been consulted but nonetheless welcomed them, setting them to work for the military as laborers, finding land for them, appointing officers among them, and giving these longtime warriors uniforms.

All this did not sit well with many Nova Scotians, who found the Maroons' plural wives, their bizarre burial customs, and their swaggering about in military garb offensive. Nor did the Maroons take to Nova Scotia. They hated the climate and complained (often with reason) about the commissioners who supervised their work. The governor, trying to keep the peace, persuaded the Maroons to stay another year on condition that he forward to England their petitions for removal. In 1799, the British offered to pay the costs for transporting these Maroons to Sierra Leone, settling them, and educating them, if the Sierra Leone Company would accept them. In the fall, the British dispatched a ship to pick up the Maroons, with orders to the provincial authorities to deport the lot of them. By that time, the ship was frozen in the ice of the St. Lawrence, and Nova Scotia had to pay for the Maroons' support for another winter. It finally sailed on August 3, 1800. At least 25 of the Maroons died during the voyage, and the rest came near to mutiny.

Clearly they arrived in Sierra Leone in no happy mood. Equally clearly, the "Nova Scotian" residents of Sierra Leone were not happy to see these independent, tough rowdies, as clannish as themselves. For years thereafter the two groups kept apart, doing different work and belonging to different classes.

The Third Wave: The War of 1812— The "Refugee Negroes"

In the War of 1812, American slaves again sought refuge behind British lines. They were well received; the British even entertained hopes of stirring up a slave rebellion.[5] In 1813, the first group was shipped to Nova Scotia—as before, without consultation with the authorities there. Once landed, these former slaves were sent off to the interior to find work. As these "Refugee Negroes" continued to arrive in growing numbers, Nova Scotia did its best to cope, even while questioning the wisdom of such mass immigrations.

The numbers of Refugee Negroes increased in 1814, when British vice admiral Sir Alexander Cochrane invited slaves to come to British warships and military posts. Anyone who did, he promised, would "meet with all encouragement" as a free settler. (Of course, he had not asked Nova Scotia or other possible British refuges about this; the man was trying to win a war and had little time for political niceties.) England later agreed to pay U.S. slave owners more than $1.2 million in compensation for 3,601 slaves who accepted Cochrane's invitation.[6]

Nova Scotia authorities improvised. They sent some who were both penniless and ill to the poor house. There smallpox killed many; vaccination temporarily halted the epidemic, but it broke out again on Melville Island, where new arrivals were kept. The government settled some of the refugees around Halifax, but land there was becoming scarce, and questions were being raised about concentrating the new inhabitants in one place. Nonetheless, most of the refugees arriving in 1814 and early 1815 were established as settlers and were given seeds, agricultural tools, and provisions for two years. Officials theorized that in winter they could work as woodsmen in the forests, cutting lumber for houses and firewood.

By the summer of 1815, the authorities had evolved a more efficient reception method for the Refugee Negroes at Melville Island, under the direction of the chief customs officer. He was empowered to give them the same rations as had been distributed to American prisoners of war in the recent conflict, open a hospital for them, and vaccinate them. He moved them on as fast as he could, presumably in accordance with governmental policy, which now preferred dispersing them among the white population rather than concentrating them in one place. He also discouraged the separation of families by refusing rations to absent heads of families, for many fathers were leaving their wives and children to look for work in Halifax. In June of 1816, Nova Scotia was able to close down the operation at Melville Island.

Reception and resettlement had cost the province dearly, but what was too much for its taxpayers was not enough for a successful resettlement for the Refugee Negroes. Once again, as for the blacks who had escaped during the American Revolution, and for similar reasons, conditions worsened.

The land distribution did not work. The blacks were disappointed at not receiving outright grants of land, whereas Nova Scotia hesitated to give title to parcels until the occupants had proved that they could make good use of them. The blacks thought the plots too small and the land sterile. Crops failed. They lacked sufficient skill in fishing to earn their livings that way. The closer they moved to a welfare situation, the more the government's efforts went wrong, with relief fraud and refusal of rations to the homeless.

Every now and then, someone came up with a scheme to help. For instance, the surveyor general enthused over a plan for a settlement where a gang of 30 pioneer blacks would put up two houses a day, the next arrivals would clear the fields around the houses, and everybody would plant crops in the spring. The anticipated outcome was an instant flourishing community. In the event, more people arrived than had been expected. Too little land was cleared to feed them. The ground remained frozen until June. The shacks, built of green wood, fell apart. The potatoes froze, because the storage huts for them had been constructed without floors or cellars, and the common land was soon denuded of fuel.

The Council of Nova Scotia, thoroughly weary after this four-year-long nightmare, told the refugees on April 30, 1817, that after the first of June the government would stop handing out rations except to the aged and infirm, gave single men two weeks to find work, promised those who had cleared land more seed potatoes and tools, offered transportation to any refugees who wanted to return to the United States, and pledged to conduct a survey to see who would like to go to Trinidad.

Trinidad was willing, even eager, to receive refugee blacks. But those in Nova Scotia, by this time mistrustful of governmental offers, suspected reenslavement. Ninety-five did accept the offer, and they apparently got along reasonably well in Trinidad. But being illiterate, like most of the friends they had left behind in Nova Scotia, they could not communicate their satisfaction, and their silence was interpreted as a sure sign that they had been reenslaved.

With such effort, why did things go so terribly wrong for the Refugee Negroes? Most of them had been field hands in Maryland and Virginia; they had not learned to live side by side with whites, and not all of them had even had their own garden plots, where they might learn something about farming independently. Earlier refugees, mostly Anglicans and Wesleyans, had fitted more easily into the religious environment, but most of the Refugee Negroes were Baptists, an affiliation that Nova Scotian leaders associated with ignorance. Also, the former slaves had hard luck in their timing. They arrived at a time of especially severe winters and plentiful cheap, white labor. In their inexperience, some of them thought that freedom promised no work and no responsibility. As conditions worsened, instead of cooperating, they stole from each other and quarreled among themselves. The shiftless, poverty-stricken ways of life into which they drifted and the growing racial prejudices of their new white neighbors fed on each other.

Ultimately, most of the Refugee Negroes became permanent wards of the state. Seemingly unassimilable—with the exception of a community in Hammond's Plains—they remained an identifiable group within Nova Scotia until the end of the 19th century.

The 500 Refugee Negroes in New Brunswick fared no better, possibly worse. A settlement at Loch Lomond failed, acquiring a reputation among whites as a source of trouble. Nearby Loyalist blacks tried to help, but the Refugee Negroes hesitated to cooperate with them because of religious differences. White missionaries and philanthropists succeeded no better. These Refugee Negroes refused the province's offer to resettle them in smaller groups elsewhere. They worked at menial jobs in the cities rather then entering the more stable and better-paying trades of farming, fishing, and lumbering—from which they were in any case blocked by the refusal of master workmen to train them, for fear of possible quarrels among black and white apprentices. So most took jobs as stable boys or hotel servants. Others went to live with Indians.

The Fourth Wave: Fugitive Slaves (1815–1861)

As the number of slaves in the United States grew, as white fears of blacks swelled, and as the laws restricting the actions of slaves tightened, American slaves dreamed of the freedom they might find "under the British lion" in Canada. One by one or in small groups, but in increasing numbers, they "followed the North Star" to a new life in a new land. By the late 1820s, fugitive slaves were arriving in Canada in substantial numbers—which continued to grow right up to the Civil War, eventually constituting the largest group of black immigrants.

Most of those who entered Canada up until 1850 were self-selected, people with the courage and enterprise to flee into the unknown and intelligent enough to make their way through multifarious dangers. Many of them before they went to Canada had lived for a time in northern states, where they had had time to adjust to independent life in a predominantly white community. Ultimately they *chose* Canada. After 1850, when the harsh federal Fugitive Slave Law made it well-nigh impossible for black fugitives to live securely in the free American states and endangered even blacks born free, a more heterogeneous lot of blacks fled to Canada.

Like most refugees, these fugitives were driven by mixed motives, mostly negative. Above all they wanted to escape the miseries and cruelties of their lives as slaves. Like most refugees, they entertained unrealistic hopes for the land to

Fugitives Mr. and Mrs. Samuel Harper *(Siebert, Underground Railroad)*

which they fled, envisioning it as a promised land where they would be equal not only before the law but also within the society, where they would be free not only from slavery but also from racial prejudice.

In 1856 black historian Benjamin Drew, having collected narratives of fugitives in Canada, optimistically reported the formation beginning in 1854 of "True Bands" of black men and women there, aiming "to pursue such plans and objects as may be for their mutual advantage; to improve their schools and induce their race to send their children into the schools; to break down prejudice; to bring the churches, so far as possible, into one body, and not let minor differences divide them; to prevent litigation by referring all disputes among themselves to a committee; to stop the begging system [going to the United States and raising large sums of money, of which the fugitives never received the benefit]; to raise such funds among themselves as may be necessary for the poor, the sick and the destitute fugitives newly arrived; to prepare themselves ultimately to bear their due weight of political power. . . . Small monthly payments are made by the members. The receipts have enabled them to meet all cases of destitution and leave a surplus in the treasury. . . . There were in 1856 fourteen True Bands organized in various sections of Canada West.[7]

Until the 1830s, white Canadians did on the whole receive fugitives well. But with the fugitives' increasing numbers, their welcome faded. In the pattern of racial prejudice everywhere, white Canadians began to fear mass migrations. They transmuted dislike of the actions of individual erring blacks into contempt for all blacks. After the frontier closed and with the arrival of Irish immigrants, Canada needed black labor less. Disputes with the United States over the extradition of fugitive slaves dismayed some, who feared that blacks might prove disloyal to Canada in any conflict with the United States—though in fact blacks were consistently loyal to the British government, sometimes serving in provincial militias.

On the other hand, anti-Americanism led some white Canadians to sympathize with black fugitives. But some Canadians, believing that the United States had always wanted to annex Canada (news to most Americans), thought that the presence of blacks might make Canada less desirable to it.

If Canadians were ambivalent about the migration of blacks into Canada, so were the blacks. Many of them remained expatriate Americans rather than Canadians. They went to Canada less because they wanted to live there than because they could no longer live in the United States. In 1830, for instance, well-established blacks were forced out of Cincinnati by Ohio's threat to enforce harsh laws against them. More dramatically, the Fugitive Slave Law of 1850 pushed out of northern American cities blacks who had planned to live out their days there.

So it was that during the Civil War many Canadian blacks went south to join the Union army and never returned. When the Civil War ended slavery in the United States, thousands of blacks then living in Canada returned to the States, including some of those who had served in the Canadian military, voted there, and acquired property there.

Canadian officialdom acquitted itself most impressively in its refusal to return fugitive slaves to their American masters, despite strong pressures from the U.S. government. This stance was not always easy to maintain. Sometimes fugitive slaves had committed serious crimes, including theft and murder. But Canadian justices consistently maintained that since slavery did not exist in Canada, escaping from slavery certainly did not constitute a crime in Canadian courts, and neither did an act necessary to its success. In 1842, the Webster-Ashburton Treaty between Canada and the United States similarly protected fugitives.

A Ripple (1859)

Very late in the history of American slavery, the city of Vancouver offered sanctuary to a small number of free blacks who had been living in California. About 1850, that constitutionally free state had begun restricting blacks, first disqualifying them from giving evidence against white men, then toying with laws that would have permitted newly arrived slaveholders to continue to hold slaves, and in 1852 mandating the return of fugitive slaves to their owners.[8] The blacks of San Francisco, reading the handwriting on the wall, in the spring of 1858 investigated the possibility of emigration to British Columbia, and in April of that year 35 of them sailed. Later that year, perhaps another 400 families followed.

They were potential citizens that any country not dead set against all blacks would welcome—literate, skilled, intelligent, prosperous, and determined not to segregate themselves. Once arrived, instead of participating in the gold rush and then going on in the province, many of them bought property in Vancouver, property that appreciated rapidly.

These blacks were protected in part by their small numbers. But their very success aroused jealousy, and by 1862 racially discriminatory remarks were already appearing in the press.

Organized Black Communities

Beginning in 1830, private efforts organized black communities in Canada, partly to ease the transition to independent life and work there and partly to afford individuals mutual insurance. To some degree, white philanthropy supported all of them. Some blacks disapproved, arguing that the very existence of these communities implied that blacks could not make their own way without the help of whites. For example, beginning in 1854 the black True Band Societies were formed to protest the practice of begging support for black communities among whites and to advocate black autonomy, self-help, and responsibility. A freeborn black American, Mary Ann Shadd Cary, editor of the *Provincial Freeman* (a newspaper devoted to the interests of blacks in Canada), denounced the Refugee Home Society as a "begging scheme."

None of these organized black communities lasted long. Good intentions led to disastrous outcomes. The starry-eyed white reformers in charge of some of them lacked management skills or integrity or both. The communities were torn by strife, jealousy, and distrust.

Dawn, in Canada West (as Ontario and the unsettled lands to its west were known from 1841 to 1867), exemplified the problem. About 1836 a group of Oberlin students, with the support of the American Anti-Slavery Society and other American philanthropists, began a series of schools within growing black communities. This British-American Institute eventually sponsored 15 schools for the "Education Mental Moral and physical of the Colored inhabitants of Canada not excluding white persons and Indians."

The Dawn community grew around the first of these manual-labor schools, of which not only the pupils but also the board were integrated. For a while it flourished, reaching a population of some 500 black settlers, who owned some 1,500 acres; it had its own saw and grist mills, brickyard, and ropewalk. Josiah Henson, a famous and prosperous fugitive slave, contributed much to both its short-lived success and its downfall. Divisions among the blacks, bad management, and religious sectarianism had by 1854 buried it in a quagmire of quarrels and lawsuits.

Ironically enough, Elgin (also in Canada West), in some ways the most successful of these communities, was the creation of a slaveholder from Louisiana, who organized and ran it with benevolent paternalism. An intelligent and dedicated man, William King founded Elgin in 1849 with his own freed slaves. He lived there and managed it himself, welcoming churches of all denominations, founding schools so good that they attracted white children from the surrounding countryside, training black teachers who went out to teach in white schools, protecting the civil rights of the black inhabitants, and teaching them to vote in their own interest. Nonetheless, many of them went off to fight in the Civil War, and after the war others sold their property and returned to the United States. Elgin closed in 1873.

Of blacks in Canada in 1862, abolitionist Samuel Gridley Howe commented, "Taken as a whole, the colonists have cost to somebody a great deal of money and a great deal of effort; and they have not succeeded as well as many who have been thrown entirely upon their own resources."[9]

All in all, though Canada was no Utopia for blacks, and although many blacks left it when they could, it afforded thousands—perhaps as many as 40,000 in Canada West alone—physical safety, the protection of law, and political equality.[10] The promise of Sir John Colborne, the lieutenant governor of Upper Canada, to the Cincinnati blacks was kept insofar as the government was concerned: "Tell the Republicans on your side of the line that we do not know men by their color. If you come to us, you will be entitled to all the privileges of the rest of his Majesty's subjects." In the words of Lewis Richardson, once a slave owned by Henry Clay, "[O]n British soil . . . the Government knows me as a man."[11] At great expense, that government tried to help African Americans when the United States was making their lives a misery. The United States remains in debt to Canada for the haven it provided to so many Americans.

Other Refuges for Fugitives

Although over the years Canada sheltered many more fugitives from American slavery than any other foreign nation, other areas also provided havens. Where a slave fled depended a great deal on his or her location and knowledge. Most runaways stayed close to home, hiding in the woods or in maroon colonies. Although until 1850 many former slaves lived in the northern free states, surprisingly few made new homes in the vast free territories owned by the United States. Despite efforts to suggest the Northwest Territory as a more desirable site for colonization than Africa, before 1815 few blacks took refuge there. Soon, however, their numbers soared—in Ohio from 1,890 in 1810 to 4,723 in 1820 and 25,279 in 1850. On a single day a Virginia owner settled there 70 slaves whom he had freed.[12] This influx was far from welcome, and restrictions on blacks' civil liberties, court battles, and race riots ensued, forcing some to depart for Canada, but those who stayed established churches, schools, and industries.

As we have seen, while Spain held Florida, it openly invited American slaves to freedom there. Slaves accepted, fleeing individually or trying to march there in groups. Often those who made it wound up living among the Seminole, in the mild form of slavery common among them or as members of the tribe.

When it had the power, Mexico afforded a haven to Indians and African-American slaves. Its efforts were countered by the vigorous actions of Sam Houston and other Texans to protect the institution of slavery in Texas throughout its history as part of Mexico, as an independent country, as an American state, and as a member of the Confederacy.

The Colonization/Emigration Movement

From the Revolutionary War period until the 1830s, many people in the United States, North and South, agreed that slavery did not belong in a country founded on liberty. Even though many of the founding fathers held slaves and had excluded from the body politic women, blacks, and Indians, the contradictions between slavery and the country's professed ideals were uncomfortable.

Many slaveholders declared their willingness to free their slaves—if only they could think of what to do with them. Perhaps the freed slaves could be put to work on roads and other public works. Was it fair simply to liberate them and leave them to their own devices? What would happen to white people, particularly in states where blacks outnumbered whites?

For a good many white people for a good many years, right up to the Civil War, the answer was colonization: to ship free blacks off somewhere, preferably somewhere far away.

But where, precisely? Colonizationists suggested several possible locations. Haiti was near at hand, with a black government (after Toussaint Louverture brought a series of rebellions to a successful conclusion). Trinidad had indicated its interest in welcoming black settlers. Could they go to Jamaica or Panama? Surely somewhere to the west, in the vast stretches of unsettled North America, land for free blacks could be found. What about Canada? Better still, Central and South America stretched southward, with a tropical climate presumably congenial to blacks. But Africa was the most popular choice. In a sense, one suspects, Americans were trying to undo what they had done in removing slaves from their homeland. Then, too, they pointed to the example of British abolitionists in founding Sierra Leone.

The idea of establishing remote black colonies appealed to white people of different persuasions about slavery. Moderate antislavery advocates saw it as a way of encouraging slaveholders to free their slaves. Few thought that *immediate* emancipation could be achieved or would work; colonization at least would afford a start toward *gradual* emancipation. In any case, the individual slave freed and sent to a new colony would be better off. It was a peaceable process that would make few waves. The plan also relieved fears of invading slaveholders' rights to hold property. Churchmen argued that the presence of Christianized African Americans among them might help convert neighboring Africans and discourage the slave trade in the vicinity.

Southern states eager to rid themselves of free blacks supported colonization. Every slave insurrection inspired fresh enthusiasm. Defenders of slavery argued that colonization would at once appease antislavery forces and raise the value of slaves by decreasing the black population. Whites who worried about a black majority in the southern states openly argued that through colonization they could ship off enough blacks to hold down their numbers while allowing the proportion of whites to rise by "natural increase." Colonization spoke also to those who, like Abraham Lincoln, believed that blacks and whites were better off living apart—not to mention those who wished to protect the jobs of whites against black laborers.

Some white abolitionists detested the colonization movement as a slaveholders' conspiracy to protect their slave property by getting rid of free blacks. William Lloyd Garrison fought passionately against it, arguing that to remove black people, those best suited to cultivate the plantations, would be suicidal for the country. Others asserted that it would never work: Slaveholders were not about to free their slaves and send them to West Africa.

What of the people most concerned? Many black leaders opposed colonization, particularly in the early years of the 19th century. Some of these were successful people who saw no reason why African-Americans should be driven from what had by now become their native land. They still entertained hopes for emancipation, equality, and integration. African American Tunis Campbell (1812–1891), however, had been trained in an all-white school in New Jersey for missionary service with the American Colonization Society. By 1832 rising abolitionist feeling had so changed his thinking that he founded an anticolonization society, swearing "never to leave this country until every slave is free."[13]

Other blacks—*emigrationists*—advocated the establishment of separate black communities, some insisting on a location in North America, some choosing other sites. They doubted that the United States would soon emancipate slaves, let alone offer blacks political and social equality and integration. Black migrations actually began among themselves, commencing as early as 1815 and lasting at least until 1880.[14] In 1821 the all-black Richmond African Baptist Missionary Society sent to Sierra Leone missionaries led by Lott Cary, a former slave who had bought himself and believed fiercely in independent black action. To gain true liberty, he thought, blacks must leave the United States, but he scorned the American Colonization Society. As the years dragged by, with proslavery forces gaining ground in such measures as the Fugitive Slave Act of 1850, the battles over free and slave territories in the West, and especially the *Dred Scott* decision (see Appendix A), even some of the African Americans who had originally opposed colonization (such as Frederick Douglass) came to see emigration as the only hope for their people. The radical black leader Martin Delany insisted that "Central and South America are evidently the ultimate destination and future home of the colored race on this continent. . . . Go we must, and go we will, as there is no alternative. . . . To remain here in North America, and be crushed to the earth in vassalage and degradation, we never will."[15]

Over the years, both black and white individuals and groups experimented with colonies of former slaves in various locations. For instance, British abolitionist Frances Wright, who had proposed that the United States use public lands for slave labor and employ the profits to buy the slaves' freedom, in the 1820s founded a 640-acre community named Nashoba in Tennessee. There she settled slaves whom she bought from neighboring farmers, promising them eventual emancipation. This well-intentioned but ill-conceived, ill-located, and ill-managed scheme soon foundered. Wright did her best for the remaining blacks, transporting them to Haiti, setting them free, and helping them find homes and jobs.

The American Colonization Society, organized in 1817, immediately set about its avowed task of shipping free blacks to Liberia, in West Africa. The society had its work cut out for it. It had at once to try to meet the objections of its opponents and yet not offend its own heterogeneous members, some of whom opposed slavery categorically and others of whom owned slaves. It had to organize and provide for the management of a new colony in hostile surroundings—an undertaking that had defeated many another group. It had to populate that colony, raising the funds to transport the emigrants and support them there until they could fend for themselves. Fugitive slaves who, of their own free will and against enormous odds, fled to Canada did not always like it there. What was to be the response of the blacks who theoretically went to Liberia voluntarily but in actuality had been confronted by their owners with the choice between remaining slaves or going to a colony of which they knew almost nothing?

In the end, of course, colonization did not work. As a solution to the overwhelming problem of slavery it had never had any validity. It did not and could not begin to address the basic evils of that terrible institution or repair the damage done to the 4 million black people trapped in it in 1860. In this respect, colonization was a mere placebo.

As the Belgian-born editor Jean-Charles Houzeau remarked after the Civil War, the impracticality of colonization was obvious to anyone not deluding himself with hopes of a "painless" solution. How many ships would it take? And what countries would welcome such immigrants? Uncultivated land can support only three or four colonists per square league, and where was land available? What developed country would have them, or could furnish them work? "Yes, indeed, you lack workers in the United States and you talk of sending, at an immense expense, five million of them, five million persons belonging to your working class, to countries that do not want them!"[16]

Its supporters argued that the colonization effort diminished the international slave trade. It did, they said, encourage manumission. It did serve free blacks.

The idea survived. Many, including Abraham Lincoln, advocated colonization during the Civil War. Some slave owners freed their slaves and paid for a fresh start for them as free citizens of Liberia. Other masters who wanted to free their slaves could not afford the money to ship them off and furnish them with supplies for several months. The American Colonization Society could not begin to raise enough money to meet the demand, even with some support from the federal government. Altogether the society managed to send off only some 11,000 emigrants—over more than 40 years.[17]

The African Americans who reached Liberia encountered all the problems of pioneers in a new country, and more. Some emigrants did moderately well there. Others did not, wishing themselves back in the United States. The little colony was set down in unfriendly territory, subject to attack from neighboring tribes. Even in the 21st century its people live a troubled existence. Liberia survives, but it has never flourished.

Chronicle of Events

1501
- Portuguese explorer Gaspar Côrte-Real enslaves 50 Indian men and women in Labrador or Newfoundland.

1607
- The lieutenant governor of Acadia (New France) tries to enslave Indians to run his gristmill.

1628
- David Kirke brings a slave boy (later Olivier le Jeune) to Quebec.

1629
- Kirke sells his slave—the first sale of a slave in New France.

1670
- *Panis* (Indian slaves) are reported in Montreal; Indians on the northwest coast also are keeping slaves of their own.

1687
- The governor of New France seizes 40 Iroquois, whom he has invited to a peace conference, and ships them to France as slaves.

1689
- The attorney general of New France sends a memorandum to Louis XIV arguing that slavery would be profitable. Louis assents to slavery in New France, but his assent is virtually nullified by the outbreak of King William's War.

1701
- Louis XIV again authorizes slavery in New France.

1704
- New France's reversion to a fur-based economy ends the need for many slaves.

1705
- The New York legislature passes an "Act to prevent the running away of Negro slaves out of the City and County of Albany to the French at Canada."

1709
- The intendant of New France ordains that "all the *panis and Negroes who have been purchased and who will be purchased,*

shall be the property of those who have purchased them and will be their *slaves.*"

1716
- The intendant of New France pleads for the slave trade, to provide labor for agriculture, fishing, lumbering, shipbuilding, and mining.

1720
- The intendant of New France asks the king of France to send African slaves to work in the hemp market; he forwards a memorial in which the inhabitants of New France undertake to buy 101 Africans from French slavers.

1736
- The intendant of New France provides a uniform means of manumission, involving a notary's certificate and registration with the royal registry office.

1745
- The king of France decrees that slaves from enemy colonies who flee into French territory may be sold, the proceeds belonging to the king.

1752
- In Halifax, Joshua Mauger, victualler to the navy, advertises several black slaves for sale.

1763
- Slavery is specifically protected by the Treaty of Paris between Britain and France, in which France cedes its mainland North American empire east of the Mississippi to Great Britain.
- The British military governor of Quebec writes to a friend in New York asking for four slaves.

1764
- In a treaty with the superintendent of Indian affairs for New York, several Huron agree to return all "negro's, Panis or other slaves . . . who are British property" and to turn over any slaves who may subsequently seek refuge with them. The treaty introduces English law to Quebec, depriving slaves of legal protections.

1772
- In Great Britain, Lord Mansfield holds in *Somerset* v. *Stewart* that slavery cannot exist in England in the absence of specific legislation providing for it.

1773

- Dr. Samuel Hopkins of Rhode Island corresponds with Rev. Ezra Stiles about the possibility of sending a few blacks to a colony on the coast of Guinea.

1774

- With the Quebec Act, Britain restores French civil law to Quebec while retaining the English criminal code. The act also extends the boundaries of Quebec to the Ohio River, bringing under its aegis those few slaves living in the old Northwest.

1780

- A number of slaves captured in Kentucky are brought into Quebec and sold, although at least 10 of them apparently belonged to a Loyalist.
- Near Detroit, Indians continue to seize blacks for themselves.

1781

- A legislative act of Isle St. Jean (later Prince Edward Island) declares that baptism of slaves does not exempt them from bondage.

1783

- In England, Granville Sharp proposes an African colony for impoverished freed slaves.
- Loyalist (Tory) migration brings the first major influx of blacks to the maritime Canadian colonies, as masters bring their slaves with them and former slaves who had fought for the British or sought protection behind British lines embark for Nova Scotia. As a result, black slaves almost supplant Indian slaves, even in Quebec.

1786

- In England, Henry Smeathman publishes a *Plan of a Settlement to be Made near Sierra Leone.*
- *December:* About 350 impoverished former American slaves and 60 white women sail from Plymouth, England, for Sierra Leone, with the assistance of the [London] Committee for the Relief of the Black Poor.

1788

- Nova Scotia clergyman James MacGregor publishes an open *Letter to a Clergyman Urging Him to Set Free a Black Girl He Held in Slavery.*

1789

- An African tribal leader, King Jimmy, burns Granville town in the African settlement of Liberated Africans to the ground.

1790

- Through an Imperial act, Britain permits free importation into Canada of all "Negroes, household furniture, utensils of husbandry or cloathing," though furniture, utensils, and clothing were not to exceed the value of £50 for every white and £2 for every black slave.

1791

- French civil law is applied to Lower Canada (modern Quebec), English civil law to Upper Canada, and English criminal law in both.
- In Great Britain, Thomas Clarkson, Granville Sharp, and William Wilberforce form the Sierra Leone Company to administer the African colony of Liberated Africans.
- Thomas Peters, a former black pioneer in the American Revolution, arrives in England with a petition on behalf of 102 Nova Scotia and 100 New Brunswick

Canadian Dr. Alexander Ross, famous for his daring invasions of the American South to help slaves escape. *(Siebert, Underground Railroad)*

black families, asking for "some establishment where [they] may attain a competent settlement for themselves and be enabled by their industrious exertions to become useful subjects to his Majesty."

1792

- Eleven hundred freed slaves who migrated to Nova Scotia after the American Revolution establish Freetown, Sierra Leone, in West Africa.

1793–1803

- Canadian abolitionists triumph over slavery, mostly by judicial decisions.

1793

- The legislature of Upper Canada, with the king's assent, provides for the gradual abolition of slavery, forbidding the importation of slaves and the enslavement of anyone thereafter but setting no present slaves free; children born to these slaves are to be freed at age 25.

1794

- Colonists rebel against the Sierra Leone Company, but peace is restored.

1796

- A band of more than 550 non-Christian, warlike Jamaican Maroons is deported to Nova Scotia.

1798

- The chief justice of Lower Canada, James Monk, frees two slaves, incidentally remarking that slavery does not exist in that province and that he will so rule henceforth.

1800

- President Thomas Jefferson and Governor James Monroe of Virginia fail in an effort to inaugurate the colonization of blacks.
- The Court of King's Bench of Lower Canada frees a slave on the ground that the Imperial Act of 1797 abolished all legislation relating to slavery in the province; the decision renders slavery virtually untenable in the province.
- *July:* Nova Scotia black immigrants to Sierra Leone rebel against the Sierra Leone Company, believing that it has broken its promises about land; their rebellion is eventually quelled by the newly arrived Jamaican Maroons.
- *August 3:* 551 Jamaican Maroons are deported from Nova Scotia to Sierra Leone.

- *September 30:* Jamaican Maroons arrive in Sierra Leone.

1801

- President Jefferson corresponds with British authorities about the incorporation of the free blacks of the United States into the Sierra Leone colony.

1808

- Paul Cuffe, a black Quaker mariner living in Massachusetts, pioneers the idea of voluntary colonization.

1811

- Black ship's captain Paul Cuffe sails the *Traveller* from Massachusetts to Sierra Leone, where he founds the Friendly Society for the emigration of free blacks from America.

1813–1816

- The "Refugee Negroes," some 2,000 former American slaves who have sought refuge with the British in the War of 1812, are transported to Nova Scotia.

1814

- *April:* In the War of 1812, British vice admiral Sir Alexander Cochrane promises American slaves who come to a British ship or military post a choice of military service or free transportation to a British possession in North America or the West Indies, where they can be free settlers.

1815

- Captain Paul Cuffe at his own expense transports from the United States to Sierra Leone 38 persons of color.

1817

- The American Colonization Society is organized.
- *April 30:* The Council of Nova Scotia warns the Black Refugees of gradual withdrawal of support, offering any who wish it the opportunity to return to the United States and ordering a survey to see whether any wish to go to Trinidad.

1820s and 1830s

- Black labor is used in Canada to fell trees, build roads, cut railroad ties, and introduce tobacco culture.

1820

- The first effort of American colonizationists to settle a colony of black Americans in Africa fails because of the climate.

1821

- American colonizationists set out to settle another colony of black Americans in Africa, eventually purchasing land at Cape Montserado and calling their colony Liberia.
- Ninety-five Refugee Negroes sail from Nova Scotia to relocate in Trinidad.

1823

- *January 4:* Mexico enacts the Imperial Colonization Law: "There shall not be permitted, after the promulgation of this law, either purchase or sale of slaves that may be introduced into the empire. The children of such slaves, who are born within the empire, shall be free at fourteen years of age."
- *February:* The Mexican Imperial Colonization law is annulled; Stephen F. Austin is allowed to continue to colonize Texas with slaveholders.

1825

- The assembly of Prince Edward Island repeals the Act of 1781, with intent to abolish slavery.
- The *African Repository and Colonial Journal,* an instrument of the American Colonization Society, begins publication.

1826

- Secretary of State Henry Clay requests extradition of American fugitive slaves from Canada; the British government refuses.

1827

- The American Colonization Society petitions Congress for assistance, saying the society lacks both funds and the authority to govern a distant colony.

1828

- Congress asks the president to reopen negotiations with the British government for the return of fugitive slaves from Canada. The British government refuses.

1829

- The administrator of Lower Canada refuses a U.S. request for extradition of a fugitive slave and of a man who had helped him escape.
- Cincinnati, with a black population of at least 2,250, enforces Ohio laws of 1804 and 1807, in effect banishing blacks who have entered the state without a certificate of freedom and without a bond of 500 dollars guaranteeing good behavior and support and signed by two white men. Cincinnati whites riot against its blacks.

- Cincinnati's blacks form a society to seek a place to relocate.

1830

- In the spring, a large group of blacks leaves Cincinnati and founds the town of Wilberforce in Ontario; the cooperative experiment fails by 1836.
- *September 20–24:* In the United States, the National Negro Convention, taking a stand against colonization, organizes the American Society of Free Persons of Color, for Improving Their Condition in the United States; for Purchasing Lands; and for the Establishing of a Settlement in Upper Canada.

1831

- The first black convention, held in Philadelphia, adopts resolutions against the American Colonization Society, recommends emigration to Canada West, and organizes to raise money to purchase a colony in Canada.

1832

- A second black convention hears reports of the purchase of 800 acres in Canada and the beginnings of its settlement by 2,000 blacks, who, however, had encountered Canadian hostility. The convention appoints an agent to investigate Canadian settlement further, expresses opposition to the American Colonization Society, and urges abolition of slavery in the District of Columbia.

1833

- Upper Canada provides for the capture and extradition of "Fugitive offenders from Foreign Countries," leaving the governor in council free not to deliver a person if he deems it unwise.
- James Birney, exemplifying a shift in public opinion, renounces colonization in a *Letter on Colonization.*

1834

- Slavery is legally abolished in all British colonies.
- The Nova Scotia Assembly passes "An Act to prevent the Clandestine landing of Liberated Slaves," in order to prevent an anticipated inundation of former slaves. This act is disallowed as discriminatory in 1836.

1835

- Texans protest against a project for settling free blacks from the United States in Texas, then forming a provisional government.

1837

- Blacks at Niagara in Canada violently defend Solomon Mosely, whose extradition is sought for the theft of a horse when he fled.
- British authorities advise that fugitives should not be surrendered to extradition without evidence of a criminal act that "would warrant the apprehension of the accused Party, if the alleged offence had been committed in Canada."
- In Upper Canada, an antislavery society is formed in Toronto but does not survive the decade.

1840s

- As the Irish begin to immigrate in large numbers and frontiers dwindle, Canadians need black labor less.

1842

- Canada for the first time grants extradition of a fugitive slave, Nelson Hacket, who while escaping had stolen items not necessary for his escape.
- The black cooperative community of Dawn, built around a manual-arts school known as the British-American Institute, is founded in Canada West.
- Joseph Jenkins Roberts (1809–76), a black man, becomes the first president of Liberia.
- The Webster-Ashburton Treaty between the United States and Canada exempts extradition for desertion, mutiny, and revolt on board ship and protects the principle that no extradition will be granted unless for an action that would be considered an offense under Canadian law.

1847

- Liberia issues its Declaration of Independence.

1849

- The Canadian government enacts a new extradition law. No fugitive slave is ever surrendered to the United States under this law or the Webster-Ashburton Treaty.
- Former slaveholder William King founds the black colony of Elgin in Canada West with his 15 freed slaves as its nucleus.

1850

- By this time Nova Scotia and Canada West, the two major centers of black settlement, have established separate schools for blacks.
- The last segregated military Colored Corps in Canada West is disbanded.

1851

- An experimental black colony is launched; it is known successively as the Sandwich Mission, the Fugitives' Union Society, and the Refugee Home Society, under the last of which it soon is destroyed by factionalism.
- *February 26:* The Anti-Slavery Society of Canada is organized "to aid in the extinction of Slavery all over the world" by any lawful and practical means.
- *September:* The North American Colored Convention meets in Toronto and approves killing pursuers in self-defense.

1852

- The Fugitives' Union Society merges with the Refugee Home Society.
- *July:* The American Continental and West Indian League is organized in Canada West to promote settlement throughout the New World.

1853

- The National Emigration Convention of Colored People begins to investigate "intertropical" sites, especially Haiti, the Niger valley, and Central America, as refuges for blacks.
- A black convention at Rochester, N.Y., pronounces against emigration.

1854

- *August 24–26:* In Cleveland, Ohio, the National Emigration Convention of Colored Men votes to send agents to the Niger Valley in Africa, Central America, and Haiti to explore the possibility of black emigration thereto.

1856

- A black emigration convention in Canada West hears the Rev. James T. Holly report on his negotiations for black emigration to Haiti.

1858

- Black physician Martin R. Delany organizes the Niger Valley Exploring Party, instructed by its sponsors to gather scientific information, not to encourage emigration.
- Delany negotiates a treaty with eight kings of the Niger Valley, Africa, offering inducements for African Americans to settle there, but the project is interrupted by the Civil War and never resumed.
- *April:* The first black settlers arrive in Victoria, on Vancouver Island, British Columbia.

1859

- Naturalist Robert Campbell of the Niger Valley Exploring Party issues a circular in London promising that if its report is favorable, a number of blacks who wish to grow cotton there may emigrate from Canada and the free states.
- Members of the Niger Valley Exploring Party sign a treaty with the Alake of Abeokuta providing that North American blacks will settle on any unoccupied land "in common with the Egba people." The Civil War defeats their plans.
- Haiti appoints James Redpath as its emigration agent in British North America and the free states of the United States.

1861

- James Redpath, as emigration agent for Haiti, offers blacks free passage to Haiti and allotments from the public domain.

- No more than a third of the 2,000 blacks Redpath sent to Haiti permanently settle there.
- *May:* A group of 111 blacks, including some from Canada West, sail from New Haven for Haiti.
- *August:* Another 113 people, including the white wives of some Canadian blacks in the May group, sail from Canada for Haiti.
- *December:* Redpath announces that he will henceforth send blacks not to Haiti but to Jamaica, but Haiti continues to encourage agricultural settlement.

1868

- The communal experiment of Dawn having failed after years of quarrels and turmoil, the British-American Institute closes.

1873

- Elgin closes down, many of its inhabitants never having returned after fighting in the Civil War and others having sold their property and returned to the United States.

Eyewitness Testimony

Slavery in Canada

[W]ithout Servants nothing can be done. . . . [I hope] by setting a good Example [to improve agriculture.] Black Slaves are Certainly the only people to be depended upon, but . . . they should be born in one or other of our Northern Colonies, [as] the Winters here will not agree, with a Native of the Torrid Zone.

British military governor of Quebec, 1763 letter, in Winks,
Blacks in Canada, 26.

Canada as a Refuge: The Black Loyalists of the American Revolution

Great Riot today. The disbanded soldiers have risen against the Free negroes to drive them out of Town [Shelburne, Nova Scotia], because they labour cheaper than they—the soldiers. [27 July] Riot continues. The soldiers force the free negroes to quit the town—pulled down about 20 of their houses.

Benjamin Marston, July 26 and 27, 1784, in Walker,
Black Loyalists, 48.

There are a great number of Black People both in this Town and in Birch town who are in the most distressing Circumstances.

Many of them have been relieved by us, otherwise it is highly probable that some of them, during this inclement Season, must have perished—But as the number of White People, whom we have constantly to supply, are very considerable it is not in our power to afford the Blacks that assistance which their pressing Necessities loudly call for—

And as it is evident they become more and more burthensome every year [we ask that you] free this Infant Settlement from a Burden which it is by no means in a Capacity to bear.

Shelburne, Nova Scotia, Overseers of the Poor,
February 1789, in Walker,
Black Loyalists, 54.

Some Part of the said Black People [Loyalists] are earnestly desirous of obtaining their due Allotment of Land and remaining in America [Nova Scotia] but others are ready and willing to go wherever the Wisdom of Government may think proper to provide for them as free Subjects of the British Empire.

Thomas Peters's Petition to the British Cabinet, 1790, in
Walker, Black Loyalists, 95.

Canada as a Refuge: The Cincinnati Blacks (1829–1830)

[T]he law of 1804, known as the Ohio black law, was revived in that State, and enforced. By this law, every colored man was to give bonds in $500 not to become a town charge, and to find bonds also for his heirs. No one could employ a colored man or colored woman to do any kind of labor, under penalty of $100. There were then about 3,000 colored people there—by this law they were thrown out of employment. I was then clearing $600 a year, and refused to give bonds. The Colored people had a meeting, and talked about a court of appeals to test the law. Some talked of going to Texas,—we knew not what to do. . . . I spoke to them of Canada, and we formed a Colonization Society, of which I was President. I wrote for the Board to Sir John Colborne, at Little York, now Toronto, to know if we could find in Canada an asylum for ourselves, our wives, and children. . . . He wrote us . . . that so long as we remained true and loyal subjects, we should have every privilege extended to us that was enjoyed by any of his majesty's subjects, no distinction being made on account of color. . . . Mr. Hammonds, our friend, editor of a daily paper in Cincinnati, published the letter at my request. . . . Two or three of us, including myself, were sent for by the city government, next day. The reason was, as Mr. Hotchkiss said, that I, as one of the leading spirits, was doing a great deal of mischief; for every one that I took off to Canada was a sword drawn against the United States. . . . He said they were taking steps to have the law repealed, and wished me to stay any action about sending people to Canada. . . .

I paid no attention to what he told me, and sent three wagon loads out to Sandusky next day. In three or four weeks I and my family left—came to Sandusky—thence I took a boat, the "Gov. Cass," and went to Little York, where I entered into a contract with the Canada Company, for a township of land, agreeing to pay $6,000 a year, for ten years. It was the township of Biddulph. The black law had now become inoperative in Cincinnati, and the colored people wrote me, that they could now walk without being pushed off the side-walks, were well used, and were living in clover. Of 2,700 who were to have come, only 460 came out. They settled promiscuously [in different places] in the province, buying land here and there, and getting work. Only five or six families of them settled in Biddulph. Three weeks after they settled, fifteen families from Boston, Mass., met them there, and settled there, where they remain. We only paid for 1,220 acres, which was divided, from 25 to 50 acres to a family. Numbers, who came afterward, had to leave for other places. These families in Biddulph are now independent. Their lands now will sell at forty to fifty dollars an acre; it cost one dollar and fifty cents. I settled in Toronto, where I could have some means of making myself useful for them among the white people, and where my trade was good.

J. C. Brown, in Drew, Refugee, *244–47.*

Canada as a Refuge:
The Negro Refugees (1812–1817)

The slaves continue to come off [to my ship] by every opportunity and I have now upward of 120 men, women and children on board, I shall send about 50 of them to Bermuda in the [ship] Conflict. . . . There is no doubt but the blacks of Virginia and Maryland would cheerfully take up arms and join us against the Americans.

British captain Robert Barnie to Admiral Warren, November 14, 1813, in Grant, "Black Immigrants into Nova Scotia," 264.

[The interests of Nova Scotia are not being served by bringing in] a separate and marked class of people, unfitted by Nature to this Climate, or to an association with the rest of His Majesty's Colonists.

Assembly of Nova Scotia to its lieutenant governor, 1815, in Winks, Blacks in Canada, *116.*

Permit me to state plainly that little hope can be entertained of settling these [Refugee Negroes] so as to provide for their families and wants, they must be supported for many years. Slaves by habit & education, no longer working under the dread of the lash, their idea of freedom is Idleness and they are altogether incapable of industry. [They should either be restored to their masters in the United States or be sent to Sierra Leone.] [E]ither of these plans I believe would be agreeable to the greater part of them; but to the West Indies they will not go.

Governor of Nova Scotia to the Colonial Office, 1817, in Winks, Blacks in Canada, *122.*

[The farms established for the Refugee Negroes are too small, and the land is] Sterile and unproductive, [so that it is impossible for] any persons to support families on them. . . . No class of Settlers, let their habits be ever so industrious could possibly maintain their families on lots of the same size and quality, without being reduced to suffering and perhaps to starvation. [So far the refugees have supported themselves] by marketing charcoal, staves, shingles and such other lumber as their limited quantity of land enabled them to produce, [but the lumber is now exhausted].

Neighbors of the Preston, Nova Scotia, blacks, June 8, 1838, in Walker, Black Loyalists, *391.*

Canada as a Refuge:
The Fugitive Slaves (1815–1861)

My father and myself went to the Queen's Bush [in Canada] in 1846. We went four and a half miles beyond the other farms, to Canestogo, where he cleared up and had a farm; for years scarcely any white people came in, but fugitive slaves came in, in great numbers, and cleared the land. Before it was surveyed, there were as many as fifty families. It was surveyed two years after we went there. The colored people might have held their lands still, but they were afraid they would not be able to pay when pay-day [the due date] came. Under these circumstances, many of them sold out cheap. They now consider that they were overreached—for many who bought out the colored people have not yet paid for the land, and some of the first settlers yet remain, who have not yet been required to pay all up. . . .

William Jackson, in Drew, Refugee, *189–90.*

[F]or years after I came here, my mind was continually reverting to my native land. For some ten years, I was in hopes that something might happen, whereby I might safely return to my old home in New Jersey. I watched the newspapers and they told the story. I found that there would be a risk in going back. . . . I then made up my mind that salt and potatoes in Canada, were better than pound-cake and chickens in a state of suspense and anxiety in the United States. . . .

Rev. Alexander Hemsley, in Drew, Refugee, *39.*

I was earnestly solicited . . . to open a school in a new settlement of fugitives, eight miles back of Windsor, where the Refugee Association had purchased government land, on long and easy terms, for fugitive slaves.

They had erected a frame house for school and meeting purposes. The settlers had built for themselves small log-houses, and cleared from one to five acres each on their heavily timbered land, and raised corn, potatoes, and other garden vegetables. A few had put in two and three acres of wheat, and were doing well for their first year.

In the Autumn of 1852 I opened school. . . .

The unbounded confidence they placed in me was surprising; for they often brought their business papers for me to examine, to see whether they were right. One man brought me a note, as the employer could not pay him for his work in money. He said it was a note for groceries; but the grocer refused to take it, and said it was not good. I told him there was neither date nor name to it. I wrote the man a letter, asking him to rectify the mistake, which he did; but he gave his employee credit for only half the days he had worked. They [the fugitive slaves] were . . . often deceived and cheated in many ways, because of their extreme ignorance.

Haviland, A Woman's Life-Work, *192, 194.*

A True Band is composed of colored persons of both sexes, associated for their own improvement. Its objects are manifold: mainly these:—the members are to take a general interest in each other's welfare; to pursue such plans and objects as may be for their mutual advantage; to improve all schools, and to induce their race to send their children into the schools; to break down all prejudice; to bring all churches as far as possible into one body, and not let minor differences divide them; to prevent litigation by referring all disputes among themselves to a committee; to stop the begging system entirely; (that is, going to the United States, and there by representing that the fugitives are starving and suffering, raising large sums of money, of which the fugitives never receive the benefit,—misrepresenting the character of the fugitives for industry, and underrating the advance of the country, which supplies abundant work for all at fair wages;) to raise such funds among themselves as may be necessary for the poor, the sick, and the destitute fugitive newly arrived; and to prepare themselves ultimately to bear their due weight of political power.

Drew, Refugee, *236.*

[I]t is fortunate for some conscience-stricken slaveholders, that Canada affords a refuge for a certain class of their household victims—their slave-wives, or slave-children, or both. If it be a crime to assist slaves in reaching a land of freedom, it is not a crime of which those terrible fellows, the northern abolitionists, alone are guilty. Slaveholders may pour contempt on the names and the deeds of northern philanthropists: but these have no slanderous epithets to hurl back upon the southerner, who snatches his children and the mother of his children from the threatening hammer of the auctioneer, and hurriedly and tearfully starts them for the North with the parting injunction, "Stop not short of Canada!"

Drew, Refugee, *322–23.*

[In the course of escaping in 1853, the fugitive William Anderson killed the man who tried to capture him, a "crime" for which he was arrested in Toronto in 1860. When the United States tried to extradict him, Canadian Governor-General Lord Elgin wrote me that] in case of a demand for William Anderson, he should require the case to be tried in their British court; and if twelve freeholders should testify that he had been a man of integrity since his arrival in their dominion, it should clear him.

Haviland, A Woman's Life-Work, *207–8.*

I have had very bad luck since I have been here [Canada]. I was sick for six or eight months after I got here. My wife came out three months after. She was taken sick, and there were three weeks that I couldn't go out, but had to stay there and just turn her over in bed. I have buried three children since I have been here, and have had six children in all. The poorest day I ever see out here, I would rather be here than be with the best slaveholder that lives in the South, and I have seen slaves out there that were better treated than they can treat themselves here.

William Cornish, 1863 interview,
American Freedmen's Inquiry Commission, in Blassingame,
Slave Testimony, *426.*

I have travelled a good deal in the Province, and have found the prejudice greater than in the States. The political influence of the colored people now has quite a tendency to moderate the prejudice. Electioneering time, they come here for me, and I must go around and stump the county with them. The lawyers come for me with a horse and buggy, and I must go out with them, and fare just as they do. But when the election is over, they speak, of course, when we meet, but nothing more. . . . I think the root of the prejudice is to be found in the fact that the colored people came in here very rapidly, & the whites got the impression that the colored people would become a majority in the Western county. The reason that the colored people have not got along better is that they came here poor, and ignorant, and with no trades to help them along.

Horace H. Hawkins, 1863 interview,
American Freedmen's Inquiry Commission, in Blassingame,
Slave Testimony, *443–44.*

Black Communities

We [in the Wilberforce colony] have erected for our accommodations comfortable log buildings, and have a portion of our land in a state of cultivation; our crops at present continue to smile upon the labor of our hands; we shall raise the present year nearly enough to supply the present number of settlers. The people are industrious, and well pleased with their present location; and it is believed that none of them could be hired to go back to the states. Two religious societies have been organized. A sabbath school . . . is in successful operation . . . [and a] day school for the instruction of the children . . . and a temperance society has been formed consisting of about thirty in number.

Austin Steward and Benjamin Paul to
The Liberator, *January 26, 1833, in Baily,*
"Antebellum Colonization," 436.

I was not the only one who had escaped from the States, and had settled on the first spot in Canada which they had reached. [About 1835] Several hundreds of coloured persons were . . . generally working for hire upon the lands of others, and had not yet dreamed of becoming independent proprietors themselves. . . . Mr. Riseley [my employer] . . . permitted me to call meetings at his house of those who were known to be amongst the most intelligent and successful of our class. . . . [I]t was agreed, among the ten or twelve of us who assembled at them, that we would invest our earnings in land, and undertake the task . . . of settling upon wild lands, which we could call our own, and where every tree which we felled, and every bushel of corn we raised, would be for ourselves; in other words, where we could secure all the profits of our own labour. . . .

[Mr. James C. Fuller, an English Quaker,] came back with fifteen hundred dollars which had been subscribed [in England] for our benefit. . . . [I]t was thought expedient to call a convention of delegates from every settlement of blacks that was within reach; that all might see that the ultimate decision [about the money] was sanctioned by the disinterested votes of those who were thought by their companions best able to judge what would meet the wants of the community. . . . [I]t was held in June, 1838.

I urged the appropriation of the money to the establishment of a manual-labour school, at which our children could gain those elements of knowledge which are usually taught in a grammar-school. I urged that the boys should be taught, in addition, the practice of some mechanical art, and the girls should be instructed in . . . domestic arts . . . ; and that such an establishment . . . would gradually enable us to become independent of the white man for our intellectual progress, as we could be for our

physical prosperity. It was the more necessary, as in many districts, owing to the insurmountable prejudices of the inhabitants, the children of the blacks were not allowed to share the advantages of the common school. . . . [W]e could find no place more suitable than that upon which I had had my eye for three or four years, for a permanent settlement, in the town of Dawn. . . .

[The white man sent from England about 1853 to run the manual-training school at Dawn] soon began to buy the most expensive cattle in the market, at fancy prices, and without any reference to the fact that he had not sufficient fodder to feed them. . . . He also bought expensive farming utensils to work the farm scientifically, and then pulled down the school-buildings, as they were too primitive to suit his magnificent ideas, and he promised to erect more substantial and commodious buildings. . . .

He supported his family and his brother-in-law's family from the farm that belonged to our coloured people. . . . The fifth, sixth, seventh, eighth, and ninth year passed, and we had no school. . . . [I said to him,] "If you really do not intend to build us a school, you ought to leave the farm, and let us manage for ourselves."

With some excitement he said, "Pay me what I have expended during the many years I have tried to make this place meet its expenses, and I will go at once. . . ."

[After a law suit of some seven years] the important case was decided in our favour. Then the Court of Chancery appointed a new board of trustees, granted a bill to incorporate the institution as the Wilberforce University, also the power to sell the land, with a stipulation that the University should be erected on a plot of ground in the same county. The town of Chatham, Canada, was selected, and for four years the school has been *self-sustaining,* and has been attended by many pupils.

Henson, on the Dawn community, Autobiography,
76–77, 90–91, 121–23.

I was quite disappointed at the general appearance of things in New Bedford [Massachusetts]. The impression which I had received respecting the character and condition of the people of the north, I found to be singularly erroneous. I had very strangely supposed, while in slavery, that few of the comforts, and scarcely any of the luxuries, of life were enjoyed at the north, compared with what were enjoyed by the slaveholders of the south. I probably came to this conclusion from the fact that northern people owned no slaves. I supposed that they were about upon a level with the non-slaveholding population of the south. I knew *they* were exceedingly poor. . . .

[But in New Bedford] I was for once made glad by a view of extreme wealth, without being saddened by seeing extreme poverty. But the most astonishing as well as the most interesting thing to me was the condition of the colored people, a great many of whom, like myself, had escaped thither as a refuge from the hunters of men. I found many, who had not been seven years out of their chains, living in finer houses, and evidently enjoying more of the comforts of life, than the average of slaveholders in Maryland.

Former slave Frederick Douglass, 1845, Autobiography, *147, 148–49.*

The [Elgin] settlement at Buxton was first projected by the Rev. Wm. King in 1849. Mr. King was formerly a slaveholder in Louisiana, but . . . he manumitted his own slaves, about fourteen in number, (for whom he had been offered nine thousand dollars,) and brought them with him to Canada, where he settled them on farms or on lands recently purchased of the government. . . .

The land is divided into farms of fifty acres each, and so situated that a road runs past each man's farm. The houses are set thirty-three feet from this road, facing streets, so that the whole settlement, when cleared up and opened, will present a uniform appearance. The land is sold to the settlers at $2.50 per acre, the government price, and is paid in ten equal annual instalments, with interest at the rate of 6 per cent. But although ten years were allowed to the settlers to pay for their farms, a number have taken out their deeds already; and there is no doubt that before the ten years shall have expired, each settler will have his deed in possession: for which he will be indebted to his own exertions—since the settlers receive no money, no grants of land, no farming implements,—nothing but protection and advice. . . .

Drew, Refugee, *291–92.*

Colonization/Emigration Projects

[We] respectfully suggest to that august body [the American Colonization Society] of talent and learning, and worth, that . . . they are pursuing the direct road to perpetuate slavery with all its unchristian concomitants, in this boasted land of freedom. . . . Many of our fathers and some of us have fought and bled for the liberty, Independence and peace which you now enjoy; and surely it would be ungenerous and unfeeling in you to deny us a humble and quiet grave in that country which gave us birth.

National Convention of Colored Men, Philadelphia, 1831, in Carroll, Slave Insurrections, *171.*

Mr. Randolph said, "He thought it necessary, being himself a slaveholder, to show that so far from being in the *smallest degree* connected with the abolition of slavery, the proposed [Colonization] Society *would prove one of the greatest securities to enable the master to keep in possession his own property.*" . . .

Thus in an Address delivered March, 1833, we are told, "It ought never to be forgotten that the slave-trade between Africa and America, had its origin in a compassionate endeavor to relieve, by the substitution of negro labor, the toils endured by native Indians. . . ."

A writer in the Kentucky Luminary, speaking of colonization, uses the following argument: "None are obliged to follow our example; and those who do not, *will find the value of their negroes increased by the departure of ours.*" . . .

An Education Society has been formed in connection with the Colonization Society, and their complaint is principally that they cannot find proper subjects for instruction. . . .

[The Education Society] pledge themselves to educate no colored persons unless they are solemnly bound to *quit the country.*

Abolitionist Lydia Child, Appeal, *123–37 passim.*

Our design [in founding the American Colonization Society] was, by providing an asylum on the coast of Africa, and furnishing the necessary facilities for removal to the people of colour, to induce the voluntary emigration of that portion of them already free, and to throw open to individuals and the States a wider door for voluntary and legal emancipation. The operation, we were aware, must be—and, for the interests of our country, ought to be gradual. But we entertained a hope, founded on our knowledge of the interests as well as the feelings of the South, that this operation, properly conducted, would, *in the end,* remove from our country every vestige of domestic slavery, without a single violation of individual wishes or individual rights.

Virginian William H. Fitzhugh, 1826, in Fox, American Colonization Society, *48.*

The great obstacles alleged [against colonization] . . . are . . . :

1. The expense of the scheme. . . .
2. [T]he difficulties attendant on colonization under the most favourable circumstances; the fearful expense of nursing an infant colony into vigor; and the very great time that must elapse before it can have attained sufficient maturity to bear an annual access of 60,000 to its numbers.
3. The habits of the negro render it doubtful whether a successful colony of that race can ever . . . be effected. . . .

4. Will the South consent to relinquish her slaves? . . .
5. [T]he tendency of the natural increase to swell with the increase of the deportation.

The South Vindicated (1836), 147–48.

We regard your assembly as the sovereign representatives of the colored people of the United States and the Canadian provinces. You have the supreme right to legislate for their interest, and adopt measures for their advancement. . . . And if other associations have been formed with the same or similar objects, it is to be hoped . . . that they will immediately rank under the banners that you will unfurl at Toronto.

Vermont delegates' message, written by black emigrationist James T. Holly, to the North American Convention of Colored Men, Toronto, 1851, in Harding, River, 168. Holly proposed that the convention set up a Canadian-based North American Union of blacks— in effect a black government-in-exile.

I believe it to be the destiny of the negro, to develop a higher order of civilization and Christianity than the world has yet seen. I also consider it a part of his "manifest destiny" to possess all the tropical regions of this continent, with the adjacent islands. . . . [There the black race could] exercise its proper influence in moulding the destiny, and shaping the policy of the American continent.

Black poet-journalist and barber J. M. Whitfield, in Harding, River, 185.

The American colonization movement, as now systematized and conducted, is, in our opinion, simply an American humane farce. At present the slaves are increasing in this country at the rate of nearly one hundred thousand per annum; within the last twelve years, as will appear below, the American Colonization Society has sent to Liberia less than five thousand negroes.

In 1847	39
In 1848	213
In 1849	474
In 1850	590
In 1851	279
In 1852	568
In 1853	583
In 1854	783
In 1855	207
In 1856	544
In 1857	370
In 1858	163
Total	4,813

The average of this total is a fraction over four hundred and one, which may be said to be the number of negroes annually colonized by the society; while the yearly increase of slaves . . . is little less than one hundred thousand? Fiddlesticks for such colonization.

North Carolinian Hinton Rowan Helper, in Impending Crisis (1860), 87–88.

You and we are different races. Whether it is right or wrong I need not discuss, but this physical difference is a great disadvantage to us both, as I think your race suffer very greatly, many of them by living among us, while ours suffer from your presence. In a word we suffer on each side. If this be admitted, it affords a reason at least why we should be separated.

Abraham Lincoln advocating colonization to a group of African Americans, August 1862, in Franklin, The Emancipation Proclamation, 33.

Sir, we were born here and here we choose to remain. . . . Don't advise me to leave, and don't add insult to injury by telling me it's for my own good. Of that I am to be the judge. It is in vain you talk to me about "two races" and their "mutual antagonism." In the matter of rights, there is but one race, and that is the *human* race. . . . Sir, this is our country as much as it is yours, and we will not leave it.

African-American abolitionist Robert Purvis, public letter to Sen. S. C. Pomeroy, New York Tribune, September 20, 1862, in McPherson, The Negro's Civil War, 97–98.

The finest specimens of manhood I have ever gazed upon in my life are half-breed Indians crossed with negroes. It is a fact . . . that while amalgamation with the white man deteriorates both races, the amalgamation of the Indian and the black man advances both races. . . . I should like to see these eighty thousand square miles [of the Indian Territory] . . . opened up to the Indian and to the black man, and let them amalgamate and build up a race that will be an improvement upon both.

U.S. senator Jim Lane during Reconstruction, quoted in Porter, Negro on the American Frontier, 75.

Africa as a Refuge: Sierra Leone

A larger body of settlers is wanted [in the Sierra Leone colony of former American slaves] to oppose the treachery of the natives, instigated by the *English slave dealers* in the neighbouring factories.

Granville Sharp, 1788, in Walker, Black Loyalists, 105.

Captain Paul Cuffe enabled the emigration of slaves to Sierra
Leone. *(Library of Congress)*

The people of the colony [Sierra Leone] are very fond
of spiritous liquors, and many of them are retailers and
dealers in that article. It appears to me there is not so
much industry as would be but for them [liquors]. They
are very fond of having a number of servants about them.
The industry on their farms are too much neglected.
Their young men are too fond of leaving the colony and
become seamen for other people. I have thought if commerce could be introduced in the colony, it might have
this good tendency of keeping the young men at home,
and in some future day qualify them to become managers of themselves. And when they become thus qualified
to carry on commerce, I see no reason why they may not
become a nation to be numbered among the historians'
nations of the world. . . .

I think of keeping open a small intercourse between
America and Sierra Leone in hopes through that channel
some families may find their way to Sierra Leone.

Paul Cuffe to William Allen, April 22, 1811, in Harris,
"An American's Impressions," 39–40.

Africa as a Refuge: Liberia

[T]he natives, here is not. very. much given to Industry.
Or the[y] would have had more land. Cleared, the most
the[y] care about is Hunting and fishing, but that is only
when the[y] have no Tobacco. nor Rum. that is the Cheaf
Articles the[y] Care about, the[y] are about the Closest
people I have ever seen, the[y] would not give one mouth-
ful if we was diing for it.

Liberian colonizer Mars Lucas, 1830–1836, quoted in Tyler-
McGraw, "Liberia," 197.

[M]e and Brothr went down to Bassa to make money and
while we was down there we had to saw out in the Bush
& there were some insinuations past on the short & the
heathens came in one night & destroyed 20 more or less
of our American people & then came into our saw pit
& took us away from our work & carried us to a native
town, kept us some space of time & used us very cruel but
throw the mercy of God we were delivered from the[m],
& afterwards Mars went back & fought in the war but I
did not.

Liberian colonizer Jesse Lucas, 1830–1836, quoted in Tyler-
McGraw, "Liberia," 198.

But, the people. get, above their trades after the[y].
come. here., the[y] won't work but live from hand to
mouth. . . .

Liberian colonizer Mars Lucas, 1830–1836, quoted in Tyler-
McGraw, "Liberia," 198.

I must Say that our Country never will improve as it ought
until the people in the United States keep their Slaves that
they have raised dumb as horses at home and Send those
here who will be A help to improve the country.

Letter of June 2, 1834, from former slave Samson Caesar to
his master, Henry Westfall, in Caesar, Letters to David S.
Haselden and Henry F. Westfal, 1834–35. *University of*
Virginia Library Web site. Available online at URL: http://
etext.lib.virginia.edu/subjects/liberia/samson.html.

I had directions from Mr. McClain to see all of the pas-
sioners [passengers] on board by three o'clock which I
did, so after I saw all on board Me and Mr. McClain
came ashore again when he advise me when I Got to
Monrovia [the capital of Liberia] to set me out some coffee trees which I has not done as yet being I has not had
the opportunity, when we arrived to the Jolucal mountin
we did not meat the Bovner [an official?], he was in the
States, but I will make it my Business to do so as soon

as he coms. I has not been up the River as yet, but I has been inform that the land up thir is very good, but I am in hopes when I Goes up that I will make a living which it is my desires, for I believe an industrious person can live here. . . . [T]h[e]y is some as smart people as I would wish to be in company with and some bad enough to pay for it since of them has been ashore th[e]y has been stealing but I am in hopes that I shall never be guilty of that th[e]y is some of them sily enough to say they wish themself Back and there is a great many a going to school, I am included in the number, but I has Regret very much that I refuse when I was there. . . .

Abram Blackford, letter of September 9, 1844, from Liberia to his former owner, in Blassingame, Slave Testimony, *61–62.*

[Free black men who had migrated North] found themselves so depressed and despised and crowded out of employment, and so much less respected than they had been in Charleston, that they could not endure it, but returned to their old homes. . . . [Thereafter, however, they concluded] that in this country they can never possess those rights and privileges which will make them men [and sailed for Liberia].

African Repository and Colonial Journal *(1847), quoted by Johnson and Roark,* Black Masters, *218.*

We have been here eight months, and we have all been very sick, with the fever, but I am happy to be able to say that we are still alive and enjoying as good health, as we might expect. For four or five months after we arrived in Africa, my children looked better than I think I ever saw them; they were so fond of palm oil and rice, and eat so much of it, that they fattened very fast. Myself and Rosabella also, enjoyed very good health for four or five months of our residence in Liberia. . . . When I arrived in Baltimore, preparatory to sailing, I had, with what you gave me, a little over one hundred dollars, but after paying board for two weeks, and buying some things necessary for house keeping and paying off all my accounts for moving, and getting a few things to the amount of $10, I found that when I got on board of Ship, I had only $33 left. When I arrived, I spent two months at Monrovia, which is a very expensive place to live in, having to pay for your wood and water. I found *this* would never do for me, so I got the favor of the agent to allow me a room, up the St. Pauls' river. . . . I went to work to cut down my lot and clear a spot for a house, not knowing at that time how I should go about it, having no means. Many persons however advised me to go to *shoemaking* . . . I took their

advice, and when the six months were out. I had a house of my own to live in. It is 22 by 13 feet and though very rough, yet it is very comfortable. I have found my trade to be very valuable to me indeed. . . . The greatest drawback, is the want of *leather.*

The only farmers here who are making anything for sale, are those who come to this country with money. Farming is more difficult now than it has been, as all the land on the St. Paul's river has been bought and the emigrants now, have to go back in the forest, some two, three and four miles, and whatever they may plant, is destroyed by the wild hog, the wild cow and many other wild animals. We hope, however, that the time will soon come, when persons will venture to settle a little back from the river, and beasts of burden will be brought into use. . . .

Letter of William C. Burke of August 20, 1854, from Liberia, to his former owners, Col. and Mrs. Robert E. Lee, in Blassingame, Slave Testimony, *100–101.*

[H]is employer suggested to [a slave who worked for many years as a lumberman] that he might *buy* his freedom, and he immediately determined to do so. . . . [U]pon collecting the various sums that he had loaned to white people in the vicinity, he was found to have several hundred dollars more than was necessary. With the surplus, he paid for his passage to Liberia, and bought a handsome outfit.

Olmsted, Cotton Kingdom, *116.*

I want to know exactly whether if I go [to Liberia] at the expense of the State of Virginia, I shall be able to return when I please, as I shall probably wish to return to bring my wife and children. My Misstress died the 1st day of last Decr and left me free to go to Liberia. . . . The provisions of the will were that if I did not leave the country in a year I was to be sold. I have a wife and four children. I have not been able to get these as they belong to a lady here, but hope to return for them. . . .

William James Henry, 1855 letter from Lynchburg, Virginia, in Starobin, Blacks in Bondage, *162.*

December 7–13, 1856

Go down to Music Hall on Monday—find Sister Mary alone—brother Jim having taken the freed servants to Norfolk, to ship them for "Africa's sunny clime."—he gets back this week & has so many amusing stories to tell of their trip down—poor things! To many of them their freedom will prove any- thing but a blessing—My kindest wishes attend them to their new home.

April 12–18, 1857

Hear some sad accounts of the servants who were sent to Africa. Some ten or fifteen of their number are already dead—Mary Lewis at home poorly—the weather quite warm again.

Diary of Louisa H. Minor [manuscript], 1855–1866.
University of Virginia Department of Special Collections,
MSS 10685. Available online at URL: http://etext.lib.
virginia.edu/subjects/liberia/samson.html.

That Emily Hooper, a negro and a citizen of the republic of Liberia, be and she is hereby permitted voluntarily to return into a state of slavery as a slave of her former owner, Miss Sallie Mallett of Chapel Hill. . . .

A bill enacted February 1859 by the North Carolina legislature
providing for the reenslavement of a free black, in Franklin,
"The Enslavement of Free Negroes," 415.

Other Refuges

[Capt. Davis was quoted as saying] that no less than nineteen Negro slaves which he had in Carolina, run away from him lately all at once, under that strong Temptation of the Spaniards . . . which he said he found verified; for he saw all his said Negroes now at St. Augustine, who laughed at him.

December 18, 1738, in Porter, Negro on the American
Frontier, *162–63.*

"But negro property isn't very secure there [in a section of Louisiana], I'm told. How is't? Know?"

"Not at all secure, sir; if it is disposed to go, it will go: the only way you could keep it would be to make it always contented to remain. The road would always be open to Mexico, it would go when it liked."

"So I hear. Only way is, to have young ones there and keep their mothers here, eh? Negroes have such at-tachments, you know. Don't you think that would fix 'em, eh? No? No, I suppose not. If they got mad at anything, they'd forget their mothers, eh? Yes, I suppose they would. Can't depend on niggers. But I reckon they'd come back. Only be worse off in Mexico—eh?"

"Nothing but—"

"Being free, eh? Get tired of that, I should think. Nobody to take care of them. No, I suppose not. Learn to take care of themselves."

Olmsted, Cotton Kingdom, *413.*

Fourteen Negro slaves [from Texas] with their families came to me this day and I sent them free to Victoria.

Mexican general José Urrea, April 3, 1836, in Campbell,
Empire, *44.*

We have often wondered why some bold and enterprizing men in our state do not club together and go into Mexico and bring away the large Number of fine likely runaways known to be not far over the line, forming a pretty respectable African colony.

San Antonio Herald *1855, in Campbell,* Empire, *63–64.*

We caught him [the fugitive slave] once, but he got away. . . . I had my six shooter handy. . . . [E]very barrel missed fire . . . shot at him three times with rifles, but he'd got too far off. . . . My dog got close to him once, but he had a dog himself, and just as my dog got within about a yard of him, his dog turned and fit [fought] my dog. . . . We run him close, though, I tell you. Run him out of his coat, and his boots, and a pistol. . . . He got into them bayous, and kept swimming from one side to another. If he's got across the river . . . the Mexicans'd take care of him.

Texan's 1855 report, Olmsted, Journey through Texas,
256–57, quoted in Tyler, "Fugitive Slaves in Mexico," 1.

CHAPTER EIGHT

Rebels
1526–1865

Outside Influences

Slavery infected North America with hatred, fury, and rebellion. It turned friendly Indians into enemies. Slaves brought from Africa might flee or fight; they might in despair commit suicide. Their new owners tried to subdue these impulses by sheer physical force—manacles and the lash. These might—or might not—suppress the behavior, but the desire for freedom persisted in slaves born on this continent. Their rage and despair sprang from their enslavement and the near impossibility of freeing themselves.

Some slaves in the American colonies in the late 18th century heard the fiery discussions of men's natural rights to life and liberty. They watched and fought in

Mob attacks the Charleston post office to destroy abolitionist literature. *(Library of Congress)*

the American Revolution. Some fought in that war alongside the British to gain these rights for themselves—so many as to make up the largest group of slaves emancipated before the Civil War. Others sided with the Americans, only to live through the making of a republic based on freedom, but a freedom it denied blacks solely because of their race. They understood the injustice the nation committed against them and the example of rebellion it had set.

Many slaveholders blamed discontent among the slaves not on their enslaved condition but on "outside agitators"—Yankees in general, abolitionists in particular, and certain religious denominations, notably Quakers and Methodists. "We are exposed to still greater perils by the swarm of missionaries white and black that are perpetually visiting us," wrote Edwin C. Holland in 1822, "who, with the sacred volume of God in one hand, breathing peace to the whole family of man, scatter at the same time with the other the firebrands of discord and destruction, and secretly disperse among our Negroes, the seeds of discontent and sedition. It is an acknowledged fact, that some of those religious itinerants, those apostolic vagabonds, after receiving charities from the philanthropy and open-hearted generosity of our people, have by means of Tracts, and other methods of instruction all professedly religious in their church, excited among our Negroes such a spirit of dissatisfaction and revolt, as has in the end brought down upon them, the vengeance of offended humanity. And given to the gallows and to exile the deluded instigators of a most diabolical unholy Insurrection."[1]

Rumors flew about the diabolical schemes of abolitionists. "[T]here is a great excitement in this country on the account of Negro rebellion," wrote Benjamin Bowman in 1860. "[A]bolition Emissarys ar going through this country instigating Negros to Burne the towns and kill there Masters[.] [T]here has all ready been some 12 or fourteen towns burnt[.] Dallasville is burnt entirely up and many others towns that I could name[.] [T]he people of Dallasville have sustained over a half Million of losses[.] [T]hey caught one of the ablitionst last Weake and hung him up to a limb without jug [judge] or jury tho they had proof sufficient to justify there course[.] [I]t is Dangros for a Stranger to travel through this Country at this time in Dallas county they ar Whipping about thirty Negros pr Day[.] [T]he Negros ar Confessing all about the plot[.] [T]hey say that the Abolisionists have promised them there freedom if they would burne all the towns Down in the State[.] [A]llso they was to break out on the Sixth Day of August when the men was all gon to the Election than kill all the Wimmin and Children that they could[.] [A]ll the likely young ladies they Was to save for Wives for themselves[.] [T]hose Secret Emmisaries promised them that they would be her with an army from Kanses about the time the Negros was to break out[.] [T]his they have proof of from hundreds of Negros, What will be the result of the strife God only knows[.]"[2]

True enough, in the latter half of the 18th century and into the 19th, antislavery sentiments prompted a few in the South and more in the North to help slaves as best they could. Free blacks in the North organized to help fugitives, create a refuge for them in Canada, and found black schools and churches. Black and white abolitionists together maintained the Underground Railroad. Abolitionists not only propagandized endlessly in the North but also tried to reach white southern ears and consciences, or even to get their materials to the few slaves who had learned to read. With rare exceptions, such as David Walker, however, abolitionists black or white rarely tried to stir slaves to insurrection. Very occasionally, a free black in the South fomented and led an uprising.

In 1818 southerners took to court the Reverend Mr. Jacob Gruber, a Methodist minister, on a charge of intent to incite insurrection. His attorney freely admitted the abolitionist hopes of the Methodists, but, he said, they planned to achieve these by peaceable means. Gruber's arguments against slavery in his sermons, said the attorney, were "directed exclusively to the whites. . . . He could not have designed . . . to influence the conduct of the slaves, but was obviously, and clearly, seeking to reform the hearts of the masters."[3]

Slaves with hopes of escape or insurrection might seize on whatever helpful information or hope for help they could pick up from what they heard in sermons or covertly read or gleaned from their masters' conversations. But probably the echoes of the successful Haitian slave revolution in 1791, led by Toussaint L'Ouverture, stirred them far more, giving them hope and inspiration to try to gain their own freedom.

The Laws of Slavery

Early on, slaves tried to sue for freedom in the courts, and some succeeded. In 1781, for instance, Mun Bett sued on the grounds that the declaration in the Massachusetts constitution of 1780 that all people are "born free and equal" negated slavery; she won her case and took the name Elizabeth Freeman. But as the institution of slavery was formalized, and as in the 1830s more and more civil rights were taken away, that legal approach was barred them.

New state laws declared them property in all respects save one: They could be punished if they broke the law. As property, they could not sue, they could not have a trial by jury, they could not testify against a white, and they would be judged by slaveholders, on the grounds that these would best protect the property interests of the owners of the accused slaves, "by infusing into the trial, that temperate and impartial feeling, which would probably exist in persons owning the same sort of property."[4]

The law did not even effectively protect slaves against the violence of their owners. True enough, their owners were not supposed to kill them, but the law recognized many mitigating circumstances for even this act. In the unlikely case that a homicide charge was brought against a master in the death of a slave, the accused might defend himself by alleging that the slave had provoked him or that the slave had been conspiring to rebel. For instance, a North Carolina law of 1774 designated the willful and malicious killing of a slave as murder and set the penalty of a year's imprisonment for a first offense and death for a second. However, this law exempted the homicide of "any Slave in the Act of Resistance to his lawful Owner or Master, or to any Slave dying under moderate correction."[5]

Protection for slaves from the violence of persons other than their owners was enacted mainly to keep masters from having their property harmed. On the whole, the law left slaves terrifyingly vulnerable. It was not until 1860 that the Mississippi legislature made it a crime for a black man to rape a black female under 10 years old.[6] The law did not recognize rape of a slave woman by a white man. Though in the course of the 19th century some states granted slaves more safeguards, for the most part they were outside the law unless they themselves violated it.

A slave found guilty of a crime presented a problem, for he could not be punished in the same way as a white. He could not be fined, for he owned no property. If the state imprisoned or executed or deported him, it would be depriving his master of his services. Courts usually resorted to beatings as punishment or, in extreme cases, executed the slave and reimbursed his master for his value. A slave found guilty, wrote R. R. Cobb in 1858, "can be reached only through his body, and hence in cases not capital, whipping is the only punishment which can be inflicted. In the case of manslaughter, some of the States prescribe branding on the cheek as an additional punishment, more particularly with a view to protect distant and innocent purchasers from negroes who have been guilty of homicide. The extremes, death and whipping, being the only available punishments, it becomes necessary, in forming a slave code, to throw all offences under the one or the other. Hence, many offences are, from public policy, necessarily made capital, which, when committed by a white person, are not."[7]

A white might commit with impunity an action labeled as a crime when committed by a black. Moreover, the mitigating circumstances that would reduce the punishment for a crime committed by a white would not help the accused slave. Slaves were supposed to bear humbly and obediently insults and injuries that would excuse retaliation in a white. "[T]he same provocation which will so reduce the offence in a citizen, will not in a slave. A legal provocation for a slave, is such as, having due regard to the relative condition of the white man and the slave, and the obligation of the latter to conform his instinct and his passions to his condition of inferiority, would provoke a well-disposed slave into a violent passion. Hence, the mere fact of an engagement, on a sudden heat of passion, would not of itself form such a provocation."[8]

In short, the courts held, "Masters and slaves cannot be governed by the same common system of laws: so different are their positions, rights, and duties."[9]

Suicide and Self-Mutilation

Some slaves turned their rage at their condition and at their masters against themselves, at the same time depriving their masters of the property they constituted. In the early days of slavery, many were prompted to suicide by the belief that in death they would return to Africa. Slaves in despair wounded themselves, suffocated themselves by drawing in their tongues to close off the passage of air, took poison, or drowned themselves. One 16-year-old, deciding that "she'd as leave be dead as to take the beatings her master gave her, . . . went into the woods and eat some poison oak. She died, too."[10]

Fear of being sold prompted some to mutilate themselves rather than leave their families and friends. Former slave Lewis Clarke in 1846 told of a carpenter named Ennis whose master bargained with a slave trader to carry him downriver: "He took a broadaxe and cut one hand off; then contrived to lift the axe, with his arm pressing it to his body, and let it fall upon the other, cutting off the ends of the fingers."[11]

Rebellions by Individual Slaves

More commonly, slaves rebelled. Usually, of course, they just flared up for a moment, refused to obey, or ran away to the woods or swamps for a while. However, thousands of slaves resisted violently. In self-defense or revenge, or maddened by cruelty and frustration, they recklessly ignored the enormous odds against them. They fought off beatings. They burned their masters' buildings, damaged their crops, and killed their livestock. They assaulted whites, robbed them, and poisoned them.

Everyday irritations chafed slaves into disobedience and defiance. A slave who had endured many beatings might refuse to take another—like Frederick Douglass, who fought the master to whom he had been hired out: "We were at it for nearly two hours. Covey at length let me go, puffing and blowing at a great rate, saying that if I had not resisted, he would not have whipped me half so much. The truth was, that he had not whipped me at all. . . . [H]e had drawn no blood from me, but I had from him."[12]

Another slave might brood on his wrongs until he exploded into fury, and suddenly a tool became a weapon. Abram first assaulted his master with a hoe and then picked up a stone, which, he said, "I hurl'd at his head face, &c. again and again, until I thought he was certainly dead."[13] The slave Battiste terrorized a whole neighborhood in Alabama: "[V]arious citizens of Mobile frequently complained to the police that they lived in terror . . . of said slave, and were afraid to leave their houses. . . . [I]t was difficult for police officers to find him, and difficult to arrest him when found; . . . he had gone greased, in order to facilitate his escape, and wore his clothes without buttons, in such a manner that he could, and did readily divest himself when seized."[14]

Women sometimes reacted with equal violence. Mary Armstrong recalled her vengeance on her mistress: "[I picked] up a rock 'bout as big as half your fist and hits her right in the eye and busted the eyeball, and tells her that's for whippin' my baby sister to death. You could hear her holler for five miles."[15] Jinny testified in court that her fellow slave Creasy had broken her plow handle and as she set off to get it fixed her mistress struck her, "whereupon Creasy seized her, and her mistress called Sall; upon which Sall came up and struck her mistress upon the forehead and knocked her down and gave her several blows with the axe and killed her.[16] Celia, bought as a concubine by her widowed Missouri owner, killed him and burned his body in her fireplace.[17]

Now and then a slave's rebellion forced the owner into respectful wariness. After his battle royal, Frederick Douglass was never again beaten. Plantation mistress Susanna Warfield acknowledged in her diary that a particular slave "exercises dominion over me—or tries to do it—one would have thought to see her in the fury she was in yesterday that I was the Servant, she the mistress."[18] Or the owner might decide to sell the slave. Alternatively, as one slave who had beaten her mistress with her fists, knocking her through the panels of a door, reminisced, "The master . . . told me that as my mistress and I got along so badly, if I would take my child and go to New Jersey, and stay there, he would give me my freedom; I told him I would go. It was late at night; he wrote me a pass, gave it to me, and early the next morning I set out for New Jersey."[19]

Ruses and Deceptions

Other slaves reacted less directly, more subtly, getting a bit of their own back whenever they thought they could do so without being detected. Most commonly, of course, they feigned sickness—women perhaps more often than men, because sometimes the owners were afraid to take chances with their reproductive abilities.

To protect themselves and each other, to gain some control over their lives, slaves lied. They covered their real emotions with a show of feelings more acceptable to their owners. They wept copiously even as they secretly rejoiced at the death of a cruel master.

Jim, who escaped to Canada, went back to the plantation for his family, "confessing" to his master, "I thought I wanted to be free, massa, so I run away and went to Canada. But I had a hard time there, and soon got tired of taking care of myself. I thought I would rather live with massa again and be a good servant. I found that Canada was no place for niggers; it's too cold, and we can't make any money there. Mean white folks cheat poor niggers out of their wages when they hire them. I soon got sick of being free and wished I was back on the old plantation. And those people called abolitionists, that I met with on the way, are a mean set of rascals. They pretend to help the niggers but they cheat them all they can. They get all the work out of a nigger they can and never pay him for it. I tell you, massa, they are mean folks. . . . Well, old massa seemed mightily pleased with my lies. He spoke pleasant to me, and said: 'Jim, I hope you will make a good missionary among our people and the neighbors.'" Jim did indeed do missionary work, but hardly of the expected kind. A few months later he led a group of 14 slaves across the Ohio River and onto the Underground Railroad.[20]

Insurrections: White Fears

Oddly enough, the records show relatively little fear among slaveholders of rebellions of individual slaves, at least until the Civil War. Time and time again, however, they reveal southern whites' deep-seated dread of the group revolts known as "insurrections." In the late 1770s Benjamin Franklin played on this fear in the debate over the Articles of Confederation. When a South Carolinian argued that slaves should not be counted for tax purposes because they were property, more like sheep than humans, Franklin responded, "There is some difference between them and sheep: Sheep will never make any insurrection."[21] Presumably southerners felt that they had less to worry about from their own slaves than from those of others. "I am afraid of the lawless Yankee soldiers," Betty Herdon Maury wrote in her diary in April 1862, "but that is nothing to my fear of the negroes if they should rise against us."[22]

Fanny Kemble, newly arrived in the South, was struck by the miasma of fear: "[A] most ominous tolling of bells and beating of drums . . . on the first evening of my arrival in Charleston, made me almost fancy myself in one of the old fortified frontier towns of the Continent, where the tocsin is sounded, and the evening drum beaten, and the guard set as regularly every night as if an invasion were expected. In Charleston, however, it is not the dread of foreign invasion, but of domestic insurrection, which occasions these nightly precautions. . . . [O]f course, it is very necessary where a large class of persons exists in the very bosom of a community whose interests are known to be at variance and incompatible with those of its other members. And no doubt these daily and nightly precautions are but trifling drawbacks upon the manifold blessings of slavery . . . ; still, I should prefer going to sleep without the apprehension of my servants' cutting my throat in my bed, even to having a guard provided to prevent their doing so."[23]

After the Stono Rebellion of 1739 in South Carolina, white fear mounted to such a point that several farmers abandoned their homes. A century later, in 1836, plantation owner Iveson Brookes wrote to his wife, "The substance of [my dream] is that in some twenty or thirty years a division of the Northern & Southern

States will be produced by the Abolitionists and then a war will issue between the Yankees & slave-holders—that the Army of Yankees will be at once joined by the N[egroe]s who will shew more savage cruelty than the blood thirsty Indians—and that Southerners with gratitude for having escaped alive will gladly leave their splendid houses & farms to be occupied by . . . those who once served them.—This all looks so plausible that I have been made to conclude that all who act with judicious foresight should within two years sell every [?] of a negro & land & vest the money in Western lands—so as to have a home and valuable possessions to flee to in time of danger."[24]

So strongly did whites fear slave insurrections that scholars still differ as to whether certain fancied conspiracies to rebel actually occurred. It was so easy to explain away a series of fires, say, by assuming that they had been set by slaves plotting to kill whites. Thus in New York City in 1712, for instance, there may or may not have been an insurrection. After several buildings burned, shaky evidence convicted some 25 African Americans, slave and free, of a plan to burn the town, destroy all its whites, and obtain their freedom, a plot in which they allegedly sealed their oath of secrecy by sucking each other's blood and rubbing conjurer's powder on their bodies to make them invincible. The convicted were burned alive, hanged, chained and starved, or broken on the wheel.

Insurrections: Their Nature

Nevertheless, groups of slaves did rebel. In 1774, Abigail Adams wrote to her husband, "There has been in town a conspiracy of the negroes. At present it is kept pretty private, and was discovered by one who endeavored to dissuade them from it. . . . I wish most sincerely there was not a slave in the province; it always appeared a most iniquitous scheme to me to fight ourselves for what we are daily robbing and plundering from those who have as good a right to freedom as we have."[25]

In the early days, both slave men and women participated in these revolts. After a revolt in Louisiana in the early 1770s, for instance, one Mariana received a hundred lashes and lost her ears, though her punishment was lighter than that handed out to her male coconspirators. But even the earliest slave revolts were primarily male. Women were more apt to rebel individually than collectively.[26]

Revolts could occur anywhere—in town, on a plantation, even in a coffle. In 1829 in Kentucky, "a white driver," by the name of Gordon, who had purchased in Maryland about sixty negroes, was taking them, assisted by an associate named Allen, and the wagoner who conveyed the baggage, to the Mississippi. "The men were handcuffed and chained together. . . . It appears that, by means of a file the negroes, unobserved, had succeeded in separating the irons which bound their hands, in such a way as to be able to throw them off at any moment. About 8 o'clock in the morning, while proceeding on the state road leading from Greenup to Vanceburg, two of them dropped their shackles and commenced a fight, when the wagoner rushed in with his whip to compel them to desist. At this moment, every negro was found to be perfectly at liberty." The slaves overcame the men in charge, killing two, pillaged the wagon, stole $2,400, and 16 of them took to the woods. "The neighbourhood was immediately rallied, and a hot pursuit given—which, we understand, has resulted in the capture of the whole gang and the recovery of the greatest part of the money. Seven of the negro men and one woman, it is said were engaged in the murders, and will be brought to trial at the next court in Greensburg."[27]

More often than not, slave revolts were unplanned. A master or overseer who inflicted an unusually severe beating, violated a tacit agreement about the length of work hours, or suddenly withdrew privileges might find himself with a revolt on his hands. For hunger, a burning sense of injustice, or just the last straw could arouse not only individual but also group rebellions. This sort of local uprising was aimed at getting even, securing privileges, or restoring the accustomed order of things that the master or overseer had transgressed.

More rarely, slaves rebelled with the intention of escaping from or even overthrowing the slavery system. As a rule, these slaves planned to withdraw into self-governing, independent communities of fugitives, known as maroons. Less realistically, a small number dreamed of reversing the power structure, with blacks claiming the power then commanded by whites. We all dream of glory, and slaves did too. Though we must always allow for the possibility that white reports reflected more of abolitionist hopes or slaveowner fears than of reality, rumors abounded of the ambitions of black rebels. The *Liberator* reported in 1856 that a Tennessee slave woman had been told "that the negroes all intended rising on the day of the election, and that their plan was to take advantage of the absence of the white men on that day, and while they were all from home at the polls voting, to kill all the women and children, get all the money and arms, and waylay the men on their return home from the election and murder them; then make for the railroad cars, take them and go to Memphis, where they could find arms and friends from up the river to carry them off to the Free States if they did not succeed in taking this country."[28] In 1835, reports circulated that blacks then rising on the Brazos River in Texas had in their plans "divided all the cotton farms and they intended to ship the cotton to New Orleans and make the white men serve them in turn."[29]

Obviously, revolts were more likely on large plantations than on small farms. The more distant the master-slave relationship, the more probable a revolt. Slaves imported from Africa were more prone to rebel than those born into American slavery. So were slaves who lived where blacks heavily outnumbered whites. Islamic culture among the slaves more encouraged revolt than Christianity, especially because it divided slaves from owners. Geography too influenced rebellions, as when slaves saw a possibility of sustaining a maroon community in mountain fastnesses, forests, or swamps. So also, hard times could encourage slaves to rebel, seeing their masters unable to provide them with food.

Whatever the intent or the immediate cause, the slaves' chances of success were almost nil. They were up against a system backed not only by the powers of the states but also by the beliefs of the community, slaveholders or not. The whites controlled the weapons. They constructed "black codes," specifically aimed at preventing rebellion by limiting the mobility and controlling the conduct of slaves. Efficient as the slave grapevine was in communicating within and among plantations and farms, isolation made secret planning difficult. Where were the leaders to come from? Free blacks were legally constrained almost as much as slaves; slave states tried vigorously to hold their numbers down, requiring that manumitted slaves leave the state. Natural leaders among slaves were frequently co-opted by being singled out for positions of privilege, such as drivers, on the plantations so that they would have more to lose by rebelling. Conspirators could not even count on the secrecy of other blacks, who might betray the plot out of fear, out of loyalty to a master or mistress or white child, or in hope of a reward. The possible reward of freedom could powerfully motivate a slave who overheard rebellious plans. In any case, conspirators had to risk everything on one stroke. They could not retreat and regroup—they would not survive for a second try. Almost all planned insurrections were discovered and put down before they began or were crushed very soon after.

This pattern of failure gradually decreased the number of rebellions. Rationally, a slave would be better off trying to run away. Slim as his chances were in that effort, he risked less. Or he might simply decide to make the best of his enslavement, seeking what control over his life and what privileges he might acquire within the system. Nonetheless, slave rebellions persisted into the Civil War.

Insurrections: Specific Uprisings

Among the many insurrections in the history of American slavery, a few stand out.

Escape attempts sometimes blurred into rebellions, as armed slaves fled in a self-protective group. Thus it was in the Stono, South Carolina, uprising of September 9, 1739. When the Spanish held what is now Florida they repeatedly encouraged American slaves to escape there, offering them freedom and protection. On that September Sunday, about 20 slaves, perhaps encouraged by a Spanish emissary, sacked and burned the armory, seized arms and ammunition, and raided stores for supplies and liquor, killing the storekeepers and leaving their heads on their doorsteps. They then marched toward a Spanish fort in Florida manned by black militia. Along the way, waving banners and beating drums, calling out "Freedom," they enlisted other slaves. They burned and plundered plantations, killing 20 or 30 whites. But about 10 miles from Stono, a group of white planters caught up with the blacks, their numbers now grown to 60–100, and overcame most of them, though a small group escaped, only to be subdued the next Saturday.

More careful planning preceded Gabriel's rebellion in and around Richmond, Virginia, in 1800. Gabriel Prosser was semiliterate and had some knowledge of tactics. He was a defiant slave. Caught stealing a pig, he had fought punishment, biting off the ear of the man who was trying to inflict it; while in jail for that offense, he planned an insurrection. He was also a deeply religious man who believed himself called by God to lead an uprising; he wanted to model himself on the biblical Samson. Upon his release, he concocted his plot with other slaves under the guise of religious meetings. They planned to kill all whites except Quakers, Methodists, and the French. He appointed a weaponsmaker and sent out emissaries into the countryside to enlist men.

The conspirators planned to seize the bridges and raid the local magazine for weapons, the mills for bread, and the state house treasury for money, dividing the money among them. Then they would crown Gabriel king of Virginia. They expected all blacks and maybe some poor whites to join them, not only in Virginia but across the continent. They also hoped for help from the Catawba Indians. Should they fail, however, they would retreat into the mountains. Alas for their dreams, two slaves betrayed them before they began operations, and the authorities set about arresting all the conspirators they could find, including Gabriel himself.

Twenty-odd years later, in about 1821, freeman Denmark Vesey organized an insurrection of slaves and free blacks in Charleston, South Carolina. Vesey, a mulatto, had spent two decades at sea as a slave on a slaving vessel until in 1800 he won a lottery. With his $1,500 prize he bought his own freedom and set himself up as a carpenter. An eccentric, a polygamist with slave wives and children, he was intelligent, ambitious, and domineering. He spent hours studying the Bible, eventually concluding that he had a religious duty to incite slaves to rebellion.

Vesey thought that he could expect aid from England and from Haiti and that all slaves would rise in his support. He planned long and carefully, over some five years. He recruited at local congregations, urging slaves to behave proudly and quoting the Bible to persuade them that acquiescence in bondage was sinful. He named as one of his lieutenants a sorcerer, a slave named Gullah Jack, who some other slaves thought could make them invulnerable. Estimates of the number of people involved in the plot run as high as 9,000.[30] But some scholars, notably Richard C. Wade, believe that "no conspiracy in fact existed, or at most that it was a vague and unformulated plan in the minds or on the tongues of a few colored townsmen. No elaborate network had been established in the countryside; no cache of arms lay hidden about the city; no date for an uprising had been set; no underground apparatus, carefully organized and secretly maintained, awaited a signal to fire Charleston and murder the whites. What did exist were strong grievances on one side and deep fears on the other."[31]

Whatever the case, too many people shared the secret for it to be safe. Two blacks reported it, the insurrection was foiled, and those convicted suffered deportation or death.

Finally, there was Nat Turner, in himself an insurrection poised to happen. From his childhood near Suffolk, Virginia, he believed himself a born prophet, "intended for some great purpose." He saw visions and heard voices, found blood on corn and hieroglyphs on leaves. An eclipse of the sun in February 1831 persuaded him, he said, that "I should arise and prepare myself, and slay my enemies with their own weapons. . . . I communicated the great work laid out for me to do, to four in whom I had the greatest confidence (Henry, Hark, Nelson, and Sam). It was intended by us to have begun the work of death on the 4th of July last. Many were the plans formed and rejected by us, and it affected my mind to such a degree that I fell sick, and the time passed without our coming to any determination how to commence—still forming new schemes and rejecting them, when the sign appeared again, which determined me not to wait longer." Thereupon the group agreed to spare no one and to "carry terror and devastation wherever we went."[32] The five and their recruits rampaged murderously through the countryside, killing some 55 whites.

Turner, like so many of his predecessors, had believed that he could raise a large black army. He could not. The militia soon overcame his band of some 60 men, capturing Turner himself a couple of weeks later.

Insurrections: Their Results

Insurrections immediately resulted in harsher controls and stiffer punishments on blacks. Whites, who complained of the barbarity of insurrectionists' actions, did not hesitate to torture and kill those whom they suspected of such plots and to display their mutilated bodies. All too typical were the reactions of the citizens of Gallatin, Tennessee, in 1856: "[T]he question was, what shall be done with the four leaders now in jail? A number of voices said, *'hang them at once.'* On this a vote was taken, and one tremendous shout of 'Aye' was interrupted by only three small voices. . . . The meeting then adjourned to the jail, and though the jailor did all in his power to prevent it, the aforesaid Sam, Jack, Ellick and Dick were taken out and executed."[33]

In the long run, however, insurrections may have led to compromises and adjustments to the slave system, with an eye to keeping it working. Just as individual rebellions sometimes taught owners not to meddle with certain slaves, so group insurrections sometimes led to accommodations and concessions on the part of white society. Almost certainly they hastened the end of the African slave trade, as whites became wary of bringing in more potential insurrectionists.

On the other hand, the string of rebellions, particularly Nat Turner's, helped defeat such organized abolitionism as had existed in the South. For a time in the second half of the 18th and the beginning of the 19th century, a number of southerners had agreed that slavery was morally wrong and seriously looked for a way to end it. But in the 1830s, in the wake of the insurrections, this feeling transmuted into passionate defenses of slavery as a system ordained by God, healthy for blacks and whites alike, and essential to the welfare of their states.

Maroon Communities

Fugitive slaves, both men and women, sometimes found their freedom for a shorter or longer time in maroon communities, or communities of "outlyers." These centered especially in the Carolinas, Virginia, Louisiana, Florida, Georgia, Mississippi, and Alabama in semitropical, sparsely settled locations. They began early. What might be called the first was founded by the 100 or so black slaves who in 1526 rebelled against the Spanish colonizer Lucas Vásquez de Ayllón. The rebels took refuge with Indians and became the first permanent inhabitants, other than Indians, of what is now the United States.[34]

Wartime offered inviting opportunities for slaves to escape and set up maroon colonies. In 1783, William Reynolds of Charleston complained that 30 of his slaves had run away to follow the British army to Georgia and thereafter had joined up with the Creek Indians.[35] Wars also left behind bands of black soldiers who had fought against the United States. After the American Revolution, for instance, blacks who had taken the British side carried on guerrilla warfare along the Savannah River until 1783. During the War of 1812, the British built a fort for themselves and their black and Indian allies. After the war, 300 fugitive slaves took it over, cultivating land for 50 miles round about. The fort was destroyed only after its defenders fired on an American gunboat. Survivors among them went on to fight in the Seminole wars. In the confusion of the Civil War, maroons flourished as never before, favoring locations invaded by Union troops, especially in Virginia, the Carolinas, Florida, and Louisiana.

Unsettled political and economic conditions also provided opportunities for slaves to found maroon colonies. Sometimes in these they allied themselves with poor whites and Indians.

Most "outlyers" were nomadic. Occasionally, though, a group established itself on a permanent site, preferably one easily defended. When they could, outlyers chose places near disputed borders or friendly Indian tribes. In the early 18th century, some outlyers tried to re-create African villages, choosing as chief a slave who had been an African prince, building homes of grasses and branches, and planting crops. The most noted of the established communities was that in the Great Dismal Swamp between Virginia and North Carolina, founded before 1800. There some

2,000 fugitives and their descendants lived, more or less accepted, trading with their white neighbors on the borders of the swamp. So long did some of these colonies last that children born in them grew up to become their leaders. Some maroons never saw a white person.

Many maroons supported themselves by raiding and stealing. The insecure and difficult conditions under which they lived turned some of them into desperadoes. Their guerrilla activities, of course, aroused the inhabitants on whose property they preyed. States might respond to pleas for protection by paying Indians so much for each maroon scalp taken.

Residents also feared that the maroons would lure away their slaves or foment insurrection among them. In the early days, maroon colonies did indeed depend on slaves for support and encouraged them to desert and rebel. But their interests were not identical. Slaves sometimes went in fear of the maroons, who seized their supplies and their women. Colonial powers would sometimes allow a maroon enclave to exist in peace if it would capture runaway slaves and help them put down slave revolts. Similar tactics on the part of the whites eventually made maroons into enemies of the Indians, on whom they had originally relied for help.

Slavery, with all its indignities and cruelties, failed to quell the spirit of all the African Americans on whom it was inflicted. In small ways and large, daring the lash and death itself, many of them fought for at least some degree of control over their own fates. The record on slave escapes and rebellions is too murky to allow us ever to know precisely how often they occurred. But it does clearly reveal that these risings figured significantly in the history of the country during the dreadful days of slavery. One small illustration: In February 1841, Congressman Joshua Giddings complained "that Congress had appropriated $250,000 in 1821 to pay Georgia slaveholders for slaves who had fled to the Seminole tribes of Florida between 1770 and 1790; that an unused portion of this sum, amount[ing] to $141,000, was prorated to these slaveholders by special act of Congress as 'compensation for the offspring which they would have borne their masters, had they remained in servitude'; that the fugitives had intermarried with the Seminoles, and the latter could not come out of the swamps without surrendering their wives and children to slavery; that bloodhounds were imported from Cuba at a cost of $5,000 to track them down; that by order of the commanding General all Negroes, cattle and horses belonging to the Indians were the property of the army unit capturing them; that $20 each was paid to the soldiers from the United States Treasury for more than 500 of these slaves, who were turned over to claimants."[36]

Chronicle of Events

1526

- Black slaves of the Spanish colonizer Lucas Vásquez de Ayllón (in what is now South Carolina) rebel, fleeing to the Indians, with whom they remain as the first permanent inhabitants other than Indians of what is now the United States.

1640

- In the Chesapeake region black indentured servant John Punch is sentenced to service for life for running away.

1657

- In Hartford, Connecticut, Africans and Indians are said to have joined in an uprising and destroyed some buildings.

1676

- In Virginia, blacks join white indentured servants, unemployed workers, and other whites in Bacon's Rebellion, a fairly long-lived political and economic movement led by an aristocrat but largely composed of disaffected whites.

1682

- Virginia requires that church wardens must read the act of 1680 "on Negro insurrection" twice a year during divine service and forbids a master or overseer to allow a slave of another to remain on his plantation more than four hours without permission of the slave's owner.

1687

- A slave insurrection is attempted at Northern Neck, Virginia.

1708

- In Queen's County, New York, an Indian slave and his black wife kill their master and his family, for which they and two black accomplices are put to death.

1710

- A plan of insurrection on foot in Surrey City, Virginia, is revealed by the slave Will, in return for his freedom.

1712

- Violence resulting from an alleged New York City slave revolt results in the deaths of nine whites and the execution of 18 slaves. It provokes even harsher conditions for all blacks, slave or free; new restrictions permit manumission only after a master guarantees the slave's ability to be self-supporting, prohibit the harboring of any slaves, forbid slaves to carry arms or to testify against free people, and make arson by a slave a capital offense.

1720

- In Charleston, South Carolina, slaves attack whites in their homes and on the street.

1722

- In Virginia near the mouth of the Rappahannock River, two hundred blacks arm themselves, intending to kill whites in church, but flee upon discovery.

1723

- When fires break out in Boston, Indian and black slaves are suspected of arson.

1728

- In Savannah, slaves plan an insurrection but quarrel among themselves.

1730

- Slaves in Williamsburg, Virginia, hearing a rumor that the king has ordered that all baptized persons be freed, plan to rebel.
- A black insurrection arises in the plantations around New Orleans.
- South Carolina slaves allegedly conspire to destroy all the whites.
- A slave plunders and burns a house in Malden, Massachusetts, complaining that his master had sold him to a man whom he does not like.

1734

- In Burlington, Pennsylvania, slaves allegedly conspire to kill every master and his sons and their draft horses, set the masters' property on fire, and secure their saddle horses for flight to the Indians.

1738

- When 23 runaway slaves arrive in St. Augustine, the Spanish governor announces that he will establish them at a well-fortified settlement at Mosa, at the mouth of the St. Johns River.

1739

- Slaves sack and burn the armory at Stono, South Carolina, and then march toward a Florida fort manned by a black militia company. On the way they enlist more runaways, gather arms, kill whites, and stir expectations of freedom. The colonial militia crushes the rebellion.

- In South Carolina, the militia is called out to pursue a group of runaway slaves committing robberies around Dorchester.

1740

- *May–July:* In the "Inglorious Expedition," Georgia and Carolina troops attempt to invade Florida in retaliation for "the Protection our deserted Slaves have met with" there.
- *June:* 150 unarmed slaves gather near Charleston; 50 are captured and hanged.

1740–1741

- A series of fires in New York City sets off hysterical suspicions of slave insurrection, resulting in severe punishment of 154 free and slave blacks.

1751

- South Carolina prescribes punishment for any black who instructs another about poisons.

1754

- Black women allegedly burn the buildings of C. Croft of Charleston, South Carolina.

1755

- Slaves Mark and Phillis are executed for poisoning their master, Mr. John Codman of Charlestown, Massachusetts—he by hanging and she by being burned alive.

1768

- British captain John Wilson allegedly attempts to incite Boston slaves to insurrection, assuring them that the British troops have come to secure their freedom.

1775

- In New Jersey the slave Titus runs away from his Quaker owner to fight for Loyalists, during which service he liberates his family and friends and kidnaps key Patriot leaders.

1782

- A white man, a notorious robber, gathers about 50 blacks and whites and terrorizes a community in Georgia.

1791

- Toussaint-Louverture, a former slave, leads a successful (and bloody) rebellion against French rule in Santo Domingo, eventually establishing the Republic of Haiti and abolishing slavery. In the United States, Toussaint-Louverture becomes a symbol of slave rebellion.

1793

- In Albany, New York, three blacks are executed for setting a major fire.

1795

- The Pointe Coupee uprising in Louisiana results in the hanging of 26 slaves.
- The "General of the Swamps," leader of a group of outlyers, is caught and killed.

1796

- Fires, allegedly set by blacks, break out in South Carolina, New York, Savannah, Baltimore, Charleston, and Newark and Elizabeth, New Jersey.

1800

- Led by visionary blacksmith Gabriel Prosser and his preacher brother Martin, slaves unsuccessfully try to march on Richmond to kill the city's white inhabitants (except the Quakers, Methodists, and French).
- The Virginia legislature asks the governor to correspond with the president of the United States about purchasing lands outside the state for a penal colony to which to transport slaves involved in insurrection.

1807

- A number of Africans brought to Charleston, South Carolina, for sale starve themselves to death in the slave pens.

1811

- Free mulatto Charles Deslondes from Haiti leads a slave rebellion in Louisiana. One hundred eighty or more poorly armed slaves strike toward New Orleans, only to be defeated by slaveholders, free black militia, and federal troops.

1812

- Insurrections are crushed in Virginia, Louisiana, and Kentucky.

1813

- Insurrections are crushed in the District of Columbia, South Carolina, and Virginia.

1814
• Insurrections are crushed in Maryland and Virginia.

1816
• White storekeeper George Baxley leads an unsuccessful slave insurrection in Spottsylvania City, Virginia.

1822
• Denmark Vesey, a former slave, allegedly conspires to organize a slave revolt in South Carolina. His plans are betrayed by followers, and he is executed along with 37 slaves; 30 others are sold out of the state.

1826
• Seventy-seven slaves mutiny on a Mississippi River steamer, kill five, and escape to Indiana.
• On the *Decatur*, going from Baltimore to Georgia, 29 slaves rebel, throw the captain and the mate overboard, put a white crew member in command, and order him to steer for Haiti.
• Inhabitants of New Bern, Tarborough, and Hillsborough, in North Carolina, informed that 40 slaves whom they suspect of insurrectionary intention are assembled in a nearby swamp, surround it and kill all the slaves.

1828
• Four slave artisans being carried by ship from Charleston to New Orleans commit suicide during the voyage.

1829
• Slaves in a coffle from Maryland to the South attack their guards, killing two.
• The governor of Georgia talks of a conspiracy in Georgetown, South Carolina, and of fires set by slaves in Augusta and Savannah.

1831
• *August 22:* Nat Turner's rebellion begins in the home of his master, Joseph Travis, and spreads through Southampton County, Virginia. The killing spree is ended by a band of white men, who hang Turner and a number of his fellows.

1835
• Texas revolts against Mexico, at least partly over the slavery issue; slaves unsuccessfully attempt an insurrection.

1837
• Slaves plot insurrection in Alexandria, Louisiana; vigilantes hang nine.

1841
• One hundred thirty-five slaves on the *Creole* out of Richmond rise and take the ship to Nassau, where the British authorities free them.

1845
• Seventy-five Maryland slaves arm and begin to march toward Pennsylvania; some are killed, and 31 are recaptured.

1849–1850
• In Philadelphia, blacks attacked by white mobs defend themselves with bricks and paving stones.

1851
• Blacks in Lancaster, Pennsylvania, riot for freedom.

This image canonizes John Brown. The legend reads: "Meeting the Slave-mother and her child on the steps of Charleston jail on his way to execution. The Artist has represented Capt. Brown regarding with a look of compassion a Slave-mother and Child who obstructed the passage on his way to the Scaffold.—Capt. Brown stooped and kissed the Child—then met his fate. From the original painting by Louis Ransom." *(Library of Congress)*

1854

• Texas forbids either blacks or whites to aid, plan, or incite a slave rebellion.

1856

• In Colorado City, Texas, a large group (perhaps four hundred) of free and hired-out blacks, assisted by Mexicans, plan for slaves to rise and fight their way to Mexico.
• One hundred fifty black men march on Dover, Tennessee, attempting to liberate the black iron workers jailed for trying to seize the mines where they work.

1858

• John Brown proposes the organization of a biracial, armed movement to uproot slavery, moving down from northern Virginia into the Deep South to form a provisional government of black and white people in a kind of guerrilla territory within the United States, under the formal aegis of the U.S. government.

1859

• *October 16:* John Brown leads a small biracial group attempting to capture the armory at Harpers Ferry, Virginia. His hanging makes him an abolitionist martyr.

1860

• White authorities in Waxahachie, Texas, claim to uncover a plan for a black uprising, and a Committee of Vigilance leads a mob in lynching the supposed leaders: Sam Smith, Cato, and Patrick.
• In Alabama, 25 blacks and four whites are executed for allegedly participating in a plot to take over the area.

1861

• Forty black men are hanged in the Natchez, Mississippi, area for allegedly plotting insurrection.
• Two black men and a black woman are hanged in northern Arkansas for allegedly plotting insurrection.
• *December:* Sixty slaves march through New Castle, Kentucky, "singing political songs and shouting for Lincoln," and no one dares stop them.

Eyewitness Testimony

Laws Governing Slaves: Enslavement

[W]hatsoever freeborn woman shall intermarry with any slave, from and after the last day of the present assembly, shall serve the master of such slave during the life of her husband; and . . . all issue of such free woman, so married, shall be slaves as their fathers were.

Maryland law of 1663, in Olexer, Enslavement of the American Indian, *48.*

And be it further enacted, That if any slave hereafter emancipated shall remain within this commonwealth more than twelve months after his or her right to freedom shall have accrued, he or she shall forfeit all such right, and may be apprehended and sold by the overseers of the poor of any county or corporation in which he or she shall be found, for the benefit of the poor. . . .

Virginia law, 1805, in Finkelman, Law of Freedom, *111.*

Laws Governing Slaves: Slave Codes

In order to show the true aspect of slavery among us, I will state distinct propositions, each supported by the evidence of actually existing laws:

1. Slavery is hereditary and perpetual, to the last moment of the slave's earthly existence, and to all his descendants, to the latest posterity.

2. The labor of the slave is compulsory and uncompensated; while the kind of labor, the amount of toil, and the time allowed for rest, are dictated solely by the master. . . .

3. The slave being considered a personal chattel, may be sold, or pledged, or leased, at the will of his master. . . .

4. Slaves can make no contracts, and have no legal right to any property, real or personal.

5. Neither a slave, nor free colored person, can be a witness against any white or free man, in a court of justice. . . .

6. The slave may be punished at his master's discretion—without trial. . . .

7. The slave is not allowed to resist any free man under any circumstances. . . .

8. Slaves cannot redeem themselves, or obtain a change of masters, though cruel treatment may have rendered such a change necessary for their personal safety.

9. The slave is entirely unprotected in his domestic relations.

10. The laws greatly obstruct the manumission of slaves, even where the master is willing to enfranchise them.

11. The operation of the laws tends to deprive slaves of religious instruction and consolation.

12. The whole power of the laws is exerted to keep slaves in a state of the lowest ignorance.

13. There is in this country a monstrous inequality of law and right. . . . [T]he same offences which cost a white man a few dollars only, are punished in the negro with death.

Abolitionist Lydia Child, Appeal *(1836), 41–42.*

The tribunal for the trial of slaves [in South Carolina] . . . is the worst system which could be devised. The consequence is, that the passions and prejudices of the neighborhood arising from a recent offense, enter into trial, and often lead to the condemnation of the innocent.

Judge John Belton O'Neall, 1848, in Higginbotham, In the Matter of Color, *180.*

The slave, who is but *"a chattel"* on all *other* occasions, with not one solitary attribute of personality accorded to him, becomes *"a person"* whenever he is to be *punished!* He is the only being in the universe to whom is denied all self-direction and free agency, but who is, nevertheless, held responsible for his conduct, and amenable to law. Forbidden to *read* the law, and kept as ignorant and as unenlightened as possible, he is nevertheless accounted criminal for acts which are deemed innocent in others, and punished with a severity from which all others are exempted. He is under the *control* of law, though *unprotected* by law, and can know law only as an enemy, and not as a friend.

Goodell, Slave Code *(1853), 309.*

Laws Governing Slaves: Concerning Slaves as Victims

Be it enacted . . . if any slave resist his master . . . and by the extremity of the correction should chance to die, that his death shall not be accompted ffelony, but the master . . . be acquit from molestation, since it cannot be presumed that prepensed malice . . . should induce any man to destroy his owne estate.

Virginia act, 1669, in Finkelman, Law of Freedom, *17.*

For the prevention and restraining of inhuman severities which by evil masters or overseers, may be used towards their Christian servants, that from and after the publication hereof, if any man smite out the eye or tooth of his man servant or maid servant, or otherwise maim or disfigure them much, unless it be by mere casualty, he shall let him or her go free from his service, and shall allow such further recompense as the court of quarter sessions shall adjudge him. . . . That if any person or persons whatever in this province shall wilfully kill his Indian or negroe servant or servants he shall be punished with death.

New Hampshire law, 1718, in Williams,
History of the Negro Race, *I:311.*

They further informed me . . . that for killing a negro, ever so wantonly, as without provocation, there could be nothing but a fine; they gave a late instance of this; that (further) to *steal* a negro was death, but to *kill him* was only fineable.

Bostonian Josiah Quincy Jr., visiting South Carolina, 1773,
in Bell, Major Butler's Legacy, *67.*

Be it enacted . . . That the offence of Killing a Slave shall hereafter be denominated and considered homicide, and shall partake of the same degree of guilt when accompanied with the like circumstances that homicide now does at common law.

North Carolina law, 1817, in Finkelman,
Law of Freedom, *201.*

The prisoner was put upon his trial . . . for the murder of his own female slave, a woman named Mira. The witnesses . . . testified to a series of the most brutal and barbarous whippings, scourgings and privations, inflicted by the prisoner upon the deceased, from about the first of December, to the time of her death in the ensuing March, while she was in the latter stages of pregnancy, and afterwards, during the period of her confinement and recovery from a recent delivery. A physician . . . called to view the body of the deceased, stated that there were five wounds on the head of the deceased, four of which appeared to have been inflicted a week or more before her death; that the fifth was a fresh wound, about one and a half inches long, and to the bone, and was, in his opinion, sufficient to have produced her death; that there were many other wounds on different parts of her body, which were sufficient independent of those on the head, to have caused death. The reasons assigned by the prisoner to those who witnessed his inhuman treatment of the deceased, were, at one time, that she stole his turnips and sold them to the worthless people in the neighborhood, and that she had attempted to burn his barn, and was disobedient and impudent to her mistress; at another, that she had attempted to burn his still house, and had put something in a pot to poison his family. There was no evidence except her own confessions, extorted by severe whippings, that the deceased was guilty of any of the crimes imputed to her; nor did it appear that she was disobedient or impertinent to her master or mistress; on the contrary, she seemed, as some of the witnesses testified, to do her best to obey the commands of her master, and that when she failed to do so, it was from absolute inability to comply with orders to which her condition and strength were unequal. . . .

[Chief Justice Ruffin:] [T]he prisoner employed himself from day to day in practising grievous tortures upon an enfeebled female. . . . He beat her with clubs, iron chains, and other deadly weapons, time after time; burnt her; inflicted stripes over and often, with scourges, which literally excoriated her whole body; forced her out to work in inclement seasons, without being duly clad; provided for her insufficient food; exacted labour beyond her strength, and wantonly beat her because she could not comply with his requisitions. These enormities, besides others too disgusting to be particularly designated, the prisoner, without his heart once relenting or softening, practised from the first of December until the latter end of the ensuing March; and he did not relax even up to the last hour of his victim's existence. . . .

North Carolina case State v. Hoover, *1839,*
in Finkelman, Law of Freedom, *227–29.*

Individual Rebels: Fighting Back

[G]reat disorders, insolences and burglaries are oft times raised and committed in the night time by Indians, negro and mulatto servants and slaves, to the disquiet and hurt of her majesty's good subjects.

1703 Massachusetts act establishing a curfew, in
Higginbotham, In the Matter of Color, *77.*

Shall a man be deem'd a rebel that supports his own rights? It is the first law of nature, and he must be a rebel to God, to the laws of nature, and his own conscience, who will not do it.

Reverend Isaac Skillman, Oration upon the Beauties of
Liberty, *1772, in Aptheker,* One Continual Cry, *24.*

At first the quarrel began between my wife and her mistress. I was then at work in the barn, and hearing a racket in the house, induced me to run there and see what had broken out. When I entered the house, I found my mistress in a violent passion with my wife, for what she informed me was a mere trifle. . . . I earnestly requested my wife to beg pardon of her mistress for the sake of peace, even if she had given no just occasion for offence. But whilst I was thus saying, my mistress turned the blows which she was repeating on my wife to me. I reached out my great black hand, raised it up and received the blows of the whip on it which were designed for my head. Then I immediately committed the whip to the devouring fire.

Some days after his [my master's] return, in the morning as I was putting on a log in the fireplace, not suspecting harm from any one, I received a most violent stroke on the crown of my head with a club two feet long and as large around as a chair post. This blow very badly wounded my head. . . . The first blow made me have my wits about me . . . , for as soon as he went to renew it I snatched the club out of his hands and dragged him out of the door. He then sent for his brother to come and assist him, but I presently left my master, took the club he wounded me with, carried it to a neighboring justice of the peace, and complained of my master. He finally advised me to return to my master and live contented with him till he abused me again, and then complain. . . . But before I set out for my master's, up he came and his brother Robert after me. The Justice improved this convenient opportunity to caution my master. He asked him for what he treated his slave thus hastily and unjustly, and told him what would be the consequence if he continued the same treatment towards me. After the justice had ended his discourse with my master, he and his brother set out with me for home, one before and the other behind me. . . . [T]hey both dismounted . . . and fell to beating me with great violence. I . . . immediately turned them both under me, laid one of them across the other, and stamped them both with my feet. . . .

Venture, Life and Adventures *(1798), 14–15.*

[Sarah is] the biggest devil that ever lived, having poisoned a stud horse and set a stable on fire, also burnt Gen. R. Williams stable and stock yard with seven horses and other property to value of $1500. She was handcuffed and got away at Ruddles Mills on her way down the river, which is the fifth time she escaped when about to be sent out of the country.

Kentucky planter's 1822 advertisement, in Blassingame, Slave Community, *116.*

[Sinda] passed at one time for a prophetess among her fellow slaves on the plantation, and had acquired such an ascendancy over them that, having given out . . . that the world was to come to an end at a certain time, and that not a very remote one, the belief in her assertion took such possession of the people [slaves] on the estate that they refused to work, and the rice and cotton fields were threatened with an indefinite fallow in consequence of this strike on the part of the cultivators. Mr. K[ing], who was then overseer of the property . . . acquiesced in their determination not to work; but he expressed to them his belief that Sinda was mistaken, and he warned her that if, at the appointed time, it proved so, she would be severely punished. . . . [P]oor Sinda was in the wrong. Her day of judgment came indeed, and a severe one it proved. . . . [T]he spirit of false prophecy was mercilessly scourged

This image depicts an individual slave rebellion—a more frequent occurrence than an insurrection. *(Library of Congress)*

out of her, and the faith of her people of course reverted from her to the omnipotent lash again.

Kemble, Journal *(1839), 118–19.*

Then there was the unruly slave, whom no master particularly wanted for several reasons: first, he would not submit to any kind of corporal punishment; second, it was hard to determine which was the master or which the slave; third, he worked when he pleased to do so. . . . This class of slaves were usually industrious, but very impudent. There were thousands of that class, who spent their lives in their master's service doing his work undisturbed, because the master understood the slave. . . . [T]here were thousands of high-toned and high spirited slaves, who had as much self-respect as their masters, and who were industrious, reliable, and truthful, and could be depended on by their masters in all cases. . . . These slaves knew their own helpless condition. . . . But . . . they did not give up in abject servility.

Ex-slave Henry Clay Bruce, in Blassingame,
Slave Community, *215–16.*

[My mother] was a black African an' she sho' was wild an' mean. [Nobody could whip her unless she was tied up, so] sometimes my master would wait 'til de next day to git somebody to he'p tie her up, den dey'd fergit to whip 'er. [She was the cause] of my ol' masser firin' all de overseers. . . . [S]he was so mean he was afraid dey'd kill her. She'd work without no watchin' an' overseers wa'n't nothin' nohow.

Susan Snow, in Fox-Genovese, Plantation Households, *187.*

[Having heard a slave say] that if he ever struck her [as he had just struck another], it would be the day he or she would die, [the overseer struck her; she knocked him from his horse with her hoe and then] pounced upon him and chopped his head off. . . . [Then she] proceeded to chop and mutilate his body; that done to her satisfaction, she then killed his horse, [then] calmly went to tell the master of the murder. . . . [He said,] "You are free from this day and if the mistress wants you to do anything for her, do it if you want to."

Ex-slave Irene Coates, in Fox-Genovese,
Plantation Households, *317.*

At this, Ma [Fannie] took the baby by its feet, one foot in each hand, and with the Baby's head swinging downward, she vowed to smash its brains out before she'd leave it. Tears were streaming down her face. . . . It was seldom

that Ma cried and everyone knew that she meant every word. Ma took her baby with her.

Fannie's daughter, describing her mother's reaction when told that she was to be sold for attacking her mistress and could not take her baby with her, in Lerner, Black Women, *38.*

Individual Rebels: Ruses and Revenges

After that I again refused to eat anything, at all; but pretended to be sick all of the time. I also told Frankee to tell my master that I was subject to such turns every spring, and I should not live through this. . . . He then again tried to make me eat . . . , often leaving victuals by my bedside at night, or order Frankee to do it. He would then inquire of her if I had eaten anything yet. She replied, no, sir, I have not seen him eat anything since last Friday noon. I had his horse to water every day; and as I went out of, or across the yard, where I knew he would see me, I would pretend to be so weak that I could scarcely go. . . . I would, however, have it understood that during all this time I did not go without victuals. . . . One morning he sent me to eat my breakfast. I went, and returned. When I came back, he asked me if I had eaten my breakfast? I told him, no, sir, I thank you, I did not wish for any. You did not, did you? Gad dam you, you are sick, are you? You may die and be damned, by Gad;—you may die and be damned;—your coffin shall not cost me a quarter of a dollar, by Gad;—you shall be buried on your face, by Gad;—you may die and be damned. . . .

I went to one Major Lewis, a free black man, and very cunning. I gave him money to go to my master and run me down, and endeavor to convince him that I was really sick, and should never be good for anything. In a few days from this, my master came down in the kitchen and says, boy get up; there, boy, (holding it out in his hand,) there is the very money I gave for you; I have got my money again, and you may go and be damned; and don't you never step into my house again; if you do, I will split your damned brains out.

William Grimes, Life *(1855), 82–83.*

[A Virginia planter complained of] the liability of women, especially to disorders and irregularities which cannot be detected by exterior symptoms, but which may be easily aggravated into serious complaints. . . . "They don't come to the field and you go to the quarters and ask the old nurse what's the matter and she says, 'Oh; she's not . . . fit to work, sir'; and . . . you have to take her word for it that

something or other is the matter with her, and you dare not set her to work; and so she will lay up till she feels like taking the air again, and plays the lady at your expense."
Olmsted, Seaboard Slave States, *190.*

About four years ago a negro who gave the impression of being a good subject, and even wanting to appear religious, came to see me for about a month, making me fine promises and begging me, almost on his knees to free him by buying him from a bad position. I was foolish enough to agree to this . . . and, in all of this, I was duped by a first-class knavery, either on the part of those who sold him to me well guaranteed, while he had been fraudulently brought into the state, or by the negro himself who . . . did not give me even one hundred dollars . . . and who finally by negligence or bad will on the part of Mr. Soule my lawyer, succeeded in having himself recognized as free, while it would have been so easy to prove the opposite. Hence I lost the negro, and, besides, I was condemned to pay him twelve Hundred dollars for *His work.*
Clothile Bornet, February 14, 1846, in Owens, Property, *220.*

[My mother] often hid us all in the woods. . . . When we wanted water, she sought for it in any hole or puddle formed by falling trees or otherwise. It was often full of tadpoles and insects. She strained it, and gave it round to each of us in the hollow of her hand. For food, she gathered berries in the woods, got potatoes, raw corn, etc. After a time, the master would send word to her to come in, promising he would not sell us.
Ex-slave Moses Grandy, quoted in Webber, Deep like the Rivers, *166.*

Ole Marsa would spell out real fas' anything he don't want me to know 'bout. One day Marsa was fit to be tied, he was in setch a bad mood. Was ravin' 'bout de crops, an' taxes, an' de triflin' niggers he got to feed. "Gonna sell 'em, I swear before Christ, I gonna sell 'em," he says. Den ole Missus ask which ones he gonna sell an' tell him quick to spell it. Den he spell out G-A-B-E and R-U-F-U-S. 'Course I stood dere without battin' an eye, an' makin' believe I didn't even hear him, but I was packin' dem letters up in my haid all de time. An' soon's I finished dishes I rushed down to my father an' say 'em to him jus' like marsa say 'em. Father say quiet-like: "Gabe and Rufus," an' tol' me to go back to de house an' say I ain't been out. De next day Gabe and Rufus was gone—dey had run away. Marsa nearly died, got to cussin' an' ravin' so he

took sick. Missus went to town an' tol' de sheriff, but dey never could fin' dose two slaves.
Ex-slave, quoted in Webber, Deep like the Rivers, *228–29.*

[O]ld Aunt Delia, the cook who had been in the family for years and completely bossed the kitchen, came right out and said, "How many times I spit in the biscuits and peed in the coffee just to get back at them mean white folks."
Murray, Proud Shoes, *159–60.*

All the slaves were allowed to stop at home that day [when the master died] to see the last of him, and to lament with mistress. After all the slaves who cared to do so had seen his face, they gathered in groups around mistress to comfort her; they shed false tears, saying "Never mind, missus, massa gone home to heaven." While some were saying this, others said, "Thank God, massa gone home to hell."
Ex-slave Jacob Stroyer, in Raboteau, Slave Religion, *297.*

Individual Rebels: Suicides and Self-Mutilations

[When the wife learned of her imminent sale, she and her husband] resolved to put an End to their lives, rather than be parted; and accordingly, at seven o'clock (the Wench being at the House of her countryman), they went up Stairs into the Garret, where the Fellow, as is supposed, cut out the Wench's Throat with a Razor, and then shot himself with a Gun prepared for the Purpose. They were both found lying upon the Bed, she with her Head cut almost off, and he with his Head shot all to Pieces.
Boston Evening Post, *December 8, 1746, quoted in Gutman,* Black Family, *349.*

At night [the newly arrived slaves] would begin to sing their native songs. . . . In a short while they would become so wrought up that, utterly oblivious to the danger involved, they would grasp their bundles of personal effects, swing them on their shoulders, and setting their faces towards Africa, would march down into the water [of Lake Phelps] singing as they marched till recalled to their senses only by the drowning of some of the party.
Trotter, overseer for the rice-producing Lake Company in North Carolina, ca. 1785, in Redford, Somerset Homecoming, *132.*

When the bidding started [for a slave on the auction block] she grabbed a hatchet, laid her hand on a log and chopped it off. Then she threw the bleeding hand right in her master's face.

Nancy Bean, in Fox-Genovese,
Plantation Households, *329.*

He [a master] was so mean they [his slaves] got up a plot to run off and they never come in till after twelve o'clock that night. They had plotted to go and jump in the Mississippi River and drown themselves. . . . [A]fter that he quit beating and knocking on 'em, and if he got an overseer that was too mean he would turn him off. . . . They said they meant to drown, too, but they thought about their little children and come on home.

Ex-slave, in Johnson, God Struck Me Dead, *199.*

Group Rebellions: Insurrections

[Suppose the slaves rebel,] will these masters and mastrisses take the sword at hand and warr against these poor slaves, licke, we are able to believe, some will not refuse to doc; or have these negers not as much right to fight for their freedom, as you have to keep them slaves?

Germantown Quaker protest, 1688, in Aptheker,
One Continual Cry, *22.*

[Virginia lacks adequate slave-control laws,] in consequence of which, negroes have run together in certain parts of the Colony, causing assemblages so dangerous as to threaten the peace of the whole community.

Sir Edmund Andros, royal governor of Virginia, 1694,
in Harding, River, *31.*

"In the year 1712," says the Rev. D. Humphreys, "a considerable number of negroes of the Carmantee and Pappa Nations formed a plot to destroy all the English, *in order to obtain their liberty;* and kept their conspiracy so secret, that there was no suspicion of it till it came to the very execution. However, the plot was by God's Providence happily defeated. The plot was this. The negroes sat fire to a house in York city. . . . The fire alarmed the town, who from all parts ran to it; the conspirators planted themselves in several streets and lanes leading to the fire, and shot or stabbed the people as they were running to it. Some of the wounded escaped, and acquainted the Government, and presently by the firing of a great gun from the fort, the inhabitants were called under arms and pretty easily scattered the negroes; they had killed about 8 and wounded 12 more. In their flight some of them shot them, others their wives, and then themselves; some absconded a few days, and then killed themselves for fear

of being taken; but a great many were taken, and 18 of them suffered death."

Joshua Coffin, Account of . . . Slave Insurrections,
10–11.

[The] fires [in Boston] have been designedly and industriously kindled by some villanous and desperate negroes, or other dissolute people . . . it being vehemently suspected that they have entered into a combination to burn and destroy the town.

Massachusetts governor, 1723, in Higginbotham,
In the Matter of Color, *76.*

[In the firing during the Stono Rebellion] One Negroe fellow [advanced upon his master. H]is Master asked him if he wanted to kill him the Negroe answered he did at the same time snapping a Pistoll at him but it mist fire and his master shot him thro' the Head about fifty of these Villains attempted to go home but were taken by the Planters who Cutt off their heads and set them up at every Mile Post they came to.

In Porter, Negro on the American Frontier, *168.*

[During the Stono Rebellion some slaves] shewed so much Integrity and Fidelity, that it was at that Time a Service to the Province, as well as to their Masters' Families, and saved them from the Fate of several of their unfortunate Neighbors; and bravely withstood that barbarous Attempt at the Hazard of their own Lives.

South Carolina lieutenant governor Bull, November 1739,
in Wax, "The Great Risque," 141.

[Five slave] conspirators, after their master [Henry Ormond of Beaufort County] was abed, went up to his room and with an handkerchief attempted to strangle him, which they thought they had effected, but in a little time after they left him, he recovered, and began to stir, on hearing which they went up and told him he must die, and that before they left the room; he begged very earnestly for his life, but one of them, his house wench, told him it was in vain, that as he had no mercy on them, he could expect none himself, and immediately threw him between two feather beds, and all got on him till he was stifled to death.

Virginia Gazette, *September 6, 1770, quoted in Kay and*
Cary, Slavery in North Carolina, *79.*

My brother Gabriel was the person who influenced me to join him and others in order that (as he said) we might conquer the white people and possess ourselves of their property. I enquired how we were to effect it. He said by falling upon them (the whites) in the dead of night, at which time they would be unguarded and unsuspicious. I then enquired who was at the head of the plan. He said Jack, alias Jack Bowler. I asked him if Jack Bowler knew anything about carrying on war. He replied he did not. He said a man from Carolina who was at the siege of Yorktown, and who was to meet him (Gabriel) at the Brook and to proceed on to Richmond, take, and then fortify it. This man from Carolina was to be commander and manager the first day, and then, after exercising the soldiers, the command was to be resigned to Gabriel. If Richmond was taken without the loss of many men, they were to continue for some time, but if they sustained any considerable loss they were to [head] for Hanover or York, they were not decided which, and continue at that place as long as they found they were able to defend it, but in the event of a defeat or loss at those places they were to endeavor to form a junction with some negroes which, they had understood from Mr. Gregory's overseer, were in rebellion in some quarter of the country. This information which they had gotten from the overseer, made Gabriel anxious, upon which he applied to me to make scythe-swords, which I did to the number of twelve. Every Sunday he came to Richmond to provide ammunition and to find where the military stores were deposited. Gabriel informed me in case of success, that they intended to subdue the whole of the country where slavery was permitted, but no further.

The first places Gabriel intended to attack in Richmond were, the Capitol, the Magazine, the Penitentiary, the Governor's house and his prison. The inhabitants were to be massacred, save those who begged for quarter and agreed to serve as soldiers with them. The reason I think insurrection was to be made at this particular time was, the discharge of the number of soldiers, one or two months ago, which induced Gabriel to believe the plan would be more easily executed.

Given under our hands this 15th day of September 1800.

Gervas Storrs
Joseph Selden

Confession of Solomon, in Starobin, Blacks in Bondage, *127–28.*

I have nothing more to offer than what George Washington would have had to offer had he been taken by the British and put to trial by them. I have adventured my life in endeavoring to obtain the liberty of my countrymen, and am a willing sacrifice to their cause.

Courtroom testimony of an anonymous black insurrectionist, 1804, in Harding, River, *52.*

This gentleman . . . mentioned, that his servant had informed him, that A—[a witness who was promised that his name would not be divulged] had stated, that about three months ago, Rolla, belonging to Governor Bennett, had communicated to him the intelligence of the intended insurrection [Denmark Vesey's], and had asked him to join—That he remarked, in the event of their rising, they would not be without help, as the people from San Domingo and Africa would assist them in obtaining their liberty, if they only made the motion first themselves.

J. Hamilton, Jr., intendant, Charleston, August 16, 1822, in Carroll, Slave Insurrections, *9.*

On Thursday the 27th, DENMARK VESEY, a free black man, was brought before the Court for trial,

Assisted by his Counsel, G. W. Cross, Esq. . . . There is ample reason for believing, that this project was not, with him, of recent origin, for it was said, he had spoken of it for upwards of four years.

These facts of his guilt the journals of the Court will disclose—that no man can be proved to have spoken of or urged the insurrection prior to himself. All the channels of communication and intelligence are traced back to him. His house was the place appointed for the secret meetings of the conspirators, at which he was invariably a leading and influential member; animating and encouraging the timid, by the hopes of prospects of success; removing the scruples of the religious, by the grossest prostitution and perversion of the sacred oracles, and inflaming and confirming the resolute, by all the savage fascinations of blood and booty.

J. Hamilton, Jr., intendant, Charleston, August 16, 1822, in Carroll, Slave Insurrections, *16.*

The Court tried JESSE, the slave of Mr. Thomas Blackwood.

The testimony against *Jesse* was very ample. His activity and zeal . . . were fully proved. He had engaged with Vesey to go out of town on Sunday the 16th, to bring down some negroes from the country, to aid in the rising on that night; and remarked, to the witnesses, on his way to Hibbens' ferry, "if my father does not assist I will cut off his head." All the particulars in proof against him, he confirmed after receiving his sentence, by his own full and satisfactory Confession. . . .

This man excited no small sympathy, not only from the apparent sincerity of his contrition, but from the mild and unostentatious composure with which he met his fate.

J. Hamilton, Jr., intendant, Charleston, August 16, 1822, in Carroll, Slave Insurrections, 18.

[N]o description can accurately convey . . . the impression which his [Gullah Jack Pritchard's] trial, defence and appearance made on those who witnessed the working of his cunning and rude address. Born a conjurer and a physician, in his own country (for in Angola they are matters of inheritance) he practised *these arts* in this country for fifteen years, without its being generally known among the whites. . . . It does not appear that Jack required much persuasion to induce him to join in a project, which afforded him the most ample opportunities of displaying his peculiar art, whilst it is very obvious that his willingness, to do all that Vesey might require, was in no little degree stimulated, by his bitterness and his gall against the whites. . . . If the part which he was to play in this drama, bespoke that the treacherous and vindictive artifices of war in his own country, existed in unimpaired vigour in his memory, his wildness and vehemence of gesture and the malignant glance with which he eyed the witnesses who appeared against him, all indicated the savage, who indeed had been *caught*, but not *tamed*. . . . Such was their belief in his invulnerability, that his charms and amulets were in request, and he was regarded as a man, who could *only* be harmed but by the *treachery* of his fellows.

J. Hamilton, Jr., intendant, Charleston, August 16, 1822, in Carroll, Slave Insurrections, 23–24.

[Bacchus, allegedly a Denmark Vesey conspirator] went to the gallows, *laughing and bidding his acquaintances in the streets* "good bye"; on being hung, owing to some mismanagement in the fall of the trap, he was not thrown off, but the board canted, he slipped; yet he was so hardened that he *threw himself forward, and as he swung back he lifted his feet, so that he might not touch the board!*

Confession, quoted in Bracey, Meier, and Rudwick, American Slavery, 130.

Friends and brothers, we are to commence a great work to-night! Our race is to be delivered from slavery, and God has appointed us as the men to do his bidding; and let us be worthy of our calling. I am told to slay all the whites we encounter, without regard to age or sex. We have no arms or ammunition, but we will find these in the houses of our oppressors; and, as we go on, others can join us. Remember, we do not go forth for the sake of blood and carnage; but it is necessary that, in the commencement of this revolution, all the whites we meet should die, until we have an army strong enough to carry on the war upon a Christian basis. Remember that ours is not a war for robbery, nor to satisfy our passions; it is a *struggle for freedom*. Ours must be deeds, not words. Then let's away to the scene of action.

Nat Turner, 1831, in Williams, History of the Negro Race, 87–88.

I heard a loud voice in the heavens, and the Spirit instantly appeared to me and said. . . . I should arise and prepare myself, and slay my enemies with their own weapons . . . for the time was fast approaching when the first should be last and the last should be first.

Nat Turner, 1831, in Harding, River, 75.

THE BANDITTE. They [Nat Turner's insurrectionists] remind one of a parcel of blood-thirsty wolves rushing down from the Alps; or, rather like a former incursion of the Indians upon the white settlements. Nothing is spared; neither age nor sex respected—the helplessness of women and children pleads in vain for mercy. . . . The case of Nat. Turner warns us. No black-man ought to be permitted to turn a Preacher through the country.

Enquirer, August 30, 1831, quoted in Williams, History of the Negro Race, 90.

The predictions of Mr. Randolph some years since are now becoming true; the whites are running away from the blacks, the masters from the slaves, in lower Virginia, the place of insurrection. I received an intimation from a gentleman yesterday to go to his house to advize his negroes, 8 in number, most young ones, to embark for Liberia, as he was willing to emancipate them.

Collin H. Minge, October 1831, in Fox, American Colonization Society, 25.

I never did intend murder, or treason, or the destruction of property, or to excite or incite slaves to rebellion, or to make insurrection. The design on my part was to free the slaves.

John Brown, after the incident at Harper's Ferry, in Williams, History of the Negro Race, 222.

The Harpers Ferry affair [John Brown's rebellion] proves to be more serious than at first it appeared to be—not in reference to the Negro population, for that had nothing to do with it; but in reference to the hostility of large numbers of men of all classes in the free states to the slave-holding states, even unto blood, and their readiness to aid and abet such attempts with counsels and money, and to employ reckless agents to carry them out. Such sparks as these, struck to produce a universal conflagration, should be stamped out immediately. Such enemies should be met and overwhelmed without quarter in a moment. A decision of this sort is demanded by our circumstances, and brings the free and the slave states to a perfect understanding on the whole subject.

Slaveholder Reverend Charles C. Jones, November 7, 1859, in Myers, Children of Pride, 527–28.

Group Rebellions: Maroon Communities (Outlyers)

[In the 1650s in Virginia fugitive Africans are rumored to be attempting] to form small armed groups in various sections of the colony and to harass neighboring plantations, at the same time creating bases to which others might flee.

Harding, River, 30.

[I applied] for the assistance of some Notchee Indians in order to apprehend some runaway Negroes, who had sheltered themselves in the Woods, and being armed, had committed disorders. . . .

Governor James Glen of South Carolina, 1744, in Aptheker, "Maroons," Maroon Societies, 153.

We have had most alarming times this Summer all along shore, from a sett of Barges manned mostly by our own negroes who have run off—These fellows are dangerous to an individual singled out for their vengeance whose property lay exposed—They burnt several houses.

Virginia resident, 1781, in Aptheker, Revolts, 207.

The safety of our frontier I conceive requires this course [sending troops against the Indians in Georgia]. They have, I am informed, several hundred fugitive slaves from the Carolinas and Georgia at present in their Towns and unless they are checked soon they will be so strengthened by desertions from Georgia & Florida that it will be found troublesome to reduce them.

Lt. Col. Thomas Smith, U.S. Army, July 30, 1812, in Aptheker, "Maroons," Maroon Societies, 155.

A nest of runaway negroes were lately discovered in the fork of the Alabama and Tombeckbee rivers, and broken up,

after a smart skirmish by a party from Mobile county. Three of the negroes were killed, several taken and a few escaped. They had two cabins and were about to build a fort. Some of them had been runaway for years, and had committed many depredations on the neighboring plantations.

Charleston Observer, July 21, 1827, in Bracey, Meirer, and Rudwick, American Slavery, 15.

This much I can say that old Hal . . . and his men [outly-ers] fought like spartans, not one gave an inch of ground, but stood, was shot dead or wounded fell on the spot.

White attacker of outlyers, 1827, in Harding, River, 81.

[Our] slaves are become almost uncontrollable. They go and come when and where they please, and if an attempt is made to stop them they immediately fly to the woods and there continue for months and years Committing depreda-tions on our Cattle hogs and Sheep. . . . [P]atrols are of no use on account of the danger they subject themselves to.

Complaint of North Carolina planters, December 1830, in Aptheker, Revolts, 289.

Many deserters [from the Confederate army] . . . are col-lected in the swamps and fastnesses of Taylor, La Fayette, Levy and other counties [in Florida], and have organized, with runaway negroes, bands for the purpose of com-mitting depredations upon the plantations and crops of loyal citizens and running off their slaves. These depreda-tory bands have even threatened the cities of Tallahasee, Madison, and Marianna.

Confederate officer John K. Jackson, quoted in Aptheker, "Maroons," Maroon Societies, 164–65.

[It is] difficult to find words of description . . . of the wild and terrible consequences of the negro raids in this ob-scure . . . theatre of the war. . . . In the two counties of Currituck and Camden, there are said to be from five to six hundred negroes, who are not in the regular military organization of the Yankees, but who, outlawed and dis-owned by their masters, lead the lives of banditti, roving the country with fire and committing all sorts of horrible crimes upon the inhabitants.

This present theatre of guerrilla warfare has, at this time, a most important interest for our authorities. It is described as a rich country, . . . and one of the most im-portant sources of meat supplies that is now accessible to our armies. . . .

Richmond Daily Examiner, January 14, 1864, quoted in Aptheker, "Maroons," Maroon Societies, 165.

CHAPTER NINE

Indians as Slaves, as Friends and Enemies of Black Slaves, and as Slaveholders

1529–1877

Slavery among Indians

Slavery existed in North America long before the arrival of the European explorers and settlers. The idea of slavery did not outrage Indians any more than it outraged Europeans or Africans. In North America, as in Africa and Europe, it was a condition of life that few questioned.

Indian tribes enslaved—sometimes for a limited period, sometimes for life—male prisoners of war whom they did not torture or kill outright. The Iroquois, for instance, usually killed their prisoners of war, but if they felt contempt for a captive, they might make him a slave, cutting off part of his foot to prevent his running away and forcing him to do "woman's work." These practices led to slave raids on neighboring tribes, particularly among the Illinois and Iroquois, as young braves vied to prove their skills as warriors by taking scalps or captives. Some Indian nations also punished crime and debt with slavery. Enslavement dishonored the slave, denying him a warrior's death or marking him as a violator of tribal rules. Before the Europeans came, most tribes refused to accept back a member who had been captured and enslaved. (Later, when they realized that such a reaction in the face of mass enslavements might prove the death of the tribe, they reversed the practice.)

Indians enslaved Indians, then, to gain honor and preserve order, not to benefit by their labor. Even those nations that practiced agriculture farmed only on a small scale, for which the women sufficed as labor. Before whites came, Indians did not buy or sell slaves, for their cultures were not built on a market economy. But a tribe might barter slaves to placate an unfriendly neighboring tribe or in exchange for its own captured members. After Europeans established a market in slaves, Indians began to seize members of other tribes as bargaining chips, neither using them as slaves nor adopting them as members of their own tribe but accumulating them as means of exchange.

Though Indian masters had complete power of life and death over their slaves, treatment of slaves varied widely from tribe to tribe. In many ways, slavery among Indians paralleled slavery among Africans. A few Indian nations treated their slaves harshly, even killing them on a whim, but relations between masters and slaves were generally relaxed. Seminole masters, perhaps the most liberal, demanded little more than a tribute of corn or hogs from their slaves, allowing them to live apart more or less as they pleased and to own property—even other slaves. Most Indian groups considered their slaves eligible for adoption into the tribe. They intermarried with them. Some treated slaves' children as free. Children of Creek fathers and slave mothers were brought up in practical equality with the Creek's full-blooded offspring.

The Enslavement of Indians by Whites

Early European settlers of North America, like the Indians, usually took slavery for granted, though now and then they displayed a need to justify it on the grounds that as masters they were improving the lot of slaves and saving their souls by Christianizing them. But, true to the European tradition, white colonists thought of slaves also as a source of labor and profit.

When white explorers first ventured into North America, they kidnapped Indians to act as informants and interpreters, guide them through the deserts and wildernesses, and help them communicate with other Indians. When the settlers came, they faced a more complex problem. They wanted Indians for servants or for concubines, but they feared to alienate neighboring tribes, on whom they might well depend for advice, help, and safety—indeed, their very survival. If they dared not kidnap, however, they sometimes could bargain. Indians wanted the white men's goods. When they did not have war captives to trade, they might sell erring members of their own tribes for a limited time as a punishment. They might even offer themselves or their children as security for loans, with default bringing enslavement. These practices were risky for the Indians, however, for colonists sometimes broke the terms of the agreements, selling the Indians abroad or refusing to release them at the end of their terms.

As the whites came to appreciate the size of the continent and how much labor would be needed to develop it, such arrangements no longer sufficed. The record of 16th-, 17th-, and 18th-century Europeans in North America dismayingly parallels that in Africa, in that the Europeans in both cases tried to exploit the labor of the natives. In the New World, however, whites were also determined to establish permanent settlements: They were after land as well as slaves. Their ambitions soared. Why not use Indians as slaves to till and develop the vast unsettled continent, or as trading goods for black slaves? As Emanuel Downing argued in a 1645 letter to John Winthrop, "A warr with the Narraganset is verie considerable to this plantation, ffor I doubt whither yt be not synne in vs, hauing power in our hands, to suffer them to maynteyne the worship of the devill which their paw wawes [powwows?] often doe; 2lie, If vpon a Just warre the lord should deliuer them into our hands, wee might easily haue men woemen and children enough to exchange for Moores [blacks], which wilbe more gaynefull pilladge for vs then wee conceive, for I doe not see how wee can thrive vntill wee get into a stock of slaves sufficient to doe all our buisines, for our children's children will hardly see this great Continent filled with people, soe that our servants will still desire freedome to plant for them selues, and not stay but for verie great wages. And I suppose you know verie well how wee shall maynteyne 20 Moores cheaper then one Englishe servant."[1]

For such purposes and to get land, Europeans provoked wars with the Indians, sometimes directly, sometimes indirectly. As a missionary to the Mohawks commented in 1715, "The Indians have Lately done a great deale of mischief in South Carolina having cut off a great many inhabitants but as we are very well informed, it is what they [the settlers] have brought upon themselves by abus[in]g the Indians with drink and then cheat them in Trading with them and Stealing Even their Child[re]n away and carry them to other places and sell them for slaves."[2] In 1636–37, in the Pequot War, whites descended to attacks on Indian property and noncombatants to gain their ends, burning Indian villages and crops and massacring the Indians they could find. They had brought with them the custom of enslaving prisoners of war—the Mayflower Compact included just such a proviso. They seized on every excuse. In 1622, for instance, a Virginia settler declared that after the Good Friday massacre of whites, Indians might now "most justly be compelled to servitude and drudgery, and supply the roome of men that labour, whereby even the meanest of the plantation may imploy themselves more entirely in their Arts and Occupations, which are more generous whilest Savages performe their inferiour workes of digging in mynes, and the like."[3]

The colonists made slaves, too, of Indians whom they convicted as criminals for violating white laws. Thus, for example, in 1636 an Indian named Chousop of Block Island was sentenced to "bee kept as a slave for life to worke. . . ."[4] In 1646, the New England Confederation of Colonies (Massachusetts, Plymouth, Connecticut, and New Haven) feared that "it will be chargeable keeping Indians in prison, and if they should escape, they are like to prove more insolent and dangerous after." So they further extended slavery by providing that if an Indian harmed any white citizen's property, the inhabitants of the Indian's village or of any that harbored him might be seized "either to serve or to be shipped out and exchanged for negroes as the cause will justly beare."[5] Such a law encouraged whites to kidnap Indians as slaves and to raid Indian villages.

In December 1675 Carolinians found another way to justify enslaving Indians. They would buy Indian prisoners of war from friendly tribes. "[T]he said Indian prisoners," the Carolinians assured their British proprietors, "are willing to work in this Country, or to be transported fren hence," so enslaving them would not violate the proprietors' order that "no Indian upon any occasion or pretense whatsoever is to be made a Slave, or without his own consent be carried out of Carolina."[6] Besides, they said, only by buying the prisoners could the Carolinians save them from death.

But the settlers' relations with Indians were not monolithic. They treated different tribes differently, some as enemies, some as allies. Thus in King Phillip's War (1675–76), whites and their Indian allies fought against the Wampanoag. André Penicaut's account of a 1702 expedition against the Alabama also illustrates how whites allied themselves with some Indians while attacking others: "Going up the Rivière des Alibamons [Alabama River], seventy leagues upstream on the left side he [Boisbriant] came upon six Alibamon boats, which made him believe that there must be Alibamons off hunting in the vicinity. He sent a French soldier with a Canadian to reconnoiter. . . . He quickly led his men up close to them without making any noise. At once he had us fire a volley. All the savages were killed, only women and their children being spared; they were taken away as slaves to Mobile along with their boats loaded with their game. The Mobiliens, our neighbors six leagues away and allies of the Alibamons, saw us pass with these slaves on our way back to Mobile. They came to M. de Bienville and asked him for them, begging him to kindly give them to them, as these captives were their kin. M. de Bienville granted their request. This act of generosity . . . caused the Mobiliens later on to unite with us in the wars we carried on against the Alibamons."[7] In 1715, South Carolina agreed to reward any Tuscarora who captured any of the colony's Indian enemies with the return of a Tuscarora slave. Whether allies or enemies, the Indians suffered, as war's havoc was multiplied by starvation and deaths from the diseases that the Europeans brought with them, diseases to which the Indians had no immunity.

Alliances with Indians, the dependence of some early colonists on Indians for survival, and white respect for Indians as warriors produced an attitude toward Indians different from attitudes toward blacks. Whites held themselves superior to all other races, but they had higher opinions of Indians generally than of blacks. Their feelings about interracial sexual relationships demonstrate this contrast. Officially—though certainly not in practice—black-white relationships were taboo, but until the 19th century some whites argued for Indian-white intermarriage, insisting that it would improve the character of Indians. The ardent American patriot Patrick Henry called for governmental tax incentives and cash stipends to encourage it, and during his presidency Thomas Jefferson proposed, "Let our settlements and [Indians] meet and blend together, to intermix, and become one people."[8] Such sentiments did not encourage the enslavement of Indians.

Nevertheless the colonies, North and South, continued the practice. For instance, in Bacon's Rebellion, which began in a conflict over how to treat with the Indians, the Virginia Assembly in 1676 in effect granted Nathaniel Bacon a slave-hunting license by "providing that any enemy Indians [whom his soldiers] caught were to be their slaves for life," and in 1677 by ordering that these soldiers should "reteyne and keepe all such Indian slaves or other Indian goods as they either have taken *or hereafter shall take*."[9] In 1685, Chief Caruee reported an incident in a dispute between the Spanish and the British for the Indian trade: "[A]bout 3 months agoe the Scotts settled at Port Royal did send Caleb Westbrooke & Aratomahan, a chieftain among them, to the Yamasses to encourage them to make warr with the Timecho Indians who are Christians and had a Spanish Fryer [friar] and a Chappell among them which they agreeing to the Scotts furnished them with 23 fyre Arms in order to distroye the sd [said] Timechos that thereupon they proceeded and burnt several Towns and in particular the said Chappell and the Fryer's house and killed fifty of the Timechoes and brought away Two and Twenty prisoners which they delivered to the Scotts as slaves."[10]

American colonists thus incited wars among Indians. In 1715, a missionary commented on such provocations: "It is certain many of the Yammousees and Creek Indians were against the war all along. But our military men were so bent upon revenge, and so desirous to enrich themselves by making all the Indians slaves that fall into yr [their] hands . . . that it is in vain to represent the cruelty and injustice of such a procedure."[11]

Even when colonial and state governments sporadically tried to prevent them, white traders encouraged Indians to raid other tribes for slaves, whom the traders then bought, often cheating the Indians in the process. The Carolina proprietors (holders of royal grants, through 1729) seem at least from time to time to have tried especially hard to prevent such raids. In 1680, they issued instructions that "[P]eace and a friendly correspondence with the Indians that are our Neighbors . . . cannot be expected long to continue without due care be taken for the equall Administration of Justice to them and to preserve them from being wronged or oppressed. . . . [T]ake special care not to suffer any Indian that is in League or friendly correspondence with us and that lives within 200 miles of us to be made slaves or sent away from the country without special directions from us."[12] But the very frequency of such messages suggests how little they were heeded. Captain Moore of North Carolina in 1760 reported a direct defiance of orders. After his soldiers had captured some Cherokees, he said, "I allowed that it was our Duty to Guard Them to prison, or some place of safe Custody till we got the approbation of the Congress Whether they should be sold Slaves or not, and the Greater part [of my men] Swore Bloodily that if they were not sold for Slaves upon the spot, they would Kill & Scalp them Immediately. Then the 3 prisoners was sold for £242. . . . Our men was Very spirited & Eager for Action, and is Very Desirous that your Honour would order them upon a second Expedition."[13] Even orders of the French king to Louisiana colonials in 1720 failed to stop the raids.

Individual whites also kidnapped Indians whom they enslaved, just as they did blacks. In an 1862 letter to the *Liberator,* Rosa Barnwell told of her family's experience: "I was born in Charleston S.C. I was a slave for more than twenty years. My mother was of Indian descent, and a free woman, but was kidnapped by a man named Leo Edwards, and doomed to a life of servitude. She had twelve children, one of whom was sold to Texas. God alone knows her fate. Five others now sleep between the sod, while the rest are still in slavery, and I . . . have escaped to a land of freedom, through the mercy and goodness of God."[14] A Creek Indian, Susan, was betrayed by the family her mother trusted: "A blacksmith, by the name of Jeremiah Taylor, went among the Creek nation, to work for them at smithing," testified a fellow slave. "Susan's mother, a poor woman, gave her to the blacksmith's wife to raise, when she was a little girl: and she became so much attached to the family, that when they left the tribe, she went with them. She says that Mrs. Taylor always told her she would be free, when she was a woman; but before that time arrived, Mr. and Mrs. Taylor both died. Their son John sold Susan, and she has been a slave ever since."[15]

Indians are hunted in Florida with bloodhounds. *(Library of Congress)*

Indian slavery, like black slavery, developed at different rates and resulted in different numbers in different colonies, with more slaves in the South, both Indian and black, and more indentured servants in the North. Other local conditions also modified the practice of slavery. The English colonists in Virginia enslaved fewer Indians than did Carolina settlers, simply because the Virginians needed the food that nearby Indians supplied.

Both a domestic and an international trade in Indian slaves developed. Domestically, masters felt safer if slaves came from farther away, local Indians being far too likely to escape back home. Toward the end of the 17th century, North American settlers experimented with importing Indians from Spanish colonies as slaves. Much more often, however, the North American colonists exported Indian slaves to other places in the New World. In 1520, Spaniards in Carolina tried using North American Indian slaves to work the gold mines of Hispaniola. When, in 1637, Massachusetts settlers captured slaves in the Pequot War, they distributed the females in the towns of Massachusetts and Connecticut but shipped off some of the young boys on the Salem ship *Desire*, which then brought back from the tropics a cargo of tobacco, cotton, and blacks. New England settlers sold into slavery in the West Indies thousands of Indians captured in King Philip's War (1675–76). In 1706, slave owners in Louisiana sought permission from the French king to export Indian slaves in exchange for blacks; when the king repeatedly refused, the settlers began the trade anyway.

In 1707, Florida governor Francisco de Corcoles y Martinez speculated that the Indians that slavers had taken there "must number more than ten or twelve thousand persons."[16]

Indian enslavement, however, contained the seeds of its own destruction. It never proved as successful as early white colonists hoped. It diminished the settlers' chances of maintaining peace and trade with the Indian nations. The Indian slaves they took into their houses or tried to use on their farms were, after all, close to home and knowledgeable about getting around in the countryside. They found escape relatively easy. Whites, in whom slavery inspired a multitude of fears, worried about alliances among Indians, indentured servants, and slaves. Since Indian slaves knew how to run away, might they not teach the blacks, who picked up Indian lore more readily than the whites? Also, true or not, the idea spread that Indians did not work as productively as blacks. The males among them, trained to hunt, fish, and fight, deemed other work proper only for women. In any case, free Indians could be hired for such low wages that it was hardly worthwhile to enslave them.

Even when Indian slaves were shipped so far from home that they could not readily escape, they proved unsatisfactory. For one thing, many Indians thrust into the mines died even faster than the African slaves they worked beside. For another, so strongly did slaveholders prefer blacks to Indians that they would accept Indian slaves only at the rate of two for one black slave. In time, some whites experienced pangs of conscience about enslaving Indians, who had welcomed them to North America and helped them to live in the New World. As white territory moved nearer to them, the powerful tribes and confederations of Appalachians ferociously discouraged Indian enslavement. It also became apparent that the numbers of Indian slaves available, whatever the machinations of the European settlers, could not meet the rapidly rising demands for more workers.

What with all these difficulties, well before 1700 whites gave up on the idea of using Indian slaves as their core workforce. Indian slavery had largely ended by the 1750s, though Indians were occasionally sold in slave markets up into the 1770s, and descendants of Indians who had borne children with blacks continued to be held in slavery.

Even when Indian slavery was at its height, numbers were probably relatively small. In Louisiana, for instance, in 1726 there were 229 Indian slaves but 1,540 black slaves. By the 1760s, the number of Indian slaves had declined to about 225, while the number of black slaves had grown to perhaps 5,000.[17]

Indians Meet Blacks

How soon Indians met blacks depended on their location on the continent and the practices of European explorers and settlers. Spanish explorers in the Southwest and Florida often were accompanied by black slaves. Spanish residents in St. Augustine imported black slaves in 1581. In these ways western and southern Indians met and grew accustomed to blacks early on, so that when Los Angeles was founded in 1781, of the 44 settlers only two were European and the rest African, Indian, or of mixed blood.[18]

Thus in 1529, his Spanish master took black Arab Estevanico on an expedition to Florida, where they were shipwrecked. Four black survivors of the wreck wandered for several years among the Indians of what is now Texas, first as slaves, and after 1535 as medicine men. In 1539, Estevanico, who had by then distinguished himself by his ability to learn languages, reached Spanish settlements in Mexico. There he lived in some luxury, collecting women and gems, until he was sent later that year with two friars to discover the fabled Kingdom of Quivira—carrying with him his harem and accumulated wealth. The North American Indians whom he met on that trip preferred him to the Europeans, so the friars sent him ahead to pacify them. Maybe success went to his head; at any rate the Indians of the Zuni pueblo of Cibola killed Estevanico instead of giving him the women and jewels he demanded. A few years later, in 1541, blacks also accompanied Coronado in his search for the same golden cities.

Farther east and north, however, most Indians encountered blacks only after slavery had grown commonplace in the United States. The mulatto York, who acted as an interpreter on the Lewis and Clark expedition of 1803–6, entertained the Indians by exhibiting feats of strength and telling them that he had been a wild animal, caught and tamed by his master. York may have been a St. Louis black who had picked up some French in Missouri. Apparently he spoke bad French and worse English. The expedition managed after a fashion by having Shoshone guide Sacajawea translate the Indians' speech to her husband, French-Canadian trader Toussaint Charbonneau, who apparently translated it into French for York, who then transmitted it in English to Lewis and Clark.[19] York may even have had a smattering of Indian dialects, for the expedition also employed him to trade with the Indians for food.

The reactions of American Indians to these and later first encounters with blacks varied from fascination to outright terror. The tribes in Virginia, according to a late-18th-century report, were awed, thinking the blacks "a true breed of Devils, and therefore they called them *Manitto* for a great while: this word in their language signifies not only God but likewise the Devil."[20] As late as the mid-19th century a group of runaway blacks led by fugitive Henry Bibb met young Indian warriors, who ran from them. Mrs. Bibb was frightened, sure that the Indians were preparing to attack the family. It turned out, however, that they had fled in fear, never having seen black people before. Their chief reassured his young men, and the tribe received the Bibbs kindly, giving them food, shelter, rest, and advice about the best way to go on.

Indians and Black Slaves

Indians and blacks in North America interacted with each other in every imaginable way—except that as far as we know, blacks did not own Indian slaves. Indians were both enemies and friends of blacks. They both succored black fugitives and hunted them down. They held blacks as slaves, and Indians and blacks toiled side by side as slaves of white masters. They intermarried. Indians married their slaves. In some nations, widows chose black prisoners of war to replace Indian husbands who had died in battle. Indian slaves of whites married black slaves. Black male slaves sometimes preferred to marry free Indian women, knowing that their children would be free. On the other hand, Hugh Jones reported in 1724 that the Virginia Indians "hate, and despise the very sight of a *Negroe*. . . . Such as are born of an *Indian* and *Negroe* are called Mustees."[21]

The complexities of Indian-black relationships are illustrated by a series of questions posed among census officials in 1832: "Sir: We the commissioners engaged in taking the census of the Creek Indians, . . . beg leave to respectfully propose the following questions. . . . If an Indian have living with him as his wife a negro slave, the property either of himself or of another, is he to be considered as the head of a family in the sense contemplated in the instructions transmitted to us and to be enrolled as entitled to a reservation? . . . Is one of mixed blood of Indian and Negro, free, keeping a separate house and having a negro slave for a wife, to be ranked and enrolled in like manner as the Indian is? . . . There is a number of free black families that seem to be in every way identified with these people and the only difference is color. I have taken their number in all cases, but am I to take them as heads of families for reservations or not?"[22]

Bewildered white settlers often could not penetrate Indian attitudes toward blacks. In the early 1850s, for instance, a missionary reported, "Within the past few years the Comanches have (for what reason I could not learn) taken an inveterate dislike to the negroes, and have massacred several small parties of those who attempted to escape from the Seminoles and cross the plains for the purpose of joining Wild Cat upon the Rio Grande. Upon inquiring of them the cause of their hostility to the blacks, [they] replied that it was because they were slaves to the whites and they were sorry for them."[23]

Indians frequently befriended blacks, especially fugitive slaves. In the late 18th century, a black fugitive, Betty, encountered the Indians of Agawam, Connecticut, who sympathized with and sheltered her because they themselves had been slaves.[24] An 1834 account tells of a black fugitive who escaped from his master on the Arkansas River and wandered on the prairies until an Indian hunting party found him. He said that "after he was taken he came ten days with those Indians without anything to eat save some plumbs, berries &c but since he had been living among them they had treated him well and had given him corn mellons Buffaloe meat &c to eat—he appeared very well satisfied with his situation [they] requireing of him nothing but to grave [graze?] their horses."[25] In 1858, Edinbur Randall spoke of the underground railroad conducted by Indians on Martha's Vineyard: "I told them that I thought the sheriff was after me, whereupon the Indians told me to go into a swamp near by. I took their advice, and went into the thickest bushes about one hundred yards, and remained there some time; at length Beaulah Vanderhoof, the Indian woman who took me in to her house, came to the swamp, called me out, and put a gown, shawl, and bonnet upon me, and took me some distance to the house of her grandmother, Mrs. Peters, hid me in the garret, and then went to engage a boat to take me from the island. This aged woman, Mrs. Peters, entered into their plans for my escape, with a will: she declared that she would have a large kettle of hot water ready to scald the sheriff, or any of his understrappers who crossed her threshold."[26]

Blacks learned wilderness survival skills from Indians, and Indians learned about whites from the blacks whom the whites had enslaved. These alliances alarmed whites. "The [black] Slaves that are now come up talk good English as well as the Cherokee Language and . . . too often tell falcities to the Indians which they are very apt to believe," warned one Colonel Chicken in 1725.[27] In 1763, during Pontiac's rebellion: "[T]he Indians are saving and caressing all the negroes they take; should it produce an insurrection, it may be attended with the most serious consequences."[28] It is hard to discern how much or how often these white fears of blacks and Indians joining together against them had any real basis. Such alliances did help individual slaves make their escapes and strengthen Indian tribes in their resistance to white incursions. The presence of the sympathetic Yamasees near St. Augustine helped induce runaway black slaves to leave Carolina for Spanish-ruled Florida. But Indian-black cooperation did not result in the major uprisings of white imaginings.

To the contrary—why, we wonder, did the maroon communities so rarely seek Indian collaboration? Instead, they frequently became antagonists. Some Indians helped whites conquer maroon colonies, just as occasionally maroons joined whites in overcoming Indians.[29]

Nonetheless, white fears persisted, as in a trader's 1751 deposition: "Three runaway Negroes of Mr. Gray's told the Indians, as they said that the white people were coming up to destroy them all, and that they had got some Creek Indians to assist them so to do. Which obtained belief and the more for that the old Warriour of Kewee said some Negroes had applied to him, and told him that there was in all Plantations many Negroes more than white people, and that for the Sake of Liberty they would join him."[30]

In the later days of slavery, Indian friendship for blacks now and then led to Indian advocacy for them. In 1848, for instance, the *Cherokee Advocate* reported the arrest of a Cherokee man on a charge of having sold free blacks as slaves. "At best," the editor wrote, "the situation of the colored race is an unenviable one, and he who rises up in defense of any right they may have, especially the right of freedom, against the cupidity of those who would deprive them of it by unjust means, deserves the thanks of all friends of humanity and justice among us."[31]

Until Europeans came to North America, Indians had not based slavery on race. True enough, Indians usually inflicted slavery only on people who differed from themselves by belonging to different tribes. Indeed some tribes had no concept of race. However, as whites and blacks arrived, Indians, soon observing that whites looked down on blacks, backed away from being identified with a despised race. This new attitude was reinforced by whites who, fearing an alliance between Indians and blacks, strove to make them mutually hostile.

During the American Revolution British agents gave black slaves to Creek chiefs allied with them. Then in the 1790s the new federal government of the United States decided to "civilize" Indians, indoctrinating them with white values. This pressure continued after the founding in 1824 of the bureau-level Office of Indian Affairs, most of whose agents were southern and strongly proslavery. For instance, Elias Rector, superintendent of southern Indian affairs, believed in Indians' owning slaves as a "civilizing" force. Slaves, he thought, "could teach them to cultivate the soil and properly prepare and cook their foods."[32]

Moreover, agents feared that Indians might help runaways. On November 27, 1854, agent Douglas H. Cooper wrote to the Indian Affairs southern superintendent warning, "[S]omething must be done speedily to arrest the systematic efforts of the Missionaries to abolitionize the Indian Country. Otherwise we shall have a great runaway harbor, a sort of Canada—with 'underground rail-roads' leading to & through it—adjoining Arkansas and Texas. . . . I see . . . no way except secretly to induce the Choctaws & Cherokees & Creeks to allow slave-holders to settle among their people & control the movement now going on to abolish slavery among them."[33]

Some Indians, especially in the South, accordingly adopted both racial prejudice and white economic ideas of property—whether of land or of people. Motivated by both this prejudice and economic advantage, Indians recaptured black fugitives for whites, in exchange for either goods or the return of Indian slaves of their own nations. They quickly grasped and profited by the greater worth of capturing blacks over capturing whites, for blacks, having a market value, could always be sold, whereas white captives might or might not be ransomed. By the end of the 18th century, Indians were raiding to capture black slaves and eventually even free blacks to sell.[34]

As whites forced Indians to emigrate westward, more of them moved South, where they learned the status bestowed on owners of black slaves. Numbers of Indians, especially in the more settled and less nomadic tribes of the South, also learned to use black slaves to do the agricultural work hitherto assigned to Indian women. By 1824, the Cherokee owned 1,277 black slaves; by 1861, the Choctaw and Chickasaw laid claim to 5,000 blacks.[35] During the 1820s and 1830s, Indians were some of Georgia's biggest slaveholders; later Greenwood Lefore, a half-white Choctaw chief, owned 400 slaves. By 1860, black slaves constituted 12.5 percent of the population of the Indian Territory.[36]

Among the larger slaveholders were many mustees—people of both white and Indian blood. As plantation owners, some of them sought to obtain more and more land. Their tribes prospered and gained political influence; among Indians, they became a sophisticated elite.

Treatment of black slaves by Indian masters varied from tribe to tribe as well as from individual to individual. Seminoles offered slaves more opportunities, both economic and social, than any other slaveowners. Their slaves lived independently, apart from the masters, cultivating fields cooperatively and tending open-range livestock. They owed their masters only an annual tribute.[37] Some Seminoles and slaves intermarried, and many blacks not only were adopted into the tribe but achieved high position as respected counselors, interpreters, and negotiators with Europeans. The arrangement benefited both Seminole and blacks, for the runaway slaves of whites whom the Seminole accepted as their own slaves had had longer and closer relationships with whites, spoke European languages better, and understood the thinking and customs of their former masters more thoroughly than the Indians.

The other four of the Five Civilized Tribes (so-called because they had developed constitutions, law codes, and judicial systems)—the Cherokee, Choctaw, Chickasaw, and Creek—adopted slave codes, some of them as harsh as those of whites, which grew more severe over time. Indian slaveowners too dealt harshly with mutiny, as when in November 1842 the Cherokee recaptured and executed rebellious slaves.[38]

Slave memories reflect a spectrum of treatment by Indian masters, from lenient to harsh. Of the Creek: "We [slaves] all lived in good log cabins we built. We worked the farm and tended to the horses and cattle and hogs, and some of the older women worked around the owner's house, but each Negro family looked after a part of the fields and worked the crops like they belonged to us."[39] Of a Cherokee: "Young Master never whip his slaves, but if they don't mind good he sell them off sometimes. He sold one of my brothers and one sister because they kept running off."[40]

The Impact of Slavery on Indians

Slavery damaged the Indians: Enslavement disrupted family and tribal relations; their adoption of the white system of black slavery altered their culture and their very character. These changes are most obvious among the Seminole, by tradition the gentlest of slaveholders. For years they lived in amity with their black slaves, mostly fugitives who had sought refuge among them. They shared many descendants. During the Seminole Wars with the United States, Indians and blacks fought side by side. Some in the U.S. military thought of the Second Seminole War as more a war with blacks than with the Indians, noting that blacks counseled the Indians never to make peace unless the terms guaranteed that blacks would not be returned to their former white masters. Indian teams of negotiators for peace included blacks not only as interpreters but also in positions of influence and power. One of them, Abraham, impressed all who saw him. "Abraham is a non-committal man, with a countenance which none can read, a person erect and active and in stature over six feet. He was a principal agent in bringing about the peace, having been a commander of the negroes during the war, and an enemy by no means to be despised. . . . Abraham made his appearance bearing a white flag on a small stick which he had cut in the woods, and walked up to the tent of General Jesup with perfect dignity and composure. He stuck the staff of his flag in the ground, made a salute or bow with his hand, without bending his body, and then waited for the advance of the General with the most complete self-possession. He has since stated that he expected to be hung, but concluded to die, if he must, like a man, but that he would make one more effort to save his people."[41]

As the U.S. government moved Indians willy-nilly off lands the whites wanted, it interfered with the relationships between Indians and their black slaves. Notoriously, this interference hopelessly damaged the relations between the Seminole and their respected black

Abraham was a fugitive slave who escaped to the Seminole, for whom he became an interpreter and negotiator. *(Library of Congress, Prints and Photographs Division, LC-USZ62-75977)*

advisors. After they went west to the Indian Territory, disputes and distrust arose between them. Whites tried to steal some of the Seminole slaves. The Seminole began to fear the blacks and sought to disarm the very allies at whose sides they had fought.

The Civil War and Reconstruction

As historian Annie Abel writes, Indians from Arkansas to Texas "were slaveholding tribes, . . . yet [as the Civil War began] were supposed by the United States government to have no interest whatsoever in a sectional conflict that involved the very existence of the 'peculiar institution.' Thus the federal government left them to themselves at the critical moment and left them, moreover, at the mercy of the South, and then was indignant that they betrayed a sectional affiliation."[42]

Meanwhile, the Confederacy wooed these potential allies, situated in strategically vital areas. Approaching Indians diplomatically with respect for their power to negotiate as separate nations, Confederate representatives offered political equality and a bona fide protectorate. They were aided by U.S. Bureau of Indian Affairs agents, mostly Southerners, who told the Indians that the Union would again violate treaties to seize Indian lands and that they would lose the money that the U.S. government held in trust for them, most of it invested in Southern bonds. These arguments had the force of fact: Northerners indeed wanted Indian lands, whereas Southerners cared mainly that they be settled by slaveholders.

By early April 1861, Confederates had won over most of the slave-holding tribes.[43] Other tribes stayed loyal to the Union, partly because they had never adopted white ideas of enslavement, but also because they remained faithful to the treaties that the United States was even then dishonoring. Arguments split several tribes, like the Cherokee, whose Chief John Ross fought to keep the nation neutral. The slaveholding elite of the Cherokee, Chickasaw, Choctaw, and Creek elected to support the Confederacy, whereas many Indian small farmers, like their Southern white counterparts, chose the Union in protest against class divisions.

Of course Indian decisions to ally with the Confederacy did not ensure the compliance of their slaves. A slave of the Creek, Mary Gibson, whose master supported the South, remembered how in her childhood "we Negroes got word somehow that the Cherokees over back of Fort Gibson was not going to be in the war and that there were some Union people over there who would help slaves to get away. . . . Some upper Creeks came up into the Choska bottoms talking around among the folks there about siding with the North." One morning she awoke to find that her father and all the other male slaves had disappeared. They had been smuggled into Missouri and then into Kansas, where they joined the Union army.[44]

The Confederacy proved no more faithful to its promises to the Indians than had the United States. Consequently, beginning in 1862, many Indians shifted their loyalties from South to North, as nations or individually—in growing numbers as Confederate fortunes waned. On both sides some Indians fought on, despite lack of equipment, inefficient officers, and white prejudice against them. Toward war's end, some tribes began guerilla warfare, particularly in the West, and some of their slaves became desperadoes. Enmities arose between Indians and blacks.

By then impoverished tribes were torn apart by Civil War divisions, by dispersal, and by depredations of their lands and property. Most accepted black emancipation without question, but many balked at incorporating their former slaves into their tribes, for membership meant sharing in the tribal lands and wealth. Tribes declining in numbers while blacks multiplied by natural increase were wary of black domination. They also feared black colonization, for some U.S. officials saw transfer into Indian territory as a painless solution to the problem of what to do with some of the millions of freed slaves. At an 1865 peace council of the federal government and many tribes, the Osage asked, "You told [us red children] also that no white man, except officers, should be allowed in the Indian country. Now you have prohibited the white man, and why do you say that the negro may come in?"[45]

The U.S. government, eager to evade responsibility for the Indians' former slaves, wanted the tribes to admit them as members if the freedmen so opted. John B. Sanborn, sent to deal with this situation, warned the Indians that "the policy of the Government . . . is fixed . . . , and a race famous for its prowess and shrewdness will at once see that they have no interests that can be subserved by placing themselves in a position of antagonism or hostility to the mightiest power of Earth."[46]

Some Indian tribes complied, others dillydallied, and still others flatly refused. The United States compounded the confusion by making different treaties with different tribes. Thus in early 1866, the federal government signed a treaty with the Seminole confiscating their lands for 15 cents an acre, resettling them in a much smaller area of formerly Creek land purchased at 30 cents an acre, and forcing them to incorporate with full tribal rights not only their own former slaves but also other freedmen admitted into the territory. However, the U.S. treaty with the Choctaw and Chickasaw did not require incorporation of blacks, but only a grant of Indian land to blacks and limited civil and political rights.[47]

Freed Indian slaves complained to Congress that they were being denied a share of the U.S. payment for Indian land—even though "the unrequited toil of your petitioners went toward up-building the millions of Cherokee National wealth."[48] Hatred flared. In some tribes blacks fought in vain for the suffrage, protection of their civil rights, and school admission for their children. In desperation some freedmen stole from their former masters, and Indians retaliated by vigilante justice, whipping and killing their captives. Both blacks and Indians terrorized and preyed on white settlers. Right after the Civil War these roving bands and U.S. troops warred, but by 1875 most of the "outlaws" had surrendered.

Relationships between Indians and blacks ranged from affectionate kinship and interdependence to bitter enmity and cruelty. Take, for instance, Cow Tom, a slave who in the 1830s traveled west with his master, Upper Creek Chief Yargee, negotiating for him in several languages and eventually earning his freedom and acquiring property. During the war the settlement of Confederate-allied Lower Creek into his neighborhood forced Cow Tom and his family to take refuge in Union-held Fort Gibson (in what is now Oklahoma), where his importance as interpreter and negotiator with the Union army made him a chief. After the war, as their nation reunited, the Lower Creek tried to remove blacks completely from the nation. With other black interpreters Cow Tom went to Washington to protect black interests in federal payments to the Creek nation, establishing rights that held until the 1970s.[49]

Despite all these difficulties, during Reconstruction and thereafter freedmen dwelling among the Seminole, Creek, Cherokee, and even the Choctaw became the envy of blacks situated among whites, sizable numbers of whom surged into the Oklahoma and Indian territories.

Chronicle of Events

1513

• Ponce de León, the Spanish explorer of Florida, seeks slaves.

1520

• Spaniards in Carolina try to secure Indians as slaves to work in the gold mines of Hispaniola.

1529

• Perhaps the earliest contact between Indians and blacks in North America is made when an Arab, Estevanico, black slave of a Spaniard, accompanies his master on an expedition to Florida.

1540

• Spanish explorer Hernando de Soto forces Indians to serve as carriers for his expedition.

1542

• In Louisiana, the French king's protection is extended to Indians, and their enslavement is forbidden.

1618

• Colonial *Lawes Divine, Morall and Martiall*, authorizing execution of all recaptured servants who have fled to Indian settlements, are repealed.

1620

• The first school for blacks and Indians in North America is established.

1622

• The Powhatan uprising enables colonists to justify enslaving Indians by defining them as enemies.

1637

• The colonial government of Massachusetts and the Narragansett tribe divide Pequot women and children captured in war; the Narragansett apparently adopt theirs, while Massachusetts enslaves those it takes.

1641

• Massachusetts provides for the enslavement of Indians taken in "just wars."

1644

• Governor Willem Kieft of New Netherlands sends two Indian prisoners as a gift to the governor of Bermuda.

1646

• Plymouth declares it legal to seize any Indians.

• The United Colonies (Massachusetts, Plymouth, Connecticut, and New Haven) resolve that if any citizen's property is harmed by an Indian, the inhabitants of his village or any that harbors him may be seized "either to serve or to be shipped out and exchanged for negroes as the cause will justly beare."

1655

• Virginia declares that Indian children brought into the colony by friendly Indians shall not be treated as slaves but as indentured servants, to be instructed in the trades and Christianity.

1656

• A Virginia law promises Indians that their hostages will not be used as slaves.

• A Massachusetts law forbids arming blacks and Indians or permitting them to train with the colony's military companies.

1657

• Virginia forbids masters to sell Indian children bound to them for education or instruction; these children are to be freed at age 25.

• Virginia forbids buying Indians from Englishmen, as the English have "corrupted" [wrongly persuaded] Indians to bring them the children of other Indians "to the great scandall of Christianitie and of the English nation."

1659

• Rhode Island authorizes the enslavement and sale of any Indian who steals cattle or goods exceeding 20 shillings, unless restitution is made.

1660

• The New Netherlands Council resolves to transport to Curaçao recently captured Esopus Indians, "to be employed there, or at Buenaire, with the negroes in the Company's service."

1662

• The Virginia assembly orders the release of a Powhatan Indian wrongly enslaved, because he speaks English perfectly and desires baptism.

- A Virginia law declares that "all Indian servants male or female however procured being adjudged sixteen years of age shall be . . . tythable [taxable]."

1664
- South Carolina settlers begin slave raids against the Stono and Westo Indians.

1667
- Virginia rules that baptism no longer will affect the slave status of either Indians or blacks.

1670
- Virginia divides non-Christian servants into two classes: those imported by ship, who "shall be slaves for their lives," and those, like Indians, who come by land, who "shall serve, if boys or girles, untill thirty yeares of age; if men or women twelve yeares and no longer."
- Virginia forbids frce blacks and Indians, though baptized, to own Christian servants.

1671
- The South Carolina council orders open war on Indians; captives are to be sold abroad as slaves.

1674
- In *re Indian Hoken,* a Massachusetts court orders magistrates to "cause [Hoken] to be apprehended and sold or sent to Barbadoes."

1675
- Massachusetts colonists provoke King Philip's War, in which most of the Wampanoag are killed.
- *August 4:* Colonists sell into slavery about 160 Indians captured in King Philip's War.
- *October:* Colonists sell into slavery 144 Narragansett because their tribe has given sanctuary to Wampanoag old men, women, and children.

1676
- Indians kill a "Negro Servant" belonging to Andrew Harris at Patuxet.
- At Newport, Rhode Island, a bill is passed stating, "No Indian in this colony be a slave but only to pay their debts, or for their bringing up, or courtesy they have received, or to perform covenant, as if they had been countrymen not in war."

- The Virginia assembly provides that enemy Indians caught by Nathaniel Bacon and his soldiers shall be their slaves for life.

1677
- In *re Indian Popannooie,* a Massachusetts court condemns Popannooie, his wife, and his children to perpetual servitude.
- The Virginia assembly orders that soldiers who have captured Indians shall keep them and also any they shall take in the future.

1679
- In Virginia an act is passed declaring that *"for the better encouragement of soldiers,"* whatever Indian prisoners are taken in a war shall be the property of the soldiers taking them.
- New York abolishes Indian slavery, declaring all free except "such as have been formerly brought from the Bay of Campeachy [Compeche, Mexico] and other foreign parts."

1680
- Morgan Godwyn writes *The Negro's and Indians Advocate,* a treatise on the duties of masters of slaves.

1682
- The Virginia assembly makes slaves for life of all imported non-Christian (i.e., Indian or black) servants.

1684
- Louis XIV orders the marquis de la Barre to send all Iroquois prisoners to France to serve in the royal galleys, because "these savages are strong and rebust."

1685
- A New York vessel kidnaps four Indians near Cape Fear and carries them to New York to sell.

1688
- Louis XIV repeats his order for Indian galley slaves.

1689
- Louis XIV returns surviving Indian galley slaves to New France.

1691
- Virginia passes a law repealing the acts of 1679 and 1682 that enslaved Indians, ruling that no Indian may thenceforth be made a slave.

1694

• Carolina decrees that Indians and slaves guilty of setting adrift a boat shall for a first transgression receive 39 lashes and for a second have their ears cut off; Englishmen for the same offense will merely be fined.

1697

• Smallpox from a slave ship spreads 500 miles from Charlestown through the Indian tribes, by way of contaminated trade goods.

Early 1700s

• Especially in the South, some Indians take up a European definition of racial slavery, as a few buy black slaves to use as laborers or translators.

1700–1710

• In the South, British and allied Indian slavers organize large armies and small parties to capture other Indians for the slave trade.

1704

• Indians attacking the house of the Reverend John Williams at Deerfield, Massachusetts, kill his black woman-servant, Parthena, and later his black manservant.

1705

• The death penalty is prescribed for any slave apprehended 40 miles north of Albany without a pass.
• Pennsylvania passes a law forbidding the importation of Indian slaves from North Carolina.
• Virginia declares "Negro, Mulatto, and Indian slaves within this dominion, to be real estate."

1706

• Louisiana settlers request of France that they be allowed to trade Indian slaves in the West Indies for black slaves, at the rate of three Indians for two blacks.
• About this time, against the orders of the French throne, Louisiana residents begin a slave trade with the West Indies, sometimes exchanging two Indian slaves for one black slave.

1708

• A South Carolina law rewards with a gun every friendly Indian who takes prisoner or kills an enemy Indian and empowers commanding officers to buy all captive enemy Indians above 12 years of age and ship them to the West Indies as slaves.
• A Connecticut law forbids trading with any Indian, mulatto, or black servant or slave without the master's approval.

1708

• The number of Indian slaves in the Carolinas is nearly half that of African slaves.

1709

• At Quebec, Jacques Raudot decrees that "all the Pawnis [Indian slaves] and Negroes, who have been brought and who shall be purchased hereafter, shall belong in full proprietorship to those who have purchased them as their slaves."

1711

• The Tuscarora, Coree, and Pamlico Indians, exasperated by trader abuses, war on North Carolina settlers.

1712

• In New York City, 25 Coromantee and Paw Paw blacks, joined by mestizoes captured at sea and enslaved, set fire to a house and kill 10 or 12 whites. They are routed by gunfire.
• Massachusetts prohibits the importation of Indian slaves.

1715

• The South Carolina colony's violation of promises to stop selling Indians into slavery triggers a war with several tribes, in which black slaves fight against the Indians. The colonists' victory pushes the Indian slave-catching field farther inland.

1717

• A complaint is made that New York colony slaves run away, are hidden by the Minisink, and intermarry with Indian women.
• The South Carolina Indian trade is declared a government monopoly.

1718

• The founding of New Orleans ends the struggle between the French and the Chitimachas, in which many Indians had been captured and enslaved.

1719

• A Carolina law rules that owners are to be taxed for Indian slaves at a rate half that for black slaves.

1720

- France orders that Indian raids on other tribes for slaves be stopped in Louisiana; to enforce this order, the Crown later decrees that offending traders are to be seized and their merchandise confiscated.

1721

- The governor of Virginia negotiates with the Iroquois for the return of runaway black slaves.
- The Cherokee are forced to sign a treaty with the South Carolina colony agreeing to return all runaway slaves.

1723

- The Iroquois deny to the governor of New York the presence of runaway slaves among them.

1724

- Trade in Indian slaves in the Carolinas is dying, though occasional instances occur.

1727

- A maroon camp called Natanapalle is discovered in Louisiana, leading the governor to request the termination of the Indian slave trade.

1728

- Louis XV taxes the owners of slaves in Louisiana.

1729

- The governor of Louisiana uses black slaves to exterminate the Choucha, though some of these slaves are recruited to the Indian side by the promise of freedom.
- Blacks support the rising of the Natchez in Louisiana.

1732

- Virginia allows blacks, Indians, and mulattoes to testify in the trials of slaves.

1735

- Louis XV forbids in Louisiana the sale of a female slave or her child if a free colonist has fathered the child. He

An artist's conception of the methods used by patrollers and bounty hunters to capture fugitives *(Library of Congress)*

decrees that after a certain time both mother and child shall be free.

1738

• Indians on patrol for Louisiana's governor capture La Fleur, a runaway black, who accuses his owners of not giving him enough food.

1740

• The Spanish, Indians, and blacks repel Georgia general James Oglethorpe's invasion of Florida.
• The South Carolina Assembly declares all blacks, Indians, mulattos, and mestizos to be slaves "unless the contrary can be made to appear," but the act effectively frees Indian slaves, because, whereas it exempts Indians in amity with the colonists, it assumes already enslaved Indians to be in amity with the colonists.

1748

• Jean Deslandes hires an Indian to accompany 10 of his slaves on an attack against a camp of armed runaways.

1750

• Connecticut rules that any Indian brought into the colony shall be forfeited to its treasury, unless the importer gives security to transport the Indian out within one month.

1751

• South Carolina enjoins traders from taking slaves or free blacks into Indian territory.
• South Carolina prohibits traders from employing "Indians, Negroes, or Slaves."

1760s

• The Lower Creek of Georgia [Seminole] begin to establish settlements in Florida in which runaway black slaves take refuge.

1760

• The South Carolina assembly decides by a margin of one vote not to arm 500 blacks to serve against the Cherokee.
• At the surrender of Montreal, the English guarantee the French colonists their right to hold their black and Indian slaves.
• A North Carolina law rules that Indian prisoners of war are slaves belonging to their captors.

1763–1783

• Florida, under British rule, no longer functions as a haven for runaway slaves, but some slaves flee to or are captured by the Seminole there, who treat them more as vassals and allies than as slaves.

1764–1765

• The Huron, Iroquois, and Delaware (Lenni Lenape) promise once again to give up any runaway slaves, but no record shows any such transaction.

1769

• A 14-year-old black captured by the Cherokee is sentenced to death by torture but is spared thanks to the intervention of an Indian girl.
• *December 7:* Governor Alexander O'Reilly prohibits the enslavement of Indians in the Spanish colonies; the decree does not affect those already enslaved but orders masters to declare before local authorities the number of slaves held and their age, sex, tribe, and market value.

1776

• In the American Revolution colonial forces attack towns of the Cherokee, who have sided with the British. The colonists kill, scalp, or sell into slavery almost every inhabitant.
• A few Cherokee prisoners of war are still auctioned off as slaves in the Carolinas.

1779

• Governor O'Reilly outlaws Indian slavery in Florida.

1781

• Los Angeles is founded by 44 people: two Europeans and the rest African, Indian, or of mixed blood.

1785

• "Negroes, Indians and Mulattoes" are "exempted" from service in the new U.S. Army.
• A posse of Indians receives a reward from the New Orleans *cabildo* [municipal council] for killing a black highwayman.

1790s

• The U.S. government "civilization" program to persuade Indians to adopt white values and lifestyles leads to increasing Indian adoption of racial slavery.

1790

• The Creek agree to return black slaves they have captured.

1790–1794

• A few Indian slaves in the Spanish colonies successfully bring suit against their masters for their freedom.

1794

• The U.S. agent says that the Creek cannot return their black prisoners and suggests that instead the United States compensate their former owners.

1797

• A New Jersey court rules that Indians may be slaves in the state.

1800

• Indian slavery has almost ceased in Lower Canada.

1803

• The slave York travels as manservant to William Clark on the Lewis and Clark expedition, arousing the curiosity and awe of the Indians because of his color.

1806

• The Virginia Court of Appeals holds that it was lawful to enslave Indians only until 1691; thereafter, only Indians descended from a female enslaved lawfully before that date could be slaves.
• The slave York wins his freedom at the end of the Lewis and Clark expedition.

1812–1814

• Spanish, Indians, and blacks repel the so-called American Patriot invasion of East Florida.

1812

• In the Patriot invasion of East Florida, Americans try to take land from the Indians and Spanish. In reaction, black sergeants are sent into South Carolina to instigate slave insurrections and desertions.
• Some Creek form a war party under the name "Red Stick," some blacks participate in these battles, probably as slaves of white enemies.

1813

• *August 30:* In the Creek War, Red Sticks attack Fort Mimms in Alabama, killing almost 500 mestizos and whites, but no blacks.

1814

• General Andrew Jackson crushes the Red Sticks, but a faction of Creek decline to accept the treaty and flee to kin in Florida.
• Runaway black slaves take over a British fort, with its abandoned arms and ammunition, in Spanish territory on the Appalachicola River for their own use and that of their Indian allies; it becomes known as the "Negro Fort."
• After the Creek War the Red Stick Creek transport their slaves with them to join the Seminole in Florida.

1817

• A British agent is reported to be stirring up Seminole and blacks at the mouth of the Appalachicola River, signaling the start of the First Seminole War.

1818

• The First Seminole War (a slave-hunting invasion of Florida) ends informally after Gen. Andrew Jackson captures Bowleg's Town on the Suwanee River; Seminole and black survivors retreat into swamps.

1819

• When the sovereignty of Florida passes from Spain to the United States, Americans face the problem of the Seminole and their black slaves and allies.

1820

• The Cherokee council prohibits the purchase of goods from slaves and forbids masters to allow their slaves to buy or sell liquor.

1823

• The Seminole sign a treaty at Fort Moultrie, agreeing to return all runaway black slaves entering their territory.

1824

• The Cherokee council grants tribe member Shoe Boots's petition for recognition of the legitimacy and citizenship of his three children by a black slave, on condition that "Capt. Shoe Boots cease begetting any more children by his said Slave *woman.*"
• *March 11:* A bureau-level Office of Indian Affairs is established in the U.S. War Department.

1826

• The Seminole return many runaway slaves but complain that some of their own slaves have been seized by whites and that whites are selling blacks to Indians and then claiming them again.

1827

- The Cherokee Nation grants all adult males the vote, excepting "negroes, and descendants of white and Indian men by negro women who may have been set free. . . . No person who is of negro or mulatto parentage, either by the father or mother side, shall be eligible to hold any office or trust under this government. . . ."

1828

- The Cherokee Nation rules that "all free negroes coming into the Cherokee Nation under any pretence whatsoever, shall be viewed and treated, in every respect as intruders, and shall not be allowed to reside in the Cherokee Nation without a permit."
- The Cherokee forbid the marriage of whites and Indians to slaves and make it unlawful for slaves to own property.

1830–1840

- The removal of the Indians from the Gulf states and the consequent opening of new cotton fields motivates many slaves to flee for fear of being sold south.

1832

- Some Seminole chiefs sign the Treaty of Payne's Landing, agreeing to move across the Mississippi into Indian Territory with the Creek, but their reluctance and that of their black allies and counselors lead to the Second Seminole War.

1833

- The United States begins compulsory removal of Indians to the country west of Arkansas and Missouri.

1835

- *March 24:* Colonel James Morgan reports that Texas blacks who wish to join the Mexicans are making overtures to Indians, apparently without result.
- *December 28:* Seminole and blacks in Florida, with the help of plantation slaves, ambush U.S. soldiers on their way to reenforce Fort King, who are betrayed by their slave guide Luis Pacheco; the Second Seminole War begins.

1836

- The Choctaw Nation exiles abolitionists.

1837

- *January 17:* John Caesar, a Seminole black leader in the Second Seminole War, is killed after an attack on a plantation west of St. Augustine.
- *March 6:* Representatives of Seminole chiefs Micanopy and Alligator sign an agreement to suspend hostilities and agree to move the entire nation west; the United States guarantees their safety on the way and allows their negroes, their *bona fide* property, to accompany them.

1838

- General Thomas Sidney Jesup promises the Seminole blacks that if they will surrender, the U.S. government will protect them against capture or kidnapping by whites and send them west as part of the Seminole nation.

1839–1842

- The Cherokee adopt a relatively harsh slave code as well as restrictions on free blacks.

1840s

- Indians east of Mississippi have become biracial.

1841

- The U.S. government decides that the 1832 Treaty of Payne's Landing has canceled all claims against the Indians for any blacks run away or captured before that treaty.
- The Cherokee make the education of blacks illegal.

1842

- More than 20 black slaves owned by Cherokee flee toward Mexican territory, fighting off pursuers until finally captured nearly 300 miles southwest of Fort Gibson.
- A Cherokee law provides that any free black who helps a slave escape shall receive 100 lashes and be exiled.
- *November 15:* Slaves mutiny against their Cherokee masters, who recapture them, punish them, and execute some.

1843

- The Second Seminole War ends.

1845

- A treaty between the Seminole and Creek fails to resolve questions of title to and control of Seminole blacks and causes distrust between blacks and Indians.

- When General Jesup on a visit to Indian Territory sends word to blacks that he considers them free although the Seminole still claim them as slaves, the blacks stop working for the Indians. Many take refuge at Fort Gibson and help in its construction.

1846

- A California magistrate orders the release of enslaved Indians but forbids any Indian who accepts employment to leave without written permission from the magistrate.

1848

- *June 28:* U.S. Attorney General John Y. Mason rules that of the slaves claimed by the Seminole, only those whom Alligator brought in under an agreement with General Jesup are free.

1849

- Marcellus Duval of the Bureau of Indian Affairs asks for troops to disarm the blacks being returned to the Seminole as slaves.
- Wild Cat leads a party of Seminole and Creek, accompanied by about 20 black slave families headed by Gopher John, to Cow Bayou in Texas and then in 1850 to Mexico, where they ask admission as settlers.

1850

- About 300 Seminole and blacks leave Indian Territory, heading across Texas for Mexico, where slavery is illegal. In Mexico, they agree to guard the border in return for grants of land; others follow.
- The U.S. government ends its protection of blacks who have claimed their freedom on General Jesup's promise to all blacks in the Second Seminole War who would give themselves up.
- Under Jim Bowlegs, about 180 blacks leave Indian Territory for Mexico; they are pursued by Creek and white slave traders, who kill some and capture most, returning them to Seminole country.
- Fifteen hundred blacks are reported to be fighting in Texas alongside Comanche resisting the encroachments of white settlers.

1856

- Seminole chiefs seek compensation for the loss of slaves occasioned by General Jesup's promise of freedom to all blacks who would come in or persuade their Indian masters to emigrate westward.

1859

- U.S. Indian Bureau agent for the Cherokee George Butler credits the increasing wealth of the Cherokee to their being slaveholders.
- Kansas whites demand that Indians vacate their territory.

1861

- *February 21:* The Provisional Congress of the Confederate States instructs the Committee on Indian Affairs to look into opening negotiations with Indian tribes.
- *February 25:* The Confederate Committee on Indian Affairs is instructed to investigate appointing agents to Indian tribes.
- *March 12:* Confederate States president Jefferson Davis recommends that the Confederate States organize a Bureau of Indian Affairs.
- *April 8:* The Creek, Cherokee, Seminole, Quapa, and Socks listen favorably to the proposals of Confederate agent James E. Harrison and his colleagues.
- *May:* The Chickasaw resolve to join with other Indian nations for mutual protection and to ally themselves with the Confederacy.
- *May 17:* Cherokee Chief John Ross issues a proclamation of neutrality.
- *May 21:* President Davis approves an act providing for the Confederate States to protect and act as trustee for Indian tribes.
- *May 25:* The Chickasaw formally express their southern sympathies.
- *June 14:* The Choctaw Nation declares itself "free and independent."
- *July 10–October 7:* The Confederate States negotiate treaties of alliance and military support with Indians of the South.

1862

- Soldiers, federal agents, and white civilians and freedmen begin stealing Indian cattle from both tribes allied with the Confederacy and those loyal to the United States.
- *May:* A Cherokee regiment is formed to fight in alliance with the Confederacy, but later that year, after a Union force penetrates their country, the Cherokee return to their loyalty to the United States.

1863

- Large and small groups of Indians from several nations return to their loyalty to the United States.
- The Cherokee abolish slavery.

1864

- *January:* The Creek, Seminole, and Chickasaw, regarding the United States as victorious, run their slaves to Texas for safety.
- *February:* The Choctaw try to resume their alliance with the United States, but the federal government regards them as defectors.
- *March:* The Choctaw try to persuade the Creek, Seminole, Cherokee, Caddo, and Osage to make a stand with them for the Confederacy.
- *October:* The federal government convokes a general council and gets a promise of loyalty from the Chickasaw, Creek, Seminole, Seneca, Quapaw, Shawnee, Osage, Western Miami, Pottawatomie, Wea, Peoria, Kaskaskia, Piankeshaw, Sac, and Fox in attendance.

1865

- The U.S. government demands the abolition of slavery among the Indians and the integration of slaves into the tribes.
- *March 21:* A treaty between the Seminole and the United States abolishes slavery and puts the freedmen on equal footing with the Seminole.
- *May:* The U.S. War Department musters out Indian troops.
- *May 22:* Southern Indians hold a Grand Council, planning to negotiate their own peace and ignoring the desire of Union Indians to penalize tribal members for their support of the Confederacy.

- *September:* At a peace council at Fort Smith the U.S. representative asserts that tribes who supported the Confederacy have "forfeited all rights to annuities, lands and protection by the United States," and promises that "those who have always been loyal, although their nations may have gone over to the enemy, will be liberally provided for and dealt with." He also demands emancipation, abolition, and the incorporation of slaves into the tribes.
- *November 16:* The Commissioner of Indian Affairs rules "that no distinction be made between members of the Cherokee tribe who were held in bondage and those who were free. That in all cases they should receive the same annuities, lands, and educational advantages."

1866

- *January 1:* The United States sends John B. Sanborn to persuade Indians to incorporate blacks into their tribes.
- *July:* The United States makes the first of a series of different treaties with various tribes, beginning with the Seminole.

1876

- By this time more than 300 black ex-slaves are voting in the Creek National Council, but Indian tribes differ widely in their treatment of freedpeople.

Eyewitness Testimony

Enmity between Indians and Blacks

[The Indians were] worse scared than hurt, who seeing a blackamore in the top of a tree looking out for his way which he had lost, surmised he was *Abamacho*, or the devil; deeming all devils that are blacker than themselves: and being near to the plantation, they posted to the English, and entreated their aid to conjure this devil to his own place, who finding him to be a poor wandering blackamore, conducted him to his master.

William Wood, New England Prospect, 1634, quoted in Williams, History of the Negro Race, 173.

We came hither naked and poor as the Worm out of the earth, but you have everything and we that have nothing must love you and can never break the Chain of Friendship that is between us.

Here stands the Governor of Carolina whom we know. This small Rope we shew you is all we have to bind our slaves with and may be broke but you have Iron Chains for yours. We shall bind them as well as we can and deliver them to our Friends again and have no pay for it.

Scalileskin Retagusta, speaking for the Cherokee chiefs in London before the British king, 1730, in Wood, Black Majority, 262.

When [the Negro slaves in North Carolina] have been guilty of these barbarous and disobedient Proceedings [mutiny or insurrection], they generally fly to the Woods, but as soon as the *Indians* have Notice from the *Christians* of their being there, they disperse them; killing some, others flying for Mercy to the *Christians* (whom they have injured) rather than fall into the others Hands, who have a natural aversion to the Blacks, and put them to death with the most exquisite Tortures, they can invent, whenever they catch them.

John Brickell, 1737, in Porter, Negro on the American Frontier, 105.

Polly, a woman of color, was brought before the circuit court [in Indiana] by Lasselle, in obedience to a writ of *habeas corpus.* He stated in his return, that he held her by purchase as his slave, she being the issue of a colored woman purchased from the Indians in the territory northwest of the river Ohio. . . .

1820, in Wheeler, Law of Slavery, 352.

[The slave Swann declares that] he was brought to this country when it was a frontier settlement and much infested with savages. He was then owned by a Mr. Henry Hambleton, whose family was attacked by the Indians and several of them butchered and made captive. Your petitioner is now able to prove that by his own intrepidity and valor he preserved and carried into the fort two of the small [white] children, being closely pursued by the savages and beating them off with a butcher knife. . . .

This day came Charles Hambleton before the undersigned, a Justice of the Peace for the said County, and made oath that he was one of the children then about thirteen years of age rescued by the Negro Swann then owned by his father. And his statement of the affair in his petition is substantially true only not representing in character sufficiently honorable to the petitioner. The affiant perfectly recollects that the Indians pursued the petitioner with this affiant and the other child in his care, and came frequently with tomahawks and knives drawn within ten steps of them, when the petitioner would urge the children on and turn and beat them [the Indians] back with his butcher knife till he got in the house and saved us.

Virginia petition, December 12, 1821, in Johnston, Race Relations, 10, text and n. 26.

Persecution has reared its hideous head, and not only threatened but bound and whipped and tortured some poor creatures who had been in the habit of worshipping the God of Heaven with us. . . . Yesterday . . . my poor family . . . as they were assembled for worship in their usual way in my absence, with a few coloured persons, a band of savage [Creek] monsters rushed in upon them, seized the poor black people, bound them with cords & belts and such other things as were convenient to them; they were then led out one by one to a post in the yard and beat unmercifully, on which post the blood yet remains as a witness against them.

Rev. Lee Compere, May 18, 1828, in "Red Indians, Black Slavery, and White Racism: Interracial Tensions among Slaveholding Indians," quoted in McLoughlin, Ghost Dance, 272.

[Nelson Jackson, one of my slaves, in 1838] was intrusted with a team and wagon for service in Florida, the place of destination being distant about nine hundred miles. [Employed in the transport service of the U.S. Army, Jackson defended two white teamsters against an attack by the Seminole, bringing one, severely wounded, and the body of the other back to camp.] I concluded to set him free not only in justice to himself but that his course through life and his reward may be referred to as an example of all men of color.

Virginia petition, December 6, 1844, in Johnston,
Race Relations, 10–11.

Indians' Enslavement of Each Other

As to ye [the] next Reason alleadged of humanity, it is nor more nor Lesse than this, yt [that] by buying Indians of ye Savanahs you induce them through Couvetousness to your gunns, Powder and shott & other European Commodities to make war upon their neighbours, to ravish the wife from the Husband, kill the father to get ye Child & burne and Destroy ye habitations of these poore people into whose country wee are charefully [cheerfully] Reced [received]. By them, Cherished and supplyed when we were weake or at least never have done us hurt & after wee have set them on worke to do all these horrid wicked things to get slaves to see ye Dealers in Indians call it humanity to buy them and thereby keep them from being murdered. . . .

Wee are further informed, ye Westohs would have peace & sent some of their people to ye Savanahs to mediate for them but their messengers were taken & sent away to be sold, so would ye poore Winahs, but wee are informed, yt their messingers were Layed hold of & sent away also, but if there be peace with ye Westohs and Waniahs, where shall ye Savannahs get Indians to sell ye Dealers in Indians so yt wee are convinced ye sending away of Indians made ye Westoh and Winiah Wars & Continue them & will not only continue them but make other Warrs if ye Indians are suffered still to be sent away. . . .

The Carolina proprietors, 1683, in Olexer, Enslavement of
the American Indian, 114.

Having got information that some French-Canadians living among the Cascassias Illinois were inciting the savage nations in the environs of this settlement to make war upon one another and that the French-Canadians themselves were participating in order to get slaves that they afterwards sold to the English, MM. Dartaguet and de Bienville dispatched M. d'Eraque with six men in a boat with letters for the Reverend Jesuit Fathers and presents for the savages to induce them to make peace among themselves. When M. d'Eraque reached the Cascassias Illinois, he delivered the letters . . . and forbade the French-Canadians to engage in further warfare with the savages or to incite them to war. He then addressed the savages, urging them . . . to live at peace with other savages, and then gave them the presents. . . .

André Penicaut's account of the 1706 situation, in Olexer,
Enslavement, 205.

There is a Nation of INDIANS call'd the YAMASEES, who formerly liv'd under the SPANISH Government, but now live under the ENGLISH, about 80 Miles from CHARLES-TOWN. Some of these INDIANS going a-hunting, about 200 miles to the Southward, met with some SPANISH INDIANS that lived about Sancta Maria, not far from AUGUSTINE, the Seat of the SPANISH Government; and taking them prisoners, brought them Home, designing to sell them for Slaves to Barbadoes or Jamaica as was usual; but I understanding thereof, sent for their King, and ordered him to bring these INDIANS with him to CHARLES-TOWN, which accordingly he did: There were three Men and one Woman; they could speak SPANISH, and I had a JEW for an Interpreter, so upon examination I found they profess'd the Christian Religion as the papists do: upon which I thought in a most peculiar manner, they ought to be freed from Slavery; and thereupon order'd the King to carry them to Augustine, to the Spanish governour with a Letter. . . .

Former Carolina governor John Archdale, 1707, in Olexer,
Enslavement, 125.

Indian Friends and Allies of Black Slaves

It was a runaway negro taught them [the Indians] to fortify thus [with hidden tree limbs, reeds, and canes set into the ground at an angle, so that advancing enemies would impale their legs on them], named Harry, whom Dove Williamson sold into Virginia for roguery & since fled to the Tuscaruros. . . . I never saw such subtill [subtle] contrivances for Defence.

Col. John Barnwell of South Carolina, 1712, in Wood,
Black Majority, 129–30 n.

Arrived at the Pallachocola Town. Two Spaniards, on[e] Negro, and four Commantle Indians. . . . The Spanyard was Shye of Comeing into the Square for Some Time but the Negro Sat in the Square in a Bould Manner. . . .

[I intend to take him since] though he has Been Taken by the Yemasees and Lived among the Spanyards Yet that dis [does] not make him free. . . .

[The Spaniards] appeared in Behalf of the negro Assuring me that he was a Good Christian [and offering to ransom him with two Indian slaves]. . . .

There being a[nother] Negro then in the Pallachocole town Belonging to Andrew Partoson of Port-Royal, I sent five White men to take him and bring him to me. They Accordingly Took the Negro and had him, but the King of the Town Cutt the Rope and threw it into the fire and the King of sd [said] Town told the White men that they had as Good Guns as they, and Could make use of them; upon which the white man Returned unto me. . . .

Capt. Tobias Fitch, journal entries, 1725 mission to the Cherokees, in Porter, Negro on the American Frontier, *173–75.*

There was danger of the Choctaws determining to fall upon the city [New Orleans], if it should be deprived of all its troops; and the Negroes, to free themselves from slavery, might join them, as some had done with the Natchez.

Father Mathurin Le Petit, letter of July 12, 1730, in Olexer, Enslavement, *221.*

The half-Breed Fellow who came down from the Cherokee Nation in Company with James Maxwell, did seduce 6 of my Negroes to run away from me into the Cherokees, from whence they might depend on their Freedom. They proceeded on their way as far as Broad River, and there three of them receded from whom I have this Account. There is many Circumstances to coroborate [*sic*] the Truth. As he is a subtil Fellow, he may have the like Influence on many Slaves in South Carolina.

South Carolinian's account, 1751, in Perdue, Slavery and Cherokee Society, *38.*

[The Arikaras] are much pleased with my black Servent [York]. Their women verry fond of carressing our men &c. . . . I ordered my black Servent to Dance which amused the crowd [of Mandans] verry much, and Somewhat astonished them, that So large a man should be active &c. &c.

Capt. William Clark, journal entry 1804–6, in Porter, Negro on the American Frontier, *13.*

Very few of them [the Massachusetts Indians] are of unmixed blood, the number of pure Indians is very small, say fifty or sixty, and is rapidly decreasing. The mixture of blood arises far more frequently from connection with Negroes than with white.

Jedidiah Morse, report to the secretary of war, 1822, in Johnston, Race Relations, *273.*

[In Ohio on our escape to Canada in 1830, my family and I] discerned some persons approaching us at no great distance. . . . [T]he advance of a few paces showed me they were Indians. . . . I walked along coldly, till we came close upon them. They were bent down with their burdens, and had not raised their eyes till now; and when they did so, and saw me coming towards them, they looked at me in a frightened sort of a way for a moment, and then, setting up a peculiar howl, turned round, and ran as fast as they could. There were three or four of them, and what they were afraid of I could not imagine. . . . [W]e heard their wild and prolonged howl, as they ran, for a mile or more. . . . As we advanced, we could discover Indians peeping at us from behind the trees, and dodging out of sight if they thought we were looking at them. Presently we came upon their wigwams, and saw a fine-looking, stately Indian, with his arms folded, waiting for us to approach. He was, apparently, the chief; and saluting us civilly, he soon discovered that we were human beings, and spoke to his young men, . . . and made them come in and give up their foolish fears. And now curiosity seemed to prevail. Each one wanted to touch the children, . . . and as they shrunk away, and uttered a little cry of alarm, the Indian would jump back too. . . . However, a little while sufficed to make them understand whither we were going, and what we needed; and then they supplied our wants, fed us bountifully, and gave us a comfortable wigwam for our night's rest. The next day we resumed our march. . . . They sent some of their young men to point out the place where we were to turn off, and parted from us with as much kindness as possible.

Josiah Henson, describing his family's escape from slavery, Life, *66–67.*

The council decided that the Cherokee would "resist this oppression and illegal wrong attempted to be practiced on our Brother and Sister . . . in carrying into slavery Two of whom have been and are considered native Cherokee."

The "Two" were the black woman Chickaw and her son by a Cherokee father. In the 1770s, the Cherokee Deer clan had adopted Chickaw when a white trader had bought her and presented her to his in-laws, members of that clan, to replace his wife, whom he had killed. In 1833, a white woman tried to claim the two as her slaves, having inherited Chickaw from her father. Quoted in Perdue, "Mixed Blood" Indians, *5.*

Many [slaves] have escaped to and joined the Indians, and furnished them with much important information, and if strong measures were not taken to restrain our

Representation of massacres in Florida of whites by blacks and Indians, December 1835–April 1836 *(Library of Congress)*

slaves, there is but little doubt that we should soon be assailed with a servile as well as Indian war.

Major Benjamin A. Putnam, July 31, 1836, to the secretary of war, in Porter, Negro on the American Frontier, *270.*

It seemed that after the Friars I have mentioned and the Negro [Estevanico de Dorantes, black slave of a Spanish master,] had started [on an 1838 excursion to find the seven legendary golden cities of Cibola, with Estevanico as guide], the Negro did not get on well with the Friars because he took the women that were given him and collected turquoises and got together a stock of everything. Besides, the Indians in those places through which they went got along better with the Negro because they had seen him before. . . . [Estevanico] thought he could get all the reputation and honor himself, and that if he should discover those settlements with such famous high houses, alone, he would be considered bold and courageous. . . . For three days [the Cibolans] made inquiries about him and held a council. The account which the Negro gave them of two white men who followed him, sent by a great lord, who knew about the things in the sky, and how these were coming to instruct them in divine matters, made them think that he must be a spy or a guide from some nations who wished to come to conquer them, because it seemed to them unreasonable to say that the people were white in the country from which he came and that he was sent by them, he being black.

Soldier-chronicler Castaneda, member of the excursion, in Berlin, Reidy, and Rowland, Black Military Experience, *12, 13, 15.*

Now he [Wild Cat] come back [from Mexico] with enticing news, and want to carry his people in that nation; and the negroes, he told them if they emigrate to that country,

they will all be freed by the government. This is good news to the negroes. I am told some are preparing to go.

Chief McIntosh, September 23, 1850, in Littlefield, Africans and Seminoles, *154.*

Indian Masters and Black Slaves

My parents were slaves in New York State. My master's sons-in-law . . . came into the garden where my sister and I were playing among the currant bushes, tied their handkerchiefs over our mouths, carried us to a vessel, put us in the hold, and sailed up the river. . . . The white men sold us at Niagara to old Indian Brant, the king. . . .

Brant's third wife, my mistress, was a barbarous creature. She could talk English, but she would not. She would tell me in Indian to do things, and then hit me with any thing that came to hand, because I did not understand her. I have a scar on my head from a wound she gave me with a hatchet: and this long scar over my eye, is where she cut me with a knife. The skin dropped over my eye; a white woman bound it up. . . . Brant was very angry, when he came home, at what she had done, and punished her as if she had been a child. Said he, "You know I adopted her as one of the family, and now you are trying to put all the work on her."

Sophia Pooley, in Drew, Refugee, *192, 194.*

When a barbarian has split the head of his slave with a hatchet, he says, "It is a dead dog—there is nothing to be done but to cast it upon the dung hill."

Saying of Jesuit missionaries about the Iroquois, in Lauber, Indian Slavery, *41.*

[Cherokees take their slaves on hunting trips, where they are] employ'd to carry Burdens, to get bark for the Cabins, and other Servile Work; also to go backward and forward to their Towns, to carry News to the old People, whom they leave behind them.

John Lawson, A New Voyage to Carolina, *1709, quoted in Perdue,* Slavery and Cherokee Society, *15.*

A white man sells us a Negro, and then turns around and claims him again, and our big father [the U.S. government] orders us to give him up.

Seminole chief John Hicks, 1829, in Porter, Negro on the American Frontier, *243.*

Abraham was the most noted and for a time an influential man in the [Seminole] nation. He dictated to those of his own color, who to a great degree controlled their [Seminole] masters. They were a most cruel and malignant enemy. For them to surrender would be servitude to the whites; but to retain an open warfare, secured to them plunder, liberty, and importance.

U.S. Army officer, 1837, quoted in Porter, Negro on the American Frontier, *62.*

The negroes exercised a wonderful control. They openly refused to follow their [Seminole] masters, if they removed to Arkansas. Many of them would have been reclaimed by the Creeks, to whom some belonged. Others would have been taken possession of by the whites, who for years had been urging their claims through the government and its agents. In Arkansas, hard labor was necessary for the means of support, while Florida assured them of every means to indulge in idleness, and enjoy an independence corresponding with their masters. In preparing for hostilities they were active, and in the prosecution blood-thirsty and cruel. It was not until the negroes capitulated, that the Seminoles ever thought of emigrating.

U.S. Army officer in the Seminole War, quoted in Porter, Negro on the American Frontier, *58–59.*

Most of the labor among the wealthier classes of Cherokees, Chocktaws, Chickasaws, Creeks, and Seminoles, is done by negro slaves; for they have all adopted substantially the Southern system of slavery.

Trader Josiah Gregg, after 1838, in Perdue, Slavery and Cherokee Society, *72.*

Comanches steal negroes sometimes from Texas and sell them to Cherokees and Creeks. The latter have been known to pay $400 and $500 for a negro.

U.S. government investigator, 1841–42, quoted in Porter, Negro on the American Frontier, *69.*

My pappy was a kind of a boss of the negroes that run the [river]boat, and they all belong to old Master Joe [Vann, a Cherokee]. Some had been in a big run-away and had been brung back, and wasn't so good, so he kept them on the boat all the time mostly. . . . My pappy run away one time, four or five years before I was born, mammy tell me, and at that time [in 1842] a whole lot of Cherokee slaves run off at once. They got over in Creek Country and stood off the Cherokee officers that went to git them, but pretty soon they give up and come home. Mammy says they was lot of excitement on old Master's place and all the negroes mighty scared, but he didn't sell my pappy off. He jest kept him, and he was a good negro after that. He had to work on the boat, though, and never got to come home but once in a long while.

Ex-slave Betty Robertson, in Perdue, Slavery and Cherokee Society, *83.*

[A surviving Vann slave] said that [in the fall of 1844] my grandfather was on the top deck [of his boat the *Lucy Walker*], entertaining the passengers at a ball and dinner and there was a good deal of drinking. They were having a race with another boat on the river and though they were a little ahead of the other boat my grandfather came down to the boiler deck drunk and he told the negro to throw another side of meat on the fire in order to get more steam so that they could gain on the other boat. The negro told him that the boat was carrying every pound of steam it could stand and Joe Vann [a Cherokee] pulled his pistol on the negro and told him that if he did not obey him he would shoot him. The negro threw the side of meat on the fire as he was ordered and then turned and ran to the stern of the boat and jumped into the river, and he had not much more than got into the water when the boilers blew up.

Memoirs of R. P. Vann, the grandson of Joe Vann, in Perdue, Slavery and Cherokee Society, *103.*

One time he [Cherokee Ben Johnson] whipped a whole bunch of the men on account of a fight in the quarters, and then he took them all to Fort Smith to see a hanging. He tied them all in the wagon, and when they had seen the hanging he asked them if they was scared of them dead men hanging up there. They all said yes, of course, but my old uncle Nick was a bad negro and he said, "No, I ain't a-feared of them nor nothing else in this world," and old Master jumped on him while he was tied and beat him with a rope, and then when they got home he tied old Nick to a tree and took his shirt off and poured the cat-o-nine-tails to him until he fainted away and fell over like he was dead. I never forgot seeing all that blood all over my uncle, and if I could hate that old Indian any more I guess I would, but I hated him all I could already I reckon.

Ex-slave Sarah Wilson, in Perdue, Slavery and Cherokee Society, *117–18.*

[D]uring slave times, it was the duty of the slave women to do the spinning and weaving. Many an old Indian woman, who was used to having slaves do this work for them, learned the art . . . after we were set free. . . . The Negro men did the shearing, and the women washed the wool, carded it into small bats, and sorted it for quality, then spun it into threads or yarn. . . . The very coarsest was knit into socks, and that was a job of itself, for socks were worn out so fast, that it required all the extra time in knitting.

Eliza Whitmore, interviewed in 1938, quoted in Minges, Black Indian Slave Narratives, *37.*

[Indian] Louis Ross had not been a very kind master to his slaves . . . , but when it came time to leave they . . . were afraid the Northern soldiers could not protect them, and get them out of the country as they said they would. . . .

The soldiers told the slaves they had earned everything their masters had many times over, and told them now was the time to get it. They made us load everything we could find. . . . [When they left us] the soldiers gave us plenty to live on, and left us plenty of ox teams and wagons, and about five hundred head of cattle. The slaves were so frightened about their former masters following them and catching them with all their stuff, that they turned loose about five hundred head of cattle, and broke up all the fine furniture and looking glasses, as soon as the soldiers got out of their sight. If we had kept all the cattle they gave us, we would have fared well, but as it was we nearly starved to death before the War was over.

Moses Lonian, interviewed in 1937, describing events of 1862, quoted in Minges, Black Indian Slave Narratives, *60–61.*

After de War was over, Old Master tell me I am free, but he will look out after me 'cause I am just a little Negro, and I ain't got no sense. . . . Well, I go ahead and make me a crop of corn, all by myself, and then I don't know what to do wid it. I was afraid I would get cheated out of it, 'cause I can't figure and read, so I tell Old Master about it, and he bought it off'n me. . . . Master give me

over to de National Freedmen's Bureau, and I was bound out to a Cherokee woman. . . . But later on, [as part of the United States treaty with the Cherokee Indians] I got a Freedman's allotment. . . . I always think of my old master as de one dat freed me, and anyways, Abraham Lincoln and none of his North people didn't look after me, and buy my crop right after I was free, like old Master did. Dat was de time dat was de hardest, and everything was dark and confusion.

Morris Sheppard, interviewed in 1937, quoted in Minges, Black Indian Slave Narratives, *70–73 passim.*

Indian Slaves

[Since the Indians of Florida] can never be made submissive and become Christians, [they should be] placed on ships and scattered throughout the various islands, and even on the Spanish Main, where they might be sold as His Majesty sells his vessels to the grandees in Spain.

Interpreter Hernando de Escalante Fontanedo, 1560s or 1570s, in Lauber, Indian Slavery, *48.*

But one Thomas Hunt, the Master of this ship . . . betrayed four and twenty of those poor salvages [savages] aboard his ship, and most dishonestly and inhumanly, for their kind usage of me and all my men, carried them with him to Malaga; and there for a little private gain, sold these silly [innocent] salvages for rials of eight; but this vile act kept him ever after from any more employment to those parts. . . .

Capt. John Smith, 1614, in Olexer, Enslavement, *34–35.*

Came home and found my Indian girl had liked to have knocked my Theodorah on the head by letting her fall. Whereupon I took a good walnut stick and beat the Indian to purpose till she promised to do so no more. . . .

Peter Thatcher of Massachusetts, diary entry of about 1674, in Olexer, Enslavement, *55.*

And it shall be lawful, and is hereby warranted, for him to make sale of such prisoners as they think meet (they being such as the law allows to be kept).

Instructions of the governor of Massachusetts to Capt. Benjamin Church to attack Indians, January 15, 1676, in Lauber, Indian Slavery, *142.*

[U]pon a beare information [mere accusation] of Indians . . . without ever inquiring into the truth of ye [the] thing or ever sending to ye Waniahs to let them know ye Information had been given to ye govermt yt [that] such a murder was Comited by some of their people, demanding thereupon ye persons guilty of ye fact, a warr is proclaimed against them and pore Innocent women and Children Barberously murdered taken and sent to be sold as slaves, who in all probability had been innocent of ye fact had any such been Comited.

The Carolina proprietors, letter to the council and governor, 1683, in Olexer, Enslavement, *115.*

[The North Carolina Indians] are not of so robust and strong Bodies as to lieft [lift] great Burdens and endure Labour and slavish Work, as the Europeans are; yet some that are Slaves, prove very good and laborious; But, of themselves, they never work as the English do, taking care for nor farther than what is absolutely necessary to support Life, In Traveling and Hunting, they are very indefatigable; because that carries a Pleasure along with the Profit. . . . Most of the Savages are much addicted to Drunkeness, a Vice they never were acquainted with, till the Christians came amongst them. . . .

John Lawson, 1709, in Olexer, Enslavement, *142.*

Our Traders have promoted Bloody Warrs this last Year to get slaves and one of them brought lately 100 of those poor Souls. . . . I don't know where the fault lyes but I see 30 Negroes at Church for an Indian slave, and as for our free Indians—they goe their own way and bring [up] their Children like themselves with little Conversation among us. I generaly Pceive [perceive] something Cloudy in their looks, an Argumt. [sign] I fear, of discontent. I am allso Informed yt. [that] Our Indie Allyes [the Yamasees] are grown haughty of late.

Minister Francis LeJau, 1712, in Wood, Black Majority, *143 n.*

[These Indian wars are God's punishment upon the slave owners.] All we can doe is, to lament in Secret those Sins, which have brought this judgement upon us. Our Military Men are so bent upon Revenge, and so desirous to enrich themselves, by making all the Indians Slaves that fall into their hands, but such as they kill . . . that it is in vain to represent to them the Cruelty and injustice of Such a procedure.

Anglican vicar Gideon Johnston, 1715, in Ball, Slaves, *95.*

[T]hese Indian slaves being mixed with our negroes may induce them to desert with them, as has already happened, as they may maintain relations with them which

might be disastrous to the colony when there are more blacks.

Louisiana governor Etienne Boucher de Perier, 1727, in Usner, "American Indians," 108.

The French army re-embarked and carried the Natchez as slaves to New Orleans, where they were put in prison; but afterwards, to avoid the infection, the women and the children were disposed of on the King's plantation and elsewhere. Among these women was the Female Sun, called the Stung Arm, who then told me all she had done in order to save the French. Some time after, these slaves were embarked to St. Domingo, in order to root out the nation in the colony.

Antoine Simon LePage du Pratz, describing actions of 1730, in Olexer, Enslavement, *227.*

I am very glad that your excellency has given orders to have the Indian children returned, who are kept by the traders as pawns or pledges as they call it, but rather stolen from them (as the parents came at the appointed time to redeem them, but they sent them away before hand), and as they were children of our Friends and Allies, and if they are not returned next Spring, it will confirm what the French told the Six Nations (viz.): that we looked upon them as slaves or negroes, which affair gave me a great deal of trouble at that time to reconcile.

Indian commissioner Johnson to New York governor Clinton, 1750, in Lauber, Indian Slavery, *200–1.*

[Indian slaves] are also full of pride and resentment, and will not hesitate to kill their masters in order to gratify their revenge of a supposed injury. The girls are more docile, and assimilate much sooner into the manners of civilization.

John Long, journal of 1768–82, in Olexer, Enslavement, *87.*

The Indians from Stono came down in straggling parties and plundered the fruits of labor and industry. Being accustomed to the practice of killing whatever came in their way, they ranked the planters' hogs, turkeys, and geese among their game and freely preyed upon them. The planters as freely made use of their arms in defence of their property, and several Indians were killed during their depredations. This occasioned a war and the Indians poured their vengeance indescrimanately, as usual, on the innocent and guilty for the loss of their friends. Governor West found it necessary to encourage and reward such of the colonists as would take the field against them for the public defence. Accordingly a price was fixed on every Indian the settlers could take prisoner and bring to Charlestown. These captive savages were disposed of to the traders, who sent them to the West Indies and there sold them for slaves.

Alexander Hewatt, 1779, in Olexer, Enslavement, *103.*

Professor Dew is of opinion that the introduction of slavery among the Indians of this country, would have averted the approaching annihilation of the aboriginal race. . . . "Slavery [he says] . . . appears to be the only means that we know of, under heaven, by which the ferocity of the savage can be conquered, his wandering habits eradicated, his slothfulness—by which, in fine, his nature can be changed."

The South Vindicated *(1836), 102–3.*

I belonged to the Rev. Adam Runkin, a Presbyterian minister in Lexington, Kentucky.

My mother was of mixed blood,—white and Indian. She married my father when he was working in a bagging factory near by. After a while my father's owner moved off and took my father with him, which broke up the marriage. She was a very handsome woman. My master kept a large dairy, and she was the milk-woman. . . . A man who belonged to the [Masonic] lodge saw my mother when she was about her work. He made proposals of a base nature to her. When she would have nothing to say to him, he told her that she need not be so independent, for if money could buy her he would have her. My mother told old mistress, and begged that master might not sell her. But he did sell her. My mother had a high spirit, being part Indian. She would not consent to live with this man, as he wished; and he sent her to prison, and had her flogged, and punished in various ways, so that at last she began to have crazy turns. . . . She tried to kill herself several times, once with a knife and once by hanging. She had long, straight black hair, but after this it all turned white, like an old person's. When she had her raving turns she always talked about her children. The jailer told the owner that if he would let her go to her children, perhaps she would get quiet. . . .

At last her owner sold her, for a small sum, to a man named Lackey. While with him she had another husband and several children. After a while this husband either died or was sold, I do not remember which. The man then sold her to another person, named Bryant. My own father's owner now came and lived in the neighborhood of this man, and brought my father with him. He had had another wife and family of children where he had been living. He and my mother came together again, and finished their days together. My mother almost recovered her mind in her last days.

I never saw anything in Kentucky which made me suppose that ministers or professors of religion considered it any more wrong to separate the families of slaves by sale than to separate any domestic animals.

Lewis Hayden, 1853 autobiographical account, in Blassingame, Slave Testimony, *695–96.*

Marster only whipped when they needed it. The Indians were not whipped. They did what he wanted and worked steady, and he 'pended on them a lot.

Della Bibles, Waco, Texas, October 1937, in Minges, Black Indian Slave Narratives, *32.*

Indian Relations with Maroon Blacks

In our Quarrels with the *Indians,* however proper and necessary it may be to give them Correction, it can never be our interest to extirpate them, or to force them from their Lands: their Grounds would be soon taken up by runaway *Negroes* from our Settlements, whose Numbers would daily increase and quickly become more formidable Enemies than *Indians* can ever be, as they speak our Language and would never be at a Loss for Intelligence [news, information].

Indian policy in the colony of South Carolina, in Perdue, Slavery and Cherokee Society, *40.*

It will be difficult to form a prudent determination, with respect to the maroon negroes, who live among the [Seminole] Indians [in Florida]. Their number is said to be upwards of three hundred. They fear being again made slaves, under the American government; and will omit nothing to increase or keep alive mistrust among the Indians, whom they in fact govern. If it should become necessary to use force with them, it is to be feared that the Indians would take their part.

Indian agent reporting on plans to move the Seminole west after the United States acquired Florida in 1819, in Blassingame, Slave Community, *122–23.*

[T]here are negroes enslaved in the Indian Territory: the descendants of the bravest warriors America has produced—the hunted maroons, who, for forty years, in the swamps of Florida, defied the skill and armies of the United States. They hate slavery and the race that upholds it, and are longing for an opportunity to display that hatred. Not far from this territory, in a neighboring province of Mexico, live a nation of trained negro soldiers—the far-famed Florida Indians, who, after baffling and defying the United States, and after having been treacherously enslaved by the Creeks, incited thereto by Federal officials—bravely resisted their oppressors and made an Exodus, the grandest since the days of Moses, to a land of freedom. Already have their oppressors felt their prowess; and their historian tells us—*"they will be heard from again."*

Redpath, Roving Editor *(1859), 250.*

The Civil War and Reconstruction

If we succeed in the South . . . then your lands, your slaves, and your separate nationality are secured and made perpetual, and in addition nearly all your debts are in Southern bonds, and these we will also secure. If the North succeeds you will most certainly lose all. First your slaves they will take from you; that is one object of the war, to enable them to abolish slavery. . . . Another . . . is to get upon your rich lands and settle their squatters. . . . [T]hey will settle among you, overshadow you, and totally destroy the power of your chiefs and your nationality, and then trade your people out of the residue of their lands. . . .

Confederate commissioner of Indian affairs David Hubbard, letter to Cherokee chief John Ross, June 2, 1861, quoted in Abel, American Indian as Secessionist, *144–45.*

[T]he Choctaws . . . feared that [allying with the Confederacy] would result in the destruction of the[ir] nation. Said Joseph P. Folsom, . . . "We are choosing in what way we shall die." . . . Others said to me, "if the north was here so we could be protected we would stand up for the north but now if we do not go in for the south the Texans will come over here and kill us."

Missionary teacher S. Orlando Lee, letter to Commissioner William P. Dole, March 15, 1862, quoted in Abel, American Indian as Secessionist, *75 ff.*

[At a Choctaw meeting I said] it was of no use of us following the Confederate States Army any longer. For they have left us to fight for ourselves and . . . we ought to come to some terms of agreement with the Federals . . . and it was the wish of the people to form themselves into a home Guard to protect their homes and property against Jay Hawkers and marauding parties. . . . And Genl . . . your last scouting parties plundered a great deal of property from our people . . . , and I hope Genl that after these remarks that you will not allow it to proceed but if so we will have to bear it.

Choctaw Jackson McCurtain to Union general McNeil, December 16, 1863, in Abel, American Indian under Reconstruction, *15–16, n. 11.*

. . . The finest specimens of manhood I have ever gazed upon in my life are half-breed Indians crossed with negroes. It is a fact . . . that while amalgamation with the white man deteriorates both races, the amalgamation of the Indian and the black man advances both races; and . . . I should like to see these eighty thousand square miles . . . opened up to the Indian and to the black man, and let them amalgamate and build up a race that will be an improvement upon both.

Senator Henry S. Lane debates the Harlan Bill to give the United States new powers over the Indian Territory, February 23, 1865, quoted in Abel, American Indian under Reconstruction, *253–54.*

[Your former slaves] have gone to work in good earnest, and we are daily looking for more hands. Soloman . . . told the negroes in a public speech that he had more confidence in his old master in doing him justice than he had in all Yankee promises and other white men. . . . They said they were Indian negroes, freed by Indians, not Yankees and were a part of the Indian tribe and had nothing to do with white people.

Indian son to his plantation-owning father, January 1866, in Wickett, Contested Territory, *104.*

[The Choctaw and Chickasaws] have the bitterest feeling toward the blacks, and are determined that they shall not pass through their country; nor leave it, and . . . they hold on to their slaves with greatest tenacity, swearing . . . that if it had not been for . . . (the blacks) the federals could never have whipped the south—that they (the Indians) are not whipped and that they are going to manage and control things in their country to suit themselves.

John A. Garrett, District South Kansas, letter July 22, 1865, in Abel, American Indian under Reconstruction, *273, n. 518.*

Under Gen'l [Henry J.] Hunt's view . . . as this Territory was not included in the Emancipation Proclamation . . . the negroes are still slaves. This is the one that now obtains both with the Indians and negroes and all are acting upon it. General Hunt fears that if information is given to the negroes that they are free, they will all . . . become solely dependent upon the Government. I think however that such ideas may be communicated to them of the rights and advantages they will have with the Indian tribes . . . that they will be disposed to remain with them. . . . Hence it is my intention to inform them all and at once that they are free men.

U.S. envoy John R. Sanhorn, January 1866, in Abel, American Indian under Reconstruction, *278–79.*

On Indian-owned plantations "The rights of the freedmen are acknowledged by all; fair compensation for labor is paid; a fair proportion of crops to be raised on the old plantation is allowed; labor for freedmen to perform is abundant, and nearly all are self-supporting."

Brevet Major General John B. Sanborn, April 16, 1866, report to Freedmen's Bureau, quoted in Wickett, Contested Territory, *103.*

I think we are in a mighty bad condishion. Havin got no school. Just growin up ignerent for the want of schooling.

Former Choctaw slave J. W. Dunn to Col. Elijah Sells, October 1866, in Wickett, Contested Territory, *78.*

I was riding along alone when all at once I heard the well-known Indian war whoop and noticed not far away a large party of Indians making straight for me. They were all well mounted and they were in full war paint. . . . I decided to run for it. . . . I turned in my saddle every once in a while and gave them a shot by way of greeting, and I had the satisfaction of seeing a painted brave tumble from his horse and go rolling in the dust every time my rifle spoke. . . . Reaching Yellow Horse Canyon, I had about decided to stop and make a stand when one of their bullets caught me in the leg, passing clear through it and then through my horse, killing him. Quickly falling behind him I used his dead body for a breast work and stood the Indians off for a long time. . . .

"Deadwood Dick" (former slave Nat Love), recollecting an Indian attack on October 4, 1876, quoted in Katz, Eyewitness, *324–25.*

CHAPTER TEN

The Argument over Slavery
1637–1877

Attitudes toward Slavery until the 1830s

Americans did not argue much about slavery until they began to think about demanding liberty for themselves—liberty from Great Britain and its king. A few colonists, to be sure, raised their voices against slavery from the early 17th century on—especially the Quakers and the Mennonites. Conscience, as well as the dangers and threats that slavery brought to the dominant white population, pricked a few to propose antislavery legislation. In its earliest days, Georgia forbade slavery. In 1652, the Rhode Island legislature banned servitude for more than ten years or after the age of 24—but on paper only. Colonial Massachusetts courts occasionally heard cases in which slaves sued for their freedom. But by and large, colonists accepted slavery as a fact of life that worked better in some colonies than in others.

By the middle of the 18th century, the natural-rights theories of John Locke began to humanize the climate of ideas in Britain and France and consequently in America. All men, he said, are equal, possessed of rights that no one can take away from them, free to pursue "life, health, liberty, and possessions." Clearly, no one could reasonably accept Locke's theories and at the same time approve of slavery, embedded in the American economy though it was. The defiant American rebels who used Locke's ideas to justify their own revolution against Britain could not blind themselves to the contradiction between those ideas and the realities of slavery—or so one would think. On the other hand, many Christians who said that they believed in the equality of all people under God had nonetheless gone along quite comfortably enslaving blacks and Indians. Human beings had long since proved themselves quite capable of believing contradictory things at the same time and of believing one thing and practicing another.

Nonetheless, in the latter half of the 18th century sentiment against slavery rose in the American colonies. North and South alike were alarmed by the growth of the slave system. Even as the numbers of slaves continued to multiply, slaveholders themselves deplored the institution, and many others denounced it. In a desperate effort to form an American union, the founding fathers compromised on the issue. They implicitly sanctioned slavery's existence in the Constitution but empowered Congress to prohibit the importation of slaves after 1808. In the new nation, the opposition to slavery began to gain legal victories. In 1783, a Massachusetts court interpreted that state's constitution as outlawing slavery. In 1791, Vermont joined the Union as a free state. Between 1780 and 1804, Pennsylvania, Connecticut, Rhode Island, New York, and New Jersey passed gradual-emancipation statutes.

In the South, too, the moral climate of the post-Revolutionary years nurtured a vigorous antislavery movement. Southern newspapers published antislavery sentiments, which also infiltrated the evangelical sects of the Upper South. In 1791, Virginian Robert Carter III, a founding father of the United States, apparently motivated by both ethics and economics, provided in a "Deed of Gift" that he and his heirs would free his more than 500 slaves and rent out land to them, at the rate of 15 a year. Despite the predictable difficulties about which slaves should be freed when, the Carter family pursued this course into the 1850s.[1] Scores of other owners freed their slaves on condition that they would emigrate to Liberia, a move fueled by the founding of the American Colonization Society in 1816. In the 1820s, the slave states actually had more antislavery societies than the free states, furnishing leadership for the movement throughout the country. For example, in 1826, of the 100 societies working for voluntary manumission, colonization, and betterment for slaves, 45 were in North Carolina. As late as 1832, the Virginia legislature was hotly debating the slavery issue.[2]

The Difficulties of Ending Slavery

Condemning slavery as sinful and unchristian, Americans searched for a means of ridding the country of it. Any modification of the system would disrupt the South politically, economically, and socially; it would profoundly change the whole nation. French abolitionist Brissot de Warville observed that Americans "fear that if the Blacks become free they would cause trouble; on rendering them free they know not what rank to assign them in society; whether they shall establish them in separate districts or send them out of the country."[3]

Would freed slaves enjoy the benefits of citizenship—the rights to vote, bear arms, sit on juries, hold office, testify against whites in court cases? If denied, their demands for these rights might lead to a war between blacks and whites. If they were granted, could blacks live up to the responsibilities of citizenship? Could blacks and whites live together as equals? Could whites, trained to an arrogant sense of their own superiority, learn to accept blacks as political equals—let alone social equals? Where blacks outnumbered whites, might not they take their revenge by attempting to enslave whites?

Could blacks, trained to obedience and dependence, support themselves once freed? Would they work if no one forced them to? If they were to own property, where would they get it? Would freed slaves not desert the South in a mass migration northward? How could the North absorb large numbers of them in its labor force? How would the South get its work done without them? Who would compensate slave owners for the loss of most of their capital?

If the 13 original states had not been able to agree to abolish slavery when they ratified the Constitution, how could the greater number of states now in the Union agree? Could abolition be achieved piecemeal, one state at a time? Meanwhile, what would happen when slave owners moved from a slave state to a free state? Would a free state return fugitive slaves to their owners? Would not their differences put the slave states and the free states at sword's point?

The prospect of ending slavery in the United States brought the country face to face with terra incognita. For all anyone knew, such an action might precipitate chaos. History offered no similar situation on which Americans could base their actions—a move that would profoundly change the lives of so many people.

Even that well-informed, detached, and intelligent observer Alexis de Tocqueville hesitated: "I am obliged to confess that I do not consider the abolition of slavery as a means of delaying the struggle between the two races in the southern states. The Negroes might remain slaves for a long time without complaining; but as soon as they join the ranks of free men, they will soon be indignant at being deprived of almost all the rights of citizens; and being unable to become the equals of the whites, they will not be slow to show themselves their enemies. In the North there was every advantage in freeing the slaves; in that way one is rid of slavery without having anything to fear from the free Negroes. They were too few ever to claim their rights. . . .

"I confess that in considering the South I see only two alternatives for the white people living there: to free the Negroes and to mingle with them or to remain isolated from them and keep them as long as possible in slavery. Any intermediate measures seem to me likely to terminate, and that shortly, in the most horrible of civil wars, and perhaps in the extermination of one or other of the two races."[4]

While the nation discussed these questions, the numbers of slaves dwindled in the North and soared in the South: The two sections of the country were developing their economies on different bases. In the North, free industrial laborers wanted no competition from slaves. In the South, planters depended more and more on slave labor. Hearing the ever-louder protests of northern abolitionists, they felt increasingly besieged. The slave revolts led by men such as Gabriel Prosser, Denmark Vesey, and Nat Turner frightened all southerners and hardened the slave owners' determination to control and hang on to their slaves. They turned from denouncing slavery to defending it. By the mid-1830s, the southern antislavery movement had withered to almost nothing.

From that time on, as several prescient contemporary writers pointed out, the forces for and against slavery were on collision courses. In 1848, for instance, diarist George Stanley Fisher observed, "The slavery question is becoming more important & alarming every day. The South has made another move on the chessboard. From being defensive they have become aggressive. They declare openly that it is essential to their protection that they should govern the country. That soon they will be outvoted by the North & therefore at its mercy. To acquire this political preponderance, Texas was annexed and the Mexican War undertaken. . . . When the question comes to be fairly raised—which shall govern, South or North—then the Union will be in imminent danger. It is absurd to suppose that the South can succeed. Its domination is opposed to all the principles & opinions of the country expressed by none more strongly than by themselves. They are essentially an aristocracy, a collection of landed proprietors surrounded by serfs, their property in slaves is represented [as] the only sort of property that gives political power, and they are a small minority in population of the whole country. Numbers as well as wealth, civilization and power are enormously on the side of the North. On every democratic principle, therefore, the North should govern. It will govern or the Union will be severed. . . . [T]here is great reason to fear that ere long there will be a Northern party and a Southern party, and that the former, encouraged by the consciousness of strength & exasperated by conflict will not long continue to respect the 'Compromises of the Constitution,' but will attempt the entire abolition of slavery. This would be a signal for civil war."[5]

Slavery's advocates and its antagonists radicalized. Both sides expounded more and more extreme positions with mounting fervor and conviction; their tolerance for each other evaporated.

Proslavery Arguments

Defenders of slavery lined up one argument after another:

1. They attacked the character and abilities of blacks, who, they said, needed white men's oversight. "The African is incapable of self-care and sinks into lunacy under the burden of freedom," said John C. Calhoun. "It is a mercy to him to give him the guardianship and protection from mental death."[6]
2. Slaves in the United States were not only better off than free people in Africa but also better off than workingmen in England and the northern states. As slaves, they enjoyed the blessings of Christianity and the support and protection of their masters.
3. The South needed slave labor; indeed, American business generally depended on it, directly or indirectly. "Religion and humanity have nothing to do with this question [slavery]," a South Carolina representative to the Constitutional Convention of 1787 proclaimed bluntly. "Interest alone is the governing principle with nations."[7] In 1859, Texan Charles DeMorse was equally direct: "We want more slaves—we *need* them. We care nothing for . . . slavery as an abstraction—but we desire the practicality; the increase of our productions; the increase of the comforts and wealth of the population; and if slavery, or slave labor, or Negro Apprentice labor ministers to this, why this is what we want."[8]
4. The Bible, history, and the natural order of the universe all supported slavery. Virginia professor Thomas Drew announced, "It is as much in the order of nature that men should enslave each other as that other animals should prey upon each other."[9]
5. Neither the nation nor the individual states were entitled to interfere with slave owners' property. "The right of property exists before society," said William O. Goode in 1834. "The Legislature cannot deprive a citizen of his property in his slave. It cannot abolish slavery in a State. It could not delegate to Congress a power greater than its own."[10]
6. Slavery freed white men to cultivate their minds and concentrate on public affairs.
7. Black slavery freed white women from the servitude to which society must otherwise relegate them to get its work done and at the same time protected their virtue by providing an outlet for white men's passions in black women.
8. The welfare of society is more important than the welfare of any one person or race, so blacks ought to accept their own enslavement for the good of society. Unitarian minister Orville Dewey told slaves, "*Your right to be free is not absolute, unqualified, irrespective of all consequences. If my espousal of your claim is likely to involve your race and mine together in disasters infinitely greater than your* personal servitude, then you ought not to be free. In such a case personal rights ought to be sacrificed to the general good. You yourself ought to see this, and be willing to suffer for a while—one for many."[11]

9. Slavery may lead to abuses, but that is no reason to abandon the institution, any more than divorces are a reason to abandon the institution of marriage.

10. Southerners had not originated slavery. It had been forced upon them by England and northern traders, but they had since made of it an institution beneficial to all.

Abolitionist Arguments

Abolitionists propounded arguments as diverse for their stand.

1. If we value freedom for ourselves, we should also want it for others. "Would we enjoy liberty?" asked Reverend Nathaniel Miles of Massachusetts. "Then we must grant it to others. For shame, let us either cease to enslave our fellow-men, or else let us cease to complain of those that would enslave us."[12]

2. Slavery endangers the Union. "The existence of Slavery may be viewed as one forcible cause of a final separation of the United States," warned the *Connecticut Courant* in 1796.[13]

3. Slavery does not profit the slave owner. Those who work for wages labor more productively than slaves, and their employers do not have to support them in their nonworking years of childhood and old age.

4. Slavery damages the communities in which it exists. "Slavery is ruinous to the whites; it retards improvement; roots out our industrious population; banishes the yeomanry of the country; deprives the spinner, the weaver, the smith, the shoemaker, the carpenter of employment and support," Thomas Marshall argued before the Virginia House of Delegates in 1832. "The EVIL admits of no remedy. It is increasing, and will continue to increase, *until the whole country* will be inundated by one black wave, covering its whole extent, with a few white faces, here and there, floating on its surface. The master has no capital but what is invested in human flesh; the father, instead of being richer for his sons, is at a loss how to provide for them. There is no diversity of occupations, no incentive to enterprise. Labor of every species is disreputable, because performed mostly by slaves. Our towns are stationary, our villages almost everywhere declining; and the general aspect of the country marks the curse of a wasteful, idle, reckless population, who have no interest in the soil, and care not how much it is impoverished. Public improvements are neglected, and the entire continent does not present a region for which nature has done so much and art so little."[14]

5. Slavery causes masters to sin. "[I]t is too well known," said Judge Samuel Sewall in 1700, "what Temptations Masters are under, to connive at the Fornication of their Slaves; lest they should be obliged to find them Wives, or pay their Fines. . . . It is likewise most lamentable to think, how in taking Negroes out of *Africa*, and selling of them here, That which GOD has joined together, Men do boldly rend asunder: Men from their Country, Husbands from their Wives, Parents from their Children. How horrible is the Uncleanness, Mortality, if not Murder, that the Ships are guilty of that bring great Crowds of these miserable Men and Women."[15]

While abolitionists and proponents of slavery worked ever more ardently to persuade people to their way of thinking, the great majority of the population, of course, either took more moderate positions or remained indifferent to the whole

Illustrations of the American Anti-Slavery Almanac for 1840.

"Our Peculiar Domestic Institutions."

Northern Hospitality—New-York nine months law. [The Slave steps out of the Slave State, and his chains fall. A Free State, with another chain, stands ready to re-enslave him.]

Burning of McIntosh at St. Louis, in April, 1836.

Showing how slavery improves the condition of the female sex.

The Negro Pew, or "Free" Seats for black Christians. | *Mayor of New-York refusing a Carman's license to a colored Man.*

Servility of the Northern States in arresting and returning fugitive Slaves.

Selling a Mother from her Child.

Hunting Slaves with dogs and guns. A Slave drowned by the dogs.

" Poor things, ' they can't take care of themselves.' "

Mothers with young Children at work in the field.

A Woman chained to a Girl, and a Man in irons at work in the field.

Branding Slaves.

Cutting up a Slave in Kentucky.

Paid. | *Unpaid.*

This publication from 1840 depicts scenes of American slavery. *(Library of Congress)* issue. Most people went about their business, "going along to get along"—like young David Bush, who, having moved away from his Delaware family to Mississippi, wrote home, "Tell Pop I have not received a letter from him since I left. I expect he is angry with me for making the purchase of negroes . . . , but he must not be as it is no more for us here to purchase a servant or negro than it is for him to hire one. There is none for us to hire, and we are necessarily compelled to purchase to get our work done."[16] A good many people hoped that slavery, if left alone, would die a natural death, fading out of the South as they saw it fading out of the North—whereas, they feared, vigorous opposition might strengthen it.

Opposition to the extension of slavery, it must be understood, seldom reached to advocacy of full equality for blacks and whites. Free states and territories all too often either tried to exclude blacks completely or denied them civil rights and limited the categories of jobs open to them. Thus in 1844, the Oregon provisional government prohibited slavery and required slaveholders to remove their chattels within three years—but warned all free blacks and mulattoes to leave the territory within two years, subjecting any who remained to periodic floggings.

Many northern whites simply did not want blacks around at all, and most southern states required freed blacks to leave. Such sentiments help explain the long life of the colonization movement, which sent blacks out of the country entirely. Pennsylvania Democrat David Wilmot based his 1846 proposal against the extension of slavery into any territory acquired by the Mexican War on a plea for "the cause and the rights of [the] white freeman [and] I would preserve to free white labor a fair country, a rich inheritance, where the sons of toil, of my own race and own color, can live without the disgrace which association with negro slavery brings upon free labor." He added privately, "By God, sir, men born and nursed of white women are not going to be ruled by men who were brought up on the milk of some damn Negro wench!"[17]

Even ardent abolitionists often questioned the abilities of blacks. They might and did argue that blacks and whites are equal under God, but those like Theodore Weld and the Grimké sisters, Sarah and Angelina, who actually practiced integration, were the exception rather than the rule. So were those Quakers and others who insisted that slaveholders owed their slaves not only freedom but also compensation for their labors in the past and help in getting new starts.

Antislavery Divisions

The wearing struggle against slavery divided antislavery forces more than it united them on questions of ideology and strategy. Should they confine themselves to moral suasion? Should they reinforce it by political action? Need they resort to direct militant action?

The first split came early, with disagreements over women's role in the movement and in society as a whole. The refusal of the World Anti-Slavery Society in 1840 to seat women delegates from the United States motivated Elizabeth Cady Stanton and Lucretia Mott to organize the first woman's rights convention. But already in 1835–36, the Grimké sisters had broken with the tradition that women should neither allow their names to appear in print nor appear on public platforms. Their deep devotion to the cause of antislavery demanded that they write and speak out for it—a decision that troubled other antislavery advocates. Despite women's numbers and important work, particularly in the grassroots societies, many in the antislavery movement feared that endorsing women lecturers would attract opposition; the movement could not afford, they argued, to lose support by embracing other causes. Nonetheless, talented women like Abby Kelley Foster and Sallie Holley soon followed the Grimkés' example. William Lloyd Garrison backed them, to the point of taking up the cause of women's rights as well. In 1840, the American Anti-Slavery Society split over the issue into two organizations.

Garrison's refusal to compromise on gradual emancipation or anything else drove moderates from his side. His ideology finally moved him to declare that he could neither support nor cooperate with the U.S. government, since it helped implement slavery. In 1842, he asserted that the statements on slavery in the Constitution, together with such other federal actions as the Gag Rule (the refusal of Congress to read antislavery petitions), made the American union merely "a rope of sand—a fanciful nonentity—a mere piece of parchment—'a rhetorical flourish and splendid absurdity'—and a concentration of the physical force of the nation to destroy liberty, and to uphold slavery."[18] He opted in favor of anarchy and the dissolution of the Union. His stance horrified antislavery advocates who believed in reform, not revolution, and counted on political means within the existing system to achieve their ends.

The relations between black and white antislavery workers also caused trouble. A good many emancipationists, eager as they were to free the slaves, nevertheless were infected with the prevailing racism of the time. Few whites honestly thought of blacks as their social or intellectual equals, despite the obvious abilities of the black abolitionists they worked with. Whites treated blacks in the movement as their inferiors, assuming that they needed supervision—a particularly galling attitude, for in many ways the movement owed its very existence to the courage, sacrifices, and labors of free blacks and escaped slaves. What was more, blacks understood what many whites did not: the necessity of working not just for the end of slavery but against all forms of racial injustice. Yet as Martin R. Delany complained in 1852, "We [blacks] find ourselves occupying the very same position in relation to our Anti-Slavery friends, as we do in relation to the pro-slavery part of the community—a mere secondary, underling position, in all our relations to them, and anything more than this, is not a matter of course affair—it comes not by established anti-slavery custom or right, but . . . by mere suffrance."[19]

Blacks accordingly moved toward separatism, arranging black abolitionist conventions. They also changed their thinking about strategy. In the early years, most black abolitionists had spoken out against the use of violence to change the system, at least in part because they knew all too well the odds against slave insurrections and did not want to encourage hopeless actions.

But as the years wore on, they despaired of reform. David Ruggles, for instance, in 1841 said: "We have no right to hope to be emancipated from thralldom until we honestly resolve to be free. . . . We must remember that while our fellow countrymen of the south are slaves to individuals, *we of the north are slaves to the community*, and ever will be so, until we arise, and by the help of Him who governs the destiny of nations, go forward, and like the reformed inebriates, ourselves strike for reform—individual, general and radical reform, in every ramification of society. . . . Strike for freedom, or die slaves! . . . In our cause, mere words are nothing—action is everything. Buckle on your armour, and appear at the Black Convention, remember that our cause demands of us union and agitation—agitation and action."[20] Black writer Frances Ellen Watkins called the U.S. government "the arch traitor to liberty, as shown by the Fugitive Slave Law and the Dred Scott decision."[21] Even Frederick Douglass, who for years had insisted on moderation, began to think of violence as the only effective option: "There are three millions of slaves in this land, held by the United States Government, under the sanction of the American Constitution," he said in Boston in June 1849. "[I] would welcome the news that the slaves had risen and that the sable arms which have been engaged in beautifying and adorning the South were engaged in spreading death and devastation there."[22]

The disagreements in the antislavery movement spawned several political parties. Many had lost faith in the major parties, on the grounds that their southern members would never permit them to work effectively to end slavery. Accordingly, in 1840 antislavery forces founded the Liberty Party, including in its platform a determination to end slavery in the District of Columbia, abolish the interstate slave trade, and ban the admission of any more slave states to the Union. In 1847, a group of Liberty Party adherents, Van Buren Democrats, and Whigs united as the Free Soil Party to oppose the extension of slavery into territory won during the Mexican War. Finally in 1854, opponents of extending slavery into the territories—old-line Whigs, antislavery Democrats, and Free Soilers—founded the Republican Party. With each change, the movement expanded, thanks to its publications, agents, and grassroots auxiliary societies.

Strategy and Tactics

Just as blacks began the Underground Railroad, so they pioneered the antislavery movement in the United States. Even before the American Revolution, some slaves ended their enslavement through the courts, charging their masters with restraining their liberty. In 1773, for instance, Caesar Hendrick won his freedom from Richard Greenleaf of Newburyport, Massachusetts, collecting damages and court costs.[23] To get around the difficulties of such suits, which were expensive and slow and freed only one slave at a time, blacks resorted to a kind of class action, petitions addressed not to the courts but to the legislature. For example, in 1779, 19 New Hampshire blacks petitioned the legislature asking "from what authority they [the masters] assume to dispose of our lives, freedom and property."[24] Free blacks supported such efforts. Shipyard owner and captain Paul Cuffe signed a petition in 1780 requesting that free blacks be relieved of paying taxes, since they could not vote, and another in 1781 seeking the vote for free blacks and mulattoes. Although these petitions failed to bring about immediate action, they contributed to the antislavery sentiments that eventually moved the northern legislatures and courts to abolish slavery.

The defenders of slavery, of course, had much more political clout than blacks and early on understood its importance. In their insistence that the Constitution protect the international slave trade for 20 years and guarantee the return of fugitive slaves to their owners, they built slavery into the very foundation of the new nation. Thereafter they rammed successive fugitive slave laws through Congress. They quickly grasped the potency of enlarging slave territory. They struggled to preserve their dominance in Congress, believing it necessary to protect their agriculture. Some of them saw the production of cotton—for which they believed slave labor essential—as the primary economic prop of the nation, while the rest of the nation labored to support those who grew and processed it. In their view, cotton was king, and the representatives of the slaveholders who supervised its production must be the most powerful bloc in Washington.

The antislavery movement, though it won an occasional political victory along the way, at first depended primarily on moral suasion. Believing themselves to hold the high ground, abolitionists undertook to convert the populace North and South to their way of thinking. Slavery, they argued, was a sin, one that had to be expiated through penance and suffering.

Grassroots antislavery societies began to appear about 1775 and pledged to work to end slavery and improve the condition of blacks. They tried various methods: paying masters to free slaves, guaranteeing the support of freed slaves, protecting blacks against kidnapping, buying slaves to free them, helping freed slaves find jobs, and conducting schools. Most of all they propagandized to shape public opinion.

The American Anti-Slavery Society, founded in 1833, sent out lecturers to expound its principles. Theodore Weld, Angelina and Sarah Grimké, Frederick Douglass, and a host of others—black and white, female and male—ranged the northern countryside. It was uphill, hazardous work. All of them literally risked their lives, and the escaped slaves among them additionally risked their freedom, to spread the gospel of liberty. Many endured physical assaults and beatings. Their jobs were at least as dangerous as those of doctors in abortion clinics at the beginning of the 21st century. For their pains, the American Anti-Slavery Society paid them eight dollars a week and expenses. It instructed them to oppose compensated emancipation and colonization, not to argue about plans of emancipation, and to emphasize free and equal rights for slaves.

In the South and the border states, of course, those who opposed slavery ran risks at least as great. In 1858, diarist Sidney George Fisher noted, "In the [Philadelphia] *Evening Bulletin* is an article about a recent outrage committed in Kent Co. [Maryland] such as are common now in the South. A person named Bowers had excited the indignation of the neighborhood by expressing openly free soil opinions and by taking the *New York Tribune,* an abolition paper. A charge was fabricated against him, founded on the extorted testimony of Negroes, that he had been guilty of assisting slaves to escape. He was tried and acquitted by the jury. The public were not satisfied with this and a mob seized upon him on his farm and tarred and feathered him. This act excited the indignation of a portion of the people, who in return made an attack on those concerned in it. A meeting was then called at Chestertown of the 'most respectable' inhabitants, at which resolutions were passed supporting the proceedings of the mob, denouncing all opposed to slavery, all who expressed opinions against it, all even who refused openly to approve it and threatening them with a similar punishment."[25]

Abolitionists published scores of newspapers, notably William Lloyd Garrison's *Liberator* and Frederick Douglass's *North Star.* In these appeared many slave narratives, reports purportedly or actually written by fugitive slaves describing their enslavement and their escapes. Their editors and publishers were attacked. Bostonians dragged William Lloyd Garrison through the streets, and in Alton, Illinois, mobs several times destroyed Elijah Parish Lovejoy's press and finally shot him dead.

Antislavery propagandists also distributed reams of pamphlets, not only in the North but also in the South. Southerners tried to confiscate them, arresting travelers whom they caught with them. One group raided post offices to seize antislavery literature; the proslavery U.S. postmaster general Amos Kendall backed the raiders. While admitting that his office conferred no legal authority on him "to exclude from the mails any species of newspapers, magazines, or pamphlets," he nonetheless wrote, "By no act or direction of mine, official or private, could I be induced to aid, knowingly, in giving circulation to papers of this description [antislavery literature], directly or indirectly. We owe an obligation to the laws, but a higher one to the communities in which we live, and if the former be perverted to destroy the latter, it is patriotism to disregard them."[26]

Besides these floods of propaganda, abolitionists exerted political pressure through memorials. In 1790, for instance, Benjamin Franklin, as president of a Philadelphia antislavery society, memorialized Congress: "From a persuasion that equal liberty was originally the portion, and is still the birth-right, of all men; and influenced by the strong ties of humanity, and the principles of their institution, your memorialists conceive themselves bound to use all justifiable endeavors to loosen the bands of slavery, and promote a general enjoyment of the blessings of freedom. Under these impressions, they earnestly entreat your serious attention to the subject of slavery; that you will be pleased to countenance the restoration of liberty to those unhappy men, who alone, in this land of freedom, are degraded into perpetual bondage, and who, amidst the general joy of surrounding freemen, are groaning in servile subjection; that you will devise means for removing this inconsistency from the character of the American people; that you will promote mercy and justice towards this distressed race; and that you will step to the very verge of the power vested in you for discouraging every species of traffic in the persons of our fellow-men."[27]

Antislavery advocates also began the grassroots political maneuver of collecting thousands of signatures on petitions. When in 1836 Congress refused to read these petitions, passing the so-called Gag Rule, John Quincy Adams fought a long-drawn-out battle to protect the citizens' right of petition. In 1842 he answered a motion to censure him for having presented an antislavery petition for the dissolution of the Union by asking, "[A]m I, the representative . . . of the *free* people of the state of Massachusetts . . . —am I to come here and be tried for high treason because I presented a petition—a *petition*—to this house, and because the fancy or imagination of the gentleman from Kentucky supposes that there was anti-slavery or the abolition of slavery in it? The gentleman charges me with subornation of perjury and of high treason, and he calls upon this house, *as a matter of mercy and grace*, not to expel me for these crimes, but to inflict upon me the severest censure they can."[28]

Some abolitionists asked themselves whether they could in conscience use the products of slave labor. Henry Blackwell expended much of the earnings of his wife, Lucy Stone, in his efforts to produce sugar from sugar beets competitively with the slave-produced sugar from cane. James Mott gave up his cotton brokerage and went into the wool business. Levi Coffin bought and sold cotton from small non-slaveholding farms in the South. The American Anti-Slavery Society invited its members "diligently and prayerfully to examine the question, whether they can innocently make an *ordinary* use, or be concerned in the traffic of the productions of slave labor?"[29]

This Free-Labor (or Free Produce) movement, however, never had much support; even the most enthusiastic abolitionists had to recognize that it was not viable. Abolitionist lecturer Abby Kelley, for example, argued that "it is right for me to use any person's property for *his own benefit*—the slave's property I can use to batter down his prison door and that of the oppressed every where to draw them from under the heels of the tramplers—In one word, it is my duty to use these things

FORCING SLAVERY DOWN THE THROAT OF A FREESOILER

This cartoon depicts the Free Soil controversy. *(Library of Congress)*

[the products of slave labor], for to abstain would compel me to the life of a recluse [and to be unable to] plead the cause of the poor and needy."[30]

The Free Soil struggle over whether new states admitted to the Union should be free or slave was waged for years, fueled by the desire to protect the jobs of white laborers against blacks and by the hope on both sides of increased political power. The Ordinance of 1787 barred slavery in the vast Northwest Territory and, by extension, in any state carved out of it. The Missouri Compromise of 1820–21 forbade slavery in the Louisiana Purchase territory north of 36 degrees and 30 minutes; it tried to preserve a balance by admitting states in pairs, one slave (Missouri) and one free (Maine). In 1845, the United States provoked war with Mexico by annexing Texas, which had long battled against Mexico, largely because Texas wanted slavery and Mexico did not. The Wilmot Proviso, introduced in the House of Representatives in 1846, would have outlawed slavery in any territory acquired in the Mexican War, but it failed to pass. In 1854, the Kansas-Nebraska Act demolished the Missouri Compromise by establishing the principle of "squatter sovereignty"—the presence or absence of slavery within a new state, that is, was to be determined by the inhabitants of that state.

Challenging the right of Congress to forbid slavery—or as they put it, to tell a man what to do with his own property—southern politicians argued that such a determination belonged to the individual states, including new states seeking admission to the Union. The Kansas-Nebraska Act brought on a no-holds-barred struggle that turned Kansas into a bloody battleground. As a congressional committee reported in 1856, "In 1854 congress passed an act establishing two new territories—Nebraska and Kansas—in this region of country, where slavery had been prohibited for more than thirty years; and instead of leaving said law against slavery in operation, or prohibiting or expressly allowing or establishing slavery, congress left the subject in said territories to be discussed, agitated and legislated on. . . .

"Thus it was promulgated to the people of this whole country that here was a clear field for competition—an open course for the race of rivalship; the goal of which was the ultimate establishment of a sovereign state; and the prize, the reward of everlasting liberty and its institutions on the one hand, or the perpetuity of slavery and its concomitants on the other. . . .

"[I]n the performance of this novel experiment, it was provided that all white men who became inhabitants in Kansas were entitled to vote without regard to their time of residence, usually provided in other territories. Nor was this right of voting confined to American citizens, but included all such aliens as . . . would declare, on oath, their intention to become citizens. Thus was the proclamation to the world to become inhabitants of Kansas, and enlist in this great enterprise, by the force of numbers, by vote, to decide for it the great question [slavery]."[31]

Abolitionist emigrant aid societies, especially in Massachusetts, recruited and armed thousands of settlers to migrate to Kansas and claim farms there. Proslavery forces in neighboring Missouri not only resolved "[t]hat we will afford protection to no abolitionist as a settler of this territory" but also encouraged raids on the abolitionist settlers. The Missourians also resolved "[t]hat we recognize the institution of slavery as already existing in this territory, and advise slaveholders to introduce their property as early as possible."[32] John Brown, always ready to pour gasoline on smoldering fires, took revenge for such practices by invading the state and murdering Kansas slaveholders. The governor of Kansas failed to keep order, and President Franklin Pierce removed him from office. When the polls finally opened to determine whether the new state should be slave or free, thousands of nonresidents from Missouri poured in and registered their proslavery votes.

By 1856, passions between slavery and antislavery forces throughout the country had reached the point that on May 22 the inflammatory oratory in the Senate chamber of antislavery senator Charles Sumner of Massachusetts provoked a physical beating from Rep. Preston S. Brooks of South Carolina. Sumner was unable to resume work for three and a half years.

By 1860, the struggle between abolitionists and the defenders of slavery had brought the United States to the brink of civil war. Slavery had almost ended in Europe, Central America, and South America. The United States, in other respects so advanced, now found itself on this score in the company of Cuba, Brazil, and portions of Asia and Africa. The slave states were isolated not only from the other states but from most of the Western world, outmoded, defensive, looking toward the past rather than the future. They clung desperately to the institution of slavery, even though in 1860 only about 400,000 of the 8,500,000 whites owned the country's 4 million slaves.[33]

Woman's Rights and the Argument over Slavery

The 19th-century woman's movement was rooted in abolitionism. A sense of the immorality of slavery prompted women to struggle to end it, a process in which they became conscious of their own legal, social, and educational disadvantages. In the abolitionist movement, they learned how to fight politically. Some of the most prominent women suffragists first defied gender discrimination by speaking publicly against slavery—most famously the sisters Angelina and Sarah Grimké. Their consciences drove these daughters of a slaveholding southern family to move North and join the abolitionist movement. Their public speeches evoked the wrath of some male abolitionists but drew crowds. The sisters retired from public life after Angelina married abolitionist leader Theodore Weld in 1838, but they circulated antislavery petitions and gathered materials, mostly from southern newspapers, for Weld's revelatory book *American Slavery as It Is.* Later, although themselves poverty-stricken, they paid for the education of their black nephews (their brother's sons), one as a lawyer and one as a clergyman.

The Declaration of Woman's Rights of 1848 was fueled by the refusal of the 1840 international slavery convention to seat women delegates. Five women—Harriet Cady Stanton, Mary Ann McClintock, Jane Hunt, the Quaker preacher Lucretia Mott, and her sister Martha Pelham Wright—framed the declaration for the first woman's rights convention in the United States, held in July 1848 at Seneca Falls, New York. All the framers were active abolitionists. So, for the most part, suffragists remained throughout the Civil War, although they differed on whether as a group they should concentrate exclusively on getting the vote or should agitate for other reforms as well.

During Reconstruction, the Fourteenth and Fifteenth Amendments created a moral and political dilemma for woman suffragists. They ardently hoped that their work of two decades for their rights and their active support for the Union during the Civil War would enable the enfranchisement of black and white women as well as of black men. Many of their male supporters, however, told them that women must wait their turn: that the needs of black men must take precedence. The controversy split the movement, which in 1869 divided into two organizations, the National Woman Suffrage Association (NWSA) and the American Woman Suffrage Association (AWSA). Longtime abolitionists like Stanton and Susan B. Anthony were driven into a position where their need for the support of southern white women overcame their concern for blacks—yet another instance during Reconstruction in which politics and self-interest obscured ethics, and yet another instance in the history of the world in which two wronged groups have conflicted.

Chronicle of Events

1637
- Roger Williams, pleading for captive Pequots, protests against "perpetuall slaverie."

1640
- New Netherlands enacts an ordinance forbidding inhabitants to harbor or feed fugitive servants.

1641
- The Massachusetts Body of Liberties provides that "there shall never be any bond slaverie, villinage or Captivitie amongst us unless it be lawfull Captives taken in just warres, and such strangers as willingly selle themselves or are sold to us. . . . This exempts none from servitude who shall be Judged thereto by Authoritie."

1643
- In the Articles of Confederation, the New England Confederation of Plymouth, Massachusetts, Connecticut, and New Haven incorporate a fugitive slave law.
- The colonies of New Netherlands and New Haven agree on the mutual surrender of fugitive slaves.

1650
- Connecticut legalizes slavery.

1652
- Rhode Island bans enslavement for more than ten years or after age 24. Despite this law, slavery survives in Rhode Island for another 150 years.

1657
- Virginia enacts a fugitive slave law.

1660
- The New Netherlands Council resolves to transport to Curaçao all but two or three of a group of recently captured Esopus Indians, "to be employed there, or at Buenaire . . . in the Company's service."

1663
- Maryland legalizes slavery.

1664
- New York and New Jersey legalize slavery.

1666
- Maryland enacts a fugitive slave law.

1667
- Virginia rules that baptism no longer will affect the status of slaves.

1668
- New Jersey enacts a fugitive slave law.

1676
- Quaker William Edmondson at Newport, Rhode Island, writes an antislavery letter of advice to Friends in America.

1688
- Germantown Mennonites of Philadelphia issue a proclamation, written by Francis Daniel Pastorius, declaring slavery inconsistent with Christian principles.

1691
- Virginia requires that manumitted slaves be sent out of the colony.

1693
- George Kieth publishes *An Exhortation and Caution to Friends Concerning Buying or Keeping of Negroes.*

1696
- The Friends' Yearly Meeting opposes the importation of slaves.
- Maryland taxes the importation of black servants, slaves, and white servants.

1700
- Samuel Sewall condemns slaveholding in *The Selling of Joseph: A Memorial.*
- Pennsylvania legalizes slavery.

1701
- John Saffin defends slaveholding in *A Brief and Candid Answer to a Late Printed Sheet, Entituled, The Selling of Joseph.*

1702
- Slave Abda Jennings sues for his freedom in Hartford, Connecticut.

1703
- Massachusetts requires every master who wants to liberate a slave to furnish a bond of at least £50, to indemnify the authorities should the freedman become a charge on the public.

- Connecticut orders that slaves be whipped for disturbing the peace or offering to strike a white person.
- Rhode Island forbids blacks and Indians to walk at night without a pass.

1708
- Rhode Island taxes imported slaves.

1711
- Connecticut orders that freed slaves who become indigent must be relieved by their former masters.
- Pennsylvania prohibits the importation of blacks and Indians but says that "it is neither just nor convenient to set them at Liberty."
- Rhode Island forbids "*clandestine* importations and exportations of passengers, or negroes, or Indian slaves."

1714
- An emancipation plan, published anonymously, advocates sending all slaves back to Africa, except those who choose to go on serving their masters.

1715
- Rhode Island legalizes slavery.

1723
- Virginia abolishes manumissions.

1728
- Rhode Island requires a master freeing a slave to give bond that the slave not become a public charge.

1733
- Quaker Elihu Coleman of Nantucket publishes *A Testimony against That Anti-Christian Practice of MAKING SLAVES OF MEN.*

1735
- An English law forbids the importation and use of black slaves in the colony of Georgia.

1737
- Quakers disown Benjamin Lay for writing *All Slave Keepers That Keep the Innocent in Bondage, Apostates.*

1740
- The South Carolina Assembly declares all blacks, Indians, mulattos, and mestizos to be slaves "unless the contrary can be made to appear," but the act effectively frees Indian slaves, because it exempts Indians in amity with the colonists and so designates enslaved Indians.

1742
- The Society for the Propagation of the Gospel in Foreign Parts buys two young blacks to be trained as teachers in black schools in South Carolina, where the society offers black and Indian slave children a free Christian education.

1749
- Georgia allows slavery.

1751
- Benjamin Franklin in *Observations Concerning the Increase of Mankind* points to the evil effects of slavery upon population, industry, and the production and distribution of wealth.

1754
- Quaker John Woolman publishes the antislavery *Considerations on Keeping of Negroes.*

1755
- Salem instructs its representative to petition the General Court of Massachusetts to forbid the importing of slaves.

1758
- Philadelphia Quakers cease buying and selling slaves.

1760s
- The theory of natural rights, a spark of the American Revolution, raises questions of the morality of slavery.

1760
- *A Narrative of the Uncommon Sufferings and Surprising Deliverance of Briton Hammon, a Negro Man,* is published in Boston.

1762
- Anthony Benezet publishes the antislavery *A Short Account of That Part of Africa Inhabited by Negroes.*

1764
- James Otis's *The Rights of the British Colonies Asserted and Proved* excoriates slavery.

1765
- Massachusetts slaves begin bringing civil lawsuits for their liberty.

• Worcester, Massachusetts, instructs its representative to the colonial legislature to lobby for a law against slavery.

1766

• Boston instructs its representative to the colonial legislature to move for a law against importing and purchasing slaves.

1767

• Members of the Virginia House of Burgesses, meeting as a private body, boycott the British slave trade, resolving "[t]hat they will not import any Slaves or purchase any imported, after the First day of *November* next, until the said [Tax] Acts of Parliament are repealed." Similar boycotts are soon adopted in South Carolina, Georgia, and North Carolina.

1768

• Maryland Quakers cease buying and selling slaves.

1770

• Congregational minister Samuel Hopkins of Newport, Rhode Island, begins preaching against slavery.
• New England Quakers cease buying and selling slaves.

1772

• Reverend Isaac Skillman publishes *An Oration upon the Beauties of Liberty.*
• Some members of the Society of Friends are disowned (expelled) for not freeing their slaves.
• In London, Lord Chief Justice Mansfield rules that slavery is not supported by English law.
• The Virginia House of Burgesses tells King George III that "the importation of slaves into the colonies from the coast of Africa hath long been considered a trade of great inhumanity, and under its present encouragement, we have too much reason to fear will endanger the very existence of your Majesty's American dominions."

1773

• *Personal Slavery Established,* published anonymously, argues that slavery is a positive good.
• Benjamin Rush publishes the antislavery *An Address to the Inhabitants of the British Settlements in America, upon Slavekeeping.*
• Harvard seniors Theodore Parsons and Eliphalet Pearson debate slavery.

• Boston slaves petition for consideration of their "unhappy state and condition."
• Massachusetts slaves petition for land for settlement.
• A slave successfully sues Richard Greenleaf of Newburyport, Massachusetts, for holding him in bondage.

1774

• The First Continental Congress suspends trade with Great Britain, providing that Americans will not import or buy slaves imported after December 1, "after which time, we will wholly discontinue the slave trade."
• The Massachusetts legislature passes a bill against importing slaves, but the governor refuses to sign it.
• A Massachusetts court grants freedom to slave Caleb Dodge, who has sued his master for restraining his liberty.
• Connecticut and Rhode Island forbid the importation of slaves.
• Virginia and North Carolina take action against importing slaves.
• New York Quakers cease buying and selling slaves.

1775–1793

• In the New Jersey supreme court, 20 of 22 freedom suits are decided in favor of slaves.

1775

• Georgia takes action against importing slaves.
• The Society for the Relief of Free Negroes Unlawfully Held in Bondage is organized. (In 1787 it becomes the Pennsylvania Society for Promoting the Abolition of Slavery and for the Relief of Free Negroes Unlawfully Held in Bondage and for Improving the Conditions of the African Race.)

1776

• The Second Continental Congress votes "[t]hat no slaves be imported into any of the thirteen United Colonies."
• Delaware prohibits the further importation of slaves from Africa.
• The Society of Friends excludes all those who buy or sell a slave or refuse to emancipate their slaves.
• Pastor Samuel Hopkins, in *A Dialogue, Concerning the Slavery of Africans,* urges upon the Second Continental Congress measures for immediately abolishing slavery.
• Wealthy South Carolina merchant Henry Laurens, later president of the Continental Congress, writes a letter against slavery.

1777

- The Vermont constitution prohibits slavery, gives the franchise to all males of mature age, and extends the rights of jury trial and habeas corpus to fugitives.
- At New York's constitutional convention, delegates vote 36 to five to adopt an antislavery resolution.
- The New York State constitution enfranchises all free propertied men, without reference to color, prior condition of servitude, or religion.
- A committee of the Virginia legislature, chaired by Thomas Jefferson, proposes the gradual emancipation and exportation of slaves.

1778

- The Articles of Confederation treats the word *citizens* as interchangeable with the word *inhabitants*, declaring that the "free inhabitants" of each state shall be entitled to "all the privileges and immunities of free citizens in the several States."
- Virginia forbids the further importation of slaves.

1780

- The Massachusetts constitution declares that all men are free and equal by birth, in a clause later interpreted as abolishing slavery. It also enfranchises all males, regardless of race.
- Pennsylvania begins gradual emancipation, freeing the children of all slaves born after November 1, 1780, at their 28th birthday.
- Delaware resolves "that no person hereafter imported from Africa ought to be held in slavery under any pretense whatever."
- Elizabeth Freeman of Sheffield, Massachusetts, successfully sues for her freedom; her mistress had tried to strike Freeman's sister with a red-hot poker, and Freeman had interfered and run away.
- The Methodist Conference at Baltimore declares slavery "contrary to the laws of God, man, and nature."

1781

- Decisions in *Commonwealth* v. *Jennison* and related cases effectively end slavery in Massachusetts.

1782

- A provisional peace agreement between Great Britain and the United States stipulates that the British withdraw "without . . . carrying away any Negroes or other Property of the American Inhabitants." The British interpret this to mean that blacks with them before November 30, 1782, are free.

- Virginia repeals its law confining the power of emancipation to the legislature.

1783

- The Virginia legislature repeals a law limiting citizenship to whites and provides instead that "all free persons born within the territory of this commonwealth" shall be citizens.
- Virginia emancipates slaves who served in the American army *with the permission of their masters.*
- Maryland prohibits the importing of slaves from Africa.
- *A Serious Address to the Rulers of America, on the Inconsistency of Their Conduct Respecting Slavery, forming a Contrast between the Encroachments of England on American Liberty and American Injustice in tolerating Slavery* is published.

1784

- Thomas Jefferson's proposal to prohibit slavery in the whole region west of the Alleghenies fails in Congress by one vote. Jefferson comments, "Thus we see the fate of millions unborn hanging on the tongue of one man, & heaven was silent in that awful moment."
- Rhode Island and Connecticut pass gradual emancipation laws.
- North Carolina forbids the importation of slaves from Africa.
- The Methodist Conference, at the urging of John Wesley, adopts regulations requiring slaveholding members to manumit slaves within a brief term of years, the children of such slaves to be free at birth.

1785

- New York passes a bill for gradual emancipation but limits the legal and political rights of blacks and forbids marriage with whites.
- The New York Society for Promoting the Manumission of Slaves is established—the first antislavery society organized on a public basis.
- The Rhode Island Society for Abolishing the Slave Trade is organized.

1786

- New Jersey passes manumission acts, though it does not enact effective legislation against slavery until 1804.
- North Carolina declares the slave trade "of evil consequences and highly impolitic."
- In England, Thomas Clarkson publishes an *Essay on the Slavery and Commerce of the Human Species, Particularly the*

African, which becomes a basic handbook of the abolitionist movement.

1787

- The U.S. Constitution institutionalizes slavery by providing that a slave will be counted as three-fifths of a person in determining representation in Congress. It gives Congress the power to tax the importation of slaves and to end the international slave trade after 1808. The Northwest Ordinance excludes slavery from the Northwest Territory (including the present-day Ohio, Indiana, Illinois, Michigan, Wisconsin, and part of Minnesota) but includes a provision for the return of fugitive slaves to their masters elsewhere.
- Rhode Island prohibits its residents from participating in the slave trade—without much effect.
- Virginia decrees death without benefit of clergy to anyone who knowingly sells a free person as a slave.
- Blacks withdraw from St. George's Methodist Episcopal Church in Philadelphia to found the first black churches there: St. Thomas's African Episcopal Church, under Absolom Jones, and the African Methodist Episcopal Church, under Richard Allen.
- "Othello" (possibly Benjamin Banneker) publishes "On Slavery," an antislavery pamphlet.

1788

- Connecticut prohibits residents from participating in the slave trade.
- After three free blacks are abducted, the Massachusetts legislature enacts a total prohibition of the slave trade.
- The Delaware Society for Promoting the Abolition of Slavery and for the Relief and Protection of Free Blacks and People of Colour Unlawfully Held in Bondage is organized.

1789

- Pennsylvanians organize an abolition society, headed by Benjamin Franklin. It appeals to the public for funds.
- The Maryland Society for Promoting the Abolition of Slavery and the Relief of Free Negroes and Others Unlawfully Held in Bondage is organized.

1790–1820

- Hot local debates on slavery are conducted in Tennessee, Kentucky, Ohio, Indiana, and Illinois, culminating in the abolition of slavery in the states north of the Ohio River and entrenching it in those to the south.

1790

- Congress endorses the expansion of slavery into the Southwest.
- The Connecticut Society for the Promotion of Freedom, and for the Relief of Persons Holden in Bondage is organized.

1791

- A movement to refuse to buy the products of slave labor begins in England—the Free Produce movement.
- Vermont is admitted to the United States, with the provision in its constitution that "no male person born in this country, or brought from over sea, ought to be bound by law to serve any person as a servant, slave, or apprentice after he arrives at the age of twenty-one years, nor female, in like manner, after she arrives at the age of twenty-one years, unless they are bound by their own consent after they arrive at such age, or are bound by law for the payment of debts, damages, fines, costs, or the like."
- Kentucky is admitted to the United States. Its constitution denies the legislature the power to emancipate slaves without the owner's consent or without recompensing the owner. The constitution also forbids the legislature to pass laws prohibiting emigrants from other states from bringing their slaves with them.
- Massachusetts courts find the brigantine *Hope,* John Stanton, master, guilty of violating the statute against participation in the international slave trade.

1792

- The king of Denmark forbids his subjects to carry on the slave trade after 1802, except on the West Indies islands owned by Denmark.
- The first constitution of Kentucky does not discriminate against blacks in civil rights or suffrage.

1793

- Georgia, wary of slave insurrections, forbids importing slaves from the West Indies, the Bahamas, and Florida.
- The New Jersey Society for Promoting the Abolition of Slavery is organized.
- The American Convention for Promoting the Abolition of Slavery and Improving the Condition of the African Race is organized.
- Quaker Warner Mifflin publishes the antislavery *A Serious Expostulation with the Members of the House of Representatives of the United States.*

1794

- Congress prohibits carrying on the slave trade from the United States to any foreign place or country.
- The French National Convention abolishes slavery in all French territories, in a law repealed by Napoleon in 1802.
- An antislavery convention, with representatives from abolition societies in many states, is held in Philadelphia.
- Reverend Timothy Dwight denounces slavery in *Greenfield Hill.*
- Black bishops Richard Allen and Absolom Jones publish *An Address to Those Who Keep Slaves and Approve the Practice.*

1795–1835

- The Great Awakening, a religious revival movement, gives the antislavery movement impetus.

1796

- The first constitution of Tennessee does not discriminate against blacks in civil rights or suffrage.
- Methodists weaken their rules against slaveholding.
- The American Convention of Delegates of the Abolition Societies calls for a boycott on products of slave labor.
- St. George Tucker publishes *A Dissertation on Slavery with A Proposal for the Gradual Abolition of It, in the State of Virginia.*

1797

- New York passes a law, to take effect July 4, 1799, stating that all children born henceforth will be free, though children born to slaves must serve until the age of 28 if male and 25 if female.

1800

- The House of Representatives votes 85-1 to offer "no encouragement or countenance to petitions against slavery from Negroes."
- Indian slavery has almost ceased in Lower Canada.

1801

- Toussaint-Louverture succeeds in gaining control of the island of Hispaniola, ensuring the liberty of slaves freed officially in 1793.

1802

- Reverend Alexander McLeod publishes *Negro Slavery Unjustified.*

1803

- The House of Representatives in a resolution refers to "such American seamen, citizens of the United States, as are free persons of color."
- Ohio is admitted to the United States as a free state.

1804

- Louisiana comes under the sovereignty of the United States, with the results that the slave code becomes harsher and voluntary manumission by an owner becomes difficult.
- The United States forbids the importation of blacks from foreign territory into the Louisiana Purchase territory after October 1.
- New Jersey provides for the gradual abolition of slavery.
- Former slave trader Thomas Branigan publishes the first of his antislavery works.

1806

- Virginia passes a law requiring all slaves emancipated after May 1, 1806, to leave the state within 12 months after being freed or to be sold.

1807

- England and the United States prohibit the international slave trade.
- Ohio prohibits blacks from settling in the state unless within 26 days they have secured a 500-dollar bond ensuring their good behavior and sets a fine of 100 dollars for harboring or concealing fugitive slaves.
- Indiana enables slave owners to bring slaves into the territory.
- Thomas Branigan calls on all Christians to refuse to buy the products of slave labor.
- Reverend David Rice writes *Involuntary, Unmerited, Perpetual, Absolute Slavery, Examined.*
- Ex-slave John Gloucester becomes the first pastor of the Negro Presbyterian Church in Philadelphia.

1808–1832

- Local and state antislavery societies are established and function in the South.

1809

- Ohio allows blacks with a "fair certificate of actual freedom" from a U.S. court to settle in that state.

1813

- Argentina adopts gradual emancipation.

- Congress restricts employment on American ships to citizens of the United States and "persons of color, natives of the United States."
- When the Philadelphia legislature proposes excluding black immigrants, James Forten writes a series of letters in protest, under the signature "A Man of Color."

1814

- Colombia adopts gradual emancipation.
- The Mexican congress abolishes slavery.
- With the defeat of Napoleon, France promises to end the slave trade within five years but continues an illegal slave trade.
- Charles Osborn organizes the Tennessee Society for Promoting the Manumission of Slaves.

1815

- Benjamin Lundy organizes the Union Humane Society in Ohio.

1816

- The North Carolina Manumission Society is founded.
- *December 23:* The Virginia legislature requests the governor to ask the president to arrange for a territory abroad to which free American blacks may be sent.

1817

- Indiana rules that no blacks, mulattoes, or Indians may act as witnesses except in cases against blacks, mulattoes, or Indians, or in civil cases where blacks, mulattoes, or Indians alone are parties.
- Wealthy free black James Forten calls a meeting in Philadelphia to combat the idea of the inferiority of blacks.

1818–1822

- Congress drafts bills to strengthen the Fugitive Slave Law.

1818

- Darien, Georgia, enacts an ordinance imposing a tax of $10 for men and five dollars for women on all free "Negroes, Mullattoes, or Mustezos—persons of color." On such immigrants, a fee of $50 is to be paid in 10 days, on pain of imprisonment and public sale of their persons.
- A Maryland grand jury indicts Methodist elder Jacob Gruber for intent to incite mutiny and rebellion among blacks, because at a camp meeting attended by whites

and slaves he has preached that slaveholding is a national sin.

1819

- Georgia provides for the disposal of slaves illegally imported into the state, agreeing to turn them over to the Colonization Society if it will transport them to a foreign colony and reimburse the state for its expenses.
- Congressman James Tallmadge Jr. of New York unsuccessfully argues that Congress should prohibit the further introduction of slavery into Missouri and emancipate all children of slaves at age 25.
- Robert Walsh of Maryland defends slavery in *An Appeal from the Judgments of Great Britain Respecting the United States of America;* in *Free Remarks on the Spirit of the Constitution,* he endorses the doctrine of free soil, arguing against any extension of slavery.
- Northern defenders of slavery argue that some sections of the United States should be reserved entirely for whites, with no free blacks and no black slaves.

Early 1820s

- South Carolina produces a spate of proslavery literature.

1820

- England begins using naval power to suppress the slave trade.
- South Carolina makes it a high misdemeanor to introduce into the state any written or printed matter against slavery.

1821

- In the Missouri Compromise, Congress admits Maine as a free state and Missouri as a slave state and prohibits slavery in the territory of the Louisiana Purchase north of 36 degrees, 30 minutes. The compromise includes a fugitive slave provision.
- U.S. attorney general William Wirt issues the opinion that "No person is included in the description of citizen of the United States who has not the full rights of a citizen in the State of his residence."
- Congress receives a petition from Maryland to redress grievances caused by the underground operations of antislavery Pennsylvanians, and another from Kentucky protesting against Canada's admission of fugitive slaves.
- Spanish authorities officially permit slaveholder Moses Austin to settle a colony in Texas; Austin's son Stephen

arranges a distribution of land for the colonists that includes a grant of 50 (later 80) acres per slave.

- Quaker Benjamin Lundy begins publication of *The Genius of Universal Emancipation.*

1822

- New York abolishes property requirements for whites to vote but increases them for blacks.
- South Carolina requires every free black over 15 to obtain a white guardian.
- Antislavery Mexican authorities, newly independent from Spain, refuse to approve Austin's contract; they allow his slave-owning colonists to occupy land only provisionally.

1823

- John Rankin publishes antislavery *Letters on American Slavery, Addressed to Mr. Thomas Rankin, Merchant at Middlebrook, Augusta County, Virginia.*
- Clergyman Richard Furman publishes the proslavery *Exposition of the Views of Baptists, Relative to the Coloured Population of the United States.*
- Chile abolishes slavery.
- Congress reduces funds for aiding in the suppression of the slave trade.

1824

- Mexico decrees that "[c]ommerce and traffic in slaves proceeding from any country and under any flag whatsoever, is forever prohibited in the territory of the United Mexican States."
- Sam Austin promulgates civil and criminal regulations containing a "slave code" for his colony in Texas and instructs the Mexican authorities to enforce them.
- Englishwoman Elizabeth Heyrich writes *Immediate, Not Gradual Abolition.*
- Reverend James Duncan publishes *A Treatise on Slavery, In Which Is Shown Forth the Evil of Slaveholding.*

1825

- In Baltimore, Frances Wright publishes *A Plan for the Gradual Abolition of Slavery in the United States.*
- A North Carolina manumission society survey finds that 60 percent of the state's population favors emancipation.

1826

- Vermont sends a resolution to North Carolina offering to cooperate "in any measures which may be adopted by the general government for its [slavery's] abolition in the United States"—in response to which North Carolina tightens its slave-patrol and militia laws.
- Pennsylvania passes a fugitive slave law.
- The Massachusetts General Colored Association, dedicated to improvement of local conditions and agitation for abolition, is founded.
- Episcopalian priest William Barlow urges the preaching of the acceptability of slavery to divine law.

1827

- The people of Baltimore present a memorial to Congress asking that slaves born in the District of Columbia, after a given time and on arriving at a certain age, become free.
- In New York, African Americans Samuel Cornish and John B. Russwurm found the weekly *Freedom's Journal,* the first black newspaper in the United States.
- *March 11:* The Congress of Coahuila and Texas adopts a constitution stating, "From and after the promulgation of the Constitution . . . no one shall be born a slave in the state, and after six months the introduction of slaves under any pretext shall not be permitted." Colonization of Texas by slaveholders continues.

1828

- With the approval of the authorities, slaveholding Texas settlers begin bringing in former slaves held as indentured servants, now working to pay their masters for their freedom and for the cost of moving them into Texas; children born in Texas of these "indentured servants" must serve until age 25 without pay and then on the same terms as their fathers.

1829

- An unsuccessful attempt is made to revise the constitution of Virginia to abolish slavery.
- The Female Association for Promoting the Manufacture and Use of Free Cotton is established in Philadelphia.
- The Colored Female Free Produce Society of Pennsylvania is organized by the women of the Bethel African Methodist Episcopal Church.
- Sarah and Angelina Grimké leave Charleston for the North to become Quakers, activist abolitionists, and champions of women's rights.
- Free black New Yorker Robert Young publishes the pamphlet *The Ethiopian Manifesto.*
- Free black David Walker publishes *Walker's Appeal, in Four Articles; Together with a Preamble, to the Coloured Citizens*

of the World, But in Particular and Very Expressly, to Those of the United States of America, advocating self-improvement and violent revolt.

- *September 15:* Mexican president Vicente Guerrero decrees all slaves forever free.
- *December 2:* President Guerrero exempts Texas from the general Mexican emancipation.

1830

- *April 6:* The Mexican president prohibits further immigration into Texas from the United States and calls for strict enforcement of rules against the further introduction of slaves.

1831

- Bolivia emancipates slaves.
- U.S. attorney general John M. Berrien pronounces South Carolina's black-seamen law (1821) constitutional.
- Mississippi enacts a law saying, "It is unlawful for any slave, free Negro, or mulatto to preach the gospel upon pain of receiving thirty-nine lashes upon the naked back of the . . . preacher."
- The Massachusetts Anti-Slavery Society is founded.
- The Afric-American Female Intelligence Society is founded in Boston.
- The Colored Female Society is organized in Philadelphia.
- African American Maria W. Stewart's *Religion and the Pure Principles of Morality* is published in Boston.
- *January 1:* William Lloyd Garrison begins publication of *The Liberator* in Boston.
- *June 6–11:* The First Annual Convention of the People of Color is held in Philadelphia.
- *December:* William Lloyd Garrison organizes the New England Anti-Slavery Society (later the Massachusetts Anti-Slavery Society).

1832

- U.S. attorney general Roger B. Taney issues an opinion that free American blacks have *no* rights under the Constitution.
- The government of Coahuila and Texas decrees, "Servants and day laborers, hereafter introduced by foreign colonists, cannot be obligated by any contract to continue in the service of the latter longer than ten years."
- Maria W. Stewart makes her first public address, to the Afric-American Female Intelligence Society in Boston.
- Prudence Crandall establishes her school for "colored girls" in Canterbury, Connecticut.

- *January 1:* William Lloyd Garrison and others organize the American Anti-Slavery Society.
- *February 22:* Black women of Salem, Massachusetts, establish an antislavery society.
- *July 1:* Rhode Island women establish an antislavery society.
- *October 8:* Laura Haviland and Elizabeth Chandler organize the Logan Female Anti-Slavery Society in the Michigan Territory.
- *December 9:* Lucretia Mott establishes the Philadelphia Female Anti-Slavery Society.

1833–1837

- Black and white antislavery societies are integrated.

1833

- An agreement between London and Paris authorizes British cruisers to search and break up French slave ships.
- The Providence Anti-Slavery Society, the New York City Anti-Slavery Society, and the Boston Female Anti-Slavery Society are organized.
- Lydia Maria Child publishes *An Appeal in Favor of That Class of Americans Called Africans.*
- *December 4–6:* The first American Anti-Slavery Society convention is held in Philadelphia.
- *December 6:* The Kentucky Society for the Gradual Relief of the State from Slavery is organized.

1834

- The British government abolishes slavery in all its colonies.
- Legal immigration of Americans into Texas resumes.
- The North Carolina Manumission Society holds its last meeting.
- After a debate on slavery at Lane Theological Seminary in Cincinnati, the trustees order the students to discontinue their antislavery society and stop discussing the question; 51 students, led by Theodore Weld, withdraw (many transfer to Oberlin College) and begin intensive antislavery lecturing, under frequent mob attack.
- A Colored Female Anti-Slavery Society in Middletown (Connecticut), a Colored Anti-Slavery Society in Newark (New Jersey), the Vermont State Anti-Slavery Society, and the New Hampshire State Anti-Slavery Society are organized.
- The first antislavery fair raises 300 dollars under the leadership of Lydia Maria Child.

- The violence of townspeople forces Prudence Crandall to close the Canterbury Female Boarding School for the education of free black young women.
- *July 10:* A New York City mob riots against blacks and antislavery activists.
- *August:* The "Passover" riots of Philadelphia attack the homes of blacks, passing by houses owned by whites with lights in the windows.

1835

- Antiabolition riots multiply. Provoked by the murder of a white man by his black servant, a Philadelphia mob riots against blacks. William Lloyd Garrison is mobbed in Boston for his abolitionism.
- The Ladies' New York City Anti-Slavery Society is established. The Female Anti-Slavery Society of Ohio is organized in Muskingum County. James Birney organizes the Kentucky Anti-Slavery Society, which is almost immediately shut down, and Theodore Weld organizes the Ohio State Anti-Slavery Society. The New York State Anti-Slavery Society is organized, amid mob violence.
- *July 29:* In Charleston, South Carolina, a mob breaks into the U.S. Post Office, removes a bag of mail containing antislavery publications, and burns them; a committee then arranges to meet the mail boats, escort the mail to the post office, and remove and destroy all offensive (antislavery) publications.
- *August 10:* Dr. Reuben Crandall is jailed in the District of Columbia, charged with having published papers intended to excite insurrection; he is detained there until April 1836, when after a prosecution by Francis Scott Key he is acquitted. He dies soon thereafter.
- *October 15:* A Louisiana committee of vigilance offers $50,000 for the capture of abolitionist Arthur Tappan.
- *December 7:* Pres. Andrew Jackson asks Congress for legislation to prohibit the sending of incendiary (abolitionist) literature through the mails into the South.
- *December 19:* North Carolina formally requests other states to enact penal laws prohibiting the printing of publications that might make its slaves discontented.
- *December 20:* South Carolina requests other states to suppress all abolition societies and penalize the publication of literature that might excite slaves to revolt.

1836

- Georgia, Alabama, and Virginia ask other states to "put an end to the malignant deeds of the abolitionists."
- The Supreme Judicial Court of Massachusetts frees a six-year-old slave girl whose mistress has brought her into the state on a visit.
- Texas wins its independence from Mexico; the Constitution of the Republic of Texas permits slavery.
- The Charleston, South Carolina, postmaster confiscates abolitionist literature.
- The Methodist church, which has earlier attacked slavery, now disclaims "any right, wish, or intention to interfere with the civil and political relation between master and slave."
- By this time, Congregationalists have closed their doors to advocates of immediate abolition.
- Huge numbers of antislavery petitions are generated, mostly by women.
- In Boston, a black vigilance committee organizes a successful rescue of two women recaptured under the Fugitive Slave Act of 1793, precipitating the "Abolition Riot."
- Theodore Weld and Henry B. Stanton recruit men and women agents for the American Anti-Slavery Society, training them to lecture and to face mob violence.
- The Michigan State Anti-Slavery Society and the Rhode Island Anti-Slavery Society are organized.
- African American Charles Ball's autobiographical *Slavery in the United States* is published.
- James K. Paulding defends slavery in *View of Slavery in the United States*, the first comprehensive criticism of abolitionism.
- Sarah Grimké publishes *An Epistle to the Clergy of the Southern States.*
- *January:* James G. Birney begins publication of the antislavery *Philanthropist* in Cincinnati, under threat of mob violence.
- *February 2:* The Milledgeville Federal Union offers $10,000 for the kidnapping of abolitionist Amos A. Phelps.
- *May 14:* The Treaties of Velasco call for the return of black slaves and indentured servants who have been captured by or have taken refuge with the Mexican army.
- *May 22:* In Palmyra, Missouri, American Anti-Slavery Society agent Reverend David Nelson reads from the pulpit a parishioner's offer to contribute $10,000 toward a fund for compensated emancipation; a mob assails the parishioner and drives Nelson from the state.
- *May 23:* Editor Elijah P. Lovejoy of the St. Louis *Observer* reports the lynching of a black, under the headline, "Awful Murder and Savage Barbarity"; vandals damage his press; he continues publication from Alton, Illinois.

- *May 26:* The U.S. House of Representatives adopts the Gag Rule, tabling antislavery petitions without reading them.
- *June 8:* Princeton theological student Aaron W. Kitchell is mobbed and expelled from the state at Hillsborough, Georgia, on suspicion of talking with slaves.
- *July:* A mob pillages the printing press of James Birney's antislavery *Philanthropist* and attacks the black section of Cincinnati.
- *August 3:* The citizens of Mount Meigs, Alabama, offer $50,000 for the capture of abolitionists Arthur Tappan and LaRoy Sunderland.
- *August 6:* Congress provides a fine and imprisonment for any postmaster convicted of detaining letters, packages, pamphlets, or newspapers to prevent or delay delivery.
- *September:* Angelina Grimké publishes "An Appeal to the Christian Women of the South" in the *Anti-Slavery Examiner.*
- *December:* The Grimké sisters begin an antislavery speaking tour.

1837

- The governor of New York refuses the demand of the governor of Alabama that the publishing agent of the American Anti-Slavery Society be delivered to Georgia as a fugitive from justice for the publication of antislavery literature.
- A Virginia law allows slaves emancipated after 1806 to apply for permission to remain in the state.
- Abolitionist Elijah Lovejoy is assassinated in Illinois for protesting the lynching of Francis McIntosh, a mulatto freeman.
- The first National Anti-Slavery Society Convention is held in New York.
- No southern abolition societies remain in existence.
- The American Convention for Promoting the Abolition of Slavery, etc., is dissolved.
- The Pennsylvania State Anti-Slavery Society and the Illinois State Anti-Slavery Society are organized.
- The American Anti-Slavery Society publishes *Emancipation in the West Indies,* written by its agents James A. Thome and J. Horace Kimball.
- Catharine E. Beecher publishes *An Essay on Slavery and Abolitionism, with Reference to the Duty of American Females,* arguing that slavery is a domestic concern of the South.
- Angelina Grimké publishes *Letters to Catharine E. Beecher in Reply to an Essay on Slavery and Abolitionism,* as a series in *The Liberator.*

A mob attacks the stored printing press of Elijah Lovejoy. *(Library of Congress)*

- *An Appeal to the Women of the Nominally Free States Issued by an Anti-Slavery Convention of American Women* is published.
- *March:* Angelina Grimké addresses a "promiscuous" audience (that is, of both genders) in Poughkeepsie at a meeting called by the black community.
- *May 9–12:* The first Anti-Slavery Convention of American Women is held in New York.
- *September:* The Tappan brothers, through the American and Foreign Anti-Slavery Society, establish the *National Era* in Washington, D.C., with Gamaliel Bailey as editor.

1838

- The Pennsylvania Supreme Court holds that a black is not a freeman within the meaning of Pennsylvania's constitution and hence not entitled to vote.
- The Presbyterian church splits into North and South, having refused to take a stand on slavery.
- James G. Birney informs Congress that 225 antislavery societies existed as of May 1835; 527 in 1836; and 1,006 in 1837; an estimated 1,406 exist in 1838, with an estimated total membership of 115,000 in a population of roughly 16 million.
- Reformers start the first National Female Anti-Slavery Society in New York.
- The Indiana State Anti-Slavery Society is organized.
- Black women of Philadelphia organize the Female Vigilant Committee to support the Underground Railroad.
- Sarah Grimké publishes *Letters on the Equality of the Sexes, and the Condition of Women* as a series in the *New England Spectator.*
- *February 21:* Angelina Grimké speaks to the Massachusetts legislature, representing 20,000 Massachusetts women who have signed a petition to end slavery.
- *May 15–18:* During the Second Anti-Slavery Convention of American Women, a mob attacks and burns down the new Philadelphia Hall, dedicated to free speech.
- *May 15:* Abby Kelley and Maria Weston Chapman begin their lecture careers, speaking at the Second Anti-Slavery Convention of American Women.
- *September 6:* The American Free Produce Association is established in Philadelphia.

1839

- The British and Foreign Anti-Slavery Society is founded in London to promote international cooperation against slavery.
- New York refuses to extradite three sailors "charged with having feloniously stolen a negro slave" in Virginia.

This Free Produce store in Hamorton, Pennsylvania, sold no products of slave labor. *(Courtesy of Frances C. Taylor)*

- Ohio repeals its antikidnapping law and establishes a system by which state officers superintend the arrest, trial, and delivery of fugitive slaves to their owners.
- The Massachusetts Female Emancipation Society is established by antifeminist abolitionists. Anti-Garrisonians organize the Massachusetts Abolition Society. The organization of women's antislavery societies begins in Indiana.
- Maria Weston Chapman publishes *Right and Wrong in Massachusetts,* attributing the split among abolitionists to a dispute over women's rights.
- The Boston Female Anti-Slavery Society publishes *Liberty Bell,* an antislavery annual edited by Maria Weston Chapman.
- With the assistance of the Grimké sisters, Theodore Weld publishes *American Slavery as It Is,* incorporating the testimony of slaveholders and other eyewitnesses.
- *January 11:* An Evangelical Union Anti-Slavery Society is formed in New York with the intent of "purifying" the churches on the slavery question.
- *May 1–3:* The Third Anti-Slavery Convention of American Women is held in Philadelphia.
- *November 13:* Antislavery men favoring political action nominate James G. Birney for president and Francis J. LeMoyne for vice president of the United States.

1840

- Russia permits factory owners to emancipate their serfs.
- The American Anti-Slavery Society splits over woman's rights and political action; Garrison gains control, and

his opponents break off into the American and Foreign Anti-Slavery Society.

- New York black women establish the Manhattan Abolition Society.
- The American Anti-Slavery Society starts the *National Anti-Slavery Standard.*
- *April 1:* The National Convention of Friends of Immediate Emancipation approves the candidacy of James G. Birney and Thomas Earle for president and vice president of the United States, effectively forming the Liberty, or Human Rights, Party.
- *May 12–13:* The American Anti-Slavery Society Convention is held in New York.
- *June 12–23:* The World Anti-Slavery Convention, held in London, refuses to seat women delegates.

1841

- Uruguay emancipates its slaves.
- England, France, Russia, Prussia, and Austria agree to mutual search of ships on the high seas in order to suppress the slave trade.
- The New York legislature repeals a law that had allowed masters passing through the state to keep slaves for up to nine months.
- Ohio repeals its statute of 1839 that had established a system by which state officers cooperated in returning fugitive slaves to their owners, and it again passes its antikidnapping law of 1831.
- In Cincinnati a mob pillages the printing press of James Birney's antislavery *Philanthropist* for the third time and kills and wounds blacks.
- Ex-slave James C. Pennington publishes *A Text Book of the Origin and History of the Colored People.*
- *May:* Lydia Maria Child becomes editor of the *National Anti-Slavery Standard.*
- *May 12–13:* The Liberty Party holds its national convention in New York City, again nominating Birney for the presidency.

1842

- The U.S. Supreme Court rules in *Prigg* v. *Pennsylvania* that the federal Fugitive Slave Law of 1793 is constitutional; that state personal liberty laws unconstitutionally levy new requirements on slaveholders wishing to recover fugitive slaves; that under the Constitution's fugitive slave clause, any slave owner can capture a fugitive slave without complying with the Fugitive Slave Law of 1793, if he can do so without a breach of the peace; and that all states ought to enforce the federal

law but the federal government cannot force them to do so. Several northern states react by forbidding their officers to perform the duties imposed by the Fugitive Slave Law of 1793.

- The Georgia legislature unanimously resolves that free blacks are not citizens of the United States and that Georgia will "never recognize such citizenship."
- Black people of Troy, New York, meet to discuss action in the face of the Supreme Court's nullification of states' personal liberty laws.
- The *New York Times* alleges that abolitionist Gerritt Smith has advised slaves to raise insurrections against their masters.

1843

- Massachusetts, Vermont, and Ohio pass personal liberty (antikidnapping) laws.
- The Black Convention is held in Buffalo, New York.
- Black abolitionist Henry Highland Garnet calls on slaves to rise against their masters.
- Lewis Tappan writes *An Address to the Non-Slaveholders of the South, on the Social and Political Evils of Slavery.*

1844

- The Gag Rule, enacted annually by Congress since 1836, is defeated.
- Connecticut passes a personal liberty (antikidnapping) law.
- Justice Frederick Nash of North Carolina declares: "The free people of color cannot be considered as citizens in the largest sense of the term, or, if they are, they occupy such a position in society as justifies the legislature in adopting a course of policy in its acts peculiar to them."
- The South Carolina legislature empowers the governor to use the militia, if necessary, to prevent the release by writ of habeas corpus of any person imprisoned under the Negro Seamen Act.
- Oregon prohibits slavery and requires slaveholders to remove their chattels within three years.

1845

- Texas enters the Union as a slave state.
- The Anti-Slavery Office in Boston publishes the *Narrative of the Life of Frederick Douglass,* an escaped slave and a leader of the abolition movement.
- B. S. Jones and Elizabeth H. Jones found the *Anti-Slavery Bugle* at New Lisbon, Ohio.

1846

- Congressman David Wilmot of Pennsylvania introduces the Wilmot Proviso, prohibiting slavery in any territory acquired from Mexico. It fails in the Senate.
- German settlers of Mercer County, Ohio, formally resolve to expel blacks from the county and no longer to employ or trade with blacks.
- The Free Produce Association is organized by the Friends of Ohio Yearly Meeting. The Western Free Produce Association is organized in Indiana.
- In St. Louis, according to later oral tradition, 12 young black men form the Knights of Tabor, undertaking to organize a liberation army called the Knights of Liberty to strike for freedom by about 1856.

1847

- Pennsylvania passes a personal liberty (antikidnapping) law. The state also repeals the law that has allowed masters traveling through the state to keep slaves for up to six months.
- The idea of "squatter sovereignty" is proposed: that the settlers of a territory, not the federal government, should decide whether a new state will be slave or free.
- *The Narrative of William Wells Brown, A Fugitive Slave,* is published.
- *October:* The Liberty Party holds its third national convention, nominating John P. Hale for the presidency.
- *December 3:* The first issue of *North Star* appears. This antislavery weekly is edited by Frederick Douglass and Martin Delaney and published by William C. Nell.

1848

- Slavery is abolished in all French and Danish colonies.
- Rhode Island passes a personal liberty (antikidnapping) law.
- The Free Soil Party is created from many antislavery groups, opposing slavery in the territories acquired by the United States in the U.S.-Mexican War, and nominating Martin Van Buren for the presidency.

1849

- A Virginia law provides that any person may emancipate any of his slaves by will or by deed, and that the children of any woman so emancipated who are born between the death of the testator or the recording of the deed and the time when her right to freedom arrives shall also be free at that time, unless the deed or will forbids it.

1849

- African-American Bostonian Benjamin F. Roberts sues for the admission of his daughter to the nearest elementary school, and loses.

1850

- Congress enacts the Missouri Compromise of 1850, admitting California as a free state, leaving it to popular sovereignty to decide free or slave status for New Mexico and Utah, prohibiting the slave trade in the District of Columbia, and passing a more stringent fugitive slave law that puts the burden of enforcement on U.S. commissioners and marshals. This law strengthens the property rights of slaveholders and endangers blacks living in free states. The federal government rigorously enforces it, and some states react by passing more personal liberty laws.
- The slave Shadrach is seized by his owner in Boston but is rescued and spirited away. As a result, Congress gives the president authority to use the armed forces to enforce the new fugitive slave law.
- The Virginia constitution requires that any emancipated slave must leave the commonwealth within a year of emancipation and forbids the legislature to emancipate any slave or any slave's descendant.
- Lucy Stone begins her service as an antislavery agent.

1851

- Indiana takes away the right of male negroes and mulattoes to vote and excludes them from the militia.
- In Syracuse, New York, Liberty Party men rescue the fugitive slave Jerry from jail and send him to Canada.
- *September 11:* Whites and blacks battle in Christiana, Pennsylvania, after federal officers try to capture fugitive slaves, with the loss of four lives.

1852

- Harriet Beecher Stowe publishes *Uncle Tom's Cabin.*
- Abolitionist William Goodell publishes *Slavery and Anti-Slavery.*

1853

- Argentina frees its slaves.
- The Oregon Supreme Court rules that all blacks brought into the Oregon territory are thereby free.
- Maryland enacts a law making free blacks entering the state from the North liable to sale as slaves.
- Sallie Holley begins her career as an antislavery lecturer.

1854

- Peru and Venezuela abolish slavery.
- The Kansas-Nebraska Act creates the territories of Kansas and Nebraska, allows popular sovereignty to settle the slavery issue, and repeals the antislavery clause of the Missouri Compromise.
- The Connecticut legislature enacts an antikidnapping law, in response to the Fugitive Slave Law of 1850.
- Rhode Island extends its personal liberty law of 1848, providing, "No judge of any court of record of this State, and no justice of the peace, shall hereafter take cognizance or grant a certificate in cases" arising under the Fugitive Slave Law of 1850 "to any person who claims any other person as a fugitive slave within the jurisdiction of this state."
- In Boston, 1,100 armed federal troops and officials frustrate citizens' attempts to rescue fugitive slave Anthony Burns and place him on shipboard for return to his master in Virginia.

1855

- Michigan and Maine pass personal liberty laws opposing the Fugitive Slave Law of 1850.
- Massachusetts reenacts its 1843 personal liberty law and makes it applicable to the Fugitive Slave Law of 1850.
- The Massachusetts legislature prohibits segregation in public schools.

1856

- The Republican Party is formed on the base of the Free Soil Party.
- Advocates of slavery sack and burn the town of Lawrence, Kansas.
- *May 22:* Preston S. Brooks of South Carolina assaults Charles Sumner in the Senate chamber for his antislavery speech "The Crime against Kansas."

1857

- The U.S. Supreme Court in the *Dred Scott* decision declares that Congress has no power to limit slavery in the territories; three justices hold that a black descended from slaves has no rights as an American citizen.
- Ohio and Wisconsin pass antikidnapping laws.

- New Hampshire provides that no person because of descent from an African shall be disqualified from becoming a citizen of the state.

1858

- Vermont passes an antikidnapping law and provides that no person because of descent from an African shall be disqualified from becoming a citizen of the state.
- Texas entitles any person who captures a slave escaping to Mexico and delivers him to the sheriff at Austin to a reward of a third of the slave's value.
- Texas prohibits "the owners of slaves from placing them in charge of farm or stock ranches, detached from the home or residence of the owner or employer."
- John Brown proposes the organization of a biracial, armed guerrilla movement to uproot slavery, moving down from northern Virginia into the Deep South to form a provisional government of black and white people in a kind of guerrilla territory within the United States, under the formal aegis of the U.S. government.
- Black emigrationist Martin Delaney publishes the novel *Blake,* with the theme of pan-African revolution in the Western Hemisphere.

1859

- John Brown leads a small biracial group in capturing the federal armory at Harpers Ferry, Virginia.

1860

- The state of New York, in *Lemmon v. The People,* frees slaves in transit from Virginia to Texas by coastal vessel.
- Mississippi resolutions declare that northern states have (as in *Lemmon v. The People*) "insulted and outraged our citizens when travelling among them for pleasure, health or business, by taking their servants and liberating the same . . . and subjecting their owners to degrading and ignominious punishment."
- Black emigrationist Martin Delaney goes to Canada to organize a company of black emigrants to move toward a new homeland.

1862

- Free black Louis Roudanez begins publication of *L'Union,* the first black newspaper in the South.

Eyewitness Testimony

The Morality of Slavery: The Capabilities of Blacks

The unhappy man, who has long been treated as a brute animal, too frequently sinks beneath the common standard of the human species. The galling chains that bind his body do also fetter his intellectual faculties, and impair the social affections of his heart. Accustomed to move like a mere machine; by the will of a master, reflection is suspended; he has not the power of choice, and reason and conscience have but little power over his conduct for he is chiefly governed by the passion of fear.

Benjamin Franklin, calling for abolition, quoted in Kates, "Abolition, Deportation, Integration," 40–41.

[Because of slavery] We colored people of these United States are the most degraded, and abject set of beings that ever lived since the world began. . . . It is indeed surprising that a man of such great learning, combined with such excellent natural parts [as Thomas Jefferson], should speak . . . [of the natural inferiority] of a set of men in chains. I do not know what to compare it to, unless, like putting one wild deer in an iron cage, where it will be secured, and hold another by the side of the same, then let it go, and expect the one in the cage to run as fast as the one at liberty. . . .

The whites have always been an unjust, jealous, unmerciful, avaricious and blood thirsty set of beings, always seeking after power and authority. . . . The whites want slaves, and want us for their slaves, but some of them will curse the day they ever saw us. As true as the sun ever shone in its meridian splendor, [people of] my Colour will root some of them out of the very face of the earth. They shall have enough of making slaves of, and butchering, and murdering us in the manner which they have. . . . The whites shall have enough of the blacks, yet, as true as God sits on his throne in heaven.

Free black David Walker, Walker's Appeal (1829), in Dumond, Antislavery, 115.

The negro, constituted as he is, has such an aversion to labour, and so great a propensity for indulgence and vice, that no prospect of advantage can stimulate him. . . . Without force he will sink into lethargy, and revert to his primitive savage character, and the only feasible and effectual plan to promote his civilization is to persist in those measures which compel him to labour, inculcate morality, and tend to extirpate those vices which are inherent in the descendants of the African race.

The South Vindicated (1836), 120.

The negro requires government in every thing, the most minute . . . even in his meat and drink, his clothing, and hours of repose. Unless under the government of one man to prescribe rules of conduct to guide him, he will eat too much meat and not enough of bread and vegetables; he will not dress to suit the season, or kind of labor he is engaged in, nor retire to rest in due time to get sufficient sleep. . . . Nor will the women undress the children and put them regularly to bed. . . . They let their children suffer and die, or unmercifully abuse them, unless the white man or woman prescribe rules in the nursery for them to go by. . . .

The prognathous race require government also in their religious exercises, or they degenerate into fanatical saturnalia. . . .

S. A. Cartwright, in Elliott, Cotton Is King (1860), 727–28.

I am . . . treated as one in rebellion against the Government. Let it be so: it is one of the results of the teachings of your doctrines. Oh! the blood which has and will be spilt in consequence of the false sympathy for the negro and the Indian. I think it is a great misfortune to mankind that there is a large party, who prize the negro blood more highly than that of their own intelligent country men. Had it not been for that accursed negro question peace and prosperity would now reign, where blood flows in torrents and lives are taken by thousands. But such are the results of false and fanatical teachings. You are too tender hearted to see a deer killed for the necessities of man, which was intended by God for his use, but you can see hundreds of thousands of men go into a sister state and slay thousands of your countrymen and believe they are doing God's service because they happen to be the owners of property in slaves which you for the sake of lucre sold them.

Slaveowner William Pelham, imprisoned for refusing to take an oath of loyalty to the Union, to his abolitionist but heretofore beloved niece Marianna Pelham Mott, August 11, 1861, Women in Social Movements Web site. Available online at URL: http://womhist.binghamton.edu.

The Morality of Slavery: Defenses of the Institution of Slavery

Our Imitation of him [the biblical Abraham] in this his Moral Action [slaveholding], is as warrantable as that of [adopting] his Faith. . . . Any lawful Captives of Other Heathen nations may be made Bond men. . . . [But] Tis unlawful for Christians to Buy and Sell one another for slaves. . . . [God has ordained] some to be High and Honourable, some to be Low and Despicable; some to be Monarchs, Kings, Princes and Governours, Masters and Commanders, others to be Subjects, and to be Commanded; Servants of sundry sorts and degrees, bound to obey; yea, some to be born Slaves, and so to remain during their lives.

Massachusetts justice John Saffin, 1701, in Tise, Proslavery, *17.*

In Spight of all Endeavours to disguise this Point, it is clear as Light itself, that Negroes are as essentially necessary to the Cultivation of Georgia, as Axes, Hoes, or any other Utensil of Agriculture.

Thomas Stephens, 1743, in Tise, Proslavery, *17.*

[I should consider myself] highly favored [if I could] purchase a good number of them [slaves], in order to make their lives comfortable, and lay a foundation for breeding up their posterity in the nurture and admonition of the Lord.

Anglican evangelist George Whitefield, ca. 1750, in Tise, Proslavery, *21.*

[T]he nature of society . . . requires various degrees of authority and subordination; and while the universal rule of right, the happiness of the whole, allows greater degrees of Liberty to some, the same immutable law suffers it to be enjoyed only in less degrees by others. . . . [Africans are entitled to no more liberty than] concomitant circumstances being considered tends *to happiness on the whole.* . . . [A] vast inequality [exists between] different individuals of the human species, in point of qualification for the proper direction of conduct. . . . [S]ome are actually found so far to excell others both in respect to wisdom and benevolence, both in the knowledge of the principles of propriety, and a disposition to practice such principles, that the general end, happiness, would be better promoted by the exercise of authority in the former, though necessarily involving subordination of the latter, than by the enjoyment of equal Liberty in each. . . . [The Africans'] removal to America is to be esteemed a favor. . . . [Bringing them] from the state of brutality, wretchedness, and misery . . . to this land of light, humanity, and christian knowledge, is to them so great a blessing.

Harvard senior Theodore Parsons, 1773, in Tise, Proslavery, *30–32.*

One of the most pleasing incidents of slavery is its amelioration of the condition of the female sex. Among all savage people women are degraded into slaves, the abject drudges of their brutal lords. . . . The slave relieves the woman. Released from a condition worse than that of bondage, leisure is afforded; and with woman, in her rudest state, leisure must result in improvement. Her faculties are developed; her gentle and softening influence is seen and felt; she assumes the high station for which nature designed her; and happy in the hallowed affections of her own bosom, unwearily exerts those powers so well adapted to the task of humanizing and blessing others.

The South Vindicated *(1836), 104.*

[O]ne of the first and most essential requisites in the formation of republican character is intelligence. . . . [T]he slave-holder has, in that particular, the inestimable advantage of leisure. Relieved from the labour required for actual support, he is enabled to direct his attention to public affairs; to investigate political subjects, and exercise his privileges understandingly. This result has been fully attained at the south. . . . [N]owhere are the rights of man so fully canvassed and understood by the mass of citizens.

The South Vindicated *(1836), 110.*

Mr. May, we are not such great fools as not to know that slavery is a great evil and a great wrong. But it was consented to by the founders of the Republic. It was provided for in the Constitution of our Union. A great portion of the property of the Southerners is invested under its sanction; and the business of the North as well as of the South, has become adjusted to it.

There are millions upon millions of dollars due from the Southerners to the merchants and mechanics of this city [New York] alone, the payment of which would be jeopardized by a rupture between the North and the South. We cannot afford, sir, to let you and your associates succeed in your endeavor to overthrow slavery. It is not a matter of principle with us. It is a matter of business necessity.

Partner in a mercantile house to Reverend Samuel J. May, 1835, in Aptheker, One Continual Cry, *19–20.*

The poorest and humblest freeman of the South feels as sensibly, perhaps more sensibly than the wealthiest planter, the barrier which nature, as well as law, has erected between the white and black races. . . .

James H. Hammond, DeBow's Review, *June 1850, quoted in Lewis,* Coal, Iron, and Slaves, *225.*

The comparative evils of Slave Society and of Free Society, of slavery to human Masters, and of slavery to Capital are the issues which the South now presents, and which the North avoids. And she avoids them because the Abolitionists, the only assailants of Southern Slavery, have . . . asserted the entire failure of their own social system, proposed its subversion, and suggested an approximating millennium, or some system of Free Love, Communism, or Socialism, as a substitute. . . . [T]he profits which capital exacts from labor makes free laborers slaves, without the rights, privileges, or advantages of domestic slaves, and capitalists their masters, with all the advantages, and none of the burdens and obligations of the ordinary owners of slaves. . . .

Fitzhugh, Cannibals All *(1857), 7.*

[To argue against slavery] as a domestic institution simply because it is abused [is to be] like the socialists and free-lovers who argue against the marriage relation, because married people are always quarrelling, and running off to Indiana to be divorced. They have not the good sense to discriminate between the legitimate uses of an institution and the illegitimate abuses to which it can be subjected.

David Hundley, Social Relations in our Southern States, *1860, quoted in Tadman,* Speculators and Slaves, *182.*

[The] foundations [of the Confederacy] are laid, its corner-stone rests, upon the great truth, that the negro is not equal to the white man; that slavery, subordination to the superior race, is his natural and normal condition.

This, our new government, is the first, in the history of the world, based upon this great physical, philosophical, and moral truth. . . .

Many governments have been founded upon the principle of the subordination and serfdom of certain classes of the same race; such were and are in violation of the laws of nature. Our system commits no such violation of nature's laws. With us, all of the white race, however high or low, rich or poor, are equal in the eye of the law. Not so with the negro. Subordination is his place.

Alexander H. Stephens, vice president of the Confederacy, March 21, 1861, in Durden, Gray and the Black, *7–8.*

The Morality of Slavery: Sentiment against Slavery

It seemeth to me that to sell them away as slaves is to hinder the enlargement of His kingdom. To sell souls for money seemeth to me a dangerous merchandise. If they deserve to die it is far better to be put to death under godly persons who will take religious care that means may be used that they may die penitently. To sell them away from all means of grace when Christ hath provided means of grace for them is the way for us to be active in destroying their souls, when we are highly obliged to seek their conversion and salvation.

Puritan minister John Eliot, letter of June 13, 1675, to the Boston General Council, in Higginbotham, In the Matter of Color, *65.*

We hear that the most part of such negers are brought hither against their will and consent, and that many of them are stolen. Now, though they are black, we cannot conceive there is more liberty to have them slaves, as it is to have other white ones. There is a saying that we should do to all men like as we will be done ourselves; making no difference of what generation, descent, or colour they are. And those who steal or rob men, and those who buy or purchase them, are they not all alike.

Mennonites of Germantown, Pennsylvania, 1688, in Higginbotham, In the Matter of Color, *267.*

[Slave masters] can afford to keep them with white hands [without guilt], except at some Times they chance to be besparkled with the blood of those poor Slaves, when they fall to beating them with their *twisted Hides and Horse-whips,* . . . to go with *fine powdered Perriwigs,* and great bunched *Coats;* and likewise keep their Wives idle *(Jezebel-like)* to paint *their Faces,* and *Puff,* and *powder their Hair,* and to bring up their Sons and Daughters in *Idleness* and *Wantonness,* and in all manner of *Pride* and *Prodigality,* in *decking* and *adorning* their Carkasses. . . . All, and much more, the miserable Effects produced by the Slavery of the Negroes.

Quaker John Hepburn of New Jersey, 1714, in Locke, Anti-Slavery, *22.*

[Preachers are] a sort of Devils, that Preach more to Hell than they do to Heaven, and so they will do forever, as long as they are suffered to reign in the worst, and Mother of all Sins, Slave-Keeping. . . . What do you think of these Things, you brave Gospel Ministers? that keep poor Slaves to Work for you to maintain you and yours in Pride, Pride and much Idleness or Laziness, and Fulness of Bread, the Sins of *Sodom.* . . .

Quaker Benjamin Lay, 1737, in Locke, Anti-Slavery, *26.*

Slavery is against the gospel, as well as fundamental law of England. We refused, as trustees [of the colony of Georgia], to make a law permitting such a horrid crime.

Gen. James Oglethorpe, ca. 1738, in Locke,
Anti-Slavery, 12.

It is shocking to human Nature that any Race of Mankind, and their Posterity should be sentenced to perpetual Slavery; nor in Justice can we think otherwise than that they are thrown amongst us to be our Scourge one Day or other for our Sins; and as Freedom to them must be as dear as to us, what a Scene of Horror must it bring about.

The Scotch of New Inverness, Georgia, to Gen. James
Oglethorpe, January 3, 1739, in Locke, Anti-Slavery, 12.

I think that we Americans, at least in the Southern Colonies, cannot contend with a good grace for liberty, until we have enfranchised our slaves.

John Laurens, in a 1776 letter, in Bell,
Major Butler's Legacy, 10.

As much as I value a union of all the states, I would not admit the Southern States into the Union unless they agree to the discontinuance of this disgraceful trade, because it would bring weakness, and not strength, to the Union.

George Mason at the Virginia ratifying convention, ca. 1788,
in Dumond, Anti-Slavery, 28.

Future inhabitants of America will inevitably be Mulattoes. . . . [T]his evil is coming upon us in a way much more disgraceful, and unnatural, than intermarriages. Fathers will have their own children for slaves, and leave them as an inheritance to their children. Men will possess their brothers and sisters as their property, leave them to their heirs, or sell them to strangers. Youth will have their grey-headed uncles and aunts for slaves, call them their property, and transfer them to others. Men will humble their own sisters, or even their aunts, to gratify their lust. An hard-hearted master will not know whether he has a blood relation, a brother or a sister, an uncle or an aunt, or a stranger from Africa, under his scourging hand.

Rev. David Rice, 1792 speech in the Kentucky convention, in
Dumond, Anti-Slavery, 62.

I will be as harsh as truth, and as uncompromising as justice. On this subject [slavery] I do not wish to think, speak, or write, with moderation. No! Tell a man whose house is on fire to give a moderate alarm; tell him to moderately rescue his wife from the hands of a ravisher; tell the mother to gradually extricate her babe from the fire into which it has fallen—but urge me not to use moderation in a cause like the present. I am in earnest—I will not equivocate—I will not retreat a single inch—and I will be heard!

William Lloyd Garrison, Liberator, January 1831, quoted
in Reynolds, African Slavery, 89.

I have thus, I think, clearly proved to you seven propositions, viz.: First, that slavery is contrary to the declaration of our independence. Second, that it is contrary to the first charter of human rights given to Adam, and renewed to Noah. Third, that the fact of slavery having been the subject of prophecy, furnishes *no* excuse whatever to slave-dealers. Fourth, that no such system existed under the patriarchal dispensation. Fifth, that *slavery never* existed under the Jewish dispensation; but so far otherwise, that every servant was placed under the *protection of law,* and care taken not only to prevent all *involuntary* servitude, but all *voluntary perpetual* bondage. Sixth, that slavery in America reduces a *man* to a *thing,* a "chattel personal," *robs him of all* his rights as a *human being,* fetters both his mind and body, and protects the *master* in the most unnatural and unreasonable power, whilst it *throws him out* of the protection of law. Seventh, that slavery is contrary to the example and precepts of our holy and merciful Redeemer, and of his apostles.

But perhaps you will be ready to query, why appeal to *women* on this subject? We do not make the laws which perpetuate slavery. *No* legislative power is vested in us; *we* can do nothing to overthrow the system, even if we wished to do so. To this I reply, I know you do not make the laws, but I also know that *you are the wives and mothers, the sisters and daughters of those who do;* and if you really suppose *you* can do nothing to overthrow slavery; you are greatly mistaken.

Angelina Grimké, "Appeal to the Christian Women
of the South," September 1836, in Rossi,
The Feminist Papers, 296ff.

While we know that God lives, and governs, and always will, that he is just and has declared that righteousness shall prevail, we believe, despite all corruption and caste, we shall yet be elevated with the American people here. . . . We believe . . . that it is our duty and privilege to claim an equal place among the *American people,* to identify ourselves with American interests, and to exert all the power and influence we have, to break down the disabilities under which we labor, and look to become a happy people in this extended country.

Charles Ray, editor of the Colored American, *April 1840, in Harding,* River, *132.*

Our [Pilgrim Fathers were] men who had no communion with tyranny and oppression. . . . In consideration of the toils of our [black] fathers we claim the right of American citizenship. Our ancestors fought and bled for it. . . . With every fibre of our hearts entwined around our country, and with an indefeasible determination to obtain the possession of the natural and inalienable rights of American citizens, we demand redress for the wrongs we have suffered, and ask for the restoration of our birthright privileges.

Black abolitionist Henry Highland Garnet, 1840, in Harding, River, *134–35.*

What, to the American slave, is your Fourth of July? I answer: a day that reveals to him, more than all other days in the year, the gross injustice and cruelty to which he is the constant victim. To him, your celebration is a sham; your boasted liberty an unholy license; your national greatness swelling vanity; your sounds of rejoicing are empty and heartless; your denunciation of tyrants brass-fronted impudence; your shouts of liberty and equality hollow mockery; your prayers and hymns, your sermons and thanksgivings, with all your religious parade and solemnity, are to Him mere bombast, fraud, deception, impiety and hypocrisy—a thin veil to cover up crimes which would disgrace a nation of savages. There is not a nation on the earth guilty of practices more shocking and bloody than are the people of the United States at this very hour.

Frederick Douglass, "The Meaning of the Fourth of July for the Negro," Rochester, New York, 1852, quoted in Genovese, From Rebellion to Revolution, *132.*

I am an Abolitionist—and something more. I am in favor, not only of *abolishing* the Curse, but of making *reparation* for the Crime. . . . I more than agree with Disunion Abolitionists. They are in favor of a free Northern Republic. So am I. But as to boundary lines we differ. While they would fix the Southern boundary of their free Republic at the dividing line between Ohio and Kentucky, Virginia and the Keystone State, I would wash it with the warm waters of the Gulf of Mexico. "But what shall we do with the slaves?" Make free men of them. "And with the

slaveholding class?" Abolish them. "And with the Legrees of the plantations?" Them, annihilate! Drive them into the sea, as Christ once drove the swine; or chase them into the dismal swamps and black morasses of the South. "Anywhere—anywhere—out of the world!"

James Redpath, 1859, writing in Roving Editor, *8.*

[T]he causes which have impeded the progress and prosperity of the South, which have dwindled our commerce and other similar pursuits, into the most contemptible insignificance; sunk a large majority of our people in galling poverty and ignorance, rendered a small minority conceited and tyrannical, and driven the rest away from their homes; entailed upon us a humiliating dependence on the Free States; disgraced us in the recesses of our own souls, and brought us under reproach in the eyes of all civilized and enlightened nations—may all be traced to one common source, and there find solution in the most hateful and horrible word, that was ever incorporated into the vocabulary of human economy—*Slavery.*

Helper, Impending Crisis *(1860), 12.*

The free labouring [North Carolina] farmer remarked [in 1854], that, although there were few slaves in this part of the country, he had often said to his wife that he would rather be living where there were none. He thought slavery wrong in itself, and deplorable in its effects upon the white people. . . .

He himself never owned a slave, and never would own one for his own benefit if it were given to him, "first, because it was wrong; and secondly, because he didn't think they ever did a man much good."

Olmsted, Cotton Kingdom, *403–4.*

Alternatives to Abolition: The Free Soil Controversy

I am extremely sorry to hear the Senator from Mississippi say that he requires, first the extension of the Missouri Compromise line to the Pacific, and also that he is not satisfied with that, but requires . . . a positive provision for the admission of slavery south of that line. And now, sir, coming from a slave State, as I do, I owe it to myself, I owe it to truth, I owe it to the subject, to say that no earthly power could induce me to vote for a specific measure for the introduction of slavery where it had not before existed. . . . If the citizens of those territories choose to establish slavery, and if they come here with constitutions establishing slavery, I am for admitting them with such provisions in their constitutions; but then it will be their own work, and not ours, and their posterity will have to reproach them, and not us. . . .

Henry Clay, 1829 speech, in Helper, Impending Crisis, *99.*

But certain it is that the principle of interference [by the federal government] . . . should be limited to the creation of proper governments for new countries, acquired or settled, and to the necessary provision for their eventual admission into the Union; leaving, in the meantime, the people inhabiting them, to regulate their internal concerns in their own way. They are just as capable of doing so as the people of the states; and they can do so, at any rate as soon as their political independence is recognized by admission into the Union. During this temporary condition, it is hardly expedient to call into exercise a doubtful and invidious authority, which questions the intelligence of a respectable portion of our citizens, and whose limitation, whatever it may be, will be rapidly approaching its termination—an authority which would give to congress despotic power, uncontrolled by the constitution, over most important sections of our common country. For, if the relation of master and servant may be regulated or annihilated by its legislation, so may the regulation of husband and wife, of parent and child, and of any other condition which our institutions and the habits of our society recognize.

An assertion of "squatter sovereignty," by General Lewis Cass, December 24, 1847, in Blake, Slavery and the Slave Trade, *559.*

The political influence which [the Kansas-Nebraska] Territories will give to the South, if secured, will be of the first importance to perfect its arrangements for future slavery extension—whether by divisions of the larger States and Territories, now secured to the institution, its extension into territory hitherto considered free, or the acquisition of new territory to be devoted to the system, so as to preserve the balance of power in Congress. When this is done, Kansas and Nebraska, like Kentucky and Missouri, will be of little consequence to slaveholders, compared with the cheap and constant supply of provisions they can yield. . . . White free labor, doubly productive over slave labor in grain-growing, must be multiplied within their limits, that the cost of provisions may be reduced and the extension of slavery and the growth of cotton suffer no interruption. The present efforts to plant them with slavery, are indispensable to produce sufficient excitement to fill them speedily with a free population; and if this whole movement has been a Southern scheme to cheapen provi-

sions, and increase the ratio of the production of sugar and cotton, as it most unquestionably will do, it surpasses the statesman-like strategy which forced the people into an acquiescence in the annexation of Texas.

And should the anti-slavery voters succeed in gaining the political ascendancy in these Territories, and bring them as free States triumphantly into the Union; what can they do, but turn in, as all the rest of the Western States have done, and help to feed slaves, or those who manufacture or who sell the products of the labor of slaves.

David Christy Elliott, in Cotton Is King *(1860), 123–24.*

Alternatives to Abolition: The Free Produce Movement

I cannot help contemplating a sugar maple-tree with a species of affection and even veneration, for I have persuaded myself to behold in it the happy means of rendering the commerce and slavery of our african [sic] brethren in the sugar islands as unnecessary, as it has always been inhuman and unjust.

Dr. Benjamin Rush to Thomas Jefferson, in Locke, Anti-Slavery, *189.*

If every bale of cotton and every piece of calico were stained with the sweat and blood which has flowed so freely in raising the raw material, who would be found ready to receive, and manufacture, and vend, and wear the fabric into which slave grown cotton has been wrought?

Angelina Grimké, letter to Lewis Tappan, August 1841, in Dumond, Antislavery, *350.*

[Slave-labor products] are so mixed up with the commerce, manufactures and agriculture of the world—so modified or augmented in value by the industry of other nations,—so indissolubly connected with the credit and currency of the country—that, to attempt to seek the subversion of slavery by refusing to use them, or to attach moral guilt to the consumer of them is, in our opinion, preposterous and unjust.

William Lloyd Garrison, 1847, in Kraditor, American Abolitionism, *218–19.*

The Means to Emancipation: Gradual Emancipation

[W]e rejoice that it is in our power, to extend a portion of that freedom to others, which hath been extended to us. . . . We esteem it a peculiar blessing granted to us, that we are enabled this day to add one more step

William Lloyd Garrison was a passionate antislavery advocate. *(Holley,* A Life for Liberty*)*

to universal civilization, by removing, as much as possible, the sorrows of those, who have lived in undeserved bondage. . . .

III. *Be it enacted, and it is hereby enacted,* That all persons as well Negroes and Mulattoes as others, who shall be born within this state from and after the passing of this act, shall not be deemed and considered as servants for life, or slaves; and that all servitude for life, or slavery of children, in consequence of the slavery of their mothers, in the case of all children born within this state from and after the passing of this act as aforesaid, shall be, and hereby is, utterly taken away, extinguished, and for ever abolished.

IV. *Provided always, and be it further enacted,* That every Negro and Mulatto child, born within this state after the passing of this act as aforesaid (who would, in case this act had not been made, have been born a servant for years, or life, or a slave) shall be deemed to be, and shall be, by virtue of this act, the servant of such person, or his or her assigns, who would in such case have been entitled to the service

of such child, until such child shall attain unto the age of twenty-eight years, in the manner, and on the conditions, whereon servants bound by indenture for four years are or may be retained and holden . . .

Pennsylvania statute of 1780, in Finkelman,
Law of Freedom, *42–43.*

The Means to Emancipation: Political and Judicial Action

It is ordered by this court, and the authority thereof; that there shall never be any bond slavery, villainage or captivity amongst us, unless it be lawful captives taken in just wars, as willingly sell themselves or are sold to us, and such shall have the liberties and christian usage which the law of God established in Israel concerning such persons doth morally require; provided this exempts none from servitude, who shall be judged thereto by authority.

Massachusetts Body of Liberties, 1641, in Williams,
History of the Negro Race, *177.*

And forasmuch as great inconveniences may happen to this country by the setting of negroes and mulattoes free, by their either entertaining negro slaves from their masters service, or receiving stolen goods, or being grown old bringing a charge upon the country; for prevention thereof, *Be it enacted . . . , and it is hereby enacted,* That no negro or mulatto be after the end of this present session of assembly set free by any person or persons whatsoever, unless such person or persons, their heires, executors or administrators pay for the transportation of such negro or negroes out of the countrey within six moneths after such setting them free. . . .

Virginia law, 1691, in Finkelman, Law of Freedom, *108.*

AN ACT for rendering the Colony of Georgia more Defencible by Prohibiting the Importation and use of Black slaves or Negroes into the same. WHEREAS Experience hath Shewn that the manner of Settling Colonys and Plantations with Black Slaves or negroes hath Obstructed the Increase of English and Christian Inhabitants therein who alone can in case of a War be relyed on for the Defence and Security of the same, and hath Exposed the Colonys so settled to the Insurrections Tumults and Rebellions of such Slaves & Negroes and in case of a Rupture with an Foreign State who should encourage and Support such Rebellions might occasion the utter Ruin and loss of such Colonys. . . .

English law of 1735, quoted in Olexer, Enslavement of
the American Indians, *193.*

[A petition] of Felix Holbrook, and others, Negroes, praying that they may be liberated from a state of Bondage, and made Freemen of this Community; and that this Court would give and grant to them some part of the unimproved Lands belonging to the Province, for a settlement, or relieve them in such other Way as shall seem good and wise upon the Whole.

Petition to the Massachusetts legislature, 1773, in Williams,
History of the Negro Race, *233.*

We will neither import nor purchase any slave imported after the first day of December next, after which time we will wholly discontinue the slave trade and will neither be concerned in it nor will we hire our vessels nor sell our commodities or manufactures to those who are concerned in it.

First Continental Congress, 1774, in Harding, River, *45.*

Therefore, no male person, born in this country, or brought from over sea, ought to be holden by law, to serve any person, as servant, slave or apprentice, after he arrives to the age of twenty-one years, nor female, in like manner, after she arrives at the age of eighteen years, unless they are bound by their own consent, after they arrive to such age, or bound by law, for the payment of debts, damages, fines, costs, or the like.

Vermont Bill of Rights, 1777, in Locke, Anti-Slavery, *80.*

I was involved in several causes in which negroes sued for their freedom, before the Revolution. The arguments in favour of their liberty were much the same as have been urged since . . . arising from the rights of mankind. . . . Argument might have some weight in the abolition of slavery in Massachusetts, but the real cause was the multiplication of labouring white people, who would no longer suffer the rich to employ these sable rivals so much to their injury.

John Adams, March 21, 1795, in Higginbotham,
In the Matter of Color, *97.*

The professed object of this [Liberty] Party is to secure the rights of *colored men* in THIS country; [but] they have given no opportunity to the poor colored man to speak for him, by placing him in the legislature where he *ought* to be heard with themselves. . . . In view of this state of things, what better is this third abolition *party* for us than either of the other parties?

Black abolitionist Thomas Van Rensselaer, 1840,
in Harding, River, *135–36.*

The Means to Emancipation: Threats and Military Action

Sir, the people of the west[ern part of Virginia], I undertake to say, feel a deep, a lively, a generous sympathy for their eastern brethren. They know that the evils which now afflict them are not attributable to any fault of theirs that slavery was introduced against their will; that we are indebted for it to the commercial cupidity of that heartless [British] empire. . . . Yet we will not that you shall make our fair domain the receptacle of your mass of political filth and corruption. No, sir, before we can submit to such terms, violent convulsions must agitate this state.

Slaveholder Charles James Faulkner, speech in the
House of Delegates of Virginia, 1832, in Redpath,
Roving Editor, *99–100.*

You are not certain of heaven, because you suffer yourselves to remain in a state of slavery, where you cannot obey the commandments of the Sovereign of the universe. . . . It is your solemn and imperative duty to use every means, both moral, intellectual, and physical, that promises success [to end slavery]. . . . Promise the slaveowners renewed diligence in the cultivation of the soil, if they will render to you an equivalent for your services. . . . Point the slaveholders to the increase of happiness and prosperity in the British West Indies since the Act of Emancipation. . . . Inform them that all you desire is FREEDOM. . . . However much you and all of us may desire it, there is not much hope of redemption without the shedding of blood. . . . Brethren, arise, arise! Strike for your lives and liberties. Now is the day and the hour. Let every slave throughout the land do this, and the days of slavery are numbered. You cannot be more oppressed than you have been. . . . RATHER DIE FREEMEN THAN LIVE TO BE SLAVES. REMEMBER THAT YOU ARE FOUR MILLION! . . . Let your motto be resistance! *Resistance!* RESISTANCE! No oppressed people have ever secured their liberty without resistance.

Black abolitionist Henry Garnet, Address to the Slaves of
the United States, *1843, quoted in Harding,* River, *141.*

Resolved, that in the language of inspired wisdom, there shall be no peace to the wicked, and that this guilty nation shall have no peace, and that we will do all we can to agitate. *Agitate!* AGITATE!!! till our rights are restored and our brethren are redeemed from their cruel chains.

Resolution sponsored by Frederick Douglass at the National
Convention of Colored People, 1847, in Harding,
River, *146.*

Abolitionism

The object of this [American Anti-Slavery] Society is the entire abolition of slavery in the United States. While it admits that each State, in which slavery exists, has, by the Constitution of the United States, exclusive right to *legislate* in regard to its abolition in this State, it shall aim to convince all our fellow-citizens, by arguments addressed to their understandings and consciences, that slave-holding is a heinous crime in the sight of God, and that the duty, safety, and best interests of all concerned, require its *immediate abandonment*, without expatriation. The Society will also endeavor, in a constitutional way, to influence Congress to put an end to the domestic slave-trade, and to abolish slavery in all those portions of our common country, which come under its control, especially in the District of Columbia, and likewise to prevent the extension of it to any State that may be hereafter admitted to the Union. . . . This Society shall aim to elevate the character and condition of the people of color, by encouraging their intellectual, moral, and religious improvement, and by removing public prejudice, that thus they may, according to their intellectual and moral worth, share an equality with the whites, of civil and religious privileges; but this Society will never, in any way, countenance the oppressed in vindicating their rights by resorting to physical force.

Constitution of the American Anti-Slavery Society, 1833, in Kraditor, American Abolitionism, 5.

Abby Kelley Foster braved calumny and riot to speak in public for abolition. *(Holley, A Life for Liberty)*

As to the governments of this world, . . . we shall endeavor to prove, that, in their essential elements, and as at present administered, they are all Anti-Christ; that they can never, by human wisdom, be brought into conformity to the will of God; that they cannot be maintained, except by naval and military power; that all their penal enactments being a dead letter without an army to carry them into effect, are virtually written in human blood; and that the followers of Jesus should instinctively shun their stations of honor, power and emolument—at the same time "submitting to every ordinance of man, for the Lord's sake," and offering no *physical* resistance, to any of their mandates, however unjust or tyrranical.

William Lloyd Garrison, Liberator, December 15, 1837, quoted in Kraditor, American Abolitionism, 86–87.

[V]erily some of our northern gentlemen abolitionists are as jealous of any interference [by women] in rights they have long considered as belonging to them exclusively, as the southern slaveholder is, in the right of holding his slaves—both are to be broke up, & *human* rights alone recognized.

Quaker James Mott, on objections raised to Abby Kelley's participation in the New England Anti-Slavery Convention, 1838, in Kraditor, American Abolitionism, 46.

At an anti-slavery meeting of the citizens of Sardinia and vicinity, held on November 21, 1838, a committee of respectable citizens presented a report, accompanied with affidavits in support of its declarations, stating that for more than a year past there had been an unusual degree of hatred manifested by the slave-hunters and slaveholders towards the abolitionists of Brown County [Ohio], and that rewards varying from $500 to $2,500 had been repeatedly offered by different persons for the abduction or assassination of the Rev. John B. Mahan; and rewards had also been offered for Amos Pettijohn, William A. Frazier and Dr. Isaac M. Beck, of Sardinia, the Rev. John Rankin and Dr. Alexander Campbell, of Ripley, William McCoy, of Russellville, and citizens of Adams County.

Newspaper report, in Siebert, Underground Railway, 53.

With [abolitionists], the rights of property are nothing; the deficiency of the powers of the General [federal] Government is nothing; the acknowledged and incontestible powers of the States are nothing; civil war, a dissolution of the Union, and the overthrow of a government in which are concentrated the fondest hopes of the civilized world, are nothing. . . . Utterly destitute of constitutional or other rightful power, living in totally distinct communities as alien to the communities in which the subject on which they would operate resides, so far as concerns political power over that subject, as if they lived in Africa or Asia, they nevertheless promulgate to the world their purpose to be to manumit forthwith, . . . and without moral preparation, three millions of negro slaves, under jurisdictions altogether separated from those under which they live. . . . Does any considerate man believe it to be possible to effect such an object without convulsion, revolution, and bloodshed?

Henry Clay, 1839 Senate debate, in Fox, American Colonization Society, *147.*

[The abolitionist Dr. Hudson and I] traveled all through the eastern and western part of Connecticut, and a part of Massachusetts. We had some opposition to contend with; it made it much better for the Doctor in having me with him. Brickbats and rotten eggs were very common in those days; an anti-slavery lecturer was often showered by them. . . .

When we were in Saybrook [Connecticut] there was but one Abolitionist in the place. . . . As we could not be accommodated at his house, we stopped at a tavern; the inmates were very bitter toward us, and more especially to the Doctor. . . . [A]n old sea captain . . . asked the Doctor, "what do you know about slavery? All you know about it I suppose, is what this fellow (meaning me) has told you, and if I knew who his master was, and where he was, I would write to him to come on and take him." This frightened me very much. . . .

[At another town we had what we thought a successful meeting in the house of an abolitionist, having been denied the use of the school at the last minute.] The next morning the Doctor went to the barn to feed his horse, and found that some one had entered the barn and shaved

his horse's mane and tail close to the skin; and, besides, had cut our buffalo robe all in pieces; besides shaving the horse, the villans [sic] had cut his ears off.

Fugitive slave James Lindsay Smith, describing experiences of 1842, in his Autobiography, *62–63, 64. Available online. at URL: http://docsouth.unc.edu/neh/smithj/smithj. html#jsmith56.*

Abolitionists—about 5% of the voting population. Sober people, willing to see slavery abolished, but not by overthrowing the Constitution—70%. Highly respectable people who sympathize with the South—5%. The remainder—20%, who care less for principles than for spoils. Yet the abolitionists hold the balance of power from the nearly equal division of Democrats and Whigs. Hence the danger to the South should any party unite with the abolitionists.

John Calhoun's analysis of the political strength of the North, about 1849, in Buckmaster, Let My People Go, *172.*

I John Brown am now quite *certain* that the crimes of this *guilty, land will* never be purged away; but with Blood. I had *as I now think: vainly* flattered myself that without *verry much* bloodshed; it might be done.

Abolitionist John Brown, note handed to his guard on his way to be hanged, December 2, 1859, quoted in McPherson, "Days of Wrath," 14.

These dreadful times of mobs are thought to be the last struggle of the slave-power in the North. . . . I think it was worth living a great many years to be present at the [antislavery] meeting in Tremont Temple [in Boston] last Thursday morning [in January, 1861]. . . .

Mrs. Lydia Maria Child, as full of enthusiasm as she could express by flashing eye, glowing cheek, and waving handkerchief, as she sat by the organ on the highest seat of the platform, making everybody glad by her presence; Mrs. Maria Chapman, sitting with the calm dignity of a queen, her sister and daughter beside her; T. W. Higginson, ready with brilliant eloquence of tongue or with the revolver's bullet—so it was said—to do battle for free speech that day. . . .

Holley, A Life for Liberty, *177–78.*

CHAPTER ELEVEN

Black Soldiers in America's Wars
1635–1877

Black men, free and slave, have served as soldiers and sailors in American wars since colonial times, often with distinction. In the years up to the end of the Civil War, their participation in the military was never universally welcomed, often grudgingly solicited, and always controversial. Black labor (both free and slave) in support of military activity was commonplace, but white fears of armed blacks and racist doubts about their courage limited their acceptance into the military.

No historian can discriminate precisely between slaves and free blacks in military service. Records are vague, and many slaves were promised their freedom if they would fight: Did they, then, fight as free men or as slaves?

Colonial America

Colonial America as a rule excluded blacks from militia service and forbade them to own or use weapons. North Carolina, for example, specifically exempted slaves and free blacks from the militia service required of white males, an average of 10 to 20 days a year.[1] In 1639, Virginia slaves were "excused" from owning or carrying arms; in 1705, they were barred from holding or exercising any military office, and if found in possession of a "gun, sword, club, staff, or other weapon" they were subject to 20 lashes. On the other hand, Massachusetts for a brief period (1652–56) required "negroes" to train in the militia—though few if any actually did. Thereafter, Massachusetts barred them.[2] But militias everywhere pressed blacks, both free and slave, into military-support services—building fortifications, fixing roads, cooking, and pitching tents, thus relieving white militiamen of backbreaking labor.

Still, some black soldiers fought. The rosters of troops engaged in the French and Indian War (1754–63) identify some as blacks and mulattoes and a few as slaves.[3] During their brief occupation of New York (1621–64), the Dutch enlisted both free blacks and slaves in the militia; during the Indian Wars of 1641–43, they used slaves to track down fugitive Indians accused of what were later called "war crimes."

Even in the Deep South, where the outnumbered white population lived in perpetual terror of slave insurrections, exceptional circumstances occasionally prompted colonial legislatures to authorize the enlistment of slaves. Slaves could be used, they said, to defend against hostile Indians, or against the Spanish, who from their bases in Florida provided a haven for runaways, encouraged slave uprisings, and armed fugitive slaves for military service. In the face of such threats, training slaves as soldiers and mustering them into an auxiliary militia seemed to make sense. Both South Carolina and Georgia, for example, once provided by law for the enlistment of slaves in the militia. In both colonies, slave owners were obligated to provide suitable males for service. Slaves whose behavior in battle was exceptionally meritorious were to be rewarded with freedom. Masters were to be paid for the loss of their slaves' services and compensated for their injury or death, and the proportion of blacks to whites in each company was limited to one-third. In practice, however, slaves were never mustered for military service under these laws, except possibly in the 1740s, when James Oglethorpe successfully led Georgia and South Carolina troops, including some slaves, against Spanish forts to the south.[4] At least once, in the war against the Yamasee in Carolina (1715–16), the British mustered black men into temporary military service.[5]

The Revolutionary War

During the Revolutionary War also, the exclusionary system broke down. Crispus Attucks, a former slave, was the first American to fall when English soldiers opened fire in the Boston Massacre. Peter Salem, also a former slave, saw action at the battle of Lexington and later attained prominence for his bravery at Bunker Hill. The militias sent in 1775 by neighboring towns and colonies to besiege Boston included free blacks and slaves. At least three black soldiers in Col. John Nixon's New Hampshire regiment were identified by the muster master as slaves "inlisted with the Consent of their Masters."[6]

In the first months of the Revolutionary War, when the Continental Congress asked that all "able-bodied men in each colony form themselves into regular companies of militia," black men volunteered, and some were accepted, despite exclusionary laws.[7] Their presence did not go unchallenged. When in 1775, the Second Continental Congress created the Continental Army with George Washington as commander in chief, questions immediately arose. Should the Continental Army recruit black soldiers? Should those black volunteers already mustered in be retained? Official policy (and practice) with respect to the recruitment of blacks ran the gamut from acceptance to exclusion, but by 1776 exclusion had become the rule.

Early in 1777, however, opposition to the enlistment of blacks confronted reality. White men, despite promises of pay raises and substantial enlistment bounties, were not volunteering in numbers sufficient to meet army requirements. Under these circumstances, recruiting officers began accepting blacks even though state laws forbade it. After 1777, black recruitment, primarily of free men, prevailed in most of the northern states.

Enlisting slaves was more complicated. Unless the slave was a fugitive, enlistment typically required the owner's permission, which depended upon either the patriotism of the master or the inducements offered by the government—or both. Rhode Island, for example, inducted two battalions of slaves, paying their owners up to 200 pounds each for their freedom, and in 1785 it provided for the survivors' maintenance at public expense. New York in 1781 authorized the raising of two regiments of black soldiers, whose owners were given a grant of land for each slave who served.[8] As an additional inducement, and a most persuasive one, slave owners were frequently allowed to send their slaves as substitutes for their own military service.

In the southern states, proposals to enlist slaves rarely succeeded. In October 1780, the border state of Maryland did authorize the enlistment of slaves between the ages of 16 and 40. But an attempt in 1781 to raise an all-black regiment by requiring owners of six or more slaves to send one to the army failed. Maryland, however, continued to induct a few slaves. More telling was the rejection in 1781 by South Carolina and Georgia of a proposal by the Continental Congress (supported by Washington's best generals) that they recruit 3,000 slaves for their own safety and defense—this at a time when British forces threatened to overrun the entire region. Congress's proposal stipulated that the separate black battalions would be under white command and that slave owners would be compensated for each slave. The slaves themselves would receive subsistence and clothing but no pay for their service; upon discharge they would be given $50 and their freedom. South Carolina and Georgia flatly refused.

Military service at sea was another story. From the beginning of the Revolutionary War, slaves and free blacks served in the navies created first by states (beginning with Rhode Island in 1775) and then by the Continental Congress (1776). Blacks who sought service with these navies were almost always accepted, on a basis comparatively free of prejudice. Typically employed in the lowest ranks and ratings, they were sometimes rewarded for outstanding performance by promotion to higher positions and better pay—or even freedom. Caesar, a slave in the Virginia service, was set free when the legislature bought him from his master in recognition of his "gallant behavior." After his death, the legislature awarded his daughter Nancy 2,667 acres of land for her father's service in the war.[9]

In addition to the few slaves who fought as soldiers or sailors in the Revolutionary War, thousands contributed to the victory by their labor. Commonly, a state or army hired slaves, paying the owner for their services. If owners refused (because the price was not acceptable or the slave could not be spared at home), states sometimes would resort to impressment. In March 1776, for example, New York City empowered the commanding officer of each army corps in the city to call out all the black males in his district, slaves included, to work on the city's fortifications.

Slaves captured from the British military or from British sympathizers were typically considered spoils of war and put to work. Alternatively, they might be treated as private booty to be sold for the benefit of the regiment or retained as personal servants. Sometimes they would be turned over to states for disposition—hired out or sold. Some northern slaves obtained their freedom when their Tory masters fled to the British or when the state confiscated Tory estates. More often, particularly in the South, the slaves of Tories were sold, the proceeds going to the state. However procured, slaves were employed on roads and fortifications, as stevedores and teamsters, in mines and factories, in hospitals and kitchens. Slaves were particularly useful as guides and spies because of their intimate knowledge of the territory and sometimes in this way earned their freedom at war's end. Thus the Virginia legislature awarded one James his freedom and later a pension for his service with Lafayette as a spy and courier, duly compensating his owner, William Armistead.[10]

To weaken American forces, the British offered freedom to slaves who would escape and take refuge with the king's army. When on November 7, 1775, Lord Dunmore, the British governor of Virginia, issued such an invitation, within three weeks some 300 slaves had accepted, and more followed. Fitted out with uniforms on which the words "Liberty to Slaves" were inscribed, they were officially known as Lord Dunmore's Ethiopian Regiment. The governor's black recruits saw some action, but an epidemic of smallpox killed most of them and ended the experiment.[11] Alarmed by the loss of laborers upon whom they depended to produce food and raw materials and angered by the loss of their "property," the Americans responded indignantly, warning their slaves that the British wanted only to replenish the slave stock in the West Indies and threatening that fugitives would be severely punished unless they came back in 10 days.

The British repeated their coup in 1778, when Sir Henry Clinton, the commander in chief of British forces in North America, issued the Phillipsburg Proclamation, directed not just to able-bodied men but to the entire slave population. Blacks rushed to accept. One slave owner in South Carolina was appalled to discover that 15 of his slaves had disappeared in a single 24-hour period—and that was only the beginning.[12] What was more, some of the fugitives helped the British capture the plantations on which they had lived or held the white family prisoner until the British arrived.[13] Many a slave owner felt obliged to stay at home and keep an eye on his slaves, thus contributing to the manpower shortage plaguing American commanders.

No one knows how many slaves sought haven with the British. Some historians think it as many as 100,000; James Walker speaks of "tens of thousands," adding, "They swam, they hiked, they stowed away in boats and wagons, they carried each other to safety with the Redcoats. Many took advantage of the temporary presence of a British army in the neighbourhood to make a bid for freedom, others made a longer journey to British strongholds such as Charleston and Savannah. Boston King waded out to a British boat, risking a treacherous current as well as the possibility of recapture."[14]

British commanders were cautious about arming these fugitives as combat soldiers, although a black cavalry troop was formed in 1782, and some 200 blacks participated in the defense of Savannah (1779) and Augusta (1781). Several black pioneer (engineer) corps with their own noncommissioned officers were created to work on fortifications, roads, and bridges. A few found a place in the Royal Navy as ordinary seamen. Others served as guides, inland waterway pilots, spies, and couriers. More commonly, these former slaves were employed in garrisons as servants, orderlies, cooks, and laundresses.

Not all the slaves who fell into British hands improved their condition. Those who had been seized as war booty or taken from American plantations occupied by British troops might be sold back into slavery either to a Loyalist planter (who might have lost his own slaves to the "rebels") or into the West Indies. British officers kept some as personal servants. But for the most part, the British kept their promises, shipping most of the former slaves to refuges of their choice.

Slaves who served in the Continental Army also in most cases won their freedom. Some were cruelly disappointed, like Frederick, who had served with the consent of his master, legally remaining a slave. When as a veteran he sued for the

1,000 acres the state had promised each veteran, he lost—because a slave could not hold property. Another Revolutionary War soldier, Jehu Grant, was denied his pension on the grounds that he had been a fugitive when he fought for the Americans.[15]

How many blacks served in the Continental armies? Probably between 4,000 and 5,000.

The War of 1812

In the War of 1812, blacks were actively involved from the outset. Even before the war, when the British man-of-war *Leopard* attacked the American frigate *Chesapeake* to search it for (alleged) deserters, three of the four sailors removed were black.[16]

The military record of slaves and free blacks in the War of 1812 resembles that of the Revolution, except that whites were even more loath to arm blacks. Many blacks tried to enlist, and some succeeded, for the start of the war found an American army of 6,000 white men facing a much larger number of British soldiers.[17] Even so, only time and the fortunes of war would drive home to the government the need for black soldiers. Civil authorities eagerly used blacks to build defenses but long hesitated to give them weapons. Even after the British occupation of Washington in 1814 alerted Philadelphia to the danger it might be facing, the city's defense committee still wanted black fatigue parties to work separately from whites. Black leaders James Forten, Absalom Jones, and Richard Allen organized 2,500 black men to labor in support services. Only when peace was declared did Philadelphia have a black battalion ready to march.

Not until October 1814 did a state, New York, authorize the creation of two black regiments, officered by whites. Roughly 2,000 enlisted men were recruited from among free blacks and slaves given permission by their owners; slaves were to be freed when discharged.[18] Gen. Andrew Jackson, in a proclamation of September 21, 1814, invited "freemen of color" to enlist, promising them the same compensation as whites. Four hundred blacks fought with Jackson in the battle of New Orleans in January 1815, earning his commendation for their valor.[19]

In the War of 1812, however, most of the action for blacks was in the navy, where they were already serving at the conflict's onset. Not only during the war but for several years after it, blacks constituted 10 to 20 percent of the crews.[20] In the navy, prejudice had given way to practicality; black and white seamen fought together, ate together, and shared quarters in the limited space available. Nonetheless, relations between black and white seamen varied from ship to ship, depending on the prejudices of the commanding officer.

Early on, aboard the *Governor Tompkins,* two black crew members, John Johnson and John Davis, were shot in a battle at sea. Johnson shouted encouragement to his mates as he lay dying, and Davis asked again and again to be thrown overboard to leave space for those still fighting. After the battle of Lake Erie in 1813, Commodore Oliver Perry praised the gallantry of 100 blacks who constituted a quarter of his crews, saying that "they seem to be absolutely insensible to danger."[21]

In this war, as in the Revolution, the British invited slaves to seek refuge and eventual freedom with them. More than 3,500 responded to the Cochrane Proclamation issued by that vice admiral in April 1814. Of these, some 2,000 wound up in Nova Scotia.[22]

The "Negro Fort"

During the War of 1812, a small British force under Lt. Col. Edward Nicholas allied itself with the Seminole Indians in Florida and rebuilt an old Spanish fort on the Apalachicola River. The Seminole had long provided refuge for runaway slaves, some of whom counseled the Indian nation, particularly in its dealings with the United States. When Nicholas departed after the war, he left the fort and a store of supplies, arms, and ammunition in the charge of the Seminole and blacks. Around this "Negro Fort," by then occupied mostly by some 3,000 blacks, settled a growing community of Indians and blacks, among them some 1,000 fugitives. From it, blacks allied with the neighboring Creek raided and terrorized slave owners across the border. When the Spanish authorities refused to intervene, the United States in the summer of 1816 sent gunboats to destroy the fort and return the fugitive slaves to their owners. Fire from the gunboats set off the fort's magazine, killing 270 people, mostly blacks. Other blacks were captured and reenslaved.

Nonetheless Indians and blacks kept up their resistance from new towns they founded on the Suwanee River. The continuing border wars finally led to Andrew Jackson's invasion of Florida. When the black commander Bowlegs got wind of an immense force of Americans and Indians friendly to them advancing on the fort, most Seminole fled, but the blacks fought a rearguard action to enable their families to escape to the swamps and eventually to the Bahamas. The United States annexed Florida in February 1819.[23]

The Civil War: A White Man's War

At the outbreak of the Civil War in 1861, many free blacks attempted to enlist with the Union army, and black communities offered to organize combat regiments. These efforts were repulsed. To avoid antagonizing slave owners in the border states and in hopes of even picking up some support in the South, President Lincoln held that the war was being waged to preserve the Union, not to end slavery. In this white man's war, it was argued, blacks (free or slave) had no stake in the outcome.

Fugitive slaves from the South seeking freedom behind Federal lines often found themselves turned back or returned to their masters by Union officers. Field commanders marching into rebel territory sometimes felt obliged to reassure the local inhabitants that the sanctity of their property (slaves) would be respected. On occasion, Confederate slave owners and sheriffs were even allowed to enter Union territory and hunt for their runaway slaves.

Meanwhile antislavery commanders in the field, such as Gen. John C. Frémont, were freeing the slaves in the territories under their control—only to have their orders countermanded by Washington. But Gen. Benjamin Butler found a way to justify using the services of slaves who fled to the Union lines: He declared them contraband of war. In August 1861, Congress legitimated Butler's action with the First Confiscation Act, which made all property used to support the rebellion, including slaves, subject to prize and capture. Next, in December 1861, Congress prohibited the use of federal forces to return fugitives to their masters.[24] Six months later, the Second Confiscation Act of July 17, 1862, authorized the president, at his discretion, to recruit blacks into the army. Every slave mustered into the army would be free, and his master (if loyal to the United States) would be compensated.[25] Lincoln, however, did not begin this recruitment for some time. Full-scale active recruitment got under way only in 1863.

Military necessity pushed toward abolition and the enlistment of blacks in the armed forces of the Union, for the South's huge slave labor force enabled it to send most of its white men of fighting age into the army—eventually some 75 percent. Meanwhile, the Union was using to advantage the services of the runaway slaves flooding behind Union lines wherever Federal troops appeared. These services ranged from housekeeping functions in army camps and hospitals to heavy labor on fortifications, roads, and bridges. "Contrabands" worked as wagon masters, teamsters, washerwomen, nurses, cooks, waiters, cleaners, carpenters, and blacksmiths; they served as scouts, spies, guides, and pilots.[26] Ineluctably, the war was becoming a battle to abolish slavery as well as to preserve the Union.

The Civil War: Arming of Contrabands and Recruitment of Black Troops

In all theaters of the war, enterprising commanders in the field, faced with diminishing manpower reserves, began arming and drilling contrabands on their own authority. Washington wavered, censuring such an action of one general and endorsing that of another by ignoring it.

West of the Mississippi in late 1861, blacks associated with the Creek, Seminole, and Cherokee Indians fought their way north to Kansas to join Union regiments. Runaway slaves from the Kansas-Missouri-Arkansas frontier were being recruited—notably in Kansas by James H. Lane and James Montgomery—without official sanction of or even acknowledgment by Washington. As early as October 1862, black troops were fighting against Confederate irregulars on the Missouri border.[27]

In South Carolina, Gen. David Hunter's enlistment of black soldiers in May 1862 earned him official censure, and his black regiment was disbanded in August. The same month, the War Department authorized General Saxton, military governor of the South Carolina Sea Islands, to raise five regiments of black troops. On January 31, 1863, under the command of Col. Thomas W. Higginson, the 1st South Carolina Colored Volunteers became an official part of the Federal army—the first organization of black soldiers fully authorized by the War Department.[28] Higginson's men (and a second black regiment commanded by Col. James Montgomery) served with distinction in the interior of Georgia and Florida; in March 1863 they occupied Jacksonville.

When in May 1862 General Butler occupied New Orleans, he put to work many of the thousands of contrabands who fled there from plantations. At first, doubting the ability of blacks to fight, he refused to enlist them, rejecting the proposals of his subordinate Gen. John W. Phelps—who promptly resigned.[29] Shortly after, however, desperation for reenforcements forced General Butler to change his mind. He accepted the services of the Louisiana Native Guard, a black organization that had been formed to fight for the Confederacy. After the Confederate army retreated, the unit offered its services to General Butler. On May 27, 1863, those black soldiers fought valiantly under Butler's command at the battle of Port Hudson, sustaining great losses. They distinguished themselves once again in the battle of Milliken's Bend. Gradually field commanders, with no more sanction than the absence of an official reprimand, presented the Union government with the accomplished fact of trained and fighting black units.[30]

General Thomas recruits black troops in Louisiana during the Civil War. *(Library of Congress)*

In the North, state governors short of manpower began to enlist blacks. In July 1862, Congress dropped the requirement that state militia members be white. In January 1863, the Union secretary of war authorized states to enlist black troops. Gov. John A. Andrew of Massachusetts sent agents around the country and soon more than filled the Massachusetts quota. The famous Massachusetts 54th Regiment included 287 former slaves.[31]

Other states soon followed suit. In June 1863, Rhode Island organized a black artillery regiment, later sent to New Orleans. Pennsylvania resisted the recruitment of blacks until Gen. Robert E. Lee's invasion of the state in 1863; in the early summer of that year, a group of public-spirited citizens recruited blacks, eventually enrolling 10 full black regiments.[32] In November, in the face of the governor's resistance, black leaders and other prominent New Yorkers finally got permission from the secretary of war to organize black troops. On March 5, 1864, the 20th U.S. Colored Troops received their flag at a ceremony in which President Charles King of Columbia University said, "When you put on the uniform and swear allegiance to the standard of the Union, you stand emancipated, regenerated and disenthralled—the peer of the proudest soldier in the land."[33] The regiment then embarked for New Orleans.

Ohio, Connecticut, Michigan, Illinois, Indiana, Iowa, and Kansas each raised one or more black regiments, but recruitment was slowed because there simply were not enough blacks in their states. Congress then authorized northern governors to recruit blacks in Confederate territory occupied by Union troops. The Union commanders there resisted, lest they lose the labor of the contrabands. So the results were unimpressive until the federal government took over.

In May 1863, the War Department established the Bureau for Colored Troops to control recruitment and training of blacks. Thereafter, the U.S. government began intensive recruiting of black soldiers directly into federal service. In some cases, the Union resorted to impressment, particularly of outlyers, but by and large blacks volunteered, often despite vigorous local white opposition. Federal agents also recruited significant numbers from the black settlements in Canada.[34] Gen. Lorenzo Thomas signed up many blacks in the Mississippi Valley. Special commissioners were appointed to recruit in the border states, where "white opposition to their recruitment was at times so fierce that black men and boys had to run and fight their way past armed posses and other white gauntlets on their way to the Union enlistment stations. Many blacks did not make it, and were left hanging on trees by the road, while others paid the price of a sheared-off ear or a bloodied head to join the federal forces." Despite these dangers, in Tennessee and Kentucky an astonishing 40 to 50 percent of the eligible black male population eventually served in the military.[35]

Recruitment of blacks ended soon after Lee's surrender. By then, the number of enlisted blacks had soared to 178,975, or approximately one-eighth of the entire Union army.[36]

The Civil War: Black Soldiers Fighting for the Union

The Union seemed to have little to offer black soldiers but blood, sweat, tears, and inequities. They could hardly look forward to promotion above the noncommissioned ranks. Usually whites officered black units. Only about 100 blacks were commissioned, 90 of whom were combat officers, almost all in the Louisiana Native Guard. That Guard was recruited among free blacks.[37]

Black troops of Company E, 4th U.S. Colored Infantry, Fort Lincoln, D.C., Civil War *(Library of Congress)*

Black regiments were not always properly equipped. Obsolete arms were issued them. Sometimes the bayonets would not fit their muskets. More often than white troops, blacks were assigned fatigue duty like unloading ships, filling sandbags, and draining marshes. They could not avoid feeling singled out for menial labor, as indeed they often were.[38]

Medical care was inadequate throughout the Civil War armies, North and South, partly because of the relatively primitive state of medicine and partly because no provisions had been made before the war for nurses. Too many of the surgeons were incompetent even by the standards of the day, and black units were likely to receive the worst of the lot—for few white doctors were willing to serve with them, and only eight black physicians were commissioned in the Union army.

Black soldiers did not at first receive equal pay, so that often their families were reduced to poverty. Racial prejudice all too often manifested itself in the assumption that blacks, no matter how gallantly they served, somehow deserved less than whites. This attitude so galled some black soldiers that month after month they refused to take any pay at all rather than take less than whites. Others came near to mutiny. For instance, Sgt. William Walker of the 3d South Carolina Volunteers was court-martialed and shot because he ordered his company to stack arms and resign from an army that broke its contract with them.[39] Not until June 15, 1864, did Congress authorize equal pay for black troops.

Finally, blacks had every reason to fear being taken prisoner, for the Confederacy thought of them not as soldiers but as rebelling slaves and therefore not prisoners of war. Blacks could never hope to be included in prisoner exchanges. At one point, the Confederate Congress ruled that captured blacks or those who gave aid and comfort to the enemy should be dealt with according to the laws of the state in which they were captured—that is, they would probably be killed or enslaved. In an effort to retaliate and protect black troops, Lincoln in July 1863 announced that for every Union soldier enslaved a Rebel prisoner of war would be sentenced to hard labor; for every Union soldier killed in violation of the laws of war, a Rebel would be executed. Such records as exist indicate that captured black Union soldiers in fact were seldom enslaved, but in some cases they were killed rather than taken prisoner, as in the notorious "massacre" at Fort Pillow in April 1864.[40] Fort Pillow was not the only battle in which black troops were allegedly massacred, but it was the most notorious, and its memory inspired black soldiers to fear being left wounded on the field or taken prisoner. Thereafter they engaged the enemy with shouts of "Remember Fort Pillow," and sometimes retaliated in kind.[41]

The Civil War: Black Sailors Fighting for the Union

As in earlier wars, black sailors fared better than black soldiers. In September 1861, the navy adopted a policy of signing up former slaves. Contrabands fled to Union warships, where many saw active duty as cooks, coal heavers, firemen, and gunners. Their service as pilots was particularly critical, whatever their ratings, for their years of experience as boatmen in the winding channels of South Carolina, Georgia, and the Sea Islands had familiarized them with the coastal waters. In May 1862, the young Carolina slave Robert Smalls, a seaman on the Confederate gunboat *Planter*, with a black crew and white officers, managed a daring escape. In the absence of the officers, he smuggled aboard his family and that of his brother, and then under the Confederate flag he steamed out to open sea, where he hoisted a flag of truce and turned the gunboat over to the Union ships blockading the Charleston harbor. His skills and courage made his personal services as valuable as the gunboat he surrendered; eventually, he rose to the rank of captain in the Union navy.

On the Mississippi too, contrabands, both women and men, surged onto riverboats and were put to work. Women contraband nurses were the first women in history to serve aboard American naval vessels. They were rated as regular crew members.[42]

Eventually, blacks constituted about a quarter of the Union seamen; perhaps overall as many as 29,000 blacks served in the navy.[43] On some Union vessels, the crews were predominantly black: That of the gunboat *Glide*, for example, comprised 30 contrabands and only eight whites. Black casualties were estimated at 800, about a quarter of the total, and another 2,000 black seamen died of disease. At least four black sailors won the Navy Medal of Honor.[44]

Bigoted naval captains on some ships tried to reduce blacks to Jim Crow status and to make their lives as miserable as possible.[45] Nonetheless, the prospects for a black sailor were better than those for a black soldier.

The Civil War: Confederate Slavery

Throughout the war the Confederacy had to learn and relearn that slaves differed from other property in having wills of their own. Although their discontent and rage never erupted into a major insurrection, they damaged the war effort at every turn. Confederate troops wasted untold time and energy trying to recapture escaping slaves.

The South, long dependent on slave labor, could no longer rely on it. Thousands upon thousands of slaves fled behind Union lines or followed in the wake of Union armies. When they did not flee, they often shirked or ignored or resisted orders. Soldiers fighting in the Confederate armies heard from their relatives at home of the problems thus created, and sometimes they deserted to attend to their farms and plantations. When they did, they might find no able-bodied laborers at all, or they might find themselves "betrayed" by their slaves, who guided Yankees to their hidden treasure-troves. They might lock up their slaves at night, they might redouble their patrols, but their harshest punishments only hastened the stampede of slaves northward. Sometimes the owners' inability even to feed their slaves caused a complete breakdown in discipline. From day to day, the masters' power declined, and the slaves' expectations of freedom heightened. Unable to work their wills as in the past by physical force, owners began to bargain with slaves to persuade them to work at all, offering them better conditions, a share of the crops, or even wages. Other whites simply abandoned their plantations and some of their slaves.

As Ira Berlin notes, "To prevent the transformation of plantations into federal recruiting stations, Confederate commanders ordered able-bodied black men removed deep into the interior of the South or to Texas. But attempts to tear black men from their families, rather than ending unrest, further stimulated flight."[46] The efforts of hard-pressed masters to "refugee," to move their most valuable slaves to the interior or even to Texas, motivated more slaves to escape, while those left behind on the abandoned plantations began to farm independently, establishing communities sympathetic to fugitives and to Union scouts.

By November 1864, the situation had grown so grave that President Jefferson Davis proposed that the Confederate Congress consider emancipation.

The Civil War: Blacks and the Confederate Military

Arming blacks, free or slave, raised hackles in most southern souls. All whites had grown up in fear of black insurrections. Moreover, white Confederate soldiers thought that fighting alongside blacks would demean them. Nonetheless, emerging research reveals instances of a greater acceptance of blacks in the Confederate forces than has been thought. The number is and probably will remain in dispute.

Efforts to determine these numbers are impeded by conflicting views of the Civil War. Most mainstream historians interpret it as a war intended by President Lincoln and by many Northern soldiers to save the Union, in the course of which emancipation became inevitable. In the face of known black resistance to and flight from slavery during the war, they find it difficult to believe that any significant number of blacks willingly supported the Confederate cause. Some Southerners, however, insist that the war was not about slavery, not about a moral issue, but about economic dominance. They point to the military service of blacks in Confederate forces as proof. Southern revisionist historians' estimates of the numbers of blacks there range from 30,000 to 100,000. Civil War historian Ed Kennedy believes that 7 to 8 percent of the Confederate military may have been black.[47] Moreover, historians disagree because so much depends on the status of the blacks associated with the Confederate military.

Some free blacks, particularly the slaveholders among them, had internalized white values and sought higher status by identification with whites. They may well have seen their own best interest as casting their lot with the reigning power structure, the white establishment. Moreover, they thought of the South as their homeland, which was now being invaded. In some cases these black men had the option of enlisting not in the Confederate army but in one of the state militias or state-organized regiments. The Louisiana Native Guards, for example, organized two regiments to defend their state—mostly free, well-educated, prosperous men of mixed black and European heritage. The Confederacy accepted them as militia units and used them for public display and propaganda but had no intention of honoring them as regular soldiers or permitting them to fight. Frustrated by such treatment, after the fall of New Orleans many Guard officers and enlisted men joined the Union army.[48]

Masters ordered slaves to support the military in two capacities. First, the Confederacy required slave owners to furnish slaves for manual labor, such as constructing forts and breastworks. Indeed, Confederates had used both slaves and free blacks to construct defenses even before the war. They needed them, for the white southern ethos disdained physical labor. But as owners discovered that slaves working on fortifications might be killed, lost, or incapacitated or that they might escape, the owners balked at sending them, sometimes demanding compensation for loss or injury to them, sometimes sending them only if forced. Even if owners were willing to hire out slaves, military demands for labor drove the market sky high. Beginning in 1862, Confederate states enacted legislation to impress slaves, with compensation to owners, for work mostly on fortifications but also on salt works, mines, railroads, and haulage. Its enforcement caused complaint all during the war.[49] The question of the use of slaves in the war effort divided Confederates, pitting "state officials against national officials, national officials against army officers, army officers against slaveholders, and slaveholders against nonslaveholders."[50]

Second, masters took slaves to war with them as body servants. Records show many a slave who rescued and cared for his master after the white man was wounded. Some of these slaves in the heat of battle probably picked up weapons and fought. As contraband and Union intelligence records show, others seized the chance to escape, often taking with them Confederate property and valuable information about Confederate positions and supplies.

Then too, as black war correspondent Thomas Morris Chester pointed out, the early Union policy of returning fugitive slaves to their owners and the memory of the resultant torture prompted rumors that "the Yankees would sell them to Cuba, and other stories which worked equally upon their fears, [inducing] many to cling to the cause of the South under protest, and suffer the evils they have than fly to others they know not of. These, however, are the exception."[51]

As the war dragged on, the Confederacy grew desperate for manpower. It had drained the South of able-bodied white men and had little choice but to arm blacks. Union victories and the desertions of white soldiers forced the Confederate Congress in February 1864 to declare "free black men between eighteen and fifty universally liable to impressment."[52] Despite the advocacy of General Robert E. Lee and other officers, not until mid-March 1865, when the war was already as good as lost, could the Confederate Congress bring itself to enact the Negro Soldier Law to enlist slaves as soldiers.

The Reconstruction Era: Black Veterans

Black men's Civil War military service had offered them a liberating experience, providing opportunities for self-improvement and opening doors to respectability and upward mobility. Becoming a soldier, a traditionally masculine role, had enabled both free blacks and former slaves to prove their manhood and validate their claim to equal citizenship. Despite galling instances of injustice and mistreatment, black troops had performed well. They had deserted less often than their white comrades. Their valor in combat had won high praise from their commanders and 25 Congressional Medals of Honor.[53] As historian Donald Shaffer notes, their service "helped many acquire schooling, self-confidence, [and] leadership skills" that facilitated the former slaves' transition to freedom and citizenship.[54] During Reconstruction at least 41 black veterans served as delegates to state constitutional conventions, 64 as legislators, three as lieutenant governors, and four as congressmen.[55]

Like their white comrades, black veterans were entitled to bounties (lump sums offered to encourage enlistments) and pensions (regular payments for those eligible). Congress had at first denied bounties to former slaves, holding that the freedom that came with enlistment was reward enough. Not until March 1873 did it fully equalize bounties, but it did grant pensions to all, regardless of previous condition of servitude.[56] Besides the money coming to them in bounties and pensions, the government also owed some veterans wages and allowances earned during the war.

Claiming their money was another matter. Robbed of recorded personal history, kept illiterate by slavery, and inexperienced in dealing with bureaucratic procedures, former slaves often could not produce the documents needed to establish their entitlements. Those who had enlisted under their masters' last names might have chosen other surnames after emancipation; fugitive slaves often used names other than their masters' to avoid recapture. Few had marriage or birth certificates or for that matter even knew their own birthdays. Photographs were rare, and family Bibles—if they had ever existed—were often destroyed in the carnage of war. The illiterate and semiliterate had trouble with paperwork. Poverty barred some from even getting to the pension office. In their frustration the Pension Bureau agents dealing with these nightmarish tangles inevitably roused suspicions of fraud among a clientele all too experienced in being cheated. Some received what was owed them as late as the end of the 19th century, some never.

The Reconstruction Era: Buffalo Soldiers

At war's end the military services were closed to blacks, even to black Civil War veterans. Only in July 1866, some 15 months later, did Congress authorize the creation of six black regiments, two cavalry and four infantry. All their commissioned officers were white, though some white officers accepted these non-career-enhancing posts only reluctantly, while others simply refused.[57]

The military life was hard and dangerous. In the early postwar years troops were ill-provisioned and ill-equipped. Often they had to fend for themselves, right down to cutting logs and making adobe bricks to build their own forts and corrals. Yet in an environment where freedmen with no capital and few skills had to make their own way, the military looked attractive. Military life at least offered status, equal pay for equal work, job security, opportunities to learn to read and write, and a chance, however limited, for promotion as noncommissioned officers.

The black regiments were ordered to the Southwest, then swarming with cattle thieves, marauders from Mexico, "petty, scheming, and sometimes murderous politicians, greedy land and cattle barons, crooked government contractors, heartless Indian agents, and land-hungry homesteaders."[58] Indians warred against the eastern settlers invading their lands. The army had its hands full keeping the peace; guarding railroad lines, waterholes, and stage coaches from Indian and outlaw raiders; and constructing forts as bases for the protection of settlers. Black soldiers as well as whites escorted stage coaches and cattle drives, built roads and telegraph lines, and explored and mapped. The Ninth and Tenth Cavalry of black troops won special notice for outstanding performance on the western frontier. After Indians as a term of respect began to call blacks "buffalo soldiers," the Tenth Cavalry adopted a buffalo head as its logo.[59]

Often Seminole-Negro Indian Scouts served with the buffalo soldiers. These sturdy frontiersmen were recruited in 1870 to help protect settlers and travelers against Apache and Comanche defending their homelands. They were descended from slaves who had escaped their white masters to serve and gradually to intermarry with the Seminole in Florida. With the Seminole they had been forced to move to Indian Territory (later Oklahoma) in the late 1830s and early 1840s. Still fearing recapture and reenslavement, they had moved on to Mexico, where their young men learned to "ride, hunt, track, trap and shoot" and become so tough and daring that they attracted U.S. army recruiters.[60]

Chronicle of Events

1656

- Massachusetts repeals the law of 1652 admitting blacks to military training.

1704

- The South Carolina legislature passes an act "for raising and enlisting such slaves as shall be thought serviceable to this Province in times of Alarms." It is reenacted in 1708.

1708

- In the colonial South, a law requires each militia captain "to enlist traine up and bring into the field for each white, one able Slave armed with gun or lance."

1715

- Black slaves constitute part of the military force that in South Carolina meets and routs the Yamasee Indians.

1755

- The Georgia legislature authorizes the enlistment of slaves in the militia under carefully controlled conditions.

1760

- New Jersey prohibits the enlistment in the militia of "any slaves who are so for terms of life" without leave of their masters.

1768

- British captain Wilson urges Boston slaves to rise, declaring that British troops have come to free them.

1770

- *March 5:* In the "Boston Massacre," British soldiers shoot down several colonists, including Crispus Attucks, allegedly an escaped slave.

The American Revolution (1775–1783)

1775

- *April:* Blacks are among the minutemen battling the British at Lexington and Concord.
- *May:* The Massachusetts Committee on Public Safety excludes slaves from the army being raised by the Continental Congress but permits the enlistment of free blacks.
- *June 17:* Former slave Peter Salem is among the blacks who fight the British at the Battle of Bunker Hill; Peter Salem shoots British major Pitcairn.
- *July 9:* General George Washington announces a ban on further enlistment of blacks, slave or free, a policy endorsed by the Continental Congress in October.
- *November 7:* Governor Lord Dunmore of Virginia urges male slaves to desert their masters and join the British forces, promising good treatment and freedom.
- *December 31:* General Washington rescinds the ban on the recruitment of free blacks, ordering their acceptance into the Continental army.

1777

- The states begin to admit nonwhite men into the army as draft substitutes and volunteers. Massachusetts leads the way early in the year by including blacks among those draft-eligible.
- *July:* Prince, a black soldier with Colonel Barton, captures British major general Prescott.
- *October:* The Connecticut General Assembly authorizes the enlistment of slaves as substitutes for their masters, if the masters consent.

1778

- *February:* The Rhode Island legislature votes to raise two battalions of slaves.
- *August 29:* Black soldiers distinguish themselves at the battle of Rhode Island.

1779

- *March 29:* The Continental Congress recommends to South Carolina and Georgia that they raise and train 3,000 slaves for service with the Continental Army, with the promise of emancipation at the end of the war. Neither state adopts the plan.
- *June 30:* General Sir Henry Clinton, British commander in chief, offers slaves freedom if they desert their masters, and he invites male slaves to join his forces.

1781

- *March 20:* The New York General Assembly authorizes the raising of two regiments of black troops.
- *May 14:* Black soldiers defend Colonel Greene at Points Bridge, New York.

1783

- Virginia emancipates Virginia slaves who have served as soldiers in the Revolutionary War, effective at war's end.

Integrated troops fight in the Battle of New Orleans, War of 1812. *(Library of Congress)*

1785

- "Negroes, Indians and Mulattoes" are "exempted" from the army organized under the Articles of Confederation.

1786

- *October:* The Virginia legislature votes to free James Armistead in recognition of his service as spy during the Revolutionary War, his master to be compensated from the state treasury.

1792

- Congress excludes blacks from the U.S. military services.

War of 1812 (1812–1815)

1812

- The British transport many American slaves who seek refuge with them to the Bahamas, Bermuda, Nova Scotia, and New Brunswick.

1813

- Black sailors contribute to Admiral Perry's victory against the British fleet in the Battle of Lake Erie.

1814

- Blacks Richard Allen, James Forten, and Absalom Jones raise a force of 2,500 black men to protect Philadelphia against the British.
- *April 4:* British Vice Adm. Sir Alexander Cochrane invites American slaves to take refuge with the British, promising an opportunity to become free British subjects and settlement in one of the British possessions in North America or the West Indies.
- *September 21:* American general Andrew Jackson invites the "Free Colored [male] inhabitants of Louisiana" to enlist in his forces.
- *October 24:* The New York legislature authorizes the raising of two black regiments.

1815

- *January 14:* The troops (including black soldiers) of General Andrew Jackson defeat the British decisively at the Battle of New Orleans, two weeks after the treaty ending the war is signed in Ghent on December 24, 1814.

1817

- The First Seminole War begins. Fugitive slaves support the Indians.

1835

- The Second Seminole War begins. Black forces fight alongside the Indians against the U.S. Army.

1857

- New Hampshire and Vermont repeal their laws against black enlistments in the state militia.

The Civil War (1861–1865)

1861

- *February:* In Montgomery, Alabama, the seceded states adopt the constitution of the Confederate States of America and elect Jefferson Davis provisional president.
- *April 12:* The Civil War begins when Confederates fire upon Fort Sumter in Charleston, South Carolina. Free blacks respond to President Lincoln's call for 75,000 volunteers but are rejected.
- *April 19:* Black leader Frederick Douglass calls for recruitment of black troops.
- *April 23:* Black men meeting in Boston offer to fight for the Union.
- *May:* At Fortress Monroe in Virginia, Union general Benjamin Butler declares fugitive slaves "contraband of war," refuses to surrender them, and frees them to be employed by the Union army.
- *August 6:* Congress passes the First Confiscation Act, which provides that all property used in support of the rebellion, specifically including slaves, is subject to prize and capture.
- *August 30:* General John C. Frémont declares martial law in Missouri and frees slaves taken from disloyal owners. President Lincoln orders Frémont to modify his emancipation order to conform to existing law.

- *September:* Secretary of the Navy Gideon Welles authorizes enlistment of fugitive slaves for naval service when that service is useful.
- *October 14:* Secretary of War Simon Cameron authorizes Gen. Thomas W. Sherman to employ fugitive slaves as Union soldiers if needed in his campaign against the coast of South Carolina.
- *December:* Secretary of War Simon Cameron recommends to Lincoln that slaves should be emancipated and armed. Lincoln disagrees.

1862

- *January 15:* Union general Thomas Sherman requests that the War Department send teachers for former slaves at Port Royal, South Carolina.
- *February 4:* The Virginia House of Delegates debates enrolling free blacks in the Confederate army but fails to take action.
- *March:* General David Hunter begins to issue certificates of emancipation to all slaves who have been employed by the Confederacy.
- *March 13:* An addition to the Articles of War prohibits Union forces to aid in the capture or return of runaway slaves of disloyal masters.
- *April:* General David Hunter, without authorization, raises a black regiment at Hilton Head, South Carolina.

The gunboat *Planter,* was run out of Charleston, South Carolina, and surrendered to the Union navy by Robert Smalls, May 1862. *(Engraving from* Harper's Weekly, *1862, courtesy of the U.S. Naval Historical Center)*

It is disbanded in August after the War Department refuses to pay or equip the regiment.
- *April:* A black gunner at the Battle of New Orleans distinguishes himself and is awarded the Congressional Medal of Honor.
- *May:* Slaves Robert and John Smalls seize the Confederate steamer *Planter,* run it out of Charleston harbor, and deliver it to the Union navy.
- *May:* General David Hunter declares free the slaves within the Department of the South. President Lincoln countermands this order, reserving to himself the power to free slaves.
- *May:* General David Hunter's efforts to recruit black men into the army provoke a national debate.
- *July 17:* Passage of the Second Confiscation Act authorizes the president to employ "persons of African descent" in any capacity to suppress the rebellion. Slaves owned by disloyal masters are declared "forever free of their servitude" as soon as they cross Union lines. Slaves seeking refuge in Union army camps are to be protected against recapture and enslavement, welcomed, and put to work. The act also forbids military personnel to surrender fugitive slaves to disloyal owners.
- *July 17:* Passage of the Militia Act authorizes the president "to receive into the service of the United States, for the purpose of constructing entrenchments, or performing camp service, or any other labor, or any military or naval service for which they may be found competent, persons of African descent." They will be paid $10 a month, of which three dollars will be deducted for clothing.
- *August:* Union general Benjamin Butler in New Orleans accepts into his command existing "Native Guard" regiments composed of free black soldiers and begins to recruit free blacks and former slaves for additional regiments.
- *August 6:* President Lincoln agrees to the recruitment of black men as laborers with the army.
- *August 25:* Congress authorizes recruitment of black soldiers in South Carolina.
- *September:* Three regiments, constituting the "Black Brigade," are organized in Cincinnati to construct fortifications but are neither armed nor given uniforms. They are disbanded when the threat of Confederate attack ends.
- *September 27:* The 1st Regiment of Louisiana Native Guards is mustered into Federal service, followed on October 12 by the 2d Regiment and on November 24 by the 3d Regiment.

These four fugitives, led by Robert Small, sailed the steamer *Planter* to the Union navy. *(Library of Congress)*

- *October:* The 1st Regiment of the Kansas Colored Volunteers, recruited by James Lane, engages in combat at Island Mount, Missouri.
- *October 3:* Virginia authorizes the impressment of slaves to work on fortifications and for other military labor. Other Confederate states soon follow suit.
- *October 11:* The Confederate Congress exempts from conscription one white man on each plantation with more than 20 slaves.
- *November 15:* The Union organizes Company A, 1st South Carolina Volunteers—the first black regiment raised with full War Department authorization.
- *December 23:* Confederate president Davis orders that captured black Union soldiers and their white officers not be treated as prisoners of war but remanded to state authorities for disposition according to state law.

1863

- *January 1:* President Lincoln issues the Emancipation Proclamation, freeing all slaves "in areas still in rebellion," and announces plans to recruit black soldiers and

sailors throughout the North and in Union-occupied states of the Confederacy.
- *January 13:* The First Regiment of the Kansas Colored Infantry is mustered into Federal service.
- *January 20:* Secretary of War Edwin Stanton asks Massachusetts governor John Andrews to recruit and organize black soldiers.
- *January 26–31:* The 1st South Carolina Colored Regiment is mustered into the Union army and engages the enemy at Township, Florida.
- *March 25:* Union general Lorenzo Thomas is sent to the Mississippi Valley to recruit as many black regiments as possible.
- *March 26:* The Confederate Congress authorizes military commanders to impress private property, including slaves, for public service.
- *April 30:* The Confederate Congress affirms that black soldiers captured by the Confederate army will be dealt with according to the laws of the state in which they are seized, not as prisoners of war.
- *May:* Organization of the 54th Massachusetts Colored Infantry, the first black regiment in the free states, is completed.
- *May 18:* The 1st Regiment Kansas Colored Infantry engages Confederate troops at Sherwood, Missouri.
- *May 22:* The Federal War Department establishes the Bureau of Colored Troops to regulate and supervise the enlistment of black soldiers and the selection of white officers to command them.
- *May 27:* The black soldiers of the 1st Louisiana Native Guards distinguish themselves fighting for the Union in the battle of Port Hudson, the last Confederate fortification on the lower Mississippi. They fight valorously and sustain great losses.
- *June:* Recruitment of black soldiers begins in Pennsylvania.
- *June 7:* In the Battle of Milliken's Bend, a Union camp on the Mississippi, black soldiers repel a Confederate attack, defeating 2,000 Texans in hand-to-hand combat.
- *June 14:* The black 14th Rhode Island Heavy Artillery Regiment is organized.
- *June 17:* At the battle of Honey Springs (Elk Creek), Indian Territory, the 1st Kansas Colored Infantry fights along with Union forces.
- *July 18:* The 54th Massachusetts Colored Infantry leads the assault on Fort Wagner, South Carolina, losing half its men. In this battle Sgt. William H. Carney wins the Congressional Medal of Honor.

- *July 30:* President Lincoln threatens retaliation if Confederates enslave or kill captured black soldiers.
- *October 30:* The War Department orders recruitment of black soldiers in Maryland, Missouri, and Tennessee, owners loyal to the Union to be compensated for their slaves.
- *November:* The Connecticut General Assembly authorizes the recruitment and training of black troops.
- *November:* The regimental quota of the 5th U.S. Colored Regiment in Ohio is completed.
- *December 25:* Former slave Robert Blake earns the Congressional Medal of Honor for his conduct as a powderboy on the USS *Marblehead* on the Stono River, in South Carolina.

1864

- Black Union soldiers at Vicksburg complain that their wives have been sent to an unknown destination. By this time, 10 full black regiments have been mustered in.

- *January 2:* Confederate general Patrick R. Cleburne and a group of fellow officers in the Army of Tennessee propose "that we immediately commence training a large reserve of the most courageous of our slaves."
- *February:* The Union failure to award black soldiers equal pay provokes near mutiny in the 54th Massachusetts and other black regiments.
- *February 17:* The Confederate Congress authorizes the employment of 20,000 slaves at the same wages as privates and eventually enrolls one-fifth of all black males aged 18–45. By this act, the Confederate Congress intends "to increase the efficiency of the Army by employment of free negroes and slaves in certain capacities," also empowering the secretary of war to impress an additional 20,000 if need be.
- *February 20:* At the battle of Olustee, Florida, Union forces include the black troops of the 54th Massachusetts Infantry Regiment and the 8th and 35th U.S. Colored Infantry Regiments.

Mustered-out Union soldiers reunite with their families in Little Rock, Arkansas, in 1866. *(Library of Congress, Prints and Photographs Division, LC-USZ62-175)*

- *April:* Union army surgeon A. W. Kelly, on grounds of public health, tries to expel from Natchez all ex-slaves except those employed by and living with whites. Black soldiers swear revenge, some desert, and within a few weeks Kelly is relieved.
- *April 12:* Confederate troops commanded by Gen. Nathan Bedford Forrest massacre captured black Union soldiers after the battle of Fort Pillow, Tennessee.
- *June 7:* The Union recruits male slaves in Kentucky into the army with or without the consent of their owners, but it compensates loyal owners.
- *June 15:* Congress passes the Equalization Bill, granting black Union troops the same pay as white.
- *July:* Black infantrymen and cavalry fight in the sieges of Petersburg and Richmond. Thirteen win the Medal of Honor for valor.
- *September 29:* A black cavalry regiment and 12 black infantry regiments participate in the battle of Chaffin's Farm, Virginia. Thirteen of these men are awarded the Congressional Medal of Honor.
- *October 2–3:* At the Battle of Saltville, Virginia, the victorious Confederates allegedly massacre black cavalry soldiers.
- *December:* Two brigades of black troops contribute to the Union victory at the battle of Nashville.

1865

- By this time, some 180,000 blacks have served in the Union army, more than 20 percent of the adult black male population under 45.
- *January:* General Robert E. Lee recommends the employment of blacks in the Confederate army.
- *February 18:* Men of the 21st U.S. Colored Infantry are the first Union troops to enter Charleston after its evacuation by the Confederate army.
- *March–April:* An estimated 6,000–9,000 black troops participate in the Union victory at Fort Blakeley, Alabama, the last major battle of the Civil War.
- *March 13:* The Confederate Congress passes and President Davis signs the "Negro Soldier Bill," authorizing the enlistment of slaves as soldiers. Emancipation, however, requires the consent of the owners and of the states of their residence.
- *April 9:* The Civil War effectively ends when General Lee surrenders his Army of Northern Virginia to Gen. Ulysses S. Grant at Appomattox Court House, Virginia. The last Confederate troops surrender May 10.
- *May:* Union recruitment of black soldiers is terminated.
- *July:* Congress creates six black regiments, with white officers, as part of the regular army.

Eyewitness Testimony

Colonial Period

We account all generally from Sixteen to Sixty that are healthfull and strong bodys, both House-holders and Servants fit to beare Armes, *except Negroes* and slaves, whom wee arme not.

Massachusetts governor Bradstreet, 1680,
in Williams, History *1:195.*

[Any slaves who] manfully Behave themselves in fight with the enemy . . . so as to deserve public Notice . . . shall be entitled to and receive from the public Tresury Yearly, and every Yr. A Livery Coat, and pair of Breeches, made of good red Negro Cloth turn'd up with Blue, and a Black Hat and pair of Black Shoes, and shall that Day in every Year (during their Lives) on which such Action Shall be perform'd be free'd and exempted from all personal Labour & Service to their owner or Manager.

Georgia legislature, in Higginbotham,
In the Matter of Color, *260–61.*

The Revolutionary War

Resolved, That it is the opinion of this committee, as the contest now between Great Britain and the colonies respects the liberties and privileges of the latter, which the colonies are determined to maintain, that the admission of any persons, as soldiers, into the army now raising, but such as are freeman, will be inconsistent with the principals [sic] that are supported, and reflect dishonor on this colony; and that no slaves be admitted into this army upon any consideration whatever.

Committee of Safety of Massachusetts, May 29, 1775,
in Williams, History *1:334.*

Resolved, That the colonels of the several regiments of militia throughout the Colony have leave to enroll such a number of able male slaves, to be employed as pioneers and laborers, as public exigencies may require; and that a daily pay of seven shillings and sixpence be allowed for the service of each such slave while actually employed.

South Carolina legislature, 1775, in Wilson,
Black Phalanx, *42.*

TO THE HONORABLE GENERAL COURT OF THE MASSACHUSETTS' BAY.

The subscribers beg leave to report to your Honorable House, (which we do in justice to the character of so brave a man), that under our own observation, we declare that a negro man named Salem Poor, of Col. Frye's regiment, Capt. Ame's company, in the late battle at Charleston, behaved like an experienced officer, as well as an excellent soldier. . . . [I]n the person of this said negro, centers a brave and gallant soldier. The reward due to so great and distinguished a character, we submit to Congress.
[14 signatures]
Cambridge, Dec. 5, 1775.

Wilson, Black Phalanx, *37.*

Your Lordship will observe by my letter, No. 34, that I have been endeavoring to raise two regiments here— one of white people, the other of black. The former goes on very slowly, but the latter very well, and would have been in great forwardness, had not a fever crept in amongst them, which carried off a great many very fine fellows.

Lord Dunmore, royal governor of Virginia to the secretary of
state in London, March 30, 1776, in Wilson,
Black Phalanx, *45.*

Whereas, for the preservation of the rights and liberties of the United States, it is necessary that the whole powers of government should be exerted in recruiting the Continental battalions; and whereas, His Excellency Gen. Washington hath enclosed to this state a proposal made to him by Brigadier General Varnum, to enlist into the two battalions, raising by this state, such slaves as should be willing to enter into the service; and whereas, history affords us frequent precedents of the wisest, the freest, and bravest nations having liberated their slaves, and enlisted them as soldiers to fight in defence of their country; and also whereas, the enemy, with a great force, have taken possession of the capital, and of a greater part of this state; and this state is obliged to raise a very considerable number of troops for its own immediate defence, where it is in a manner rendered impossible for this state to furnish recruits for the said two battalions, without adopting the said measure so recommended.

It is voted and resolved, that every able-bodied negro, mulatto, or Indian man slave, in this state, may enlist into either of the said two battalions, to serve during the continuance of the present war with Great Britain.

It is further Voted and Resolved, That every slave so enlisting shall, upon his passing muster before Col. Christopher Greene, be immediately discharged from the service of his master or mistress, and be absolutely free, as though he had never been encumbered with any kind of servitude or slavery.

Rhode Island legislature, 1778, in Williams, History
1:347–48.

Whereas the enemy have adopted a practice of enrolling Negroes among their Troops, I do hereby give notice That all Negroes taken in arms, or upon any military Duty, shall be purchased for [the public service at] a stated Price; the money to be paid to the Captors.

But I do most strictly forbid any Person to sell or claim Right over any Negroe, the property of a Rebel, who may take Refuge with any part of this Army: And I do promise to every Negroe who shall desert the Rebel Standard, full security to follow within these Lines, any Occupation which he shall think proper.

*The Phillipsburg Proclamation, issued by the British
commander in chief, June 30, 1779, in Williams,* History
1:357.

[My slave] sometime in the month of July 1776, made his elopement and afterwards . . . entered the service of the United States in the 14th Virginia regiment, under the fictitious name of William Ferguson, and served until discharged from thence by Col. William Davies.

*Virginia slave owner asking compensation for his slave, October
22, 1789, in Johnston,* Race Relations, *14.*

I. *Whereas* . . . during the course of the war, many persons in this state had caused their slaves to enlist in certain regiments or corps raised within the same . . . as substitutes for free persons, whose lot or duty it was to serve in such regiments or corps, at the same time representing to such recruiting officers that the slaves so enlisted by their direction and concurrence were free; and . . . that on the expiration of the term of enlistment of such slaves that the former owners have attempted again to force them to return to a state of servitude, contrary to the principles, and to their own solemn promise.

II. And whereas it appears just and reasonable that all persons enlisted as aforesaid . . . have thereby of course contributed towards the establishment of American liberty and independence, should enjoy blessings of freedom as a reward for their toils and labours; *Be it therefore enacted,* that each and every slave, who by the appointment and direction of his owner hath enlisted in any regiment or corps raised within this state, either on continental or state establishment, . . . and hath served faithfully during the term of such enlistment, or hath been discharged from such service by some officer duly authorized to grant such discharge, shall . . . be fully and compleatly emancipated. . . .

New York legislature, 1783, in Wilson,
Black Phalanx, *68–69.*

To The General Assembly of the State of North Carolina

The Petitioner of Ned Griffin a Man of mixed Blood Humbley Saieth that a Small space of Time before the battle of Gilford a certain William Kitchen then in the Service of his countrey as a Soldier Deserted from his line for which he was Turned in to the Continental Service to serve as the Law Directs—Your petitioner was then a Servant to William Griffin and was purchased by the said Kitchen for the purpose of Serving in His place, with a Solom Assurance that if he your Petitioner would faithfully serve the Term of Time that the said Kitchen was Returned for he should be a free man—Upon which said Promise and Assurance your Petitioner Consented to enter in to the Continental Service in said Kitchens Behalf and was Received by Colo: James Armstrong At Martinborough as a free Man[.] Your Petitioner further saieth that . . . at the Time that I was Received into Service by said Colo: Armstrong said Kitchen Openly Declared me to be free Man—The Faithfull purformance of the above agreement will appear from my Discharge,—some Time after your Petitioners Return he was Seized upon by said Kitchen and Sold to a Certain Abner Roberson who now holds me as a Servant—Your Petitioner therefore thinks that by Contract and merit he is Intitled to his Freedom. . . .

N Carolina   his

Edgecomb County   Ned X Griffin

April 4th 1784   mark

Aptheker, Documentary History of the Negro
People *1: Doc. 4-b.*

In the beginning of the late war which gave America freedom, your petitioner shouldered his musket and repaired to the American standard, regardless of invitations trumpeted up by British proclamations for the slaves to emancipate themselves by becoming the assassins of their owners. Your petitioner avoided the rock that too many of his colour were shipwrecked on. He was taught that the war was levied on Americans not for the emancipation of the blacks, but for the subjugation of the whites, and he thought that the number of bondmen ought not to be augmented. Under these impressions he did actually campaign in both armies—in the American army as a soldier, in the British as a spy.

Virginia petition, October 9, 1792, in Johnston,
Race Relations, 12.

From an estimate I made at that time, on the best information I could collect, I supposed the State of Virginia lost [to the British], under Lord Cornwallis' hand, that year, about thirty thousand slaves; and that, of these twenty-seven thousand died of the small-pox and camp fever; the rest were partly sent to the West Indies, and exchanged for rum, sugar, coffee and fruit; and partly sent to New York, from whence they went, at the peace, either to Nova Scotia or to England.

Thomas Jefferson, on the treatment of blacks who went with
the British army, in Wilson, Black Phalanx, 70.

Indian Wars

At fifteen, I was hired to Capt. George Smith, who volunteered to go to Tippecanoe [scene of an 1811 battle with Tecumseh]. I was a fifer in his company. The freedom of myself, Moses, and some others was promised us on our return. But the last time I saw Moses, he was bowed down in hellish slavery in Little Rock, Ark., and I had the misfortune to have to pay N. eighteen hundred dollars for my freedom.

J. C. Brown, in Bontemps, Four Fugitive
Slave Narratives, 168.

The [maroon] Negroes, from the commencement of the Florida [Second Seminole] war, have, for their numbers, been the most formidable foe, more blood-thirsty, active, and revengeful than the Indian. . . . Ten resolute negroes, with a knowledge of the country, are sufficient to desolate the frontier, from one extent to the other.

U.S. Army officer, about 1840, in Blassingame,
Slave Community, 124.

War of 1812

Whereas it has been represented to me that many persons now resident in the United States have expressed a desire to withdraw therefrom with a view to entering His Majesty's service, or of being received as free settlers into some of His Majesty's colonies.

This is therefore to give notice that all persons who may be disposed to migrate from the United States, will with their families, be received on board of His Majesty's ship or vessels of War, or at the military posts that may be established upon or near the coast of the United States,

when they will have their choice of either entering into His Majesty's sea or land force, or of being sent as free settlers to the British possessions in North America or the West Indies where they will meet with due encouragement. Given under my hand at Bermuda this second day of April 1814, by command of Vice Admiral Alex Cochrane.

In Grant, "Black Immigrants into Nova Scotia," 264–65.

Our Negroes are flocking to the enemy from all quarters, which they convert into troops, vindictive and rapicious [*sic*]—with a minute knowledge of every byepath. They leave us as spies upon our strength, and they return upon us as guides and soldiers and incendiaries. . . . The example too which is held out in these bands of armed negroes and the weakness of the resistance which as yet has been made to oppose them, must have a strong effect upon those blacks which have not as yet been able to escape.

Virginian J. P. Hungerford, August 3, 1814, in Grant, "Black
Immigrants into Nova Scotia," 266.

SECT. 6. *And be it further enacted,* That it shall be lawful for any able-bodied slave, with the written assent of his master or mistress, to enlist into the said corps; and the master or mistress of such slave shall be entitled to the pay and bounty allowed him for his service; and, further, that the said slave, at the time of receiving his discharge, shall be deemed and adjudged to have been legally manumitted from that time, and his said master or mistress shall not thenceforward be liable for his maintenance.

New York law, October 24, 1814, in Wilson,
History 2:23–25.

Texas War of Independence

Fourteen Negro slaves [from Texas] with their families came to me this day and I sent them free to Victoria.

Mexican general José Urrea, April 3, 1836,
in Campbell, Empire, 44.

The Civil War: The Confederacy

Some of our people are fearful that when a large portion of our fighting men are taken from the country, that large numbers of our negroes aided by emissaries will ransack portions of the country, kill numbers of our inhabitants, and make their way to the black republicans. There is no doubt but that numbers of them believe that Lincoln's intention is to set them all free. Then, to counteract this idea, and make them assist in whipping the black republicans, which by the by would be the best thing that could be done, could they not be incorporated into our armies, say ten or twenty placed promiscuously [at random] in each company?

John J. Cheatham, Confederate patriot, to the secretary of war, May 4, 1861, in Berlin, Freedom 2: Doc. 114.

Genl Magruder directs that you will make a call upon the citizens of Gloucester, Middlesex and Mathews counties for one half of their male force of slaves to finish the works around Gloucester Point—They will be allowed fifty cents a day and a ration for each negro man during the time he is at work. . . . The free negroes will be impressed if they refuse to come and a force will be sent to bring them in. . . .

Orders to the Confederate commander at Gloucester Point, Virginia, July 28, 1861, in Freedom 1: Doc. 260A.

According to instructions which you gave me by telegraph, I have detached militia men who are overseeing on plantations to do police and patrol duty upon the same. . . . [T]here is a great disposition among the Negroes to be insubordinate, and to run away and go to the federals. Within the last 12 months we have had to hang some 40 for plotting an insurrection, and there has been about that number put in irons.

The provost marshal of Adams County to the governor of Mississippi, July 17, 1862, in Aptheker, "Notes on Slave Conspiracies in Confederate Mississippi," 76.

Tyrone died this morning about four o'clock—another death from the sickness contracted on the batteries in Savannah last spring. Three out of the seven men [slaves sent to work on the fortifications] have died.

Rev. Charles C. Jones, October 2, 1862, in Myers, Children of Pride, 972.

My name is John Parker. . . . [When] the excitement about the expected battle at Bull Run arose, [t]hey [the Confederates] said that all the colored people must then come and fight. I arrived at the Junction two days before the action commenced. They immediately placed me in one of the batteries. There were four colored men in our battery, I don't know how many there were in the others. We opened fire about ten o'clock on the morning of Sunday the 21st; couldn't see the Yankees at all and only fired at random. . . . My work was to hand the balls and swab out the cannon; in this we took turns. The officers aimed this gun; we fired grape shot. The balls from the Yankee guns fell thick all around. In one battery a shell burst and killed twenty, the rest ran. . . . We wish to our

hearts that the Yankees would whip [the Confederates], and we would have run over to their side but our officers would have shot us if we had made the attempt.

Reading Journal, quoted in Douglass' Monthly (March 1862), in McPherson, Negro's Civil War, 25, 28.

[S]lavery is a source of great strength to the enemy in a purely military point of view, by supplying him with an army from our granaries. . . . All along the lines slavery is comparatively valueless to us for labor, but of great and increasing worth to the enemy for information. It is an omnipresent spy system, pointing out our valuable men to the enemy, revealing our positions, purposes, and resources. . . .

Adequately to meet the causes which are now threatening ruin to our country, we propose . . . that we immediately commence training a large reserve of the most courageous of our slaves, and further that we guarantee freedom within a reasonable time to every slave in the South who shall remain true to the Confederacy in this war.

Proposal of a group of Confederate officers, January 2, 1864, in McPherson, Negro's Civil War, 245–46.

The time has come to put into the army every able-bodied Negro as a soldier. . . . He must play an important part in the war. He caused the fight, he will have his portion of the burden to bear.

Governor Allen of Louisiana to Confederate secretary of war, September 1864, in DuBois, Black Reconstruction, 117.

Until our white population shall prove insufficient for the armies we require and can afford to keep the field, to employ as a soldier the Negro, who has merely been trained to labor, and as a laborer under the white man accustomed from his youth to the use of firearms, would scarcely be deemed wise or advantageous by any; and this is the question before us. But should the alternative ever be presented of subjugation or of the employment of the slave as a soldier, there seems no reason to doubt what should be our decision.

President Jefferson Davis to the Confederate Congress, November 1864, in DuBois, Black Reconstruction, 117.

For a year past I have seen that the period was fast approaching when we should be compelled to use every resource at our command for the defense of our liberties. . . . The negroes will certainly be made to fight against us if not armed for our defense. The drain of that source of our strength is steadily fatal, and irreversible by any other expedient than that of arming the slaves as an auxiliary force.

I further agree with you that if they are to fight for our freedom they are entitled to their own. . . .

General Lee . . . is strongly in favor of our using the negroes for defense, and emancipating them, if necessary, for that purpose. Can you not yourself write a series of articles in your papers, always urging this point as the true issue, viz, is it better for the negro to fight for us or against us?

> *Letter from the Confederate secretary of war, December 21, 1864, in McPherson,* Negro's Civil War, *247–48.*

Slavery is lost or will be, & we had better as well emancipate if we can make anything by it now. . . . We can certainly live without negroes better than with yankees and without negroes both.

> *James Branch O'Bryan, January 20, 1865, in McPherson,* For Cause, *231.*

Mother, I did not volunteer my services to fight for a free negroes country but to fight for a free white mans country & I do not think I love my country well enough to fight with [alongside] black soldiers.

> *Confederate sergeant, February 18, 1865, reacting to the Confederate decision to recruit slaves as soldiers and offer them freedom at war's end, in McPherson,* For Cause, *172.*

The Civil War: The Union—Contrabands

The [Union] guard on the bridge across the Anacostia arrested a negro who attempted to pass the sentries on the Maryland side. He seemed to feel confident that he was among friends, for he made no concealment of his character and purpose. He said he had walked sixty miles, and was going North. He was very much surprised and disappointed when he was taken into custody, and informed that he would be sent back to his master. He is now in the guard-house, and answers freely all questions relating to his weary march. Of course, such an arrest excites much comment among the men. Nearly all are restive under the thought of action as slave-catchers.

> *New York Herald, 1861(?), quoted in Brown,* American Rebellion, *57.*

In a loyal State I would put down a servile insurrection. In a state of rebellion I would confiscate that which was used to oppose my arms, and take all that property, which constituted the wealth of that State, and furnished the means by which the war is prosecuted, besides being the cause of the war; and if, in so doing, it should be objected that human beings were brought to the free enjoyment of life, liberty, and the pursuit of happiness, such objection might not require much consideration.

> *Gen. Benjamin Butler, July 30, 1861, in Dumond,* Antislavery, *370.*

You will . . . avail yourself of the services of any persons, whether fugitives from labor or not, who may offer them to the National Government. You will employ such persons in such services as they may be fitted for—either as ordinary employees, or, if special circumstances seem to require it, in any other capacity, with such organization (in squads, companies, or otherwise) as you may deem most beneficial to the service[,] . . . this, however, not being a general arming of them for military service. . . . You will assure all loyal masters that Congress will provide just compensation to them for the loss of the services of the persons so employed.

> *Secretary of war to Gen. Thomas W. Sherman, October 14, 1861, in Cornish,* Sable Arm, *19.*

The contrabands . . . will hereafter be placed in the employ of the Government upon the following terms, viz.

1. Men will receive $10 per month, one ration, and soldier's allowance of clothing.
2. Women will receive $4 per month, one ration, and soldier's allowance of clothing.
3. Boys between the ages of twelve and sixteen will receive $4 per month, one ration, and soldier's allowance of clothing.
4. All children under the age of twelve will receive one ration and remain with their parents.
5. The above regulations apply only to contrabands in the public service. When in the employ of officers or any other persons . . . , they will be paid by the person in whose employ they are an amount in money equal to the sum total of the clothing allowance, rations, and money expressed in the above regulations.

> *U. S. War Department, "War of the Rebellion." Available online at URL: http://www.bjmjr.com/contrabands/contrabands3.htm.*

We had fifteen miles to go before we could get to the Federal blockade, and on the way we had to pass a rebel gunboat and a fort. I meant to wait till the tide fell, so that the gunboat would go back in the Cut where she lay at low water, but I did not see her till I got close upon her, and heard the men talking, and looked up and saw them on the deck. I kept close to the marsh, so they might not see me, and managed to get round the point. About a mile and a half above this point was the fort which I had to pass. I passed the fort in the same way as I passed the boat. After I got a little beyond, I crossed on to the same shore that she was, and after I got a little way along the shore, day broke as clear as could be. I looked back and could not see the fort, and I knew I was out of their reach.

About two hours and a half later we reached the Federal gunboats in Stono river. When I got in sight of the Union boats, I raised a white flag, and when I came near, they cheered me, and pointed to the flagship Pawnee. There I had the pleasure of a breakfast of hot coffee, ham, nice butter, and all under the American flag—all strange things in Charleston. There I gave the Almighty praise and glory for delivering me so far. On board the Pawnee I told the Captain about the Charleston harbor, and how the vessels run the blockade, and the next day but one they took two vessels from the information I gave them. Then we were put on board a transport vessel for Port Royal and reached there in safety. Capt. Elwell, Chief Quartermaster, gave me a piece of land, and I built me a little house. I waited on Capt. Elwell, and my wife washed for him and other officers. My wife used to sew for Gen. Hunter's wife, and about a week before we came North Gen. Hunter gave me a paper that made me forever free.

William Summerson in the National Anti-Slavery Standard, *December 27, 1862, quoted in Blassingame,* Slave Community, *701–2.*

Contrabands building stockades, Civil War. *(Library of Congress)*

A few days after the arrival of the contrabands, their services were needed in an important expedition in the interior. These negroes, upon being told what was wanted of them, although knowing that the enterprise would be attended with the greatest danger, and would require the utmost skill, volunteered their services. . . . [T]hey succeeded in penetrating the enemy's country, arresting three very important rebels, and conveying them to the fleet. In the return march, the rebels complained at their being made to walk so far and so fast; but Bob, the captain of the company, would occasionally be heard urging them along after this style: "March along dar, massa; no straggling to de rear: come, close up dar, close up dar! we're boss dis time."

Brown, American Rebellion, *213.*

There followed me back to Corinth, almost the entire Negro population of that valley. They came in every conceivable conveyance; from the master's private carriage to a wheelbarrow and they hitched to the conveyances, carts, haywagons, and sometimes a cow and a horse, and sometimes a fine team of horses, or a cow and an ox. Hundreds were on foot with their household goods packed on a mule, a horse, or a cow. They made a picturesque column, much larger than my command. At night our camp spread over a large territory. . . . We all arrived safely at Corinth, where I established the great contraband camp and guarded it by two companies of Negro soldiers that I uniformed, armed, and equipped without any authority to. . . .

Union general Grenville Dodge, 1863, in Horton, "Submitting to the 'Shadow of Slavery,'" 130.

Losing patience at the failure of all orders and exhortations to these poor people [slaves] to stay at home, General Davis . . . ordered the pontoon bridge at Ebenezer Creek to be taken up before the refugees who were following that corps had crossed, so as to leave them on the further bank of the unfordable stream and thus disembarrass the marching troops. . . . The poor refugees had their hearts so set on liberation, and the fear of falling into the hands of the Confederate cavalry was so great, that, with wild wailings and cries, the great crowd rushed, like a stampeded drove of cattle, into the water, those who could not swim as well as those who could, and many were drowned in spite of the earnest efforts of the soldiers to help them. . . . [T]here were many ignorant, simple souls to whom it was literally preferable to die freemen rather than to live slaves.

Cox, March, *37–38, in Bell,* Major Butler's Legacy, *382–83.*

The Civil War: The Union—Recruitment of Blacks

The Department finds it necessary to adopt a regulation with respect to the large and increasing number of persons of color, commonly known as contraband, now subsisted at the navy yard and on board ships of war. . . . You are therefore authorized, when their services can be made useful to enlist them for the naval service, under the same forms and regulations as apply to other enlistments. They will be allowed, however, no higher rating than "boys" [apprentices, the lowest rank in the Navy], at a compensation of $10 per month and one ration a day.

Secretary of the navy, September 20, 1861, in Aptheker, "The Negro in the Union Navy," 175–76.

The negroes are mistaken if they think white men can fight for them while they stay at home. We have opened the pathway. We don't want to threaten, but we have been saying that you would fight, and if you won't fight we will make you.

Abolitionist state senator James Lane, recruiting speech in Leavenworth, Kansas, August 6, 1862, in Castel, "Civil War Kansas," 132–33.

In these journeys through the country the recruiting officer often met with strange experiences. Recruits were taken wherever found, and as their earthly possessions usually consisted of but what they wore upon their backs, they required no time to settle their affairs. The laborer in the field would throw down his hoe or quit his plow and march away with the guard, leaving his late owner looking after him in speechless amazement. On one occasion the writer met a planter on the road, followed by two of his slaves, each driving a loaded wagon. The usual questions were asked and the whilom slaves joined the recruiting party, leaving their teams and late master standing in the highway.

Historian of the 7th New York Regiment, in Wilson, Black Phalanx, 130–31.

If I could have carried a gun, I would have gone personally, but I thought it was my duty to talk to the people. I told them "that the young and able-bodied ought to go into the field like men, that they should stand up to the rack, and help the government." My oldest son, Tom, who was in California, enlisted on a man-of-war in San Francisco, and I suppose he must have been killed, as I have not heard from him since that time.

My son-in-law, Wheeler, enlisted in Detroit. I advised the people, in general terms, to do the same, and said that if any of them wished to go to enlist early, so as to secure the bounty offered, I would provide for their families till they could send the bounty-money to them. A number went, and some lost their bounty-money through "sharpers" lying in wait for them. . . .

Many in the States, both white and coloured, enlisted merely to receive the bounty, and then they "jumped the bounty," as it was termed—that is, they took the money and did not go into the army.

Rev. Josiah Henson, an escaped slave, in Four Fugitive Slave Narratives, 128–29, 133.

The Civil War: The Union—Black Soldiers

. . . the Rebels have sent into the fields all their available fighting men—every man capable of bearing arms; and you know they have kept at home all their slaves for the raising of subsistence for their armies in the field. In this way they can bring to bear against us all the strength of their so-called Confederate States; while we at the North can only send a portion of our fighting force, being compelled to leave behind another portion to cultivate our fields and supply the wants of an immense army. The administration has determined to take from the rebels this source of supply—to take their Negroes and compel them to send back a portion of their whites to cultivate their deserted plantations. . . .

All of you will some day be on picket duty; and I charge you all, if any of this unfortunate race come within your lines, that you do not turn them away. . . . They are to be encouraged to come to us; they are to be received

Recruiting poster, Civil War *(Library of Congress)*

with open arms; they are to be fed and clothed; they are to be armed.

Adjutant-General Lorenzo Thomas, March 1863, speaking to Union officers in Louisiana, quoted in DuBois, Black Reconstruction, *98–99.*

[T]he rebels drove our force towards the gunboats, taking colored men prisoners and murdering them. This so enraged them that they rallied, and charged the enemy more heroically and desperately than has been recorded during the war. It was a genuine bayonet-charge, a hand-to-hand fight. . . . One brave man took his former master prisoner, and brought him into camp with great gusto. A rebel prisoner made a particular request, that *his own* negroes should not be placed over him as a guard.

Eyewitness account of a battle on June 7, 1863, in the Mississippi valley, in Brown, American Rebellion, *137–38.*

The Battle of Olustee, or Ocean Pond, on the 20th of February, will be long remembered by the Eighth, which suffered terribly in the conflict. . . . It looked sad to see [black] men wounded coming into camp with their arms and equipments on, so great was their endurance and so determined were they to defend themselves till the death. . . . The order from the War Department, giving authority in this department to enroll and draft all male colored persons, is to be put into effect in a few days. It creates some excitement among those who prefer to be servants instead of soldiers. They are not very numerous here, as the Rebels have sent them far away.

Sgt.-Maj. Rufus Jones, 8th U.S. Colored Infantry, April 16, 1864, in Redkey, Grand Army of Black Men, *41–42.*

On the march the Colored Soldiers as well as their white Officers were made the subject of much ridicule and many insulting remarks by the White Troops and in some instances petty outrages such as the pulling off the Caps of Colored Soldiers, stealing their horses etc was practiced by the White Soldiers. These insults as well as the jeers and taunts that they would not fight were borne by the Colored Soldiers patiently or punished with dignity by their Officers but in no instance did I hear Colored soldiers make any reply to insulting language used towards [them] by the White Troops.

On the 2d of October the forces reached the vicinity of the Salt Works and finding the enemy in force preparations were made for battle. . . . The point to be attacked was the side of a high mountain, the Rebels being posted about half way up behind rifle pits made of logs and stones to the height of three feet. All being in readiness the Brigade moved to the attack. The Rebels opened upon them a terrific fire but the line pressed steadily forward up the steep side of the mountain until they found themselves within fifty yards of the Enemy. Here Col. Wade ordered his force to charge and the Negroes rushed upon the works with a yell and after a desperate struggle carried the entire line killing and wounding a large number of the enemy and capturing some prisoners. . . . Out of the four hundred engaged, one hundred and fourteen men and four officers fell killed or wounded. . . .

Such of the Colored Soldiers as fell into the hands of the Enemy during the battle were brutally murdered. The Negroes did not retaliate but treated the Rebel wounded with great kindness, carrying them water in their canteens and doing all they could to alleviate the sufferings of those whom the fortunes of war had placed in their hands. . . .

James S. Brisbin, October 20, 1864, in Berlin, Freedom 2: *Doc. 219.*

In battle's wild commotion
I won't at all object
If a nigger should stop a bullet
Coming for me direct.
Marching ditty among some Union troops, in Burchard, One Gallant Rush, *73.*

Sergt. William Walker, of Company A, Third South Carolina colored troops, was yesterday killed, in accordance with the sentence of a court-martial. He had declared he would no longer remain a soldier for seven

Black troops liberate slaves in North Carolina during the Civil War. *(Library of Congress)*

dollars per month, and had brought his company to stack their arms before their captain's tent, refusing to do duty until they should be paid thirteen dollars a month, as had been agreed when they were enlisted by Col. Saxon. He was a smart soldier and an able man, dangerous as leader in a revolt. . . . He met his death unflinchingly. Out of eleven shots first fired, but one struck him. A reserve firing-party had been provided, and by these he was shot to death.

The mutiny for which this man suffered death arose entirely out of the inconsistent and contradictory orders of the Paymaster and the Treasury Department at Washington.

Beaufort (S.C.) Cor. Tribune, *1864(?), in Brown,*
American Rebellion, *253.*

[M]y wife and children came with me [in October, 1864, to Camp Nelson, Kentucky], because my master said that if I enlisted he would not maintain them, and I knew they would be abused by him when I left. I had then four children, aged respectively ten, nine, seven, and four years. On my presenting myself as a recruit, I was told by the lieutenant in command to take my family into a tent within the limits of the camp. My wife and family occupied this tent by the express permission of the aforementioned officer, and never received any notice to leave until Tuesday, November 22, when a mounted guard gave my wife notice that she and her children must leave camp before early morning. This was about six o'clock at night. My little boy, about seven years of age, had been very sick. . . . My wife had no place to go. I told him that I was a soldier of the United States. He told me that it did not make any difference; he had orders to take all out of camp. He told my wife and family if they did not get up in the wagon he had, he would shoot the last one of them.

Affidavit of Joseph Miller, in Gutman, Black Family, *373.*
The little boy died.

[I]n case of ultimate defeat, the Northern troops, black or white, would go home, while the First South Carolina must fight it out or be re-enslaved. This was one thing that made the St. John's River so attractive to them and even to me;—it was so much nearer the Everglades. I used seriously to ponder, during the darker periods of the war, whether I might not end my days as an outlaw,—a leader of Maroons.

T. W. Higginson, white commander of a black regiment,
Army Life in a Black Regiment, *251.*

On the 29th of Oct., 1862, twenty-four men of the 1st Regiment of Kansas, Colored Volunteers, having advanced beyond the limits prescribed, were charged upon by one hundred and twenty of the Rebel cavalry. There was a desperate hand-to-hand encounter. . . . Out of the twenty-four men, only six escaped unhurt. The Rebels were armed with shot-guns, revolvers and sabres; our men with Austrian rifles and sabre bayonets. This last is a fearful weapon, and did terrible execution. Six Killer, the leader of the Cherokee negroes, shot two men, bayoneted a third, and laid the fourth with the butt of his gun. Another was attacked by three men. He discharged his rifle and had no time to load again. When asked to surrender, he replied by a stunning blow from the butt of his rifle, which knocked the Rebel off his horse.

So ended the battle of Island Mounds, which resulted in a complete victory to the. . . . negro regiment. . . . [Y]et four months passed and they were not mustered—still they adhered to their organization through every discouragement and disadvantage.

Autobiography of James L. Smith, ex-slave, in Bontemps,
Five Black Lives, *222–23.*

My dear husband
I have just this evening received your letter. . . . [Y]ou can imagin how anxious and worry I had become about you. And so it seems that all can get home once in awhile . . . but you[.] . . . [Y]our poor old Mother is hear delving and working like a dog to try to keep soul and body together and here am I with to little children and myself to support. . . . I do think if your officers could see us they would certainly let you come home and bring us a little money[.]

Letter from Letty Barnes, n.d., quoted in Weidman, "Preserving the Legacy of the United States Colored Troops." Available online at URL: www.bjmjr.com/contrabands/
contrabands3.htm.

The difficulty of colored troops being discharged from the service is illustrated in the cases of about a dozen men in the 3rd U.S.C.T. [United States Colored Troops], whom the surgeon has declared unfit for duty, and sent to the base hospitals for exam to that effect. . . . the surgeons at the hospitals have refused to examine them, and returned them to their regiment with the consolation that they will be sent back as often as the surgeon forwards them to the hospitals. Should there be an attack, these helpless persons would only tend to create a panic, as in their inability to defend themselves they would have to seek safety as best they could in flight.

War correspondent Thomas Morris Chester to the Philadelphia Press, December 6, 1864, quoted in Blackett, Thomas Morris Chester, 202–3.

Sir I have the honor to call your attention To the neccesity of having a school for The benefit of our regement We have never Had an institution of that sort and we Stand deeply in need of instruction the majority of us having been slaves We wish to have some benefit of education To make of ourselves capable of business In the future. . . . We wish to become a People capable of self support as we are Capable of being soldier. . . .

First Sgt. John Sweeny to Tennessee Freedman's Bureau assistant commissioner, Nashville, Tennessee, October 8, 1865, in Berlin, Freedom 2: Doc. 248.

After the war started, I ran off and joined the army. During the war I saw my mistress. She came to me and said, "Don't you remember how I nursed you when you were sick, and now you are fighting against me." I said, "No, Ma'am, I am not fighting against you. I am fighting for my freedom." . . . I was sent to Tullahoma for training. This was the biggest thing that ever happened in my life. I felt like a man, with a uniform on and a gun in my hand. . . .

Ex-slave in Johnson, God Struck Me Dead, 102.

Civil War:
The Union: Spies and Scouts

James Lawson . . . made his escape last December. . . . [He] shipped on board of "The Freeborn," flag-gun-boat. . . . He furnished Capt. Magaw with much valuable intelligence concerning the rebel movements. . . .
On Thursday, week ago, it became necessary to obtain correct information of the enemy's movements. . . . "Jim," said the general [Sickles], "I want you to go over to-night and find out what forces they have at Aquia Creek and Fredericksburg. If you want any men to accompany you, pick them out." . . .

Away went Jim over to the contraband camp, and returning almost immediately, brought two very intelligent-looking darkies. . . .

"Well, here, Jim, you take my pistol," said Gen. Sickles, unbuckling it from his belt; "and, if you are successful, I will give you $100." . . .

Capt. Foster . . . landed them a short distance below the Potomac-Creek Batteries. They were to return early in the morning, but were unable, from the great distance they went in the interior. Long before daylight on Saturday morning, the gunboat was lying off at the appointed place. As the day dawned, Capt. Foster discovered a mounted picket-guard near the beach, and almost at the same instant saw Jim to the left of them, in the woods, sighting his gun at the rebel cavalry. He ordered the "gig" to be manned and rowed to the shore. The rebels moved along slowly, thinking to intercept the boat, when Foster gave them a shell, which scattered them. Jim, with only one of his original companions, and two fresh contrabands, came on board. Jim had *lost the other.* He [Cornelius] had been challenged by a picket when some distance in advance of Jim, and the negro, instead of answering the summons, fired the contents of Sickles's revolver at the picket. . . . [A]t that time the entire picket-guard rushed out of a small house near the spot, and fired the contents of their muskets at Jim's companion, killing him instantly. Jim and the other three hid themselves in a hollow, near a fence and, after the pickets gave up pursuit, crept through the woods to the shore. From the close proximity of the rebel pickets, Jim could not display a light, which was the signal for Capt. Foster to send a boat.

New York Times, quoted in Brown, American Rebellion, 62–64.

This fearless woman [Harriet Tubman] was often sent into the rebel lines as a spy, and brought back valuable information as to the position of armies and batteries; she has been in battle when the shot was falling like hail, and the bodies of dead and wounded men were dropping around her like leaves in autumn; but the thought of fear never seems to have had place for a moment in her mind.

Bradford, Harriet, 102.

The Civil War:
Blacks and the Confederate Military

The enemy [the Confederacy] is doing a rushing business in recruiting their depleted troops with Negro troops. Some twenty thousand are already assembled at Camp Lee in the vicinity of Richmond, and the number is rapidly increasing. Twenty-two regiments are in progress of formation. . . . The officers of colored troops in [the Union] army, knowing the merits of the race as soldiers, are a little anxious to learn whether the negroes can be induced to fight for the South. . . . The negroes thoroughly understand this war, and no fears need be entertained for them, as they will, without doubt, turn right side up with care at the earliest practicable moment.

Dispatch from black war correspondent T. M. Chester to the Philadelphia *Press, March 26, 1865, cited in Blackett,* Thomas Morris Chester, *282–83.*

Levi Miller [a slave who accompanied his master] stood by my side [at Spotsylvania Courthouse] and man never fought harder and better than he did and when the enemy tried to cross our little breastworks and we clubbed and bayoneted them off, no one used his bayonet with more skill and effect than Levi Miller.

Captain J. E. Anderson, quoted in Dean, "The Black and the Gray." Available online at URL: www.37thtexas.org/html/Wshcitypaper.html.

Reconstruction

Genl We the soldiers of the 36 U.S. Col Regt Humbly petition you to alter the Affairs at Roanoake Island. . . .
1 . . . The rations for our wifes and family's have been . . . cut down) to one half the regular ration. . . . [O]ur ration's are stolen from the ration house by Mr Streeter the Asst Supt at the Island (and others). . . .
2nd Mr Streeter . . . takes no care of the colored people and has no Simpathy with the colored people. . . .
3rd . . . Captn James has not paid the Colored people for their work for near a year and at the same time cuts the ration's off to one half. . . . [S]ome soldiers are sick in Hospitals that have never been paid a cent. . . .
4th . . . the white soldiers break into our houses act as they please steal our chickens rob our gardens and if any

one defends their-Selves against them they are taken to the gard house. . . .

North Carolina veterans to the Freedmen's Bureau Commissioner, May or June 1865, in Freedom. *Available online at URL:* http://www.history.umd.edu/Freedmen/sampdocs.htm.

I landed in Shreveport, Caddo Parish, La., September 25th, 1869, and went about trying to rent a house, but it was rumored all over town that a boat load of discharged Union soldiers had come, and the whites would not rent us their houses. Finally we came up with a Baptist preacher, and he let us have his house. After we had been there a few months the white people began saying they were going to kill . . . all the discharged Negro soldiers; that these discharged men were going to spoil all the other Negroes, so that the whites could do nothing with them. . . .

Black Union veteran Henry Adams, reporting events of September 1869, quoted in Painter, Exodusters, *74.*

The case of the colored cadet [James W.] Smith [the first black admitted to West Point] who has been on trial before a court-martial at West Point for breaking a cocoanut dipper over the head of another cadet named Wilson has been closed. . . . He appears to have been too prompt in breaking the cocoa-nut over cadet Wilson's head; but that member doubtless represented to him for the time the collective heads of the white cadets who had subjected him to humiliating ill treatment.

New National Era, *November 3, 1870, quoted in Katz,* Eyewitness, *352.*

CHAPTER TWELVE

The End of Slavery
1861–1877

The Union: The Rocky Road to Emancipation

By the time the Civil War erupted, feeling for and against slavery ran high in the North as well as in the South. The newly inaugurated Abraham Lincoln believed it his prime duty to hold the Union together, with or without slavery. The United States had still to prove to the world that such a democracy could survive.

Although Lincoln personally thought slavery an evil, he doubted that blacks and whites could live peaceably together as equals. With reason, he worried about what was to become of blacks, once freed. Well into the war, he still saw colonization as the best possible solution. He edged toward emancipation hesitantly, basing his decisions about it on military and political advantage. Would proclaiming emancipation cause the border states to secede from the Union and join the Confederacy? Would it weaken the Union's military position by alienating soldiers who had enlisted to save the Union, not to free the slaves? Would it strengthen the Union's military position by depriving the South of its labor force and recruiting soldiers for the North? This last was a powerful argument, for the South's ability to consign almost all nonmilitary labor to blacks freed three-fourths of white men of military age to serve in the Confederate army.[1]

Abolitionists urged upon the president the moral, political, and military advantages of emancipation. Abolitionist generals in the Union army repeatedly took matters into their own hands. Some of them insisted that slaves in territory they captured were contrabands of war, subject like any other enemy property to seizure. Others, on their own authority, declared the slaves in captured territory free. Repeatedly Lincoln voided such orders. But every one of them encouraged more slaves to think of freedom as near at hand or to try to seize it for themselves by following Union troops or fleeing to Union forts or ships.

Until the summer of 1862, Lincoln's actions discouraged abolitionists, particularly when he insisted that the government must as a matter of law and duty return fugitive slaves to their owners. When, for instance, in September of 1861 Lincoln countermanded General Frémont's emancipation order in Missouri, Thomas Hamilton, the editor of the *Anglo-African*, wrote, "[T]he man who had reduced back to slavery the slaves of rebels in Missouri would order the army of the United

Contrabands escape to a Union ship. *(Library of Congress)*

States to put down a slave insurrection in Virginia or Georgia."[2] In fact, though, emancipation no longer depended on the will of one man, even the president of the United States. Willy-nilly, thousands of slaves claimed their own freedom, sometimes assisted by abolitionist Union soldiers. Independently of governmental action, they attained a kind of gradual emancipation. Slaves, wisely, did not rise up in a mass rebellion, but in their multitudes they left their owners' plantations and farms, either on their own or encouraged by Federal troops.

True enough, slaves could not count on assistance from these troops, for the more racist among them treated the blacks abominably. But some intended to free them as a matter of conscience; others wanted their services as drivers, cooks, or construction workers on fortifications. Slaves also brought to the aid of the Union an intimate familiarity with the countryside and waterways, as well as knowledge of where commodities had been hidden. "A big drove of soldiers comes into town," reminisced Mary Reynolds. "They say they's Federals. More'n half the niggers goes off with them soldiers, but I goes on back home 'cause of my old mammy. Next day them Yankees is swarming the place. Some the niggers wants to show them something. I follows to the woods. The niggers shows them soldiers a big pit in the ground, bigger'n a big house. It is got wooden doors that lifts up, but the top am sodded and grass growing on it, so you couldn't tell it. In that pit is stock, hosses and cows and mules and money and chinaware and silver and a mess of stuff them soldiers takes."[3] Slave owners looked at their slaves with new eyes, seeing them now not as beasts of burden or as devoted servants but as potential spies.

Lincoln twisted and turned, looking for alternatives to outright emancipation. In August 1861, he signed the First Confiscation Act, providing that when slaves were engaged in hostile military service, their owners forfeited claims to their labor, thus enabling the Union to accept the services of former slaves previously employed by the Confederacy. In March 1862, he got through the Congress provision for money to compensate slave owners of any state abolishing slavery, in the hope that border states would avail themselves of this face-saving possibility.

Slaves flee toward Union lines. *(Library of Congress)*

July 1862 saw a burst of similar presidential efforts. Lincoln proposed but failed to get through Congress a bill providing that "whenever the President of the United States shall be satisfied that any State shall have lawfully abolished slavery . . . [he] is to pay the State in 6% interest bearing bonds equal to the aggregate value, at X dollars per head."[4] He appealed to congressmen from the border states to support gradual, compensated emancipation, with colonization of freed slaves outside the United States. The Second Confiscation Act freed the slaves of all traitors to and rebels against the Union. The Militia Act freed not only any enemy-owned slave who rendered military service to the Union but also his mother, wife, and children.

Only after all that did Lincoln, that same month, inform his cabinet that he intended to issue an emancipation proclamation—after a major military victory. Abolitionist lobbying, the pressure of events, and perhaps the successes of blacks in the Union army had gradually persuaded him that the advantages to the Union of emancipation exceeded its hazards. He announced his intention to the public in September in the Preliminary Emancipation Proclamation, after the Battle of Antietam, formally declaring his intention to free the slaves in the rebel states on January 1, 1863, and to offer financial assistance to loyal slave states if they would free their slaves. Moreover, he promised to begin enforcement of the Confiscation Acts.

The Emancipation Proclamation itself freed the slaves of all rebels against the Union—but, significantly and confusingly, not those of the loyal border states. The impact of the proclamation far outweighed that of its specific terms. Many slaves, unsure of what freedom involved, with no access to accurate information, took the wish for the fact. Border state slaves understandably assumed that they were free—to the point that the Louisville *Journal* asked black leaders to explain to slaves that the proclamation did not affect slavery in Kentucky.[5] Annie Davis of Belair, Maryland, resorted to writing President Lincoln in August 1864: "Mr president It is my Desire to be free, to go to see my people on the eastern shore. My mistress wont let me you will please let me know if we are free, and what I can do. I write to you for advice. Please send me word this week, or as soon as possible and oblidge."[6]

The Union: Fugitives and Contrabands

If emancipation lay only at the end of an uncharted road, so also no plan existed for a fresh start for freed slaves. They themselves could not see beyond attaining freedom, and those who dealt with them were operating catch as catch can. For 250 years, Americans had sown the wind of slavery. Now they were reaping the whirlwind.

Accustomed as Americans are today to pictures of refugees streaming through war-torn countries, it is hard for most to imagine such things in their own land. The Civil War overturned the southern economy and the southern way of life; ironically, no one suffered and endured as much in the process as the slaves whom it freed. Masters went off to fight in the Confederate army, leaving in charge of the slaves overseers or wives inexperienced in managing farms and plantations. Masters tried to move slaves out of the path of the advancing Union armies, sometimes upcountry, sometimes farther south, sometimes all the way to Texas. If slaves were too old, too sick, or too young to work, some masters abandoned them. Masters in retreat would shoot down their fleeing slaves rather than let them go free. Masters sent slaves to work for the very Confederate army that fought to keep them enslaved, or took them along as servants when they themselves joined up.

Amid all these uncertainties, slaves trained to obedience and passivity were suddenly confronted with the necessity of choice. Should they try to escape to the North or to follow Union troops? Escape was a difficult and dangerous effort. Many who tried did not make it. Consider those who tried to follow Sherman's army in its sweep through Georgia. Sherman, no abolitionist, saw the black men, women, and children in his wake as impediments to his military objective. He would not, perhaps could not, turn from that objective to provide for them, and hundreds suffered and died trying to keep up with his army.

In the words of Mary Livermore, an agent of the Union's Sanitary Commission traveling up the Mississippi on a riverboat laden with wounded soldiers and contrabands: "One afternoon, as the sunset was deepening into twilight, we made a bend in the river, when we received a momentary fright from a huge fire blazing red, straight before us, close at the water's edge. A great crowd was hovering about it, waving flags, gesticulating, and signalling us. As we came nearer, we found they were negroes, of all sizes, and had their little bundles in their hands or on their heads and backs.

"The captain dared not, or would not, stop. As the poor creatures saw us steaming directly by, they redoubled their exertions to attract our attention. Catching up blazing firebrands, they ran up the shore with them, waved them, threw them in air, and with the most frantic pantomime sought to convey to us a sense of their eagerness to be taken aboard. It seemed pitiful not to stop for them. . . . Doubtless they had signalled other boats ahead of us; and still they were left on the river banks, amid the gray moss-draped cottonwoods, as far from the land of freedom as ever."[7]

Or think of the bewilderment of a 12-year-old slave. When the fighting came near one night, his mother sent a man to fetch him. "[W]e left for town about

Contraband children entertain Union troops in Louisiana. *(Library of Congress)*

twelve o'clock. After we had gone some distance, the man showed me the way and left me. I went along half scared to death. All at once somebody said, 'Halt! Who goes there?' I said, 'Me.' He asked me again who I was, and I just said, 'Me.' He told me to advance. I went up, and they got around me and asked me who I was and where I was going.

"I told them that I had been working, and that I was trying to find my mother. I was cold, so they made a big fire and told me to sit there by the fire until day, because it would be dangerous for me to go on that night.

"The next day they let me go on my way, and I found my mother. She hid me around until she got a chance to take me to a lady's house. All the slaves were running off about this time. I didn't know what the war was all about, but I used to hear the white people talking about the slaves getting ready to rise up against the white folks."[8]

Even if slaves escaped into free territory, where were they to go, and what were they to do? Many locations in the North, far from welcoming the contrabands—a term soon extended to former slaves generally—banned them. Hancock County, Illinois, for example, in February 1863 sold into service five blacks and a mulatto found guilty of remaining in the county for more than 10 days. The bidder who offered the shortest time of service won.[9] Race riots and violent labor demonstrations against blacks occurred in northern cities throughout the war.

More liberal communities often found themselves overwhelmed by the sheer numbers of contrabands. Levi Coffin wrote, "Many of the slaveholders fled farther South, taking their able-bodied slaves with them, and leaving the women and children, aged and sick ones, to take care of themselves. In many cases there was nothing for this helpless class to live upon. . . . Thousands gathered within the Union lines and were sent to various points up the river. Some were brought on boats to Cincinnati and left on the wharf without food and shelter or means of obtaining them. . . . The colored people here acted nobly, taking as many as they could and caring for them."[10]

The contrabands' best hope of succor lay in the camps operated by the Union military or by the semigovernmental, semiprivate freedmen's aid organizations. For the military, before the Emancipation Proclamation, uncertainty about the status of the contrabands complicated the problem. Were they free? Who should pay for their support? Should those who worked for the military receive the same wages as others, or should those wages be applied to the support of other contrabands?

Moreover, the numbers of contrabands outran the available supplies. They had to live in deserted houses, in huts, in old army tents, in brush shelters, in the open fields. In the fall of 1862, Coffin visited a camp in Cairo, Illinois, where former slaves lived "in their crowded huts and sick rooms. . . . Many were sick from exposure and for want of sufficient clothing; they had no bedding nor cooking utensils. . . . The scanty rations issued by Government were their only subsistence. The weather being quite chilly, many of them were suffering with coughs and colds; that dreadful suffering—small-pox—was quite prevalent among them. . . ."[11] The hospitals hardly eased their suffering. As one superintendent reported, "Hospital not under charge of Superintendent. Its condition wretched in the extreme. Lack of medicines, of utensils, of vaccine matter. . . . No attention to sick in camp by surgeon. . . . *Diseases*—Pneumonia, fevers, small pox."[12] In a camp at Memphis where three large colonies of contrabands had set about cultivating the ground, it was necessary for the men to maintain a strong picket guard against Confederate raids.

Undoubtedly, many of the contrabands were physically worse off in these camps than they had been in slavery. They could not see into the uncertain future. Yet one of them preached, "We have been in the furnace of affliction, and are still, but God only means to separate the dross, and get us so that like the pure metal we may reflect the image of our Purifier, who is sitting by to watch the process. . . . We have need of faith, patience and perseverance, to realize the desired result. There must be no looking back to Egypt. Israel passed forty years in the wilderness, because of their unbelief. What if we cannot see right off the green fields of Canaan,

Contrabands go to work. *(Library of Congress)*

Moses could not. . . . We must snap the chain of Satan, and educate ourselves and our children."[13]

Endless problems confronted the freed slaves. Years of dependence and enforced ignorance had ill fitted most of them for the responsibilities of liberty The naïve among them had expected money and an easy life as part of the freedom package. Few of them owned anything besides the clothes on their backs—certainly not means of production. Yet in a contraband camp near Washington, D.C., every morning they set off to work, the men for the government, the women to find what tasks they could as laundresses and housecleaners. In the camps, contrabands assisted by northern aid societies organized schools and churches. They reunited families. Former slave Susie King Taylor devoted herself to improving the lot of black soldiers: "I taught a great many of the comrades [of the South Carolina Volunteers] in Company E to read and write, when they were off duty. Nearly all were anxious to learn. . . . I was very happy to know my efforts were successful in camp, and also grateful for the appreciation of my services. I gave my services willingly for four years and three months without receiving a dollar. I was glad, however, to be allowed to go with the regiment, to care for the sick and afflicted comrades."[14]

Supporting Contrabands

For most of the war, contrabands had to depend for help on the military or on volunteers, some of them in societies established for the purpose, others from long-existing abolitionist groups, and still others from associated organizations like the Sanitary Commission. These northern volunteer groups included the Freedmen's Aid Societies, the American Missionary Association, various church groups, the National Freedmen's Relief Association, the American Freedmen's Union, and the Western Freedmen's Aid Commission—some 50 or more. To aid the freedmen they sent clothes, money, books, and teachers. Abolitionist Laura Haviland, for example, worked for a freedmen's aid commission: "In September [of 1864] I had a car-load of supplies ready, and $400 in money. Of this amount, $298 was placed in my hands by friends at Adrian [Michigan], with the request of the donors that it should be retained in my own hands for disbursement on reaching the scene of suffering. At Chicago appeals were made to the Soldiers' Aid Society and Christian Commission for aid in the freedmen's department, and also to myself personally, on account of the great distress in Kansas after General Price's raid through Missouri, followed by Colonels Lane and Jennison, who drove thousands of poor whites and freedmen into that young State. I decided to hasten thither, with . . . an assistant.

"At Leavenworth we met J. R. Brown, . . . who had charge of both white refugees and freedmen and a sort of soldiers' home. . . . He kindly offered me headquarters in his establishment. . . . General Curtis . . . telegraphed for my supplies to be forwarded in preference to other army supplies, and gave me passes through the State to Fort Scott. . . . He also gave me liberty . . . to call upon quarter-masters for half, whole, or quarter rations, wherever suffering for food existed."[15]

But the military bore the brunt of dealing with the contrabands. Unprepared for this difficulty, officers had to improvise, with more or less success. "Said some, 'We have nothing to do with slaves.' 'Hereafter,' commanded [Major General Henry Wage] Halleck, 'no slaves should be allowed to come into your lines at all; if any come without your knowledge, when owners call for them, deliver them.' " But others said, "We take grain and fowl; why not slaves?" No matter what a general's attitude, however, he could not escape the problem of abandoned or fleeing black slaves behind the lines of the Union army.[16]

So as early in the war as July 1861 General Benjamin Butler in occupied Louisiana adopted the obvious solution of setting them to military tasks, under the direction of Private Edward L. Pierce, in civilian life an abolitionist attorney. They also were sent to work on abandoned plantations, thus providing them with the necessities of life and helping them move toward self-sufficiency. The military also responded to the black people of the region, who in late 1862 had seized on their new status to refuse to harvest cotton unless the Union army started schools for their communities; by 1865, 13,000 students were attending some 120 federal schools.[17]

Throughout the war, Union commanders had to come up with solutions, fitting them as best they could to the military situation. As the numbers of fugitives mounted and as women, children, and the elderly joined the hordes, officers could neither ignore them nor simply utilize the services of the able-bodied. In fall 1862, General Ulysses S. Grant assigned John Eaton to set freedmen to work on deserted plantations and hire them out to planters. "At once," Grant wrote in his memoirs, "the freedmen became self-sustaining. The money was not paid to them directly, but was expended judiciously and for their benefit."[18]

The War Department made intermittent efforts to shift the problem to the Treasury Department, none of which succeeded. However, secretaries of the treasury did become involved, most famously in the Sea Islands experiments, which historian Willie Lee Rose has called in the title of her book a "rehearsal for Reconstruction." In January 1862, the abolitionist secretary of the treasury Salmon P. Chase sent attorney Edward L. Pierce to survey the situation of the hundreds

In 1861–1862, workers on a black-run cotton plantation in Port Royal, South Carolina, stand in front of the gin house. *(Library of Congress, Prints and Photographs Division, LC-0159)*

of slaves left on 16 abandoned cotton plantations on islands off the coast of South Carolina after the Union had captured the area. Pierce reported favorably on the willingness and ability of blacks to work, to learn, and to organize—a burning question in the minds of many whites. Accordingly the Treasury Department with the support of the War Department and several volunteer societies instituted the Port Royal experiment. Under northern white superintendents, former slaves took over the plantations. In March, northern missionaries traveled to Port Royal to set up a hospital and schools with black and white teachers for the freedmen.

The history of the Roanoke Island, North Carolina, settlement again demonstrates the determination with which slaves freed themselves at the first opportunity and then labored to take care of themselves. Union forces occupied the island in February 1862; by the end of the year 1,000 slaves had taken refuge there, and by the end of the war about 3,500. Although many of them did not know one another, they established a community that included a school and several churches. In April 1863, Major General John G. Foster appointed the evangelical Congregationalist minister and abolitionist Horace James "Superintendent of all the Blacks" in the Department of North Carolina. A little later Foster instructed James to organize a contraband colony on Roanoke Island as a safe sanctuary for the families of black men soon to be recruited into the Union army.

James tried to make the colony a permanent settlement in a new social order based on free (not slave) labor. He laid out a settlement like a New England village, constructed community buildings, gave freedpeople lots for homes, encouraged domestic manufacturing, brought in northern missionary teachers to educate the inhabitants for independence and citizenship, and projected shad fisheries and a sawmill. "It would gratify their friends at the north could they see the energy and zeal with which the freedmen enter upon the work of clearing up their little acre of land," James wrote, "by cutting the timber upon it and preparing it for their rude log-house. . . . [They] ask nothing more than a decent chance to make themselves wholly independent of government aid, and be thrifty, wealthy citizens." His dreams of permanence were not fulfilled; by 1870 the community had disintegrated.[19]

Early in 1863, General Lorenzo Thomas encouraged private enterpreneurs to operate black colonies on plantations along the Mississippi River leased for that purpose. Although 15 such plantations leased to freedpeople worked well, the white speculators and adventurers who rented the other plantations exploited their black laborers to gain profits for themselves.[20]

The Freedman's Village established in May 1863 on the estate of Confederate general Robert E. Lee, now the site for Arlington National Cemetery, provided a model for such settlements elsewhere in the South.[21] Under the sponsorship of the Union military and later of the Freedmen's Bureau (which Congress finally founded in March 1865), the village was intended as a temporary refuge where residents would learn basic literacy and a trade. However, as its residents built the village from a tent city into a thriving community, it attracted other blacks, especially members of the Union army—first to attend its religious services and political meetings and then to move there with their families. Residents constructed wooden homes housing two to four families, churches, homes for the aged and infirm, and a hospital. Soon after the village opened, they built its first school, which started with 150 students and grew to 900, both adults and children. Its industrial school trained freedpeople as blacksmiths, wheelwrights, carpenters, shoemakers, and tailors; in turn the trainees made clothes and shoes for village residents and furniture for the school. Farmers grew produce both to help feed the residents and to sell for profit. Of the $10 a month workers were paid, they had to pay half into a general fund for village maintenance. Despite the usual conflicts with their "landlord," the federal government, residents so cherished the village that they successfully fought off efforts to close it from 1868 to 1900, when the United States agreed to compensate them $75,000 for the improvements they had made and the contraband tax they had paid.

In summer 1864, Secretary of the Treasury William Pitt Fessenden worked out a plan whereby he appointed agents responsible for freedpeople in given areas, who were to form Freedman's Home Colonies on abandoned estates. In these colonies, the supervisors provided buildings, work animals, tools, and supplies. They also guaranteed food and clothing at cost. Freedpeople worked under contracts by which they received wages from $10 to $25 a month, depending on gender and the kind of work they did. Some of these operated under the military and others independently.[22]

For Union commanders, the problem of contrabands swelled as the war went on. General William Tecumseh Sherman tried at first to ignore the "dark and human cloud that clung like remorse on the rear" of his columns on his march through Georgia, "swelling at times to half their size, almost engulfing and choking them." After seeking the advice of 20 black leaders in Savannah, Georgia, and consulting with Secretary of War Edwin M. Stanton, on January 16, 1865, he issued Field Order #15 (the Sea Island Circular), extending the Sea Islands experiments by reserving "for the settlement of Negroes now made free by act of war" "the islands from Charleston south, the abandoned ricefields along the rivers for thirty miles back from the sea, and the country bordering the St. John's River, Florida."[23]

Tunis Campbell, the African-American supervisor of land claims and resettlement, arrived on St. Catherine's Island with his own plan to organize the freedmen flocking there to claim the 40 acres and a mule Sherman had promised them. Campbell set up an exclusively black colony, awarding land to each family and establishing a government modeled on that of the United States, with himself at its head.[24] The effort was thriving when in 1866 President Andrew Johnson ended all the Sea Island experiments by pardoning the former Confederate owners and allowing them to reclaim their lands, leaving the blacks who had rescued the plantations from abandonment with nothing to show for their labors.

The Confederacy: Managing Chaos

The southern states had not built strong, active prewar governments or communities. Southerners had devoted little effort and money to building schools, libraries, bridges, or roads. As John C. Calhoun remarked, "The Southern States are an aggregate . . . of communities, not of individuals. Every plantation is a little community, with the master at its head. . . . These small communities aggregated make the State in all."[25] Basing their economy on agriculture left most of the population, particularly the slaves, living on isolated farms and plantations. The patriarchal system had placed almost all the power in the hands not of governments but of individual men, who ruled their domains almost absolutely.

With the Civil War and the departure of many of these men, conditions deteriorated into anarchy. The aging minister and slave owner Charles C. Jones turned for advice on dealing with slaves who ran away to his attorney son, by then a lieutenant in the Confederate army. His son replied, "You ask me, my dear father, . . . whether Negroes deserting to the enemy can be summarily dealt with by the citizens themselves. . . . A trial by jury is accorded to everyone, whether white or black, where life is at stake. . . . Any punishment other than that involving a loss of life or limb could be legally inflicted without the intervention of judge or jury. If General Mercer refuses to take military cognizance of such cases, and they occur during the intervals of the sessions of the courts, I cannot see what can be done except to take the law in one's own hand. . . ."[26]

In July 1862, the provost marshal of Natchez, Mississippi, wrote in desperation to the governor: "I appeal to you for assistance, for I do assure you that if the overseers are taken off[,] this County will be left in a condition that will be by no means safe. I do not wish to except them from entire service [in the army], I only want to keep them until an emergency arises requiring their services, then let them go and do service, but don't let them be taken off as long as it can be helped—Also instructions as to the manner of proceeding against persons who will keep no overseer, and make but little provision for their Negroes, rendering it necessary for them to steal or starve and go naked. . . . [N]egroes seemingly are permitted to forage upon the Community—The owners will not look after them, will not provide for them, nor will they employ an overseer. The negroes have such large liberties, they are enabled to harbor runaways, who have fire arms, traverse the whole County, kill stock, and steal generally, supplying those who harbor them, and send to market by Negro market-men. The state of things in consequence to this in a few cases are a serious nuisance as well as dangerous to the Community. Complaints are made to me to remedy the evil. I am however at a loss how to proceed."[27]

The Confederacy also had to deal with divisions among its own population. Southerners had long trembled at the possibility of black insurrection; now they had to face the presence of a large black population that had every reason to long for a Union victory. More important, considerable numbers of white southerners, called *Unionists,* sympathized with the Union, some because they saw their best economic prospects in a Union victory, others because they believed slavery wrong or secession unconstitutional. Some Unionists and many blacks spied, furnishing the Union army with valuable information.

Often these spies, men and women, black and white, simply took it upon themselves to offer Union officials military information about Confederate positions, fortifications, and plans.[28] One of the most remarkable, Elizabeth L. Van Lew, a native of Richmond, Virginia, on her father's death had freed his slaves.[29] Known as "Crazy Bet" because she used eccentricity as a cover for espionage, she began by encoding and sending to General Ulysses S. Grant information she collected when she visited captured Union soldiers in a Confederate prison; reportedly, she also helped some of these soldiers escape. She then recruited as members of her spy ring her mother and her former slave Mary Elizabeth Bowser, whom she had sent north to be educated. Van Lew found Bowser a job as a maid in the household of Jefferson Davis, president of the Confederacy; Bowser, said to have a photographic memory, then passed to Van Lew information that she gathered from the conversations she heard and the documents she read there. In an independent operation, freed slave Mary Touvestre stole from her engineer employer plans for the first Confederate ironclad warship, the *Merrimac,* and carried them to the Union Department of the Navy in Washington, D.C. In March 1862, the free black harbor pilot Robert Smalls of Charleston, South Carolina, rowed out to a Union warship to report that Confederate troops were about to evacuate the town and destroy its harbor facilities, an action the Union forces then forestalled.

So many contrabands brought with them invaluable information that General Benjamin F. Butler ordered that all who arrived behind Union lines be debriefed. Fugitive George Scott, for instance, not only brought word about military positions, but also went on scouting trips behind Confederate lines. "If I want to find out anything hereabouts," General Rush Hawkins reportedly said, "I hunt up a Negro; and if he knows or can find out, I'm sure to get all I want."[30] The generals' faith was justified by blacks like the Dabneys, he a contraband and she a servant at General Robert E. Lee's headquarters, who allegedly worked out a system of signaling Confederate plans by her arrangement of laundry on a line that he could see from the other side of a river: Thus a red shirt might indicate General Stonewall Jackson, a pair of pants hung upside down the direction in which he was moving.[31]

Allan Pinkerton, in 1861–62 chief of intelligence for the Union Army of the Potomac, also depended for information mainly on people crossing over Confederate lines, especially former slaves, and recruited blacks who were outstanding for observing and remembering as agents. One of these, John Scobell, educated and freed by his former owner and adept at role playing, often traveled behind Confederate lines to learn about and report on local conditions, fortifications, and troop dispositions, using his membership in the black abolitionist Legal League as an entrée. In 1863, Union intelligence also recruited the famed Underground Railroad leader Harriet Tubman to organize short-term spying trips behind enemy lines, several of which she led: In June 1863, she guided a Union raid up South Carolina's Combahee River that destroyed millions of dollars worth of Confederate supplies and brought back some 800 slaves and enemy property.

The Confederacy simply did not possess the resources or the infrastructure to fight a war and protect the domestic peace as well. The task of coping with chaos fell mostly to individuals—particularly to the slaves and white women left behind on the plantations.

The Confederacy: Slaves' Experiences of the War

Slaves and white women bore the brunt of the Yankee invasion of the South. Some slaves welcomed it as an opportunity for freedom. Others tried to protect their mistresses from the Yankees. "That all changed after Massa go to war," reminisced former slave Pauline Grice. "First the 'Federate soldiers come and takes some mules and hosses, then some more come for the corn. After while, the Yankee soldiers comes and takes some more. When they gits through, they ain't much more tooking to be done. The year 'fore surrender, us am short of rations and sometime us hungry. Us sees no battling, but the cannon bang all day. Once they bang two whole days 'thout hardly stopping. That am when Missy got touch in the head, 'cause Massa and the boys in that battle. . . . Then word come Willie am kilt. . . . For her, it am trouble, trouble, and more trouble. . . . One day she tell us, 'The war am on us. The soldiers done took the rations. I can't sell the cotton, 'cause the blockade. . . . Now,' she say, 'all you colored folks born and raise here, and us always been good to you. I can't help it 'cause rations am short, and I'll do all I can for you. Will you be patient with me?' All us stay there and holp Missy all us could."[32]

Ex-slave Mom Ryer Emanuel reacted differently, hailing the arrival of the Yankees. Her master had hidden all the supplies he could in pits dug under the slave cabins and then fled to the woods, leaving the women of the plantation to confront the Union soldiers: "No, child, they didn't bother nothing much, but some of the rations they got hold of. Often times, they would come through and kill chickens and butcher a cow up and cook it right there. Would eat all they wanted and then when they would go to leave, they would call all the plantation niggers to come there and would give them what was left. O Lord, us was glad to get them victuals, too. . . . Us been so glad, us say that us wish they would come back again. . . . Old Massa, he been stay in the swamp till he hear them Yankees been leave there, and then he come home and would keep sending to the colored people's houses to get a little bit of his rations to a time. Uncle Solomon and Sipp and Leve, they been et [as] much of Boss's rations [as] they wanted 'cause they been know the Yankees was coming back through to free them. . . . I tell you, honey, some of the colored people sure been speak praise to them Yankees."[33]

Perhaps a majority of slaves found their wartime experiences confusing and disorienting, swaying now toward exaggerated hopes of freedom and riches, now toward trying to defend themselves and their families as best they could against racist Union soldiers, vengeful slave owners, and starvation.

As noted above, when the Confederacy ran short of manpower, it turned to using slaves. From the beginning of the war, white officers had taken slaves into the army to act as servants. The Confederacy had also called on or forced owners to send a certain number of their slaves for such work as building ramparts and driving wagons. Owners typically were not happy at such demands, particularly as they learned that their slaves were mistreated, overworked, likely to take sick, and returned, if at all, in a weakened condition. "I fear that I have not acted for the best," Lizzie Neblett wrote her husband, "but I did not want to send any [of your slaves to work for the Confederate military] if I could help it, but if they come again Joe will have to go, & be put under any overseer they please, etc., but I can't help it."[34]

These short-term arrangements proved unsatisfactory to the military, too. No sooner would a slave gain skill in "encamping, marching, and packing trains" than he had to be returned to his owner. Maybe, officialdom came to think, the Confederacy needed "to acquire for the public service the entire property in the labor of the slave, and to pay therefor due compensation rather than to impress his labor for short terms. . . ."[35] Moreover, to keep the slave loyal, perhaps the Confederacy should promise him freedom and the right to live in his home state once the war was over.

The Confederacy: White Women's Experiences of the War

The departure of the slave owners to fight left the women of the Confederacy with the tasks of farm and plantation management, for which few of them were prepared. The men's ownership of all property together with the traditions of the southern lady meant that few women had management experience beyond the running of their households, though wives of small farmers were probably better off in this respect than their moneyed sisters. Almost all of the plantation mistresses were horrified by the necessity of doing the housework themselves, as they had grown up believing that it should be left to inferiors and had acquired no household skills.

They had to take over at the very moment that both their way of life and their value system were under attack. Of the difficulties they met, they talked most on the record about the problems of managing slaves. Certainly they faced a harder task than their menfolk had, as the repeated rumors of freedom made the slaves less inclined to obey and to work. The women's dependence on the slaves increased as the slaves became more independent. "I tell you all this attention to farming is uphill work with me," Mrs. W. W. Boyce wrote her husband in the spring of 1862. "I can give orders first-rate, but when I am not obeyed, I can't keep my temper. . . . I am ever ready to give you a helping hand, but I must say I am heartily tired of trying to manage *free* negroes."[36] Frustrated mistresses suggested that they would be better off without the slaves than with them.

Besides, a good many of them feared their slaves. Stories of individual slave attacks on white women floated around—some true, some not. Ada Bacot was certain the fire in her neighbors' house was set by their slave Abel; Laura Lee was horrified when occupying troops released a Winchester slave convicted of murdering her mistress. In September 1862, the *Mobile Advertiser and Register* noted that a slave had succeeded in poisoning his master; the same month the *Richmond Enquirer* recorded the conviction of one Lavinia for torching her mistress's house. Abbie Brooks of Georgia described the terrible scars on the face of a woman neighbor who had been shoved into the fire by a slave. "All that saved her life was the negro taking fire and had to let go to her mistress to extinguish herself."[37]

Some women resorted to hiring overseers. But what with the shortage of manpower, it was difficult to find a good one. Women who had been insisting that what their blacks needed was a firm hand found themselves horrified by the cruelties of the overseers they hired.

Even older women who had firmly established their authority in their households could do little in the face of the destruction of the Southern economy. Mary Jones watched successive raids reduce resources until she could no longer operate her husband's plantations and needed to make other arrangements to support his slaves: "The lateness of the season makes it very difficult if not *impossible* to hire them [out to work for someone else]. *Jack* is the only one I have been able to hire as yet—for twenty-five dollars per month. Corn is now selling for twelve and twenty dollars per bushel, and I will have to purchase provisions for them at that price. . . . Your uncle has kindly offered the use of a place distant about five miles . . . that our people might plant; but as we are without mules, plows, or hoes, that would not be practicable. I must depend on hiring."[38] Such women as these, who had spent most of their adult lives supervising slaves and seeing to it that they were clothed, fed, sheltered, and nursed, experienced their departure as a betrayal.

Chronicle of Events

1861–1865

- New York City, San Francisco, Cincinnati, and Cleveland integrate streetcars.

1861

- Russia emancipates the serfs, who are to retain the land they have been working, though they do not gain complete freedom or equality.
- A Georgia code specifies that jailors and constables shall be paid one dollar "for whipping a negro," and sets a limit of 39 lashes, not "inhumanly" done.
- Texas, now a member of the Confederacy, absolutely prohibits manumission.
- Western counties secede from Virginia.
- In Hampton, Virginia, freeborn mulatto Mary Peake opens the first school for blacks.
- *March 2:* Congress adopts a constitutional amendment forbidding any subsequent amendment to "abolish or interfere . . . with the domestic institutions of the states." It is not ratified.
- *May 24:* Fugitive slaves at Fortress Monroe, Virginia, are received and put to work by Union general Benjamin F. Butler, who declares them "contraband of war."
- *July:* Congress enacts the Crittenden Resolution asserting that the war is being fought to preserve the Union and not to interfere with slavery.
- *August 6:* Congress passes (and Lincoln later signs) the First Confiscation Act, providing that when slaves are engaged in hostile military service, the owners' claims to their labor are forfeited. All property, including slaves, used in support of the rebellion is made subject to prize and capture. The Union can legally accept the services of any former slaves previously employed on behalf of the Confederacy. Fugitive slaves are thus transformed into contraband.
- *August 30:* Invoking martial law, General John C. Frémont declares free the slaves of disloyal owners in Missouri; President Lincoln asks that he modify his order so as not to exceed congressional laws respecting emancipation.
- *September 11:* General Frémont having refused to modify his emancipation order, President Lincoln orders him to do so.
- *November:* The U.S. Navy occupies Port Royal, South Carolina; almost all whites flee to the mainland; and the abandoned 10,000 slaves sack the owners' houses, destroy cotton gins, and plant subsistence crops. The Sea Island experiment begins.
- *December 1:* Secretary of War Simon Cameron issues his annual report, from which President Lincoln has required the deletion of passages advocating emancipation and the employment of former slaves as military laborers and soldiers.

1862–mid-1864

- Union general Nathaniel P. Banks installs a "free-labor" system for freedpeople in the Department of the Gulf that limits their right to control their own labor and their ability to earn a decent living.

1862

- Cuba ends the slave trade.
- Utah abolishes slavery.
- "Refugeeing"—taking slaves to Texas to keep them away from the advancing Union forces—becomes common.
- In Corinth, Mississippi, blacks in a contraband camp organize a cohesive community for work, education, and worship, which the Federal government dismantles in 1863.
- New Orleans free blacks found the newspaper *L'Union.*
- *February:* President Lincoln appoints Andrew Johnson military governor of Tennessee.
- *March:* Lincoln proposes and Congress passes a resolution to provide money "to compensate for the inconveniences, public and private, produced by such change of system" to any state abolishing slavery.
- *March 13:* Congress adopts an additional article of war forbidding members of the army and navy to return fugitive slaves to their owners.

Contrabands arrive at Fortress Monroe, Virginia. *(Library of Congress)*

- *April 3:* General David Hunter tries to arm blacks for military service but fails for lack of support from the War Department.
- *April 10:* A joint resolution of Congress offers monetary assistance to any state that will begin emancipation of its slaves
- *April 16:* Congress abolishes slavery in the District of Columbia, appropriating money to compensate owners up to $300 dollars for each slave and providing for the removal and colonization of the freedmen to Haiti, Liberia, or other countries.
- *May:* The Superior Court of the District of Columbia rules that the Fugitive Slave Law is as applicable to the District of Columbia as to any of the states.
- *May 9:* General David Hunter declares free all slaves in South Carolina, Georgia, and Florida.
- *May 19:* President Lincoln nullifies General David Hunter's emancipation edict and urges the border states to embrace gradual, compensated emancipation.
- *June 19:* Congress abolishes slavery in the territories.

- *July:* Lincoln proposes, but Congress does not act on, a bill providing that "whenever the President of the United States shall be satisfied that any State shall have lawfully abolished slavery . . . [he] is to pay the State in 6% interest bearing bonds equal to the aggregate value, at X dollars per head."
- *July 12:* Lincoln appeals to congressmen from the border states to support gradual, compensated emancipation, with colonization of freed slaves outside the United States.
- *July 17:* Congress passes and Lincoln signs the Second Confiscation Act, providing that the slaves of anyone committing treason are free and that slaves of all persons supporting rebellion are "forever free of their servitude, and not again held as slaves." Congress also passes a law saying that no slave escaping from one state into another will be delivered up except for a crime, unless he belongs to a loyal owner; the law also frees disloyal owners' slaves who come into the Union lines. Lincoln signs the Militia Act, freeing any enemy-owned slave who renders military service (for one ration and pay of

This poster celebrates the Emancipation Proclamation. *(Library of Congress)*

$10 per month, less three dollars for clothing) and also freeing the slave's mother, wife, and children.

- *July 22:* Lincoln tells his cabinet that he intends to free the slaves in the Confederate states.
- *August 22:* General Benjamin F. Butler takes over Louisiana Native Guard units of free blacks and later recruits other blacks.
- *August 25:* The War Department agrees to recruit blacks in the South Carolina Sea Islands.
- *September 22:* In the Preliminary Emancipation Proclamation, Lincoln formally declares his intention to free the slaves in the rebel states on January 1, 1863, and to offer financial assistance to loyal slave states if they will free their slaves.
- *November:* General Ulysses S. Grant appoints chaplain John Eaton, Jr., superintendent of freedmen to deal with the contrabands fleeing behind Union lines.
- *Late 1862:* The black people of Union-occupied Louisiana refuse to harvest cotton unless the Union army opens schools for them.
- *December:* In a message to Congress, President Lincoln speaks of the possibility of compensation to slave owners and colonization for blacks.
- President Lincoln signs an agreement to settle 5,000 blacks on an island off Haiti.
- *December 23:* The Confederacy orders that captured black soldiers not be treated as prisoners of war but remanded to Confederate authorities of the states "to which they belong to be dealt with according to the laws of said States."
- *December 31:* West Virginia is admitted into the Union as a free state.

1863

- Slavery is abolished in all Dutch colonies.
- The Women's Loyal National League is founded by militant feminists to ensure the complete elimination of slavery.
- The former western counties of Virginia reenter the Union as the separate state of West Virginia, provided that it abolishes slavery.
- California permits blacks to testify in criminal cases.
- The War Department appoints an American Freedmen's Inquiry Commission to suggest ways of dealing with freedpeople.
- *January:* In Union-occupied Louisiana, General Nathaniel P. Banks institutes a "free labor" system that forces freedmen to work, mostly under a contract system that restricts their choice of employer and mobility.

- *January 1:* President Lincoln issues the Emancipation Proclamation, freeing all slaves in the Confederacy except in Tennessee, southern Louisiana, and parts of Virginia. The president also announces that the Union will recruit blacks for military service.
- *January 1:* The Southern Homestead Act of 1862 opens 46 million acres of southern public lands to homesteaders.
- *Spring:* Union general Lorenzo Thomas leases Mississippi River plantations to northerners who must hire blacks on terms set by the army, a system that soon fails.
- *March 12:* The Captured and Abandoned Property Acts of this date and July 2, 1864, make subject to seizure property owned by absent individuals who have supported the South.
- *March 16:* Secretary of War Stanton appoints the American Freedmen's Inquiry Commission to investigate the condition of former slaves and recommend measures for their employment and welfare.
- *June 18:* U.S. commissioner Walter S. Coxe remands two fugitive slaves to claimants from Maryland (a Union state)
- *July:* Led by Benjamin Montgomery, blacks on the Joseph and Jefferson Davis estates at Davis Bend above Vicksburg cultivate the plantations for their own benefit in an undertaking that flourishes.
- *July 11–14:* In New York City, draft rioters protesting being forced to fight to end slavery beat and murder blacks and burn the Colored Orphan Asylum.
- *November:* Maryland abolishes slavery.
- *December 8:* Lincoln issues the Proclamation of Amnesty and Reconstruction, offering pardon and restoration of property other than slaves to Confederates who swear allegiance to the Union and agree to accept emancipation, and proposing a plan by which loyal voters of a seceded state can begin to apply for readmission into the Union.

1864

- Charles Sumner presents to the Senate a women's antislavery petition with thousands of signatures.
- Congress enacts black soldiers' equality in compensation.
- *Early 1864:* President Lincoln begins Reconstruction in Union-occupied Louisiana.
- *January:* Missouri abolishes slavery.
- *January 2:* Confederate major general Patrick R. Cleburne proposes freeing all the slaves and arming some of them to fight for the Confederacy.

- *March:* John Eaton, superintendent of contrabands in the Department of the Tennessee and Arkansas, instructs Union army clergy to "solemnize the rite of marriage among Freedmen."
- *March:* In New York City, a huge reception is given for black soldiers.
- *March 16:* Pro-Union voters ratify a new Arkansas state constitution that abolishes slavery.
- *May:* A meeting at Beaufort, South Carolina, elects 16 black delegates to the Republican National Convention.
- *June 28:* President Lincoln signs the repeal of the Fugitive Slave Law.
- *July:* Congress passes the Wade-Davis Bill, stiffening President Lincoln's requirements for readmission of secessionist states, but the president pocket vetoes the bill.
- *September 3:* Pro-Union voters ratify a new Louisiana state constitution that abolishes slavery.
- *October:* A national convention of 145 free black leaders establishes the National Equal Rights League to work for abolition, equality before the law, and suffrage.
- *November:* Belgian scientist Jean-Charles Houzeau becomes the crusading editor of the black newspaper the *New Orleans Tribune,* urging alliance between free blacks and freedmen to demand black suffrage, equality before the law, school and transportation desegregation, and land distribution.
- *December:* Two blacks and a white demand black suffrage at a New Orleans meeting.
- *December:* When General Sherman captures Savannah, Georgia, local black ministers organize the Savannah Educational Association to start black schools.

1865

- Blacks in Vicksburg petition Congress not to seat Mississippi's delegates while blacks are denied the vote.
- Hundreds of freedmen on southern plantations refuse either to sign labor contracts or to leave.
- Missouri delegates write a new state constitution, abolishing slavery, mandating racial equality in property rights and access to the courts, enabling the legislature to establish schools for blacks, and guaranteeing the right of blacks to testify
- In St. Louis, the Western Sanitary Commission operates a high school for blacks and offers classes for black soldiers.
- Illinois repeals its laws barring blacks from entering the state, serving on juries, and testifying in court.

- Ohio repeals the last of its "black laws."
- Minnesota, Wisconsin, and Connecticut deny their black residents suffrage.
- Although most freedpeople do not leave their homes and those who do usually travel only short distances, thousands removed to Texas by their former owners now return to Mississippi and Louisiana; others go back to the homes they fled during the Civil War; some emigrate to the Southwest in search of higher pay; many move to southern towns and cities; and separated family members seek one another.
- *January:* At a New Orleans Equal Rights League convention, blacks demand black suffrage and equal access to the city's streetcars.
- *January:* Sentiment against segregation in public transportation rises when the black war hero Robert Smalls is thrown off a Philadelphia streetcar.
- *January:* In a New Orleans convention, the Equal Rights League demands black suffrage and integrated public transportation.
- *January:* In New Orleans, free black James Ingraham chairs a convention of the Equal Rights League that calls for black suffrage and integrated streetcars.
- *January:* In Georgia, formerly secret black schools are operating openly.
- *January 9:* Fisk Free Colored School opens in Nashville, Tennessee.
- *January 12:* Twenty black leaders meet with Gen. William T. Sherman and Secretary of War Stanton to discuss the future of freedmen.
- *January 16:* General Sherman sets aside part of coastal South Carolina, Georgia, and Florida for settlement exclusively by blacks, settlers to receive title to 40-acre plots.
- *January 31:* Congress approves the Thirteenth Amendment.
- *February:* The last 10,000 Confederate soldiers evacuate Charleston, South Carolina, and black Union troops take over the city.
- *February 1:* Boston attorney John S. Rock becomes the first black admitted to practice before the U.S. Supreme Court
- *February:* Twenty-five thousand white Tennessee voters approve a state constitutional amendment abolishing slavery.
- *February 8:* Martin Robinson Delany becomes the first black major in the U.S. Army.
- *February 12:* Henry Highland Garnet, Washington pastor, becomes the first black man to speak in the

House of Representatives when he delivers a sermon there; he is one of the first blacks allowed to enter the Capitol.

- *February 22:* An amendment to the Tennessee state constitution abolishes slavery.
- *March:* President Lincoln signs a bill to establish the National Asylum for Disabled Volunteer Soldiers, later called the National Home for Disabled Volunteer Soldiers. Eventually 11 branches are built.
- *March:* Andrew Johnson assumes the U.S. vice presidency.
- *March:* Four thousand blacks parade in Charleston, South Carolina, in a "grand jubilee" of freedom.
- *March:* In New Orleans, a mass meeting denounces the U.S. Army's "free labor" system, under which blacks must sign yearly contracts, work for fixed wages, and carry passes.
- *March 3:* Congress charters the Freedmen's Savings Bank.
- *March 3:* Congress establishes the Bureau of Refugees, Freedmen, and Abandoned Lands to provide health care, education, and technical assistance to emancipated slaves.
- *March 3:* Congress frees the wives and children of black soldiers.
- *April 9:* Confederate general Robert E. Lee surrenders to Union general Ulysses S. Grant.

Eyewitness Testimony

The Union: The Rocky Road to Emancipation

Not only will we abstain from all interferences with your slaves, but we will, with an iron hand, crush any attempt at insurrection on their part.

Union general George B. McClellan, "Proclamation to the People of Western Virginia," May 26, 1861.

God's ahead ob Massa Linkum. God won't let Massa Linkum beat de South till he do the right thing. Massa Linkum he great man, and I'se poor nigger; but dis nigger can tell Massa Linkum how to save de money and de young men. He do it by setting de niggers free.

Harriet Tubman, in Quarles, "Harriet Tubman's Unlikely Leadership," in Hine, Black Women in American History *4:1145.*

[The Emancipation Proclamation] gave a new direction to the councils of the Cabinet, and to the conduct of the national arms. . . . [I took it] for a little more than it purported, and saw in its spirit a life and power far beyond its letter. Its meaning to me was the entire abolition of slavery, and I saw that its moral power would extend much further.

Frederick Douglass, in Franklin, The Emancipation Proclamation, *143.*

[Slavery] is a *national* evil, for which to a large extent the *nation* and all its parts are responsible, and which to a large extent the *nation* may remove. [The nation has a direct responsibility for slavery in the District of Columbia,

the territories, the slave trade between states, the admission of new states, returning fugitive slaves, transportation of slaves, laws of slave states affecting the liberty of free colored persons of the Northern states, the capture by federal troops of blacks held by the Seminoles, and power to amend the constitution in all points affecting slavery.] It cannot be doubted, then, that the Constitution may be amended so that it shall cease to render any sanction to Slavery. The power to amend carries with it the right to inquire into and to discuss the matter to be amended. . . .

Senator Charles Sumner, 1842, in Pierce, Memoir *II:239–40.*

The Union: Fugitives and Contrabands

On the 30th of July, [1861,] General [Benjamin] Butler, being still un-provided with adequate instructions, the number of contrabands having now reached nine hundred, applied to the War Department for further directions. . . . Assuming the slaves to have been the property of masters, he considers them waifs abandoned by their owners, in which the Government as a finder cannot, however, acquire a proprietary interest, and they have therefore reverted to the normal condition of those made in God's image, "if not free-born, yet free-manumitted, sent forth from the hand that held them, never to return." . . . the answer of the War Department, so far as its meaning is clear, leaves the General uninstructed as to all slaves not confiscated by the Act of Congress.

Edward L. Pierce, "The Contrabands at Fortress Monroe," Atlantic Monthly *8 (November 1861), 626. Available online at URL: http://www.millikensbend.org/articles-docs/atlantic-monthly/contrabands/contrabands2.html.*

I have worked by the month for six months . . . and the money is all my own; and I'll soon educate my children. But, brethren, don't be too free. . . . Don't lean on our master [the superintendent of the contraband camp]. . . . You must depend on yourselves.

Virginia contraband in Washington, D.C., January 1, 1863, in Franklin, Emancipation Proclamation, *106–7.*

One day, a negro, who was believed trustworthy, was sent out of the enemy's [Confederate] lines with a six-mule team for a big load of wood. He had got beyond the pickets, and seemed to think it worth while to venture a little farther, and so kept on towards "Uncle Sam's

Clothing of captured Confederates is distributed to contrabands in North Carolina. *(Library of Congress)*

boys." The rebel pickets saw him going, and rushed after him. Our men saw him coming, and rushed towards him. The ebony teamster whipped up his mules, shouted, hurrahed, and urged them on. Guns were fired on both sides, and the yelling and excitement were tremendous for a few minutes. But the negro gained the day, and ran out of slavery into freedom. He was taken to the quartermaster, who gave him several hundred dollars for his team, so he not only got his liberty but a good start.

Livermore, My Story of the War, *270–71.*

While our army was at Grand Gulf, Miss., an intelligent contraband gave much valuable information as to the position of the enemy, and otherwise rendered himself useful to our forces. He finally fell into the hands of the rebels, who administered one hundred and fifty lashes, and placed an iron collar around his neck, riveting it on very strongly. . . . This collar was a round rod of iron, two inches in circumference, riveted together before and behind with two iron prongs one inch wide, three fourths of an inch thick, and twelve inches long, rising from each side directly outside the ears.

Livermore, My Story of the War, *440.*

As the slaveholders fled before the advancing Union forces they took with them their able-bodied slaves, and when these tried to escape and reach the Union lines, they were pursued and fired upon by their masters who had rather shoot them down than let them go free.

Coffin, Reminiscences, *361.*

The Union: Supporting Contrabands

The Western Freedmen's Aid Commission was organized [in January, 1863]. . . . I was appointed general agent of this commission. . . .

General Grant . . . gave us free transportation for all supplies for the freedmen and for our agents and teachers. We sent efficient agents to attend to the proper and judicious distribution of the clothing and other articles, and a number of teachers, well supplied with books, to open schools among the colored people.

Coffin, Reminiscences, *359.*

With such an army of [contrabands], of all ages and both sexes, as had congregated . . . , amounting to many thousands, it was impossible to advance. There was no special authority for feeding them unless they were employed as teamsters, cooks and pioneers with the army; but only able-bodied young men were suitable for such work. . . . The plantations were all deserted; the cotton and corn were ripe: men, women and children above ten years of age could be employed in saving these crops. . . . Chaplain Eaton, now and for many years the very able United States Commissioner of Education, was suggested [to supervise this work.] . . . The cotton was to be picked from abandoned plantations, the laborers to receive the stipulated price . . . from the quartermaster, he shipping the cotton north to be sold for the benefit of the government. Citizens remaining on their plantations were allowed the privilege of having their crops saved by freedmen on the same terms.

At once the freedmen became self-sustaining. The money was not paid to them directly, but was expended judiciously and for their benefit. . . .

Later the freedmen were . . . paid for chopping wood used for the supply of government steamers [on the Mississippi River]. . . . In this way a fund was created not only sufficient to feed and clothe all, old and young, male and female, but to build them comfortable cabins, hospitals for their sick, and to supply them with many comforts. . . .

Union general Ulysses S. Grant, writing about events of 1861,
Personal Memoirs, *251–52.*

For the support of the sick and those otherwise dependent a tax was temporarily required . . . on the wages of the able-bodied. . . . [I]t compelled the employer and the employed to appear, one or both, before the officer charged with its collection, and this officer allowed no wages to go unpaid. The Negro soon saw in the measure his first recognition by government, and although the recognition appeared in the form of a burden, he responded to it with alacrity, finding in it the first assurance of any power protecting his right to make a bargain and hold the white man to its fulfilment.

Col. John Eaton, Superintendent of Freedmen, ca. 1863,
quoted in DuBois, Economic Co-operation, *36. Available*
online at URL: http://docsouth.unc.edu/church/
dubois07/dubois.html#dub.

The scenes [in freedmen's camps near Vicksburg] were appalling: the refugees were crowded together, sickly, disheartened, dying on the streets, not a family of them all either well sheltered, clad, or fed; no physicians, no medicine, no hospitals, many of the persons who had been charged with feeding them either sick or dead.

John Eaton, speaking of August 1863, quoted in Hermann,
Pursuit, *46.*

[The freedmen] have shown capacity for knowledge, for free industry, for subordination to law and discipline, for soldierly fortitude, for social and family relations, for religious culture and aspirations; and these qualities, when stirred and sustained by the incitements and rewards of a just society . . . will . . . make them a constantly progressive race, and secure them ever after from the calamity of another enslavement, and ourselves from the worse calamity of being again their oppressors.

Edward L. Pierce, "The Freedmen at Port Royal," Atlantic Monthly *12:21 (September 1863), 315. Available online at* URL: cdl.library.cornell.edu/moa/browse.journals/ atla.html.

These freedmen are now disposed of as follows: In military service as soldiers' laundresses, cooks, officers' servants and laborers in the various staff departments, 41,150; in cities, on plantations and in freedmen's villages and cared for, 72,500. Of these, 62,300 are entirely self-supporting . . . , conducting on their own responsibility or working as hired laborers. The remaining 10,200 receive subsistence from the government. Three thousand of them are members of families whose heads are carrying on plantations and have under cultivation 4,000 acres of cotton. They are to pay the government for their subsistence from the first income of the crop. The other 7,200 include the paupers, that is to say, all Negroes over and under the self-supporting age, the crippled and sick in hospital, of the 113,650, and those engaged in their care. . . . Some Negroes are managing as high as 300 or 400 acres.

Col. John Eaton, Superintendent of Freedmen, 1864, quoted in DuBois, Economic Co-operation, *38. Available online at* URL: http://docsouth.unc.edu/church/dubois07/ dubois.html#dub32.

The feeling against serving the Negro in any capacity still prevailed among the officers of our troops. . . . It was exceedingly difficult to find men adapted to the task. . . . To get a man who could be kind to the Negro and just to the Negro's master was all but impossible.

John Eaton, Report of the General Superintendent of Freedmen . . . for 1864, *7.*

[In 1864 in my work for a freedman's aid society I visited Fort Scott, Kansas.] Many of them [refugees and freedmen] had stopped here. . . . Here was a great number of the poor whites, called "Clay-eaters," who complained about government dealing rations to colored people. I

A Union general speaks to freedmen. *(Library of Congress)*

heard one of them say that "if niggers would stay where they belonged, with their masters, they would have more white-bread and beef." I told them, I had learned that many of their husbands were fighting against the [Union] government while the husbands of many of the colored women were fighting to sustain it, and I should favor those who were on the side of the government. . . .

The greatest difficulty in managing this class was to get them to do any thing. Not so with colored people; they would do any thing they could find to do.

Haviland, A Woman's Life-Work, *370–71.*

[The] best way we can take care of ourselves is to have land.

African-American Reverend Garrison Frazier, consulted by General William T. Sherman, late 1864, quoted in Alexander, "Forty Acres and a Mule," n.p.

The Confederacy: Managing Chaos

A Southern planter wrote a friend in New York that four of his runaway slaves had returned voluntarily after a spell of "Yankee freedom." But several months later he complained bitterly that the same four had run away again—this time taking with them two hundred other slaves.

1862 account, in Ottley and Weatherby, Negro in New York, *iii.*

Cato [a slave] is taken; the other two, with others, are said to be on the Island [in Union hands]. Little Andrew, who married into the family, knew all about it and has told. . . . My determination is to turn them over to the proper authorities and let them be tried and dealt with as the public welfare may require. . . . They are traitors who may pilot an enemy into your *bedchamber!* They know every road and swamp and creek and plantation in the county, and are the worst of spies

Slaveholder Rev. Charles C. Jones, July 5, 1862, in Myers,
Children of Pride, *929–30.*

I have just returned from Middle Georgia, and have purchased Mr. Henry J. Schley's Buckhead plantation containing fourteen hundred and twelve acres at ten dollars per acre, and also his present corn crop. . . .

Mr. Schley tells me if at any time danger threatens, to send the Negroes up at once. . . . We can send the Negroes either by Central Railroad . . . or we can send them with wagons, etc. . . .

Lieutenant Charles C. Jones Jr., October 8, 1862, in Myers,
Children of Pride, *974–75.*

[More than 10,000 slaves] flocked into Beaufort on the hegira of the whites, and held high carnival in the deserted mansions, smashing doors, mirrors and furniture, and appropriating all that took their fancy. After this sack, they remained at home upon the plantations and revelled in unwonted idleness and luxury, feasting upon the corn, cattle and turkeys of their fugitive masters.

General Isaac Ingalls Stevens, reporting events after whites fled
their plantations, in Bell, Major Butler's Legacy, *353.*

[Dr. Charles Carter was] obliged to go there [Louisiana & Mississippi] when the war broke out to prevent the confiscation of [his] property. . . . He says the privation & suffering around Natchez, which has not been devastated to any great extent by the armies, was chiefly among people of property, caused by the loss of articles supplied by commerce . . . and by the desertion of household servants. . . . In some cases, the stock & Negroes were carried off from plantations, by which the owners were prevented from planting a crop of cotton. He himself kept his Negroes & put in a crop last year, which, tho a small one, paid him, because of the high price as well as his average crop, 1,150 bales. He paid his Negroes wages, as other planters are glad to do. Wages are very high, $25 per month. Everyone considers slavery at an end & is preparing for the new state of things. Most of the planters in Miss. & Louisiana are Union men & have been from the first and are anxious to restore the Union.

Sidney George Fisher, diary entry for March 4, 1864, A
Philadelphia Perspective, *467.*

When the war come along, Old Master just didn't know what to do. He always been taught not to raise his hand up and kill nobody—no matter how come—. . . and he wouldn't go and fight. He been taught that it was all right to have slaves and treat them like he want to, but he been taught it was sinful to go fight and kill to keep them. . . .

Old Master come down to the quarters and say, "Git everything bundled up and in the wagons for a long trip." The Negroes all come in, and everybody pitch in to help pack up the wagons. . . . Old Master had about five wagons on that trip down into Louisiana, but they was all full of stuff and only the old slaves and children could ride in them. I was big enough to walk most of the time, but one time I walked in the sun so long that I got sick, and they put me in the wagon for most the rest of the way.

We would come to places where the people said the Yankees had been and gone, but we didn't run into any Yankees. . . . We went on down to the south part of Mississippi and ferried across the big river at Baton Rouge. Then we went on to Lafayette, Louisiana, before we settled down anywhere. . . .

I seen lots of men in butternut clothes [Confederate soldiers] coming and going hither and yon, but they wasn't in bunches. They was mostly coming home to see their folks. Everybody was scared all the time, and two-three times when Old Master hired his negroes out to work, the man that hired them quit his place and went on west before they got the crop in. But Old Master got a place, and we put in a cotton crop, and I think he got some money by selling his place in Mississippi. Anyway, pretty soon after the cotton was all in, he moves again and goes to a place on Simonette Lake for the winter. . . .

The next spring Old Master loaded up again, and we struck out for Texas when the Yankees got too close again. But Master Bill didn't go to Texas, because the Confederates done come that winter and made him go to the army. . . . Old Master was hopping mad, but he couldn't do anything or they would make him go too, even if he was a preacher. . . . About that time it look like everybody in the world was going to Texas. When we would be going down the road, we would have to walk along the side all the time to let the wagons go past, all loaded with folks going to Texas.

Pretty soon Old Master say, "Git the wagons loaded again," and this time we start out with some other people, going north. We go north a while and then turn west, and cross the Sabine River and go to Nachedoches, Texas. Me and my brother Joe and my sister Adeline walked nearly all the way, but my little sister Harriet and my mammy rid in a wagon. Mammy was mighty poorly, and just when we got to the Sabine bottoms she had another baby. . . . Old Master went with a whole bunch of wagons on out to the prairie country in Coryell County and set up a farm where we just had to break the sod and didn't have to clear off much. . . .

We raised mostly cotton and just a little corn for feed. [Old Master] seemed like he changed a lot since we left Mississippi, and seem like he paid more attention to us and looked after us better. But most the people that already live there when we git there was mighty hard on their Negroes. . . .

One day Old Master come out from town and tell us that we all be set free, and we can go or stay just as we wish.

Ex-slave Allen V. Manning, in Botkin, Lay My Burden Down, *94–97.*

The Confederacy: Slaves' Experiences of the War

[The blacks' spontaneously singing "My country, 'tis of thee" was] so simple, so touching, so utterly unexpected and startling, that I can scarcely believe it on recalling. . . . I never saw anything so electric; it made all other words cheap; it seemed the choked voice of a race at last unloosed

Colonel Thomas Wentworth Higginson, describing the Port Royal, South Carolina, celebration of the Emancipation Proclamation, in Franklin, Emancipation Proclamation, *117–18.*

I was table waiter then, and after talking over the news at table, missus would say, "Now Tom, you mustn't repeat a word of this." I would look mighty obedient,—but, well—in less than half an hour, some way, every slave on the plantation would know what had been said up at massa's house. One would see sad faces when the Yankees got whipped. . . . By and by the rebels kept getting beaten, and then it was sing, sing, all through the slave quarters. Old missus asked what they were singing for, but they would only say, because we feel so happy. One night, the report of Lincoln's Proclamation came. Now, master had a son who was a young doctor. I always thought him the best man going: he used to give me money, and didn't believe much in slavery. Next morning I was sitting over in the slave quarters, waiting for breakfast, when the young doctor came along and spoke to my brother and sister, at the front door. . . . They jumped up and down, and shouted, and sang,

and then told me I was free. I thought that very nice; for I supposed I should have everything like the doctor, and decided in a moment what kind of a horse I would ride.

Ex-slave Thomas Rutling, 1872, in Blassingame, Slave Testimony, *616–17.*

While Master Jim is out fighting the Yanks, the mistress is fiddling round with a neighbor man, Mr. Goldsmith. I is young then, but I knows enough that Master Jim's going be mighty mad when he hears about it.

The mistress didn't know I knows her secret, and I'm fixing to even up for some of them whippings she put off on me. That's why I tell Master Jim next time he come home.

"See that crack in the wall?" Master Jim says, "Yes," and I say, "It's just like the open door when the eyes are close to the wall." He peek and see into the bedroom. "That's how I find out about the mistress and Mr. Goldsmith," I tells him and I see he's getting mad.

"What do you mean?" And Master Jim grabs me hard by the arm like I was trying to get away.

"I see them in the bed."

That's all I say. The demon's got him, and Master Jim tears out of the room looking for the mistress.

Then I hears loud talking and pretty soon the mistress is screaming and calling for help, and if Old Master Ben hadn't drop in just then and stop the fight, why, I guess she be beat almost to death, that how mad the master was.

Esther Easter in Botkin, Lay My Burden Down, *195.*

[Visitor] number seven [at the office of the Sanitary Commission] was a colored woman, whose husband has been in the Fifty-fourth Massachusetts, under Col. Robert G. Shaw, from its organization. Not a cent has yet been paid by government to any colored soldier who has gone from Chicago. This woman was a slave when the war began,—is still, as far as any manumission by her master is concerned. Since her husband's absence, she has passed through hunger, cold, sickness, and bereavement. Her landlord, a rich man of the city, a German, put her out of her house on the sidewalk, in a cold rain storm, because she owed him five dollars for rent, and could not then earn it, as her child was sick unto death with scarlet fever. One of her colored neighbors, as poor as she, took her in; and the baby died on the next Sunday morning. She came to me to get the baby buried, without going to the poormaster. "It don't seem right for my child to be buried like a pauper," she said, "when her father is fighting for the country." And I agreed with her.

Livermore, My Story of the War, *599.*

There were several likely-looking negro-girls still in the cell [in a New Orleans jail], and three mothers. All of these mothers had sons in the Union army. . . . One of them had *three* sons in one regiment; the other had two sons, her only children; and the only child of the third, a boy of nineteen years, was a sergeant in a colored company. These mothers were all the *property* of rebels. . . . I asked them how they happened to be imprisoned, and was informed that their masters and mistresses had them "sent to prison for safe-keeping." One mother told me she was always treated well until her sons joined the negro regiment, since which time she had been whipped and otherwise sadly abused.

Report to The Boston Traveller, *quoted in Brown,* American Rebellion, *178–81.*

[M]istress called the colored people together and told them to pray—to pray mightily that the enemy may be driven back. So we prayed and prayed all over the plantation. But 'peared like de more de darkies prayed, de more nearer de Yankees come. Then the missus said, "stop all this praying for the enemies to come." So there was no more praying where mistress could hear it. . . . One day my mistress came out to me. "Maria, M'ria . . . what *does* you pray for?" "I prays, missus, that de Lord's will may be done." "But you mustn't pray that way. You must pray that our enemies may be driven back." "But missus, if it's de Lord's will to drive 'en back, den they will go back."

Ex-slave Maria, in Raboteau, Slave Religion, *309.*

The young mens in grey uniforms used to pass so gay and singing, in the big road. Their clothes was good, and we used to feed them the best we had on the place. Missy Angela would say, "Cato, they is our boys and given them the best this place 'fords." We taken out the hams and the wine and kilt chickens for them. That was at first.

Then the boys and mens in blue got to coming that way, and they was fine-looking men, too. Missy Angela would cry and say, "Cato, they is just mens and boys, and we got to feed them, too." We had a pavilion built in the yard, like they had at picnics, and we fed the Federals in that. Missy Angela set in to crying and says to the Yankees, "Don't take Cato. He is the only nigger man I got by me now. If you take Cato, I just don't know what I'll do." I tells them soldiers I got to stay by Missy Angela so long as I live.

The Yankee mens say to her, "Don't 'sturb youself, we ain't gwine to take Cato or harm nothing of yours." The reason they's all right by us was 'cause we prepared for them, but with some folks they was rough something terrible.

Ex-slave Cato, in Botkin, Lay My Burden Down, *87.*

[S]ince the issuing of the President's [emancipation] proclamation, Jonas H. French has stopped all of our night-meetings and has caused us to get permits to hold meetings on Sunday, and sends his police around to all of the colored churches every Sunday to examine all of the permits. He had all the slaves that were turned out of their former owners' yards re-arrested and sent back; those who belonged to rebels as well as those who belong to loyal persons. The slaves were mustered into the rebel army. He has them confined in jail to starve and die, and refuses their friends to see them. He is much worse than our rebel masters, he being the chief of police. Last night, after Gen. Banks left the city, Col. French issued a secret order to all the police-stations to arrest all the negroes who may be found in the streets, and at the places of amusement, and placed in jail. There were about five hundred, both free and slave, confined, without the least notice of cause,—persons who thought themselves free by the President's proclamation. . . .

Letter from a black man in New Orleans to the New York Tribune, *quoted in Brown,* American Rebellion, *181–82.*

Mother had lots of nice things, quilts and things, and kept 'em in a chest in her little old shack. One day a Yankee soldier climbed in the back window and took some of the quilts. He rolled 'em up and was walking out of the yard when Mother saw him and said, "Why, you nasty, stinking rascal! You say you come down here to fight for the niggers, and now you're stealing from 'em." He said, "You're a goddam liar. I'm fighting for $14 a month and the Union."

Ex-slave Sam Word, in Botkin, Lay My Burden Down, *206.*

My name is James Carter[.] I am about 44 years old[.] I was brought to Natchez Miss. . . . I belonged to George W. Fox a Druggist in Natchez. During the year I was arrested by the vigilance Committee here and tried for my life. . . . It was represented that certain colored men were in the habit of meeting in a Bayou called Mrs Boyds Bayou and drilling for the purpose of rising against the white. I was charged with getting dispatches from the enemy and reading them to these men. I was . . . tried for about three weeks almost each day. The final day they carried me out then they whipped me terribly. Several of them were whipping me at once. . . . The object in whipping me was to make me confess to something. . . . They would whip until I fainted and then stop and whip again. Dr Harper sat by and would feel my pulse and tell them when to stop and when to go on. . . . At the end of the trial they decided to hang me. . . . I was then taken to the gallows to be hung. . . . They then said to me that they had concluded not to hang me but would give me a whipping and send me home. I was told when I got back to town by Benjamin Pendleton a white man and a deacon in the Baptist Church that he had saved me from being hung. I belonged to his church and he had interfered and told them that I was a pious man and did not associate with these men who went to the Bayou.

Ex-slave testifying before the Southern Claims Commission, March 31, 1874, in Jordan, Tumult and Silence, *Document N, 328–29.*

The Confederacy: White Women's Experiences of the War

[April 26, 1863] It has got to be such a disagreeable matter with me to whip, that I haven't even dressed Kate but once since you left, & then only a few cuts—I am too troubled in mind to get stirred up enough to whip. I made Thornton [another slave] whip Tom once.

[August 18, 1863] The negros are doing nothing. But ours are not doing that job alone[.] . . . [N]early all the negroes around here are at it, some of them are getting so high in anticipation of their glorious freedom by the Yankees I suppose, that they resist a whipping. I don't think we have one who will stay with us.

[August 28, 1863] I am so sick of trying to do a man's business when I am nothing but, a poor contemptible piece of multiplying human flesh tied to the house by a crying young one, looked upon as belonging to a race of inferior beings.

[November 17, 1863. The new part-time male overseer, Meyers,] will be right tight on the negroes I think, but they need it. . . .

[December 6, 1863 Meyers] don't treat [the slaves] as moral beings but manages by brute force.

[March 20, 1864. Please hire out your slaves or] give your negroes away and, I'll . . . work with my hands, as hard as I can, but my mind will rest.

Lizzie Neblett, letters to her husband reporting her difficulties in managing his 11 slaves, in Faust, Mothers of Invention, *65–70.*

At New Orleans, where we arrived April 6, 1864, . . . we visited ten colored schools in the city, filled with eager learners. One was taught by Mrs. Brice, who had in charge sixty scholars. She had been teaching here three years, under much persecution, and stemmed the torrent of opposition, sometimes in secret, before the war. Sister Brice and her husband had been struggling in this city nearly five years, through this bitter hate to the North, contending for Unionism everywhere, through civil, religious, and political life. We called on them, and spent two hours in eating oranges and listening to the fanaticisms and wild conceptions of this misguided people and terror-stricken multitude when the "Yankee" soldiers marched up the streets from the gun-boats. Schools were dismissed; the children cried as they ran home, telling those they met that the Yankees had come to kill them and their mothers. But there were those who cried for joy at the sight of the national flag.

Haviland, A Woman's Life-Work, *320.*

[Sue] had left. She is still at the Boro, and I am told has hired Elizabeth to work at Dr. Samuel Jones's. Flora is in a most unhappy and uncomfortable condition, doing very little, and that poorly. . . . I overheard an amusing conversation between Cook Kate and herself: they are looking forward to gold watches and chains, bracelets, and *blue veils* and silk dresses! Jack has entered a boarding house in Savannah, where I presume he will practice attitudes and act the Congo gentleman to perfection. Porter and Patience will provide for themselves. I shall cease my anxieties for the race. My life long . . . I have been laboring and caring for [the family slaves], and since the war labored with all my might to supply their wants, and expended everything I had upon their support, directly or indirectly; and this is their return.

Mary Jones, in Myers, Children of Pride, *1308.*

These [Yankee] men were so outrageous at the Negro houses that the Negro men were obliged to stay at their houses for the protection of their wives; and in some instances they rescued them from the hands of these infamous creatures.

Mary Mallard, December 17, 1864, in Myers, Children of Pride, *1229, 1230.*

[Moses] slept in the house, every night while at home, & protected everything in the house & yard & at these perilous times when deserters are committing depredations, on plantations every day, I am really so much frightened at night, that I am up nearly all night.

Maria Hawkins, letter to Governor Zebulon Vance of North Carolina, requesting release of her slave Moses from working for the Confederate army, in Faust, Mothers of Invention, *62.*

The workings of Providence in reference to the African race are truly wonderful. The scourge [of the war] falls with peculiar weight upon them: with their emancipation must come their extermination. All history, from their first existence, proves them incapable of self-government; they perish when brought in conflict with the intellectual superiority of the Caucasian race. . . . I never heard such expressions of hatred and contempt as the Yankees heap upon our poor servants. One of them told me he did not know what God Almighty made Negroes for; all he wished was the power to blow their brains out.

Plantation mistress Mary Jones, January 6, 1865, in Myers, Children of Pride, *1244.*

The Aftermath

When we all gits free, they's the long time letting us know.

Isabella Boyd, in Campbell, Empire, *249.*

After the war, Master Colonel Sims went to git the mail, and so he call Daniel Ivory, the overseer, and say to him, "Go round to all the quarters and tell all the niggers to come up, I got a paper to read to 'em. They're free now, so you can git you another job, 'cause I ain't got no more niggers which is my own." Niggers come up from the cabins nappy-headed, just like they gwine to the field. Master Colonel Sims, say, "Caroline [that's my mammy], you is free as me. Pa said bring you back, and I's gwine do just that. So you go on and work and I'll pay you and your three oldest children $10 a month a head and $4 for Harriet"—that's me—and then he turned to the rest and say, "Now all you-uns will receive $10 a head till the crops is laid by." Don't you know before he got halfway through, over half them niggers was gone.

Ex-slave Harriet Robinson, in Botkin, Lay My Burden Down, *229.*

It is not too late for the [federal] Government to adopt the correct policy in this matter [ownership of captured land]. Sooner or later, this division of property must come about; and the sooner, the better. The land tillers [the former slaves] are entitled by a paramount right to the possession of the soil they have so long cultivated. . . . If the Government will not give them the land, let it be rented to them. It is folly now to deny the Rebellion and not accept all its logical results.

New Orleans Tribune, a black-owned newspaper, 1865, in Harding, River, *256.*

The way we can best take care of ourselves is to have land, and turn it and till it by our own labor. . . . We want to be placed on land until we are able to buy it and make it our own. . . .

I would prefer to live by ourselves [rather than scattered among whites], as there is prejudice against us in the South that will take years to get over; but I do not know that I can answer for my brethren.

Baptist minister Garrison Frazier speaking with Secretary of War Stanton and General Sherman, Savannah, 1865, in Harding, River, *263.*

Some of us are soldiers and have had the privilege of fighting for our country in this war. . . . We want the privilege of voting. . . . [W]e cannot understand the justice of denying the elective franchise to men who have been fighting for the country, while it is freely given to men who have just returned from four years of fighting against it.

Petition from the black community of North Carolina, 1865, in Harding, River, *291.*

Many of the negroes . . . common plantation negroes, and day laborers in the towns and villages, were supporting little schools themselves. Everywhere, I found among them a disposition to get their children into schools, if possible. I had occasion very frequently to notice that porters in stores and laboring men about cotton warehouses, and cart drivers on the streets, had spelling books with them, and were studying them during the time they were not occupied with their work.

Northern journalist Sidney Andrews, 1865, in Harding, River, *308.*

The laws which have made white men powerful have degraded us, because we were black and because we were reduced to the condition of chattels. But now that we are freemen—now that we are elevated, by the Providence of God, to manhood, we have resolved to stand up, and

From plantation to Senate. Left to right: Benjamin Turner of Alabama, H. R. Revels of Mississippi, Bishop Richard Allen of the A.M.E. Church, Frederick Douglass, Josiah T. Walls of Florida, Joseph H. Rainey of South Carolina, and Dr. William Wells Brown. *(Library of Congress)*

people; that, in short, we be dealt with as others are—in equity and justice.

Black convention, "Address to the White Inhabitants of the State of South Carolina," 1865, in Harding, River, *325.*

Of the 108 slaves at these pits only four or five left Monday evening, but the next evening there was 30 or 40, the provisions were not entirely issued & some held back to get their weekly allowance of meat &c. The negroes were slow to realize the fact that they were free. Many disclaimed any disposition to be so, particularly Alfred, Philosophy &c. &c. But by Tuesday evening the fever was so high that every soul who had legs to walk was running to Richmond.

Pit operator Christopher Q. Tompkins, April 1865, in Lewis, Coal, Iron, and Slaves, *137.*

I charge you, men, to make your homes comfortable, and you, women, to make them happy. Work industriously. Be faithful to each other; be true and honest with all men. If you respect yourselves, others will respect you. There are Northerners who are prejudiced against you; but you can find the way to their hearts and consciences through their pockets. When they find that there are colored tradesmen who have money to spend, and colored farmers who want to buy goods of them, they will no longer call you Jack and Joe; they will begin to think that you are Mr. John Black and Mr. Joseph Brown.

Speech by Judge Kelly to freedmen and freedwomen, Charleston, S.C., April 1865, in Child, Freedmen's Book, *263.*

like men, speak and act for ourselves. We fully recognize the truth of the maxim, "The gods help those who help themselves. . . ."

We simply ask that we shall be recognized as *men;* that there be no *obstructions* placed in our way; that the same laws which govern *white men* shall govern *black men;* that we have the right of trial by jury of our peers; that schools be established for the education of *colored children* as well as white; and that the advantages of both colors shall, in this respect, be *equal;* that no impediments be put in the way of our acquiring homesteads for ourselves and our

I suppose you have learned even in the more secluded portions of the country that slavery is entirely abolished. . . . I know it is only intended for a greater humiliation and loss to *us.* . . . On our plantation everything is "at sixes and sevens." One day they work, and the next they come to town. Of course no management of them is allowed. Our Yankee masters think that *their* [the slaves'] term of slavery having expired, that the shackles they have abandoned . . . will do for us their former owners.

Eva Jones, June 13, 1865, in Myers, Children of Pride, *1274.*

CHAPTER THIRTEEN

Reconstruction
1865–1877

Two opposing facts dominate the short, tragic history of Reconstruction. First, African Americans persistently tried to exercise their rights, as they struggled to learn both how to earn their livings and how to function as citizens. For instance, in Richmond, Virginia, on June 10, 1865, 3,000 freedpeople meeting at the First African Black Church formally protested mistreatment of blacks to the state governor and President Johnson; the governor then threw out the city government and appointed a provisional city manager until elections could be held.[1] Two years later, in May 1867, Richmond blacks resorted to direct action to prevent what they regarded as the unjust arrest of a freedman; a riot resulted, quelled only by infantry troops. By every means available, blacks struggled to claim their place as free and equal men and women.

Second, a majority of white southerners fought with equal passion and persistence to reestablish white dominance. In defeat they remained determined to restore their former way of life. As German-American general and politician Carl Schurz observed on his tour of the South in summer 1865, "The emancipation of the slaves is submitted to only in so far as chattel slavery in the old form could not be kept up. But although the freedman is no longer considered the property of the individual master, he is considered the slave of society."[2] For another century whites combined ruthlessness with their greater sophistication in the ways of government to frustrate black dreams of full citizenship. The white establishment, constituted mainly of planters, survived the defeat of the South. Aided by the sympathetic actions of President Johnson, many of its members held onto or soon regained their property and power.

Black leaders emerged in a remarkably short time, thanks to freedpeople's determination to learn and practice politics. Some leaders were northern free blacks who moved south after the war. Some were free blacks from Washington, Richmond, Charleston, and especially New Orleans, relatively well-off, accustomed to independence and a degree of power. Many emerged from the ranks of Union veterans, some of whom had benefited from lessons in literacy, and all of whom wore the authority of members of the military. Still other leaders were nurtured within the black church. With the coming of freedom this first and strongest black institution quickly rid itself of white clergy, separated from white congregations, erected buildings, and expanded in size and activities, including political meetings.

Almost unanimously blacks allied with the Republican Party and in turn received its support, particularly that of the wing known as "Radical Republicans." Their coalition was joined by two other groups, whom establishment southerners scornfully named *scalawags* and *carpetbaggers.*

Scalawags were southern supporters of Union policy. Some had remained loyal to the Union throughout the war, and others adopted a postwar policy of citizenship for blacks. A motley group, scalawags included prominent men and unknowns, wealthy planters and semisubsistence farmers, businessmen who wanted to modernize the economy, and pragmatists who recognized defeat. Schurz described the last group as saying, " 'We cannot be expected at once to give up our principles and convictions of right, but we . . . desire to be reinstated as soon as possible in the enjoyment and exercise of our political rights.' "[3] Scalawags shared one common characteristic: They believed that a Republican South offered better chances of advancing their own interests.

Carpetbaggers were northerners, both white and black, many of them Union veterans or Freedmen's Bureau agents, who saw opportunity in the postwar South. Some were genuinely interested in justice for blacks and in rebuilding the area, others opportunists out for their own gain. All were vilified by southerners as outside troublemakers, and only a few managed to settle there permanently.[4] Many were violently expelled, like Marshall H. Twitchell, who married into a distinguished southern family, helped them get out of debt, brought other members of his birth family south, and for a time succeeded in politics. In the end he lost to southern white hatred several members of his family, his property, and both his arms.[5] Albert T. Morgan, a white Union veteran who believed that "deep down in the heart of all men is a sense of the *law* of right and of love," was also forced to flee. In Mississippi he had dared to marry a black teacher, of whom Morgan's brother commented, "She'd make a better member of the legislature than any of those you saw in that august body."[6]

Because the Radical-Republican vision of equal protection of all required abandoning white supremacy, many southerners experienced Republican deeds as an extension of the Civil War. According to Schurz, they "would grumblingly insist upon the restoration of their 'rights,' as if they had done no wrong, and indicated plainly that they would submit only to what they could not resist and as long as they could not resist it. . . . whenever they look around them upon the traces of the war, they see in them, not the consequences of their own folly, but the evidences of 'Yankee wickedness.' "[7] They used their hatred of the new order to justify violence against blacks, carpetbaggers, and scalawags.

To the astonishment of many whites, freedpeople did not exact vengeance for their enslavement and mistreatment. However, many insisted on being treated as people, not chattel, and whites often mistook this show of independence as calculated insult.[8] Accustomed to ordering blacks about, convinced of their inferiority, whites flinched when they had to look at them on parade in military dress or to deal with them in positions of authority. Lawyers suffered when they had to address blacks as "gentlemen of the jury."

Freedpeople and their allies entered Reconstruction with high hopes. Some naive blacks absurdly anticipated the wealth and leisure in which they believed their former masters and mistresses had luxuriated, but a majority more realistically worked and sacrificed for independence, education, citizenship, control over their own labor, and a modest living. Their expectations were shared by Belgian-born

Jean-Charles Houzeau, the sophisticated editor of the mulatto-owned New Orleans *Tribune*. Houzeau understood the divisions among black people, particularly between freedpeople and blacks free before the Civil War. He also recognized northern white indifference to the fate of blacks and southern white intentions to make blacks pariahs, standing midway between citizens and slaves. Yet he wrote, "The coming to power of this new class—numerous, powerful, hardworking, yet only a few years before so severely and deeply downtrodden—was a magnificent sight. . . . On March 18, 1868, when the Louisiana [Constitutional] Convention adjourned, all that we could have conceived and asked for in the legal sphere had been accomplished."[9]

The Political Situation: Postwar Chaos

The end of the Civil War left the South in near-anarchy, its government no longer functioning, the preservation of law and order left to the Union military. Its economy, always mainly dependent on agriculture, was destroyed. It had never had public school systems nor more than a few public institutions to care for the ill and the helpless; it had no transportation system adequate to an industrial economy. It had always been a society in which millions labored to provide a decent standard of living for the few.

Confederate supporters were traumatized by the violations of war and resentful of their enormous losses—in lives, in real and personal property, and in slaves. The dollar value of those slaves in 1860 had amounted to more than that of all the nation's banks, railroads, and manufacturing combined.[10] Despite military defeat, most whites hung doggedly onto their way of life. In Scottsborough, Alabama, for instance, a sheriff arrested Union soldiers on a charge of murder because they fought guerrillas thereabouts: Only the prompt action of the Union district commander defeated the sheriff's efforts.[11]

Freedpeople arrive in Baltimore in September 1865. *(Library of Congress, Prints and Photographs Division, LC-USZ62-37023)*

The 4 million freedpeople were displaced, many ignorant of the whereabouts of their relatives, few knowing how or where they were to get food, clothing, and shelter. Already robbed by slavery of their ancestral histories, they had now lost their personal histories, only a few scattered remnants of which existed, and their very identities. With no birth certificates, no exact knowledge of their birth dates, no record of their marriages, and no last names, they lacked the means to claim even the little to which they were entitled. Seizing their new freedom to move about, many of them roamed, looking for their families and seeking better job opportunities and living conditions. They wanted to live like the whites they had so long envied, governing their own hours, pace, and terms of labor; owning land; and enjoying a modicum of leisure. Their productivity dropped, reinforcing white convictions about black laziness and need of white supervision.

At the end of a soul-wrenching war, its president assassinated, the Union had to cope with these crises—immediately, even while it dealt with its triumph and its grief. It was ill-prepared. White northerners, even activists who had struggled for years to end slavery in the United States, had exhausted their supply of energy and passion. War weary after four bloody years—the Union preserved and emancipation an accomplished fact—they wanted most to look away from the conflict between blacks and southern whites. They did not even begin to fathom the depths of anger and desire in those two groups.

The Political Situation: Presidential Reconstruction (April 1865–March 1867)

Abraham Lincoln's dream of a Reconstruction period during which the United States would act "with malice toward none, with charity toward all" failed to be realized. His assassination brought to the presidency Andrew Johnson, whose refusal as Democratic senator for Tennessee to vote for secession had deluded many into thinking that he agreed with the antislavery views of the Republican Party and into nominating him Republican candidate for vice president in 1864. In fact he had so voted only because he believed secession unconstitutional. When after Lincoln's assassination on April 14, 1865, Johnson became president, his southern sympathies and personal ambition dominated his decisions. He battled stubbornly to keep power in the hands of southern whites, even though in 1864 he had presented himself as a "Moses" who would lead blacks into the promised land. He was to insist that no state had ever seceded from the Union, on the grounds that the Constitution forbade secession: Therefore, he said, it had never happened. With similar logic he held that slaves in alliance with their owners had oppressed whites who did not own slaves.[12]

Eager to restore peace and make the Union whole again, Johnson wooed the South with leniency. As soon as late May 1865, he began authorizing constitutional conventions in the secessionist states, the delegates to be elected by the voters of 1861—all, of course, white. In August and September, declaring that "white men alone must manage the South," he ordered the restoration of land to its former owners, including land set aside for freedmen in January 1865 by General William T. Sherman in Field Order 15.[13] In the fall, the president announced the removal of black troops from the South, and before 1865 ended he pulled out all but 152,000 Union troops. In December, he pardoned those Confederates who would swear allegiance to the United States, restoring their voting rights and property, excepting only certain leaders and wealthy men.

In all this the president ignored the warnings of the abolitionist Carl Schurz, whom he had commissioned in summer 1865 to survey conditions in the South: "Treason does, under existing circumstances, not appear odious in the south. . . . [T]here is, as yet, among the southern people an utter absence of national feeling. . . . While admitting that, at present, we have perhaps no right to expect anything better than [their] submission—loyalty which springs from necessity and calculation—I do not consider it safe for the government to base expectations upon it."[14]

Encouraged by the president's stance, many former Confederates set about to restore prewar conditions as nearly as possible. They could not reimpose slavery, but they could and did strive to keep blacks in poverty and ignorance, cramping their liberties at every turn. They enacted Black Codes that not only regulated such rights as marrying and holding property but also required blacks to work, on pain of arrest for vagrancy, while limiting them to employment as agricultural laborers or domestics. In South Carolina, to work in any other capacity a black had to obtain a special license and a certificate from a local judge vouching for her or his skill in the desired occupation.[15] Throughout the southern states, the codes dictated the hours, duties, and conduct of agricultural workers.

Then too the codes restricted the mobility of blacks, depriving them of a chance to look for better jobs elsewhere. Many southern towns denied them residency unless an employer guaranteed their conduct. Even to enter Opelousas, Louisiana, blacks had to present a note from their employer stating the reason for and length of the visit.[16] States criminalized blacks' collective action to raise wages. Mississippi forbade them to rent urban land and inflicted fines or involuntary labor on blacks who "misspend what they earn." In Florida, blacks who broke labor contracts could be sold for a year.[17] Though blacks had to pay taxes, some state and local governments barred them from poor relief and public institutions. Some made punishable "insulting" gestures or language and preaching without a license. Some even forbade blacks to hunt and fish, depriving them of means of feeding themselves.

Whites also delayed ratifying the Thirteenth Amendment abolishing slavery, refused blacks the vote, attacked them, and burned their schools and churches. By the time Congress reconvened in December 1865, such men had begun a reign of terror. "In many districts," Schurz advised the president, "robbing and plundering was going on with perfect impunity. . . . [I]t is difficult to conceive how, in the face of the inefficiency of the civil authorities, the removal of the troops can be thought of. . . . [T]he perpetration of [murderous assaults on blacks] is not confined to that class of people which might be called the rabble."[18]

By the end of 1865, Johnson had almost pulled off his coup. Radical Republicans were appalled by southern efforts to restore white supremacy, and members of Congress were infuriated with the president for what they saw as his usurping of their powers, especially after he announced in December that Reconstruction was complete. Thereupon Congress refused to recognize the new southern governments, nor would it seat the congressional delegates-elect from the South, who included high-ranking Confederate officers and the vice president of the Confederacy. A 15-member Congressional Joint Committee on Reconstruction was formed. In February 1866, overruling Johnson's veto, Congress extended the life of the Freedmen's Bureau, created before Lincoln's death to care for freedpeople, and increased its powers, enabling it to build and maintain schools and to adjudicate cases in which state officials refused blacks the same civil rights as whites.

In June, Congress approved the Fourteenth Amendment. Recognizing the citizenship of all persons born or naturalized in the United States and subject to the nation's jurisdiction, it forbade the states to abridge citizens' privileges or immunities or to deprive them of life, liberty, or property without due process of law and extended the equal protection of the laws to any person within U.S. jurisdiction. The amendment empowered Congress alone to restore the right to hold office to any person who engaged in insurrection or rebellion.

For the rest of Johnson's term, through 1868, congressional Radical Republicans and the president battled, as Congress fought to raise the requirements for readmission to the Union and make emancipation something more than a legal fiction. In 1867, Congress weakened the president's authority as commander in chief by requiring that all orders to subordinate commanders pass through General

This 1867 sketch shows blacks and whites voting peaceably together in Washington, D.C. *(Library of Congress, Prints and Photographs Division, LC-USZ62-100971)*

Ulysses S. Grant. The Tenure of Office Act of 1867 further limited Johnson by requiring Senate consent for him to remove Cabinet members he had appointed. On March 2, 1867, the first Reconstruction Act set up military governments in the South and provided that for readmission states must ratify the Fourteenth Amendment and guarantee adult male suffrage. The second, enacted on March 23, authorized military commanders to run elections for delegates to write new state constitutions. Also that month, in the Habeas Corpus Act, Congress helped citizens move cases into federal courts and abolished peonage—the practice that forced a debtor to labor until he had paid what he owed.

Overestimating his own support, Johnson threw out several military commanders and fired Secretary of War Edwin Stanton. On February 24, 1868, Congress impeached him. A chastened president promised to stop resisting Republican Reconstruction policy, and on May 16 he was acquitted by one vote—but the acquittal sapped Radical Republican strength.

The Political Situation: Radical Reconstruction (March 1867–1877)

However, in many areas Republican policies seemed to be working, thanks in large part to the freedmen, who were organizing in their churches, Union Leagues, Equal Rights Leagues, and other groups to advance educationally, politically, and economically. Next to the churches, the Union Leagues constituted the most important of these groups. Curiously, they had originated during the war as northern white patriotic organizations. After the war, but particularly in 1867, southern blacks poured into them, often joining with Unionist hill-country whites—so many freedmen that by the end of 1867 almost every black voter belonged to a Union League or a similar organization. Their members pledged to uphold the Republican Party and the principle of equal rights. The Leagues aimed mainly to foster political education and develop black political leaders, but they also formed self-defense groups, held rallies and parades, promoted the building of schools and churches, collected funds for the care of the sick, drafted petitions, and emboldened laborers to assert themselves with their employers and even to strike.[19]

By 1867, blacks had startled some secessionist southerners into trying to win their political support, which went, however, to Republicans, including blacks, carpetbaggers, and scalawags. Ironically enough, in the fall elections of 1867 Republicans triumphed in the South and Democrats gained in the North, where some were becoming uncomfortable about the "confiscation" of white-owned property that would open lands to blacks.

In 1868, new Reconstruction state governments began operating in the South, except in Alabama and Mississippi. Black members appeared in state legislatures. In all, 600 blacks served during Reconstruction, most of them former slaves,[20] but only in the South Carolina legislature did they ever form a majority. In most legislatures, whites dominated important committees, and most black-sponsored bills failed. Blacks also served as local and federal officials: a few as mayors; more as members of city and town councils, justices of the peace, sheriffs, overseers of the poor, and school commissioners; and yet others as state militia officers, postmasters, land-office clerks, and internal revenue collectors.

Congress readmitted state after state to the Union, beginning with Tennessee in 1866 and ending with Mississippi, Texas, and Virginia in 1870. In 1868, the election of President Ulysses S. Grant guaranteed the survival of Reconstruction. In 1870 and 1871, Enforcement Acts intended to quell violence became the law of the land.

Finally, in February 1869, Congress enacted the Fifteenth Amendment, ratified on March 30, 1870, at long last constitutionally protecting the rights of black men over age 21 to vote. The Fourteenth Amendment had promoted these rights within the southern states by threatening to reduce the congressional representation of states that kept their male inhabitants from voting and by requiring for readmission that state constitutions allow black suffrage. On paper, at least, that had worked well enough that the former Confederate states granted blacks the right to vote, but 16 loyalist states did not. Now the Fifteenth Amendment forbade each and every state as well as the United States itself to deny or abridge "the right of citizens" to vote "on account of race, color, or previous condition of servitude." The amendment did not offer all that was hoped. It failed to guarantee black rights to hold office, nor did it address state requirements for the payment of poll taxes, property ownership, and literacy as a condition of voting. Like the Fourteenth Amendment, it bitterly disappointed woman suffragists by not extending the vote to women, black and white.

Despite the Thireenth, Fourteenth, and Fifteenth Amendments and the other measures taken by Republican Congresses, all was not well for freedmen in these years. In the South, assaults still raged against them and their property. White merchants, employers, and landlords used their economic clout for political advantage, denying blacks credit, firing them, and evicting them. Democrats made electoral gains, and Republicans compromised their beliefs and practices to stay in power. Because blacks had to vote for Republicans to protect their own interests, they had only limited influence within that party, attaining neither the highest offices nor the numbers of offices proportionate to their population—a situation personally damaging in that most southern Republican politicians, white and black, depended on their offices for their livelihood.

Still, Republicans were transforming southern governments and southern life generally, striving to promote industry and build the infrastructure to sustain it. They broadened state responsibilities to provide schools and hospitals and to protect the rights of women and children. They enacted civil rights laws—though usually they could not enforce them. They gave a modicum of protection and power to laborers. They humanized harsh penal codes. They tried to limit the dominance of plantation owners and make land available to blacks.

All this took money, hard to come by in an area only slowly recovering from war's devastation. By 1872, these governments were experiencing economic troubles. The Panic of 1873 threw the nation into a deep depression that lasted until 1878, defeating southern governments' hopes of attracting northern capital. Political corruption spread. Freedpeople lost hope of land ownership, independence, and even the safety of their persons and property.

Meanwhile, the shadow of what southerners called "Redemption" darkened black's prospects. In this era of "home rule," which culminated in the 1890s with black disfranchisement, southern Democrats seized control of state and local governments, sapped black voting power, and restored white supremacy. Only two years after war's end Redemptionists governed Maryland; in 1869, Tennessee; and in 1870, Virginia, North Carolina, and Missouri. They presented themselves as reasonable New Democrats, or "Redeemers," who in a "New Departure" were moving toward the political center. Nonetheless, they used whatever tactics came to hand, from repeal of Republican-passed laws to castration, rape, torture, arson, and murder. Individuals and some Republican state governments courageously opposed them. But by 1870, rednecks and "respectable citizens" in the Ku Klux Klan, the Knights of the White Camellia, Red Shirts, rifle clubs, and the White Brotherhood were riding roughshod over the rights of freedpeople and of white Republicans.

Gradually, such determination to preserve white supremacy was blunting the northern will to deal justly with blacks. Exaggerated rumors of corruption and inefficiency among southern Republicans spread. Reformers, short of both energy and funds, wearied of black woes. Many abolitionists felt that they had achieved their goal with the end of slavery, and many other northerners believed that they had already done enough for the freedmen. Defeated in their hopes for the vote, some woman suffragists courted southern white support, ignoring the predicament of black women. The social Darwinism coming into fashion in the 1870s nurtured latent racist belief that whites were "natural rulers," the surviving fittest. Most northerners desired above all a "return to normalcy," especially "business as usual." During the Panic of 1873 and the long depression that followed, economic issues preoccupied the nation. The economic breakdown eroded trust in the free-labor system and reawakened racism.

President Grant was committed to Republican principles, but he had been elected under the motto, "Let us have peace." Moreover, he owed a political debt to moderates and to businessmen impatient to restore trade with the South. As northern public support for federal intervention waned, even after the Senate had been told that 50,000 murders had been committed in the South since the war, he

This campaign poster for Thomas Seymour, Democratic presidential candidate in 1866 who lost to General U.S. Grant, asserts that Grant is pulling the Republican wagon toward "Salt River" (defeat), that Republicans are bummers (carpetbaggers and party hangers-on), and that whites have been slaughtered to emancipate blacks, who really long to return to "old massa." (*Library of Congress, Prints and Photographs Division, LC-USZ62-7186*)

wavered.[21] Then in October 1871 he broke the power of the Ku Klux Klan, in effect forcing it to disband.[22] He dramatically reduced violence by proclaiming a "condition of lawlessness" in parts of South Carolina, suspending habeas corpus, and sending in troops. These decisive actions made the election of 1872 the most peaceful of the whole Reconstruction. At other times, however, particularly in his second term, Grant flinched before the political dangers, party splits, and public criticism that followed intervention in the South.[23]

The U.S. Supreme Court aided white supremacists with two astonishing decisions. In 1873, it ruled in the *Slaughterhouse* cases that the Fourteenth Amendment protected only federal rights, which it instanced as the right to run for federal office, travel to the seat of government, and be protected at sea and abroad—all other rights remaining under state control. Three years later the Court said in *U.S.* v. *Cruikshank* that the Thirteenth, Fourteenth, and Fifteenth Amendments applied only to violations of black rights by states, not by individuals.

By the mid-1870s, most reformers were focusing not on equality for blacks but on putting the "best men" into office. In a sharp about-face, the American Missionary Society, earlier a major donor to black institutions, alleged that black suffrage had failed and that freedpeople were ungrateful.[24] In 1874, the Freedmen's Bank closed, its mismanagement having robbed freedpeople of at least 40 percent of their small savings. Both the remaining Reconstruction state governments and freedpeople staggered under the blows inflicted by the 1873–78 depression. Riots in the South had become endemic, and weary northern Republicans decided that Reconstruction was a political liability.

As white supremacists more openly embraced racism, black discouragement turned into despair. Some impoverished blacks considered migration, and some of the better-off joined interracial conservative coalitions.

The 43rd Congress (1873–75), the last under Republican control for a decade, managed to pass some legislation to increase protection of blacks. For instance, the Civil Rights Bill of 1875 required equal accommodations for blacks with whites in public facilities, except schools. In the same year, the Jurisdiction and Removal Act eased the transfer to federal courts of suits to exert citizens' federal rights. But the Civil Rights Act never really worked, and in 1883 the Supreme Court declared it unconstitutional.

In the hotly disputed presidential campaign of 1876, the Republican candidate Rutherford B. Hayes's promise to bring the South "honest and capable local self government"—in other words, to end Reconstruction—left southern Republicans "abandoned," as one wrote, "to the tender mercies of the Ku Klux Klan."[25] The campaign, carried on amid southern race riots and strikes, resulted in a popular majority for the Democratic candidate, Samuel J. Tilden, but a one-vote victory in the electoral college for Hayes. Well aware of fraud in Florida, South Carolina, and Louisiana, Democrats challenged the count. In the negotiated "Compromise of 1877," which freedpeople called the "Great Betrayal," Hayes took the presidency and Republicans agreed to remove federal soldiers from the South, enact federal legislation to help industrialize the South, appoint Democrats to patronage positions in the South, and appoint a Democrat to the cabinet.

Reconstruction had ended. Democrats assumed control of southern state governments. Southern blacks, deserted by the federal government, were left at the mercy of their former owners. The next federal bill to protect their civil rights would not take effect until 1957. Southern Democrats now recriminalized the violation of labor contracts and began a long process of disfranchising black men, not to be reversed until the 1960s. In the words of black leader and historian W. E. B. DuBois, "The slave went free: stood a brief moment in the sun; then moved back again toward slavery."[26]

The Freedmen's Bureau: Aims and Organization

During the Civil War Congress usually left it up to the military to deal with contrabands and fugitive slaves. It did empower the Treasury Department to lease confiscated and abandoned lands to blacks, but the supervision of these lands fell to the generals in the field.

In March 1865, it finally created a catchall "Bureau of Refugees, Freedmen, and Abandoned Lands" with the power to distribute food, fuel, clothing, and medical supplies; regulate labor and contracts; help establish schools and churches; try to ensure justice in the courts for freedpeople; and rent and sell abandoned and confiscated Confederate lands to them. It situated the Freedmen's Bureau in the War Department, authorized it to exist for the duration of the war plus one year, and, fatefully, made it subject to presidential authority. In 1866, overriding two presidential vetoes, Congress enlarged the bureau's powers so that it could make, interpret, and enforce laws; collect taxes; define and punish crime; and use military force. As DuBois commented, "The very name of the Bureau stood for a thing in the South which for two centuries and better men had refused even to argue,—that life amid free Negroes was simply unthinkable, the maddest of experiments."[27]

The wonder is that the agency accomplished so much, given that it was placed under the thumb of a president who believed in the virtues of slavery and the inferiority of blacks. At every turn, Andrew Johnson undermined its workings. Had

The Freedmen's Union Industrial School, Richmond, Virginia, 1886. *(Library of Congress, Prints and Photographs Division, LC-USZ62-33264)*

Congress not overridden him, he soon would have ended its life. Frustrated in that effort, he did all he could to impede its operation, depriving it of funds, countermanding the bureau commissioner's orders, and replacing agents whom he thought too sympathetic to freedpeople with his own men. His open opposition encouraged white southerners to hamper the bureau's efforts.

Theoretically, the bureau was to support itself by leasing and selling some 800,000 acres of abandoned or confiscated property to freedmen in 40-acre parcels. In actuality, the president's restoration of property to secessionists robbed the bureau of that potential income. Some bureau agents tried to help blacks homestead some of the 46 million acres of southern public land available under the Southern Homestead Act of 1862, only to be defeated by the poor quality of the available land, local obstructionism, and corporate competition for the land. Most freedpeople would never realize the hope of 40 acres and a mule raised by Sherman's wartime order and sustained by the wording of the act creating the Freedmen's Bureau.

Commissioner Major General Oliver Howard, known for his abolitionist and humanitarian views as "the Christian general," confronted the gigantic task of serving white indigents and more than 4 million freed slaves with inadequate funds and personnel. Howard laid down the policy of helping freedpeople to independence as soon as possible and inviting the aid of volunteer agencies. Blacks soon were building their own schools, contributing to their support, and teaching in them. Black churches nurtured black political leaders and supported bureau undertakings. Northern charities filled in some of the gaps left by government.

The bureau employed only 2,441 men in total, no more than 900 at any one time.[28] Most, appointed by military commanders, were soldiers, officers, and camp hangers-on, who could at least claim military pay. Others were local whites; still others were veterans, including Reserve Corps officers eager to perform their duties well to protect their records. Agents varied from selfish, greedy men, on the lookout to acquire land or enter politics, to a few idealists dedicated to a mission, with a selfless desire to help the freedmen and rebuild the southern economy.

All agents faced crisis and catastrophe. Good or bad, they were vulnerable to the handicaps of their position: overwork, lack of authority, lack of a support system, lack of protection for their property and indeed their lives, isolation, the need to win over the local population, and most of all the stubborn opposition of many southern whites, ranging from obstruction to violence. They had to begin functioning at once, with no time for training. They had to operate on isolated posts, in areas where war had smashed the economy. Many whites hated them because they were conquerors, because they were trying to shift power from those who had held it so long, and because the southerners thought them carpetbaggers out to make their fortunes, as some, but by no means all, indeed were. Freedpeople on the move were creating unemployment in some areas and a shortage of labor in others. They feared—often justly—signing labor contracts with former slave owners.

In such a situation, the agents had to improvise ways to restore order, feed the hungry, house the homeless, care for the old and sick, find jobs for millions, reunite families, protect and defend freedpeople legally and physically, and educate them. Withal, the agents struggled to introduce a free-labor economy into a system based on slave labor. As time wore on, deprived of their power to help blacks to acquire land—the best economic hope for most of them in a still primarily agricultural society—agents concentrated on functioning as relief providers, labor mediators, and school builders.

Conscientious agents worked through fatigue, illness, and personal danger to do the best they could. They achieved something of a miracle, thanks to the generosity of white volunteers and even more to the determination of freed-people to earn economic independence. As General Howard wrote in 1869 in his final report, "[O]f the four millions of people thrown suddenly upon their own resources only one in about two hundred has been an object of public charity; and nearly all who have received aid have been persons who, by reason of age, infirmity or disease, would be objects of charity in any state at any time."[29] By no means could the bureau have restored the southern economy had not freedpeople proved what so many whites, North and South, doubted: that they were willing and competent to work.

The Freedmen's Bureau was an unusual agency in that it did not advocate its own permanence. In line with its consistent emphasis on black independence, it sought instead black suffrage as the best protector of black rights. Most dramatically of all, agents endeavored to change attitudes as they struggled to demonstrate that slavery was dead, that black people had rights, and that the old assumptions about race relations and local power would no longer hold.

The Freedmen's Bureau: Achievements

When the bureau was disbanded in July 1870, it had distributed 21 million free rations, transported 30,000 blacks from refuges and relief stations back to farms, and operated 60 hospitals and asylums. Its physicians and surgeons had treated more than half a million patients. It had expended $6 million for education, of which $750,000 was contributed by freedmen. And it had disbursed $6 million to 5,000 black Union veterans.[30] The bureau had helped only a few blacks own their own land, but it had opened some public land to those who had tools and capital—often money derived from army pay and bounties.[31] Before it closed it had to transfer to state and local governments some half a million sick and infirm people, black and white, still under its care.

It had aided thousands of freedpeople in finding jobs, when necessary transporting them to areas that needed laborers. It had written and tried to enforce 50,000 labor contracts. One way and another, it had jumpstarted the South's stalled economy. As Carl Schurz observed, "[N]ot half of the labor that has been done in the south this year [1865], or will be done there next year, would have been or would be done but for the exertions of the Freedmen's Bureau."[32]

In its judicial efforts, the agency had failed more often than it had succeeded—failed to protect blacks from attacks on their lives, their civil rights, and their properties and failed to protect whites from discourtesy and repeated punishment. In DuBois's words, "Bureau courts tended to become centers simply for punishing whites, while the regular civil courts tended to become solely institutions for perpetuating the slavery of blacks."[33] One has to ask, however, whether in the chaotic, hate-filled, demoralized South of early Reconstruction any organization could have done better.

The bureau's most lasting and significant accomplishment resulted from its educational work. Despite white southerners' ruinous efforts to continue to keep blacks in ignorance, the bureau helped catapult the black literacy rate upward. And in cooperation with freedpeople, the agency introduced the idea of free elementary public education throughout the South.

The Economy: Labor

War's end left southern agriculture—almost its only source of revenue—without a stable labor force. Displacement, flight, and migration had moved many freedpeople far from their former owners. In any case, many blacks wanted nothing more to do with the whites they had served or the kind of work they had done. On the other hand, how else were they to earn their bread? How else was the economy to be restarted? Cotton, almost everyone agreed, was the mainstay of that economy; it remained the nation's most important export.

Freedpeople wanted and expected land, and the Freedmen's Bureau had expected to make it available to them. In fact, however, even the few who had claimed abandoned property were being evicted, as President Johnson restored it to its previous owners. To survive, most freedpeople were driven to hire themselves out.

In their efforts to find jobs for freedpeople, Freedmen's Bureau agents often copied the "contract system" established during the war by such military officers as General Nathaniel P. Banks in Louisiana—a system that had the advantages of restoring order and getting the economy to working again. Under this plan, blacks contracted with plantation owners and other farmers for a year under specified conditions and for specified wages—sometimes cash, sometimes a share of the crop. Endless difficulties arose with both writing contracts and enforcing them, difficulties that agents had to try to settle. They could not regularly compel fairness. To be effective, they had to get along with white employers—no easy undertaking with men long accustomed to life-and-death control over their workers who were feeling the stigma of loss and defeat and who wanted to insert terms into labor contracts demanding the political loyalty of freedpeople. Blacks who had never worked for pay also had much to learn about the obligations of free labor, lacked experience in bargaining with employers, and resented signing contracts to which they had no real alternative. Moreover, the uneven supply of labor caused the bureau to move workers around in what must have seemed arbitrary ways.

Neither the black workers nor the planters liked the contract labor system. For the freedmen, contract labor resembled slavery all too closely—the same work, the same subjection to the orders of overseers and owners, the same subsistence standard of living. Even the practice of whipping long survived slavery, albeit illegally. As the crusading white editor Jean-Charles Houzeau wrote, "What became of the principle of freedom of contract if a master refused to give his workers the *permit* necessary to seek work elsewhere? Moreover, what effect did this regulation have on the right to negotiate salaries? The worker was put on a salary schedule according to whether he was *good*, *average*, or *bad*, and the employer was the judge. . . . The wage scale was set excessively low, and the planter had to feed and lodge his workers just as in the days of slavery. He was forbidden to use corporal punishment. But . . . to whom could the black man complain?"[34] Nonetheless, economic necessity, pressure from Freedmen's Bureau agents, and the Black Codes coerced workers into signing contracts, while dependence on black labor impelled plantation owners.

Neither the authorities nor the courts protected black workers against violence and the all-too-frequent fraud imposed on them by their employers, who might fire them or harass them until they quit just before harvest time, when they were entitled to a share of the crop. As one South Carolina freedman described such tactics, "There's a many masters as wants to git de colored peoples away, ye see; an' dey's got de contrac's, an' dey can't do it, ye see, lawful; so dey 'buses dem, an' jerks 'em up by de two fums, an' don't give 'em de bacon, an' calls on 'em to do work in de night time an' Sun'ay, till de colored people dey . . . goes off."[35] Employers were horrified when laborers organized, as when in 1871 in Marion County, Alabama, freedmen formed a labor union and threatened to emigrate unless they were offered better contracts.[36]

For the most part, however, the planters obstructed such efforts. They effectively wielded the Black Codes. Although as the era of presidential Reconstruction drew to a close in late 1866 most of these codes were repealed, the white attitudes that had prompted their passage remained unchanged, and southern courts used other state laws against freedpeople.

The codes were aimed directly at black men, though their provisions were also invoked against black women. Southern whites expected freedwomen to return to the housework or fieldwork they had done as slaves. The Freedmen's Bureau was torn. It wanted both to make freedwomen independent and to strengthen black families. Many of these women wanted to stay home with their children, as the white mistresses they had long envied did. Bureau agents tried to help women hold men responsible as fathers and husbands. They encouraged blacks to formalize their marriages. When agents transported the unemployed able-bodied to areas where labor was needed, they often exempted women with working husbands or small children.

Some agents treated able-bodied freedwomen more permissively than able-bodied freedmen, as agents became sensitized to the special problems of these women. In the employment market, they were even worse off than freedmen. They had little chance of acquiring a skill or moving to a place that afforded better jobs. They were paid less for the same jobs, even when they labored in the fields alongside men. Accordingly numbers of them refused bureau efforts to move them from the city back to the country, knowing that there they would be paid wages below subsistence level and would be even more vulnerable to employers' harassment than they were in the cities.[37]

Single mothers were always the last ones hired. Many of them had inherited from slave days their status as single parents, the only support and protection of their children. What was a woman to do when she had six or seven children whom whites regarded as illegitimate, fathered either by a slave who had been sold away and whose whereabouts were unknown or by a white master whose willingness to support his offspring ended with their emancipation?

Remarkably, some of these often illiterate freedwomen fought as common-law wives in the Freedmen's Bureau and in the courts to claim dower, inheritance, and bastardy rights. In 1866, for instance, former slave Eliza Cook claimed support for herself and her seven children from their white father, whose white wife demanded their removal from the plantation. Despite the support of the bureau, the courts refused to hear her case, and she and her children were evicted.[38]

Additionally, freedwomen daringly sued for a right that white women did not have: the right to custody and control of their own children. Most of the time they went down to defeat, but now and then they won. Often they were motivated by white attempts to "apprentice" black children, 'binding them out' for terms as long as eight years and teaching them no trades. In North Carolina, for example, the Freedmen's Code of 1866 empowered county courts to apprentice the children of newly freed slaves when their parents did not "habitually employ their time in some honest industrious occupation" and instructed courts to give priority in these efforts to the former masters of these children, who became the children's guardians, entitled to their services until they were legally adults.[39] Plantation owners desperate for labor hunted out black adolescents to use as field laborers and domestic workers.

Thus on September 24, 1866, Lucy Ross complained to the bureau that her daughters, Maria and Delia, had been kidnapped to be apprenticed to their former master, state legislator Daniel Lindsay Russell. She described the children as able to "earn good wages for themselves"; moreover, she testified, she could support them, an assertion that her brothers and a neighbor backed up. The bureau agent voided the indentures, but Russell kept the girls anyway. Despairing of winning a state court case for Ross because she was unmarried, the bureau took to court a similar case in which a married black man, Wiley Ambrose, complained against Russell. In early 1867, the North Carolina Supreme Court canceled the Ambrose children's apprenticeships, but only on the technicality that Russell had not notified their parents; the court thus failed to sustain Ambrose's claim to the right to protect his children. Nevertheless, the court decision created a confusion that freedwomen used to demand full custody of their children.[40]

The Economy: Artisans

Before the Civil War, many of the skilled workers—barrel makers, barbers, cooks metalworkers, and mechanics—were blacks, both slave and free. As Nell Irwin Painter has remarked, "There were many more skilled black people in 1865 than there were skilled white people. And when skilled work became wage work, then white workers moved into that niche."[41] White artisans, some of them unionized, wanted these higher-paying jobs, and they did not want to work alongside blacks. They fought for the jobs, often violently, and their violence, combined with prejudiced employers' preference for white workers, pushed blacks out of skilled work.

The Economy:
Black Landowning and Sharecropping

The land ownership for which freedpeople yearned never materialized for the majority. Most had no capital, many whites refused to lend them any, and many whites would not sell to them. The venturesome chose sharecropping as the only alternative to paid employment—to such an extent that by 1870 sharecropping dominated the southern labor scene.

In this system, blacks and poor whites independently farmed perhaps 20 to 50 acres, agreeing to give the landowners a certain amount of produce at harvest. If the owner provided the necessary tools, fertilizer, animals, and feed, he usually took two-thirds of the crop; if the sharecropper supplied his own, they divided the crop equally.[42] Unless as slaves they had participated in farm management, freedmen had never had to plan how to survive after a poor harvest, or none. All too often illiterate, ignorant of even basic arithmetic, they were in no position to drive a bargain, and unscrupulous whites took advantage of them. Contracts might assign an unfair portion of the harvest to the landowner; they might require that a certain amount be delivered to him regardless of the size of the harvest. Outright fraud was common. Beyond that, the very system of using future crops as collateral was flawed, leading to overproduction of cotton and low prices. At the same time, world demand for cotton was slowing.

Much southern land had already been depleted by overuse, lack of crop rotation, and inadequate fertilizer, organic or chemical. The sharecropping system perpetuated these practices, so that the soil yielded less and less. The depression of 1873–78 lowered cotton prices further. Toil as the whole sharecropping family might, most sharecroppers soon were mired in debt, dependent on credit from the landowner or the local merchant, with harvests insufficient to pay off the loan and its mounting interest, at rates often higher than 50 percent.[43] Desperation drove sharecroppers to plant ever more cotton, at the expense of space to grow food.

Still, many blacks, especially those who raised cotton, preferred the modicum of independence of sharecropping to contract labor. There were no bosses. They gained control over their own time, their work methods, and their pace—even, as far as economics permitted, their own consumption. They had privacy; their nuclear families could live together—by themselves.

The Economy: The Freedmen's Bank

Well before the Civil War, free black mutual aid societies in cities had encouraged saving. Some individual black entrepreneurs had used money they had earned as barbers or carpenters to lend to others who needed capital. During the war, some Union commanders had established banks to accommodate black soldiers and contrabands.[44] Toward war's end, at the suggestion of philanthropists, the federal government chartered a bank to inculcate thrift in freedpeople. On March 3, 1865, President Lincoln signed a bill incorporating the Freedmen's Savings and Trust Company.

This bank, for black depositors only, staffed by blacks, and with local black leaders as members of branch advisory boards, founded 37 branches in 17 states and Washington, D.C. Black organizations entrusted their treasuries to it.[45] It aggressively pursued and attracted the savings of thousands of freedpeople, mostly in accounts under $50; its passbooks and literature featured slogans and poems "on temperance, frugality, economy, chastity, the virtues of thrift & savings."[46] It went into the schools to persuade black children to set up their own accounts with a few pennies. At its New York headquarters, it offered blacks training in business and loaned them money to get started. Its advertisements led many to believe, falsely, that the federal government was backing their deposits.

Things went well for a while, but in the early 1870s the directors speculated in real estate and made unsecured loans to railroads and other large companies. In the Panic of 1873, they tried to cover up by installing the respected black abolitionist Frederick Douglass as president, concealing the true condition of the bank from him and even persuading him to invest $10,000 of his own money in it.[47] He lost it all. As he later said, he had been "married to a corpse."

In June 1874, the bank suspended operations. According to black educator Booker T. Washington, when the bank failed some 60,000 freedmen had deposits amounting to $57 million.[48] About half of them lost everything; the others were able to collect about 60 percent of their money. The federal government did nothing for them. This economic nightmare so devastated freedpeople's trust in banks (and to some extent in the federal government) that years had to elapse before other black banks were founded.

African-American leader Frederick Douglass was U.S. Marshal of the District of Columbia in 1877. *(Library of Congress, Prints and Photographs Division, LC-USZ62-93268)*

Education

By 1860, all but 91,736 of the 488,070 free blacks were literate; they supported clandestine black schools in the slave states attended that year by 3,651 black children.[49] Even before the war, some slaves, understanding literacy as the key to liberty, had risked beatings and torture to learn to read and write. Here and there a member of a slave-owning family, often a child or a woman, taught a slave to read. What one slave managed to learn, he taught others, in the fields and woods, wherever they could work secretly. Even as a slave Lily Ann Granderson, having learned to read from her master's children, managed to conduct a covert night school in Kentucky for seven years, teaching 12 students at a time. School opened around midnight, with all doors and windows shut and with minimal light. In 1863 when Union troops took over the area, Granderson went on teaching, then for the American Missionary Society.[50]

During the war, some black soldiers in the Union army and some contrabands learned to read in facilities furnished by the army, which also opened schools for blacks in occupied areas of the South. When northern missionaries arrived in the Sea Islands in 1862, they found two black schools already operating.[51] Before the war ended, such schools were emerging into sight elsewhere: Georgia blacks in January 1865 were openly conducting their own formerly clandestine schools.[52] By emancipation, perhaps 150,000 of the 4 million slaves could read.[53]

Freedpeople yearned for literacy—some simply to read the Bible, some to possess the key to independence, political power, and upward mobility. As the war ended, blacks held classes for other blacks in abandoned warehouses, billiards rooms, former slave markets, deserted hotels, and even on the waysides. Children taught parents; laborers taught each other. Elected black representatives in Reconstruction legislatures enrolled in law schools as soon as they were permitted. Black churches, Union Leagues, and other groups built schoolhouses. Despite antagonism and repression, black enthusiasm for education jammed schoolrooms for 20 to 30 years after the Civil War.[54]

As Union victories opened up areas of the South, the American Missionary Association (AMA) and other northern groups sent money, supplies, and educators for blacks. With such help, Avery Normal Institute was founded in Charleston, South Carolina, the only educational institution there to offer a classical curriculum preparing black students for college and enabling them to become doctors, lawyers, and teachers.

Under presidential Reconstruction, state governments tried to evade any responsibility for the welfare of blacks, let alone for providing schools for them. Indeed, so widespread was southern white opposition that Chaplain Joseph Warren, superintendent of education under the Freedmen's Bureau in Mississippi, wrote: "I have no doubt but that, if our protection be withdrawn, negro education will be hindered in every possible way, including obstructions by fraud and violence. I have not the smallest expectation that, with the State authorities in full power, a northern citizen would be protected in the exercise of his constitutional right to teach and preach to the colored people, and shall look for a renewal of the fearful scenes in which northerners were whipped, tarred and feathered, warned off, and murdered, before the war."[55]

The Freedmen's Bureau, however, set up schools and colleges to educate blacks—by far too few for the need, but enough to help thousands to whom even literacy had been denied and to introduce into the South the concept of a public education system. In cooperation with the American Missionary Society, other northern black aid organizations, and local black churches, the bureau founded and supported more than 4,300 schools for black children and adults—elementary schools and universities, schools for all days of the week and all hours of the day and evening, schools for the study of liberal arts and the industrial arts; in the process the bureau spent $5 million.[56] It rented buildings and oversaw construction of new ones, provided books, appealed to private agencies for teachers, superintended the schools, and tried to protect students, teachers, and schools against attacks. It discovered and supported such educators as Edmund Asa Ware, the bureau's superintendent of schools for Georgia and later president of Atlanta University; Erastus Cravath, founder of Fisk University; and Samuel Armstrong, principal of Hampton Institute. Each institution has trained thousands of African-American teachers and other skilled and professional people.

Even bureau schools, however, depended heavily on black support. Freedpeople contributed by paying tuition, providing teachers' room and board, buying land for schools, and actually building schools. They also continued to create and support schools independent of white efforts—even as some states taxed them to support the white schools from which they were excluded.

Courageous northerners taught in bureau schools in the face of white ostracism and at the risk of attack. The stream of schoolmistresses who went South to teach blacks during the war swelled during Reconstruction, so that in the early years they constituted more than half of the teachers in black schools. Often teachers had to find their own classrooms. The desperate eagerness of blacks old and young to learn drove their instructors to set up class after class, in which they tried to teach the Puritan ethic—piety, cleanliness, punctuality, thrift, honesty, and the dignity of labor along with the ABCs, just as in the northern schools they knew. Instructors also organized temperance societies, lectured on paternal obligations, and helped their students with contracts and in court, so that they had almost no rest. A smaller number of southern whites also taught in black schools—some racists among them. Of the nearly 600 teachers in Georgia's freedmen's schools during Reconstruction, more than one-fifth were native Georgians, including nearly 50 white Georgians.[57] Although contemporary teachers seldom had completed high school, many of the northern teachers of freedmen had graduated from postsecondary institutions, including Dartmouth College, Yale College, Oberlin College, and Mount Holyoke Female Seminary.

Northern blacks, including students and graduates of such institutions as Oberlin, Kimball, Wilberforce, and Lincoln, also arrived in significant numbers to teach the new freedmen. Their presence encouraged local blacks to take control over their own schools and gradually to install their own teachers, some of them trained in institutions established by mission groups and the Freedmen's Bureau. By 1869, black teachers outnumbered whites in black schools.[58]

The black/carpetbag state governments of Radical Reconstruction began to set up public schools: Alabama, Mississippi, Louisiana, South Carolina, and Arkansas in 1868; Florida and North Carolina in 1869; Virginia in 1870; and Georgia in 1873. They faced public opposition, of course, from officials who believed that parents had the responsibility to educate their own children. On the other hand, some whites argued that at least public schools would help rid the South of Yankee teachers instilling their ideas in black children. In Atlanta, former priest Daniel O'Keefe, who had changed denominations, become a physician, married, and been elected president of the city council, had to cajole its reluctant members into issuing bonds to fund a public school system, which opened in 1872.[59]

Few tried to integrate schools. Southern whites detested the very thought. Most northern whites took segregation for granted. After all, in 1834 a mob of townspeople in Canterbury, Connecticut, had assaulted and forced the closing of Prudence Crandall's school for black girls, founded in defiance of an 1833 Connecticut law making it illegal to provide blacks free education.[60]

Blacks expended little energy on integration: They wanted first and foremost to learn and to be able to send their children to school. Of course, most wanted a share in public school tax funds, and most objected to state constitutions' mandating segregated schools. As one educator foresaw, "Make this distinction in your organic law and in many places the white children will have good schools . . . while the colored people will have none."[61] Some black mothers and fathers believed that they could exert more control in black schools, which would probably also hire more black teachers. Parents worried about white teachers because so many of them rated black children as "naturally inferior."

So most southern schools, were to remain segregated until at least the 1960s. Louisiana's 1868 constitution provided that its general assembly must establish in every parish at least one free public school open without distinction of race, color, or previous condition of servitude.[62] That did not happen elsewhere, but New Orleans had an integrated system, with an attendance by 1874 of several thousand black and white children. Public institutions of higher learning in the South followed the same pattern of segregation, again with one exception, the University of South Carolina, which admitted its first black student in 1873 and held fast to the decision against student and parental resistance.[63]

For a few years, at least in cities, freedpeople successfully laid claim to the education that was their due. The Freedmen's Bureau was killed off before it could really begin to serve rural black children, for most of whom schools were either nonexistent or open for only a few months a year. When the bureau closed, poverty still kept nine out of 10 freedmen's children out of school.[64] All too soon "Redeemers"—whites eager to "redeem" the South from Radical Reform—began in 1869 to erode educational gains in Tennessee, Delaware, Kentucky, and Maryland, repealing state education laws and ordering that black schools be financed by taxes on black parents.[65] As these conservatives regained power, the erosion crept throughout the South. In 1870, Congress tried to stop it by new requirements for readmission of seceded states. But at the end of Reconstruction in 1877, with 70 percent of blacks still illiterate,[66] most southern blacks were locked into a system that denied them decent schooling. The southern white society used this system not to open opportunity but to block it.

Reconstruction had made possible schools for blacks, and even under the Redeemers these schools were better than none. During Reconstruction and long after, northern philanthropy and valiant black effort sustained 16 colleges and 84 normal and high schools in the South,[67] from which emerged black teachers and other professionals and leaders.

Religion and Community

In the United States, from its beginnings the black church, the first and most important black institution, not only provided a place for blacks to worship but also improved their opportunities, particularly for education. Over the years, it nurtured black leaders who contributed to the progress of the race economically, culturally, and politically. Before the Civil War, it was confined to cities where numbers of free blacks lived.[68] For instance, African American George Liele, licensed to preach to slaves on plantations, began founding black churches in and near Savannah, Georgia, in 1778.[69] With emancipation, the black church grew rapidly both in numbers and in the work it undertook, which included the founding and operation of schools and colleges, hospitals, orphanages, beneficial societies, insurance societies, banks, cooperative businesses, building societies, and newspapers.

The largest black denomination, the African Methodist Episcopal (AME) church, originated in protest against the Philadelphia St. George Methodist Episcopal Church's treatment of its black members. Richard Allen, later an AME bishop, led these blacks to form their own church, which immediately began night classes to teach them to help themselves. In 1816, other black churches in Delaware, Pennsylvania, Maryland, New Jersey, and elsewhere joined with this church as the AME denomination.[70] After the Civil War, membership leapt from 19,914 in 1856, to 73,000 in 1866, to 206,331 in 1876.[71] The African-American Baptist churches, mostly founded by local blacks after the Civil War, increased similarly.

The community action sponsored by black churches had originated, wrote DuBois, in "the spirit of revolt which tried to co-operate by means of insurrection." Such cooperation "led to widespread organization for the rescue of fugitive slaves among Negroes themselves, and developed . . . into various co-operative efforts toward economic emancipation and land-buying. Gradually these efforts led to co-operative business, building and loan associations and trade unions."[72] By such means, blacks helped and cared for one another during Reconstruction and the terrible years that followed.

The first of the beneficial societies, known as The Christian Progress, was formed soon after the war in Warsaw, Georgia, to care for the sick and pay for burial. Such societies usually charged an initiation fee of $2.50 to $5, plus sick dues ranging from $1.50 to $5 a week.[73] In the same period, blacks in Baltimore experimented with co-operative businesses—grocery stores, coal yards, and others. After a brief period of success, they all failed for lack of either capital or trained personnel.[74] Efforts to organize labor met a similar fate. In New Orleans soon after war's end, black and white levee workers together struck for higher wages, but the police suppressed their attempts to prevent scabs from taking over their jobs. Color prejudice among workers and the tendency of governments to support employers further obstructed labor protests.[75]

Blacks also began efforts at state and national cooperation before the Civil War. In October 1864, 145 black men met at Syracuse, New York, in a national black convention and formed a National Equal Rights League, with branches in every state, to press for abolition, equality before the law, and suffrage. They succeeded in broadening black civil liberties in some northern states, as when in 1865 Ohio and Illinois repealed their discriminatory "black laws" and Massachusetts enacted the first comprehensive public accommodations law.[76] After the war, black men convened in the southern states as well, demanding equal rights and denouncing violence against blacks.

Colonization and Migration

Before, during, and soon after the Civil War, a few colonies run by blacks were started in the southern states—by the federal government, by contrabands, or by other individuals, as at Davis Bend, Mississippi.[77] Davis Bend was owned by Joseph Davis, one of several paternalistic owners who strove to establish model plantations. Davis had invested the money he earned as an attorney in land on the Mississippi River.[78] He took good care of his slaves physically and offered them a degree of self-government and opportunities to learn, earn money, and establish businesses. The slave Ben Montgomery became an exemplar of Davis's system, learning to draw architectural plans, survey land, and function as an engineer and a mechanic. He profitably operated his own store, which catered to both blacks and whites, and participated in plantation management, including planting experimental crops.

When in 1862 the hazards of war forced Davis to flee, the federal government took over the plantation as a haven for freedmen to lease and farm land there. Ben Montgomery and his family, who had gone to Ohio to work in 1862, resumed business at the Bend in early 1864, became leaders of the black lessees, and soon thereafter first leased and then contracted to buy the Bend. They operated it successfully for several years, but in 1876 they had to sell it at auction. The next year Ben's son Isaiah Montgomery founded another black settlement at Mound Bayou, Mississippi, which grew to a self-governing and self-sustaining community of some 4,000 inhabitants.[79]

People migrate out of despair or in the hope of a golden future. After the war, some freedpeople searching for better jobs turned toward the Southwest, where Mississippi, Louisiana, Arkansas, and Texas desperately needed workers. However, few could afford the trip on their own. The Freedmen's Bureau helped many, but others could make the move only through labor agents.[80] Meanwhile, President Johnson was vetoing proposal after proposal that would have opened land for blacks—even one to settle freedpeople along the route of the Union Pacific then being built, thus providing the transcontinental railroad with a constant supply of labor.

Few freedpeople headed to the North, which offered them few jobs, but perhaps 10,000 Kentucky black veterans seized on their commanding officer's offer of transportation for themselves and their families to Ohio, which needed farm workers.[81] Unhappily, during the early 1870s northern employers recruited freedmen as strikebreakers, without warning them of the nature of their employment.

In Shreveport, Louisiana, in 1870 a group of black veterans formed "the Council" or "the Committee," with some 500 members. From 1870 to 1874, it secretly gathered information on the condition of black people. In 1876, the Council appealed to the federal government for protection; if that were impossible, they asked for a territory within the United States to which to move. Next they planned to appeal to foreign governments for refuge.[82]

As Reconstruction waned, blacks despairing of life in the South began to reexamine the possibility of emigration to Africa. Most decided against it, still reluctant to abandon their claim to U.S. citizenship, arguing that if they could not achieve equal rights among whites, the federal government ought to grant them land somewhere else within its borders—in New Mexico or Arizona, perhaps, or homesteads in Nebraska.

Freedmen building railroads were the first to glimpse opportunity in Kansas, where, according to an association of black residents, people remembered their struggle to enter the Union as a free state, when Kansas had "shed too much blood for this cause now to turn back from her soil these defenseless people fleeing from the land of oppression."[83] In the 1870s, a black "Exodus" to that state began, mostly of "Exodusters" from the border states of Kentucky and Tennessee. This movement westward was impelled by men like the former fugitive slave Benjamin "Pap" Singleton, who spent a decade from 1869 to 1879 touting opportunities in Kansas, eventually recruiting 7,432 settlers.[84] In the winter of 1874–75, rumors flew in Tennessee of free transportation, land, and supplies in Kansas. A report authorized by a black convention in Nashville in May 1875 estimated that a prospective settler would need about $1,000, though others optimistically reported that $200 would suffice. During the late 1870s, the governor of Kansas received so many inquiries about black immigration that he developed a standard reply, enclosing a Kansas agricultural report describing farming opportunities and available land types and prices. Excited groups formed emigration clubs.[85] By 1879 freedpeople had established four black colonies in the state, the best known of them Nicodemus. At the start they lived in dugouts amid the prairie grass.[86] Life was far from easy, but the blacks who settled there preferred suffering and freedom to the life forced upon them by "Redeemers." In 1860 Kansas had 627 black inhabitants; in 1870, it had 17,108; and in 1880, the number had grown to 43,107.[87]

DuBois interpreted all these efforts to find black homes as an outcome of the Underground Railroad, which, he wrote, "led directly to various efforts at migration, especially to Canada, and in some cases to Africa. These migrations . . . led to certain Negro towns and settlements."[88]

Chronicle of Events

1865

- In Wilmington, North Carolina, freedpeople form an Equal Rights League.
- *January 16:* Union general William Tecumseh Sherman issues Special Field Order 15, setting aside part of coastal South Carolina, Georgia, and Florida to be settled by blacks.
- *March:* Congress creates the Bureau of Refugees, Freedmen, and Abandoned Lands (the Freedmen's Bureau).
- *March 3:* Congress charters the Freedmen's Bank.
- *April:* Confederate general Robert E. Lee surrenders to Union general Ulysses S. Grant, ending the Civil War.
- *April 14:* President Lincoln is assassinated; Andrew Johnson succeeds him.
- *May:* Massachusetts passes the first comprehensive public accommodations law in the United States.
- *May:* President Johnson announces his plan of Reconstruction.
- *May 9:* President Johnson recognizes the governments of Arkansas, Louisiana, Tennessee, and Virginia.
- *May 12:* Major General Oliver O. Howard is appointed commissioner of the Freedmen's Bureau.
- *May 29:* President Johnson offers amnesty and the return of property to Confederates who will swear allegiance and begins to authorize state constitutional conventions.
- *June:* Mulatto Francis L. Cardozo takes charge of the American Missionary Association's largest school.
- *June 10:* White Louisianan Thomas J. Durant founds the integrated Friends of Universal Suffrage party and calls for total assimilation of blacks.
- *August:* President Johnson announces that black troops will be removed from the South.
- *August–September:* President Johnson orders the restoration of land to its former owners.
- *December:* Congress establishes a Joint Committee on Reconstruction and refuses both to recognize new southern state governments and to seat southern delegates-elect.
- *December 6:* The Thirteenth Amendment is ratified.
- *December 31:* By this time black newspapers are established in Louisiana, Alabama, Tennessee, South Carolina, and Georgia.
- *December 31:* Only 152,000 Union soldiers remain in the South.

1866–1867

- Under the auspices of the American Colonization Society, more than 1,000 blacks sail from Georgia and South Carolina to Liberia.

1866

- Freedmen's Bureau courts are dismantled.
- The Ku Klux Klan is organized in Pulaski, Tennessee.
- For want of money the Savannah Educational Association surrenders its black schools to the American Missionary Association, which replaces black teachers with whites.
- In Pine Bluff, Arkansas, a group sets fire to a black settlement and hangs 24 black women, men, and children.
- In Orangeburg, South Carolina, armed blacks capture and take to the county jail three white terrorists.
- Sharecropping emerges, with both freedmen and poor whites as tenant farmers.
- More than 2,000 freed families acquire title to lands in the Sea Islands of South Carolina and Georgia.
- *January:* Black Georgians organize the Georgia Educational Association.
- *February:* Congress extends the life and powers of the Freedmen's Bureau.
- *March 2:* Congress incorporates Howard University in Washington, D.C., open to all races.
- *April 9–July:* In its first overriding of a presidential veto on a major bill, Congress passes the Civil Rights Act of 1866.
- *May 1:* In Memphis, Tennessee, 46 blacks are killed when their schools and churches are burned.
- *June 13:* Congress approves the Fourteenth Amendment.
- *June 21:* By passing the Southern Homestead Act, Congress opens to both blacks and whites 46 million acres of public lands in Alabama, Mississippi, Louisiana, Arkansas, and Florida, but only about 1,000 freedmen ever gain title.
- *July 16:* Overriding two vetoes by President Johnson, Congress strengthens and enlarges the Freedmen's Bureau, extending its existence to July 1868.
- *July 24:* Tennessee becomes the first state readmitted to the Union.
- *July 30:* A white mob and police in New Orleans storm a Louisiana Republican constitutional convention, killing more than 40 blacks and whites.
- *August:* On a lecture tour through the nation, President Johnson attacks the Freedmen's Bureau.
- Fall: Only 38,000 Union troops remain in the South.

- *September:* The National Loyalist Convention in Philadelphia passes a resolution advocating black suffrage introduced by Frederick Douglass.
- *September:* A National Union Convention in Philadelphia fails to respond to President Johnson's call to form a new national party of moderates and conservatives, but it calls for the election of congressmen to support Johnson's policies.
- *October 2–6:* The Freedmen's Convention in Raleigh, North Carolina, forms an Equal Rights League.
- *November 6:* Texas enacts a law providing separate railroad cars for freedpeople.
- *December:* The U.S. Supreme Court rules in *ex parte Milligan* that military courts cannot try civilians in areas where civil courts remain open and unobstructed.

1867–1868

- The Freedmen's Bureau medical system all but stops functioning.
- President Johnson replaces "radical" commissioners in the Freedmen's Bureau with conservatives.

1867

- In Nashville, Tennessee, convention delegates organize the Ku Klux Klan into the "Invisible Empire of the South."
- Philadelphia integrates public transportation.
- In South Carolina, black Aaron A. Bradley leads armed freedmen in refusing to surrender their claims to land.
- Congress places 10 "unreconstructed" states under military jurisdiction.
- Congress authorizes manhood suffrage in the territories.
- *January:* Tennessee enfranchises blacks but still bars them from office and jury duty.
- *January 1:* Jacksonville, Florida, freedpeople petition Congress for help in getting homesteads and other benefits.
- *January 8:* Over President Johnson's veto, Congress grants black suffrage in the District of Columbia.
- *February 6:* George Peabody, father of modern philanthropy, establishes the Peabody Fund to give challenge grants to local communities for freedmen's schools.
- *March:* Congress passes the Habeas Corpus Act, enabling citizens more easily to take cases to federal courts.
- *March:* Congress abolishes peonage.
- *March 1:* Nebraska acquires statehood.

- *March 2:* Radical Reconstruction begins. Over President Johnson's veto, the Congress passes the Tenure of Office Act, requiring Senate consent to remove officeholders appointed by the president with Senate advice.
- *March 2:* The first Reconstruction Act, passed over President Johnson's veto, sets up military governments in the South and requires states to ratify the Fourteenth Amendment and guarantee universal male suffrage in order to rejoin the Union.
- *March 2:* President Johnson unwillingly signs a bill reducing his authority over the army.
- *March 23:* Congress passes the second Reconstruction Act, instructing military commanders on holding state constitutional conventions, and later overrides President Johnson's veto.
- *May:* The first students enter Howard University, which receives support from the Freedmen's Bureau.
- *May:* Colonel Alcibiade DeBlanc organizes the Knights of the White Camellia, a secret organization whose members support white supremacy.
- *May 1:* After black ride-ins, the Charleston (South Carolina) City Railway Company integrates its streetcars.
- *July:* Congress passes the third Reconstruction Act, empowering military district commanders to remove state officials from office.
- *Fall:* In the constitutional convention elections in Confederate states, 70–90 percent of eligible blacks vote, electing 265 black delegates. The last 10 unreconstructed states vote to hold constitutional conventions.

1868

- The life of the Freedmen's Bureau is extended to 1869.
- Former slave Oscar J. Dunn is elected lieutenant governor of Louisiana.
- When black congressman-elect John W. Menard of Louisiana is barred from his seat, he pleads his case—the first black representative to speak in the House.
- The Avery Normal Institute opens, offering blacks both vocational training and a classical education.
- More rioting erupts in Georgia and Louisiana.
- The governor of Texas organizes a 200-member state police, 40 percent of them black, to suppress the Ku Klux Klan.
- The governor of Arkansas restores order and destroys the Klan by placing 10 counties under martial law and deploying a state militia of blacks and scalawags.
- *February 21:* With congressional support, Secretary of War Edward M. Stanton defies President Johnson's attempt to remove him from office.

- *March:* Congress passes the Fourth Reconstruction Act, permitting state constitutions to be ratified by a simple majority vote.
- *March 28:* The House of Representatives impeaches President Johnson.
- *April:* Founded by Union general Samuel Armstrong to educate blacks and Indians, Hampton Normal Agricultural Institute (later Hampton Institute) opens.
- *May 26:* The Senate acquits President Johnson by one vote.
- *June:* Arkansas and Florida are readmitted to the Union.
- *July 4:* North Carolina is readmitted to the Union.
- *July 7* President Johnson extends his grants of amnesty to include all Confederates.
- *July:* South Carolina, Louisiana, and Alabama are readmitted to the Union.
- *July:* The Fourteenth Amendment is ratified.
- *September:* Georgia's legislature expels its black members.
- *September 19:* In Camilla, Georgia, white townspeople attack a Republican rally, killing nine freedmen and wounding 25–30.
- *September 28:* An estimated 200–300 blacks are massacred in Opelousas, Louisiana.
- *November:* General Ulysses S. Grant is elected president.
- *December 25:* President Johnson again extends his grant of amnesty to include all Confederates.

1869
- Grand Wizard General Nathan B. Forrest disbands the Ku Klux Klan, but its local activities continue.
- The Freedmen's Bureau expires, except for its educational and bounty departments.
- Black undertaker Benjamin "Pap" Singleton begins to lead groups of Tennessee blacks to settle in Kansas.
- South Carolina begins to enact laws requiring equal treatment by places of public accommodation and government-licensed businesses.
- Tennessee replaces its biracial Republican state government with a Democratic "Redeemer" government.
- *January or February:* Tennessee's governor declares martial law in nine counties in the middle and west of the state that were beset by violence.
- *January 13:* Politicians and professional men meet at the Colored National Labor Convention in Washington, D.C.
- *February 26:* Congress approves the Fifteenth Amendment, guaranteeing black Americans the right to vote.

- *April:* In *Texas* v. *White* the U.S. Supreme Court upholds the constitutionality of Congressional Reconstruction.
- *April 6:* President Grant appoints Ebenezer Don Carlos Bassett minister to Haiti, the first black American diplomat and the first black American presidential appointee.
- *July:* Black tradesmen convene in Baltimore, Maryland, to form a state organization.

1870–71
- House and Senate committees investigate the Ku Klux Klan.

1870–1884
- Eleven southern states ban miscegenation.

1870
- The Ku Klux Klan and similar organizations probe new depths of terrorism against blacks and white Republicans.
- President Ulysses S. Grant signs a proclamation demanding respect for the civil rights of all Americans.
- The Knights of the White Camellia effectively ceases to exist.
- Freeborn Susan M. Smith (later McKinney-Steward) becomes the first black woman to earn a medical degree in New York.
- Congress imposes new conditions for readmission to the Union, barring attempts to constitutionally abridge the right to vote, hold office, or deny citizens access to education.
- James W. Smith becomes the first African American to enter West Point.
- *January 26:* Virginia is readmitted to the Union.
- *February 23:* Mississippi is readmitted to the Union.
- *February 25:* Hiram R. Revels of Mississippi takes his seat as the first black U.S. senator.
- *March 30:* Texas is readmitted to the Union.
- *March 30:* The 15th Amendment is ratified.
- *April:* Congress passes the Ku Klux Klan Act, designating as federal offenses certain crimes committed to deny civil rights.
- *April 9:* The American Anti-Slavery Society dissolves.
- *May:* Congress passes the first Enforcement Act, authorizing election supervisors to sue state officials who discriminate racially against voters.
- *July 15:* Georgia is readmitted to the Union.
- *October:* Whites assault a Republican rally at Eutaw, Alabama, killing four blacks and wounding 54.

This poster celebrates the signing of the Fifteenth Amendment. Frederick Douglass is seated at the far right of the table. Robert Smalls stands behind Abraham Lincoln and U. S. Grant. Hiram Rhoades Revels, elected to the U.S. Senate in 1870, is the third black man. Note the celebration of black troops in the Union navy and army and at the battles of Port Hudson and Petersburg. *(Library of Congress)*

- *October:* In Laurens County, South Carolina, whites drive 150 freedpeople from their homes and murder 13.
- *December 12:* Joseph H. Rainey of South Carolina becomes the first black member of the U.S. House of Representatives.

1871

- Frederick Douglass accepts the presidency of the Freedmen's Bank.
- Texas requires state railroads to integrate.
- *March:* In Meridian, Mississippi, a Republican judge and some 30 blacks are murdered.
- *April:* Congress passes the second Enforcement Act (Ku Klux Klan Act) to protect black suffrage and target anti–civil rights conspiracies.
- *May 12:* In Louisville, Kentucky, a black teenager's sit-in leads to streetcar integration.

- *September:* In Nashville, Kentucky, Carl Schurz voices liberal Republican opinions, advocating amnesty, no more federal intervention, and local government by propertied businessmen.
- *October 6:* The Jubilee Singers of Fisk University tour the nation to support the financially failing black university.
- *October 12:* President Grant orders the Ku Klux Klan in South Carolina to disperse and surrender arms.
- *October 17:* President Grant suspends habeas corpus in nine South Carolina counties and thereafter sends federal troops to the state and prosecutes white supremacist terrorism.

1872

- The educational work of the Freedmen's Bureau ends, and its responsibility for paying veterans' bounties is transferred to the adjutant general's office.

In this 1871 southern view of Reconstruction, President Ulysses S. Grant and Congress ignore the "Murder of Lousiana sacrificed on the altar of radicalism." Carpetbagger William P. Kellogg holds up the heart that he has extracted from the female figure of Louisiana, who is held down by two freedmen. At right women representing secessionist states mourn, with the kneeling South Carolina in chains. *(Library of Congress, Prints and Photographs Division, LC-USZ62-8788)*

- George Pullman integrates railroad sleeping cars after public protests when the Fisk University Jubilee Singers are refused accommodation.
- *February 27:* Professor Charlotte Ray of Howard University is admitted to the District of Columbia Bar, becoming the first certified black woman lawyer in the United States.
- *April:* The National Convention of Colored Men meets in New Orleans.
- *May 22:* The Congressional Amnesty Act restores the right to hold office to almost all southern leaders excluded from office by the Fourteenth Amendment.
- *November:* President Grant is reelected.
- *December:* Louisiana's black lieutenant governor Pinckney Benton Stewart Pinchback serves as acting governor during the governor's impeachment trial.

1873
- Black lawmakers in Florida, Louisiana, and Mississippi manage to enact civil rights laws.
- *January:* Among southern state governments, Republicans firmly control only Arkansas, Louisiana, Mississippi, and South Carolina.
- *April:* In Louisiana, many white parishes [counties] refuse to recognize the state government and to collect state taxes.

- *April 13:* In Colfax, Louisiana, a clash between blacks and whites over 1872 elections kills three white men and some 100 black militiamen, of whom nearly half are shot or hanged after they surrender.
- *April 14:* In the *Slaughterhouse* cases the U.S. Supreme Court rules that the Fourteenth Amendment has "nothing to do" with rights remaining under state control.
- *June:* At Boston's World's Peace Jubilee, the Fisk University Jubilee Singers perform Julia Ward Howe's "Battle Hymn of the Republic" with a thousand-piece orchestra, a chorus of 10,000 and a battery of cannon.
- *August:* In Red River Parish, Louisiana, a reign of terror culminates in the murder of six Republican officials.
- *September:* The Panic of 1873 begins an economic depression that bottoms out in 1878.

1874
- The New England Freedmen's Aid Society disbands.
- *January 14:* African American I. D. Shadd is elected speaker of the Mississippi House of Representatives.
- *April:* The paramilitary white-supremacist White League forms.
- *May:* President Grant refuses to help local Arkansas Republicans in a struggle over the governorship.
- *May:* The U.S. Senate passes a civil rights bill outlawing racial discrimination in public places, jury selection, public schools, and cemeteries, but the House of Representatives postpones consideration.
- *June 28:* The Freedmen's Bank suspends operations.
- *summer:* Vicksburg, Mississippi, residents organize a White Man's party, while White Leagues strive to clear out "all bad and leading Negroes . . . and control . . . more strictly our tenants and other hands."
- *September 14:* In New Orleans, 3,500 White Leaguers defeat black militia and metropolitan police to take over the city hall, statehouse, and arsenal and are dislodged only by federal troops.
- *November:* Mid-term elections end Republican control of the U.S. House of Representatives.
- *November 3:* In Eufaula, Alabama, whites kill seven unarmed would-be black voters, wound some 70 others, kill a scalawag judge's son, and burn the ballot box.
- *December:* In Vicksburg, Mississippi, black sheriff Peter Crosby is forced to flee, setting off a battle in which whites murder about 300 blacks.
- *December 2:* A black convention in Montgomery, Alabama, organizes an emigration association to settle colored families in the Far West.

1875–1876

- In Mississippi, whites control black voting by attacking black political rallies and killing Republican leaders.

1875

- Race riots break out in Yazoo City, Mississippi.
- The founding of *The Negro World* ends Missouri's status as the only former slave state lacking a black paper.
- Eight blacks serve in Congress, a Reconstruction peak.
- In the Jurisdiction and Removal Act, Congress makes it easier for citizens to assert federal rights in federal courts.
- *January:* After whites murder some 300 blacks in Vicksburg, Mississippi, federal troops restore black sheriff Peter Crosby to office.
- *February:* A congressional committee effects a compromise in a disputed Louisiana election but deplores the "premature" enfranchisement of blacks.
- *March 1:* Congress enacts a civil rights act guaranteeing equal rights to blacks in public accommodations and jury duty, but it is never enforced and in 1883 the Supreme Court declares it unconstitutional.
- *September:* In Clinton, Mississippi, Democrats assault a Republican barbecue and whites roam the countryside shooting blacks.
- *October:* Former Mississippi governor James L. Alcorn organizes an attack on a Republican meeting, killing six blacks and two or three whites.
- *October:* The Grant administration fails to respond to Mississippi governor Adelbert Ames's requests for federal intervention to subdue violence.

1876

- Nearly half of all southern children are now in school.
- South Carolina's public Land Commission has settled 14,000 black families, a seventh of the black population, on their own homesteads.
- The Electoral College fails to elect either Samuel Tilden (Democrat) or Rutherford B. Hayes (Republican).
- Mississippi whites impeach their black lieutenant-governor and oust their white Republican governor.
- Aiming to control vagrant blacks, Mississippi enacts a "Pig Law," making stealing a pig grand larceny.
- Blacks are excluded from crews constructing the Philadelphia Centennial Exposition.
- In *U.S. v. Reese* the U.S. Supreme Court rules unconstitutional an Alabama law that would send a convict unable to pay his fine or court costs to a chain gang or release him into the custody of someone willing to pay his debt.

- In *U.S. v. Cruikshank*, the U.S. Supreme Court overturns the convictions of three whites accused of participating in the Colfax Riot.
- Race riots break out in Charleston and Cainhoy, South Carolina.
- Edward Bouchet earns a doctorate in physics from Yale University, becoming the first black to earn a Ph.D. from any American university.
- *March:* Black emigration from Tennessee to Kansas increases.
- *April:* In Nashville, Tennessee, the National Convention of Colored Men debates migration.
- *May:* Day laborers on several plantations in South Carolina successfully strike for higher wages and payment in cash.
- *May:* Congress repeals the Southern Homestead Act of 1866.
- *summer:* President Grant sends federal troops to end race riots and black terrorism in South Carolina.
- *July 8:* In a Hamburg, South Carolina, clash, six black militiamen and one white Democrat are killed, and a mob vandalizes black homes and shops.

THE NEW ERA.

GENERAL WADE HAMPTON (*to influential colored voter*). "Of course you'll *Dine* with me on Thursday?"

COLORED VOTER. "Not on Phursday, Massa HAMPTON. On Phursday I'se promised to *Sleep* with Massa PINCKNEY."

This 1867 drawing, called "The New Era," ridicules the dilemma of white southern politicians, now forced to woo the black voter. The freedman refuses the dinner invitation of former slave owner and Confederate general Wade Hampton. *(Library of Congress, Prints and Photographs Division, LC-USZ62-33264)*

- *September:* Black Republicans in Charleston, South Carolina, assault black and white Democrats.
- *October:* Blacks fire at a meeting in Cainhoy, South Carolina; five blacks and one white are killed.
- *October and November:* South Carolina Democratic candidate Confederate General Wade Hampton is elected governor after his supporters impose a reign of terror.
- *October 17:* President Grant orders white terrorist "rifle clubs" in South Carolina to disperse.

1877

- Reconstruction ends as the Compromise of 1877 makes Republican Rutherford B. Hayes president, in exchange for the withdrawal of federal troops from the South and the cessation of federal efforts to protect black civil rights.
- President Hayes appoints African American Frederick Douglass marshall of the District of Columbia.
- North Carolina's Landlord and Tenant Act places the entire crop in the planter's hands until rent has been paid and allows him to determine when that point is reached.
- *June 15:* Henry O. Flipper becomes the first black American to graduate from West Point.
- *July:* Thirty black Kentuckians settle at Nicodemus, Kansas.

Eyewitness Testimony

Postwar Chaos

History does not record where four millions of people had been held in slavery so long, that they had lost all knowledge of the way to provide for their own support, to expend their earnings to advantage, to use economy in purchasing necessaries of life and to lay up for another day. This was the condition of the Colored people at the close of the war. They were set free without a dollar, without a foot of land, and without the wherewithal to get the next meal even. . . . It does seem to me, that a Christian Nation, which had received such wealth from the labor of a subjugated people, upon setting them free would, at least, have given them a square meal. Justice seems to demand one year's support, forty acres of land and a mule each. . . . Four million people turned loose without a dollar and told to "Root hog or die!"

Freedman Henry Bruce, describing conditions in 1865, in Bruce, New Man, *116–17. Available online at URL:* http://docsouth.unc.edu/bruce/bruce. html#bruce112.

With her [North Carolina's] homesteads burned to ashes, with fields desolated, with thousands of her noblest and bravest children sleeping in beds of slaughter; innumerable orphans, widows, and helpless persons, reduced to beggary and deprived of their natural protectors; her corporations bankrupt and her own credit gone; her public charities overthrown, her educational fund utterly lost, her land filled from end to end with her maimed and mutilated soldiers; denied all representation in the public councils, her heart-broken and wretched people are not only oppressed with the weight of their own indebtedness, but are crushed into the very dust by taxation for the mighty debt incurred as the cost of their own subjugation! The very race of beasts of burthen,—by which alone we could extort bread from the half-tilled earth,—was, at the close of hostilities, almost destroyed; leaving us destitute of even the means of labor! . . . The best test of the best heroism *now,* is a cheerful and loyal submission to the powers and events established by our defeat, and a ready obedience to the Constitution and laws of our country.

Former governor of North Carolina Zebulon Vance, "The Duties of Defeat," 1866. Available online at URL: http:// docsouth.unc.edu/nc/vance/vance.html.

On March 22, 1866, my father and myself left the North. . . . I can hardly give a true idea of how crushed and sad the people are. You hear no bitterness towards the North; they are too sad to be bitter; their grief is overwhelming. . . . [T]he women live in the past, and the men only in the daily present, trying, in a listless sort of way, to repair their ruined fortunes. . . .

. . . [My father] had found the negroes all on the place, not only those who were there five years ago, but many who were sold three years before that. . . . They received him very affectionately, and made an agreement with him to work for one half the crop, which agreement it remained to be seen if they would keep. . . . Our overseer, who was responsible for all our property, has little or nothing to give us back, while everything that was left in charge of the negroes has been taken care of and given back to us without the hope or wish of reward. . . . [W]hat is to be done with the old people who are too old, and the children who are too young, to work? . . . [M]ost of the planters are utterly ruined and have no money to buy food for their own families.

Plantation mistress Frances Butler Leigh, Ten Years, *5–25, passim. Available online at URL:* http://docsouth.unc. edu/leigh/leigh.html.

Reconstruction Government

Political reconstruction is inevitable now, but social reconstruction, we have in our hands, and can prevent.

Mary Lee, Winchester, Virginia, Spring 1865, quoted on Public Broadcasting System program "American Experience: Reconstruction: White Men Unite." Available online at URL: http://www.pbs.org/wgbh/amex/reconstruction/ kkk/sf_klan.html.

I think the utter subversion of our political and social systems and sudden enfranchisement of four million slaves a great crime, and one of the most terrible calamities that ever befell any people. . . . [N]othing but intense hatred and vindictive rage could have so blinded the North to its own interests and [to] those of humanity, as to induce the consummation of this act of wickedness and folly. I look for nothing but evil to both blacks and whites in the South . . . ; intestine feuds and tumults; torpid indolence and stealthy rapacity on the part of the blacks; jealousy, distrust and oppression of them on the part of the whites; mutual outrage and injury, disquiet, apprehensions, alarms, murders, robberies, house-burnings, and other crimes; the blighting of hearts and homes and the destruction of industry, arts, literature, wealth, comfort and happiness. . . . *Their professed deliverers will prove the real destroyers of the negroes in the end.* [italics in original]

> *Imprisoned Confederate senator and agent Clement C. Clay, Jr., letter to his wife, August 11, 1865, in Sterling,* Belle of the Fifties, *294–95.*

Slavery . . . is so strong that it could exist, not only without law, but even against law. Custom, manners, morals, religion, are all on its side everywhere in the South; and when you add the ignorance and servility of the ex-slave to the intelligence and accustomed authority of the master, you have the conditions . . . under which it is impossible for the Federal government to wholly destroy it, unless the Federal government be armed with despotic power, to blot out State authority, and to station a Federal officer at every cross-road.

This, of course, cannot be done, and ought not even if it could. The true way and the easiest way is to make our government entirely consistent with itself, and give to every loyal citizen the elective franchise,—a right and power which will be ever present, and will form a wall of fire for his protection.

> *Frederick Douglass, "Reconstruction," Atlantic Monthly 1866. Available online at URL:* http://classiclit. about.com/library/bl-etexts/fdouglass/bl-fdoug-reconstruction.htm.

The great issue has been and still is the question of reconstruction. Lifting the Negro from slavery to citizenship and establishing governments with the colored man as a voter has aroused the dying hate of the kuklux democracy. . . . Had I seen fit . . . to pander to their prejudices, by betraying the principles of the republican party and shutting my eyes to a palpable violation of the laws and the wrong and injustice done by their expulsion of the colored members of the legislature . . . I would not only have escaped this ordeal, but these persons would have been as loud and intemperate in their praise, as they are now in their denunciation of me.

> *Northern-born Confederate veteran Rufus Brown Bullock, governor of Georgia 1868–70, at the 1876 trial that exonerated him of charges of corruption, conspiracy to defraud, and malfeasance. Available online at URL:* http://www. georgiaencyclopedia.org/nge/Article.jsp?id=h-2892.

General Chalmers . . . said . . . that the president was without power and influence in his party, that the legislature had made a mistake in refusing to ratify the fourteenth amendment, that it would be forced on the state, and indeed it was only the logical sequence to the freedom of the negro, and the success of the federal government, and resistance to the policy of the dominant party in this matter, was more like a childish display of spite, than a thoughtful, earnest desire and purpose to bring the state into full accord with the government as it was hereafter to be conducted; and that the certain consequence of this course would be to bring harsher and severer measures, since it would be construed to mean that we were still in a rebellious mood . . . , [that the legislature] was weakening the influence of our friends and of the moderate men in the Republican party, and giving our enemies just what they wanted, an excuse for the violent and extreme course they had determined on.

> *Confederate veteran Mississippian Frank A. Montgomery, remembering the late 1860s, in* Reminiscences, *264. Available online at URL:* http://docsouth.unc.edu/ montgomery/montgom.html#montgomery262.

The passage of the Fifteenth Amendment will give a legal finish to the Anti-Slavery work; but if the soldiers of Freedom disband and lay aside their uniform, they should be careful to turn their telescopes very frequently toward the country of the old enemy. . . . The experience of many years shows the necessity of distrusting the professions of Southerners, and of watching their policy very closely; not because they are worse than other men would be under similar circumstances, but simply because the effects of a system so despotic and so false as Slavery cannot be wiped away by legal enactments from the souls of a generation that have grown up under its malign influence.

> *Abolitionists David L. and Lydia Maria Child, "A Few Words about the Standard," December 25, 1869, quoted in Karcher,* The First Woman in the Republic, *537–38.*

[The Fourteenth and Fifteenth amendments] may stand forever, but we intend . . . to make them dead letters on the statute-book.

> *A Southern newspaper, 1875, quoted in Foner,* Reconstruction, *590.*

Certainly reconstruction is null and void in Georgia. . . . That there have been instances of glaring injustice practiced on both sides no fair-minded man can for an instant doubt. The Republican administration lasted scarcely three years; and the legitimate results of the war were not maintained so long as that after 1868. Out of the 90,000 colored voters in the State, scarcely 30,000 vote to-day; free schools are almost unknown outside the large cities and towns; and there has not been a Republican inspector of election since the Democrats assumed power. To judge from the testimony of native Georgians who are Republicans, and who have never been suspected of any dishonesty or untruth, the negroes are very grossly intimidated; and the Ku-Klux faction still exists as a kind of invisible empire.

Traveler Edward King, 1875, The Great South, *354. Available online at URL:* http://docsouth.unc.edu/nc/ king/king.html#p204.

I, of course, am an ignorant man, of African descent, but I have learned many things from the white folks. I learned one thing from Judge Redding, who was my paid attorney; that was, that a Northern Yankee lawyer is very uncertain when he could rob a poor ignorant colored man, his wife and children, to enrich his pompous son-in-law, L. B. Ray, the man I voted for to go to the Legislature to make laws. I am mighty sorry now I did it, but you see they fools me, as they are foolin' all our colored people, and makes us believe they freed us, and that they are our special friends. Well, they is not, only to get our labor; they's no friend of the colored man. They gets us here, and makes great big promises, and when we gets something they comes in and steals it—gets us to sign papers we don't understand, and then takes all. . . .

Freedman Norvel Blair, writing about the years following 1863, Book for the People, *11–12. Available online at URL:* http://docsouth.unc.edu/neh/blair/blair.html.

Carpetbaggers

[T]hese same laborers [artisans?] or mechanics in search of a job, will go South, where the Colored men have charge of such work, or nearly so, and will not only work with them, but hire to them and be bossed by them. Foreigners, seeking employment, have gone to the South in large numbers during the last five years, and finding there the typical poor whites, who are the ancient enemies of the Colored people and ever ready to do them harm, have united with them on the color line and raised that old familiar cry that "this is a white man's country, that white men must and shall rule it; no Negro domination over white men."

Freedman Henry Bruce, describing postwar conditions, New Man, *121–22. Available online at URL:* http:// docsouth.unc.edu/bruce/bruce.html#bruce112.

Shortly after the war, old man Roebuck came from Ohio. . . . Roebuck came down to shed the light of

the gospel on poor benighted freedmen and southern whites, teach them religion by example, and incidentally make a little money by farming. . . . He farmed the year through and the darkeys stole his corn and cotton from the fields at night, so that the old man lost money, and . . . faith in his ability to change the leopard's spots, so that he sold out and went back to Ohio a wiser and sadder man.

Southern attorney W. R. Houghton, "An Incident of the Reconstruction Era," in Houghton and Houghton, Two Boys, *97–99. Available online at URL:* http://docsouth.unc. edu/houghton/houghton.html.

Is it not time for the colored race to stop playing baby? The whites of America have done nobly in outgrowing the old prejudices against them. They cannot hurry this process by law. Let them obtain social equality as every other man, woman, and child obtain it—by showing themselves in their lives the social equal of those with whom they wish to consort.

Chicago Tribune, *early 1870s, quoted on Public Broadcasting System, "The American Experience: Reconstruction, The Negro Question." Available online at URL:* http://www.pbs.org/wgbh/amex/ reconstruction/nast/index.html.

[N]o one not brought up with the negroes can understand their peculiarities, and a Northern man, with every desire to be just and kind, invariably fails from not understanding their character.

Plantation mistress Frances Butler Leigh, Ten Years, *225. Available online at URL:* http://docsouth.unc.edu/ leigh/leigh.html.

Our leading men [near Darien, Georgia,] are the timber merchants, amongst whom are a Northerner, an Irish Canadian, a German, and a Scotchman. They have all come here to make their fortunes, and when they have made them mean to pack up their chattels and go off. . . . Whilst residing here they do a good deal for the place, and not the least of their meritorious acts is the building of a Protestant Episcopal Church.

J. W. Leigh, British husband of plantation mistress Frances Butler Leigh, 1870s, "Appendix," in Ten Years, *300–1. Available online at URL:* http://docsouth.unc.edu/ leigh/leigh.html.

And as for the "carpet baggers," so called, I cannot understand how the reconstruction of the Southern States could have taken place in accordance with legal requirements without their assistance; and the South is to this day indebted to these same men for some of her most substantial improvement, and much of the energy and business vitality enjoyed by her.

Free black Ohio-bred John Patterson Green, who lived in the Reconstruction South for three years, Recollections, *116–18. Available online at URL:* http://docsouth.unc.edu/southlit/green/green.html.

Freedmen's Bureau

Since we are to be remarried and obtain new lisence, I wish to know if we have the same right to make a marriage contract as a white couple would.

Freedman Philip H. Jones, letter to Freedmen's Bureau commissioner O. O. Howard, 1865, quoted in Zipf, "Reconstructing 'Free Woman,'" 6.

People say that you are too lazy to work, that you have not the intelligence to get on for yourselves. They have often told you, Sam, you lazy nigger, you don't earn your salt. . . . You men and women, every one of you around me, made thousands and thousands of dollars. Only you were the means for your master to lead the idle and inglorious life, and to give his children the education which he denied to you.

Freedman Bureau black representative Major Martin Delany, address on St. Helena Island, South Carolina, July 23, 1865. Available online at URL: http://www.pbs.org/wgbh/amex/reconstruction/40acres/ps_delany.html.

Slavery has passed away, and you are now placed on trial. . . . Some of you have the mistaken notion that freedom means liberty to be idle. . . . You must not believe the idle and malicious stories that have been told you by bad men as to what the Government intends to do for you. . . . Neither rations, nor clothing, nor mules, nor working implements will be given to you hereafter. *No land will be given to you.* [italics in original]

General James S. Fullerton, director of the Louisiana Freedman's Bureau appointed by President Johnson, "Address to the Freedmen of Louisiana," November 1865, quoted in Tunnell, Edge, 95.

The Rebbles are going a bout in many places through [Mississippi] and robbing the colered peple of arms money and all they have and in many places killing. . . . [T]he safety of this country depenes upon giving the Colered man all the rights of a white man, and especialy the Rebs

In this 1894 Thomas Nast cartoon captioned "The Union as it was—The lost cause, worse than slavery," white supremacist figures shake hands above a shield depicting an African-American couple cradling a baby—perhaps dead. *(Library of Congress, Prints and Photographs Division, LC-USZ62-128619)*

and let him know that their is power enough in the arm of the Government to give Justice, to all her loyal citizens. . . . [N]ow if you have any true harted men send them down here to carry out your wishes through the bureau . . . [or] get Congress to stick in a few competent colered men as they did in the army.

Black private Calvin Holly to Freedmen's Bureau's O. O. Howard, December 1865, in Berlin et al., Free at Last, 523–25 passim.

I find without exception the vicious and idle [whom the employing planters want to dismiss] are those who have the largest families of small children, for many of whom I can only see starvation without government aid.

Freedmen's Bureau agent Marshall Twitchell, December 1, 1865, in Tunnell, Edge, 97.

I am *tired out* and *broke down.* . . . Every day for 6 months, day after day, I have had from 5 to 20 complaints, *generally trivial* and of no moment, yet requiring consideration & attention coming from both Black & White. . . . The result is my time is consumed, and I virtually become a "pack horse" for the whole county.

Freedmen's Bureau Georgia agent James Davison, ca. 1866, quoted in Cimbala, Under the Guardianship of the Nation, *64–65.*

No labor is to be performed by hand that can better be done by animal labor or machinery. All damage for injury or loss of property by carelessness is to be paid by fair and legal assessments. All Thanksgiving, Fast Days, "Holidays" and National Celebration Days are to be enjoyed . . . without being regarded as a neglect of duty or violation of contract. Good conduct and good behavior of the Freedmen toward the proprietor; good treatment of animals; and good care of tools, utensils, etc; and good and kind treatment of the Proprietor to the Freedmen, will be strictly required by the Authorities. No stores will be permitted on the place and nothing sold on account except the necessaries of life. . . . Spirituous liquors will not be permitted. In all cases where an accusation is made against a person, the Proprietor or his Agent, [and] one of the Freedmen selected by themselves, and a third person chosen by the two shall be a council to investigate the accused.

Freedmen's Bureau black agent Martin Delany, model provisions for sharecropping contracts, ca. 1866. Available online at URL: http://www.pbs.org/wgbh/amex/ reconstruction/sharecrop/ps_delany2.html.

Should the [Freedmen's] Bureau be withdrawn, not ten colored men would take notice of it or find anything changed. Planters alone would lose. For the machinery of the Bureau is now used by them to intimidate the uneducated blacks, and to make the most of their contracts.

New Orleans Tribune, *April 29, 1866, quoted in Houzeau,* Passage, *45.*

The Misses Cooke's school, Freedmen's Bureau, Richmond, Virginia, is shown in *Frank Leslie's Illustrated Newspaper. (Library of Congress, Prints and Photographs Division, LC-USZ62-121633)*

In many counties . . . there is still great bitterness of feeling against the schools . . . and bands of K.K.K. armed and disguised men, have committed most atrocious outrages. About the last of November Mr. R. H. Gladdings who has been teaching . . . at Greensboro, Green Co. [Georgia] was driven away.

Agent J. K. Lewis, letter to the Freedmen's Bureau, 1870, quoted in Katz, Eyewitness, *278.*

We do not object, to the presence of the negro in the parish jury, we complain because nine out of ten who sit upon the jury are ignorant and have no property at all, and yet are permitted to judge of what is best for the interests of property-holders. We are often compelled to submit questions of vital importance to the judgment of irresponsible and suspicious fellows, who . . . seem to think it their bounden duty to do nothing for our material well-being. But such men as Dave Young do some good. They are teaching the negroes a little prudence and moderation. I would rather have a nigger like David, than a white man like—[a carpetbagger].

Louisiana planter's comment, quoted by traveler Edward King, 1875, The Great South, *296. Available online at URL:* http://docsouth.unc.edu/nc/king/king.html#p204.

Freedpeople: Politics

I saw no chance, of bettering the condition of the freedman, until he should . . . become a citizen, and . . . there was no safety for him or for anybody else in America, outside of the American government. . . . if the Negro knows enough to fight for his country, he knows enough to vote; if he knows enough to pay taxes to support the government, he knows enough to vote; if he knows as much when sober as an Irishman knows when he is drunk, he knows enough to vote.

Frederick Douglass, n.d., quoted in Washington, Frederick Douglass, *258–59. Available online at URL:* http://docsouth.unc.edu/neh/doug1906/doug1906.html.

I shall have to admit that I was a "Sherman Cutloose" (. . . a term applied in derision by Some of the Negroes who were *free before* the war,—To those who were *freed* by the war).

Sam Aleckson, speaking of 1865, in his [alleged] autobiography, Before the War. *Available online at URL:* http://docsouth.unc.edu/neh/aleckson/aleckson.html#aleck17.

At my last road working, when I dismissed the hands for the year, I informed them that they (the colored men) would be allowed to vote and that when the time came, they would be in great danger from two extreme parties. One party would put them back in slavery if they could; the other would crowd them forward into position so much faster than their education and experience of affairs of government would justify that the injury would be nearly as great.

Union veteran and former Freedmen's Bureau agent Marshall Twitchell, speaking of March 1867, quoted in Tunnell, Edge, *120.*

But the Congress passed [the Reconstruction Bill of March 1867], providing for a registration of Negroes, with the avowed purpose of conferring on them the right to vote and hold office, and at the same time depriving many of the white people of these rights. . . . This filled to overflowing the cup of bitterness the south was called upon to drink, for it is impossible to conceive that the ingenuity of hate could have devised anything which would have so humiliated the white people of the state.

Mississippian Frank Alexander Montgomery, Reminiscences, *263 69. Available online at URL:* http://docsouth.unc.edu/montgomery/montgom.html#montgomery262.

We used to go into the swamps to hold [meetings], and we had a house where we could meet, with no lamps or anything. . . . Some said not to go to the polls; some said they would go; some said they were afraid to go, and some said they . . . would go if they got killed. . . . [The next day the clerk of the election] told me, "We beat you badly yesterday." I says, "No, you didn't; you polled forty-seven votes." He says, "It was you polled forty-seven votes, and we polled three hundred. You all voted democratic votes." . . . [At the election the whites] . . . met the colored people, and would not allow them to come with arms; and the white people kept on theirs, and that scared the colored people. . . . Mr. Henderson told me that I would have to shut my mouth, and I told him that I thought they were going to let us have a fair election; and they said it was a fair election, only the fuss I was making.

D. J. Foreman, black Republican leader, testifying to a Senate committee about his district, which registered 300 Republicans and 47 Democrats, n.d., in Katz, Eyewitness, *283–84.*

The constitution was ratified and a legislature formed in which were several colored members. The Fourteenth

Entitled "Everything points to a Democratic victory this fall–Southern Papers," this 1874 cartoon shows White League members ready to drive freedmen away from the polls. *(Library of Congress, Prints and Photographs Division, LC-USZ62-127754)*

Amendment was adopted, and Georgia was ready for formal admission into the Union. In July, 1868, . . . the Republican Party of the State was organized. I wrote the platform, and in November of that year I cast my first ballot for President . . . "for Grant and Colfax, the Republican nominees. . . ." Georgia went Democratic, for by that time the enemies of reconstruction had adopted an active policy.

The Republican Party of Georgia attempted a conciliatory program [trying to hold] the "wool hat" boys, the non-slave-holding whites of north Georgia. . . . The compromise ended as might have been easily forecast. The colored members were expelled from the legislature, and ku-kluxism became a terror and a power. Floggings and assassinations were frequent; leaders in politics were served with notices to leave the State. Although by no means prominent as a political leader, I had attracted sufficient attention to be favored with one of these missives.

Black pastor Theophilus G. Steward, remembering 1868,
Fifty Years, *128. Available online at URL:* http://
docsouth.unc.edu/church/steward/steward.html.

It seemed to me two thirds [of the 1870 Mississippi legislature] were negroes, including in that term every shade of color which showed a trace of negro blood. A few of these had been slaves, and were without education, but the majority I think, were carpet-baggers, like the most of their white associates. White men and negroes walked arm in arm or side by side, and the sight was stranger to me than the transformation of King George's portrait into that of General Washington. . . .

Confederate veteran Mississippian Frank A. Montgomery,
remembering 1870, Reminiscences, *274–75.*
Available online at URL: http://docsouth.
unc.edu/montgomery/montgom.
html#montgomery262.

In 1871 I went South to organize schools and teach the freedmen, and in 1873 took up my residence in Newberry County, South Carolina, where, in January of the following year, after a rigid examination, and in the face of strong opposition from the Southern white lawyers, I was licensed to practise law in the courts of that state. About the same time I was appointed a trial justice for the county. . . . I had neither attended a law school nor received private instruction; yet I am led to believe that my success at the bar was not altogether discreditable.

In the autumn of 1876 I was elected a member of the legislature of South Carolina, and when that body convened I was made chairman of its leading committees. It may be added, as an historical fact, that during the stormy period that ensued, my services contributed in no slight measure to the settlement of the presidential issue of that year. About the same time that I was elected a state representative I was admitted to practise before the state Supreme Court, and also commissioned a colonel of the National Guard.

I have never regarded the political rights of the freedman as essential to his well-being. . . . When . . . the existing Republican governments of the South were overthrown, . . . I gave up the practice of law, and withdrew from active participation in politics, [to] devote my chief attention to the educational and social advancement of the freedmen. . . . I built churches, established schoolhouses, and created facilities for primary instruction in localities where such were before unknown.

Free black William Hannibal Thomas, 1871–76,
in Thomas, The American Negro, *xvi–xviii. Available*
online at URL: http://docsouth.unc.edu/church/
thomas/thomas.html.

But with us, while of course everyone did the best he could for his party, there was not the least ill-feeling between the blacks and the whites, and the election [of 1872] passed off without any trouble of any sort, which is a noteworthy fact in itself, as our county is one of the two in Georgia where the negroes outnumber the whites ten to one, and in more than one instance a negro was elected to office by the white democratic votes.

Plantation mistress Frances Butler Leigh, Ten Years, *221–22. Available online at URL:* http://docsouth.unc. edu/leigh/leigh.html.

[T]he negroes do not vote; on some [plantations] they are even hired with the distinct understanding that they shall *not,* unless they wish to be discharged. But sooner or later the politicians reach them.

Traveler Edward King, 1875, The Great South, *273–75. Available online at URL:* http://docsouth.unc.edu/nc/ king/king.html#p204.

[T]he era of carpet bag and negro rule lasted for ten years [1865–1877]. . . . [To] break up this infamous domination the southern people resorted in many places to taking forcible possession of the ballot boxes, substitution and destruction of ballots and many other devices. In many precincts where the negroes were in the majority the whites would not open the polls and they did not have sufficient intelligence to conduct an election themselves. However they never failed to turn out in great numbers to vote or try to vote. It was only a question of time after the withdrawal of military authority that the intelligent white man would overcome the brutal and ignorant black. . . . [Reconstruction was] more diabolical than the emancipation proclamation during hostilities which seemed intended to incite insurrection in the south and cause the slaughter of the women and children while their protectors were at the front fighting back the invaders of their country.

M. B. Houghton, "Reconstruction," in Houghton and Houghton, Two Boys, *56. Available online at URL:* http:// docsouth.unc.edu/houghton/houghton.html.

Cato ran away and was gone over two months before they knew what had become of him. . . . [H]e wrote back to a friendly white man that lived in the neighborhood. . . . The white man was from the North, and was very friendly to us colored people, but he had to be mighty careful about showing it. . . . He was the one that helped Cato to make his escape. . . . He bargained with a ship-master to take Cato from Charleston to Boston, . . . packed in a box and shipped for a box of cabbage. . . . [He] notified the Underground Railroad people in Boston of the time when Cato would reach Boston, so that they might get him and run him off into Canada. . . .

[There Cato] fell in among good people. . . . He soon got a good education and plenty of property. When the war broke out he came back to Boston, joined the Union army, and came South and fought in some of the hardest battles of the war. . . . [Two years ago I learned] that Cato was then living in Vicksburg, and was one of the greatest leaders of his race in Mississippi. He had been sheriff of his county, had been a senator, and had served his State in Congress and in several other stations of honor and trust.

Freedman "Uncle Cephas," n.d., in Albert, House of Bondage, *121–22. Available online at URL:* http://docsouth.unc.edu/neh/albert/albert. html#albert119.

The negroes came into power [in Natchez, Mississippi,] in 1867. The present Sheriff, the County Treasurer and Assessor, the majority of the magistrates, and all the officers managing county affairs, except one, are negroes. The Board of Aldermen has three negroes in it. There is the usual complaint among the Conservatives that money has been dishonestly and foolishly expended; but the government of the city seemed, on the whole, very satisfactory. About a thousand children are at school in the public schools, and four hundred of them,—the colored pupils,—have a handsome new school-house.

Traveler Edward King, reporting 1875, The Great South, *293–95. Available online at URL:* http://docsouth.unc. edu/nc/king/king.html#p17.

Freedpeople: Economic Conditions

I always kept master and me. Guess I can keep me.

Response of a freedman, when urged to support himself, n.d., quoted in DuBois, Economic Co-operation, *35. Available online at URL:* http://docsouth.unc.edu/church/ dubois07/dubois.html#dub24.

[W]hile Edward [Hill, a freedman,] throve and accumulated property, he did it at a fabulous cost, namely: the utter sacrifice of his manhood; the subjection of all his civil and political convictions to the dictates of those whom he dared not deny as his superiors. He did it by eschewing all political discussions, and even the ballot-box, except when, for the sake of satisfying his neighbors, he voted the

Democratic ticket, against which his soul and convictions rebelled within him.

Story of a freedman, 1865–74, in Green, Recollections, 53–54. Available online at URL: http://docsouth.unc. edu/southlit/green/green.html.

Dear Sirs We the Tobacco mechanicks of this city and Manchester is worked to great disadvantages. In 1858 and 1859 our masters hiered us to the Tobacconist at a price ranging from $150 to $180. The Tobacconist furnished us lodging food and clothing. They gave us tasks to performe. [A]ll we made over this task they payed us for. We worked faithful and they paid us faithful. They then gave us $2 to $2.50, and we made double the amount we now make. The Tobacconist held a meeting, and resolved not to give more than $1.50 cts. Per hundred, which is about one days work—in a week we make 600 lbs apece with a ste[a]mer. This weeks work then at $1.50 amounts to $9—the steamers wages is from $4 to $4.50 cts. Which leaves from $5 to $4.50 cents per week about one half what we made when slaves. Now to Rent two small rooms we have to pay from $18 to $20. We see $4.50 cts or $5 will not more than pay Rent say nothing about food clothing medicin Doctor Bills. Tax and Co. They say we will starve through laziness that is not so. But it is true we will starve at our present wages.

Demand of Richmond, Virginia, tobacco workers, September 18, 1865, in Katz, Eyewitness, 302.

Mag genrl howard has . . . beutifly addressed the freedmen of this island. . . . [N]othing did apier at that time to bee very opressing upon us but the one thing that is wee freedmen should work for wages for our former oners or eny other man. . . . [M]an that have stud upon the feal of battle & have shot there master & sons now Going to ask ether one for bread or for shelter or Comfortable for his wife & children sunch a thing the u st [United States] should not aught to Expect a man to do. . . .

Freedpeople of Edisto Island, October 25, 1865, quoted in Ames, Diary of a New England Woman, 99–103. Available online at URL: http://docsouth.unc.edu/ ames/ames.html.

A host of miserable women, with large families of children, besides old, crippled, blind and sick persons, have been driven out of Maryland and sought refuge here [in Washington, D.C.]. Most of the people have exhibited industry and thrift beyond the expectation of their friends, paying, generally by day's labor—often difficult to ob-

tain—for shanties, garrets, cellars and stables—unfit for human beings to live in—an average rent of $5 to $6 per month.

At the commencement of the winter of 1864 . . . I found nine hundred families, with an average number of five children, without wood or the means to obtain it; half that number without beds or blankets, and as many without bread. . . . [T]housands of women and children of the latest arrivals were without a change of clothing, and large numbers had no under clothing at all. A number of infants . . . perished from the cold. Hundreds of old persons and children . . . being badly frost bitten, several had their limbs amputated in consequence. . . .

The bureau of Freedmen has no appropriation from Congress to meet the[se] wants. . . . Maj. Gen. Howard . . . also invites the benevolent public, and associations already organized for Freedmen's aid, to cooperate in giving the needed relief to these sufferers until compensating labor can be found for them.

Antislavery and woman's rights reformer Josephine Griffing, "Appeal on Behalf of the Freedmen of Washington, D.C." The Liberator (November 3, 1865): 174–75. Available online at URL: http://womhist.binghamton.edu.

In my judgment you and others who wish to befriend the blacks crowded into Washington, do them great injury. Had they been told years ago, "You must find work; go out and seek it," they would have been spared much misery. . . . If there be any woman capable of earning wages who would rather some one else than herself should pay her passage to the place where she can have work, then she needs reconstruction and awakening to a just and honest self-reliance.

Horace Greeley, editor of the New York Tribune and 1872 Liberal-Democratic candidate for president, September 7, 1870, responding to reformer Josephine Griffing's work. Available online at URL: http://womhist.binghamton. edu/teacher/DBQaid6.htm.

The prospect of getting in the crop did not grow more promising as time went on. The negroes talked a great deal about their desire and intention to work for us, but their idea of work, unaided by the stern law of necessity, is very vague, some of them working only half a day and some even less. I don't think one does a really honest full day's work, and so of course not half the necessary amount is done and I am afraid never will be again. . . . I was mistaken. In the years 1877 and 1880 upwards of thirty thousand bushels of rice was raised on the place

This 1866 racist poster, one of a series, attacks Radical Republicans on the issue of black suffrage and advocates the policies of President Andrew Johnson. The labels say, "In the sweat of thy face shalt thou eat thy bread" and "The white man must work to keep his children and pay his taxes. The black man asks, "Whar is de use for me to work as long as dey make dese appropriations." The building at right top represents the alleged vision of freedom of the black man, with labels such as "No Work," "Rum, Gin, Whiskey," "Sugar Plums," and "White Women." *(Library of Congress, Prints and Photographs Division, LC-USZ62-40764)*

by these same negroes. [Leigh's note.] Our contract with them is for half the crop; that is, one half to be divided among them, according to each man's rate of work, we letting them have in the meantime necessary food, clothing, and money for their present wants (as they have not a penny) which is to be deducted from whatever is due to them at the end of the year.

Frances Butler Leigh, letter, April 12, 1866, Ten Years, 5–25, passim. Available online at URL: http://docsouth.unc.edu/leigh/leigh.html.

[A] year of hard endeavor to raise a crop, reconstruct the place with the problem of hired labor, high water, and cotton worms. . . . Cotton is so high that merchants are anxious to advance to put in a crop, and there is much Northern capital seeking investment in that field. . . . The Negroes demanded high wages, from $20 to $25 for men, in addition to the old rations of sugar, rice tobacco, molasses, and sometimes hams. Many of the old hands left, and My Brother went to New Orleans and brought back a number of ex-Negro soldiers, who strutted around in their uniforms and were hard to control. I was deadly afraid of them. . . . [T]he water came up and we were nearly overflowed. The cotton planted was very late, and when it was looking . . . luxuriant and promising . . . the worms came. In a few days the fields were blackened like fire had swept over them. We made about twenty bales and spent $25,000 doing it. What most distresses me is that none of that money went for our personal comfort. All of it went to the Negroes.

Kate Stone, diary entry, September 22, 1867. Available online at URL: http://www.pbs.org/wgbh/amex/ reconstruction/plantation/ps_stone.html.

In a single day, in our Charleston [S.C.] Savings Bank, I took the record of seventeen freedmen who were drawing their money to pay for farms they had been buying, generally forty or fifty acres each, paying about $10 per acre. I met at a cotton merchant's in that city, ten freedmen who had clubbed together with the proceeds of their crop and bought a whole sea island plantation of seven hundred acres. The merchant . . . told me that the entire purchase price was paid in cash from the balance due them on the crop of the season. Here, then, besides supporting their families with provisions raised, these men had each, by the profits of a single year bought a farm of seventy acres.

J. W. Alford, Letters from the South, *n.d., but speaking about 1870(?), quoted in DuBois,* Economic Co-operation, *43–44. Available online at URL:* http:// docsouth.unc.edu/church/dubois07/dubois. html#dub32.

We have just leased a neighbouring island to an energetic young planter, who has brought down thirty Chinamen to work it. It remains to be seen whether they will do the work better than the negroes—they could not do it much worse. Our two small islands now represent the four quarters of the globe, as we have inhabitants on them from Europe [Irish workers, English owner], Asia [Chinese workers], Africa [freedpeople], and America [freedpeople and American owner].

British husband of plantation mistress Frances Butler Leigh, 1870s, "Appendix," in Leigh, Ten Years, *269. Available online at URL:* http://docsouth.unc.edu/leigh/leigh. html.

[W]e depend upon our dykes for our livelihood, and the chief expense in connection with such property is keeping up the banks and clearing the canals and drains every year; if this were neglected for two or three years, the plantation would relapse into its original uncivilized state, and become once more a desolate marsh, fit only for wild duck, snipe, frogs, water snakes, and mud turtle to live in. Hence the reason that, since the war, owing to want of capital and labour, much of the country in the Southern States has returned to its normal condition,

and that whereas formerly, in six of the Southern States, 186,000,000 bushels of rice were sent to market, in 1870 only 72,000,000 were raised. The original planters having been completely ruined by the war, the planting in many cases has been carried on by negroes on their own account in small patches.

J. W. Leigh, letter, n.d., "Addenda," Ten Years, 263–64. Available online at URL: http://docsouth.unc.edu/ leigh/leigh.html.

Recapitulation of a Laborer's Account
• Total from all sources.....$387.31
• Total outlay.....$306.20
• Profits.....$81.11

Out of this amount ($81.11), the laborer must clothe himself and family, feed the little ones, and furnish medical attendance for the same. Hence his inability to accumulate property. Mr. McKiel then introduced the following resolution, which was adopted: . . .

Be it resolved, that this convention memorialize the Congress of the United States to pass the bill now pending before that honorable body, known as "a bill to incorporate the Freedmen's Homestead Company," thinking as we do that such a bill would do much good, by assisting many poor men to obtain homes, thereby rendering him a free and independent citizen.

Minutes of a black labor convention at Montgomery, Alabama, in 1872, quoted in Du Bois, Economic Co-operation, *51. Available online at URL:* http://docsouth.unc.edu/ church/dubois07/dubois.html#dub24.

The entire crop raised in Texas . . . was gathered and saved by the 1st of December. Most assuredly no white man in Texas had anything to do with the gathering . . . , except to look on and give orders. . . . The freedmen, I am well convinced, had something to do with it; and yet there is a fierce murmur of complaint against them everywhere that they are lazy. . . .

Two-thirds of the freedmen in the section of the country which I traveled over have never received one cent of wages since they were declared free. . . . [I]nstances of prompt payment of wages are very rare. . . .

Union general W. Swayne reporting to a congressional committee, 1872, quoted in Katz, Eyewitness, *253–54.*

It was not my good fortune to receive an education. . . . But I learned all that was practicable for one in my situation. . . . I can navigate a vessel on our sound. Yet I cannot stand an exam in geometry, in scientific engineering, in mathematics, or even in artistic penmanship. . . . I think, without vanity, that I am qualified to keep a Light House. . . . If this test be the rule, you will exclude every colored man on this seaboard from position.

Letter from Mississippi freedman Pinckney Ross to John R. Lynch, March 7, 1873, quoted in Foner, Reconstruction, 507–08.

[A New Orleans gentlemen said,] "I actually know ladies of culture and refinement, whose incomes were gigantic before the war, who are 'washing' for their daily bread. . . .

Many lovely plantations . . . are entirely deserted; the negroes will not remain upon them, but flock into the cities, or work on land which they have purchased for themselves." He would not believe that the free negro did as much work for himself as he formerly did for his master. . . .

Traveler Edward King, reporting a conversation of 1873 or 1874, The Great South, *31–33. Available online at URL:* http://docsouth.unc.edu/nc/king/king.html#p17.

The colored citizens of Little Rock and of Arkansas in general, number many gentlemen of education and refinement, [among them] [t]he Superintendent of the Penitentiary, the Commissioner of State Lands, the Superintendent of Public Instruction, some . . . [s]tate senators, police judges, and many preachers. . . . At Helena and Little Rock there have been many noteworthy instances of progress among the negroes. This is not so common in the back-country. . . . One of the most intelligent . . . told me that the negroes had, as a rule, a horror of clearing up new land, and that they had been a good deal hindered from undertaking cotton-farming by the lack of means to begin with. . . . The large landholders, too, have generally been averse to selling land in small parcels. For these reasons the country negroes are mainly hired laborers, working on shares, or tenants by rental, payable in produce. . . . A very reliable colored man told me that if the freedmen of Arkansas had made less progress since the war than those of the elder States since emancipation, he believed it to be because the white population of Arkansas was also, in many respects, behind that of the other States.

Traveler Edward King, 1875, The Great South, *281–82. Available online at URL:* http://docsouth.unc.edu/nc/king/king.html#p204.

[S]ome of the planters along the river near Natchez said, "Give the negro his due. The merchant will ordinarily stand a better chance of collecting all his advance from fifty small black planters than from fifty whites of the same class, when the crop is successful." But if the negro's crop fails, he feels very loth to pay up, although he may have the means. He seems to think the debt has become outlawed. . . .

Densely ignorant as these negroes are, they . . . have sound sense, and some idea of manners, seem well-inclined toward their employers, and appear to appreciate their own defects.

Traveler Edward King, 1875, The Great South, *273–75. Available online at URL:* http://docsouth.unc.edu/nc/king/king.html#p204.

In the days of slave labor, planters did not make more than a fraction of their present per cent. . . . .

The testimony of most of the planters in Louisiana, as elsewhere throughout the South, is that the free negro works well, and earns his wages, save when he is distracted by politics. Indeed, there are none who are willing to assert that free labor has not been a success; and the majority would prefer it to the most arbitrary days of ownership, if the State were otherwise in a settled condition.

Traveler Edward King, reporting 1875, The Great South, *53, 89. Available online at URL:* http://docsouth.unc.edu/nc/king/king.html#p17.

If it were true that rottenness was sitting in all the high places, it was equally true that many of the "respectable people of the South" winked at it and even encouraged it. For instance the Land Commission of the State of South Carolina was formed by law, and had placed at its disposal more than half a million dollars, for the avowed purpose of purchasing large tracts of land within the State, to be parcelled out to such of the ambitious freedmen as were able and willing to buy land, but who owing to the indisposition on the part of the Southern land owners to sell to them, had not the opportunity. . . . A land owner having a piece of worn out or swamp land unfit for ordinary agricultural purposes and worth in fact not more than from a dollar and fifty cents to three dollars per acre, would palm the same off upon the Land Commissioners, . . . for an exorbitant price. . . . Say of the colored people of the South that they were in some instances ignorant; that in connection with their white brethren and with the connivance of the property holding element there, they sometimes abused their respective trusts; . . . it must still be admitted . . . that they were then as now, loyal to the core and would rather die of starvation and the lash in the hands of their white oppressors than cast a ballot for the Democratic party or betray their country into the hands of traitors.

Free black Ohio-bred John Patterson Green, who lived in the Reconstruction South for three years, Recollections, *116–18. Available online at URL:* http://docsouth.unc.edu/ southlit/green/green.html.

Freedpeople: Education

When the collection of a general tax for colored schools was suspended in Louisiana by military order, the consternation of the colored population was intense. Petitions began to pour in. I saw one from the plantations across the river, at least thirty feet in length, representing 10,000 Negroes. It was affecting to . . . note the names and marks (X) of such a long list of parents, ignorant themselves, but begging that their children might be educated; promising that from beneath their present burdens and out of their extreme poverty, they would pay for it.

Inspector of Schools Report, speaking of events of ca. 1865, quoted in DuBois, Negro Common School, *25.*

The loyal white people—the Irish and German population, have shown that they are quite willing to let their children attend the same school with the loyal blacks; although it is true, that no attempt to unite them in the same room or classes would have been tolerated at the time. But in the play-grounds, white and black boys joined in the same sports as they do in the public streets; . . . now that this great step has been made, all the prejudice against equal educational advantage will speedily vanish, and indeed, it is the veriest hypocrisy in the city where old families have aided in obliterating all the complexional distinctions in mingling their blood with that of their slaves.

New York Tribune, *March 10, 1865, when the military government opened the schools of Charleston, South Carolina, to blacks. Quoted in DuBois,* Black Reconstruction, *643.*

I have a . . . constantly growing day school, a night school, and, a glorious Sabbath School of near one hundred scholars . . . wholly self-supporting. The majority of my pupils come from plantations, three, four and even eight miles distant. . . . Every scholar buys his own book and slate, etc. . . . I am trying to carry on an Industrial school on Saturday, for that I greatly need material. There are some aged ones here to whom I read the bible. . . . There has been much opposition to my school. Twice I have

been shot at in my room. My night scholars have been shot but none killed. . . . The rebels here threatened to burn down my school and house in which I board. . . . The nearest military Jurisdiction is two hundred miles distant at New Orleans. . . . The great sin of Sabbath breaking I am trying to make them see in its proper light. But they urge so strongly its absolute necessity in order to keep from suffering—that I am almost discouraged of convincing them.

Edmonia Highgate, northern black teacher in Louisiana, letter dated December 17, 1866. Available online at URL: http:// www.pbs.org/wgbh/amex/reconstruction/schools/ ps_highgate.html.

Beside carrying on church and Sunday school, my wife and I conducted a day school, which we called Union School. During the month of August, 1867, we enrolled 53 girl students and 30 males. We made a charge of 50 cents a month for each pupil, but kept none out for lack of payment; consequently we collected but a small proportion of the money earned. During the month of August, 1867, although our enrollment was 83, we collected only $13.00, and of this we paid $8.00 for printing and $3.00 for books, leaving just $2.00 apiece for our salaries.

Black pastor Theophilus G. Steward, remembering 1867, Fifty Years, *98. Available online at URL:* http:// docsouth.unc.edu/church/steward/steward.html.

A few days after the contract was signed I started the school, which I hoped would be a success. The teacher was a young country lad just fresh from college; clever enough, but very conceited, with no more manners than a young bear, which, however, I hoped he might learn in time from the negroes . . . , as they generally are singularly gentle and courteous in their manners. I had school in the morning for the children, and in the evening for the young people who worked in the fields. This is decidedly the most popular, and we have over fifty scholars, some of them quite old men—much too old to learn, and much in the way of the younger ones, but so zealous that I could not bear to turn them away.

Plantation mistress Frances Butler Leigh, Ten Years, *95, describing an event of 1867 or 1868. Available online at URL:* http://docsouth.unc.edu/leigh/leigh.html.

Seeing Mr. White among us, word soon traveled that he was a "Yankee nigger school teacher." Threatenings began near evening. We prayed through song for deliverance. Mr. White stood between us and the men and directed the singing. One by one the riotous crowd left off their jeering and swearing and slunk back, until only the leader stood near Mr. White. He finally took off his hat [and] begged us, with tears falling, to sing again.

Fisk University Jubilee Singer Ella Sheppard, describing the stranded group at a small town depot surrounded by a mob, ca. 1871, quoted in Public Broadcasting System program "The Jubilee Singers." Available online at URL: http://www. pbs.org/wgbh/amex/singers/filmmore/transcript/ transcript1.html.

Is it not significant that after the lapse of one hundred and forty-four years since the settlement [of Beaufort, North Carolina,] the Freedmen are building the first public school-house ever erected here?

Northern educator E. C. Rainey, October 3, 1872, quoted in Foner, Reconstruction, 98.

It is very pleasing, gentlemen, to witness how rapidly the schools are springing up in every portion of our State, and how the number of competent, well trained teachers are increasing. . . . Our State University has been renovated. . . . New Professors, men of unquestionable ability and erudition, now fill the chairs once filled by men who were too aristocratic to instruct colored youths. . . . The State Normal School is also situated here, and will have a fair attendance of scholars. We have, also, Claflin University, at Orangeburg, which is well attended, and progressing very favorably; and in the different cities and large towns of the State, school houses have been built. . . . the people are becoming daily more enlightened.

House Speaker S. J. Lee to the South Carolina House of Representatives, "Final Report to the South Carolina House, 1874." Available online at URL: http://www.pbs.org/ wgbh/amex/reconstruction/schools/ps_report.html.

I visited the University [of South Carolina] . . . after the revolution caused there by the entrance of the first colored student, the Secretary of State himself. In the library, . . . I saw the book from whose lists the white students had indignantly erased their names when they saw the Secretary's round, fair script beneath their own. The departure of the old professors and scholars was the signal for a grand onward movement by the blacks, and a great number entered the preparatory and the law schools. . . . I was informed that dozens of [black legislators] were occupied every spare moment outside of the sessions in faithful study. . . .

Except in the large towns, however, the educational prospects throughout the State are not very good. . . . There are, at least, two hundred thousand children in the commonwealth; and it is safe to assert that not more than seventy-five thousand have been afforded school facilities.

Traveler Edward King, reporting 1875, The Great South, 462–63. Available online at URL: http://docsouth.unc. edu/nc/king/king.html#p17.

Freedpeople: Religion

The white planters of this neighborhood [in Marion, S.C.] were generally wealthy and kind. One Major Gibson donated land for our church; another, Colonel Durant, I think, gave timber for the frame; and many contributed in money and material in aid of the building. There were of course, some who were not pleased with the new conditions and who tried to impede my work. An old building was granted us for use as church and school house; but we had not occupied it long before it was burned down.

Black pastor Theophilus G. Steward, reporting 1866, Fifty Years, 67–68. Available online at URL: http://docsouth. unc.edu/church/steward/steward.html.

Well, now, we have all something to sell that is our labor. . . . 'Tis getting money honestly to give labor—work—for it. That is the meaning of the contract in which you agree to give a certain kind, and a certain amount of labor for a certain share in, or portion of, what the labor with the assistance of land produces. . . . The crop may be good; or it may be poor; . . . if one suffers loss, all must; and if one reaps gain, all must. . . .

This 1874 photograph shows the First African Church in Richmond, Virginia. *(Library of Congress, Prints and Photographs Division, LC-USZ62-117891)*

... [I]f ... you are lazy and slothful, and negligent, it is very likely before the year is out that you may lose your place and a great part of your wages; and next year you will stand a poor chance to get a good place or good wages; ... be a good man in the place and give good labor.... [B]e economical; live according to your condition.... Don't take in at the spigot to let out by the bung. Have your houses as clean as possible and as comfortable as you can afford.... Dress as neatly and as tidily as you can, but also as cheap as you can.

Black pastor Theophilus G. Steward in a March 1866 sermon in Marion, S.C., Fifty Years, 81–83. Available online at URL: http://docsouth.unc.edu/church/steward/ steward.html.

[W]e were pretty generally black-listed so far as buying a lot for our church was concerned.... I did not complain but continued my search for a site and with the assistance of the wide-awake members of the church finally found a very suitable lot....

... Arrangements were made for Clark [a barber and church member] to meet the seller in his office at night, bringing the money, and concluding the purchase. Confiding in Clark and handing him the money, at the same time impressing upon him the necessity of having a properly-worded receipt describing the lot and reciting the terms, I waited on the outside, at a considerable distance away from the building, until he should go in and pay over the money. As we began work on the lot almost immediately, the seller discovered that he had not only sold the lot but that he himself had been sold.... He stood grandly upon the honor of his word, remarking: "Well, you beat me. I would not have sold the lot to your church; but now that you have bought it, send your trustees to me and I will make the deed directly to them." He did so and gave a subscription of ten dollars to our work.

Black pastor Theophilus G. Steward, remembering 1868 in Macon, Georgia, Fifty Years, 134–35. Available online at URL: http://docsouth.unc.edu/church/steward/ steward.html.

This winter [1872] we had the pleasure of seeing a very nice church started in Darien for the negroes. For three years my husband [a Church of England priest] had been holding services for them regularly on the Island in a large unoccupied room which we had fitted as a chapel; but we found this hardly large enough to accommodate outsiders, and as many wished to attend who were not our own people, we thought Darien the best place for the church.

Plantation mistress Frances Butler Leigh, 1872, Ten Years, 217. Available online at URL: http://docsouth.unc. edu/leigh/leigh.html.

Freedpeople: Colonization and Emigration

[I had come from St. Louis to Illinois in 1863; to my surprise white men who claimed to be friends of the colored man cheated me.] After being robbed of all I had ..., I moved, with my family, south of the river...., there I bought 80 acres of land on credit, and lived on it two years and improved it, and then sold it to the man I purchased of. Then I moved to the old Hopkins farm.... After I got started and had farmed about three years, I made money, because I worked night and day. Then comes to me this James N. Redding, and he asked me who did I owe? I told him Mr. M. K. Keller was the only man I owed anything, as I knowed of. He, Redding; then said: "I was mistaken; and that he held a note against me for five hundred and fifty dollars, in favor of McNellis," and said that he was McNellis's attorney. This was all news to me, and I told him I owed McNellis nothing, but that McNellis was largely indebted to me.... Now, when Collins and myself was in dispute, Collins wanted a receipt, he claiming my corn; but McNellis forbid his clerk giving him a receipt, and also forbid him giving me a receipt, and, therefore I lost my thirteen hundred dollars' worth of corn, because McNellis failed shortly after.

Freedman Norvel Blair, writing about the years beginning in 1863, Book for the People, 4–5. Available online at URL: http://docsouth.unc.edu/neh/blair/blair.html.

It is impossible to suppose, ... that there can ever come a time when [the black man] can be removed from this country without a terrible shock to its prosperity and peace. Besides, the worst enemy of the nation could not cast upon its fair name a greater infamy than to admit that Negroes could be tolerated among them in a state of the most degrading slavery and oppression, and must be cast away, driven to exile, for no other cause than having been freed from their chains.

Frederick Douglass, responding to arguments advanced by President Johnson, at a meeting on March 7, 1866, quoted in Washington, Frederick Douglass, 263. Available online at URL: http://docsouth.unc.edu/neh/doug1906/ doug1906.html.

The peace of the quiet villages and towns was soon disturbed by night-raiders. Law-abiding citizens were torn from their beds at midnight, hung, robbed and flogged. This was not alone confined to black men, but white men also suffered. . . . This, together with the unjust treatment by the planters in relation to paying wages, renting land, etc., forms the cause of the exodus.

Freedman James L. Smith, describing conditions in the South in the Reconstruction era, Autobiography, *140–41. Available online at URL:* http://docsouth.unc.edu/neh/smithj/smithj.html#jsmith56.

God of high heaven will put a curse should we continue to live with our former masters and ex-slaveholders. . . .

Black veteran Henry Adams, speaking of a decision he made in 1875, quoted in Painter, Exodusters, *84.*

The freeing of the American slaves and their partial migration to [Northern] states, seeking employment, excited the enmity of the white laborers, particularly the Irish, because at that time they constituted fully seventy-five per cent of the laboring class, and who imagined that the influx of Negro laborers from the South, would divide the labor monopoly which they held. . . . [T]hey would have done almost anything calculated to extirpate them. They were always ready to incite a riot and take the lead in it. . . .

Freedman Henry Bruce, describing conditions after emancipation, New Man, *119. Available online at URL:* http://docsouth.unc.edu/bruce/bruce.html#bruce112.

By the winter of 1867–1868, I had, . . . saved up five hundred dollars, with which I bought out a small business fronting on the levee at Leavenworth, Kansas, and [improved it.] I could get but two hundred dollars insurance on my stock, and it was good that I got that much, for within sixty days . . . it was destroyed by fire. I had the two hundred dollars only. I then secured another location, and with the assistance of the firm of Haas & Co., merchants of that city, I was partly on my feet again. . . . I succeeded in paying off my debts and getting a fair living out of the business, and continued it until the fall of 1870, when I transferred it to Atchison, Kansas, where I still continued in the same business until the fall of 1875, when it, too, was destroyed by fire. . . . I then rented the brick building on the corner of Fourth and Commercial streets . . . and continued the business until the fall of 1878, when I was forced to close for want of cash. I had bills due me for groceries amounting to thirty-three

hundred dollars, which I could not collect [because of drought and farm failures].

Freedman Henry Bruce, recording events of 1867–1878, New Man, *155–56. Available online at URL:* http://docsouth.unc.edu/bruce/bruce.html#bruce112.

The white people said, "you are right; take your people away." And let me tell you, it was the white people—the ex-governor of the State, felt like I did. And they said to me, "You have tooken a great deal on to yourself, but if these Negroes, instead of deceiving one another and running for office, would take the same idea that you have in your head, you will be a people."

Black migrationist Benjamin "Pap" Singleton, describing conditions in Tennessee in the 1870s, quoted in Painter, Exodusters, *111.*

In 1870, . . . or about that year, after I had left the army . . . a parcel of us got together . . . [to] look into affairs and see the true condition of our race, to see whether it was possible we could stay under a people who had held us under bondage or not. . . . Some of the members of the committee [went] into every state in the South where we had been slaves. . . . we seed that there was no way on earth . . . that we could better our condition there. . . . [T]here were many organizations; I can't tell you how many immigration associations, and so forth, all springing out of our colonization council. We had a large meeting, some five thousand people present, and made public speeches in 1877 on immigration. . . .

Black Louisianan Henry Adams, reporting his Reconstruction era movement for emigration, quoted in DuBois, Economic Co-operation, *49–50. Available online at URL:* http://docsouth.unc.edu/church/dubois07/dubois.html#dub24.

The emigrants adopted a plan of action to appeal to President Hayes, for him to enforce the laws to protect their rights. Then they appealed to Congress to set apart a territory, or aid them to emigrate to Liberia. . . . In 1877 they petitioned Congress and President Hayes. Not hearing from this petition, the colored emigrants became exasperated, saying, "let us go any where in God's world to get away from these men who once enslaved us." Many of the white republicans of the South are treated not much better than the colored people, because they are republicans. Since they have emigrated many children, fathers and mothers have died from starvation and exposure, for they were without shelter and nothing to wear, lying on the cold ground, exposed to the winter blasts with only the sky for a covering.

James L. Smith, speaking of 1877, Autobiography, *146–47. Available online at URL:* http://docsouth.unc. edu/neh/smithj/smithj.html#jsmith56.

Violence against Blacks

Some planters held back their former slaves on their plantations by brute force. Armed bands of white men patrolled the county roads to drive back the Negroes wandering about. Dead bodies of murdered Negroes were found on and near the highways and byways. Gruesome reports came from the hospitals—reports of colored men and women whose ears had been cut off, whose skulls had been broken by blows, whose bodies had been slashed by knives or lacerated with scourges.

Carl Schurz, "Report," 39th Congress, First Session (1865), Senate Executive Documents No. 2., cited in DuBois, Black Reconstruction, *671.*

No doubt that the firing of the Colored League was very deliberate & very accurate as nearly as many Conservatives were killed or wounded as there were arms in the hands of the colored men and it was evident that none of the arms were reloaded and fired a second time. It is worthy of remark that the 27 colored men whose wounds were dressed by Dr. D. B. Cliff of Franklin were all wounded in the back or in the back part of the limbs s[h]owing clearly that they were fired upon from the rear & flank by the Conservative party while marching in procession, or after they had broken ranks and were running away from the Conservative mob. There was nothing in the conduct of the League or any member of it to justify the murders and or assault on it. There is no doubt that some of the banners borne in the procession were in bad taste. For example on one was inscribed "Remember Fort Pillow when you go to the polls;" on another "The Radicals build school houses, the Conservatives burn them."

Bvt. Major General W. Martin's report of the Franklin, Tennessee, riot on July 6, 1867, in Records of the Assistant Commissioner of the State of Tennessee. *Available online at URL:* http://www.freedmensbureau. com/tennessee/outrages/franklinriot.htm.

Johnny had a fight with a young Negro in the field, shot and came near killing him, and was mobbed in return. Johnny would have been killed but for the stand one of the Negroes made for him and Uncle Bo's opportune

arrival just as the Negroes brought him to the house—a howling, cursing mob with the women shrieking, "Kill him!" and all brandishing pistols and guns. . . . Johnny had to be sent away . . . and the Negroes quieted down and after some weeks the wounded boy recovered, greatly to Johnny's relief. He never speaks now of killing people as he formerly had a habit of doing.

Kate Stone, diary entry, September 22, 1867. Available online at URL: http://www.pbs.org/wgbh/amex/ reconstruction/plantation/ps_stone.html.

[Such organizations as the Ku Klux Klan, the Constitutional Union Guards, and the White Brotherhood] were at first purely political in their character, and many good citizens were induced to join them. But gradually, . . . under the pretext that society needed to be regulated by some authority outside or above the law, their character was changed, and these secret Klans began to commit murder, to rob, whip, scourge and mutilate unoffending citizens. . . . [T]hey authorized the use of force, with deadly weapons, to influence the elections. [Their oaths] ignored or repudiated the ordinary oaths or obligations resting upon all other citizens to respect the laws and to uphold the government. . . . They met in secret, in disguise, with arms, in a dress . . . intended to conceal their persons and their horses, and to terrify those whom they menaced or assaulted. . . . This organization, under different names, but cemented by a common purpose, is believed to have embraced not less than forty thousand voters in North Carolina. . . . The members were sworn to obey the orders of their camps even to assassination and murder. They were taught to regard oaths administered before magistrates and in Courts of Justice, as in no degree binding when they were called upon to give testimony against their confederates. They were sworn to keep the secrets of the order—to obey the commands of the Chief—to go to the rescue of a member at all hazards, and to swear for him as a witness and acquit him as a juror.

W. W. Holden, governor of North Carolina, message to the General Assembly, November 22, 1870, Memoirs, *138–40. Available online at URL:* http://docsouth.unc.edu/ holden/holden.html#holden94.

They made me and my children wrap our heads up in bed-quilts and come out of the house, and they then set it on fire, burning it up, and my husband in it, and all we had. . . . There were about fifty or sixty of them terrorists. They killed him because he refused to resign his

HARPER'S WEEKLY.
A
JOURNAL OF CIVILIZATION.

Vol. X.—No. 491.]   NEW YORK, SATURDAY, MAY 26, 1866.   [SINGLE COPIES TEN CENTS.
[$4.00 PER YEAR IN ADVANCE.

Entered according to Act of Congress, in the Year 1866, by Harper & Brothers, in the Clerk's Office of the District Court for the Southern District of New York.

THE MEMPHIS RIOTS.

THERE was in Memphis, on the first two days of May, an excitement unequaled since the close of the war. The origin of the disturbance between the whites and negroes of that city was highly discreditable to the colored soldiers, and the riotous proceedings which followed were a disgrace to civilization. For the riot the lower class of white citizens were as responsible as were the soldiers of the Third United States Colored Infantry for the original difficulty. This regiment, whose reputation has been a bad one, had been mustered out, since which they had frequented whisky-shops in the southern part of the city, and had been guilty of excesses and disorderly conduct. On the evening of May 1 some drunken members of the regiment were on South Street, talking noisily, when in an insolent manner they were ordered by two policemen to cease their noise and disperse. Words ensued, followed by blows, throwing of missiles, and firing of revolvers.

To understand what followed it must be remembered that the police force of Memphis is composed mostly of Irishmen, whose violent prejudice against negroes was so shamefully displayed in the New York riots of 1863. The *Times* correspondent thus described the riot:

Word was sent to police head-quarters, and the whole force at once proceeded to the scene of the fray, being joined on the way thither by armed and excited citizens. Meanwhile the firing had brought other negroes to the spot, some armed with clubs and some with revolvers, so that by the time the police force came up the two parties were about equal in number. The negroes held the original

position, and, upon the approach of the police, showing no determination to abandon it, were fired upon by the police and citizens who accompanied them. This fire was returned, and for a while both parties busied themselves in discharging their revolvers as rapidly as possible. Meanwhile word was sent to General STONEMAN, who promptly dispatched to the scene of action a company of Regulars (white), when the negroes were quickly dispersed and driven in every direction.

During the evening the wildest and most exaggerated reports soon spread throughout the city. Every communicator of the intelligence of the fight told a different story, and the highest excitement prevailed. Each rumor placed a worse aspect upon the affair than the preceding one, and only served to develop the pent-up prejudices against the negro. Soon after dark this excitement and prejudice found vent. Large numbers of armed citizens repaired to the scene of the fight and commenced firing upon every negro who made himself visible. One negro upon South Street, a quiet, inoffensive laborer, was shot down almost in front of his own cabin, and after life was extinct his body was fired into, cut and beat in a most horrible manner. In all parts of the city, wherever they could be seen, negroes were fired upon by policemen as well as citizens. They were shot while driving hacks, and quietly walking in the streets about their business. The police seemed to make it their special business to shoot every negro they could see, no matter where he was or what he was doing. The result was that by 9 o'clock the colored population were in-doors trembling with wild alarm. How many negroes were killed during the night it is impossible to ascertain, as firing was constantly heard during the earlier hours in all parts of the city. It is estimated that from 15 to 20 were killed. So far as I have been able to learn, not a white man was fired upon by a negro during the whole night.

After the fight of Tuesday evening the negro soldiers and most of the colored people residing in the vicinity of the fight fled to the fort for security. They were perfectly quiet—in fact, were terribly frightened for their own safety. At an early hour yesterday morning every thing

SCENES IN MEMPHIS, TENNESSEE, DURING THE RIOT—BURNING A FREEDMEN'S SCHOOL-HOUSE.
[SKETCHED BY A. R. W.]

SCENES IN MEMPHIS, TENNESSEE, DURING THE RIOT—SHOOTING DOWN NEGROES ON THE MORNING OF MAY 2, 1866.—[SKETCHED BY A. R. W.]

In a race riot in Memphis, Tennessee, whites burn a black school and shoot down blacks. *(Library of Congress, Prints and Photographs Division, LC-USZ62-111152)*

List of Murders in Counties of Maury and Marshall, Tennessee, July 1, 1867–July 1, 1868

Date of Murder	Name of Person Murdered	Color	Name of Murderer	Color	Action Taken by Civil Courts
Dec. 1867	John Courtney, hung	White	Ku Klux Klan	White	No arrests made
Feb. 29, 1868	Bicknell, shot	White	Pitts alias Waters	White	Arrested by volunteer squad & lodged in Jail
March 3rd, 1868	Pitts alias Waters, hung	White	Ku Klux Klan	White	No arrests made
March 13th, 1868	Ruth Jones, shot	Colored	McKinley	White	In Jail awaiting trial
April 7th, 1868	Henry Fitzpatrick, hung & shot	Colored	Ku Klux Klan	White	No arrests made
April 7th, 1868	Rev. Littleton Lincoln, hung	White	Ku Klux Klan	White	No arrests made
May 1868	Colored field hand, shot	Colored	Jas. Campbell	Colored	No arrests made, warrant issued. Fled
Date not known	John Washington, shot	Colored	Lou Perry	Colored	In Jail awaiting trial
Date not known	Tom Jourdan, shot	Colored	Ku Klux Klan		No arrests made
Date not known	Alf Rainey, hung	Colored	Ku Klux Klan		No arrests made
Date not known	Tom Kelley	Colored	Ku Klux Klan		No arrests made

Note: Four other murders in the county by "Ku Klux" have been reported but dates and names cannot be procured.
Source: Freedmen's Bureau agent H. A. Eastman, "List of Murders," ca. 1868. Available online at URL: http://www.freedmensbureau.com/tennessee/outrages/columbia.htm.

office as constable, to which he was elected on the Republican ticket. . . . [T]hey burnt him to death; at least they thought he was dead, but he was not quite dead; he got out and fell into a hole of water and lay there; but all the skin was burnt off of him. So the white men saw him and shot him, and he lived four days and died, and leaves me, a poor widow with a houseful of children, and no one to help me. . . . O, Lord God of Hosts, help us to get out of this country and get somewhere where we can live.

Louisianan Mrs. Joe Johnson, 1876, quoted in Painter,
Exodusters, *85–86.*

Appendix A
Documents

1. From a Virginia act of 1661
2. Virginia act of 1669 "About the Casuall Killings of Slaves"
3. From the charter of the Royal African Company, 1672
4. From a Virginia act of 1680
5. From a Virginia act of 1691 against miscegenation
6. From a British act to settle the trade to Africa, 1698
7. From the Virginia act of 1705 on the status of slaves
8. From a New York law of 1706
9. Circular letter from the [British] Board of Trade to the governors of the English colonies, relative to black slaves
10. Reply of Governor Cranston of Rhode Island
11. From a South Carolina law of 1740
12. From Lord Mansfield's decision in the *Sommersett Case*, 1772, in support of the doctrine that "As soon as a Negro comes into England he becomes free"
13. From Thomas Jefferson's early draft of the Declaration of Independence, a clause rejected by the Continental Congress
14. From the constitution of the Republic of Vermont, 1777
15. Massachusetts Chief Justice Cushing's charge to the jury in *Jennison* v. *Caldwell*, 1781
16. From the Northwest Ordinance of 1787
17. The Constitution of the United States, 1787
    From Article I, Section 2
    From Article I, Section 9
    From Article IV, Section 2
18. From the antislavery petition to the U.S. Congress of the Pennsylvania Antislavery Society, February 1790, signed by its president, Benjamin Franklin
19. From the Fugitive Slave Act of 1793
20. From an act of Congress, March 22, 1794, to prohibit the carrying on the slave-trade from the United States to any foreign place or country
21. From an act of Congress, March 2, 1807, to prohibit the importation of slaves into any port or place within the jurisdiction of the United States, from and after January 1, 1808
22. Black commentary on the speech of Mr. John Randolph, of Roanoke at the organizational meeting of the American Colonization Society, 1816
23. From an act of Congress, May 15, 1820
24. From *Walker's Appeal . . . to the Coloured Citizens of the World, but in Particular . . . to Those of the United States of America*, 1829

1. From a Virginia Act of 1661

[I]n case any English servant shall run away in company of any negroes who are incapable of making satisfaction by addition of a time [because they are already in life-long servitude]: . . . the English soe running away in the company with them shall at the time of service to their owne masters expired, serve the masters of the said negroes for their absence soe long as they should have done by this Act if they had not beene slaves, every christian in company serving his proportion; and if the negroes be lost or dye in such time of their being run away, the christian servants in company with them shall by proportion among them, either pay fewer [four?] thousand five hundred pounds of tobacco and caske or fewer yeares service for every negro so lost or dead.

2. Virginia Act of 1669 "About the Casuall Killings of Slaves"

Whereas the only law in force for the punishment of refractory servants resisting their master, mistress or overseer cannot be inflicted on negroes [because the punishment is extension of time, and the "negroes" are already enslaved for life], Nor the obstinacy of many of them by other than violent meanes supprest. *Be it enacted and declared by this grand assembly,* if any slave resist his master . . . and by the extremity of the correction should chance to die, that his death shall not be accompted Felony, but the master (or that other person appointed by the master to punish him) be acquit from molestation, since it cannot be presumed that propensed malice (which alone makes murther Felony) should induce any man to destroy his own estate.

3. From the Charter of the Royal African Company, 1672

Charles the Second by the Grace of God King of England Scotland France and Ireland, Defender of the Faith, etc., To all to whom these presents shall come, Greeting: Whereas all and singular the regions, countrys, dominions and territories, continents, coasts and places, now or at any time heretofore called or known by the name of names of Guinny, Buiny [Benin], Angola and South Barbary, or by any of them, or which are or have been reputed esteemed or taken to be parcel or member of any region country dominion territory or continent called Guinny or Binny, Angola or South Barbary and all and singular ports and havens, rivers, creeks, islands and places in the parts of Africa to them or any of them belonging, and the sole and onely trade and traffic thereof,

are the undoubted right of Us our heirs and successors and are and have been enjoyed by Us and by our predecessors for many years past as in right of this our Crown of England.

And whereas the trade of the said regions, countries and places is of great advantage to our subjects of this Kingdom, . . .

Now know ye that We graciously tendering the encouragement and advancement of the said trade and to the end the new Company or Corporation hereafter erected and constituted may be the better enabled to maintain and enlarge the said trade and traffic . . . We have given and granted, and for Us our heirs and successors do hereby give and grant unto our dearest Brother James, Duke of York, Anthony, Earl of Shaftesbury, Mr. John Buckworth, Sir John Banks, John Bence, Esquire, William Earl of Craven, Mr. Jarvis Cartwright, Mr. Samuel Dashwood, Sir Richard Ford, Mr. Thomas Farrington, Captain Ferdinando Gorges, Mr. Edward Hoopegood, Mr. John Jeffries, Sir Andrew King, Charles Modyford, Esquire, Mr. Samuel Moyer, Mr. Peter Proby, Mr. Gabriel Roberts, Sir John Shaw, Mr. Benjamin Skutt, Sir Robert Vyner, Mr. Thomas Vernon, Mr. Nicholas Warren and Mr. Richard Young, their executors and assigns, all and singular the regions, countrys dominions, territories, continents, coasts and places lying and being within the limits and bounds hereafter mentioned (that is to say), beginning at the port of Sallee in South Barbary inclusive, and extending from thence to Cape De Bona Esperanza inclusive, with all the Islands near, adjoining to those Coasts and comprehended within the limits aforesaid, which regions, countrys, dominions, territories, continents, coasts, places and Islands have been heretofore called or known by the name of South Barbary, Guinny, Binny or Angola or by some or any other name or names, which are or have been reputed, esteemed or taken to be part, parcel or member of any Country, region, dominion, territory or continent within the limits aforesaid, and all and singular Ports, Harbours, Creeks, Islands, Lakes, and places in the parts of Africa, to them, or any of them, belonging or being under the obedience of any King, State, or Potentate of any Region, Dominion or Country within the limits aforesaid.

To have and To hold all and singular the said Regions, Countries, Dominions, Territories, Continents, Islands, Coasts and places aforesaid, and all and singular other the premises within the limits aforesaid, to the said James, Duke of York, Anthony, Earl of Shaftesbury, Mr. John Buckworth, Sir John Banks, John Bence, Esquire, William Earl of Craven, Mr. Jarvis Cartwright, Mr. Samuel Dashwood, Sir Richard Ford. Mr. Thomas Farrington, Captain Ferdinando Gorges, Mr. Edward Hoopegood, Mr. John Jeffries, Sir Andrew King, Charles Modyford, Esquire, Mr. Samuel Moyer, Mr. Peter Proby, Mr. Gabriel Roberts, Sir John Shaw, Mr. Benjamin Skutt, Sir Robert Vyner, Mr. Thomas Vernon, Mr. Nicholas Warren and Mr. Richard Young, their ex'ors and assigns, from the making of these, our Letters Pattent, for and during the term, and unto the full end and term of one thousand years, yielding and rendering therefore unto Us, our heirs and successors, two Elephants, whenever we, our heirs and successors, or any of them, shall arrive, land or come into the Dominions, Regions, Countrys, Territories, Plantations and places before mentioned, or any of them.

Nevertheless, our Will and pleasure is, And we do hereby declare the true intent and meaning of these presents to be, that this, our present grant and demise . . . and all the benefits, comodity, profits, and advantages made and to be made and gotten out of the same, or by reason of the term aforesaid, shall be and shall be interpreted to be in Trust and for the sole use, benefit and behoof of the Royal African Company of England hereafter mentioned, and their Successors, and after, in and by these presents Incorporated, or mentioned to be Incorporated, And, therefore, for the setting forward and furtherance of Trade intended, in the parts aforesaid, and the incouragement of the undertakers [entrepreneurs] in the discovering the Golden Mines and settling of Plantations. . . . We do will, ordain, constitute, appoint, give and grant unto our said dearest Brother James, Duke of York, His Highness, Prince Rupert, Anthony Earl of Shaftesbury, Henry, Earl of Arlington, [and 199 others] that they and all such others, as they shall from time to time think fit and convenient to receive into their Company and Society to be traders and adventurers with them to the said Countries, shall be one body Politick and Corporate of themselves, in deed and in name, by the name of the Royal African Company of England. . . .

And further, of Our more especial Grace, certain knowledge and mere motion, We do hereby, for us, our heirs and Successors, grant unto the said Royal African Company of England and their Successors, that it shall and may be lawful to and for the said Company and their Successors, and none others, from time to time to set to Sea such and so many shipps, pinnaces, and barks as shall be thought fitting . . . prepared and furnished with Ordnance, Artillery and Ammunition or any other habiliments in warlike manner fitt and necessary for their

defence; And shall for ever hereafter have, use and enjoy all mines of Gold and Silver . . . which are or shall be found in all or any the places above mentioned, And the whole, entire and only Trade, liberty, use and privilege of Trade and Traffic into and from the said parts of Africa above mentioned. . . .

And likewise that it shall and may be lawful to and for the said Royal African Company of England and their Successors, and none others, from henceforth, at any time or times, from time to time, after the date of these presents, to use, prepare and set to Sea such and so many Ships, Barks and Pinnaces and such number of men to sail therein for the further discovery of the said Rivers and places before mentioned, and all Lands, Dominions and Territories within the compass of the same, paying always unto us, our heirs and Successors such customs, subsidies, imposts and other duties as shall be due and payable for and in respective of the exportation and importation of any goods, Wares and Merchandizes by them or any of them, to be exported or imported by virtue of these presents.

. . . . .

And we do of our more especial grace and favour certain knowledge and mere motion for us our heirs and Successors give and grant unto the said Royal African Company of England, that the Governor, Sub-Governor, Deputy Governor and Assistants of the said Company for the time being . . . shall and may have the ordering rule and government of all such forts, factories and plantations as now are or shall be at any time hereafter settled by or under the said Company within the parts of Africa aforementioned, and also full power to make and declare peace and war with any of the heathen nations that are or shall be natives of any countries within the said territories in the said parts of Africa as there shall be occasion. . . .

. . . . .

In Witness etc. Witness the king at Westminster the seven and twentieth day of September [1672].

4. From a Virginia Act of 1680

Act X. Whereas the frequent meetings of considerable numbers of Negro slaves under pretense of feasts and burials is judged of dangerous consequence [it is] enacted that no Negro or slave may carry arms, such as any club, staff, gun, sword, or other weapon, nor go from his owner's plantation without a certificate and then only on necessary occasions; the punishment twenty lashes on the bare back, well laid on. And further, if any Negro lift up his hand against any Christian he shall receive thirty lashes, and if he absent himself or lie out from his master's service and resist lawful apprehension, he may be killed. . . .

5. From a Virginia Act of 1691 against Miscegenation

[Act XVI]. . . . whatsoever English or other white man or woman, bond or free, shall intermarry with a Negro, mulatto, or Indian man or woman, bond or free, he shall within three months be banished from this dominion forever.

And it is further enacted, that if any English woman being free shall have a bastard child by a Negro she shall pay fifteen pounds to the church wardens, and in default of such payment, she shall be taken into possession by the church wardens and disposed of for five years and the amount she brings shall be paid one-third to their majesties for the support of the government, one-third to . . . the parish where the offense is committed and the other third to the informer. The child shall be bound out by the church wardens until he is thirty years of age. In case the English woman that shall have a bastard is a servant she shall be sold by the church wardens (after her time is expired) for five years, and the child serve as aforesaid.

6. From a British Act to Settle the Trade to Africa, 1698

I. Whereas the Trade to Africa is highly beneficial and advantagious to this kingdom, and to the Plantations and Colonies thereunto belonging: and whereas Forts and Castles are undoubtedly necessary for the preservation and well carrying on the said Trade. . . . Be it therefore enacted by the King's most Excellent Majesty. . . . That from and after the Four and twentieth Day of June in the Year One thousand six hundred ninety and eight the said Royal African Company their Successors and Assigns by and with their Stock, and Duties herein after appointed to be paid, shall maintain, support and defend all such Forts and Castles as the said African Company now have in their Possession or shall hereafter purchase or erect . . . and at all times hereafter as occasion shall require shall supply with Men Artillery, Ammunition and Provision, and all other Necessaries and incident Charges whatsoever.

II. . . . That it shall and may be lawfull to and for any of the Subjects of His Majesties Realm of England as well as for the said Company from and after the said Four and Twentieth Day of June to trade from England, and from and after the First of August One thousand six hundred ninety and eight from any of His Majesties Plantations and Colonies in America, to and for the Coast of Africa between Cape Mount and the Cape of Good Hope, the said Company and all other the said Subjects answering and paying for the Uses aforesaid a Duty of Ten Pounds per Centum ad Valorem for [of the value of] the Goods and Merchandize to be exported from England or from any of His Majesties Plantations or Colonies in America to and for the Coast of Africa between Cape Mount and the Cape of Good Hope and in proportion for a greater or lesser Value in Manner and Forme as herein after expressed. . . .

XIV. Provided always . . . That all Persons being the natural born Subjects of England trading to the Coast of Africa as aforesaid and paying the Duties by this Act imposed, shall have the same Protection Security and Defence for their Persons Ships and Goods . . . and the like Freedom and Security for their Negotiations and Trade to all Intents and Purposes whatsoever as the said Company their Agents Factors and Assigns and their Ships and Goods have, may or shall have, and that all and every person and Persons trading to Africa and paying the Duties as aforesaid may and are hereby impowered at their own Charge to Settle Factories [establishments for traders carrying on business in a foreign country] on any part of Africa within the Limits aforesaid . . . , and that all Persons not Members of the said Company so trading and paying the said Duties as aforesaid shall, together with their Shipps and Goods, be free from all Molestations Hindrances Restraints Arrests Seizures Penalties or other Impositions whatso[e]ver from the said Company. . . .

. . . . .

Provided that this Act shall continue and be in Force Thirteen Years and thence to the end of the next Sessions of Parliament and no longer.

7. From the Virginia Act of 1705 on the Status of Slaves

XXIII. All Negro, mulatto, and Indian slaves within this dominion shall be held to be real estate and not chattels and shall descend unto heirs and widows according to the custom of land inheritance, and be held in *"fee simple."* . . .

Nothing in this act shall be construed to give the owner of a slave not seized of other real estate the right to vote as a freeholder. . . .

XXXIV. And if any slave resist his master, or owner, or other person, by his or her order, correcting such slave, and shall happen to be killed in such correction, it shall not be accounted felony; but the master, owner, and every such other person so giving correction, shall be free and acquit of all punishment and accusation for the same, as if such accident had never happened.

8. From a New York Law of 1706

All and every, Negro, Indian, Mulatto and Mestee Bastard child and children who is, are, and shall be born of any Negro, Indian, Mulatto or Mestee shall follow ye state and condition of the mother and shall be esteemed reputed taken & adjudged a Slave & slaves to all intents and purposes whatsoever.

9. Circular Letter from the (British) Board of Trade to the Governors of the English Colonies, Relative to Black Slaves

April 17, 1708

. . . However, it being absolutely necessary that a trade so beneficial to the kingdom should be carried on to the greatest advantage, there is no doubt but the consideration thereof will come early before the Parliament at their next meeting; and as the well supplying of the plantations and colonies with sufficient number of negroes at reasonable prices, is in our opinion the chief point to be considered in regard to that trade, and as hitherto we have not been able to know how they have been supplied by the company, or by separate traders, otherwise than according to the respective accounts given by them, which for the most part are founded upon calculations made from their exports on one side and the other, and do differ so very much, that no certain judgment can be made upon those accounts.

Wherefore, that we may be able at the next meeting of the Parliament to lay before both houses when required, an exact and authentic state of that trade, particularly in regard to the several plantations and colonies; we do hereby desire and strictly require you, that upon the receipt hereof, you do inform yourself from the proper officers or otherwise, in the best manner you can, what number of negroes have been yearly imported directly from Africa into Jamaica, since the 24th of June, 1698, to the 25th of December, 1707, and at what rate per head they have been sold each year, one with another, distinguishing the numbers that have been imported on account of the Royal African Company, and those which have been imported by separate traders; as likewise the rates at which such negroes have been sold by the company and by separate traders. We must recommend it to your care to be as exact and diligent therein as possibly you can, and with the first opportunity to transmit to us such accounts as aforesaid, that they may arrive here in due time. . . .

Lastly, whatever accounts you shall from time to time send us touching these matters of the negro trade, we desire that the same may be distinct, and not intermixed with other matters; and that for the time to come, you do transmit to us the like half yearly accounts of negroes, by whom imported and at what rates sold; the first of such subsequent accounts, to begin from Christmas, 1707, to which time those now demanded, are to be given. . . .

P.S. We expect the best account you can give us, with that expedition which the shortness of the time requires.

Memorandum. This letter, mutatis mutandis, was writ to the Governors of Barbados, the Leeward Islands, Bermuda, New York, New Jersey, Maryland, the President of the Council of Virginia, the Governor of New Hampshire and the Massachusetts Bay, the Deputy Governor of Pennsylvania, the Lords proprietors of Carolina, the Governors and Companies of Connecticut and Rhode Island.

10. Reply of Governor Cranston of Rhode Island

May it please your Lordships: In obedience to your Lordships' commands of the 15th of April last, to the trade of Africa.

We, having inspected into the books of Her Majesty's custom, and informed ourselves from the proper officers thereof, by strict inquiry, can lay before your Lordships no other account of that trade than the following, viz.:

1. That from the 24th of June, 1698, to the 25th of December, 1707, we have not had any negroes imported into this colony from the coast of Africa. . . .
2. That on the 30th day of May, 1696, arrived at this port from the coast of Africa, the brigantine Seaflower,

Thomas Windsor, master, having on board her forty-seven negroes, fourteen of which he disposed of in this colony, for betwixt £30 and £35 per head; the rest he transported by land for Boston, where his owners lived.

3.   That on the 10th of August, the 19th and 28th of October, in the year 1700, sailed from this port three vessels, directly for the coast of Africa; the two former were sloops, the one commanded by Nicho's Hillgroue, the other by Jacob Bill; the last a ship, commanded by Edwin Caster, who was part owner of the said three vessels, in company with Thomas Bruster, and John Bates, merchants, of Barbadoes, and separate traders from thence to the coast of Africa; the said three vessels arriving safe to Barbadoes from the coast of Africa, where they made the disposition of their negroes.

4.   That we have never had any vessels from the coast of Africa to this colony, nor any trade there, the brigantine above mentioned, excepted.

5.   That the whole and only supply of negroes to this colony, is from the island of Barbadoes; from whence is imported one year with another, betwixt twenty and thirty; and if those arrive well and sound, the general price is from £30 to £40 per head.

According to your Lordships' desire, we have advised with the chiefest of our planters, and find but small encouragement for that trade to this colony; since by the best computation we can make, there would not be disposed in this colony above twenty or thirty at the most, annually; the reasons of which are chiefly to be attributed to the general dislike our planters have for them, by reason of their turbulent and unruly tempers.

And that most of our planters that are able and willing to purchase any of them, are supplied by the offspring of those they have already, which increase daily; and that the inclination of our people in general, is to employ white servants before Negroes. . . .

Newport, on Rhode Island, December 5, 1708.

11. From a South Carolina Law of 1740

All Negroes, Indians (free Indians in amity with this government, and Negroes, mulattoes, and mestizoes, who are now free, excepted), mulattoes, and mestizoes, who are or shall hereafter be in this province and all their issue and offspring born or to be born, shall be and they are hereby declared to be and remain forever after absolute slaves, and shall follow the condition of their mother.

12. From Lord Mansfield's Decision in the Sommersett Case, 1772, in Support of the Doctrine That "As Soon as a Negro Comes into England He Becomes Free"

The state of slavery is of such a nature, that it is incapable of being introduced on any reasons, moral or political, but only by positive law, which preserves its force long after the reasons, occasion, and time itself from whence it was created, is erased from memory. It is so odious that nothing can be suffered to support it, but positive law [no such law existing in England]. Whatever inconveniences, therefore, may follow from the decision, I cannot say this case is allowed or approved by the law of England; and therefore the black must be discharged [freed].

13. From Thomas Jefferson's Early Draft of the Declaration of Independence, a Clause Rejected by the Continental Congress

[George III] has waged cruel war against human nature itself, violating its most sacred rights of life and liberty in the persons of a distant people who never offended him, captivating and carrying them into slavery in another hemisphere, or to incur miserable death in their transportation thither. This piratical warfare, the opprobrium of infidel powers, is the warfare of the Christian king of Great Britain. Determined to keep open a market where Men should be bought and sold, he has prostituted his negative veto for suppressing every legislative attempt to prohibit or to restrain this execrable commerce.

14. From the Constitution of the Republic of Vermont, 1777

No male person, born in this country, or brought from over sea, ought to be holden by law, to serve any person, as a servant, slave, or apprentice, after he arrives at the age of twenty-one years, nor female in like manner, after she arrives to the age of eighteen years, unless they are bound by their own consent, after they arrive at such age, or bound by law, for the payment of debts, damages, fines, costs, and the like.

15. Massachusetts Chief Justice Cushing's Charge to the Jury in *Jennison v. Caldwell,* 1781

The defense . . . is founded on the assumed proposition that slavery had been by law established in this province: that rights to slaves, as property, acquired by law, ought not to be divested by any construction of the [1780] Constitution [of Massachusetts] by implication; and that slavery in that instrument is not expressly abolished. It is true . . . that [slaves] had been considered by some of the Province laws as actually existing among us; but nowhere do we find it expressly established. It was a usage. . . . But whatever usages formerly prevailed . . . , they can no longer exist. Sentiments more favorable to the natural rights of mankind, and to that innate desire for liberty which heaven, without regard to complexion or shape, has planted in the human breast—have prevailed since the glorious struggle for our rights began. And these sentiments led the framers of our constitution of government—by which the people of this commonwealth have solemnly bound themselves to each other—to declare—*that all men are born free and equal; and that every subject is entitled to liberty,* and to have it guarded by the laws as well as his life and property. . . . [S]lavery is in my judgment as effectively abolished as it can be by the granting of rights and privileges wholly incompatible and repugnant to its existence. The court are therefore fully of the opinion that perpetual servitude can no longer be tolerated in our government. . . .

16. From the Northwest Ordinance of 1787

Art. 2. The inhabitants of the said territory shall always be entitled to the benefits of the writ of *habeas corpus,* and of the trial of jury; of a proportionate representation of the people in the legislature; and of judicial proceedings according to the course of the common law. . . . No man shall be deprived of his liberty or property, but by the judgment of his peers or the law of the land; and, should the public exigencies make it necessary, for the common preservation, to take any person's property, or to demand his particular services, full compensation shall be made for the same. And, in the just preservation of rights and property, it is understood and declared, that no law ought ever to be made, or have force in the said territory, that shall, in any manner whatever, interfere with or affect private contracts or engagements, *bona fide* [in good faith], and without fraud, previously formed. . . .

Art. 5. There shall be formed in the said territory, not less than three nor more than five States; . . . And, whenever any of the said States shall have sixty thousand free inhabitants therein, such State shall be admitted, by its delegates, into the Congress of the United States, on an equal footing with the original States in all respects whatever, . . . *Provided,* the constitution and government so to be formed, shall be republican, and in conformity to the principles contained in these articles. . . .

Art. 6. There shall be neither slavery nor involuntary servitude in the said Territory, otherwise than in the punishment of crimes, whereof the party shall have been duly convicted; *provided,* always, that any person escaping into the same, from whom labor or service is lawfully claimed in any one of the original States, such fugitive may be lawfully reclaimed and conveyed to the person claiming his or her labor or service aforesaid.

17. The Constitution of the United States, 1787

From Article I, Section 2

Representatives and direct Taxes shall be apportioned among the several States which may be included within this Union, according to their respective Numbers, which shall be determined by adding to the whole Number of free Persons, including those bound to Service for a Term of Years, and excluding Indians not taxed, three fifths of all other persons.

From Article I, Section 9

The Migration or Importation of such Persons as any of the States now existing shall think proper to admit, shall not be prohibited by the Congress prior to the Year one thousand eight hundred and eight, but a Tax or duty may be imposed on such Importation, not exceeding ten dollars for each person.

From Article IV, Section 2

No person held to Service or Labour in one State, under the Laws thereof, escaping into another, shall, in Consequence of any Law or Regulation therein, be discharged from such Service or Labour, but shall be delivered up on Claim of the Party to whom such Service or Labour may be due.

18. From the Antislavery Petition to the U.S. Congress of the Pennsylvania Antislavery Society, February 1790, Signed by Its President, Benjamin Franklin

From a persuasion that equal liberty was originally the portion, and is still the birthright of all men; and influenced by the strong ties of humanity, and the principles of their institution, your memorialists conceive themselves bound to use all justifiable endeavors to loosen the bonds of slavery, and promote a general enjoyment of the blessings of freedom. Under these impressions, they earnestly entreat your serious attention to the subject of slavery; that you will be pleased to countenance the restoration of liberty to those unhappy men, who alone, in this land of freedom are degraded into perpetual bondage, and who, amidst the general joy of surrounding freemen, are groaning in servile subjection; that you will devise means for removing this inconsistency from the character of the American people; that you will promote mercy and justice towards this distressed race, and that you will step to the very verge of the power vested in you for discouraging every species of traffic in the persons of our fellowmen.

19. From the Fugitive Slave Act of 1793

That when a person held to labor in any of the United States or in either of the Territories on the Northwest or South of the river Ohio, under the laws thereof, shall escape into any other of the said States or Territory, the person to whom such labor or service may be due, his agent or attorney, is hereby empowered to seize or arrest such fugitive from labor, and to take him or her before any Judge of the Circuit or District Courts of the United States, residing or being within the State, or before any magistrate of a county, city, or town corporate, wherein such seizure or arrest shall be made, and upon proof to the satisfaction of such judge or magistrate, either by oral testimony or affidavit taken before and certified by a magistrate of any such State or Territory, that the person so seized or arrested, doth, under the laws of the State or Territory from which he or she fled, owe service or labor to the person claiming him or her, it shall be the duty of such Judge or magistrate to give a certificate thereof to such claimant, his agent, or attorney, which shall be sufficient warrant for removing the said fugitive from labor to the State or Territory from which he or she fled.

20. From an Act of Congress, March 22, 1794, to Prohibit the Carrying on the Slave-trade from the United States to Any Foreign Place or Country

SECTION I. BE *it enacted by the Senate and House of Representatives of the United States of America, in Congress assembled,* That no citizen or citizens of the United States, or foreigner, or any other person coming into, or residing within the same, shall, for himself, or, any other person whatsoever, either as master, factor or owner, build, fit, equip, load or otherwise prepare any ship or vessel within any port or place of the said United States, nor shall cause any ship or vessel to sail from any port or place within the same, for the purpose of carrying on any trade or traffic in slaves, to any foreign country; or for the purpose of procuring, from any foreign kingdom, place or country, the inhabitants of such kingdom, place or country, to be transported to any foreign country, port or place whatever, to be sold or disposed of, as slaves: And if any ship or vessel shall be so fitted out, as aforesaid, for the said purposes, or shall be caused to sail, so as aforesaid, every such ship or vessel, her tackle, furniture, apparel and other appurtenances, shall be forfeited to the United Sates; and shall be liable to be seized, prosecuted and condemned, in any of the circuit courts or district court for the district, where the said ship or vessel may be found and seized.

SECTION II. *And be it further enacted,* That all and every person, so building, fitting out, equipping, loading, or otherwise preparing, or sending away, any ship or vessel, knowing, or intending, that the same shall be employed in such trade or business, contrary to the true intent and meaning of this act, or any ways aiding or abetting therein, shall severally forfeit and pay the sum of two thousand dollars, one moiety thereof, to the use of the United States, and the other moiety thereof, to the use of him or her, who shall sue for and prosecute the same.

SECTION III. *And be it further enacted,* That the owner, master or factor of each and every foreign ship or vessel, clearing out for any of the coasts or kingdoms of Africa, or suspected to be intended for the slave-trade, and the suspicion being declared to the officer of the customs, by any citizen, on oath or affirmation, and such information being to the satisfaction of the said officer, shall first give bond with sufficient sureties, to the Treasurer of the United States, that none of the natives of Africa, or any other foreign country or place, shall be taken on board the said ship or vessel, to be transported, or sold as slaves, in any other foreign port or place whatever, within nine months thereafter.

SECTION IV. *And be it further enacted,* That if any citizen or citizens of the United States shall, contrary to the true intent and meaning of this act, take on board, receive or transport any such persons, as above described in this act, for the purpose of selling them as slaves, as aforesaid, he or they shall forfeit and pay, for each and every person, so received on board, transported, or sold as aforesaid, the sum of two hundred dollars, to be recovered in any court of the United States proper to try the same; the one moiety thereof, to the use of the United States, and the other moiety to the use of such person or persons, who shall sue for and prosecute the same.

21. From an Act of Congress, March 2, 1807, to Prohibit the Importation of Slaves into Any Port or Place within the Jurisdiction of the United States, from and after January 1, 1808

Be it enacted . . . That from and after the first day of January, one thousand eight hundred and eight, it shall not be lawful to import or bring into the United States or the territories thereof from any foreign kingdom, place or country, any negro, mulatto, or person of colour, with intent to hold, sell, or dispose of such negro, mulatto, or person of colour, as a slave, or to be held to service or labour.

SEC. 2. *And be it further enacted,* That no citizen or citizens of the United States, or any other person, shall, from and after the first day of January, in the year of our Lord one thousand eight hundred and eight, for himself, or themselves, or any other person whatsoever, either as master, factor, or owner build, fit, equip, load or otherwise prepare any ship or vessel to sail from any port or place within the same, for the purpose of procuring any negro, mulatto, or person of colour, from any foreign kingdom, place, or country, to be transported to any port or place whatsoever, within the jurisdiction of the United States, to be held, sold, or disposed of as slaves, or to be held to service or labour; and if any ship or vessel shall be so fitted out for the purpose aforesaid, or shall be caused to sail so as aforesaid, every such ship or vessel, her tackle, apparel, and furniture, shall be forfeited to the United States, and shall be liable to be seized, prosecuted, and condemned in any of the circuit courts or district courts, for the district where the said ship or vessel may be found or seized.

22. Black Commentary on the Speech of Mr. John Randolph, of Roanoke at the organizational meeting of the American Colonization Society, 1816

Said he:—

"There is no fear that this proposition would alarm the slave-holders; they had been accustomed to think seriously of the subject.—There was a popular work on agriculture, by John Taylor of Caroline, which was widely circulated, and much confided in, in Virginia. In that book, much read because coming from a practical man, this description of people were pointed out as a great evil. They had indeed been held up as the greater bug-bear to every man who feels an inclination to emancipate his slaves, not to create in the bosom of his country so great a nuisance. If a place could be provided for their reception, and a mode of sending them hence, there were hundreds, nay thousands of citizens who would, by manumitting their slaves, relieve themselves from the cares attendant on their possession. The great slave-holder . . . was frequently a mere sentry at his own door—bound to stay on his plantation to see that his slaves were properly treated, &c. (Mr. R. concluded by saying,) that he had thought it necessary to make these remarks being a slave-holder himself, to shew that, so far from being connected with abolition of slavery, the measure proposed would prove one of the greatest securities to enable the master to keep in possession of his own property."

Here is a demonstrative proof, of a plan got up, by a gang of slave-holders to select the free people of colour from among the slaves, that our more miserable brethren may be the better secured in ignorance and wretchedness, to work their farms and dig their mines, and thus go on enriching the Christians with their blood and groans.

If any of us see fit to go away, go to those who have been for many years, and are now our greatest earthly friends and benefactors—the English. If not so, go to our brethren, the Haytians, who, according to their word, are bound to protect and comfort us. . . .

And now brethren, . . . Should tyrants take it into their heads to emancipate any of you, remember that freedom is your natural right. You are men, as well as they, and instead of returning thanks to them for your freedom, return it to the Holy Ghost. . . . If they do not want to part with your labours, which have enriched them, let them keep you, and my word for it, that God Almighty, will break their strong band. . . . Whether you believe it or not, I tell you that God will dash tyrants, in combination with devils, into atoms, and will bring you out from your wretchedness and miseries under these *Christian People!!!!!*

Those philanthropists and lovers of the human family, who have volunteered their services for our redemption from wretchedness, have a nigh claim on our gratitude, and we should always view them as our greatest earthly benefactors. . . .

In conclusion, I ask the candid and unprejudiced of the whole world, to search the pages of historians diligently, and see if the Antideluvians—the Sodomites—the Egyptians—the Babylonians—the Ninevites—the Carthagenians—the Persians—the Macedonians—the Greeks—the Romans—the Mahometans—the Jews—or devils, ever treated a set of human beings as the white Christians of America do us, the blacks, or Africans. I also ask the attention of the world of mankind to the declaration [of Independence] of these very American people, of the United States. . . .

See your Declaration Americans!!! Do you understand your own language? . . . Compare your own language . . . with your cruelties and murders inflicted by your cruel and unmerciful fathers and yourselves on our fathers and on us—men who have never given your fathers or you the least provocation!!!!!

The Americans may be as vigilant as they please, but they cannot be vigilant enough for the Lord, neither can they hide themselves, where he will not find and bring them out.

23. From an Act of Congress, May 15, 1820

If any citizen of the United States, being of the crew or ship's company of any foreign ship or vessel engaged in the slave trade, or any person whatever, being of the crew, or ship's company of any ship or vessel, owned in the whole or in part, or navigated for, or in behalf of, any citizen or citizens of the United States, shall . . . seize any negro or mulatto not held to service or labour by the laws of either of the states or territories of the United States, with intent to make such negro or mulatto a slave, or shall decoy, or . . . forcibly confine or detain, or aid and abet in forcibly confining or detaining, on board such ship or vessel, any negro . . . , such citizen or person shall be adjudged a pirate; and . . . shall suffer death.

24. From *Walker's Appeal . . . to the Coloured Citizens of the World, but in Particular . . . to Those of the United States of America,* 1829

[A]s the inhuman system of *slavery,* is the *source* from which most of our miseries proceed, I shall begin with that *curse* to *nations.* . . . [T]he labour of slaves comes too cheap to the avaricious usurpers, and is (as they think) of such great utility to the country where it exists, that those who are actuated by sordid avarice only, overlook the evils, which will as sure as the Lord lives, follow after the good. In fact, they are so happy to keep in ignorance and degradation, and to receive the homage and labour of the slaves, they forget that God rules in the armies of heaven and among the inhabitants of the earth, having his ears continually open to the cries, tears and groans of his oppressed people; and being a just and holy Being will at one day appear fully in behalf of the oppressed. . . .

I promised . . . to demonstrate . . . that we, (coloured people of these United States of America) are the *most wretched, degraded,* and *abject* set of beings that *ever lived* since the world began, and that the white Americans having reduced us to the wretched state of *slavery,* treat us in that condition *more cruel* (they being an enlight[en]ed and Christian people,) than any heathen nation did any people whom it had reduced to our condition. . . .

I saw a paragraph . . . in a South Carolina paper, which, speaking of the barbarity of the Turks, it said: "The Turks are the most barbarous people in the world—they treat the Greeks more like *brutes* than human beings." And in the same paper was an advertisement, which said, "Eight well built Virginia and Maryland *Negro fellows* and four *wenches* will positively be *sold* this day, *to the highest bidder!*" . . .

I have been for years troubling the pages of historians, to find out what our fathers have done to the *white Christians of America,* to merit such condign punishment as they have inflicted on them. . . . I have therefore, come to the immoveable conclusion, that they have, and do continue to punish as for nothing else, but for enriching them and their country. . . .

Ignorance, my brethren, is a mist, low down into the very dark and almost impenetrable abyss in which, our fathers for many centuries have been plunged. The Christians, and enlightened of Europe, and some of Asia, seeing the ignorance and consequent degradation of our fathers, instead of trying to enlighten them, by teaching them that religion and light with which God had blessed them, they have plunged them into wretchedness ten thousand times more intolerable, than if they had left them entirely to the Lord, and to add to their miseries, deep down into which they have plunged them tell, that they are an *inferior* and *distinct race* of beings, which they will be glad enough to recall and swallow by and by. . . .

[W]hen I view that mighty son of Africa, HAN-NIBAL, one of the greatest generals of antiquity, who defeated and cut off so many thousands of the white Romans or murderers, and who carried his victorious arms, to the very gate of Rome, and I give it as my candid opinion, that had Carthage been well united and had given him good support, he would have carried that cruel and barbarous city by storm. But they were dis-united, as the coloured people are now, in the United States of America, the reason our natural enemies are enabled to keep their feet on our throats. . . .

Beloved brethren—here let me tell you, and believe it, that the Lord our God . . . will give you a Hannibal. . . .

But what need have I to refer to antiquity, when Hayti, the glory of the blacks and terror of tyrants, is enough to convince the most avaricious and stupid of wretches. . . .

Ignorance and treachery one against the other—a grovelling service and abject submission to the lash of tyrants, we see plainly, my brethren, are not the natural elements of the blacks. . . .

[T]hey [whites] would die to a man, before they would suffer such things from men. Yes, how can our friends but be embarrassed, as Mr. Jefferson says, by the question, "What further is to be done with these people?" For while they are working for our emancipation, we are, by our treachery, wickedness and deceit, working against ourselves and our children—helping ours, and the enemies of God, to keep us and our dear little children in their infernal chains of slavery!!! . . .

Men of colour, who are also of sense, for you particularly is my APPEAL designed. Our more ignorant brethren are not able to penetrate its value. I call upon you therefore to cast your eyes upon the wretchedness of your brethren, and to do your utmost to enlighten them—*go to work and enlighten your brethren!*—Let the Lord see you doing what you can to rescue them and your selves from degradation. Do any of you say that you and your family are free and happy, and what have you to do with the wretched slaves and other people? So can I say, for I enjoy as much freedom as any of you, if I am not quite as well off as the best of you. Look into our freedom and happiness, and see of what kind they are composed!! They are of the very lowest kind—they are the very *dregs!*—they are the most servile and abject kind, that ever a people was in possession of. If any of you wish to know how FREE you are, let one of you start and go through the southern and western States of this country, and unless you travel as a slave to a white man . . . or have your free papers, . . . if they do not take you up and put you in jail, and if you cannot give good evidence of your freedom, sell you into eternal slavery, I am not a living man. . . .

I advance it therefore to you, not as a *problematical.* but as an unshaken and for ever immoveable *fact,* that your full glory and happiness, as well as all other coloured people under Heaven, shall never be fully consummated, but with the *entire emancipation of your enslaved brethren all over the world.*

There is great work for you to do. . . . You have to prove to the Americans and the world, that we are MEN, and not *brutes,* as we have been represented, and by millions treated. Remember, to let the aim of your labours among your brethren, and particularly the youths, be the dissemination of education and religion. . . .

I would crawl on my hands and knees through mud and mire, to the feet of a learned man, where I would sit and humbly supplicate him to instil [sic] into me, that which neither devils nor tyrants could remove, only with my life—for coloured people to acquire learning in this country, make tyrants quake and tremble on their sandy foundation? . . . Why, they know that their infernal deeds of cruelty will be made known to the world. Do you suppose one man of good sense and learning would submit himself, his father, mother, wife and children, to be slaves to a wretched man like himself, who, instead of compensating him for his labours, chains, hand-cuffs and beats him and family almost to death, leaving life enough in them, however, to work for, and call him master? No! no! he would cut his devilish throat from ear to ear, and well do slave-holders know it. . . .

It is a notorious fact, that the major part of the white Americans, have, ever since we have been among them, tried to keep us ignorant, and make us believe that God made us and our children to be slaves to them and theirs. *Oh! My God, have mercy on Christian Americans!!!* . . .

[Colonization is] a plan to get those of the coloured people, who are said to be free, away from among those of our brethren whom they unjustly hold in bondage, so that they [whites] may be enabled to keep them [slaves] the more secure in ignorance and wretchedness, to support them and their children, and consequently they would have the more obedient slave. For if the free are allowed to stay among the slave, they will have intercourse together, and, of course, the free will learn the slaves *bad habits,* by teaching them that they are MEN, as well as other people, and certainly *ought* and *must* be FREE. . . .

25. Excerpts from "Nero's" 1831 Letter to the South Received in Virginia Soon after Nat Turner's Insurrection

I have just been informed that my worthy friend has just arrived at N. York from his perilous and philanthropick enterprize at the South. Yes, he *has* arrived, and safe too, though he had many hair breadth escapes from the bullets of the modern Vandals of *Christian* Virginia. . . . He is a modern Leonidas, and the adored Chief of some *more* than three hundred men of colour (or *Negroes* if you please to denominate us) who have pledged ourselves with spartan fidelity to avenge the indignities offered to our race from the Slave holding Tyrant in the U. States. We have sworn in the most Solemn manner that we will not shrink from our holy and laudable purpose of vengeance, although we have to meet suffering and bear tortures that would have made the ghastly inquisitors of Spain and Portugal felt and *shown* pity. . . . [K]now ye coward race, that each of us . . . knows *how* to suffer and with a grace too. Our beloved Chief is a Native of Virginia; where he lived a slave till he was almost sixteen years old, when he found an opportunity to escape to St. Domingo, where his noble soul became warned by the spirit of freedom, and where he imbibed a righteous indignation, and an unqualified hatred for the oppressors of his race. His person is large and athletick; his deportment and manners dignified and urbane, his eye piercing, and at pleasure, can assume a fiendish malignity, which can wither any one in his presence, and which, I trust, will one day have its desired effect upon the coward hearts of many a Nabob, who now wields the sceptre of cruel domination. He is acquainted with, and speaks fluently most of the living European languages—he is a scholar and genius—he is acquainted with every avenue to the human heart   but more especially is he acquainted with all the feelings of a Slave; for he has himself been a slave. For more than three years he has been travelling, and has visited almost every Negro hut and quarters in the South States. Although he has travelled incog.[nito] both among you and your slaves, yet he knows all about the latter, and not a little of their masters. . . . O how would the boasted and bloated courage of some of your pompous great ones, have quailed had they known in whose presence they were, when in the

garb and character of a mendicant negro he examined and scrutinized with an unerring ken their persons and characters. Notwithstanding *he* has returned; he has not left the field of our future enterprize unguarded—there are now among you souls of heroick daring who are reckless of their own fate can they but subserve our vindictive purpose. In addition to this band of worthies, who are among you, we have about thirty five chosen ones in Hayti, who are learning the French and Spanish languages and at the same time taking lessons from the venerable survivors of the Haytian Revolution[;] from this quarter the people of N. Orleans and Florida may expect some realities. . . . They will know how to use the knife, bludgeon, and the torch with effect—may the genius of Toussaint stimulate them to unremitting exertion. . . . We have no expectation of conquering the whites of the Southern States—our object is to seek revenge for indignities and abuses received—and to sell our live[s] at as high a price as possible. . . . Publick opinion at the North is in our favour—we have here the generous sympathies of White people—they wish us success—nay more; they contribute largely to our enterprize—true it is not publickly done, neither is there much effort to conceal it. . . . [L]ook at the Boston Patriot of the 20th Sept. and there you will see with zeal a college for people of colour is urged—such an Institution *will be established* in N. England. Already more than one hundred and sixty seven thousand dollars has been collected for that benevolent purpose in St. Domingo. We can obtain one hundred thousand doll[ars] from our own people in N. England and N. York. We have encouragement of assistance to a considerable amount from the White people in Pennsylvania and the States North[;] our spies and agents in Ohio and Upper Canada report favourably. We hope for much from the effort of agents lately sent to Europe. . . . Knowledge and information must move our machinery—our wrongs and sufferings will give sufficient excitement. We have already a printing press in agitation, indeed, we have one purchased, and are only waiting to ascertain *where* will be the most eligible situation for its location. From this engine we hope and most sanguinely expect to work wonders; by the assistance of the Mail, we shall be able to throw fire brands on your combustibles, that we trust, will not only make a blaze but scorch your very bones to a crisp. Of physical force we have no lack—when our plans are matured we shall be able to bring into the field three hundred thousand men who will be al[l] willing to hazard their lives in defence of our common rights—we have assurance of arms and ammunition from Non-Slaveholding States—I mean from individuals in those states, and Hayti offers an asylum for those who survive the approaching carnage.

Notwithstanding our agents are indispensably important to us, yet we put no confidence, or rather no dependence upon their help in the approaching day of carnage . . . , which will require all the sternness, cool determination, and ferocity that the human character, in its most savage state, is capable of—the white men (for they are white) we well know have not personal malignity sufficient to fit them for our use—a promiscuous slaughter of women and children would produce misgivings; and that would ruin us—we *have* men, *however,* to our liking; men that can perform deeds of death and destruction that would have made . . . a Tecumseh weep. Would to Heaven, we could enlist the Indians of Georgia in our common cause—and we are not without hopes that we shall. But you will say, are not such anticipations more than savage? I answer yes; yet the punishment will come far short of the demerit of your crimes—therefore bear it with fortitude[,] bear it as we have born[e] to see our race made more abject than the Helots of Greece. [A]nd is not Slavery a greater curse than any torture that terminates with death? . . . [W]e prefer to see every person of colour headless, and their "heads on poles" if you please than to see them servants to a debauched and effe[min]ate race of whites. . . . Believe, if you please, that this is mere windy boasting—yet we know to the contrary—we know that there is a heavy charge that lies securely buried beneath you and though it may hereafter, as it has, frequently flash, yet be assured that the vindictive match of vengeance, will one day reach it, and tremendous will be the explosion—woe, to those who are within its influence—I should have been more explicit, were it not that I am fearful of communicating something that would lead to a discovery of some of our worthy agents among you. There are people in Boston, N. York, Philadelphia and Hartford who know more of the circumstances of the late insurrection than any Slave holder in Virginia or North Carolina. Our handbills and placards will soon be found in your streets, and there will be enough to read them; this you cannot prevent—the Post Office is free for anyone—any one has a right to receive communications through the medium of it—there is most surely machinery of vast power in the Press and Post Office. Believe or affect to believe that this long episle is all humbug—so much the better. . . . [M]y object in writing is hereafter to tantalize

over you—for our revenge will be more sweet, if you know, that all the calamities you are to suffer, have been premeditated—I have just heard that the good work is going on in Delaware—You will make some allowance for my barbarous chirography and the incongruity of my composition, when you are informed that since the 1st of Sept. I have written twenty nine letters almost as long as this, and written too in cypher which is slow work, and requires great accuracy. . . .

26. From Maria Stewart, "Religion and the Pure Principles of Morality: The Sure Foundation on Which We Must Build," October 1831

I was born in Hartford, Connecticut, in 1803; was left an orphan at five years of age; was bound out in a clergyman's family; had the seeds of piety and virtue early sown in my mind, but was deprived of the advantages of education, though my soul thirsted for knowledge. Left them at fifteen years of age; attended Sabbath schools until I was twenty; in 1826 was married to James W. Stewart; was left a widow in 1829; was, as I humbly hope and trust, brought to the knowledge of the truth, as it is in Jesus, in 1830; in 1831 made a public profession of my faith in Jesus Christ.

From the moment I experienced the change, I felt a strong desire, with the help and assistance of God, to devote the remainder of my days to piety and virtue, and now possess that spirit of independence that, were I called upon, I would willingly sacrifice my life for the cause of God and my brethren.

All the nations of the earth are crying out for liberty and equality. Away, away with tyranny and oppression! And shall Afric's sons be silent any longer? Far be it from me to recommend to you either to kill, burn, or destroy. But I would strongly recommend to you to improve your talents; let not one lie buried in the earth. Show forth your powers of mind. Prove to the world that

Though black your skins as shades of night, your hearts are pure, your souls are white.

. . . . .

Never Will Virtue, Knowledge, And True Politeness Begin To Flow, Till The Pure Principles Of Religion and Morality Are Put Into Force. My Respected Friends, I feel almost unable to address you; almost incompetent to perform the task; and at times I have felt ready to exclaim, O that my head were waters, and mine eyes a fountain of tears, that I might weep day and night [Jeremiah 9:1], for the transgressions of the daughters of my people. Truly, my heart's desire and prayer is, that Ethiopia might stretch forth her hands unto God. But we have a great work to do. Never, no, never will the chains of slavery and ignorance burst, till we become united as one, and cultivate among ourselves the pure principles of piety, morality and virtue. . . . O, ye daughters of Africa, awake! Awake! Arise! No longer sleep nor slumber, but distinguish yourselves. Show forth to the world that ye are endowed with noble and exalted faculties. O, ye daughters of Africa! What have ye done to immortalize your names beyond the grave? What examples have ye set before the rising generation? What foundation have ye laid for generations yet unborn? Where are our union and love? And where is our sympathy, that weeps at another's woe, and hides the faults we see? And our daughters, where are they? Blushing in innocence and virtue? And our sons, do they bid fair to become crowns of glory to our hoary heads [Proverbs 16:31]? Where is the parent who is conscious of having faithfully discharged his duty, and at the last awful day of account, shall be able to say, here, Lord, is thy poor, unworthy servant, and the children thou hast given me? and where are the children that will arise and call them blessed? Alas, O God! Forgive me if I speak amiss; the minds of our tender babes are tainted as soon as they are born; they go astray, as it were, from the womb. Where is the maiden who will blush at vulgarity? And where is the youth who has written upon his manly brow a thirst for knowledge; whose ambitious mind soars above trifles, and longs for the time to come, when he shall redress the wrongs of his father and plead the cause of his brethren? . . .

. . . . .

O, ye great and mighty men of America, ye rich and powerful ones, many of you will call for the rocks and mountains to fall upon you, and to hide you from the wrath of the Lamb [Revelation 6:16], and from him that sitteth upon the throne; whilst many of the sable-skinned Africans you now despise will shine in the kingdom of heaven as the stars forever and ever. Charity begins at home, and those that provide not for their own are worse than infidels. We know that you are raising contributions to aid the gallant Poles, we know that

you have befriended Greece and Ireland; and you have rejoiced with France, for her heroic deeds of valor. You have acknowledged all the nations of the earth, except Hayti, and you may publish, as far as the East is from the West, that you have two millions of negroes, who aspire no higher than to bow at your feet, and to court your smiles. You may kill, tyrannize, and oppress as much as you choose, until our cry shall come up before the throne of God; for I am firmly persuaded, that he will not suffer you to quell the proud, fearless, and undaunted spirits of the Africans forever; for in his own time, he is able to plead our cause against you, and to pour out upon you the ten plagues of Egypt. We will not come out against you with swords and staves, as against a thief [Matthew 26:55]; but we will tell you that our souls are fired with the same love of liberty and independence with which your souls are fired. We will tell you that too much of your blood flows in our veins, too much of your color in our skins, for us not to possess your spirits. We will tell you that it is our gold that clothes you in fine linen and purple, and causes you to fare sumptuously every day [Luke 16:19]; and it is the blood of our fathers, and the tears of our brethren that have enriched your soils, AND WE CLAIM OUR RIGHTS. . . .

27. From Angelina Grimké's Appeal to the Christian Women of the South, 1836

I have thus, I think, clearly proved to you seven propositions, viz.: First, that slavery is contrary to the declaration of our independence. Second, that it is contrary to the first charter of human rights, given to Adam, and renewed to Noah. Third, that the fact of slavery having been the subject of prophecy, furnishes *no* excuse whatever to slavedealers. Fourth, that no such system existed under the patriarchal dispensation. Fifth, that *slavery never* existed under the Jewish dispensation; but so far otherwise, that every servant was placed under the *protection of law,* and care taken not only to prevent all *involuntary servitude,* but all *voluntary perpetual* bondage. Sixth, that slavery in America reduces a *man* to a thing, a "chattel personal," *robs him* of *all* his rights as a *human being,* fetters both his mind and body, and protects the *master* in the most unnatural and unreasonable power, whilst it *throws him out* of the protection of law. Seventh, that slavery is contrary to the example and precepts of our holy and merciful Redeemer, and of his apostles. . . .

I know you [women] do not make the laws, but I also know that *you are the wives and mothers, the sisters and daughters of those who do;* and if you really suppose *you* can do nothing to overthrow slavery, you are greatly mistaken. You can do much in every way. . . .

1. Read . . . on the subject of slavery. Search the Scriptures daily. . . .

2. Pray over this subject.

3. Speak on this subject. . . . Speak then to your relatives, your friends, your acquaintances on the subject of slavery; be not afraid if you are conscientiously convinced it is *sinful,* to say so openly, but calmly, and to let your sentiments be known. If you are served by the slaves of others, try to ameliorate their condition as much as possible; never aggravate their faults . . . ; remember their extreme ignorance. . . . Discountenance *all* cruelty to them, all starvation, all corporal chastisement; these may brutalize and *break* their spirits, but will never bend them to willing, cheerful obedience. If possible, see that they are comfortably and *seasonably* fed, whether in the house or in the field; it is unreasonable and cruel to expect slaves to wait for their breakfast until eleven o'clock, when they rise at five or six. Do all you can, to induce their owners to clothe them well, and to allow them many little indulgences which would contribute to their comfort. Above all, try to persuade your husband, father, brothers and sons, that *slavery is a crime against God and man,* and that it is a great sin to keep *human beings* in such abject ignorance; to deny them the privilege of learning to read and write . . . And lastly, endeavour to inculcate submission on the part of the slaves, but whilst doing this be faithful in pleading the cause of the oppressed. . . .

4. Act on this subject. Some of you *own* slaves yourselves. *If* you believe slavery is *sinful,* set them at liberty, "undo the heavy burdens and let the oppressed go free." If they wish to remain with you, pay them wages, if not let them leave you. Should they remain, teach them, and have them taught the common branches of an English education. . . . [E]ncourage them to believe it is their *duty* to learn, if it were only that they might read the Bible.

But some of you will say, we can neither free our slaves nor teach them to read, for the laws of our state forbid it. Be not surprised when I say such wicked laws *ought to be no barrier* in the way of your duty, and I appeal to the Bible to prove this position. . . .

But some of you may say, if we do free our slaves, they will be taken up and sold, therefore there will be no use in doing it. . . . Duty is ours, and events are God's. If you think slavery is sinful, all *you* have to do is to set your slaves at liberty, do all you can to protect them, and in

humble faith and fervent prayer, commend them to your common Father. . . .

But you will perhaps say, such a course of conduct would inevitably expose us to great suffering. Yes! my christian friends, I believe it would, but this will *not* excuse you or any one else for the neglect of *duty.* . . .

But you may say, we are *women,* how can our hearts endure persecution. And why not? Have not women stood up in all the dignity and strength of moral courage to be the leaders of the people, and to bear a faithful testimony for the truth whenever the providence of God has called them to do so. Are there no *women* in that noble army of martyrs. . . . ?

The *women of the South can overthrow* this horrible system of oppression and cruelty, licentiousness and wrong. Such appeals to your legislatures would be irresistible, for there is something in the heart of man which *will bend under moral suasion.* There is a swift witness for truth in his bosom, which *will respond to truth* when it is uttered with calmness and dignity. If you could obtain but six signatures to such a petition in only one state, I would say, send up that petition, and be not in the least discouraged by the scoffs and jeers of the heartless, or the resolution of the house to lay it on the table. It will be a great thing if the subject can be introduced into your legislatures in any way, even by *women,* and *they* will be the most likely to introduce it there in the best possible manner, as a matter of *morals* and *religion,* not of expediency or politics. You may petition, too the different ecclesiastical bodies of the slave states. Slavery must be attacked with the whole power of truth and the sword of the spirit. You must take it up on *Christian* ground, and fight against it with Christian weapons, whilst your feet are shod with the preparation of the gospel of peace. And *you are now* loudly called upon by the cries of the widow and the orphan, to arise and gird yourselves for this great moral conflict, with the whole armour of righteousness upon the right hand and on the left.

28. From the Constitution of the Republic of Texas, 1836: General Provisions

Sec. 9: All persons of color who were slaves for life previous to their emigration to Texas, and who are now held in bondage, shall remain in the like state of servitude: *provided,* the said slave shall be the bona fide property of the person so holding said slave as aforesaid. Congress shall pass no laws to prohibit emigrants from bringing their slaves into the republic with them, and holding them by the same tenure by which such slaves were held in the United States; nor shall congress have power to emancipate slaves; nor shall any slave holder be allowed to emancipate his or her slave or slaves without the consent of congress, unless he or she shall send his or her slave or slaves without the limits of the republic. No free person of African descent, either in whole or in part, shall be permitted to reside permanently in the republic, without the consent of congress; and the importation or admission of Africans or negroes into this republic, excepting from the United States of America, is forever prohibited, and declared to be piracy.

29. From the Opinion of Chief Justice Shaw of Massachusetts in *Commonwealth* v. *Aves*, 1836

How, or by what act particularly, slavery was abolished in Massachusetts, whether by the adoption of the opinion in Sommersett's case, as a declaration and modification of the common law, or by the Declaration of Independence, or by the Constitution of 1780, it is not now very easy to determine, and it is rather a matter of curiosity than utility; being agreed on all hands, that if not abolished before, it was so by the declaration of rights.

30. From the Ruling of the U.S. Supreme Court in *Prigg* v. *Pennsylvania*, January 1842

[The power of legislation under the fugitive slave clause of the Constitution is] exclusive in the national government [and] not concurrent in the states. . . . [No state is bound to provide means to carry out the provisions of this clause] either by its courts or magistrates; but . . . the national government is bound, through its own proper departments, legislative, judicial, and executive, to enforce all the rights and duties growing out of this clause in the constitution. . . . [The object of this provision is] to secure to the citizens of the slaveholding states the complete right and title of ownership in their slaves, as property, in every state in the union into which they might escape. . . . We have not the slightest hesitation in holding, that . . . the owner of a slave is clothed with entire authority in every State in the Union, to seize and recapture his slave, whenever he can do it without any breach of the peace, or any illegal violence. . . .

31. From the Fugitive Slave Act of 1850

SEC. 5. *And be it further enacted,* That it shall be the duty of all marshals and deputy marshals to obey and execute all warrants and precepts issued under the provisions of this act, when to them directed; and should any marshal or deputy marshal refuse to receive such warrant, or other process, when tendered, or to use all proper means diligently to execute the same, he shall, on conviction thereof, be fined in the sum of one thousand dollars, to the use of such claimant . . . ; and after arrest of such fugitive, by such marshal or his deputy, or whilst at any time in his custody under the provisions of this act, should such fugitive escape, whether with or without the assent of such marshal or his deputy, such marshal shall be liable, on his official bond, to be prosecuted for the benefit of such claimant, for the full value of the service or labor of said fugitive in the State, Territory, or District whence he escaped . . . ; and all good citizens are hereby commanded to aid and assist in the prompt and efficient execution of this law, whenever their services may be required. . . .

SEC. 6. *And be it further enacted,* That when a person held to service or labor in any State or Territory of the United States, has heretofore or shall hereafter escape into another State or Territory of the United States, the person or persons to whom such service or labor may be due, or his, her, or their agent or attorney, duly authorized, by power of attorney, in writing, acknowledged and certified under the seal of some legal officer or court of the State or Territory in which the same may be executed, may pursue and reclaim such fugitive person, either by procuring a warrant from some one of the courts, judges, or commissioners aforesaid, of the proper circuit, district, or county, for the apprehension of such fugitive from service or labor, or by seizing and arresting such fugitive, where the same can be done without process, and by taking, or causing such person to be taken, forthwith before such court, judge, or commissioner, whose duty it shall be to hear and determine the case of such claimant in a summary manner; and upon satisfactory proof being made, by deposition or affidavit, in writing, to be taken and certified by such court, judge, or commissioner, or by other satisfactory testimony, duly taken and certified by some court, magistrate, justice of the peace, or other legal officer authorized to administer an oath and take depositions under the laws of the State or Territory from which such person owing service or labor may have escaped, with a certificate of such magistracy or other authority, as aforesaid, . . . and with proof, also by affidavit, of the identity of the person whose service or labor is claimed to be due as aforesaid, that the person so arrested does in fact owe service or labor to the person or persons claiming him or her, in the State or Territory from which such fugitive may have escaped as aforesaid, and that said person escaped, to make out and deliver to such claimant, his or her agent or attorney, a certificate setting forth the substantial facts as to the service or labor due from such fugitive to the claimant, and of his or her escape from the State or Territory in which such service or labor was due, to the State or Territory in which he or she was arrested, with authority to such claimant, or his or her agent or attorney, to use such reasonable force and restraint as may be necessary, under the circumstances of the case, to take and remove such fugitive person back to the State or Territory whence he or she may have escaped as aforesaid. In no trial or hearing under this act shall the testimony of such alleged fugitive be admitted in evidence; and the certificates in this . . . section mentioned, shall be conclusive of the right of the person or persons in whose favor granted, to remove such fugitive to the State or Territory from which he escaped, and shall prevent all molestation of such person or persons by any process issued by any court, judge, magistrate, or other person whomsoever.

SEC. 7. *And be it further enacted,* That any person who shall knowingly and willingly obstruct, hinder, or prevent such claimant, his agent or attorney, or any person or persons lawfully assisting him, her, or them, from arresting such a fugitive from service or labor, either with or without process as aforesaid, or shall rescue, or attempt to rescue, such fugitive from service or labor, from the custody of such claimant, his or her agent or attorney, or other person or persons lawfully assisting as aforesaid, when so arrested, pursuant to the authority herein given and declared; or shall aid, abet, or assist such person so owing service or labor as aforesaid, directly or indirectly, to escape from such claimant, his agent or attorney, or other person or persons legally authorized as aforesaid; or shall harbor or conceal such fugitive, so as to prevent the discovery and arrest of such person, after notice of knowledge of the fact that such person was a fugitive from service or labor as aforesaid, shall, for either of said offences, be subject to a fine not exceeding one thousand dollars, and imprisonment not exceeding six months, by indictment and conviction before the District Court of

the United States for the district in which such offence may have been committed, or before the proper court of criminal jurisdiction . . . ; and shall moreover forfeit and pay, by way of civil damages to the party injured by such illegal conduct, the sum of one thousand dollars, for each fugitive so lost as aforesaid, to be recovered by action of debt, in any of the District or Territorial Courts aforesaid, within whose jurisdiction the said offence may have been committed. . . .

SEC. 9. *And be it further enacted,* That, upon affidavit made by the claimant of such fugitive, his agent or attorney, after such certificate has been issued, that he has reason to apprehend that such fugitive will be rescued by force from his or their possession before he can be taken beyond the limits of the state in which the arrest is made, it shall be the duty of the officer making the arrest to retain such fugitive in his custody, and to remove him to the State whence he fled, and there to deliver him to said claimant, his agent, or attorney. . . .

32. From Justice Roger Taney's Opinion in the *Dred Scott* Case, 1857

Note: In Missouri in 1833 the owner of Dred Scott sold him to Dr. John Emerson, a military surgeon, who in the pursuit of his career took Scott to the free state of Illinois and to the free Wisconsin Territory. In 1842 Scott and his wife Harriet returned to Missouri with Mrs. Emerson. In 1846, the Scotts instituted a suit for freedom against Mrs. Emerson, under Missouri law, where, according to precedent (especially Rachael v. Walker, *1837), if a slave returned to Missouri after having sojourned in a free state or territory, that slave was entitled to freedom by virtue of residence in the free state or territory.*

The question is simply this: Can a negro, whose ancestors were imported into this country and sold as slaves, become a member of the political community formed and brought into existence by the Constitution of the United States, and as such become entitled to all the rights and privileges and immunities guaranteed by that instrument to the citizen? One of which rights is the privilege of suing in a court of the United States in the cases specified in the Constitution.

It will be observed that the plea applies to that class of persons only whose ancestors were negroes of the African race, and imported into this country, and sold and held as slaves. The only matter in issue before the court, therefore, is, whether the descendants of such slaves, when they shall be emancipated, or who are born of parents who had become free before their birth, are citizens of a State, in the sense in which the word citizen is used in the Constitution of the United States. And this being the only matter in dispute on the pleadings, the court must be understood as speaking in this opinion of that class only, that is, of those persons who are the descendants of Africans who were imported into this country and sold as slaves. . . .

We proceed to examine the case as presented by the pleadings.

The words "people of the United States" and "citizens" are synonymous terms, and mean the same thing. They both describe the political body who, according to our republican institutions, form the sovereignty, and who hold the power and conduct the government through their representatives. They are what we familiarly call the "sovereign people," and every citizen is one of this people, and a constituent member of this sovereignty. The question before us is, whether the class of persons described in the plea in abatement compose a portion of this people, and are constituent members of this sovereignty. We think they are not, and that they are not included, and were not intended to be included, under the word "citizen" in the Constitution, and can therefore claim none of the rights and privileges which that instrument provides for and secures to citizens of the United States. On the contrary, they were at that time considered as a subordinate and inferior class of beings, who had been subjugated by the dominant race, and, whether emancipated or not, yet remained subject to their authority, and had no rights or privileges but such as those who held the power and the government might choose to grant them.

It is not the province of the court to decide upon the justice or injustice, the policy or impolicy, of these laws. . . .

In discussing this question, we must not confound the rights of citizenship which a State may confer within its own limits, and the rights of citizenship as a member of the Union. It does not by any means follow, because he has all the rights and privileges of a State, that he must be a citizen of the United States. He may have all of the rights and privileges of the citizen of a State, and yet not be entitled to the rights and privileges of a citizen of any other State. For, previous to the adoption of the Constitution of the United States, every State had the undoubted right to confer on whomsoever it pleased the character of citizen, and to endow him with all its rights. But this character of course was confined to the boundaries of the State, and gave him no rights or privileges in other States beyond those secured to him by the laws of nations and the comity of States. Nor have the several States surrendered the power of conferring these rights and privileges by adopting the Constitution of the United States. Each State may still confer them upon an alien, or any one it thinks proper, or upon any class or description of persons; yet he would not be a citizen in the sense in which that word is used in the Constitution of the United States, nor entitled to sue as such in one of its courts, nor to the privileges and immunities of a citizen in the other States. The rights which he would acquire would be restricted to the State which gave them. The Constitution has conferred on Congress the right to establish an uniform rule of naturalization, and this right is evidently exclusive, and has always been held by this court to be so. Consequently no State, since the adoption of the Constitution, can, by naturalizing an alien, invest him with the rights and privileges secured to a citizen of a State under the Federal Government, although, so far as the State alone was concerned, he would undoubtedly be entitled to the rights of a citizen, and clothed with all the rights and immunities which the Constitution and laws of the State attached to that character.

It is very clear, therefore, that no State can, by any act or law of its own, passed since the adoption of the Constitution, introduce a new member into the political community created by the Constitution of the United States. It cannot make him a member of this community by making him a member of its own. And, for the same reason, it cannot introduce any person or description of persons who were not intended to be embraced in this new political family, which the Constitution brought into existence, but were intended to be excluded from it.

The question then arises, whether the provisions of the Constitution, in relation to the personal rights and privileges to which the citizen of a State should be entitled, embraced the negro African race, at that time in this country, or who might afterwards be imported, who had then or should afterwards be made free in any State; and to put it in the power of a single State to make him a citizen of the United States, and indue him with the full rights of citizenship in every other State without their consent. Does the Constitution of the United States act upon him whenever he shall be made free under the laws of a State, and raised there to the rank of a citizen, and immediately clothe him with all the privileges of a citizen in every other State and in its own courts?

The court think the affirmative of these propositions cannot be maintained. And if it cannot, the plaintiff in error could not be a citizen of the State of Missouri, within the meaning of the Constitution of the United States, and, consequently, was not entitled to sue in its courts.

33. From an Act of Congress, August 6, 1861, to Confiscate Property Used for Insurrectionary Purpose

Be it enacted . . . That if, during the present or any future insurrection against the Government of the United States, after the President of the United States shall have declared by proclamation, that the laws of the United States are opposed, and the execution thereof obstructed by combinations too powerful to be suppressed by the ordinary course of judicial proceedings, or by the power vested in the marshals by law, any person or persons, his, her, or their agent, attorney, or employee, shall purchase or acquire, sell or give, any property of whatsoever kind or description, with intent to use or employ the same, or suffer the same to be used or employed, in aiding, abetting, or promoting such insurrection or resistance to the laws, or any person or persons engaged therein; or if any person or persons, being the owner or owners of any such property, shall knowingly use or employ, or consent to the use or employment of the same as aforesaid, all such property is hereby declared to be lawful subject of prize and capture wherever found; and it shall be the duty of the President of the United States to cause the same to be seized, confiscated, and condemned. . . .

SEC. 3. *And be it further enacted,* That the Attorney-General, or any district attorney of the United States in which said property may at the time be, may institute the proceedings of condemnation, and in such case they shall be wholly for the benefit of the United States; or any person may file an information with such attorney, in which case the proceedings shall be for the use of such informer and the United States in equal parts.

SEC. 4. *And be it further enacted,* That whenever hereafter, during the present insurrection against the Government of the United States, any person claimed to be held to labor or service under the law of any State, shall be required or permitted by the person to whom such labor or service is claimed to be due, or by the lawful agent of such person, to take up arms against the United States, or shall be required or permitted by the person to whom such labor or service is claimed to be due, or his lawful agent, to work or to be employed in or upon any fort, navy yard, dock, armory, ship, entrenchment, or in any military or naval service whatsoever, against the Government and lawful authority of the United States, then, and in every such case, the person to whom such labor service is claimed to be due shall forfeit his claim to such labor, any law of the State or of the United States to the contrary notwithstanding. And whenever thereafter the person claiming such labor or service shall seek to enforce his claim, it shall be a full and sufficient answer to such claim that the person whose service or labor is claimed had been employed in hostile service against the Government of the United States contrary to the provisions of this act.

34. From the Constitution of the Confederate States of America, 1861

Article I, Section 9

[The Confederate Congress is explicitly prohibited from passing any law] denying or impairing the right of property in negro slaves.

Article IV, Section 2

The citizens of each State shall be entitled to all the privileges and immunities of citizens in the several States, and shall have the right of transit and sojourn in any State of this Confederacy, with their slaves and other property; and the right of property in said slaves shall not be thereby impaired. . . .

No slave or other person held to service or labor in any State or Territory of the Confederate States, under the laws thereof, escaping or lawfully carried into another, shall, in consequence of any law or regulation therein, be discharged from such service or labor; but shall be delivered up on claim of the party to whom such slave belongs, or to whom such service or labor may be due. . . .

The Confederate States may acquire new territory; and Congress shall have power to legislate and provide governments for the inhabitants of all territory belonging to the Confederate States, lying without the limits of the several States; and may permit them, at such times and in such manner as it may by law provide, to form States to be admitted into the Confederacy. In all such territory, the institution of negro slavery, as it now exists in the Confederate States, shall be recognized and protected by Congress and by the territorial government; and the inhabitants of the several Confederate States and Territories shall have the right to take to such Territory any slaves lawfully held by them in any of the States or Territories of the Confederate States. . . .

35. From an Act of Congress, April 16, 1862, for the Release of Certain Persons Held to Service or Labor in the District of Columbia

Be it enacted . . . That all persons held to service or labor within the District of Columbia by reason of African descent are hereby discharged and freed of and from all claim to such service or labor; and from and after the passage of this act neither slavery nor involuntary servitude, except for crime, whereof the party shall be duly convicted, shall hereafter exist in said District.

SEC. 2. *And be it further enacted,* That all persons loyal to the United States, holding claim to service or labor against persons discharged therefrom by this act, may, within ninety days from the passage thereof, but not thereafter, present to the commissioners hereinafter mentioned, their respective statements or petitions in writing, verified by oath or affirmation, setting forth the names, ages, and personal descriptions of such persons, the manner in which said petitioners acquired such claim, and any facts touching the value thereof, and declaring his allegiance to the Government of the United States during the present rebellion, nor in any way given aid or comfort thereto: *Provided,* That the oath of the party to the petition shall not be evidence of the facts therein stated.

SEC. 3. [Appointment of commissioners to investigate and determine validity of claims for compensation.] . . . *And provided, further,* That no claim shall be allowed for any slave or slaves brought into said District after the passage of this act, nor for any slave claimed by any person who has borne arms against the Government of the United States in the present rebellion, or in any way given aid and comfort thereto, or which originates in or by virtue of any transfer heretofore made, or which shall hereafter be made by any person who has in any manner aided or sustained the rebellion against the Government of the United States. . . .

SEC. 8. *And be it further enacted,* That any person or persons who shall kidnap, or in any manner transport or procure to be taken out of said District, any person or persons discharged and freed by the provisions of this act, or any free person or persons with intent to re-enslave or sell such person or persons into slavery, or shall re-enslave any of said freed persons, the person or persons so offending shall be deemed guilty of a felony, and on conviction

thereof in any court of competent jurisdiction in said District, shall be imprisoned in the penitentiary not less than five nor more than twenty years. . . .

SEC. 10. *And be it further enacted,* That the said clerk [of the Circuit Court for the District of Columbia] shall, from time to time, on demand, and on receiving twenty-five cents therefor, prepare, sign, and deliver to each person made free or manumitted by this act, a certificate under the seal of said court, setting out the name, age, and description of such person, and stating that such person was duly manumitted and set free by this act.

SEC. 11. *And be it further enacted,* That the sum of one hundred thousand dollars, out of any money in the Treasury not otherwise appropriated, is hereby appropriated, to be expended under the direction of the President of the United States, to aid in the colonization and settlement of such free persons of African descent now residing in said District, including those to be liberated by this act, as may desire to emigrate to the Republics of Hayti or Liberia, or such other country beyond the limits of the United States as the President may determine: *Provided,* The expenditure for this purpose shall not exceed one hundred dollars for each emigrant.

SEC. 12. *And be it further enacted,* That all acts of Congress and all laws of the State of Maryland in force in said District, and all ordinances of the cities of Washington and Georgetown, inconsistent with the provisions of this act, are hereby repealed.

36. From an Act of Congress, July 17, 1862, to Suppress Insurrection, to Punish Treason and Rebellion, to Seize and Confiscate the Property of Rebels, and for Other Purposes

Be it enacted . . . That every person who shall hereafter commit the crime of treason against the United States, and shall be adjudged guilty thereof, shall suffer death, and all his slaves, if any, shall be declared and made free; or, at the discretion of the court, he shall be imprisoned for not less than five years and fined not less than ten thousand dollars, and all his slaves, if any, shall be declared and made free; said fine shall be levied and collected on any or all of the property, real and personal, excluding slaves, of which the said person so convicted was the owner at the time of committing the said crime, any sale or conveyance to the contrary notwithstanding.

SEC. 2. *And be it further enacted,* That if any person shall hereafter incite, set on foot, assist, or engage in any rebellion or insurrection against the authority of the United States, or the laws thereof, or shall give aid or comfort thereto, or shall engage in, or give aid and comfort to, any such existing rebellion or insurrection, and be convicted thereof, such person shall be punished by imprisonment for a period not exceeding ten years, or by a fine not exceeding ten thousand dollars, and by the liberation of all his slaves, if any he have; or by both of said punishments, at the discretion of the court.

SEC. 3. *And be it further enacted,* That every person guilty of either of the offences described in this act shall be forever incapable and disqualified to hold any office under the United States. . . .

SEC. 6. *And be it further enacted,* That if any person within any State or Territory of the United States, other than those named as aforesaid, after the passage of this act, being engaged in armed rebellion against the government of the United States, or aiding or abetting such rebellion, shall not, within sixty days after public warning and proclamation duly given and made by the President of the United States, cease to aid, countenance, and abet such rebellion, and return to his allegiance to the United States, all the estate and property, moneys, stocks, and credits of such person shall be liable to seizure as aforesaid, and it shall be the duty of the President to seize and use them as aforesaid or the proceeds thereof. And all sales, transfers, or conveyances, of any such property after the expiration of the said sixty days from the date of such warning and proclamation shall be null and void; and it shall be a sufficient bar to any suit brought by such person for the possession or the use of such property, or any of it, to allege and prove that he is one of the persons described in this section.

SEC. 9. *And be it further enacted,* That all slaves of persons who shall hereafter be engaged in rebellion against the government of the United States, or who shall in any way give aid or comfort thereto, escaping from such persons and taking refuge within the lines of the army; and all slaves captured from such persons or deserted by them and coming under the control of the government of the United States; and all slaves of such persons found or being within any place occupied by rebel forces and afterwards occupied by the forces of the United States, shall be deemed captives of war, and shall be forever free of their servitude, and not again held as slaves.

SEC. 10. *And be it further enacted,* That no slave escaping into any State, Territory, or the District of Columbia, from any other State, shall be delivered up, or in any way impeded or hindered of his liberty, except for crime, or some offence against the laws, unless the person claiming said fugitive shall first make oath that the person to whom the labor or service of such fugitive is alleged to be due is his lawful owner, and has not borne arms against the United States in the present rebellion, nor in any way given aid and comfort thereto; and no person engaged in the military or naval service of the United States shall, under any pretence whatever, assume to decide on the validity of the claim of any person to the service or labor of any other person, or surrender up any such person to the claimant, on pain of being dismissed from the service.

SEC. 11. *And be it further enacted,* That the President of the United States is authorized to employ as many persons of African descent as he may deem necessary and proper for the suppression of this rebellion, and for this purpose he may organize and use them in such manner as he may judge best for the public welfare.

SEC. 12. *And be it further enacted,* That the President of the United States is hereby authorized to make provision for the transportation, colonization, and settlement, in some tropical country beyond the limits of the United States, of such persons of the African race, made free by the provisions of this act, as may be willing to emigrate, having first obtained the consent of the government of said country to their protection and settlement within the same, with all the rights and privileges of freemen.

37. From Lincoln's Proclamation of the Act to Suppress Insurrection, July 25, 1862

In pursuance of the sixth section of the act of Congress entitled "An act to suppress insurrection and to punish treason and rebellion, to seize and confiscate property of rebels, and for other purposes" Approved July 17, 1862, and which act, and the Joint Resolution explanatory thereof, are herewith published, I, Abraham Lincoln, President of the United States, do hereby proclaim to, and warn all persons within the contemplation of said sixth section to cease participating in, aiding, countenancing, or abetting the existing rebellion, or any rebellion against the government of the United States, and to return to their proper allegiance to the United States, on pain of the forfeitures and seizures, as within and by sixth section provided.

38. The Preliminary Emancipation Proclamation, September 22, 1862

I, Abraham Lincoln, President of the United States of America, and Commander-in-Chief of the Army and Navy thereof, do hereby proclaim and declare that hereafter, as heretofore, the war will be prosecuted for the object of practically restoring the constitutional relation between the United States, and each of the states, and the people thereof, in which states that relation is, or may be suspended, or disturbed.

That it is my purpose upon the next meeting of Congress to again recommend the adoption of a practical measure tendering pecuniary aid to the free acceptance or rejection of all slave states, so called, the people whereof may not then be in rebellion against the United States, and which states may then have voluntarily adopted, or thereafter may voluntarily adopt, immediate or gradual abolishment of slavery within their respective limits; and that the effort to colonize persons of African descent with their consent upon this continent, or elsewhere with the previously obtained consent of the Governments existing there will be continued.

That on the first day of January in the year of our Lord, one thousand eight hundred and sixty-three, all persons held as slaves within any state, or designated part of a state, the people whereof shall be in rebellion against the United States shall be then, thenceforward, and forever free; and the executive government of the United States including the military and naval authority thereof will recognize and maintain the freedom of such persons, and will do no act or acts to repress such persons, or any of them, in any efforts they may make for their actual freedom.

That the executive will, on the first day of January aforesaid, by proclamation, designate the States, and parts of states, if any, in which the people thereof respectively, shall then be in rebellion against the United States; and the fact that any state, or the people thereof shall, on that day be, in good faith represented in the Congress of the United States, by members chosen thereto, at elections wherein a majority of the qualified voters of such state shall have participated, shall, in the absence of strong countervailing testimony, be deemed conclusive evidence that such state and the people thereof, are not then in rebellion against the United States.

That attention is hereby called to an Act of Congress entitled "An act to make an additional Article of War"

approved March 13, 1862, and which act is in the words and figure following:

Be it enacted by the Senate and House of Representatives of the United States of America in Congress assembled, That hereafter the following shall be promulgated as an additional article of war for the government of the army of the United States, and shall be obeyed and observed as such:

Article—All officers or persons in the military or naval service of the United States are prohibited from employing any of the forces under their respective commands for the purpose of returning fugitives from service or labor, who may have escaped from any persons to whom such service or labor is claimed to be due, and any officer who shall be found guilty by a court-martial of violating this article shall be dismissed from the service.

Sec. 2. *And be it further enacted,* That this act shall take effect from and after its passage.

Also to the ninth and tenth sections of an act entitled, "An Act to suppress Insurrection, to punish Treason and Rebellion, to seize and confiscate property of rebels, and for other purposes," approved July 17, 1862, and which sections are in the words and figures following:

Sec. 9. *And be it further enacted,* That all slaves of persons who shall hereafter be engaged in rebellion against the government of the United States, or who shall in any way give aid or comfort thereto, escaping from such persons and taking refuge within the lines of the army; and all slaves captured from such persons or deserted by them and coming under the control of the government of the United States; and all slaves of such persons found *on* or being within any place occupied by rebel forces and afterwards occupied by the forces of the United States, shall be deemed captives of war, and shall be forever free of their servitude and not again held as slaves.

Sec. 10. *And be it further enacted,* That no slave escaping into any State, territory, or the District of Columbia, from any other State, shall be delivered up, or in any way impeded or hindered of his liberty, except for crime, or some offence against the laws, unless the person claiming such fugitive shall first make oath that the person to whom the labor or service of such fugitive is alleged to be due is his lawful owner, and has not borne arms against the United States in the present rebellion, nor in any way given aid and comfort thereto; and no person engaged in the military or naval service of the United States shall, under any pretence whatever, assume to decide on the validity of the claim of any person to the service or labor of any other person, or surrender up any such person to the claimant, on pain of being dismissed from the service.

And I do hereby enjoin upon and order all persons engaged in the military and naval service of the United States to observe, obey, and enforce within their respective spheres of service, the act, and sections above recited.

And the executive will in due time recommend that all citizens of the United States who shall have remained loyal thereto throughout the rebellion shall (upon the restoration of the constitutional relation between the United States, and their respective states, and people, if that relation shall have been suspended or disturbed) be compensated for all losses by acts of the United States, including the loss of slaves.

In witness whereof, I have hereunto set my hand, and caused the seal of the United States to be affixed.

Done at the City of Washington, this twenty second day of September, in the year of our Lord, one thousand, eight hundred and sixty two, and of the Independence of the United States, the eighty seventh.

Abraham Lincoln
William H. Seward
Secretary of State

39. The Emancipation Proclamation, January 1, 1863

Whereas, on the twenty-second day of September, in the year of our Lord one thousand eight hundred and sixty two, a proclamation was issued by the President of the United States, containing, among other things, the following, to wit:

"That on the first day of January, in the year of our Lord one thousand eight hundred and sixty-three, all persons held as slaves within any State or designated part of a State, the people whereof shall then be in rebellion against the United States, shall be then, thenceforward, and forever free; and the Executive Government of the United States, including the military and naval authority thereof, will recognize and maintain the freedom of such persons, and will do no act or acts to repress such persons, or any of them, in any effort they may make for their actual freedom.

"That the Executive will, on the first day of January aforesaid, by proclamation, designate the States and parts of States, if any, in which the people thereof, shall on that day be, in good faith, represented in the Congress of the United States by members chosen thereto at elections wherein a majority of the qualified voters of such State shall have participated, shall in the absence of strong countervailing testimony, be deemed conclusive evidence that such State, and the people thereof, are not then in rebellion against the United States."

Now, therefore, I, Abraham Lincoln, President of the United States, by virtue of the power in me invested as Commander-in-Chief, of the Army and Navy of the United States in time of actual armed rebellion against authority and government of the United States, and as a fit and necessary war measure for suppressing said rebellion, do, on this first day of January, in the year of our Lord one thousand eight hundred and sixty three, and in accordance with my purpose so to do publicly proclaimed for the full period of one hundred days, from the day first above mentioned, order and designate as the States and parts of States wherein the people thereof respectively, are this day in rebellion against the United States, the following, to wit:

Arkansas, Texas, Louisiana, (except the Parishes of St. Bernard, Plaquemines, Jefferson, St. Johns, St. Charles, St. James Ascension, Assumption, Terrebonne, Lafourche, St. Mary, St. Martin, and Orleans, including the City of New-Orleans) Mississippi, Alabama, Florida, Georgia, South-Carolina, North-Carolina, and Virginia, (except the forty-eight counties designated as West Virginia, and also the counties of Berkley, Accomac, Northampton, Elizabeth-City, York, Princess Ann, and Norfolk, including the cities of Norfolk and Portsmouth; and which excepted parts are, for the present, left precisely as if this proclamation were not issued.)

And by virtue of the power, and for the purpose aforesaid, I do order and declare that all persons held as slaves within said designated States, and parts of States, are, and henceforward shall be free; and that the Executive government of the United States, including the military and naval authorities thereof, will recognize and maintain the freedom of said persons.

And I hereby enjoin upon the people so declared to be free to abstain from all violence, unless in necessary self-defence; and I recommend to them that, in all cases when allowed, they labor faithfully for reasonable wages.

And I further declare and make known that such persons of suitable condition, will be received into the armed service of the United States to garrison forts, positions, stations, and other places, and to man vessels of all sorts in said service.

And upon this act, sincerely believed to be an act of justice, warranted by the Constitution, upon military necessary, I invoke the considerate judgment of mankind, and the gracious favor of Almighty God.

In witness whereof, I have hereunto set my hand and caused the seal of the United States to be affixed.

Done at the City of Washington, this first day of January, in the year of our Lord one thousand eight hundred and sixty three, and of the Independence of the United States of America the eighty-seventh.

By the President: Abraham Lincoln
William H. Seward, Secretary of State

40. Lincoln's Order to Protect Black Prisoners of War, 1863

Executive Mansion, Washington, July 30, 1863

It is the duty of every government to give protection to its citizens of whatever class, color, or condition, and especially to those who are duly organized as soldiers in the public service. The law of nations and the usages and customs of war, as carried on by civilized powers, permit no distinction as to color in the treatment of prisoners of war as public enemies. To sell or enslave any captured person on account of his color, and for no offence against the laws of war, is a relapse into barbarism and a crime against the civilization of the age. The Government of the United States will give the same protection to all its soldiers; and if the enemy shall sell or enslave any one because of his color, the offence shall be punished by retaliation upon the enemy's prisoners in our hands.

It is therefore ordered that for every soldier of the United States killed in violation of the laws of war, a Rebel soldier shall be executed, and for every one enslaved by the enemy or sold into slavery, a Rebel soldier shall be placed at hard labor on the public works, and continue at such labor until the other shall be released and receive the treatment due a prisoner of war.

41. From President Lincoln's Proclamation of Amnesty and Reconstruction, December 8, 1863

I, Abraham Lincoln, President of the United States, do proclaim . . . to all persons who have . . . participated in the existing rebellion . . . , that a full pardon is hereby granted to them and each of them, with restoration of all rights of property, except as to slaves, . . . and upon the condition that every such person shall take and subscribe an oath, and thenceforward keep and maintain said oath. . . .

"I,___ ___, do solemnly swear, in presence of Almighty God, that I will henceforth faithfully support, protect, and defend the Constitution of the United States and the Union of the States thereunder; and that I will, in like manner, abide by and faithfully support all acts of congress passed during the existing rebellion with reference to slaves, so long and so far as not repealed, modified, or held void by congress, or by decision of the supreme court; and that I will, in like manner, abide by and faithfully support all proclamations of the President made during the existing rebellion having reference to slaves, so long and so far as not modified or declared void by decision of the supreme court. So help me God."

42. From an Act to Increase the Efficiency of the (Confederate) Army by the Employment of Free Negroes and Slaves in Certain Capacities, February 17, 1864

Whereas, the efficiency of the Army is greatly diminished by the withdrawal from the ranks of able-bodied soldiers to act as teamsters, and in various other capacities in which free negroes and slaves might be advantageously employed: Therefore,

The Congress of the Confederate States of America do enact, That all male free negroes and other free persons of color, not including those who are free under the treaty of Paris of eighteen hundred and three, or under the treaty with Spain of eighteen hundred and nineteen, resident in the Confederate States, between the ages of eighteen and fifty years, shall be held liable to perform such duties with the army, or in connection with the military defenses of the country, in the way of work upon fortifications or in Government works for the production or preparation of material of war, or in military hospitals, as the Secretary of War or the commanding general of the Trans-Mississippi Department may, from time to time, prescribe, and while engaged in the performance of such duties shall receive rations and clothing and compensation at the rate of eleven dollars a month. . . .

SEC. 2. That the Secretary of War is hereby authorized to employ for duties similar to those indicated in the preceding section of this act, as many male negro slaves, not to exceed twenty thousand, as in his judgment, the wants of the service may require, furnishing them, while so employed, with proper rations and clothing, under rules and regulations to be established by him, and paying to the owners of said slaves such wages as may be agreed upon with said owners for their use and service, and in the event of the loss of any slaves while so employed, by the act of the enemy, or by escape to the enemy, or by death inflicted by the enemy, or by disease contracted while in any service required of said slaves, then the owners of the same shall be entitled to receive the full value of such slaves. . . .

SEC. 3. That when the Secretary of War shall be unable to procure the service of slaves in any military department in sufficient numbers for the necessities of the Department, upon the terms and conditions set forth in the preceding section, then he is hereby authorized to impress the services of as many male slaves, not to exceed twenty thousand, as may be required, from time to time, to discharge the duties indicated in the first section of this act . . . *Provided,* That if the owner have but one male slave between the age of eighteen and fifty, he shall not be impressed against the will of said owner: *Provided further,* That free negroes shall be first impressed, and if there should be a deficiency, it shall be supplied by the impressment of slaves according to the foregoing provisions: *Provided further,* That in making the impressment, not more than one of every five male slaves between the ages of eighteen and forty-five shall be taken from any owner. . . .

43. From American Freedmen's Inquiry Commission Final Report, May 15, 1864

[T]he Commission regard it of great importance that, . . . in the constitutions of the States when taken back, all freemen shall be secured in equal rights. . . .

[T]he enfranchised negro is as capable of taking care of himself and his family as any other portion of our people. . . .

There is no disposition in these people to go North. . . . They are equally averse to . . . emigrating to Africa. . . . A few years will probably see half the free negro population now residing among us crossing Mason and Dixon's line to join the emancipated freedmen of the South. . . .

[T]he personal prejudice against negroes as a race is stronger in the Northern than in the Southern States, and at least as strong in Canada as in any portion of the Union. . . .

It will have a tendency to increase harmony between the two races if the colored people . . . refrain from settling in colonies or suburbs by themselves. . . .

[T]here seems a probability in favor of the opinion . . . that "the mulatto, considered in his animal nature, lacks the innervation [energy, initiative] and spring of the pure blacks and whites," and that "the organic inferiority is shown in less power of resisting destructive agencies; in less fecundity and less longevity." If this be so, then amalgamation of these two races is in itself a physical evil injurious to both. . . . The Commission believe that the effect of general emancipation will be to discourage amalgamation.

Aside from this . . . , the social influence of the two races on each other, so soon as their reciprocal relations shall be based on justice, will, beyond question, be mutually beneficial. . . . The Anglo-Saxon race, with great force of character, much mental activity, an unflagging spirit of enterprise, has a certain hardness, a stubborn will, only moderate geniality, a lack of habitual cheerfulness. Its intellectual powers are stronger than its social instincts. . . .

The African race is [g]enial, lively, docile, emotional, the affections rule; the social instincts maintain the ascendant. . . . It is well fitted to occupy useful stations in life; but such as require quick observation rather than comprehensive views or strong sense. It is little given to stirring enterprise. . . . It is not a race that will ever take a lead in the material improvement of the world. . . . As regards the virtues of humility, loving kindness, resignation under adversity, reliance on Divine Providence, this race exhibits these, as a general rule, in a more marked manner than does the Anglo-Saxon. . . .

What amount of aid and interference is necessary or desirable? . . . [T]here is as much danger in doing too much as in doing too little. . . .

The essential is that we secure to them the means of making their own way. . . . If, like whites, they are to be self-supporting, then, like whites, they ought to have those rights, civil and political. . . .

The sum of our recommendations is this: Offer the freedmen temporary aid and counsel until they become a little accustomed to their new sphere of life; secure to them, by law, their just rights of person and property; relieve them, by a fair and equal administration of justice, from the depressing influence of disgraceful prejudice; above all, guard them against the virtual restoration of slavery in any form, under any pretext, and then let them take care of themselves.

44. From Black Codes of Mississippi, 1865: An Act to Confer Civil Rights on Freedmen. . . .

Section 1. All freedmen, free negroes and mulattoes may sue and be sued, implead and be impleaded, in all the courts of law and equity of this State, and may acquire personal property, . . . by descent or purchase, and may dispose of the same in the same manner and to the same extent that white persons may: Provided, That the provisions of this section shall not be so construed as to allow any freedman, free negro or mulatto to rent or lease any lands or tenements except in incorporated cities or towns, in which places the corporate authorities shall control the same. . . .

Section 3. All freedmen, free negroes or mulattoes who do now and have herebefore lived and cohabited together as husband and wife shall be taken and held in law as legally married, and the issue shall be taken and held as legitimate . . . ; and it shall not be lawful for any freedman, free negro or mulatto to intermarry with any white person; . . . and those shall be deemed freedmen, free negroes and mulattoes who are of pure negro blood, and those descended from a negro to the third generation, inclusive. . . .

Section 4. . . . freedmen, free negroes or mulattoes shall be competent in civil cases, when a party or parties to the suit, either plaintiff or plaintiffs, defendant or defendants; also in cases where freedmen, free negroes and mulattoes is or are either plaintiff or plaintiffs, defendant or defendants. They shall also be competent witnesses in all criminal prosecutions where the crime charged is alleged to have been committed by a white person upon or against the person or property of a freedman, free negro or mulatto. . . .

Section 5. Every freedman, free negro and mulatto shall, on the second Monday of January, one thousand eight hundred and sixty-six, and annually thereafter, have a lawful home or employment, and shall have written evidence thereof. . . .

Section 10. It shall be lawful for any freedman, free negro, or mulatto, to charge any white person, freedman, free negro or mulatto by affidavit, with any criminal offense against his or her person or property. . . .

45. From Gen. W. T. Sherman's Field Order 15, Savannah, Georgia, January 16, 1865 (President Lincoln later invalidated this order.)

I. The islands from Charleston, south, the abandoned rice fields along the rivers for thirty miles back from the sea, and the country bordering the St. Johns river, Florida, are reserved and set apart for the settlement of the negroes now made free. . . .

II. At Beaufort, Hilton Head, Savannah, Fernandina, St. Augustine and Jacksonville, the blacks may remain in their chosen or accustomed vocations—but on the islands, and in the settlements hereafter to be established, no white person whatever, unless military officers and soldiers detailed for duty, will be permitted to reside; and the sole and exclusive management of affairs will be left to the freed people themselves. . . .

III. Whenever three respectable Negroes, heads of families, shall desire to settle on land, and shall have selected for that purpose an island or a locality clearly defined, within the limits above designated, the Inspector of Settlements and Plantations will . . . give them a license to settle such land or district, and afford them such assistance as he can. . . . each family shall have a plot of not more than (40) forty acres of tillable ground. . . .

46. From an Act to Increase the Military Force of the Confederate States, March 23, 1865

The Congress of the Confederate States of America do enact, That in order to provide additional forces to repel invasion, maintain the rightful possession of the Confederate States, secure their independence, and preserve their institutions, the President be, and he is hereby, authorized to ask for and accept from the owners of slaves, the services of such number of able-bodied negro men as he may deem expedient, for and during the war, to perform military service in whatever capacity he may direct. . . .

Sec. 3. That while employed in the service the said troops shall receive the same rations, clothing and compensation as are allowed to other troops in the same branch of the service. . . .

Sec. 5. That nothing in this act shall be construed to authorize a change in the relation which the said slaves shall bear toward their owners, except by consent of the owners and of the States in which they may reside, and in pursuance of the laws thereof.

47. From an Address to the Loyal Citizens and Congress . . . Adopted by a Convention of Negroes Held in Alexandria, Virginia, From August 2 to 5, 1865

Well, the war is over, the rebellion is "put down," and we are declared free! Four fifths of our enemies are paroled or amnestied, and the other fifth are being pardoned, and the President has, in his efforts at the reconstruction of the civil government of the States, late in rebellion, left us entirely at the mercy of these subjugated but unconverted rebels, in everything save the privilege of bringing us, our wives and little ones, to the auction block. . . . We know these men—know them well—and we assure you that, with the majority of them, . . . their professions of loyalty are used as a cover to the cherished design of getting restored to their former relations with the Federal Government, and then . . . to render the freedom you have given us more intolerable than the slavery they intended for us.

. . . [O]ur only safety is in keeping them under Governors of the military persuasion until you have so amended the Federal Constitution that it will prohibit the States from making any distinction between citizens on account of race or color. In one word, the only salvation for us besides the power of the Government, is in the possession of the ballot. Give us this, and we will protect ourselves. . . .

48. The Thirteenth Amendment, Ratified December 18, 1865

Section 1. Neither slavery nor involuntary servitude, except as a punishment for a crime whereof the party shall have been duly convicted, shall exist within the United States, or any place subject to their jurisdiction.

Section 2. Congress shall have power to enforce this article by appropriate legislation.

49. From the Civil Rights Act of 1866, April 9, 1866 (Its constitutionality called into question, the measures in this law were reenacted as the Civil Rights Act of 1870.)

. . . all persons born in the United States and not subject to any foreign power, excluding Indians not taxed, are hereby declared to be citizens of the United States; and such citizens, of every race and color, without regard to any previous condition of slavery or involuntary servitude, . . . shall have the same right, in every State and Territory in the United States, to make and enforce contracts, to sue, be parties, and give evidence, to inherit, purchase, lease, sell, hold, and convey real and personal property, and to full and equal benefit of all laws and proceedings for the security of person and property, as is enjoyed by white citizens, and shall be subject to like punishment, pains, and penalties, and to none other, any law,

statute, ordinance, regulation, or custom, to the contrary notwithstanding.

50. From the Reconstruction Act, March 2, 1867

. . . *Whereas* no legal State governments or adequate protection for life or property now exist in the rebel States of Virginia, North Carolina, South Carolina, Georgia, Mississippi, Alabama, Louisiana, Florida, Texas, and Arkansas . . . : Therefore

Be it enacted, &c., That said rebel States shall be . . . made subject to the military authority of the United States. . . .

Sec. 3. That it shall be the duty of each officer assigned [to command these districts] to protect all persons in their rights of person and property, to suppress insurrection, disorder, and violence, and to punish, or cause to be punished, all disturbers of the public peace and criminals. . . .

. . . . .

Sec. 5. That when the people of any one of said rebel States shall have formed a constitution of government in conformity with the Constitution of the United States in all respects, framed by a convention of delegates elected by the male citizens of said State twenty-one years old and upward, of whatever race, color, or previous condition, who have been resident in said State for one year previous . . . and when such constitution shall provide that the elective franchise shall be enjoyed by all such persons as have tried without unnecessary delay, and no cruel or unusual punishment . . . , and when . . . Congress shall have approved the same, and when said State, by a vote of its legislature elected under said constitution, shall have adopted the [recently passed 14th amendment], said State shall be declared entitled to representation in Congress. . . .

Sec. 6. That until the people of said rebel states shall be by law admitted to representation in the Congress of the United States, any civil governments which may exist therein shall be . . . in all respects subject to the paramount authority of the United States. . . .

51. From Andrew Johnson's veto of the first Reconstruction Act, March 2, 1867

. . . The bill places all the people of the ten States therein named under the absolute domination of military rulers. . . .

. . . the States in question have each of them an actual government, with all the powers—executive, judicial, and legislative—which properly belong to a free state. . . . [T]hey make, administer, and execute the laws which concern their domestic affairs. An existing de facto government, exercising such functions as these, is itself the law of the state upon all matters within its jurisdiction. . . .

The military rule which [the bill] establishes is plainly to be used, not for any purpose of order or for the prevention of crime, but solely as a means of coercing the people into the adoption of principles and measures to which it is known that they are opposed, and upon which they have an undeniable right to exercise their own judgment.

The power thus given [in the bill] to the commanding officer [of the military government] over all the people of each district is that of an absolute monarch. . . . Such a power . . . reduces the whole population of the ten States—all persons, of every color, sex, and condition, and every stranger within their limits—to the most abject and degrading slavery.

. . . Have we the power to establish and carry into execution a measure like this? I answer, Certainly not. . . .

. . . [I]n the Southern States the ordinances of secession were treated by all the friends of the Union as mere nullities and are now acknowledged to be so by the States themselves. . . .

The negroes have not asked for the privilege of voting; the vast majority of them have no idea what it means. . . .

52. From The Ku Klux Klan Organization and Principles, 1868

Interrogations to Be Asked

3d. Are you opposed to the principles and policy of the Radical party, and to the Loyal League, and the Grand Army of the Republic . . . ?

5th. Are you opposed to negro equality, both social and political?

6th. Are you in favor of a white man's government in this country?

53. The Fourteenth Amendment, Ratified July 28, 1868

Section 1. All persons born or naturalized in the United States, and subject to the jurisdiction thereof, are citizens of the United States and of the State wherein they reside. No state shall make or enforce any law which shall abridge the privileges or immunities of citizens of the United States; nor shall any State deprive any person of life, liberty, or property, without due process of law; nor deny to any person within its jurisdiction the equal protection of the laws.

Section 2. Representatives shall be apportioned among the several States according to their respective numbers, counting the whole number of persons in each State, excluding Indians not taxed. But when the right to vote at any election for the choice of electors for President and Vice President of the United States, Representatives in Congress, the Executive and Judicial officers of a State, or the members of the Legislature thereof, is denied to any of the male inhabitants of such State, being twenty-one years of age, and citizens of the United States, or in any way abridged, except for participation in rebellion, or other crime, the basis of representation therein shall be reduced in the proportion which the number of such male citizens shall bear to the whole number of male citizens twenty-one years of age in such State.

Section 3. No person shall be a Senator or Representative in Congress, or elector of President and Vice President, or hold any office, civil or military, under the United States, or under any State, who, having previously taken an oath, as a member of Congress, or as an officer of the United States, or as a member of any State legislature, or as an executive or judicial officer of any State, to support the Constitution of the United States, shall have engaged in insurrection or rebellion against the same, or given aid or comfort to the enemies thereof. But Congress may by a vote of two-thirds of each House, remove such disability.

Section 4. The validity of the public debt of the United States, authorized by law, including debts incurred for payment of pensions and bounties for services in suppressing insurrection or rebellion, shall not be questioned. But neither the United States nor any State shall assume or pay any debt or obligation incurred in aid of insurrection or rebellion against the United States, or any claim for the loss or emancipation of any slave, but all such debts, obligations and claims shall be held illegal and void.

Section 5. The Congress shall have power to enforce, by appropriate legislation, the provisions of this article.

54. Report of the Commissioner of the Freedmen's Bureau, 1870

One year ago there were on duty in this bureau one hundred and forty-one (141) commissioned officers, four hundred and twelve civilian agents, and three hundred and forty-eight (348) clerks. At present there are fifteen (15) commissioned officers, seventy-one (71) civilian agents, and seventy-two clerks. . . .

We have under our care no less than five hundred and eighty-four thousand one hundred and seventy-eight (584,178) sick and infirm persons, for whom no provision was made by local authorities, and who had no means themselves of procuring the attendance and comforts necessary to health and life. It has not been possible to provide for the proper treatment of the insane. For some of this unfortunate class admission has been gained by earnest correspondence to state asylums, but the majority have been of necessity retained in the bureau hospitals, and all that could be done for them was to supply them with food and clothing and prevent them from doing injury.

For more than a year our principal aim has been to relieve the general Government by transferring to the civil authorities all these dependent classes. . . . [M]edicine and hospital stores have been furnished as an outfit where state or municipal governments have consented to assume charge of destitute sick and disabled freedmen within their borders. . . . [Our] hospitals, at one time numbering fifty-six (56), have been reduced to two (2), and one (1) of these is about to be closed. . . .

The wonder is not that so many, but that so few, have needed help; that of the four millions of people thrown suddenly upon their own resources only one in about two hundred has been an object of public charity; and nearly all who have received aid have been persons who, by reason of age, infirmity or disease, would be objects of charity in any state at any time.

. . . [E]mployment [has] been found for a great multitude of able-bodied men and women. . . .

They were uniformly assisted by us in finding good places and in making reasonable bargains. To secure fairness and inspire confidence on both sides, the system of written contracts was adopted. No compulsion was used. . . . The nature and obligations of these contracts were carefully explained to the freedmen, and a copy filed in the office of the agent approving it; this was for their use in case any difficulty arose between them and their employers. . . . [I]n a single state not less than fifty thousand (50,000) such contracts were drawn in duplicate. . . . To the freedman, the Bureau office in this way became a school in which he learned the first practical business lessons of life, and from year to year

he has made rapid progress in this important branch of education.

. . . [M]uch litigation and strife were prevented. It could not be expected that such a vast and complicated machinery would work without friction. The interests of capital and labor very often clash in all communities. . . . Some employers have been dishonest and have attempted to defraud the freedmen of just wages. Some laborers have been unfaithful and unreasonable in their demands. But in the great majority of cases brought before us for settlement, the trouble and misunderstanding have arisen from vague verbal bargains and a want of specific written contracts. . . .

. . . [A] good degree of prosperity and success has already been attained. To the oft-repeated slander that the Negroes will not work, and are incapable of taking care of themselves, it is a sufficient answer that their voluntary labor has produced nearly all the food that supported the whole people, besides a large amount of rice, sugar and tobacco for export, and two millions of bales of cotton each year, on which was paid into the United States treasury during the years 1866 and 1867 a tax of more than forty millions of dollars ($40,000,000). . . . [I]t is safe to say, as it has been said repeatedly by intelligent Southern white men, that without the Bureau or some similar agency, the material interests of the country would have greatly suffered, and the Government would have lost a far greater amount than has been expended in its maintenance. . . .

Of the nearly eight hundred thousand (800,000) acres of farming land and about five thousand (5,000) pieces of town property transferred to this Bureau . . . , enough was leased to produce a revenue of nearly four hundred thousand dollars ($400,000). Some farms were set apart in each State as homes for the destitute and helpless, and a portion was cultivated by freedmen prior to its restoration. . . .

Our expenditures from the beginning . . . , from January 1, 1865, to August 31, 1869, have been eleven million two hundred and forty-nine thousand and twenty-eight dollars and ten cents ($11,249,028.10). In addition to this cash expenditure the subsistence, medical supplies, quartermaster stores, issued to the refugees and freedmen prior to July 1, 1866, were furnished by the commissionary, medical and quartermaster's department, and accounted for in the current expenses of those departments. . . . They amounted to two million three hundred and thirty thousand seven hundred and eighty-eight dollars and seventy-two cents ($2,330,788.72) in original cost; but a large portion of these stores being damaged and condemned as unfit for issue to troops, their real value to the Government was probably less than one million of dollars ($1,000,000). Adding their original cost to the amount expended from appropriations and other sources, the total expenses of our Government for refugees and freedmen to August 31, 1869, have been thirteen millions five hundred and seventy-nine thousand eight hundred and sixteen dollars and eighty-two cents ($13,579,816.82). And deducting fifty thousand dollars ($50,000) set apart as a special relief fund for all classes of destitute people in the Southern states, the real cost has been thirteen millions twenty-nine thousand eight hundred and sixteen dollars and eighty-two cents ($13,029,816.82). That the economic co-operation of the freedmen under outside leadership made the Freedmen's Bureau thus possible goes without saying. . . .

55. The Fifteenth Amendment, Ratified March 30, 1870

Section 1. The right of citizens of the United States to vote shall not be denied or abridged by the United States or by any State on account of race, color, or previous condition of servitude.

Section 2. The Congress shall have power to enforce this article by appropriate legislation.

56. From the Civil Rights Act of 1871

Every person who, under color of any statute, ordinance, regulation, custom or usage of any state or territory, subjects or causes to be subjected any citizen of the United States or other person within the jurisdiction thereof to the deprivation of any rights, privileges, or immunities secured by the Constitution and laws shall be liable to the party injured in any action at law, suit in equity, or other proceedings.

57. From the Civil Rights Act of March 1, 1875 (Declared unconstitutional in 1883, this act was the last congressional effort to protect black civil rights until 1957.)

. . . [A]ll persons within the jurisdiction of the United States shall be entitled to the full and equal enjoyment of the accommodations, advantages, facilities, and privileges of inns, public conveyances on land or water, theaters, and other places of public amusement; . . . applicable alike to citizens of every race and color, regardless of any previous condition of servitude.

SEC. 4. . . . [N]o citizen . . . shall be disqualified for service as grand or petit juror in any court of the United States. . . .

Appendix B
Biographies of Major Personalities

Abraham (ca. 1787–ca. 1871) *black leader, counselor to the Seminole*

Abraham fled from his master in Pensacola as a boy. He was possibly recruited by the British in the War of 1812 and landed on the Apalachicola River in Florida to help build the "Negro Fort." He eventually became the slave of the Seminole chief Mikonopi, whom in 1826 he accompanied as an interpreter in a delegation to Washington, for which service Mikonopi freed him. His emancipation was formally recorded on June 18, 1835. A shrewd and intelligent man, Abraham was Mikonopi's principal counselor and married the widow of the former chief of the Seminole nation. He fathered two or three sons and at least one daughter. A contemporary account described him as a "good soldier and intrepid leader," cunning and avaricious, with polished manners: "Abra'm, or Yobly, as the Indians call him, is the chief Interpreter, and latterly succeeded Jumper as 'sense carrier' to Miconope. This high chancellor and keeper of the king's conscience, also heads about five hundred negroes of whom he is legislator, judge, and executioner through his influence with the governor. . . . [u]nder an exterior of profound meekness [he] cloaks deep, dark, and bloody purposes. He has at once the crouch and spring of the panther. . . ."

Throughout the negotiations for the removal of the Seminole from Florida to Indian Territory (now Oklahoma) in the West, Abraham counseled resistance but kept open the lines of communication with the U.S. government. Meanwhile, he gathered arms and ammunition and rallied plantation slaves to join with the Indians. In the early years of the Second Seminole War, he fought ardently, retreating with the Indians to the swamps when the battles turned against them. His negotiating skills enabled the 1837 treaty by which the Seminole agreed to removal

on the condition that their black allies accompany them. The bad faith of the American whites led to his imprisonment and that of his family; General Jesup threatened, "I have promised Abraham the freedom of his family if he be faithful to us, and I shall certainly hang him if he will not be faithful." Abraham then acted for the U.S. government in urging the Seminole and their black allies to surrender and accept transport to the West.

After his removal to the Indian Territory in 1839, he apparently lived there quietly raising cattle, though some authorities assert that in 1850 he went with some Seminole into Mexico. In any case in 1852 he interpreted for an unsuccessful delegation sent to Florida to induce Seminole leader Billy Bowlegs to surrender with his people for transportation westward, a task that included a tour of the major eastern cities and a meeting with the president of the United States.

Adams, John Quincy (July 11, 1767–February 23, 1848) *public servant*

After his term as president of the United States (1824–28), Adams rounded out a distinguished career in government with eight terms in the House of Representatives (1831–48). Although not an abolitionist, he led the fight against the Gag Rule, which in 1836 had been passed by Congress to suppress the right of petition against slavery. In 1844 the rule was finally defeated, though not before Adams endured a move by southern congressmen to discipline him. In 1836, he argued that should civil war break out, the war powers of the Congress would enable it to interfere with slavery in every possible way. Later he extended this principle to say that in a state of war the military authority might order universal emancipation of the slaves.

Adams also fought against the annexation of Texas. In his memoirs he said, "This [opposition to the extension of slavery] is a cause upon which I am entering at the last stage of life, and with the certainty that I cannot advance in it far; my career must close, leaving the cause at the threshold. To open the way for others is all that I can do. The cause is good and great."

In 1841, Adams argued for the freedom of the slave ship *Amistad* mutineers before the Supreme Court of the United States, winning his case. Adams acted consistently as a man of principle, intensely devoted to the cause of freedom for all and his belief in the inalienable rights of human beings.

Allen, Richard (February 14, 1760–March 26, 1831) *founder and bishop of the African Methodist Episcopal church*

Born a slave, Allen preached his way into freedom by converting his master, who then enabled him and his family to obtain their liberty. He then supported himself through manual labor while continuing to preach to blacks and whites. In 1784, the Methodist Church in Baltimore recognized him as a minister. In the integrated St. George Methodist Church in Philadelphia, where he occasionally preached, whites angered blacks by ordering them to sit in the gallery. The blacks left in 1787, some to follow Absalom Jones in founding the African Protestant Episcopal Church, some to go with Richard Allen in organizing an independent Methodist church. In 1816, 16 similar black congregations formed the African Methodist Episcopal Church, electing Allen bishop. To this labor he devoted the rest of his life.

Anthony, Susan B. (February 15, 1820–March 13, 1906) *suffrage leader*

Known chiefly as a woman suffragist, Anthony worked also to abolish slavery. From 1856 to 1865 she served as the principal New York agent for William Lloyd Garrison's American Anti-Slavery Society. She and the group of abolitionist speakers she led encountered hostile mobs in upstate New York. In the Kansas-Nebraska controversy, she spent months trying to promote the entry of Kansas into the Union as a free state. During the Civil War, she and Elizabeth Cady Stanton organized the Women's Loyal National League, gathering hundreds of thousands of signatures on petitions for emancipation.

Woman suffragists, including Anthony, suffered defeat when the Fourteenth Amendment for the first time introduced the word "male" into the Constitution, demol-ishing suffragist hopes that women might be enfranchised along with black men. Ironically, their struggle against the exclusion of women as full citizens in the Fourteenth and Fifteenth Amendments forced Anthony and many other abolitionist women into competition against the black men whom they had long sought to liberate.

Attucks, Crispus (ca. 1723–March 5, 1770) *American patriot, martyr*

Attucks was apparently an escaped slave who had worked around the wharves in Boston, Massachusetts, and on whalers. A William Brown of Framingham, Massachusetts, advertised the loss of a slave named Crispus, whom he described as a mulatto six feet two inches tall, with short, curly hair, and about 27 years old at the time he ran away; he also offered a reward of £10 for his capture and return. Attucks may have been of mixed Indian and black ancestry. When in March 1770 the frequent quarrels between Boston citizens and occupying British soldiers erupted into what came to be known as the Boston Massacre, Crispus Attucks was the first to fall to British fire. His body was placed in Fanueil Hall before burial with the three other victims in Boston's Middle Burying Ground.

Bailey, Gamaliel (December 3, 1807–June 5, 1859) *journalist, antislavery spokesperson*

During his adventurous life, Bailey worked as a teacher, editor, sailor, and physician. Converted to abolitionism in 1834 by the Lane Seminary debates, he served as an editor of the *Cincinnati Philanthropist*, the first antislavery paper in the West. His office there was mobbed three times, the last time evoking enough sympathy to enable him to begin a daily publication, the *Herald*. In 1847, he took over the editorship of the *National Era*, a weekly sponsored by the American and Foreign Anti-Slavery Society. The next year, when he was accused of helping fugitive slaves escape, he faced down an angry mob. Ill health first interrupted and then ended his antislavery work and his life.

Banneker, Benjamin (November 9, 1731–October 26, 1806) *self-taught mathematician, astronomer*

Banneker, son and grandson of freed slaves, was born, grew up, and spent most of his life on a Maryland farm. His grandmother taught him to read and write, and the family sent him to a country school for several seasons. A man of great mathematical gifts, he taught himself literature, history, mathematics, and astronomy. When he was almost sixty, he assisted in surveying the Federal

Territory (now the District of Columbia). Soon after, with the support of abolition societies, he published *Benjamin Banneker's Pennsylvania, Delaware, Maryland and Virginia Almanack and Ephemeris, for the Year of Our Lord, 1792.* He sent the manuscript for this almanac to Thomas Jefferson, along with a letter urging the abolition of slavery; publication of the subsequent correspondence between Banneker and Jefferson helped sales. Banneker retired from tobacco farming to devote himself to his studies, publishing more almanacs that brought him an international reputation. It is said that when the French architect Pierre L'Enfant fled with the plans for Washington, D.C., Banneker was able to reconstruct them through his prodigious memory.

Barrow, David (1753–1819) *activist, antislavery Baptist minister*

Barrow preached in southern Virginia and northern North Carolina. In 1795, he founded the integrated Portsmouth-Norfolk church, installing the black Jacob Bishop as its pastor. Violent opposition to this action drove Barrow to Kentucky. There in 1805, the North District Association of Baptists expelled him for his views on slavery. For many years he presided over the Kentucky Abolition Society. He published a pamphlet, *Involuntary, Unlimited, Perpetual, Absolute, Hereditary Slavery Examined on the Principles of Nature, Reason, Justice, Policy, and Scripture.*

Beecher, Catharine (September 6, 1800–May 12, 1878) *author, educator*

Catharine Beecher was a member of the famous Beecher family of clergymen and a sister of Harriet Beecher Stowe. She benefited women of her day by pioneering teaching as a woman's profession, crusading against the exploitation of women factory workers and the indolence and subjection to fashion of wealthy women, and developing a pragmatic approach to housework and domestic architecture. At the same time, she preached that women should adopt a conventional social role, avoiding any activity that "throws woman into the attitude of a combatant, either for herself or others." Unlike most of her family, she did not embrace abolitionism. Accordingly, when the Grimké sisters defied tradition by speaking against slavery before audiences of both women and men, Beecher in 1837 took it upon herself to reproach them in *An Essay on Slavery and Abolitionism, with Reference to the Duty of American Females.* The next year, Angelina Grimké replied in the spirited *Letters to Catharine Beecher,* converting the exchange into more grist for the abolitionist mills.

Bibb, Henry (1815–after 1851) *fugitive slave, operator on the Underground Railroad, Canadian colonist*

After his flight from Kentucky slavery in 1837 and many recaptures and escapes in trying to rescue his wife, Bibb worked prominently in the mainline abolitionist movement. Despite his long opposition to colonization, the Fugitive Slave Law of 1850 drove him to Canada, where he at once organized blacks and whites to help the thousands of incoming fugitives form black communities, to which end he edited the *Voice of the Fugitive.* In 1851, he convoked the North American Convention of Colored Men in Toronto.

Birney, James Gillespie (February 4, 1792–November 25, 1857) *antislavery attorney*

Once a prominent citizen and a slaveholding planter in Alabama, Birney moved north to educate his sons in the free states. In 1832, he became an agent for the American Colonization Society in Tennessee, Alabama, Mississippi, Louisiana, and Arkansas. But in 1833 he resigned from the colonization society and from the Kentucky Society for the Gradual Relief of the State from Slavery, publicly freed his slaves, and in a *Letter on Colonization* renounced colonization as a failed effort that led to oppression. In October 1834, he became an agent for the American Anti-Slavery Society, soon thereafter organizing the Kentucky Anti-Slavery Society and announcing his intention of publishing an antislavery newspaper there—but local forces prevailed, driving him from the state and shutting down the Kentucky Anti-Slavery Society. In January 1836, Birney established his newspaper, the *Philanthropist,* in Cincinnati.

Bourne, George (June 13, 1780–November 20, 1845) *abolitionist clergyman*

An English-born pastor of a Virginia church, Bourne in 1816 advocated immediate emancipation in *The Book and Slavery Irreconcilable,* for which he was convicted of heresy by a Presbyterian council. Compelled to leave the South, he moved north, where he served Presbyterian churches in New York and Quebec. In 1833, he switched to the more tolerant Dutch Reformed Church and continued to advocate abolitionism, helping found the Anti-Slavery Society. That year he also published *An Address to the Presbyterian Church, Enforcing the Duty of Excluding All Slaveholders from the "Communion of Saints."* Four years later, he offered to its convention a resolution censuring clergymen who defended slavery. He protested to Garrison about the latter's advocacy of nonviolence, arguing that it ill served the antislavery cause. His many works included several other diatribes against slavery.

Bowditch, Henry Ingersoll (August 9, 1808–January 14, 1892) *abolitionist physician*

Beginning practice in Boston in 1834, Bowditch was converted by Garrison to the antislavery cause, joining a committee to assist the fugitive George Latimer. He ardently helped other slaves and encouraged antislavery sentiment in the North.

Brown, John (May 9, 1800–December 2, 1859) *militant abolitionist*

A tanner by trade, Brown envisioned himself as the slaves' savior, destined to lead them out of bondage into freedom in Appalachia. In 1855, he moved to Kansas during the struggle over whether that new state should be slave or free. On May 24, 1856, he led a small band (mostly his own sons) in massacring five non-slaveholding men from a proslavery Kansas community and mutilating their bodies. God had so decreed, he said. Then, in 1858, he proposed to coconspirators in Canada a "Provisional Constitution and Ordinances for the People of the United States"—a military dictatorship under Brown, to be established by an insurrection of armed slaves. For this unlikely project he attracted the support of certain highly respectable abolitionists (the Secret Six), who helped him buy guns, ammunition, and 950 pikes for the slaves he planned to rouse to rebellion. On October 16, 1859, with a handful of men, including just five blacks, he attempted to capture the U.S. arsenal at Harpers Ferry, Virginia, defended by marines under the command of Col. Robert E. Lee, U.S. Army. In the process, many were killed: a marine, a black freeman, three other civilians, and two of Brown's sons, along with eight others of his band. His efforts at rousing a black insurrection had failed, for most blacks recognized him as a man of words trying to be a man of deeds, and they knew better than to follow him. At his trial, while the public debated his sanity, Brown defended himself by saying that he had intended only a peaceful demonstration but that in any case slavery is an "unjustifiable War of one portion of its citizens upon another"—and in war anything goes. He was hanged on December 2, 1859. Although President Lincoln, Secretary of State Seward, and Senator Edward Everett condemned Brown's actions, such avowedly peace-loving citizens as Ralph Waldo Emerson and Henry Thoreau glorified him into martyrdom.

Brown, William Wells (ca. 1816–November 6, 1884) *writer, lecturer*

The son of a slave mother and a white slaveholder in Kentucky, Brown was hired out to a slave trader, sold to a merchant, and then sold to a riverboat captain. Escaping into Ohio, he worked on a lake steamer, in one year helping 60 fugitives to Canada, at the same time educating himself. In 1843, he became an agent for the New York Anti-Slavery Society. He published his *Narrative of William Wells Brown, a Fugitive Slave* in 1847. He lectured in Great Britain for five years, visited the Continent four times, and wrote three books. Back in the United States, he contributed both to the London *Daily News* and to American antislavery journals.

Bruce, Blanche K. (March 1, 1841–March 17, 1898) *first black to serve a full term in the U.S. Senate*

Born a slave in Virginia, Bruce was educated in Missouri and at Oberlin College. He settled in Mississippi, where he held several local offices, then became a state senator. He served in the U.S. Senate from 1874 to 1881, in his maiden speech protesting against the removal of federal troops from the South. In 1880 his name was proposed for vice president, but he was not nominated. Later he served in the federal treasury.

Buffum, Arnold (December 13, 1782–March 13, 1859) *inventor, antislavery lecturer*

Raised in an abolitionist Quaker family, his home a station on the Underground Railroad, as a boy Buffum learned the trade of hatter. In 1832, the New England Anti-Slavery Society, over which he presided, commissioned him as its lecturing agent. His acceptance of this position damaged him socially and economically, but he proved effective in it. In 1833, he helped found the American Anti-Slavery Society in Philadelphia, where he moved the next year. In 1840 he went to Ohio and Indiana, lecturing against slavery and editing the *Protectionist*. In later years, disagreeing with more radical abolitionists, Buffum championed the Liberty, Free-Soil, and Republican Parties as one succeeded the other.

Burleigh, William Henry (February 2, 1812–March 18, 1871) *journalist, reformer*

Apprenticed as a boy to a printer, Burleigh in 1833 with his brother Charles edited the *Unionist*, a paper founded to support Prudence Crandall's Connecticut school for young black women. Interested in a variety of reforms, in 1836 he undertook to lecture for the American Anti-

Slavery Society while also editing various papers. In 1843, he took over the *Christian Freeman* (later the *Charter Oak*), published by the Connecticut Anti-Slavery Society. Several times he barely escaped mob violence, as when he protested against the Mexican War as a conflict fought for the "slave power."

Burns, Anthony (May 31, 1834–July 27, 1862)
fugitive slave

Born a slave in Virginia, Burns learned to read and write as a boy. When his owner hired him out, he gained some degree of control over his own life, and in 1854 he stowed away on a ship bound for Boston. His owner learned his whereabouts from a letter Burns sent his brother and followed him to Boston. There he had Burns jailed on a false charge of theft. An antislavery mob stormed the jail, killing a policeman but failing to release Burns. Under the Fugitive Slave Law of 1850, federal troops were called out, along with state militia and the Boston police, all of whom confronted an angry crowd of some 50,000 antislavery agitators. Nonetheless, Burns was returned to Virginia, at an estimated cost to the government of $100,000.

This episode, at the height of the Kansas-Nebraska controversy, hardened northern sentiment against slavery. No other fugitive was ever removed from Boston. A group of Bostonians, mostly black, raised enough money to buy Burns's freedom. He went to the abolitionist town of Oberlin, Ohio, and then to Canada, where he became the minister of a small Baptist church.

Campbell, Tunis G. (1812 or 1813–1891) *black educator, Reconstruction politician*

Born free in New Jersey, Campbell was trained as a missionary by the American Colonization Society but then came to oppose black emigration. Working as a hotel steward, he preached against slavery and founded several northern black schools. By 1861, he had married, had three children, and become a partner in a New York bakery.

In 1865, as a government official, he established an independent colony of some 400 blacks on Georgia's St. Catherine's Island, developing a community of 40-acre black-owned farms and teaching self-sufficiency. After the U.S. government in early 1866 drove the blacks off and fired Campbell, he organized another 100 freedpeople as an independent community in McIntosh County, Georgia.

During Reconstruction, Campbell passionately engaged in Georgia politics, serving at the constitutional convention and as a justice of the peace and state senator, working to protect freedpeople, encouraging them to vote, and enabling them to serve on juries. White enemies threw him out of the senate, brought charges, and sentenced him to work on a chain gang. Released, he reentered politics but was driven out of the state and spent the rest of his life in Boston.

Carney, William H. (1840–1908) *black soldier, probably the first African American to earn the Congressional Medal of Honor*

Born free in New Bedford, Massachusetts, Carney enlisted at age 23 in the Morgan Guards, later part of the 54th Massachusetts regiment. In the regiment's disastrous attack on Fort Wagner, South Carolina, in July 1863, depicted in the movie *Glory*, he was severely wounded but nonetheless rescued the flag while under heavy fire, according to legend later proudly reporting, "The Old Flag never touched the ground!" He survived to work for 31 years in the New Bedford postal service; after 1901, he was employed at the state capitol. During all those years he often spoke at patriotic events and led Memorial Day parades. In 1900, Congress recognized Carney's valor by awarding him the Congressional Medal of Honor.

Cary, Mary Ann Shadd (October 9, 1823–June 5, 1893) *teacher, journalist, lawyer*

Born free, Cary early dedicated herself to elevating and freeing her race. Between 1839 and 1855, she founded or taught in schools for blacks in Delaware, Pennsylvania, and New York. In the 1850s, she led and spoke for black refugees from the Fugitive Slave Law of 1850 who had fled to Canada, where she opened a school for the American Missionary Society. However, she repudiated their Refugee Home Society, which "begged" funds to buy land and sell it to blacks: blacks could already, as Cary pointed out, buy government land at lower cost. In 1853, she helped found the *Provincial Freeman*, a nonsectarian, nonpartisan newspaper devoted to the interests of blacks in Canada, acting (in the nominal role of publishing agent) as its real editor. During the Civil War, she recruited black soldiers in the United States.

In 1869, widowed after a marriage of 13 years, Cary moved with her daughter to Washington, D.C., where she studied law and taught in the public schools. She retired from teaching in 1884.

Chace, Elizabeth Buffum (December 9, 1806–December 12, 1899) *antislavery and woman suffrage leader*
Born into an antislavery Quaker family and educated at Quaker schools, in 1828 Elizabeth Buffum married Samuel Buffington Chace, a textiles manufacturer. After their first five children died in childhood, in 1835 she turned to antislavery work, helping organize and officiating in the Fall River (Massachusetts) Female Anti-Slavery Society. In the 1840s and early 1850s, while bearing and rearing five more children, Chace arranged antislavery meetings, raised funds, circulated petitions, wrote letters, and entertained antislavery leaders—the nuts-and-bolts work of the movement. Her home was a station on the Underground Railroad. In 1843, she resigned from the Society of Friends because of its "pro-slavery position."

After the Civil War, she served as a vice president of the American Anti-Slavery Society. In 1877, she and her daughters resigned from the Rhode Island Woman's Club because it refused to admit a black member. In 1891, she published her *Anti-Slavery Reminiscences.*

Chandler, Elizabeth Margaret (December 24, 1807–November 2, 1834) *author, abolitionist*
Reared and educated a Quaker, Chandler began writing at 16, and at 18 she won a prize for her poem "The Slave-Ship." Benjamin Lundy then urged her to write in a similar vein for his newspaper, *The Genius of Universal Emancipation,* to which she regularly contributed for the rest of her short life, soon taking charge of its "Ladies Repository." Feeling strongly the moral duty of opposing slavery, she urged other women to fight against it, particularly by supporting the Free Produce movement. In 1836 she published two volumes of her writings. Antislavery meetings sang songs with her words.

In 1832, Chandler instigated the organization of the first antislavery society in Michigan.

Chapman, Maria Weston (July 25, 1806–July 12, 1885) *abolitionist*
At the cost of social ostracism and personal danger, in 1832 Chapman and twelve other women organized the Boston Female Anti-Slavery Society, which she led and for which she edited an annual report entitled *Right and Wrong in Boston.* The society labored to educate Boston's free blacks and to abolish slavery in the District of Columbia. Chapman helped edit the *Liberator* and also the *Non-Resistant,* the publication of Garrison's New England Non-Resistance Society. In the disputes among ab-

olitionists she sided with Garrison, in 1839 publishing a pamphlet *Right and Wrong in Massachusetts,* attributing the split in antislavery ranks to disagreement over woman's rights. She and her three sisters ran the Boston antislavery fairs that provided models for other cities, and she edited the fair's annual gift book, the *Liberty Bell.* In 1840, the American Anti-Slavery Society elected Chapman to its executive committee. She helped finance, found, and edit the *National Anti-Slavery Standard.* After the Emancipation Proclamation, she busied herself in her son's brokerage office, and in 1877 she edited a two-volume autobiography of her friend Harriet Martineau, to which she added lengthy memorial tributes and reminiscences.

Chester, Thomas Morris (May 11, 1834–September 30, 1892) *African-American activist, Civil War correspondent*
Chester was born free in Harrisburg, Pennsylvania, the fourth child of George and Jane Marie Chester; his mother was an escaped slave. He supported black colonization in Liberia, which he came to call "home," living and working there for several years. For a time, he ran a school in Monrovia for Africans recaptured from American slave ships; there he also published and edited a newspaper and acted as correspondent of the *New York Herald.* In 1862, he returned to the United States and assisted in recruiting blacks for the 54th and 55th Massachusetts infantry regiments. In fall 1863, he went to England, where he lectured on the Civil War and its impact on blacks. Back in the United States in spring 1864, he became a war correspondent for the Philadelphia *Press,* attached to the Army of the James. He covered the fall of Richmond, Virginia.

After the war, Chester raised funds in England for freedpeople. He also continued to advocate black emigration to Liberia. In 1873, he was appointed brigadier general in the Louisiana state militia. After a lifetime of devotion to black rights, he returned to Harrisburg, where he died and was buried in the segregated Lincoln Cemetery.

Child, Lydia Maria Francis (February 11, 1802–October 20, 1880) *author, reformer*
Beginning her literary career at the age of 22, with the publication of a successful novel narrating the love of a white woman and a noble Indian, Francis continued it by publishing the bimonthly *Juvenile Miscellany,* the first American children's periodical. In 1828 she married the

reformer David Lee Child. His earnings as a lawyer and editor dwindled even as hers increased, but he led the way into abolitionism, with Lydia Child following only after she met William Lloyd Garrison. In 1833, she published the important antislavery book *An Appeal in Favor of That Class of Americans Called Africans,* tracing the history of slavery, describing its evils, and rejecting colonization. The book converted to antislavery such important leaders as Wendell Phillips and Charles Sumner, and it provoked the ostracism of its author in Boston. Defiantly, and at the expense of sales of her books on other subjects, she went on to edit and write other antislavery books, including an *Anti-Slavery Catechism.*

In the mid-1830s, David Child tried to buoy the Free Produce movement by raising beet sugar on a farm the couple bought in Massachusetts, an effort that predictably failed. In 1841, already a member of the executive committee of the American Anti-Slavery Society, Lydia Child began to edit its weekly, the *National Anti-Slavery Standard.* Her stormy tenure there ended in her resignation in 1843. Her husband succeeded her with equal lack of success, while she ventured into various kinds of journalism and books on a variety of subjects, constantly hampered by the unpopularity of her abolitionist convictions.

In 1850, the couple once again failed as farmers. By 1852, Lydia Child was once more writing, publishing the three-volume *The Progress of Religious Ideas, through Successive Ages* in 1855 and a volume of inspirational selections, *Autumn's Leaves,* in 1857. Again her antislavery beliefs interrupted this work. In 1859, she offered to care for John Brown in prison, thereby evoking a harsh public scolding from the wife of the senator who had introduced the Fugitive Slave Act of 1850. Child responded by denouncing the slave system; she published the exchange as a pamphlet in 1860. She followed this with more abolitionist pamphlets and books, including a novel about two beautiful quadroons (persons of one-quarter black ancestry).

Christy, David (1802–unknown) *geologist, antislavery writer*
In early life a newspaperman, in 1848 he became an agent of the American Colonization Society in Ohio, where he collected money to purchase land in Africa between Sierra Leone and Liberia for free American blacks, a colony he called "Ohio in Africa." He lectured on colonization before the Ohio legislature in 1849 and 1850, later publishing these lectures in a pamphlet *On the Present*

Relations of Free Labor to Slave in Tropical and Semi-Tropical Countries and *The Republic of Liberia: Facts for Thinking Men.* His major work, *Cotton Is King: Or the Economical Relations of Slavery,* was intended to persuade abolitionists that their plans had completely failed.

Clay, Cassius Marcellus (October 19, 1810–July 22, 1903) *politician, abolitionist*
A belligerent, crusading Kentuckian, the pugnacious Clay pursued careers in the army and in politics. His already-established aversion to slavery was increased in his college days at Yale when he heard William Lloyd Garrison. Although he thrice served in the state legislature, his antislavery stance defeated him when he ran in 1841—an event that made him determined to abolish slavery in his state. To that end, in 1845 he started the *True American,* a newspaper, taking the precaution of arming his office with two cannons, lances, rifles, and a keg of powder ready to be set off—only to have his fellow Lexingtonians ship his armament to Cincinnati, where he moved his paper; later he published it as the *Examiner* from Louisville.

Opposing the annexation of Texas, Clay nonetheless served with honor in the Mexican War. When he returned to Kentucky after a period as a prisoner of war, for a time he supported his cousin Henry Clay, but in 1844 they quarreled over abolitionism. In 1849, he convened an emancipation party in Frankfort and ran on its ticket for governor. Joining the Republican Party at its inception, he accepted a diplomatic post in Russia, only to be recalled in 1862 to serve as a major general; he refused to fight unless the government abolished slavery in the rebel states. In 1863 he did fight briefly, and then he returned to Russia.

Coffin, Levi B. (October 28, 1789–September 16, 1877) *abolitionist*
Proudly known as "president of the Underground Railroad," a title first given him by slave hunters, Coffin with his wife Catherine helped more than 3,000 slaves escape over a period of more than 30 years. He earned his living as, successively, a schoolteacher, a merchant, a wholesaler, and a boardinghouse keeper. Throughout their lives, the Coffins devoted themselves to helping blacks, most famously through their daring work for the Underground Railroad, but also by laboring for the education of free blacks, assuming responsibility for individuals brought to them for assistance and raising money in the United States and England for the thousands of blacks in need. During

the Civil War, Coffin headed the Western Freedmen's Aid Commission, which looked after newly freed slaves.

Coles, Edward (December 15, 1786–July 7, 1868) *abolitionist, governor of Illinois*

Born in Virginia of a slaveholding family, Coles early on, out of principle, embraced antislavery. In 1808, he inherited his father's plantation and slaves. In 1819, after considerable investigation of the Northwest, he moved to the new state of Illinois with his slaves; on the way, he told them that they were free. In their new home, he helped them make a fresh start.

In 1822, he ran for office against the proslavery forces in Illinois. As governor he urged the legislature to abolish the slavery that existed even though the state was nominally free. After a bitter fight, Coles triumphed, averting the possibility of a convention to amend the state constitution to allow slavery.

Collins, John Anderson (1810–1879) *abolitionist reformer*

A rather impractical idealist, Collins left Andover Theological Seminary before graduating, possibly because the seminary disapproved his helping abolitionists. He then took a post as general agent of the Massachusetts Anti-Slavery Society. In that capacity he traveled to England to raise funds for the cause. There, and on his return, he was accused of plotting to destroy the U.S. government.

For a short time in 1840 and 1841, Collins edited the *Monthly Garland*, an antislavery magazine. He saw abolition as a part of a larger social reform to free humankind. In 1843, he formed a grandiose plan of multiple picnics and conventions to rally the country against slavery. His backers, however, were dismayed at his support of other causes, and he resigned to start a utopian community, fated soon to fail.

Colman, Lucy Newhall (July 26, 1817–January 18, 1906) *abolitionist feminist lecturer*

Twice widowed by age 35, Colman with difficulty got a job at "the colored school" of Rochester, New York. The next year she managed to end racial discrimination in the schools there. She soon gave up teaching to lecture against slavery, in the face of vigorous and even dangerous opposition, for a time traveling with a young black woman.

During the Civil War, as matron of the National Colored Orphan Asylum at Washington, she introduced sanitation, kindness, and organization into the previously mismanaged institution. She also superintended black schools, supported by the New York Aid Society, in the District of Columbia.

Cowles, Betsey Mix (February 9, 1810–July 25, 1876) *educator, reformer*

Cowles grew up in Ohio, where she began her teaching career in 1825. In the 1830s, she worked in the "infant school" movement (to teach very young children "right conduct" and the three Rs) while she continued her education at Oberlin College. After graduation she taught and worked as an administrator in grammar and high schools, in time involving herself in teacher training. In 1858, she became superintendent of schools in Painesville, Ohio. She finished her career in education in Delhi, New York, where she taught until about 1862.

Besides engaging in the peace and temperance movements, Cowles from 1835 on worked against slavery through women's groups, antislavery fairs, and perhaps the Underground Railroad. She raised money for the cause and wrote against slavery. She, her sister Cornelia, and her brother Lewis sang antislavery ballads and hymns at abolition meetings. She fought against prejudice in the schools. Her advocacy of woman's rights and her friendship with Abby Kelley Foster made her a Garrisonian.

Cox, Hannah Peirce (November 12, 1797–April 15, 1876) *Quaker antislavery worker*

Cox and her second husband, Quaker farmer John Cox, were attracted to the antislavery cause by Garrison's *The Liberator* and John Greenleaf Whittier's poems. After the burning of Pennsylvania Hall in 1838 during a women's antislavery convention, she dedicated herself to emancipation. The Coxes operated a station on the Underground Railroad and generously entertained antislavery advocates, including Garrison, Whittier, and Lucretia Mott.

Craft, William (1827–1900) and Ellen Craft (ca. 1826–ca. 1897) *fugitive slaves*

Born into slavery in Georgia, the two met and married when their respective masters settled near Macon. They are known particularly because of their escape from slavery during the Christmas holidays in 1848, in which the light-skinned Ellen, daughter of her master, disguised herself as a sickly, deaf young white man traveling north with his servant for medical treatment. They settled in

Boston, where Ellen worked as a seamstress and William as a carpenter. After the passage of the Fugitive Slave Act of 1850, two agents of their owners pursued them to Boston, thwarted only by the Boston Vigilance Committee and the local black community.

The Crafts were then persuaded to leave the country for their safety. Along with fugitive William Wells Brown, they toured England and Scotland, delivering lectures against slavery and for temperance. During the mid-1850s, the Crafts attended Ockham Agricultural College in Surrey, their tuition paid by British abolitionists. They studied academic subjects and taught carpentry and sewing. In 1860 they published their autobiography, *Running a Thousand Miles for Freedom*. From 1862 to 1867, William made several extended visits to Africa to promote cotton production and trade with Britain. After their return to the United States in 1869, they founded a cooperative farm and school in Bryan County, Georgia.

Crandall, Prudence (September 3, 1803–January 28, 1890) *abolitionist educator*
When in 1833 Crandall's Canterbury Female Boarding School in Connecticut failed because she had admitted a black student, she established a teacher-training boarding school for black girls. The citizens of Canterbury, particularly those who belonged to the American Colonization Society, reacted in outrage. Stores refused to sell her food. The Congregational church barred her pupils, and the town threatened to prosecute them as paupers. The state outlawed any school that accepted out-of-state blacks without the town's consent. Civil authorities put Crandall in jail. Although abolitionists, including William Lloyd Garrison and Arthur Tappan, rallied to her rescue, the court convicted Crandall, ruling that blacks were not citizens; the conviction was reversed on appeal.

Frustrated in their attempts to stop Crandall legally, the townspeople turned to vigilantism, breaking school windows, poisoning the school well, even resorting to arson. In the fall of 1834 Crandall was forced to close the school. Eventually she and her new husband, abolitionist Calvin Philleo, moved to Illinois, where Crandall turned to other reforms.

Cuffe, Paul (January 17, 1759–September 9, 1817) *shipowner, navigator, pioneer in the colonization movement*
The son of a free black father and an Indian mother, Cuffe went to sea on a whaling vessel at 16. Despite set-backs, including pirate attacks, he established his own shipping business. By 1806 he owned several vessels and a good bit of property on land.

Throughout his career Cuffe worked actively for the rights of blacks. In 1780, he and his brother John unsuccessfully sued Massachusetts for denying suffrage to taxpaying citizens. In 1783 they helped lead a movement that obtained legal rights and privileges for blacks in that state. In 1797 he built a public school and hired a teacher.

He long advocated black emigration to Africa, using his own money to assist it. In 1811 he sailed to Sierra Leone and there formed the Friendly Society to encourage immigration from the United States. In 1815, at his own expense, he moved 38 blacks to Sierra Leone.

Davis, Paulina Wright (August 7, 1813–August 24, 1876) *feminist, reformer, suffragist*
Known primarily for her work for woman's rights and woman's health, Davis also worked against slavery. The home she shared with her husband, merchant Francis Wright, was attacked by a mob after they helped arrange the Utica, New York, antislavery convention of October 1835. After her husband's death, she married the antislavery Democrat Thomas Davis, who in 1852 was elected to Congress. In May 1850, at a Boston antislavery meeting, Davis and other suffragists planned the first national woman's rights convention, and she took charge of the arrangements.

Deitzler, George Washington (November 30, 1826–April 10, 1884) *Kansas antislavery leader*
In 1855, Deitzler engaged in organizing a free-state government to oppose the proslavery government of the territory of Kansas, collecting arms given by Bostonians and forming military companies among free-state advocates. In the "Wakarusa War" that November, he served as aide-de-camp to the commander of these companies, sometimes assuming command himself. Consequently, he was indicted with other leaders on a charge of treason, but after he spent a few months under arrest, the charge was dropped. Deitzler continued his free-state activities, including writing for the press and serving as a member of the free-state territorial legislature of 1857–58, speaker of the House of Representatives, and a senator under the Topeka constitution.

During the Civil War he organized the first regiment of Kansas volunteer infantry, eventually attaining the rank of general.

Delany, Martin R. (May 6, 1812–January 24, 1885) *abolitionist, critic, first black major in the U.S. Army*
Born free in what is now West Virginia, Delany learned pride in his African heritage from his family. Something of a Renaissance man, during his lifetime Delany engaged in a variety of occupations while continuing to work for the rights of blacks.

In 1831, he entered a school established by Pittsburgh's African Educational Society. In 1843 he founded the paper the *Mystery,* and from 1847 to 1849 he worked with Frederick Douglass on the *North Star,* during which period he was mobbed. In 1852 Delany published *The Condition, Elevation, Emigration and Destiny of the Colored People of the United States Politically Considered.* Educated in medicine at Harvard, he served in the Pittsburgh cholera epidemic of 1854.

In the disputes as to the best course for black people, Delany was something of a radical. Believing that blacks would never be fully accepted as free citizens in this country, Delany early argued for emigration. In 1854 he issued a call for a national emigration convention, of which he became an important officer. Another such convention commissioned him to explore the Valley of the Niger "for the purpose," the official record states, "of science and for general information and without any reference to, and with the Board being entirely opposed to, any Emigration there as such." He sailed on this mission in 1859.

Back in the United States, Delany recruited black soldiers and acted as an examining surgeon in Chicago. In 1865 he was commissioned a major. After the war, among other positions, he served on the Freedmen's Bureau. In 1879, his *Principia of Ethnology: The Origin of Races and Color* appeared.

Frederick Douglass once observed that he thanked "God for making me a man simply; but Delany always thanks him for making him a *black man.*"

De Wolf, James (March 18, 1764–December 21, 1837) *slave trader, manufacturer, senator*
As a boy, DeWolf adventured on pirate-ridden seas and fought in the American Revolution. By age 20 he was a ship's master, and by 25 he had made a fortune. Backed by wealthy Rhode Island merchants, he traded in African slaves, often personally supervising their sale in southern ports of the United States, though he landed most of them in the West Indies. Apparently without a qualm, he stayed in the slave trade at least until 1808. By 1812 he was investing in cotton mills, and his ventures there shifted his interest away from slaves to white millworkers.

In the Senate, where he advocated protection for cotton manufacture, he opposed extending slavery to the West.

Dickinson, Anna (October 28, 1842–October 22, 1932) *orator*
Daughter of an abolitionist father, Dickinson grew up in poverty after he died but was educated at a Quaker school for five years. At 14 she wrote an article for William Lloyd Garrison's *Liberator.* She was, successively, a copyist, a schoolteacher, and a worker in the U.S. Mint. And at 18 she made her first speech before the Pennsylvania Anti-Slavery Society. Her success there led to further lecturing, which turned into a full-time career. Her speeches for the Republicans contributed to the reelection of Abraham Lincoln.

In peacetime, Dickinson became one of the stars of the lyceum lecture circuit.

Douglas, Stephen Arnold (April 23, 1813–June 3, 1861) *statesman, orator*
This Democratic congressman (1843–47) and U.S. senator (1847–61) from Illinois argued that the question of whether a territory or state should be slave or free ought to be left to its settlers—to "squatter sovereignty." This idea underlay the Compromise of 1850 and the Kansas-Nebraska Act (1854). Douglas opposed Abraham Lincoln in 1858 in the Lincoln-Douglas debates and in the 1860 presidential race.

Douglass, Frederick (born Frederick Augustus Bailey) (ca. February 1817–February 20, 1895) *prominent abolitionist, orator, journalist*
The son of a white father and Harriet Bailey, a slave of mixed African and American Indian descent, from whom he was early separated, Douglass was born and raised in harsh slavery, against which he fought determinedly. He spent time in jail for conspiring to escape.

He taught himself secretly to read and studied oratory. He learned shipbuilding, hired his own time, and in 1838 managed to escape. With his wife, a free black woman, he settled in New Bedford, Massachusetts, and for a time he supported himself as a common laborer.

In 1841 an abolitionist friend asked him to speak at the convention of the Massachusetts Anti-Slavery Society, which at once offered him a job as its agent. He became a prominent abolitionist, a brave and moving lecturer whose activities provoked attacks on his person. To answer doubts that a man of his stature, bearing, and ability could ever have been a slave, in 1845 he published his autobiography, *Narrative of the Life of Frederick Douglass*—a daring move that might easily have led to his recapture. He then visited Great Britain and Ireland for two years; in 1847, to protect him against reenslavement, British friends enabled him to buy his freedom.

They also made it possible for him to establish his abolitionist paper *North Star* in Rochester, New York. All this set him at odds with Garrison and other white abolitionists, who did not see the necessity for the *North Star,* disapproved of anyone's buying freedom, and disagreed with the tactics Douglass endorsed.

Nonetheless, Douglass edited the *North Star* for 17 years, during which he also lectured, supported woman suffrage, and participated in politics. When John Brown was arrested, Douglass was one of several abolitionists who had to flee to Canada lest they be indicted for conspiracy; he then returned to England for six months of lecturing.

During the Civil War he recruited blacks, including two of his own sons, for the Union military. Lincoln consulted him. Reconstruction, during which he agitated for civil rights and suffrage for black men, brought him several posts of honor in the government and in private business.

Douglass, Sarah Mapps Douglass
(September 9, 1806–September 8, 1882) *teacher, abolitionist*
The daughter of a well-off black family of Philadelphia, Douglass (her maiden name as well as her married) was privately educated. In the 1820s she founded a school for black children, later supported by the Philadelphia Female Anti-Slavery Society, of which she was a member—as were Lucretia Mott and the Grimké sisters. Her interracial relationships enabled her to teach her white friends the cruel effects of racial prejudice—including that of the Philadelphia Society of Friends, to which she belonged.

In 1853, Douglass took a position at the Quaker-supported Institute for Colored Youth, where she stayed until she retired in 1877. In 1855 she married an Episcopalian priest. After the Civil War, she served as vice chair of the Women's Pennsylvania Branch of the American Freedmen's Aid Commission.

Edgerton, Sidney (August 17, 1818–July 19, 1900) *abolitionist congressman, governor of Montana*
Two years after graduating from law school in 1846, Edgerton served as a delegate to the Free-Soil Convention. In 1856, he participated in the first Republican National Convention. As a congressman, he worked to abolish slavery in the territories, in the District of Columbia, and on U.S. public property.

Embree, Elihu (November 11, 1782–December 4, 1820) *Quaker abolitionist*
Living in eastern Tennessee, amid widespread opposition to slavery, Embree freed his slaves shortly before 1815 and joined the Society of Friends. He became a leader of the Manumission Society of Tennessee, in 1819 beginning publication of the weekly *Manumission Intelligencer* (later the *Emancipator*), perhaps the first American periodical completely devoted to antislavery. In it he advocated not only universal freedom, calling upon masters to free their slaves, but also racial equality. He sent a memorial for abolition to the state legislature, excoriated states that excluded free blacks, and vigorously opposed the admission of Missouri as a slave state.

Fairbank, Calvin (November 3, 1816–October 12, 1898) *abolitionist, Methodist clergyman*
As a boy in rural New York, Fairbank became acquainted with two escaped slaves, an experience that taught him to detest slavery. As an adult he worked ardently and fearlessly to free blacks, venturing into slave states as far south as Arkansas to abduct them, learning the tricks of disguise and deception. As an agent for the Underground Railroad, he smuggled some 47 runaways into freedom. In 1842 he was sentenced to 15 years for assisting in the escape of the Lewis Hayden family; he served four before the governor pardoned him.

When Fairbank again took up his work, he was kidnapped from Indiana into Kentucky and again sentenced to 15 years, serving under miserable conditions from 1851 until 1864, when he was again pardoned. In later life, as an employee of missionary, benevolent, and educational institutions, he lectured or preached on the cruelty of slaveholders, relating his own adventures.

Fee, John Gregg (September 9, 1816–January 11, 1901) *abolitionist, educator*
Kentuckian Fee's conversion to abolitionism at Lane Seminary prompted his slaveholding family to disinherit him. Fee founded and served three antislavery Presbyterian churches in Kentucky, the best known of these being the Berea Union Church. Though his synod censured him and mobs shot at, clubbed, and stoned him, he went on to establish and run an abolitionist school, now Berea

College. False reports of his involvement in John Brown's raid on Harpers Ferry drove him from his native state, to which he returned only in 1863, to work with black soldiers. He devoted his postwar life to the Berea church and college.

Fessenden, Samuel (July 16, 1784–March 19, 1869) *abolitionist lawyer*

Fessenden officiated in the Anti-Slavery Society and served in the Maine state legislature. Disagreeing with both major political parties, he ran for Congress and the governorship on the Liberty Party ticket, a stratagem to demonstrate and strengthen antislavery sentiment. Throughout his career he insisted on the necessity of preserving the Union.

Follen, Charles (September 4, 1796–January 13, 1840) *abolitionist professor, Unitarian minister*

Emigrating to the United States as a political refugee from Germany in 1824, he was appointed to teach German at Harvard, where he later taught in the divinity school. By 1830, Follen was speaking against slavery. When he became active in the New England Anti-Slavery Society, Harvard refused to renew his contract. He then took a Unitarian pastorate in New York City but lost it within a year because of his abolitionism. Nonetheless he continued his abolitionist work and supported other causes that he believed would strengthen democracy in this country.

Follen, Eliza Lee Cabot (August 15, 1787–January 26, 1860) *author, antislavery advocate*

A member of a prominent Boston family, Cabot was well educated and deeply religious. In 1828, she married Charles Follen. After his death in 1840, she wrote and edited to support her son and herself, mostly in the fields of juvenilia and religion. Throughout her life she was dedicated to antislavery. Her tracts included *A Letter to Mothers in the Free States* and *Anti-Slavery Hymns and Songs*. She officiated in both the Massachusetts and the American antislavery societies.

Forten, Charlotte (Charlotte Grimké) (August 17, 1837–July 23, 1914) *teacher, author*

Forten was born free into a wealthy black abolitionist family in Philadelphia. In 1856, she began teaching in a white school while continuing her studies on her own and working against slavery. Problems with her health kept her at home from 1858 until 1861. Late in 1862,

however, she went to the sea islands off South Carolina and Georgia, where Union forces were trying to demonstrate that with the proper help blacks could function as free citizens. As a volunteer teacher for former slaves, Forten found her task frustrating, partly because of the suspicions of local blacks but also because of the climate and her own bad health. She wrote about her experiences for the *Atlantic Monthly* in "Life on the Sea Islands." She returned to Philadelphia in 1864 and spent several years reading and occasionally writing and teaching. In 1873, she was appointed to a federal clerkship.

In 1878, at 41, Forten married black minister Francis Grimké, nephew of Sarah and Angelina Grimké.

Forten, James (September 2, 1766–March 4, 1842) *wealthy, free black sailmaker, advocate of abolition, temperance, peace, women's rights*

Forten enlisted in the colonial navy at 14 as a drummer boy, was captured by the English, and exchanged. After another voyage to London, he was apprenticed to a sailmaker in Philadelphia. In time, he set up in business for himself, eventually hiring 40 whites and blacks. In 1814, with Richard Allen and Absalom Jones, he raised a force of 2,500 black volunteers to protect the city against the British.

Forten consistently worked for the welfare of blacks, opposing colonization. He always refused to sell rigging to the owners of slavers. He also furnished William Lloyd Garrison with critical support for the *Liberator*.

Foster, Abigail Kelley (January 15, 1810–January 14, 1887) *abolitionist, women's rights lecturer*

Born a Quaker and educated by Quakers, Kelley began her career by teaching in a Friends school. Garrison's *Liberator* inspired her to work in antislavery societies. In September 1838, she helped Garrison found the New England Non-Resistant Society.

Following the example of the Grimké sisters, whom she met at an antislavery convention, she first addressed a mixed audience of women and men at the second women's antislavery convention in May 1838 in Philadelphia. Impressed with her ability, Theodore Weld and other abolitionists urged Kelley to devote all her time to lecturing against slavery. Her family objected, presumably because of the stigma against women who spoke in public. Nonetheless, in May 1839 she started on that course, announcing, "Whatever ways and means are right for men to adopt in reforming the world, are right also for women to adopt in pursuing the same object." In 1840, opposition to her appointment to the business committee of the American Anti-Slavery Society led to a protest that split that organization, with Garrisonians insisting on woman's rights.

For more than 15 years Kelley traveled as an agent, lecturing and organizing antislavery societies and fairs, and setting an example for Paulina Wright Davis, Jane Elizabeth Hitchcock Jones, Lucy Stone, Betsey Mix Cowles, Sallie Holley, and Susan B. Anthony. She withstood numerous attacks on her reputation, as well as the many hardships of traveling in the mid-19th century on a limited budget. In 1845, she married fellow agent Stephen Symonds Foster, who eventually assumed most of the care of their only child so that she might continue lecturing against slavery and for temperance and women's rights. The farm they purchased became a station of the Underground Railroad. In the late 1850s, the Fosters parted company with Garrison over their demands for an abolitionist political party.

In 1870, poor health and a fading voice curtailed Abby Foster's lectures, though she continued her advocacy of women's rights.

Foster, Stephen Symonds (November 17, 1809–September 8, 1881) *abolitionist reformer, farmer*
Converted to the antislavery cause in his student days, Foster broke off his theological training when he came to doubt that churches upheld Christian principles. He scrounged a living lecturing against slavery. A Garrisonian, he advocated disunion. He always insisted that the political, religious, and business establishments all over the United States, not just in the South, bore the responsibility for supporting slavery. About 1841 he began interrupting church services to ask the congregations to listen to him; most congregations did not respond favorably. He again attacked the stance of the churches on slavery in his 1843 pamphlet *The Brotherhood of Thieves; or a True Picture of the American Church and Clergy.* In 1845, he married abolitionist lecturer Abigail Kelley.

Free Frank (1771–1857) *entrepreneurial slave*
His master, George McWhorter, took Frank at age 24 to the frontier in Pulaski County, Kentucky, between the Appalachian highlands and the Cumberland River. Frank helped his master clear and run two farm homesteads, becoming skilled in animal husbandry, dairying, land improvement, the use and maintenance of equipment and machinery, and the construction of buildings. He also established a reputation for honesty and industry. When the second farm was operating well enough not to need his full-time labor, some time between 1801 and 1808, McWhorter allowed Frank to hire his own time, although technically that was illegal.

Pulaski County at that time was a land of opportunity for an enterprising slave. A labor shortage created a need for his services, and the relatively low proportion of blacks in the population lulled white fears and allowed blacks to carry guns and move about. Some time before 1810, McWhorter moved on, leaving Frank in charge of his farm. Frank made the most of his opportunities. He not only managed the farm but also appropriated land to raise crops of his own and began to manufacture saltpeter, a component of gunpowder.

In 1815, McWhorter died. The heirs not only left Frank in charge of the farm but promised him that he could buy his freedom for $500. First, though, in 1817 he bought for $800 his wife Lucy, whom he had married in 1799. Once she was free, she added to the family income through household crafts (like making cloth, candles, and soap), so that in just two years they were able to buy his freedom—after which he registered himself in the census as "Free Frank."

At once they set themselves another goal—liberating their four children born in slavery. (Three younger children, born after their mother was freed, never knew slavery.) In the 1820s, the couple invested in land and expanded their farming operation. In 1829 they bought Frank, their eldest son, who had run away to Canada and returned only after manumission, by trading away their saltpeter factory. The next year Frank, Lucy, young Frank, and their three youngest children moved to Illinois, where they established a new farm. In 1836 Frank founded the town of New Philadelphia, investing in real estate there. In the 1840s and 1850s, Frank and Lucy succeeded in buying the freedom of their three other children *and* their descendants. Even the money from Frank's estate was used for this purpose. Altogether, in the four decades from 1817 to 1857 Frank and Lucy bought 16 family members, for about $15,000.

Gage, Frances Dana Barker (October 12, 1808–November 10, 1884) *reformer, lecturer, author*
During her Ohio girlhood, with her family's encouragement, Barker helped fugitive slaves. In 1829 she married James L. Gage, a lawyer and iron founder. While she bore and raised their eight children, she read widely, published poems, and developed strong views on slavery, women's rights, and temperance, a "triune cause" in which she involved herself for the rest of her life. By 1850, she had

begun to establish herself as a speaker and writer, primarily of advice to women.

In St. Louis, where the Gages moved in 1853, she provoked hostility by her radicalism. The family lived through three fires, perhaps set because of her antislavery views. In 1860, homeless and without a business, they moved back to Ohio, where Gage had to support the family because of her husband's poor health.

In 1861, with four sons in the Union army, Gage and her daughter Mary joined in the effort in the Sea Islands off the coasts of Georgia and South Carolina to demonstrate that with education and economic aid freed slaves could support themselves and live independently. There, Gen. Rufus Saxton put her and her daughter to work, without pay. Called home by her husband's fatal illness, Gage lectured to raise money for her work and then returned to Parris Island. But in November 1863 she took to the road, speaking before soldiers' aid societies about the condition of the freed slaves and raising money for the freedmen's association and soldier relief. To the end of her life, she continued her reform activities in her "triune cause."

Garnet, Henry Highland (1815–February 13, 1882) *prominent black antislavery leader, missionary to Jamaica*

Born a slave, Garnet escaped to New York when his father led his whole family to freedom; he spent his boyhood pursued by agents of their former owner. Noyes Academy in Canaan, New Hampshire, admitted him and 11 other blacks, but local farmers soon drove them out. Garnet later graduated from the Oneida Theological Institute and became pastor of a black Presbyterian church in Troy, New York, an educator of black children, and a forthright spokesman for equal rights and antislavery. He and Frederick Douglass opposed one another on the means of achieving abolition, Garnet advocating militancy and Douglass persuasion. But both supported political action, the Liberty Party, and the federal government during the Civil War. Garnet preached the sermon before the House of Representatives celebrating passage of the Thirteenth Amendment, the first black to speak in public in the nation's capital. He died in Monrovia, Liberia, where he was the minister (ambassador) of the United States.

Garrett, Thomas (August 21, 1789–January 25, 1871) *abolitionist hardware merchant, toolmaker*

An outspoken red-headed Quaker, Garrett committed himself as a youth to help "God's poor escaping from the prison house of slavery." At age 24, he rescued a free black woman who had been kidnapped from his father's house. Settling in Wilmington, Delaware, in 1822, he made his home a station on the Underground Railroad, on a much-traveled escape route. Because it was only eight miles from free territory in Pennsylvania, Wilmington was haunted by sheriffs' and slave owners' representatives.

Garrett developed a network of helpers, both black and white, and informed himself about the legal protections for fugitive slaves. He contemptuously waved away slave hunters' guns and knives, saying, "On with thee. Anyone who stoops to such low methods is a coward and I will have no dealings with him." Knowing the hazards of escape attempts, Garrett never encouraged slaves to flee, but he protected all who approached him.

In 1848, two Maryland slave owners sued Garrett, claiming that he and John Hunn had harbored a family of eight slaves and helped them escape. The evidence showed that Garrett and Hunn had scrupulously followed the law, having had no indication that the fugitives they assisted were slaves. An allegedly packed jury and Chief Justice Roger Taney of the U.S. Supreme Court (later to issue the notorious *Dred Scott* decision) found them guilty notwithstanding and fined Garrett $5,400—wiping him out financially. He responded in an hour-long speech: "I have assisted fourteen hundred slaves in the past twenty-five years on their way to the North. I now consider this penalty imposed upon me as a license for the remainder of my life. I am now past sixty and have not a dollar to my name, but . . . if anyone knows of a poor slave who needs shelter and a breakfast, send him to me. . . ."

By 1863, 2,700 slaves had passed through his hands—not counting those he helped before he began to keep records.

Garrison, William Lloyd (December 10, 1805–May 4, 1879) *reformer, Christian anarchist*

Garrison, who emigrated to the United States from Nova Scotia, had little formal education, but he was apprenticed to a printer and newspaper editor. The first newspaper he edited, the *Free Press* of Newburyport, Massachusetts, failed. He then joined the staff of the *National Philanthropist*, a temperance paper. About 1828, Quaker Benjamin Lundy talked to him about the evils of slavery, and soon thereafter he delivered his first lecture against it. By the summer of 1829 he was working in Baltimore on the weekly *Genius of Universal Emancipa-*

tion, and for the next 30 years he devoted himself to abolitionism.

As a young man he favored colonization and gradual emancipation. As he matured, he grew more radical, building a significant following but eventually angering many antislavery workers by his extreme views. He attacked those who disagreed with him in strong language; he denounced the churches; eventually, he rejected the idea of government itself, repudiating the Constitution as a proslavery document. But he never advocated violence, insisting on the power of moral suasion. He advanced no plan for abolition but uncompromisingly demanded it.

In 1830, he launched the influential antislavery weekly *The Liberator,* which gave opportunity for black leaders to express their views, although circulation never exceeded 3,000. In 1831 he helped draft the constitution for the New England Anti-Slavery Society, and the next year became its paid agent. He went on to assist in organizing such societies in New York and Philadelphia. In 1835, he was seized at an abolitionist meeting and dragged through the streets with a rope around his neck.

Garrison alienated many of his fellow abolitionists, particularly by trying to link abolitionism with other reforms, such as woman's rights. In 1840, the American Anti-Slavery Society split over this issue and Garrison's opposition to political action, leaving him firmly in charge of the remnants of that organization, over which he presided for the next 22 terms. At the World's Anti-Slavery Convention in London in 1840, he refused to participate because women were excluded, although he had long been prominent in British abolitionism. He began to call upon the North to secede from the Union, arguing that the U.S. Constitution was "a covenant with death and an agreement with hell" that "should be annulled." In 1854, he publicly burned a copy of the Constitution.

When the South seceded, Garrison rejoiced, and in 1862 he praised Lincoln's Emancipation Proclamation. In 1863, the two factions of abolitionists were reconciled. With the passage of the Thirteenth Amendment he closed the *Liberator,* turning his attention to prohibition, woman suffrage, justice for American Indians, and the elimination of prostitution.

Gibbons, Abigail Hopper (December 7, 1801– January 16, 1893) *reformer, welfare worker*
Hopper grew up the daughter of a Quaker minister mother and a father who spent much of his time and money in helping blacks, whether free or fugitive slave. She adopted her parents' values, interesting herself particularly in prison reform and antislavery. As a young woman, she founded and for a decade ran a school for Quaker children. In 1833 she married James Sloan Gibbons, a Quaker merchant and banker; she spent most of her life with him in New York City. They had six children.

Gibbons worked effectively in the Manhattan Anti-Slavery Society, running fairs to raise money. When in 1842 the Yearly Meeting of the Society of Friends disowned her father and husband for their abolitionism, she resigned.

During the Civil War, she and her daughter Sarah served as nurses for more than three years. In this work she clashed with army officers, in part because she insisted on generous treatment for contrabands. During the New York draft riots of 1863, a mob vandalized her home. Gibbons spent the end of her life as she had the beginning, trying to remedy social problems.

Giddings, Joshua Reed (October 6, 1795– May 27, 1864) *abolitionist attorney, congressman*
In Congress, the stiffnecked, aggressive Giddings supported John Quincy Adams in his efforts to protect the petition rights of antislavery citizens. He denied the power of the federal government to tax in order to support slavery, and he saw the annexation of Texas and the Mexican War as power plays by proslavery forces. When the House of Representatives censured him for his opposition to any federal measure to defend the slave trade along the coast, Giddings resigned, appealed to the voters, and was reelected. In 1848 he left the Whig Party to join the Free Soil Party, and in 1854, when the Missouri Compromise was repealed, he joined the Republicans. Opposing disunion, he argued for the president's wartime powers to emancipate slaves in rebellious states. Although bad health prevented his reelection after 1858, he remained politically active and in 1861 became consul-general to Canada.

Greenfield, Elizabeth Taylor ("the Black Swan") (ca. 1817–March 31, 1876) *singer*
Greenfield was born a slave in Natchez, Mississippi. When she was a small child, her mistress took all her slaves to Philadelphia, freed them, and sent most of them to Liberia. Elizabeth remained with her and adopted her last name. Her former owner sought a musical education for her, but the teacher to whom she applied refused to ac-

cept her, for fear of offending his white pupils. Elizabeth then taught herself, with the help of a neighbor.

In 1851 her singing impressed a number of influential people, who sponsored concerts for her. That winter she went on tour throughout the Northeast, after which her sponsors sent her to tour in England, under the aegis of such prominent figures as the duchess of Sutherland. But her manager defaulted, defeating her plans for study there. She returned to Philadelphia, where she taught and gave concerts for several years. She was the first black American musician to win a wide international reputation.

Grew, Mary (September 1, 1813–October 10, 1896) *abolitionist, suffragist*

As a girl in Hartford, Connecticut, the daughter of a minister, Grew taught a Sunday school class of black children. After moving to Philadelphia, she joined the Female Anti-Slavery Society, to which Lucretia Mott and Sarah Pugh also belonged and in which she soon was elected to office. A supporter and personal friend of William Lloyd Garrison, Grew served as an officer of the state branch of the American Anti-Slavery Society and as coeditor of the *Pennsylvania Freeman*. She also worked in the Free Produce Association.

A lecturer and writer, Grew appeared prominently at the Anti-Slavery Convention of American Women of 1838, when a proslavery mob heckled the speakers and attacked Pennsylvania Hall, site of the meeting. At the World's Anti-Slavery Convention of 1840, she and the other women elected as delegates were excluded from the floor. Henceforth she added women's rights to her reform work.

Griffing, Josephine Sophia White (December 18, 1814–February 18, 1872) *reformer, welfare worker among freedmen*

Born and raised in Connecticut, White married Charles Stockman Spooner Griffing, a machinist, and in 1842 they moved to Ohio. A Garrisonian, she repudiated the Union because it permitted slaveholding. She made her home a station on the Underground Railroad. She served prominently in the Western Anti-Slavery Society both as a volunteer and, from 1851 to 1855, as a paid agent who lectured against slavery and sang abolitionist songs. She also wrote for the *Anti-Slavery Bugle*. During the Civil War she joined the Women's Loyal National League, founded to ensure the complete elimination of slavery, lecturing for it and in 1864 collecting signatures for a women's antislavery petition.

Like many another woman, through her abolitionist activities Griffing evolved into a supporter of women's rights. But she also continued to work for blacks after the Civil War. She lobbied unsuccessfully for a federally sponsored welfare program for blacks to settle them throughout the North, and successfully for the Freedmen's Bureau—only to become its frequent and vigorous critic when it came into being. She did, however, serve in the bureau on and off until it disbanded in 1869. In 1865, she became the general agent of the National Freedmen's Relief Association of the District of Columbia. In that capacity she ran a settlement program for freed blacks, helped many find jobs and homes in the North, and founded an industrial school to train women to sew.

Grimké, Archibald (August 17, 1849–February 25, 1930) *lawyer, writer, activist*

Born a slave in South Carolina, Archibald was one of three sons of slave nurse Nancy Weston and her master, Henry Grimké. In his childhood, he was taught to read and write. Cruelly treated by his white half-brother who inherited him from Henry, Archibald ran away, hiding in the home of sympathetic whites until the end of the Civil War. Toward the end of the war, he and his brother Francis, who had served as a valet to a Confederate officer, volunteered as officers' boys in the Union army. At war's end they studied in a freedman's school in Charleston, whose headmistress arranged opportunities for them in the North; they were soon enrolled in Lincoln University in Pennsylvania. In 1868, their aunts, abolitionists Sarah and Angelina Grimké, discovered their existence and identity, sponsored their continuing studies—for Archibald at Harvard Law School and for Francis at Princeton Theological Seminary—and introduced them to many influential friends, both black and white. Later, as pastor of a church in Washington, D.C., Francis gained a national reputation as a preacher and defender of blacks.

Archibald distinguished himself as a writer on racial affairs and as an activist. In 1883 he undertook the editorship of the black newspaper the *Hub*, published in Boston; in it he supported Republican candidates and the causes of racial equality and woman suffrage. In 1886, however, accusing Republicans of deserting blacks, he left the party, eventually turning to the Democrats. In 1894, President Cleveland appointed him consul to the Dominican Republic. In the early 20th century, he helped found the National Association for the Advancement of

Colored People and for some years presided over its District of Columbia branch.

Grimké, Sarah (November 26, 1792– December 23, 1873) and
Angelina Grimké (February 20, 1805– October 26, 1879) *abolitionists, women's rights pioneers*

Daughters of a wealthy slaveholding family of Charleston, South Carolina, Sarah and Angelina were raised as proper southern young ladies and educated by private tutors. Sarah protested early on at being denied the opportunity to study serious academic subjects. On a trip north as nurse for her ailing father, this deeply religious woman was impressed by the Quakers she met, especially because of their opposition to slavery. She left the Anglican Church and in 1821 moved to Philadelphia.

Angelina shared Sarah's views on slavery, horrified particularly by the beatings inflicted on slaves. In 1829 she followed Sarah north, where both of them devoted themselves to charity. Their convictions about slavery strengthened, and in 1835 Angelina felt called to oppose it actively. After William Lloyd Garrison published a letter from her in the *Liberator,* she wrote *An Appeal to the Christian Women of the South* and signed it—defying the convention that ladies' names should appear in public only when they were born, when they were married, and when they died. She also accepted an appointment as agent of the American Anti-Slavery Society, undertaking to hold meetings for small groups of women. As these meetings grew, drawing men as well as women, Angelina again broke with tradition by addressing "promiscuous" audiences—that is, of both genders. In 1836, Sarah, disturbed by discrimination against blacks in Friends' meetings, left the Society and published an *Epistle to the Clergy of the Southern States*, refuting the idea that the Bible justifies slavery.

The Grimké sisters by this time were devoting themselves to the abolitionist cause. Angelina wrote another pamphlet, *Appeal to the Women of the Nominally Free States*, and testified before a committee of the Massachusetts legislature on antislavery petitions. Though Angelina starred on their lecture tours, Sarah too spoke on occasion.

When in 1837 the Massachusetts Congregational ministerial association issued a "Pastoral Letter" condemning them for unwomanly behavior, the Grimkés had to confront their own covert feminism. What they might not have sought in their own behalf—the right of free speech—they demanded for the sake of abolitionism. Sarah wrote on the subject in *Letters on the Equality of the Sexes, and the Condition of Woman*, and Angelina defended herself in a series of letters to the *Liberator*. Many abolitionists criticized them for their stand—including the daring Theodore Weld.

The Grimkés had met Weld in 1836 at an abolitionist training course that he taught; he and Angelina had at once been drawn to each other. They married on May 14, 1838, in Philadelphia, in a simple ceremony attended by black and white abolitionist friends. On May 16, Angelina spoke before the woman's antislavery convention there, heckled by an angry mob—the last lecture she ever gave. The Welds and Sarah henceforth lived and worked together. Most notably, they compiled *American Slavery as It Is: Testimony of a Thousand Witnesses* (1839), an effort to undermine slavery by showing its horrors in reports from southern newspapers and slave owners. Their disapproval of political action separated them from many other abolitionists, and ill health and their own poverty forced them into other activities, mostly educational.

In 1868, the Grimké sisters discovered the existence of two nephews, Archibald and Francis, sons of a Grimké brother and a slave mother. The sisters immediately took them into the family and assumed responsibility for their education, at considerable personal sacrifice.

Grinnell, Josiah Bushnell (December 22, 1821– March 31, 1891) *abolitionist, clergyman*

Grinnell, a Vermont Congregationalist, may have preached the first antislavery sermon ever heard in Washington, D.C., in about 1851. At any rate, his views forced his departure for New York City, where he served another church until his voice faltered. He then pioneered as an Iowa farmer and was influential in the founding of the town of Grinnell, a church, and what is now Grinnell College. In 1856, he was elected to the state senate on a Republican ticket and a platform of no liquor, free schools, and "No Nationalizing of Slavery." Developing a reputation as a leading abolitionist, he received into his home escaped slaves rescued by John Brown. As a U.S. congressman from 1863 to 1867, he supported Lincoln, urging the enlistment of black soldiers. After the war, he fought to make black suffrage a requirement for the readmission of rebel states to the Union.

Hallowell, Richard Price (December 16, 1835– January 5, 1904) *abolitionist, merchant*

Educated as a Quaker, Hallowell early embraced the antislavery cause, refusing to work with a company that sold the products of slave labor. An activist, on occasion he helped guard William Lloyd Garrison and Wendell Phillips. In 1859, he went with an antislavery group to receive John Brown's body after his execution. During the Civil War, he recruited black soldiers and struggled to get them equal pay. When peace came he worked to help blacks, particularly by starting and financing schools for them in the South.

Harper, Frances Ellen Watkins (September 24, 1825–February 22, 1911) *black abolitionist, poet, lecturer*

Born free, Watkins was educated at the school of her uncle, Rev. William Watkins, after which she learned to sew in a Baltimore household in which she worked to support herself. In 1850, she began to teach sewing.

Under the influence of William Still and Boston abolitionists, Harper began to lecture against slavery in August 1854. The Maine Anti-Slavery Society hired her as its agent. She interspersed her talks with readings from her own book of 1854, *Poems on Miscellaneous Subjects*. She also wrote poems, stories, and articles for abolitionist papers.

In 1860 she married Fenton Harper. After his death in 1864, she resumed her lectures, speaking on blacks' need for education, temperance, and domestic morality but also against white racial violence. In later life she also tried to curb delinquency among black youth, and in 1896 she helped to organize the National Association of Colored Women.

Haven, Gilbert (September 19, 1821–January 3, 1880) *abolitionist, Methodist bishop*

Even as a student, Haven held antislavery views. As a clergyman he preached and wrote on the immorality of slavery. During the Civil War he served as an army chaplain and worked to secure both civil rights and social equality for blacks, insisting on the necessity of complete integration of the races. After the war he kept on practicing what he preached, at the cost of ostracism and threats of violence. Not only did he support black schools in the South with his own money and funds that he raised, but he recruited teachers for them. Moreover, in articles, sermons, and lectures he exposed the ways in which southern whites repressed blacks in the postwar years.

Haviland, Laura Smith (December 20, 1808–April 20, 1898) *abolitionist, worker for freedmen's welfare*

In 1829, Haviland and her husband, the Quaker farmer Charles Haviland Jr., with Elizabeth M. Chandler organized the first antislavery society in Michigan. They resigned from the Society of Friends when that group disapproved their abolitionist activity. In 1837, the couple founded a school for poor children, later making it into a manual-labor preparatory school open to all regardless of gender or race.

After the tragic death of her husband, parents, sister, and youngest child in an 1845 epidemic, Haviland devoted herself to the antislavery cause, doing missionary work among blacks both in the North and in the slave states. She also lectured for antislavery societies and escorted fugitives on the Underground Railroad, even venturing into the South. During the Civil War she visited hospitals and prison camps to work with contrabands, in 1864 signing on as an agent of the Freedmen's Aid Commission, for which she traveled through the South. In 1879, she helped to resettle blacks in Kansas.

Hazard, Thomas (September 15, 1720–August 26, 1798) *abolitionist*

In the early 1740s, a church deacon told Hazard that Quakers who held slaves were not Christians—as did he, his family (some of whom were slave traders), and almost everyone he knew. Hazard decided that the deacon was right; he began to use free labor on his farm and to convert others to antislavery. In 1774, he worked on a Quaker committee that submitted a bill to the Rhode Island legislature prohibiting the importation of blacks. In 1783, another Quaker committee on which he sat successfully petitioned the legislature to abolish slavery. In 1787, the Providence Society for Abolishing the Slave Trade, which Hazard had helped found, persuaded the legislature to act against the slave trade.

Henson, Josiah (June 15, 1789–1883) *fugitive slave, autobiographer, colonizer, allegedly the model for Harriet Beecher Stowe's Uncle Tom*

As a youth Henson endured the tyrannies of slavery, seeing his mother assaulted and his father mutilated. He was maimed for life by an enemy of one of his three successive owners. Nonetheless, he was converted to Christianity at age 18 and later became a preacher in the Methodist Episcopal Church. He married at 22 and fathered 12 children. During the many years that he toiled for his owners, he bore responsibility for the work of other slaves. Even one master's bad faith in a "contract" to allow Henson to purchase his freedom with money he had earned by preaching did not prompt him to escape. But when in 1830 he learned that he was to be sold, he fled to Canada with his wife and four of his children, assisted by Indians and a Scots steamer captain on Lake Erie.

In Canada, Henson worked for pay and shares, farmed, preached, and helped slaves escape and succeed in a new life. In 1834, he led a group of blacks to invest in land near Colchester. With the intention of instilling "the Yankee spirit . . . into my fellow slaves," he cooperated with white abolitionists in establishing the British-American Institute, a manual-labor school around which the town of Dawn grew. Several times he went to England on the community's behalf. In 1849, Henson published a well-received narrative, *The Life of Josiah Henson*. In the divisions among the abolitionist forces, he sided with those who opposed violence.

Higginson, Thomas Wentworth (December 22, 1823–May 9, 1911) *abolitionist, woman suffragist, soldier, author*

Higginson took both his undergraduate and his divinity degrees at Harvard, after which he became first a Unitarian minister and then pastor of a "free church." During his pastorates, he devoted much of his time and energy to community activities, temperance, woman suffrage, and abolitionism.

In the abolitionist movement, he joined with those who wished to dissolve the Union because it allowed and enforced slavery. A daring and adventurous activist, he served on vigilance committees to rescue fugitive slaves, including Anthony Burns. In 1856 he not only worked in the East for a free Kansas but traveled west for this cause, meeting John Brown, whom he ardently supported.

With the outbreak of the Civil War, Higginson abandoned his pulpit to recruit and train soldiers. In November 1862, he accepted the colonelcy of the First South Carolina Volunteers, a black regiment, holding it until he was invalided out because of a wound. He described his experiences in *Army Life in a Black Regiment*. He devoted his postwar life to writing sketches, a novel, memoirs, and biographies, and to working for reforms, especially woman suffrage.

Holley, Myron (April 29, 1779–March 4, 1841) *lawyer, merchant, politician, abolitionist*

In 1837, Holley began to interest himself in antislavery political action. In 1839, he failed to persuade the Cleveland antislavery convention to present a slate in the national election; he succeeded, however, at a larger convention in getting James G. Birney nominated as an antislavery candidate. His advocacy led to the formation of the Liberty Party in 1840. From 1839 almost until his death, Holley edited the *Rochester Freeman*.

Holley, Sallie (February 17, 1818–January 12, 1893) *abolitionist lecturer, teacher of freed slaves*

Daughter of Myron Holley, the principal founder of the Liberty Party, Sallie Holley was brought up on antislavery talk. In her girlhood, she refused a proposal of marriage on the grounds that her suitor had voted for Henry Clay. In 1847, she went to Oberlin College, though her brother begged her not to expose herself to insult by going to the "nigger school"—that is, a college that had begun to admit blacks in 1834. While there she responded to the call of Abby Kelley Foster for more women to speak on behalf of slave women. She soon accepted an invitation from the blacks of Sandusky, Ohio, to address a celebration of West Indian emancipation. When Oberlin's president's wife warned her against staying in a black's house, Holley responded, "Mrs. Mahan, I should certainly feel it my duty to accept any such invitation as a testimony to my principles, and, really, to those professed by this Institution." After graduation in 1851, she became an agent for the Anti-Slavery Society, a course that she vigorously pursued until emancipation, reporting on her tours with letters to Garrison's *Liberator*.

During the Civil War, Holley lectured for black suffrage and collected clothing for freed slaves. When the American Anti-Slavery Society dissolved in 1870, she joined her friend Carolina Putnam, who had founded a school for blacks. For the next 20 years they worked together, dependent on northern contributions and black labor, ostracized by the whites around them. They instructed not only in reading and writing but also in politics, housekeeping, and gardening.

Holly, James T. (October 3, 1829–March 13, 1911) *African-American Episcopal bishop, emigrationist*

Born free in Washington, D.C., as an adult Holly edited and taught until 1855, when he was ordained an Episcopal deacon, an event that eventually led to his becoming Bishop of Haiti in 1874. Early interested in black emigration, Holly eventually advocated colonization in Haiti. He investigated possibilities there for the 1856 Emigration Convention, and in 1857 he published a lecture on Haitian history. In 1861, he led some 2,000 African Americans to pioneer in that country. Although only a fraction of these remained and many died there, including members of his own family, Holly lived in Haiti for the rest of his life, devoting himself to missionary work.

Hopper, Isaac Tatem (December 3, 1771– May 7, 1852) *Quaker abolitionist, Underground Railroad operator, prison reformer*

Early sympathetic to slaves, as a member of the Pennsylvania Abolition Society Hopper began before 1800 to help blacks escape. For their protection, he educated himself in laws that affected them and pleaded for them before Philadelphia courts. When he moved to New York City in 1829, he carried on his antislavery activities there, often shipping fugitives to Providence and Boston by water. In 1841, he joined forces with Lydia Maria Child in editing the *National Anti-Slavery Standard.* He and his son were both mobbed, and with other members of his family Hopper was disowned by the New York Monthly Meeting of the Society of Friends.

Howard, Oliver Otis (November 8, 1830– October 26, 1909) *soldier, director of the Freedmen's Bureau*

Born and educated in Maine, Howard then entered West Point, graduating fourth in his class in 1854. At the beginning of the Civil War, he was a colonel, and at its end a brigadier-general with the brevet rank of major-general and the nickname the "Christian general"; but he had lost his right arm in battle. In May 1865, President Johnson appointed him commissioner of the recently created Bureau of Refugees, Freedmen, and Abandoned Land.

In that position he battled gallantly against Johnson's persistent efforts to undermine his authority and the effectiveness of the bureau, against congressional failure to fund the bureau, and against the determination of the South, often expressed in violence, to keep blacks poor and subservient. Various charges were brought against him; at one point Congress cleared him, and at another a special court appointed by President Grant exonerated him.

After the Freedmen's Bureau disbanded, he resumed his army career. In 1872, as peace commissioner, he negotiated a treaty with the Apache, and in 1877 and 1878, he commanded expeditions against first the Nez Perce and then the Bannock and Piute. In 1880, he began to serve as superintendent of West Point, and in 1884, he attended meetings of the international Young Men's Christian Association in Berlin and represented the United States at French army maneuvers. Promoted to major-general in

1886, he finished his service as commander of the Division of the East. In 1893, he was awarded the Congressional Medal of Honor.

Between 1881 and 1908, he published a number of books on various subjects, including an autobiography and three books about Indians; he also wrote extensively for magazines and newspapers. In retirement (after 1894) he also lectured and preached.

Howland, Emily (November 20, 1827–June 29, 1929) *educator, reformer, philanthropist*

Bored with housekeeping for her Quaker family, whose home was a station on the Underground Railroad, Howland began in her late teens to read widely about slavery and to attend abolitionist conventions. In 1856, she volunteered to take over Myrtilla Miner's Washington school for free black girls, which she conducted for two years with a black assistant. The experience transformed her, introducing her to influential people and helping her gain confidence, even to the point of facing down a hostile mob.

In 1863, she began to teach in contraband camps in and around Washington. In 1867 she experimented with settling former slave families on 400 acres her father bought in Virginia, founding a school there. Soon called back to family responsibilities by her mother's death, Howland devoted much time and effort to women's education and women's rights generally, as well as to the temperance and peace movements, but still focused on black education. For more than 50 years, she continued to support the Virginia school she had established. She also contributed to many other black schools, regularly visiting them.

Hutchinson, Abigail Jemima (August 29, 1829–November 24, 1892) *singer, feminist, reformer*

Hutchinson is best remembered as a member of a professional singing group known successively as the Aeolian Vocalists and the Hutchinson Family. Beginning in 1843, the family contributed its services to antislavery, at some personal risk, singing "The Slave's Lament" and other songs at abolitionist rallies.

Jackson, James Caleb (March 28, 1811–July 11, 1895) *abolitionist physician, reformer*

As a young man, under the guidance of Gerrit Smith, Jackson became in 1838 an agent of the Massachusetts Anti-Slavery Society and in 1840 secretary of the American Anti-Slavery Society. For a period he helped edit the

National Anti-Slavery Standard. Funded by Smith, in 1841 Jackson founded the *Madison County Abolitionist* in upstate New York and went on to edit other papers. In 1847 he sponsored the fourth-party Liberty League, a descendant of the Liberty Party.

Johnson, Oliver (December 27, 1809–December 10, 1889) *antislavery leader, editor, reformer*

An admirer and associate of William Lloyd Garrison, Johnson stood with him through the disagreements and divisions among the antislavery forces. Periodically he substituted for Garrison in editing *The Liberator.* In 1832 he helped found the New England Anti-Slavery Society, for which four years later he became an agent. Until the Civil War he lectured, wrote, and edited papers against slavery—including the *Anti-Slavery Bugle,* the *Pennsylvania Freeman,* and the *National Anti-Slavery Standard.*

Jones, Absalom (1746–unknown) *first African-American Episcopalian priest*

Born a slave, Jones taught himself to read. When at age 16 he was sold to a Philadelphia owner, he attended a Quaker night school for blacks. With his earnings he bought first his wife's freedom and then his own in 1784. As a lay minister in St. George's Methodist Episcopal church, he shared the outrage of his friend Richard Allen when the white members decided to relegate the blacks to the balcony. The blacks left and in 1787 founded the Free African Society, with Allen and Jones as leaders. This society used its monthly dues to help the needy. In 1794 the church built by the society became a member of the Episcopal Diocese of Pennsylvania, retaining control over its parochial affairs.

Jones was ordained as a priest on September 21, 1802. He participated actively in the civic affairs of the black community and of the city, consistently denouncing slavery.

Jones, Charles Colcock (1804–unknown) *"Apostle to the Blacks"*

A Presbyterian minister as well as a plantation and slave owner, in 1832 Jones resigned his position at the First Presbyterian Church of Savannah to become a missionary to slaves. He upheld the institution of slavery and prided himself on being a kind and just master. In Liberty County, Georgia, he helped build three churches for slaves and then rode from one church to another, preaching and teaching, stressing the slaves' "duty" of obedience to their masters. He wrote two books, *Catechism of Scripture Doctrine and Practice* and *The Religious Instruction of the Negroes in the United States.* From 1837 to 1838 and again from 1848 to 1850, he served as professor of ecclesiastical history and church polity at the Presbyterian Theological Seminary in Columbia, South Carolina. From 1850 to 1853, he worked in Philadelphia as corresponding secretary of the Board of Domestic Missions of the Presbyterian Church, where he reinvigorated the board and aroused the denomination to the plight of the blacks. In 1853 he collapsed into semi-invalidism and retreated to his Georgia plantations, teaching and preaching as his strength permitted.

Jones, Jane Elizabeth Hitchcock (March 13, 1813–January 13, 1896) *antislavery and feminist lecturer*

In the early 1840s, Hitchcock toured with Abby Kelley Foster, lecturing against slavery. In 1845 she joined with several fellow lecturers in organizing antislavery societies around Salem, Ohio. There she and the Quaker Benjamin Smith Jones, whom she married the next year, coedited the *Anti-Slavery Bugle.* She also ran an antislavery book agency and in 1848 wrote a tract for children, *The Young Abolitionists.*

After attending the first convention of Ohio women in 1850, Jones worked ardently for women's rights. She turned to lecturing on women's legal and customary disabilities and, after studying medicine, on good health and hygiene for women. But in 1856 she again picked up antislavery work, combining it with her labors for women.

Julian, George Washington (May 5, 1817–July 7, 1899) *abolitionist attorney, reformer-politician*

About 1845, already in the Indiana state legislature, Julian began to write against slavery. A few years later, he shifted from the Whig to the Free Soil Party, on whose ticket he was elected to Congress in 1848. There he fought against such measures as the Fugitive Slave Law of 1850. In 1852 he ran for the vice presidency as the Free Soil candidate. A founder of the Republican Party in 1856, he was five times elected to Congress. During the Civil War he supported Lincoln and urged him to emancipate the slaves. After the war he worked for black suffrage.

Keckley, Elizabeth (ca. 1818–May 26, 1907) *freed slave, dressmaker*

As a slave, Keckley helped support her mistress's family by her work as seamstress and dressmaker. She married the ne'er-do-well James Keckley under the impression that he was a free black but later separated from him. In 1855, borrowing from her patrons, she purchased her own freedom and that of her son, later repaying the loan in full. In 1860, she moved from St. Louis to Washington, D.C.

After Lincoln's inauguration as president she sewed for Mary Todd Lincoln, becoming her friend, confidante, and traveling companion. During the Civil War she founded and headed a Contraband Relief Association to assist fugitive slaves coming to Washington, D.C.

In 1868 a ghost-written book, *Behind the Scenes*, appeared in Keckley's name. It embarrassed Mrs. Lincoln by revealing her private opinions of people, details of the Lincolns' family life, and Mrs. Lincoln's efforts in 1867 to sell her personal effects to settle debts. Although Keckley protested that she had intended to improve Mrs. Lincoln's image, the book ended their friendship and ruined Keckley's standing in the black community.

Kemble, Frances Anne (Fanny Kemble)

(November 27, 1809–January 15, 1893) *British actress, author*

Born into an illustrious theatrical family, Kemble achieved fame as a brilliant actress in England. Her marriage in 1834 to Pierce Butler, whom she knew as a charming young Philadelphian, resulted from a successful American tour that she undertook with her father in 1832. Publication in 1835 of her flippant *Journal of a Residence in America* damaged her marriage, which later ended, in large part over slavery. The Butlers separated in 1845 when she discovered his infidelity; she resumed her career as author and actress and later as theatrical reader. In 1849 Butler divorced Kemble for desertion, "tho'," wrote her friend Rebecca Gratz, "it is well known he drove her out from her privileges of Mother & wife long before she attempted to earn a maintenance for herself in a profession she loathes [acting]."

During the Civil War she published her *Journal of a Residence on a Georgian Plantation* in 1838–1839. This book reveals her horror at discovering the realities of slavery and the knowledge that from it her husband derived his wealth. Her inability to abate the cruelties inflicted on the slaves frustrated her and made her question her husband's character. By its publication she hoped to win friends among the British for the Union. Later in her life she published autobiographical memoirs and *Notes upon Some of Shakespeare's Plays*.

Lane, Lunsford (unknown–unknown) *black abolitionist*

Born a slave in Raleigh, North Carolina, Lunsford freed himself by hiring out and manufacturing tobacco, but he had to leave the state before he could purchase his wife and children. Returning for them, he was savaged by a mob. He lectured for the American Anti-Slavery Society and served as an army nurse in the Civil War.

Leavitt, Joshua (September 8, 1794–January 16, 1873) *clergyman, reformer, abolitionist, editor*

In 1831, Leavitt began editing the *Evangelist*, which among other causes advocated abolition—the first of several newspapers he edited in opposition to slavery. For a time, he belonged to the American Colonization Society. A cofounder of the New York Anti-Slavery Society, Leavitt helped merge it into the National Anti-Slavery Society.

Lee, Luther (November 30, 1800–December 13, 1889) *abolitionist, Methodist clergyman*

Already opposed to slavery early in his career, Lee declared himself an abolitionist when Elijah Lovejoy was assassinated in 1837. Within his denomination, he worked to stimulate the growth of Wesleyan antislavery societies. He also defended other abolitionist clergy in church trials brought by Methodist conservatives. In 1843, with other abolitionists, Lee split from his denomination to found the antislavery Wesleyan Methodist Connection of America, over which he soon presided.

As an agent of the American Anti-Slavery Society, Lee spoke so expressively and effectively that he was the target of a good deal of violence from proslavery forces. Committed to political action against slavery, in 1840 he helped found the Liberty Party.

LeMoyne, Francis Julius (September 4, 1798–October 14, 1879) *abolitionist physician*

In the 1830s, LeMoyne debated against slavery and against colonization, a movement that he thought was promoted by proslavery forces. In 1840 he ran for the vice presidency on the Liberty Party ticket, and in 1841, 1844, and 1847 for the Pennsylvania Abolitionist ticket—always unsuccessfully. He made his house a station on the Underground Railroad. He also financially supported the American Missionary Association's LeMoyne Normal Institute for blacks.

Lewis, Wildfire Edmonia (ca. July 4, 1845–ca. 1909) *sculptor*

The child of a black servant father and a Chippewa mother, Lewis was born in Greenbush, New York, and raised among the Chippewa. Her only brother, Sunrise, enabled her to attend Oberlin College's preparatory department and then the college itself, but in 1862 she was accused of poisoning two white classmates. Vigilantes beat her, but a court dismissed her case. She left for Boston, where she met abolitionists William Lloyd Garrison and Lydia Maria Child and studied briefly with sculptor Edmund Brackett.

Early in her career, this mainly self-taught woman fashioned a medallion of abolitionist John Brown and a portrait bust of Robert Gould Shaw, the white commander of a black regiment. She went to Rome, where she was welcomed by sympathetic American artists and intellectuals. At first she concentrated on realistic representations of Indian and African-American subjects, and then she moved into the neoclassicism popular during that period. Exotic in appearance and charming in manner, she made a name for herself in Europe and in the United States, though her popularity waned as neoclassicism declined. She designed *Hagar in the Wilderness*, among her best works, to show her feeling "for all women who have struggled and suffered." Apparently she lived in Italy for the rest of her life, making occasional visits home.

Liele, George (ca. 1750–1820) *slave minister*

Born in Virginia, Liele was converted by a Baptist minister. He began preaching by exhorting his fellow slaves on his home plantation and the surrounding plantations. He went on to establish a church for blacks in Savannah, winning support of slave owners by baptizing only with their permission. After he left for Jamaica in the early 1780s, Andrew Bryan, one of his converts, succeeded him as pastor of the Savannah church. Liele founded churches in the West Indies as well as in the British colonies in North America, often teaching his parishioners to read.

Loguen, Jermain Wesley (ca. 1813–September 30, 1872) *bishop of the African Methodist Episcopal Zion Church, writer, lecturer*

Born in Tennessee of a slaveholding father and a black mother kidnapped from Ohio, Loguen escaped to Canada when he was about 21. There he learned to read, and after two years of hard work and thrift was able to study at the Oneida Institute in upstate New York. He became successively an elder, a pastor, and a bishop in the African Methodist Episcopal Zion Church, with pastorates in upstate New York. He opened schools for black children in Utica and Syracuse, spoke against slavery, and officiated in the Underground Railroad. Liberty Party men sought his support for their presidential candidate. He aided hundreds of fugitives, finally fleeing to Canada when he was indicted in the rescue of the fugitive slave Jerry in 1851. He published his *Narrative* in 1859.

Loring, Ellis Gray (April 14, 1803–May 24, 1858) *antislavery lawyer*

In 1831 Loring helped organize the New England Anti-Slavery Society, although he favored gradual emancipation rather than immediate abolition. The social censure and economic losses his antislavery stance brought did not deter him. He was a moderate in his views and his choices of antislavery strategies. In his 1838 *Address to the Abolitionists of Massachusetts on the Subject of Political Action*, he advocated petitions to legislatures, public interrogation of candidates, and the use of the ballot. Yet he supported Garrison's *Liberator* financially. He and his wife Louisa turned their home into an antislavery center and a shelter for fugitive slaves. In his office Loring oversaw the law studies of a young black man. As a lawyer he fought against Massachusetts efforts to silence abolitionists. He also used his skills as an attorney for blacks, notably in the case of the slave Med, for whom he won a judgment that a slave brought by his owner into the state could not be removed from it against the slave's will.

Lovejoy, Elijah Parish (November 9, 1802–November 7, 1837) *the "martyr abolitionist"*

A Presbyterian minister and editor of the Presbyterian weekly *St. Louis Observer*, Lovejoy propagandized against slavery, intemperance, and "popery." When the paper aroused protests, he moved it to Alton, Illinois, a prosperous community that favored gradual emancipation. But as Lovejoy's increasingly radical views turned his paper toward immediate abolitionism, some citizens began to have doubts about him. When his press arrived from St. Louis on a Sunday, Lovejoy's piety forbade him to move it, so he left it on the wharf, where someone dumped it in the river. Alton citizens raised money for a new one, even while proclaiming their disapproval of abolitionism, and Lovejoy promised to avoid the subject in his columns. He not only failed to keep that promise but also helped organize a state auxiliary of the American Anti-Slavery Society.

Mobs destroyed his presses repeatedly. In November 1837, when the most recent replacement press arrived, armed abolitionists gathered to defend it, as moderates begged Lovejoy to leave. He announced his readiness for martyrdom and found it on November 7, when during a battle around the warehouse where the press was stored he was shot dead.

Lovejoy, Owen (January 6, 1811–March 25, 1864)
abolitionist, Congregational clergyman, statesman

From the beginning of his brother Elijah's antislavery activities, Owen Lovejoy supported him and the cause. In his ministry he always spoke out against slavery, even when Illinois prohibited abolitionist meetings, and even under threat of violence. In 1854 he ran successfully for the Illinois state legislature on the Republican ticket, early on opting for Abraham Lincoln as a man who could hold the party together. Elected to Congress in 1856, he functioned there as an impassioned radical and in Illinois as a supporter of the conservative Lincoln, whom Lovejoy continued to support after Lincoln's election to the presidency. Lovejoy introduced the bill by which slavery was abolished in all U.S. territories.

Lundy, Benjamin (January 4, 1789–August 22, 1839) *Quaker antislavery activist*

A self-educated, prickly, restless man, a saddler by trade, in his lifetime Lundy roamed the American countryside and traveled abroad to Haiti, Canada, and Mexico. In 1815, in Ohio, he began his known activist career by organizing the Union Humane Society to combat racial prejudice, remove legal restrictions on blacks, help blacks illegally held in bondage, protect and aid free blacks, and work for the abolition of slavery. His early recognition of the importance of cooperation among antislavery societies foreshadowed the national antislavery organizations. For a time in 1817 and 1818, he assisted Charles Osborn in publishing *The Philanthropist,* and in 1821 he began publication of *The Genius of Universal Emancipation.*

About 1825 and for ten years thereafter, he investigated the possibilities of colonization. He endorsed Frances Wright's scheme of permitting slaves to purchase their freedom by cooperative labor on the land, followed by compulsory colonization. He traveled widely in search of possible sites for colonies.

In 1827, his antislavery activities provoked a beating from slave trader Austin Woolfolk, who claimed that Lundy had libeled him. In 1828, on a lecture tour through the northern states, Lundy converted William Lloyd Garrison to abolitionism and persuaded him to help edit *The Genius.* They soon parted company, however, and in 1835 *The Genius* ceased publication, giving way to *The National Enquirer and Constitutional Advocate of Universal Liberty,* in which

Lundy vociferously opposed what he thought of as slaveholders' plots to wrest Texas from Mexico.

When in 1838 a proslavery mob burned Pennsylvania Hall in Philadelphia, Lundy lost all his papers. Once again he moved, this time to Illinois, where he resurrected *The Genius.*

McKim, James Miller (November 14, 1810–June 13, 1874) *antislavery Presbyterian clergyman*

An advocate of immediate abolition, McKim at the age of 23 represented Carlisle, Pennsylvania, blacks in founding the American Anti-Slavery Society. When this action, together with his conversion of his entire congregation to antislavery, brought denominational wrath down on him, he left the ministry and became an antislavery speaker under the tutelage of Theodore Weld. Later he served as publishing agent and corresponding secretary of the Pennsylvania Anti-Slavery Society and editor of the *Pennsylvania Freeman.* He and his wife Sarah protected fugitive slaves from slave hunters. They also accompanied the group that received John Brown's body after his execution.

During the Civil War, McKim enlisted black soldiers and established the Philadelphia Port Royal Relief Committee to aid contrabands. In 1863, under the aegis of the Pennsylvania Freedmen's Relief Association, he founded schools for blacks in the South. At war's end he shifted to work for the American Freedman's Union Commission to promote black education.

Mercer, Margaret (July 1, 1791–September 17, 1846) *antislavery worker, reformer, educator*

For many years, Mercer dedicated most of her time and energy to the American Colonization Society, hoping to encourage manumission and gradually eliminate slavery. She freed the slaves she inherited on her Maryland father's death and sent those who wished it to Liberia. She also raised funds to buy the freedom of other slaves and to educate blacks in Liberia.

Miller, Jonathan Peckham (February 24, 1796–February 17, 1847) *soldier, Greek sympathizer, lawyer, antislavery advocate*

After fighting and raising money for Greek freedom from the Ottoman Empire, Miller studied law and served in the Vermont legislature. There he introduced a resolution urging Vermont congressional representatives to work for the abolition of slavery and of the slave trade in the District of Columbia. He continued to devote time and energy to the antislavery cause, lecturing, and in 1840 acting as delegate to the World's Anti-Slavery Convention in London.

Mott, James (June 20, 1788–January 26, 1868) *abolitionist, manufacturer, merchant, reformer*

A birthright Quaker, Mott sacrificed a flourishing cotton business to his principles, refusing to go on dealing in the product of slave labor. He and his wife Lucretia endured many attacks for their antislavery activities, which they continued until emancipation. Both helped organize the American Anti-Slavery Society, and both were elected delegates to the 1840 World's Anti-Slavery Convention. After 1850 they sheltered fugitive slaves in their home.

Mott, Lucretia Coffin (January 3, 1793– November 11, 1880) *Quaker minister, abolitionist, women's rights pioneer*

Both Lucretia Mott and her husband James were prominent figures in the Quaker and abolitionist communities. In the 1827 split within the Society of Friends, they took the side of Elias Hicks, whose denunciations of slavery persuaded them not to use any slave products, at least knowingly. Not only did they speak out for the free produce movement, but James Mott at considerable risk and cost shifted from the cotton to the wool business.

Lucretia Mott met William Lloyd Garrison about 1831. In 1833 she attended the Philadelphia convention that he had called to organize the American Anti-Slavery Society (AASS). Because that society did not admit women, she helped establish the Philadelphia Female Anti-Slavery Society. Later, when the AASS opened its membership to women, she joined and held office in it. She stood with Garrison in demanding immediate emancipation.

Mott repeatedly showed her courage in the abolitionist cause. Because of her "radical" stand on slavery she endured the criticism of her fellow Quakers—but not passively. When Quaker minister Rachel Barker preached against her at the Philadelphia Yearly Meeting for more than an hour, Mott preached back for another. Because of her antislavery activities, on one of her lecture and visitation tours someone tampered with her carriage, and inns refused her service. But she continued to speak against slavery both at Quaker meetings and before the state legislatures of Delaware, New Jersey, and Pennsylvania. She participated in setting up the Anti-Slavery Convention of American Women, which met in 1838 in Philadel-

phia in the brand-new Pennsylvania Hall. When mobs disturbed its sessions, Mott set an example of calm for the other participants. On May 17, proslavery advocates fired the building and started toward the Motts' home, where the family quietly awaited them; fortunately, they never reached the house. Again in 1840, when she was traveling through Delaware visiting Friends' meetings and speaking against slavery, Mott pleaded with a mob to take her rather than her male companion, whom they were intent on tarring and feathering. In 1843, she preached in a Unitarian church to an audience that included 40 congressmen.

When in 1840 the World's Anti-Slavery Convention in London refused to seat Mott and the other officially elected women delegates of the American Anti-Slavery Society, her reaction won her the title of "the *Lioness* of the Convention." This experience and Mott's meeting there with Elizabeth Cady Stanton led to the first women's rights convention, in 1848, in Seneca Falls, New York. In both these causes Mott was fighting for emancipation.

After the Civil War and the passage of the Thirteenth Amendment, Mott propagandized for black suffrage, working through the Friends Association of Philadelphia for the Aid and Elevation of the Freedmen, which provided both educational and economic aid to blacks. She labored for the rest of her life for the causes to which she had dedicated herself. At 77 she undertook to speak in all the black churches of Philadelphia.

Nelson, David (September 24, 1793–October 17, 1844) *abolitionist, Presbyterian physician, clergyman, educator*

Before 1831, Nelson freed his slaves. In 1835, Theodore Weld's oratory persuaded him to dedicate himself to the antislavery cause, accepting an appointment as agent from the American Anti-Slavery Society (AASS). Nelson preached manumission to his congregation, calling upon slaveholders to free their slaves. Marion College thereupon ended his presidency, the state of Missouri expelled him, and mobs attacked him. Nonetheless, he continued his work for the AASS in Illinois until bad health forced him to stop in 1840.

Osborn, Charles (August 21, 1775–December 29, 1850) *Quaker abolitionist preacher*

During his residences in Tennessee, Ohio, Indiana, and Michigan, and in his travels all over the country in his ministry, Osborn preached against slavery. In 1815 he organized the Tennessee Manumission Society, and in 1816 he founded other such societies in North Carolina.

He edited briefly the antislavery *Philanthropist,* denouncing colonization as a plot of slaveholders to protect slavery and rid the country of free blacks. In 1842, he helped found both the Free Produce Association of Wayne County, Indiana, and the *Free Labor Advocate and Anti-Slavery Chronicle.* That year conservative Quakers ousted Osborn and other abolitionists from the governing committee of the Indiana Yearly Meeting, on which he had long sat, causing him to break away in 1843 to help found the Indiana Yearly Meeting of Anti-Slavery Friends.

Pennington, James W. C. (1809–October, 1870) *Presbyterian pastor, author of the first history of blacks by a black man in the New World*

Born a slave, Pennington was trained as a stonemason and blacksmith. Outraged by his master's cruel treatment of his family and himself, about 1828 with the help of Quakers he escaped to the North, where Quakers taught him reading, writing, and the elements of Christianity. He continued studying on his own, supporting himself as a farmer, a teacher, and finally a minister. For many years he served a Presbyterian church in New York City.

Pennington tried vainly to purchase his parents' freedom and his own. Eventually he helped his father and two brothers escape to Canada. Some of his sisters married free men, who bought their freedom, and three of his brothers were bought by "conscience slaveholders," who held them only for a term of years.

Pennington intended his *Text Book of the Origin and History of the Colored People* (1841) primarily for schoolchildren. In 1849 he published his memoirs, as *The Fugitive Blacksmith.* While he was still legally a slave, the University of Heidelberg conferred upon him the degree of doctor of divinity. He served five terms as a member of the General Convention for the Improvement of the Free Colored People. As late as 1859 he was still writing for the *Anglo-American* magazine.

Phillips, Wendell (November 29, 1811–February 2, 1884) *wealthy abolitionist reformer, lawyer, orator*

Early in 1837, Phillips publicly announced his belief in abolition, and later that year he denounced the assassination of Elijah Lovejoy in a speech so stirring as to place him in the forefront of the movement. Encouraged by his wife, he began lecturing against slavery. On most issues he sided with William Lloyd Garrison, avoiding association with a political party and condemning the U.S.

Constitution for its compromises on slavery. Unlike Garrison, he did not eschew the use of violence in the cause. At the World's Anti-Slavery Society Convention of 1840, he supported Garrison in insisting (vainly) that women delegates be seated.

The passion of Phillips's oratory often aroused hostile responses and physical threats. Doubtless, however, it deepened his own convictions, which with time grew more extreme. He opposed the annexation of Texas and then the Mexican War, and ultimately he advocated disunion. During the Civil War he harshly criticized Lincoln, until the issuance of the Emancipation Proclamation. After the war, over Garrison's opposition, Phillips kept the American Anti-Slavery Society going, with Phillips himself its president.

Pugh, Sarah (October 6, 1800–August 1, 1884) *teacher, abolitionist, feminist*

Educated by Quakers, in 1821 Pugh began teaching at a Friends' school in Philadelphia. In 1829 she started her own elementary school, where she taught for more than 10 years. In 1835, the British George Thompson converted her to abolitionism. She launched into antislavery activities in the Philadelphia Female Anti-Slavery Society, over which she later presided; in the Pennsylvania Anti-Slavery Society, which for many years met in her home; and in the American Anti-Slavery Society, in which she remained loyal to Garrison and the cause of immediate emancipation. One of the group of women delegates denied seats at the World's Anti-Slavery Convention in 1840, Pugh wrote the formal protest of the Pennsylvanians among them. On that trip she made friends with many British abolitionists, and in 1851 at their invitation joined their antislavery work. Back in Philadelphia 17 months later, she resumed her work for the local movement, presiding over meetings and working on fund-raising fairs.

After the Civil War, Pugh devoted herself to working for the freedmen and the rights of women.

Purvis, Robert, Sr. (1810–unknown) *the richest black man in America*

A fair man who could have passed for white, Purvis chose to identify with the blacks of Philadelphia, marrying James Forten's daughter Harriet. He helped organize both the American and the Philadelphia Anti-Slavery Societies. He headed Philadelphia's Vigilance Committee, which protected fugitive slaves, and spent endless hours in the work of the Underground Railroad

Rankin, John (1793–unknown) *activist antislavery minister*
Born in Tennessee, Rankin began his ministry in 1817 in Kentucky. In 1821, he moved to the Presbyterian church of Ripley, Ohio, which he served for 44 years. His home was a station on the Underground Railroad; for his assistance to fugitive slaves he was more than once mobbed by Kentuckians. In 1823, he published *Letters on American Slavery, Addressed to Mr. Thomas Rankin, Merchant at Middlebrook, Augusta County, Virginia*. He also lectured for the American Antislavery Society and led the fight against slavery in the Presbyterian General Assemblies.

Realf, Richard (June 14, 1834–October 28, 1878) *abolitionist poet*
An 1854 emigrant from Britain to the United States, in 1856 Realf went west as a newspaper correspondent, where he associated until 1858 with John Brown. Returning the next year, he was arrested after Brown's attack on Harpers Ferry. A commissioned officer during the Civil War, he served for a time on Reconstruction duty with a black regiment.

Remond, Charles Lenox (February 1, 1810–December 22, 1873) *black antislavery leader*
The son of a wealthy Massachusetts merchant, Remond became a lecturer for the American Anti-Slavery Society in 1838. In 1840, he went to the World's Anti-Slavery Society Convention in England. Later, he lectured for 18 months in the British Isles. He returned to the United States with a petition signed by 60,000 Irish asking Irish-Americans to support the antislavery cause. Then he resumed his American tours, this time with Frederick Douglass.

Remond, Sarah Parker (June 6, 1826–after 1887) *abolitionist lecturer, physician*
Remond was the daughter of a wealthy black abolitionist Massachusetts merchant and the sister of Charles Remond. She supplemented her public school education with extensive reading.

As an adult she participated actively in antislavery societies. Often insulted because of her race, Sarah Remond in 1853 won a suit against the New York Athenaeum for refusing her a seat. In 1856, she began lecturing as an agent for the American Anti-Slavery Society, touring New England with her brother Charles. In 1858 she appeared on the platform of the National Woman's Rights Convention.

That summer she went to England, where for the first time, she said, she was cordially received by white women as a sister. Quite different was her reception at the American legation, which refused her a visa for France on the grounds that her passport was invalid: she could not be a U.S. citizen, the diplomats ruled. For some time she continued her education at Bedford College for Ladies in London, lecturing against slavery during the vacations. She was part of an important group of American blacks who swayed British public opinion toward the Union during the Civil War.

After the war she returned briefly to the United States, working for equal rights for all Americans, blacks and women included, in the integrated American Equal Rights Association, established in 1866. Then she went back to Europe. In Italy, she became a physician and apparently married.

Revels, Hiram Rhodes (September 27, 1822–January 16, 1901) *clergyman, educator, first black U.S. senator*
Of mixed black and Indian descent, Revels was born free in Fayetteville, North Carolina, where he later worked as a barber. As an adult, Revels studied at a Quaker school in Liberty, Indiana; another school in Ohio; and Knox College in Illinois. Ordained in the African Methodist Church in 1845, he worked among blacks in several states before settling in Baltimore as a pastor and as principal of a black school. In the 1850s, he married Phoebe A. Bass; the couple had six children, all daughters.

During the Civil War, he energetically recruited for black regiments in Maryland and Missouri, served as chaplain of a black regiment and as provost marshal of Vicksburg, organized several churches in Mississippi, and worked as a pastor in Kentucky and Kansas. During Reconstruction, he undertook a career in Mississippi politics, serving successively as Natchez alderman, as state senator, in 1870–71 as U.S. senator, and as interim secretary of state. Always rather conservative, in 1875 he joined with Mississippi Democrats to expel the carpetbag government.

Revels devoted the rest of his life to education and religion, as president of Alcorn Agricultural College, as pastor, as professor of theology, and as editor of the *Southwestern Christian Advocate*.

Ross, Alexander Milton (December 13, 1832–October 27, 1897) *physician, abolitionist, naturalist, reformer*
A Canadian, Ross studied medicine in New York State from 1851 to 1855 but was apparently not licensed until

1875. After his medical studies he interested himself in abolition. Harriet Beecher Stowe's *Uncle Tom's Cabin* confirmed his determination to devote himself to abolition. "To me," Ross later wrote, "it was a command. A deep and settled conviction impressed me that it was my duty to let the oppressed go free." In 1856, he visited Gerrit Smith, who agreed to introduce him to other abolitionists involved in the Underground Railroad, people who could teach him their strategies. Together Ross and Smith traveled to Boston, New York, Philadelphia, Ohio, and Indiana. On this trip, Ross said, "I was initiated into a knowledge of the relief societies and the methods adopted to circulate information among the slaves of the South; the routes to be taken by the slaves, after leaving the so-called free states; and the relief posts where shelter and aid for transportation could be obtained." The abolitionists Theodore Parker and Lewis Tappan, as well as Smith, backed Ross in his new undertakings.

Ross daringly roamed through Maryland, Tennessee, Kentucky, and Virginia, and later penetrated into the Deep South. He went to New Orleans, and thence to Selma and Huntsville in Alabama; Columbus and Vicksburg in Mississippi; Augusta, Georgia; and Charleston, South Carolina. He found that many slaves had heard of Canada from blacks brought south from the border states and from their masters' warnings against going there, but that most thought it too far away to reach.

Ross developed his own methods, adopting different pretenses for his travels. Often he stayed in one place for several weeks, sizing up slaves and inviting those he thought most intelligent and trustworthy to a meeting, perhaps at the home of a black preacher. There he might tell the 30 or 40 he had selected about the possibility of escape to Canada and ask them to pass the news along to others whom they trusted. If by the next day some of them had decided to act, he would give them more information and equip them with gear (such as a compass) and food, or he himself might lead them to an Underground Railroad station or even to Canada. Of the first group of nine that he so conducted, all reached Canada safely; in 1863, he enlisted three of these into a black regiment. Ross continued this work through the Civil War, often in danger of his life, but never captured. During the war, he also acted as Lincoln's secret agent to uncover Confederate activities in Canada.

For several years after the war, Ross turned to collecting and classifying Canadian flora and fauna. His work brought him fame among scholars, and several European princes decorated him for it. Later still he focused on public health, trying to improve sanitation and battling against compulsory vaccination for smallpox.

Ruggles, David (1810–1849) *abolitionist*

The son of free black parents and born in Norwich, Connecticut, Ruggles moved as a young man to New York City, where he ran a temperance grocery and a printing business, distributing antislavery tracts in his bookshop and reading room. In 1833, he became a traveling agent for the *Emancipator* to boost the newspaper's circulation and to raise funds for the American Anti-Slavery Society. Ruggles, who considered a free press the primary bulwark against slavery, devoted his editorial career to promoting abolitionism, racial pride, and black uplift.

As a leader of the New York Committee of Vigilance (1835–39), he searched the city for slaves illegally detained by southern masters, and he used the courts to protect fugitives, despite official connivance in the kidnapping of free blacks and despite uncooperative white judges. He personally assisted in the escape of over 600 fugitives, directing them to the Underground Railroad. He thereby attracted the enmity of kidnappers and the part of officialdom that wanted to destroy the vigilance committee. In 1839 these elements succeeded in jailing him, endangering his health. He resigned from the vigilamce committee that year.

Thereafter, with the support of other blacks and Lydia Maria Child, Ruggles founded and successfully ran the country's first hydropathic treatment center, where he also offered a "cutaneous electricity" treatment.

Russwurm, John B. (October 1, 1799–June 17, 1851) *antislavery writer*

Born in Jamaica to a white American man and black woman, Russwurm was educated in Canada and at Bowdoin College. He established in 1827 the first black newspaper, *Freedom's Journal* (later the *Rights of All*), in New York. He advocated immediate emancipation, but his support of colonization alienated many other blacks. Later, he moved to Liberia to superintend its schools.

Salem, Peter (Salem Middlesex, Salem Poor) (ca. 1750–1816) *soldier*

Salem was born into slavery in Framingham, Massachusetts. He was owned first by Capt. Jeremiah Belknap and then by Maj. Lawson Buckminister. He was given his freedom so that he could join the army. He volunteered for the Framingham militia. With his company, he fought in the battles of Lexington and Concord. He is best known for his deeds in the battle of Bunker Hill. Legend says it was he who shot the British commander, Major Pitcairn, killing him instantly and thus checking, temporarily, the advance of the Redcoats. He served unharmed in the Continental Army for seven years. He married Katie Benson at the end of the war.

Scott, Orange (February 13, 1800–July 31, 1847) *antislavery Methodist clergyman*

Scott's activity in the antislavery movement began in 1833, when he introduced a discussion of slavery into the Boston Methodist paper, *Zion's Herald*. In 1836, when an antislavery speech at the General Conference caused his bishop to refuse to reappoint him, Scott accepted a position as an agent for the American Anti-Slavery Society, even as he continued to encourage consideration of the topic in Methodist publications and conferences. A Lowell, Massachusetts, church called him to its pastorate in defiance of episcopal authority. The fight that followed involved Scott in a split from the denomination and the establishment of the antislavery Wesleyan Methodist Connection of America. For this new denomination he edited the *True Wesleyan*. His 1846 book, *The Grounds of Secession from the M. E. Church: Being an Examination of Her Connection with Slavery, and Also of Her Form of Government,* explained why he had withdrawn.

Shaw, Robert Gould (1837–1863) *commander of a black Civil War regiment*

Born into a well-to-do, antislavery family, Shaw studied abroad and at Harvard, then entered an uncle's mercantile firm in New York City. Although for some time he had favored disunion, he supported Lincoln's candidacy. As soon as the Civil War started he went south with the New York State militia, which he had already joined, and in May 1861, he was commissioned a second lieutenant in the 2d Massachusetts Regiment. After a year of service behind the lines, with such distasteful duties as apprehending runaway slaves and returning them to their masters, Shaw fought his first battle in May 1862, at Winchester in the Shenandoah Valley. Other battles, including Antietam, turned him into a seasoned veteran.

On January 30, 1863, at age 25, he was offered the command of the Massachusetts 54th Infantry Regiment,

Colored, by Gov. John Andrew. In the face of his youth, his engagement to Annie Haggerty, and the near-certainty that the Confederacy would retaliate against the Union's use of black soldiers by declaring their white officers criminals guilty of inciting insurrection, Shaw hesitated, refused, and then accepted. His mother wrote: "God rewards a hundred-fold every good aspiration of his children, and this is my reward for asking [for] my children not earthly honors, but souls to see the right and courage to follow it. Now I feel ready to die, for I see you willing to give your support to the cause of truth that is lying crushed and bleeding."

On May 28, 1863, a few weeks after his marriage, Shaw and his regiment left by sea for St. Simons Island, Georgia. There they were put under the command of Col. James Montgomery, whose brutality and hatred of the enemy horrified Shaw. Montgomery involved the 54th on June 10, 1863, in an unopposed raid on the town of Darien, Georgia; Shaw refused to allow his men to loot or to order them to burn the town. In July, for the first time, members of the regiment came under fire, fighting bravely on James Island, near Charleston. Days later, the regiment led an assault on Fort Wagner, advancing under murderous fire, with Colonel Shaw on foot at their head. Shaw was poised on the ramparts when he was killed and fell into the fort. After hand-to-hand fighting, the remnants of the regiment retreated down the slope before the fort and fired from there. Shaw's parents later requested that his body remain where the Confederates had contemptuously buried it—with his soldiers. In his memory, the Shaw family contributed large sums to the rebuilding of Darien.

Smalls, Robert (April 5, 1839–February 22, 1915) *Civil War hero, congressman*

A man of many skills, as a slave Smalls worked as a hotel waiter, a hack driver, and a rigger. In 1861, the Confederates forced him to serve on the crew of the gunboat *Planter*. The next year, in the absence of the ship's white officers, he stowed away his family and his brother's family, sailed the ship out of Charleston harbor under the Confederate flag, and surrendered it to the blockading federal squadron. He then served aboard the *Planter* in the Union navy, saving the steamer when its commander deserted under fire. This heroic action earned him the rank of captain.

During Reconstruction, Smalls served as delegate to the National Union Convention and the South Carolina constitutional convention. In 1875, after terms in the state legislature, he was elected to Congress. He never succeeded in collecting a pension from the U.S. Navy.

Smith, Gerrit (March 6, 1797–December 28, 1874) *antislavery philanthropist, reformer*

Smith wanted to use his vast wealth, partly inherited and partly of his own making, to benefit the human race. Sometimes he succeeded; sometimes he failed, as when he tried to colonize blacks in the Adirondack forest. In the antislavery movement, which he joined in 1835, he favored compensated emancipation of slaves. Though more moderate than his friend William Lloyd Garrison, Smith nonetheless helped fugitive slaves, even after authorities had arrested them. An important contributor to the New England Emigrant Aid Company of Massachusetts, set up to enable antislavery emigrants to settle in Kansas, Smith upheld the use of violence there, on the grounds that the federal government was supporting the proslavery forces. He also funded John Brown, though the failure of the raid on Harpers Ferry and fear of exposure as Brown's supporter sent Smith temporarily insane.

Smith believed in political action against slavery. He helped establish the Liberty Party, running as its candidate for governor of New York. He served briefly in Congress as an independent in 1853 and 1854. During the Civil War he wrote and spoke for the Union, joining the Republicans in time to campaign for Lincoln's reelection. After the war, he favored black suffrage and moderation toward southern whites.

Stewart, Alvan (September 1, 1790–May 1, 1849) *abolitionist lawyer*

Something of an eccentric, Stewart began his career as an antislavery activist in 1834 by joining the American Anti-Slavery Society (AASS) and founding several local antislavery societies, including the New York State Anti-Slavery Society, over which he presided. He tried unsuccessfully to revise the creed of the AASS, arguing that slavery violated the Constitution in that it deprived the slaves of their freedom without due process of law. He also disturbed the national organization by his efforts to run the New York society independently, even excluding agents of the AASS from it.

An advocate of political action, Stewart in 1840 helped organize the Liberty Party but was soon discouraged by the lack of support for its ticket. Thereafter he devoted his antislavery activities mainly to legal efforts for slaves, as when he challenged the constitutionality of slavery before the New Jersey supreme court.

Stewart, Maria W. Miller (1803–December 17, 1879) *teacher, public speaker*

Stewart was the first American-born woman and the first black to speak from a public platform. Mentored by James Walker and William Lloyd Garrison, Stewart wrote for the *Liberator*. Garrison also published some of her work in tract form, notably "Religion and the Pure Principles of Morality." In 1832 and 1833, Stewart composed and delivered four addresses in Boston: one to the First African Baptist Church of Boston, one to the Afric-American Female Intelligence Society, one at Franklin Hall, and one at the African Masonic Hall—all reprinted in the *Liberator*. Her final speech announced her decision to move to New York: She could not help her cause in Boston, she felt, because her own community had condemned her for daring to speak publicly.

Stewart saw knowledge as potential salvation. Deploring the ignorance and degradation imposed upon blacks, and despairing of help from whites, she exhorted free blacks to educate themselves and sue for their rights. She vigorously opposed the efforts of colonizationists to send blacks back to Africa, declaring, "I am a true born American; your blood flows in my veins, and your spirit fires my breast."

She taught in New York public schools until 1852 and then moved to Baltimore, where she set up a private school for black children. In 1861 she moved again, this time to Washington, D.C., where she taught for a while and then worked as a matron in the Freedmen's Hospital. In 1871 she opened a Sunday school for children in the area around the hospital. She used her pension as a widow of a soldier in the War of 1812 to publish a second edition of her speeches and writing.

Still, Peter (ca. 1800–after 1854) *driver, later freedman*

Kidnapped with his brother Levin from their Pennsylvania home as a boy, Peter Still served for 40 years as a slave, at first in Lexington, Kentucky. At nine, he was put to work in his master's brickyard; four years later he was sold, along with Levin. In 1817, Levin was sent to Alabama with a nephew of their owner, who in 1818, on the death of his uncle, inherited Peter as well.

In Alabama, Peter and Levin raised cotton on the land of their master, Levi Gist, and with his brother ran a store. Gist flourished, acquiring more land, and he made Peter, now almost 21, his personal servant. In time, Peter married a young slave, Vina, on a neighboring plantation and started a family. Their lives together were marked by losses: Levin died, Vina's mother was taken south, and Gist died. Six years later the executors of the estate sold it and hired out the slaves. For a year, in 1846, Peter hired his own time. By his own request he was hired out in 1847 to sympathetic German Jews Joseph and Isaac Friedman. About 1849 Peter asked the Friedmans to buy him, so that he might later buy himself. In April of 1850, when he was almost 50, Peter completed his payments, freed himself, and went north. An emissary sent to lead his wife and children out of slavery succeeded in getting them to Ohio, where they were recaptured. The owner demanded $5,000 for Peter's wife and children. Undaunted, Peter traveled through the North, telling his story and collecting money from antislavery sympathizers as he went. By late 1854 he had the sum in hand. His wife and children were brought north—though their former master refused to let a widowed son take his child without further payment.

Still, William (October 7, 1821–July 14, 1902) *abolitionist*

Still was born to a father who had bought his own freedom and a mother who had twice escaped. In 1847, he began work as a clerk for the Pennsylvania Society for the Abolition of Slavery, personally sheltering most of the fugitives who escaped as far as Philadelphia. He recorded their names and in 1855 toured Canada to see how they were faring. His *The Underground Railroad*, published in 1872, would relate many of their experiences. His historical sense also manifested itself in 1861, when he helped start an association to collect data about black people.

Unlike most white abolitionists, Still recognized the necessity of improving the quality of life for free blacks. For eight years, in the face of criticism from other blacks, he campaigned against segregation on Philadelphia street cars until the Pennsylvania legislature finally ended it in 1867. Against popular opposition he supported the Democratic candidate for mayor in 1874 and argued against the establishment of a black bank. Until the end of his life he imaginatively and energetically worked for the well-being of blacks, serving on the Freedmen's Aid Commission, in 1880 founding the first black YMCA, and managing homes for aged blacks, needy black children, and the orphans of black soldiers and sailors.

Stone, Lucy (August 13, 1818–October 18, 1893) *feminist, abolitionist*

Best known as an advocate of woman's rights, Stone, inspired by Abby Kelley Foster, began her public career in 1847 lecturing for the American Anti-Slavery Society, which tried to limit her feminist work. They compromised by allowing her to lecture on women's rights at her own expense during the week and to speak against slavery on weekends. Frequently threatened, she faced hostile audiences without flinching.

In 1855 Stone abandoned her resolution never to marry, accepting the proposal of Henry Blackwell, with whom she had one child, a daughter. With her moral and financial support, he experimented extensively, though unsuccessfully, with growing sugar beets, as part of the free produce movement.

She supported the Women's Loyal National League, founded by Elizabeth Cady Stanton and Susan B. Anthony to encourage the passage of the Thirteenth Amendment. After the Civil War, Stone helped found and officiated in the American Equal Rights Association in the cause of both black and woman suffrage. Stone supported the Fifteenth Amendment, unlike Stanton and Anthony, who would support it only if it included woman suffrage.

Stowe, Harriet Beecher (June 14, 1811–July 1, 1896) *author*

Stowe was born into the gifted Beecher family. Her father, Lyman Beecher, was a clergyman, a profession into which his sons followed him. Her older sister Catharine Beecher, whom in her girlhood Harriet assisted in her school, pioneered teaching as a profession for women.

In 1836 Harriet married Calvin Ellis Stowe, who taught in the Cincinnati theological seminary over which Lyman Beecher presided. Even during the years in which she was bearing seven children, she augmented his salary by writing and keeping schools.

In 1850, the year of the most severe fugitive slave law, the family moved to Maine. All her life Harriet had heard debates over slavery, had read abolitionist literature, had even opened her home to fugitive slaves. For Harriet the 1850 law was a crisis of conscience, giving her at last a theme that aroused her passions. How, she asked, could a just and loving God permit the cruelties of slavery? How could a "Christian" nation permit them within its boundaries?

In response, she wrote *Uncle Tom's Cabin*, an epic of 19th-century life that forced Americans to look hard at themselves and their country. It was sentimental, and its vision of slave life was often both stereotypical and condescending, but Stowe empathized with slave women's anguish over the separation of families. Through her own grief over the death of one of her babies, she identified with their dread of losing their children. Her courageous black women overcome despair to save themselves and their families—Cassie by "haunting" the devilish overseer Simon Legree, and Eliza by her frantic crossing of the ice-filled river. Stowe understood, too—and demonstrated in her novel—the corruption that slavery inflicted upon both slaves and slaveholders. Her book, a runaway bestseller, moved the nation one step closer to civil war.

Stuart, Charles (1783–1865) *British godfather of the American antislavery movement*
After 13 years as an officer in the forces of the British East India Company, Stuart immigrated to Canada in 1796. In 1824, as principal of a school in upper New York State, he met the young Theodore Weld, whom he mentored and adopted as his protégé, imbuing him with antislavery principles.

In 1828, Stuart returned to England to campaign for the abolition of slavery in the British West Indies. There he successfully propagandized against the American Colonization Society. His pamphlet *The West India Question* provided the basis for the creed of the American Anti-Slavery Society when it was organized in 1831, with Weld's active participation. In such ways he infused the incipient American abolitionism with the energy of the British movement. From 1834 to 1838 Stuart directly served the American cause by lecturing as its agent in Ohio, Vermont, and New York, even in the face of mob violence. From 1840 to 1842 he raised funds in England for anti-Garrisonian abolitionists.

Sumner, Charles (January 6, 1811–March 11, 1874) *abolitionist U.S. senator*
The son of a man who not only condemned slavery but also opposed the exclusion of black children from schools and the prohibition of interracial marriages, Sumner in 1845 established a reputation as an orator and a man of principle. In 1848, he ran successfully for the U.S. Senate on a ticket formed by a coalition of Free Soilers and Democrats, being seated after a prolonged election dispute in 1851.

Throughout his Senate career, Sumner excited anger and hatred among proslavery forces within his own constituency and in the South. Time and again he roused

their fury, as when he tried valiantly but vainly to nullify the effect of the notorious Fugitive Slave Law of 1850 by persuading the Senate not to appropriate funds for its enforcement but instead to repeal it. He kindled a firestorm by not only presenting petition after petition against the Kansas-Nebraska bill but attacking it in one of the most vituperative speeches ever heard in the Senate—a speech that directly and personally insulted other senators. In retaliation, Rep. Preston S. Brooks, a relative of one of the offended senators, beat Sumner on the Senate floor so badly that Sumner could not resume his duties for three and a half years. Nonetheless, on his return he continued to indict slavery as passionately as ever, and in 1861 at the Massachusetts Republican convention he called for emancipation as a means to end the war—the first prominent statesman to do so.

During the Civil War, as chairman of the committee on foreign relations, Sumner protected the Union by opposing resolutions that might have provoked war between the United States and France or England. Looking beyond emancipation, he recognized the need of blacks for civil rights. In February 1862, he began to argue that the seceded states had lost all rights under the Constitution. After the war he continued to focus on black rights, succeeding in forcing states that wished readmission to the Union to grant black suffrage, though he failed to guarantee the freed slaves free schools and free farmsteads, as he had hoped to do.

Sunderland, La Roy (April 22, 1804–May 15, 1885) *abolitionist*
As a young Methodist minister, Sunderland enlisted other clergy in the antislavery cause and organized the first antislavery society in that church—continuing his efforts even after he withdrew from its ministry in 1833. In 1836, he began to edit the new Methodist antislavery paper, *Zion's Watchman*, enduring repeated attacks from the denomination's bishops. In 1842, with other dissidents, he withdrew to found the antislavery Wesleyan Connection of America, but ultimately religious doubts prevented his joining it.

Tappan, Arthur (May 22, 1786–July 23, 1865) *silk merchant, abolitionist philanthropist*
Seeing himself as God's steward, Tappan decided to use the fortune he and his brother Lewis Tappan had earned to promote Christianity and suppress vice. When in 1835 Theodore Weld and most of the other students withdrew from the Lane Theological Seminary because it tried to

restrict their discussion of slavery, Arthur Tappan private-ly pledged his entire income to secure the establishment of Oberlin College, in whose seminary the former Lane students enrolled.

Once a supporter of colonization as a means of gradual emancipation of slaves, Tappan soon turned to abolitionism. He funded many efforts to attain that goal and to help blacks in other ways: He supported publi-cation of the *Liberator,* the *Emancipator,* the *American and Foreign Anti-Slavery Reporter,* and the *National Era;* he backed a failed attempt to found a black college in New Ha-ven; and he funded Prudence Crandall's school for young black women in Connecticut. After the 1840 division in the American Anti-Slavery Society, Tappan presided over the new anti-Garrisonian American and Foreign Anti-Slavery Society. Committed to political action, he enlisted in the Liberty Party. In 1850 he publicly announced that he would defy the new Fugitive Slave Law, continuing to help escaping blacks and repeatedly ignoring threats of kidnapping and assassination.

Tappan, Lewis (May 23, 1788–June 21, 1873) *abolitionist merchant*
As a founder of the New York Anti-Slavery Society and the American Anti-Slavery Society, Lewis shared the opinions of his brother Arthur. In retaliation for his an-tislavery activities, an 1834 mob wrecked his house and burned his furniture. He served prominently on the com-mittee to free the slave ship *Amistad* captives. Like Ar-thur, he believed that the antislavery movement should confine itself to a single cause: Accordingly, in 1840 he helped organize the American and Foreign Anti-Slavery Society (AFASS), for which he acted as treasurer. Rec-ognizing the importance to the movement of allies, he kept in close touch with English abolitionists and used his religious connections to win the cooperation of the churches and missionary societies. When the American Board, which he had financially supported, refused its cooperation, he helped found the antislavery American Missionary Association (AMA). He also financed the daring Canadian Alexander M. Ross in his work to help slaves escape.

In time choosing a more radical course and hold-ing that the federal government had the constitutional power to abolish slavery in all the states, Tappan in 1855 resigned his position as treasurer with the AFASS to offici-ate in the new Abolition Society. He also turned his ener-gies toward supporting the constructive work for blacks of the AMA.

Taylor, John W. (March 26, 1784–September 18, 1854) *New York antislavery congressman*
In the House of Representatives, where he served from 1813 to 1833, Taylor won prominence through his anti-slavery arguments, particularly on the questions of admit-ting new states and prohibiting slavery in the territories. He based his arguments on the theory that from its power to admit new states, Congress derived the power to *refuse* to admit and to set conditions on which it would admit. The constitutional power given Congress to prohibit the importation or migration of slaves after 1808, he said, meant that that body could prohibit the passage of slaves from one commonwealth to another. What was more, Congress had the duty to limit slavery as inconsistent with the republican form of government.

Taylor believed that his antislavery stance cost him reelection as Speaker of the House in 1821 and 1825 and reelection to Congress in 1833.

Taylor, Susie King (1848–1912) *Civil War nurse*
Taylor learned to read and write while still a slave. In 1863, she volunteered as a nurse in Beaufort, South Caro-lina, and served with the 1st Regiment of South Carolina Volunteers. After the war she worked as a maid.

Torrey, Charles Turner (November 21, 1813–May 9, 1846) *abolitionist*
The bristly Torrey failed in all professions he undertook—the ministry, editing, reporting, and lecturing. He began his antislavery career as a theological student at Andover, where he organized a student antislavery society. With-in the movement he opposed William Lloyd Garrison, leading Massachusetts conservative abolitionists out of the American Anti-Slavery Society in 1838 to found the *Massachusetts Abolitionist* and the Massachusetts Abolition Society, for which he briefly and unsuccessfully served as agent.

As an abolitionist, Torrey was the central figure in two trials. In 1842 he was arrested while a freelance reporter on the 1842 "Convention of Slaveholders" in Maryland, but he was not convicted. In 1844 he was again arrested in Baltimore for helping slaves escape. This time he was convicted and sentenced to six years' hard labor. He died in prison.

Towne, Laura Matilda (May 3, 1825–February 22, 1901) *educator*
Born free to well-off black parents, Towne early became an abolitionist. In her Pennsylvania girlhood, she studied

homeopathic medicine and later taught at various "charity schools."

In 1861, she responded to a call for doctors and teachers to join the "Port Royal Experiment," a Union project in the Sea Islands off the coast of Georgia and South Carolina to educate former slaves and set up a viable black economy. There she distributed clothing, practiced medicine, and taught school. With her friend Ellen Murray, she founded and taught at the highly successful Penn School for blacks on St. Helena Island. After 1870 she trained teachers there.

Towne stayed with Penn School for the rest of her life, while also serving as a public health officer and an unofficial legal adviser in blacks' struggle to gain ownership of land. Most of the time she worked as a volunteer, and the school's expenses were paid successively by the Pennsylvania Relief Association; the Benezet Society of Germantown, Pennsylvania; and the Towne family.

Truth, Sojourner (Isabella) (ca. 1797– November 26, 1883) *preacher, abolitionist, suffragist, reformer*

Truth, born Isabella, lived the first part of her life as a slave, enduring cruel treatment, forced to watch her father die neglected, and having two of her daughters sold away from her. In 1827 she fled and, with the help of Quaker friends, successfully sued for the freedom of her son Peter, who had been illegally sold.

In about 1829 she moved to New York City, taking employment as a domestic. After misadventures with religious fanatics, in 1843 she obeyed the command of voices she heard to rename herself and travel the countryside, preaching and singing. She walked through Long Island and Connecticut, proclaiming her faith at camp meetings, on the streets, and in churches. She spent that winter in a commune in Northampton, Massachusetts, where she first learned about the abolitionist movement. Abolitionist leaders promoted her travels and speeches.

About 1850, Truth moved to Salem, Ohio, using the office of the *Anti-Slavery Bugle* as headquarters for her travels in Indiana, Missouri, and Kansas and supporting herself by selling her autobiography. Slavery advocates clubbed her in Kansas and mobbed her in Missouri. In the mid 1850s she moved to Battle Creek, Michigan. During the Civil War she solicited food and clothing throughout Michigan for black soldiers. In late 1864, as "counselor to the freed people" for the National Freedmen's Relief Association, she began collecting signatures on a petition for a "Negro State," urging that blacks be settled on west-

ern public lands—a movement that failed but encouraged the migration to Kansas and Missouri of many blacks. There Truth preached to them on cleanliness and godliness. Long into her old age, she continued to lecture on religion, black rights, and woman suffrage.

Tubman, Harriet (ca. 1820–March 10, 1913) *rescuer of slaves, Civil War scout, nurse*

Enslaved from birth, threatened in 1849 with being sold out of Maryland, Tubman escaped to Philadelphia. In December 1850 she began guiding other slaves to freedom, beginning with her sister and her two children. In the decade before the Civil War she made 19 trips into Maryland, delivering slaves to the North, often to Canada, where she lived for several years. According to Sarah Bradford, Tubman's first biographer, this "Moses of her people" delivered some 300 fugitives into the promised land of freedom—not one of whom was ever recaptured. Sometimes she worked alone, sometimes with antislavery activists in the Underground Railroad. Her daring, courage, and ingenuity at one point raised the price on her head to $40,000. In the North, she defied the fugitive slave law, once leading a crowd to release a slave from custody. She was an adviser of John Brown.

Early in 1862, Tubman volunteered her services to Maj. Gen. David Hunter, commander of the Department of the South. She served throughout the Civil War as a spy and scout, getting information from blacks behind Confederate lines. She also nursed and helped freedmen who had fled north. After the war, in her Auburn, New York, home, she cared not only for her own aged parents, whom she had earlier rescued, but for other old people and black orphans. She found time also to support southern freedmen's schools and to work for woman suffrage. Not until 1897 did Congress finally award her a pension—$20 a month—for her wartime service.

Turner, Nat (October 2, 1800–November 11, 1831) *slave, revolutionary*

Brought up by a religious family that treated him as one created for a special purpose, Turner believed himself divinely appointed to free American slaves. His family and community alleged that he had learned to read without a teacher. Rumor bruited his powers as a healer. God, Turner believed, spoke to him in visions: at age 25, he said, "I saw white spirits and black spirits engaged in battle, and the sun was darkened—the thunder rolled in the Heavens, and blood flowed in streams—and I heard a voice saying, 'Such is your luck, such you are called to see, and let it come rough or smooth, you must surely bear it." He interpreted drops on a field of corn as "the blood of Christ . . . shed on this earth . . . and now . . . returning to earth. . . . It was plain to me that . . . the great day of judgment was at hand." In 1831, seeing an eclipse of the sun as a sign to rebel, he led about 60 slaves in a revolt, the Southampton Insurrection, in which 55 whites were killed. The revolt failed, and Turner was hanged.

Vesey, Denmark (ca. 1767–July 2, 1822)
revolutionary

In 1781, a slave trader, Captain Vesey of Charleston, took this young slave aboard as part of his cargo at St. Thomas. Struck by the boy's attractiveness and intelligence, the ship's officers indulged him, dubbing him "Telemaque" (later corrupted into Denmark). Vesey sold him at San Domingo but on his next voyage received Denmark back from his buyer, who complained that he had epilepsy. He served the captain faithfully until 1800, when he bought his freedom with lottery winnings. As a free man, he supported himself as a carpenter in Charleston. His great strength and activity, and perhaps his allegedly despotic temperament, aroused awe in the slave community. In 1822, he was accused of incitement to insurrection and hanged.

Walker, David (September 28, 1785–June 28, 1830) *free black leader*

Born in North Carolina of a slave father and a free mother, as a youth Walker wandered through the South, directly observing the horrors of slavery. "If I remain in this bloody land," he said, "I will not live long. As true as God reigns, I will be avenged for the sorrow which my people have suffered. This is not the place for me—no, no. I must leave this part of the country. It will be a great trial for me to live on the same soil where so many men are in slavery; certainly I cannot remain where I must hear their chains continually, and where I must encounter the insults of their hypocritical enslavers. Go, I must!" In the 1820s, he settled in Boston, where he set himself up as a dealer in second-hand clothing. There he contributed time and money to help Boston's blacks—as an agent of the Underground Railroad, an organizer and lecturer for the General Colored Association of Massachusetts, and an agent for the black newspaper *Freedom's Journal*. In 1829 he wrote *Walker's Appeal, in Four Articles: Together with a Preamble to the Colored Citizens of the World, but in Particular, and Very Expressly to Those of the United States of America*. It

deeply agitated southerners. The governor of Georgia asked the mayor of Boston to suppress the *Appeal*. When the mayor refused, a group of Georgians put a price on Walker's head. He died suddenly and mysteriously.

Ward, Samuel Ringgold (October 17, 1817–ca. 1866) *"the Black Daniel Webster"*

Born a slave in Maryland, Ward escaped with his parents when he was three. His oratorical gifts led to his working from 1839 as an agent of the American Anti-Slavery Society and later of the New York State Anti-Slavery Society. For several years he served as a pastor, in one case with an entirely white congregation. In 1846 he signed up with the Liberty Party, speaking throughout the North. After he helped a fugitive escape, he fled to Canada, where as an agent of the Anti-Slavery Society of Canada he organized new branches, lectured, and worked among fugitives from American slavery. He raised money for them in Great Britain; a British Quaker whom he met there gave him 50 acres in Jamaica, where he spent the rest of his life.

Weld, Theodore Dwight (November 23, 1803–February 3, 1895) *abolitionist*

Beginning his life's work in 1825, Weld evangelized for two years in the "holy band" of Charles Finney. A gifted and charismatic young man, he attracted the attention of Lewis and Arthur Tappan and, most influentially, Charles Stuart. Stuart paid for his education, mentored him, and above all instilled in him a zeal for abolition, for which Weld labored from 1830 on.

Weld converted to this cause many who later led the American antislavery movement, including Lewis and Arthur Tappan, politicians Joshua R. Giddings and Edwin M. Stanton, the preacher Henry Ward Beecher, Harriett Beecher Stowe, the faculty of Western Reserve College, many Presbyterian clergy, and almost the entire student body of Lane Seminary, to which Weld himself belonged. When the seminary tried to repress their debates on slavery, Weld led an exodus of sympathetic students to Oberlin College. These students then, under Weld's tutelage, acted as agents for the newly founded American Anti-Slavery Society (AASS), bravely and effectively preaching emancipation as an act of benevolence in the face of mob violence. To this group of 30-odd the AASS in 1836 added another 40 agents, including Angelina and Sarah Grimké—all of whom Weld trained. After he strained his voice in speaking, Weld wrote pamphlet after pamphlet for the AASS and conducted a national campaign for antislavery petitions addressed to Congress. He and Angelina Grimké married in 1838.

He went on to advise Whig congressmen who were breaking with their party over the slavery issue. In 1843, Weld retired from public life. With the Grimkés, he put together *American Slavery as It Is,* an effort to condemn slavery through the words of slaveholders and other proslavery advocates.

Weld stood out among abolitionists in many ways— notably for his widespread influence and his genuine desire for equality among blacks and whites.

Wheatley, Phillis (ca. 1753–December 5, 1784) *black poet*

Kidnapped as a child in Senegal and brought to Boston in 1761, Wheatley was bought by merchant-tailor John Wheatley and his wife. Impressed by her intelligence and bearing, the Wheatleys assigned her only light tasks and treated her almost as a daughter. The Wheatley's twin daughters, some 10 years older, taught her to read and write English, which she quickly mastered. In her early teens she began writing poetry, celebrating the themes of learning, virtue, and redemption through Christ. In 1770 she became a member of the Old South Meeting House and started publishing poetry.

In 1773 the Wheatleys sent her abroad for her health, accompanied by their son. For five weeks she enjoyed a triumphal tour, during which a patron arranged for the publication of her only book, *Poems on Various Subjects, Religious and Moral.* Mrs. Wheatley's illness called her home.

After the deaths of both Mr. and Mrs. Wheatley, the family disintegrated, and Phyllis dropped from fame, except for a brief period in 1776 when her poem to George Washington was published. In 1778 she married a free black, John Peters. He failed in his duties as husband and father to the three children she bore him, two of whom soon died. She was forced to work in a cheap lodging house to support herself and the other child, but soon her health gave way. Mother and child died on December 5, 1784.

Whittier, John Greenleaf (December 17, 1807– September 7, 1892) *abolitionist poet*

Under the influence of William Lloyd Garrison, Whittier became an abolitionist in 1833. He immediately attended an antislavery convention in Philadelphia, and for the next 30 years he devoted himself to writing poems on slavery. Despite the ostracism and physical attacks that his views evoked, he was elected to the Massachusetts legislature in 1835. His antislavery activities ranged from lecturing to lobbying to employment as an agent of the American Anti-Slavery Society (AASS). In 1838 a mob burned down the new Pennsylvania Hall during a woman's antislavery convention and destroyed the office of the paper that he was editing, the *Pennsylvania Freeman.*

Despite his friendship with Garrison, when the AASS split in 1840 he went with the dissidents who formed the American and Foreign Anti-Slavery Society. In 1842, the Liberty Party ran Whittier as its candidate for Congress, and in 1844 and 1845 it made him editor of its paper, in which he opposed the annexation of Texas. He continued his political activism into the 1870s, being influential in Charles Sumner's election to the Senate and helping found the Republican Party. Nonetheless, today much of his reputation rests on his abolition poems.

Woolman, John (October 19, 1720–October 7, 1772) *Quaker minister, pioneer abolitionist, tailor*

Woolman focused his Quaker ministry against slavery, which he believed inconsistent with Christianity. Wherever he went, even in the centers of the slave trade in New Jersey and Rhode Island, he denounced it. Although he lived to see few fruits of these labors, his influence lingered among abolitionists, particularly through his 1774 *Journal* and his 1754 *Some Considerations on the Keeping of Negroes.*

Wright, Frances (September 6, 1795– December 13, 1852) *writer, reformer*

A Scot by birth, Wright attracted controversy in the United States through her appearances on the lecture platform. She devoted considerable passion and energy to black rights, in 1825 publishing *A Plan for the Gradual Abolition of Slavery in the United States without Danger of Loss to the Citizens of the South,* in which she urged that blacks be permitted to labor on public land to earn money to buy their freedom. Putting her money where her ideals were, she founded a model settlement based on this principle, purchasing 640 acres in Tennessee for the purpose. She named her plantation Nashoba and put in charge her sister, a Scottish overseer, and a mulatto New Orleans schoolteacher. Only one slaveholder accepted her invitation to cooperate, leaving there a pregnant slave and her five children. Wright bought other slaves, whom she settled there. Everything went wrong, from bad health on account of the climate, through the slaves' reluctance to work, to a scandal through which the colony got a reputation as a bastion of free love. By 1828, the colony was dilapidated and unworkable.

Undaunted, Wright transported the slaves to Haiti, freed them, and arranged for housing and jobs for them. She again published her proposal and launched an attack on racially segregated schools, organized religion, taboos on interracial sexual relations, and marriage. Despite the widespread condemnation she thus earned, she continued to promote her ideas, particularly on religion and education, becoming an important figure in the emerging labor movement.

York (ca. 1770–ca. 1832) *slave who accompanied the Lewis and Clark expedition*
The son of two slaves, Rose and Old York, in 1799 York was inherited by William Clark, who employed him as his own body servant. On the Lewis and Clark expedition of 1804 to 1806, York accompanied his master as a body servant but also acted as a member of the expedition. In the Lewis and Clark diaries he is mentioned as hunting and trading with the Indians for food. Legend has it that he also interpreted, but the evidence is shaky.

Perhaps his most important contribution to the expedition was the novelty he presented to the Indians, many of whom had never seen a black man before. They thought him something inexplicable, and therefore perhaps sacred or possessed of superhuman powers. The Flathead thought him a notable warrior, because their own victorious warriors proclaimed their triumphs by blackening themselves with charcoal. Frequently, the Indians tried to rub or wash off the black from his skin, a familiarity that York usually bore patiently.

After the expedition York remained in slavery for at least another five years, but in 1811 he and Clark fell out, and he was hired out to a master who treated him badly. Eventually he was freed. Things went awry for him, and he lost the little property he had been given.

Appendix C
Maps

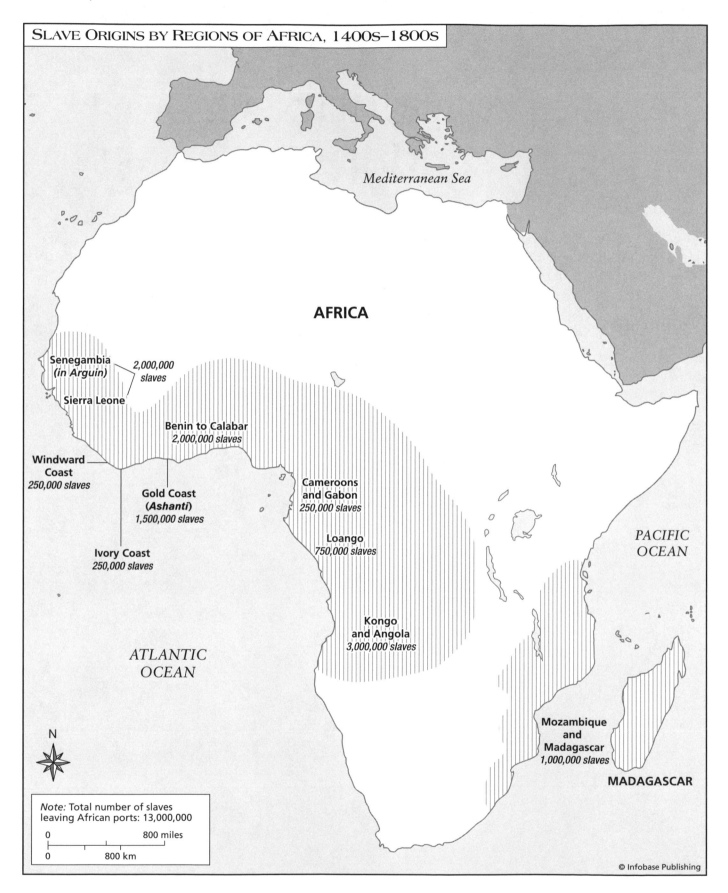

SLAVE ORIGINS BY REGIONS OF AFRICA, 1400S–1800S

Mediterranean Sea

AFRICA

Senegambia (in Arguin) — *2,000,000 slaves*

Sierra Leone

Benin to Calabar *2,000,000 slaves*

Windward Coast *250,000 slaves*

Gold Coast (Ashanti) *1,500,000 slaves*

Cameroons and Gabon *250,000 slaves*

Ivory Coast *250,000 slaves*

Loango *750,000 slaves*

Kongo and Angola *3,000,000 slaves*

ATLANTIC OCEAN

PACIFIC OCEAN

Mozambique and Madagascar *1,000,000 slaves*

MADAGASCAR

N

Note: Total number of slaves leaving African ports: 13,000,000

0 — 800 miles

0 — 800 km

© Infobase Publishing

LEGAL INSTITUTION OF SLAVERY IN THE AMERICAN COLONIES, 1641–1750

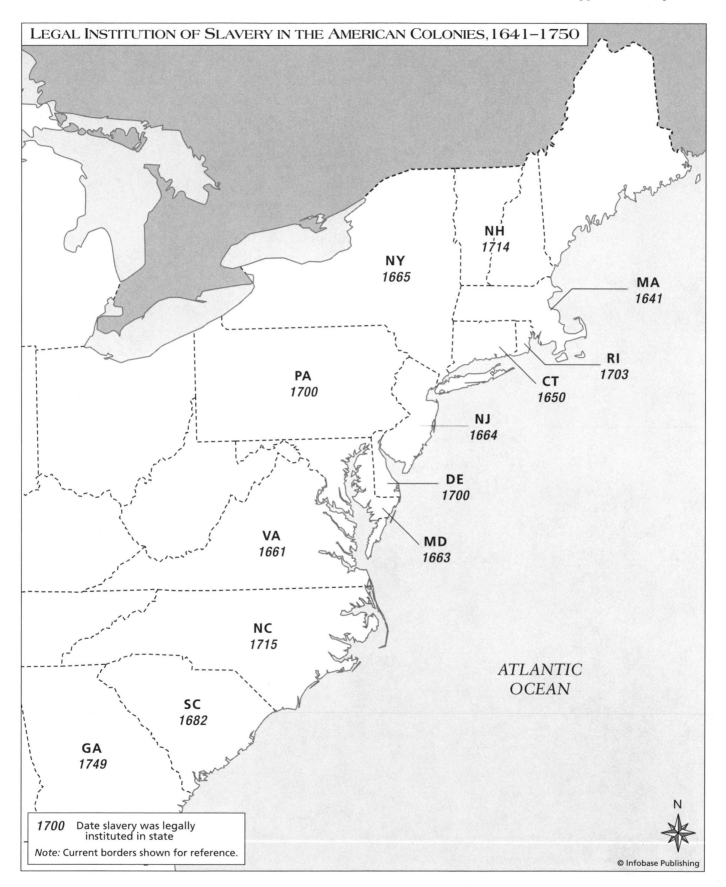

NH
1714

NY
1665

MA
1641

RI
1703

CT
1650

PA
1700

NJ
1664

DE
1700

VA
1661

MD
1663

NC
1715

*ATLANTIC
OCEAN*

SC
1682

GA
1749

N

1700   Date slavery was legally
instituted in state

Note: Current borders shown for reference.

© Infobase Publishing

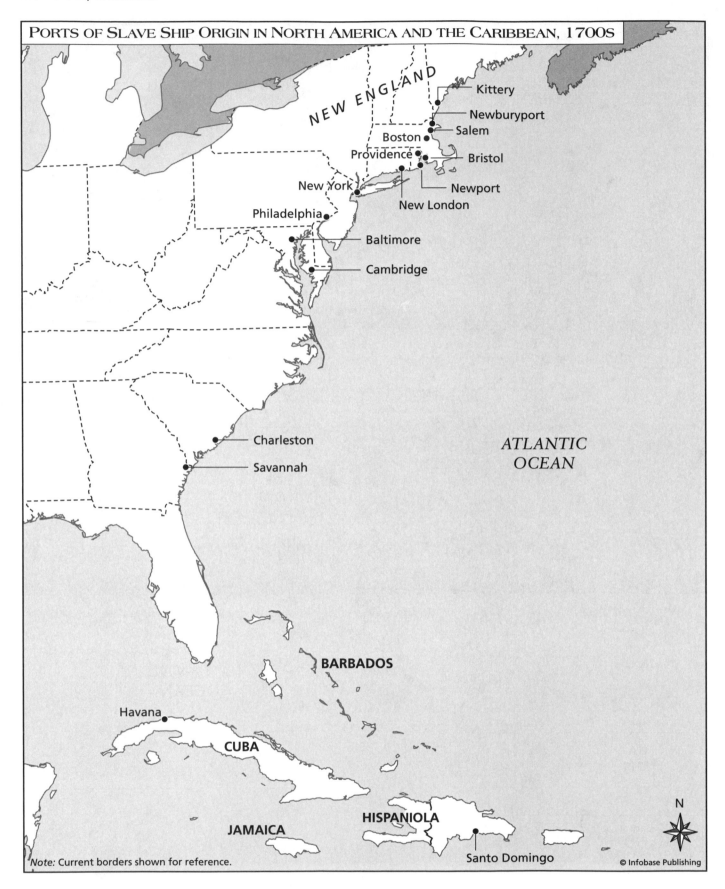

PORTS OF SLAVE SHIP ORIGIN IN NORTH AMERICA AND THE CARIBBEAN, 1700S

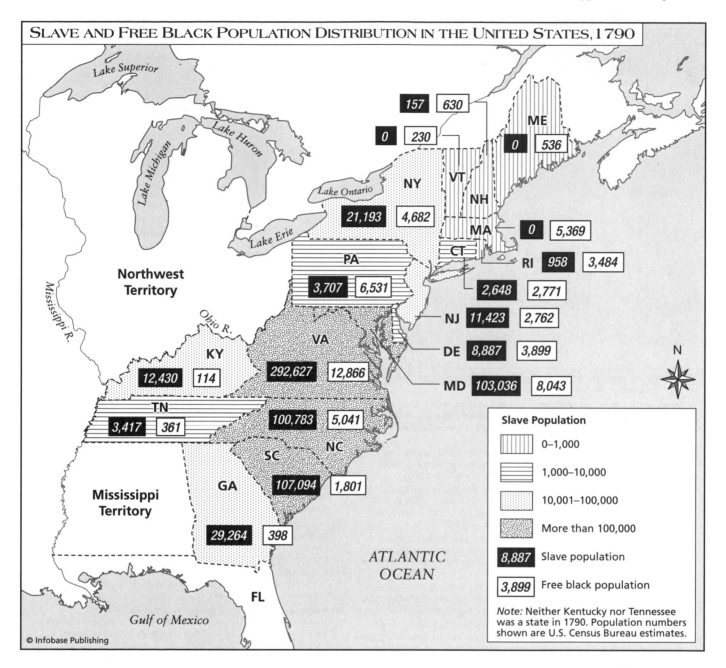

SLAVE AND FREE BLACK POPULATION DISTRIBUTION IN THE UNITED STATES, 1790

Lake Superior

Lake Michigan

Lake Huron

Lake Ontario

Lake Erie

Mississippi R.

Northwest Territory

Ohio R.

KY
12,430 | 114

TN
3,417 | 361

Mississippi Territory

GA
29,264 | 398

VA
292,627 | 12,866

NC
100,783 | 5,041

SC
107,094 | 1,801

PA
3,707 | 6,531

NY
21,193 | 4,682

VT
157 | 630

NH
0 | 230

ME
0 | 536

MA
0 | 5,369

RI   958 | 3,484

CT   2,648 | 2,771

NJ   11,423 | 2,762

DE   8,887 | 3,899

MD   103,036 | 8,043

FL

Gulf of Mexico

ATLANTIC OCEAN

N

© Infobase Publishing

Slave Population

(vertical lines)	0–1,000
(horizontal lines)	1,000–10,000
(light dots)	10,001–100,000
(dense dots)	More than 100,000
8,887	Slave population
3,899	Free black population

Note: Neither Kentucky nor Tennessee was a state in 1790. Population numbers shown are U.S. Census Bureau estimates.

SELECTED UNDERGROUND RAILROAD STATIONS AND RELATED SITES, 1822–1865

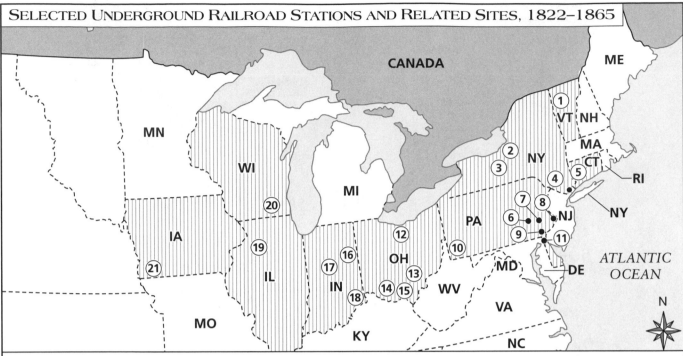

1. **Rokeby*:** Ferrisburgh, VT. Rokeby was home to the Robinson family, who harbored many fugitive slaves.

2. **Gerrit Smith Estate and Land Office*:** Peterboro, NY. During the 1840s and 1850s, Gerrit Smith acted as a conductor in the Underground Railroad. He sold farm tracts through his Land Office to runaways for one dollar each.

3. **St. James AME Zion Church:** Ithaca, NY. St. James's role as an important Underground Railroad station persuaded many former slaves to settle in Ithaca. Prominent abolitionists were associated with the church.

4. **Foster Memorial AME Zion Church:** Tarrytown, NY. This church was founded in 1860 by Amanda Foster, a free black who was active in the Underground Railroad, and her husband. Members of the church helped fugitive slaves escape to the North during the Civil War.

5. **Austin F. Williams Carriagehouse and House**:** Farmington, CT. Austin F. Williams, along with local abolitionists, harbored many fugitive slaves. Williams also housed the male Africans involved in the Amistad trial after their acquittal in 1841.

6. **Bethel AME Zion Church:** Reading, PA. The Bethel congregation was active in the Underground Railroad from 1837 through the end of the Civil War. Many members, escaped slaves themselves, opened their homes to fugitives.

7. **White Horse Farm**:** Phoenixville, PA. Built around 1770, White Horse Farm was the home of abolitionist Elijah Pennypacker. He opened the farm to fugitive slaves in 1840, personally transporting hundreds of runaways from his home to other stations in the North.

8. **Johnson House*:** Philadelphia, PA. During the 1850s the Johnson family used this house and the houses of nearby relatives to shelter fugitive slaves.

9. **Oakdale**:** Chadds Ford, PA. Oakdale, the first Underground Railroad stop north of Delaware, was built in 1940 by Quakers Isaac and Dinah Mendenhall. It contained a concealed room built especially for escaped slaves.**

10. **F. Julius LeMoyne House*:** Washington, PA. LeMoyne was part of a tightly knit Underground Railroad network in southwest Pennsylvania. His house was a center for abolitionists from the 1830s until the end of slavery in 1865.

11. **Appoquinimink Friends Meeting House:** Odessa, DE. Built in 1783, this meeting house housed a strongly antislavery congregation.

12. **Wilson Bruce Evans House***:** Oberlin, OH. Wilson Bruce Evans was a free black and a prominent abolitionist. Evans and his brother Henry participated in the 1858 rescue of an escaped slave who had been captured and was to be taken back to his master in Kentucky.

13. **Village of Mt. Pleasant Historic District:** Mt. Pleasant, OH. Mount Pleasant was home to a large Quaker abolitionist population. As a station on the Underground Railroad, the town attracted fugitive slaves and free blacks.

14. **John P. Parker House*:** Ripley, OH. John Parker, a former slave, led many fugitive slaves from Kentucky to his Ohio home. Parker delivered the runaways to Underground Railroad conductors like John Rankin, who would help them to the next depot.

15. **John Rankin House*:** Ripley, OH. John Rankin's house is believed to have been one of the first stations on the Ohio River route of the Underground Railroad. Between 1822 and 1865, Rankin assisted hundreds of slaves to freedom.

16. **Levi Coffin House*:** Fountain City, IN. Levi Coffin and his wife may have helped more than 2,000 slaves escape to freedom using his house as a station. Because of his extensive participation in the Underground Railroad, Coffin has often been called its "president."

17. **Bethel AME Zion Church:** Indianapolis, IN. Originally known as "Indianapolis Station," this church and its congregation harbored fugitive slaves en route to Canada.

18. **Eleutherian College Classroom and Chapel Building***:** Lancaster, IN. Eleutherian College was the first college in Indiana to admit students regardless of race or gender. Lancaster was a well-known stop on the Underground Railroad; some of the college trustees were conductors.

19. **Owen Lovejoy House*:** Princeton, IL. Owen Lovejoy used his home as a depot on the Underground Railroad in the 1840s and 1850s. Escaped slaves passing through Princeton were said to be riding the "Lovejoy Line."

20. **Milton House*:** Milton, WI. Joseph Goodrich built Milton House and the accompanying log cabin in the mid-1800s. Slaves escaping to communities along Lake Michigan would enter the log cabin and walk through a tunnel that led to the basement of the house, where food and shelter were provided.

21. **George B. Hitchcock House:** Lewis vicinity, IA. The Reverend Hitchcock harbored runaway slaves on their way north, as well as abolitionists travelling through Iowa.

*National Historic Landmark, **Closed to the public   © Infobase Publishing

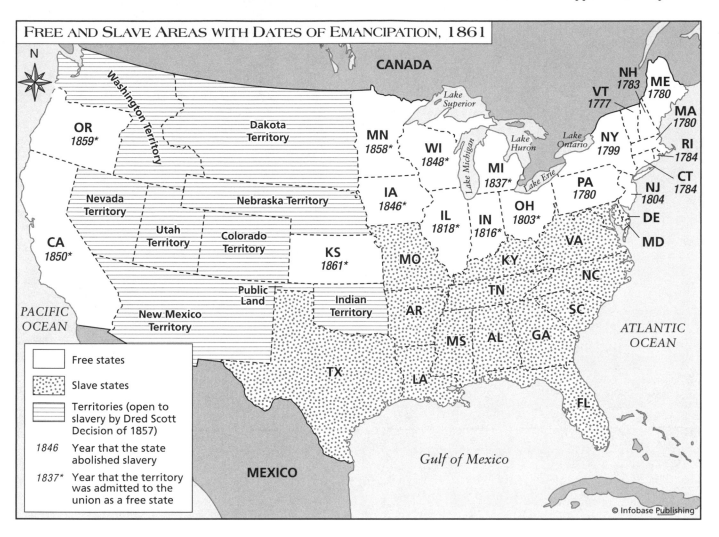

FREE AND SLAVE AREAS WITH DATES OF EMANCIPATION, 1861

N

CANADA

Lake Superior

NH 1783

ME 1780

VT 1777

MA 1780

OR 1859*

Washington Territory

Dakota Territory

MN 1858*

WI 1848*

Lake Huron

Lake Ontario

NY 1799

RI 1784

CT 1784

Nevada Territory

Nebraska Territory

MI 1837*

IA 1846*

Lake Michigan

Lake Erie

PA 1780

NJ 1804

CA 1850*

Utah Territory

Colorado Territory

KS 1861*

IL 1818*

IN 1816*

OH 1803*

DE

MD

MO

KY

VA

PACIFIC OCEAN

Public Land

Indian Territory

AR

TN

NC

ATLANTIC OCEAN

New Mexico Territory

MS

AL

SC

TX

LA

GA

FL

Gulf of Mexico

MEXICO

© Infobase Publishing

Free states

Slave states

Territories (open to slavery by Dred Scott Decision of 1857)

1846   Year that the state abolished slavery

1837*   Year that the territory was admitted to the union as a free state

Appendix D
Graphs and Tables

Graphs

1. Proportion of Blacks to the Total Population in Each of the Southern States, 1790–1880
2. Percentage of Increase in Total Population and in White and Black Populations, 1790–1880
3. Percentage of Slave-Owning Families as a Fraction of Total Free Households, 1860
4. Population of Kansas by Race, 1860–1880
5. Pension Application Success: Comparison of Black and White Civil War Veterans and Their Survivors, 1861–1934
6. Black Officeholders by State and Veteran Status, 1667–1877
7. Birthplaces of Black Kansas Residents, 1870
8. Survival Rates, Black and White Union Veterans, 1865

Tables

1. Estimated Population of American Colonies, 1610–1780
2. Value of Slaves Imported into British North American Colonies, 1768–1772
3. Population by Sex, Race, Residence, and Median Age, 1790–1880
4. Population of Regions of the United States by Sex and Race, 1790–1880
5. Black Population, by Age, Sex, and Status as Free or Slave, 1820–1860
6. School Enrollment Rates per 100 Population by Sex and Race, 1850–1880
7. Casualties in Ferrero's Division at the Battle of the Mine, July 30, 1864
8. Illiteracy in Persons 14 Years Old and Over, by Race and Nativity, 1870 and 1880

PROPORTION OF BLACKS TO THE TOTAL POPULATION IN EACH OF THE SOUTHERN STATES, 1790–1880

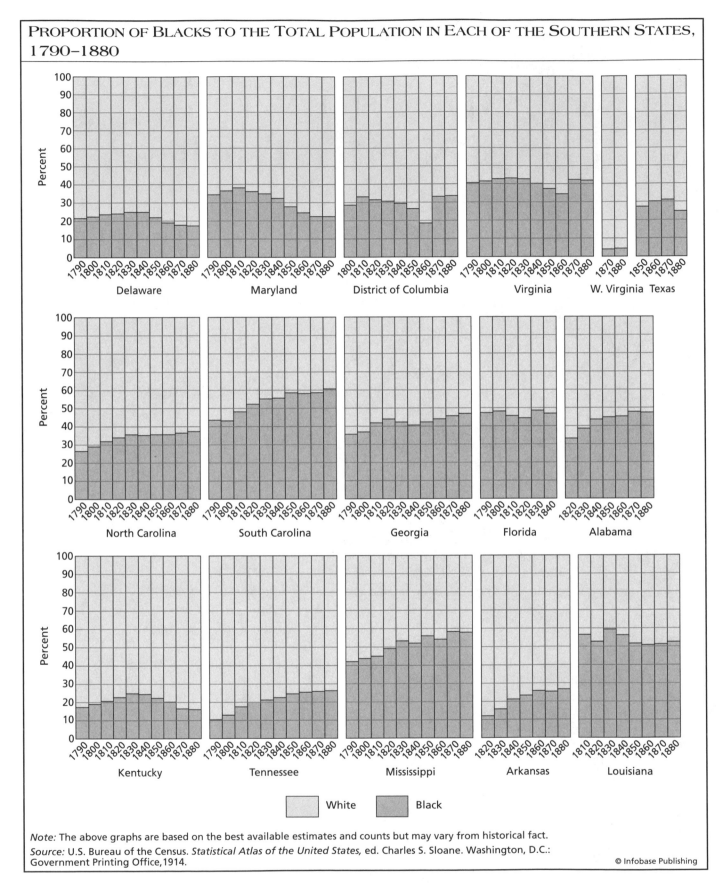

Note: The above graphs are based on the best available estimates and counts but may vary from historical fact.

Source: U.S. Bureau of the Census. *Statistical Atlas of the United States,* ed. Charles S. Sloane. Washington, D.C.: Government Printing Office, 1914.

© Infobase Publishing

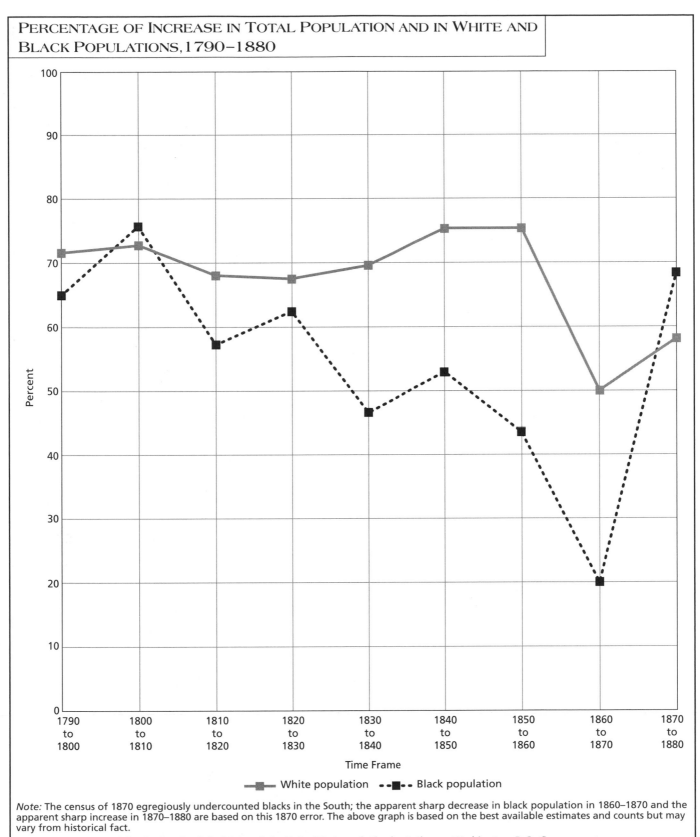

PERCENTAGE OF INCREASE IN TOTAL POPULATION AND IN WHITE AND BLACK POPULATIONS, 1790–1880

White population   Black population

Note: The census of 1870 egregiously undercounted blacks in the South; the apparent sharp decrease in black population in 1860–1870 and the apparent sharp increase in 1870–1880 are based on this 1870 error. The above graph is based on the best available estimates and counts but may vary from historical fact.

Source: U.S. Bureau of the Census. *Statistical Atlas of the United States,* ed. Charles S. Sloane. Washington, D.C.: Government Printing Office, 1914. Plate #135, fig. 2.

© Infobase Publishing

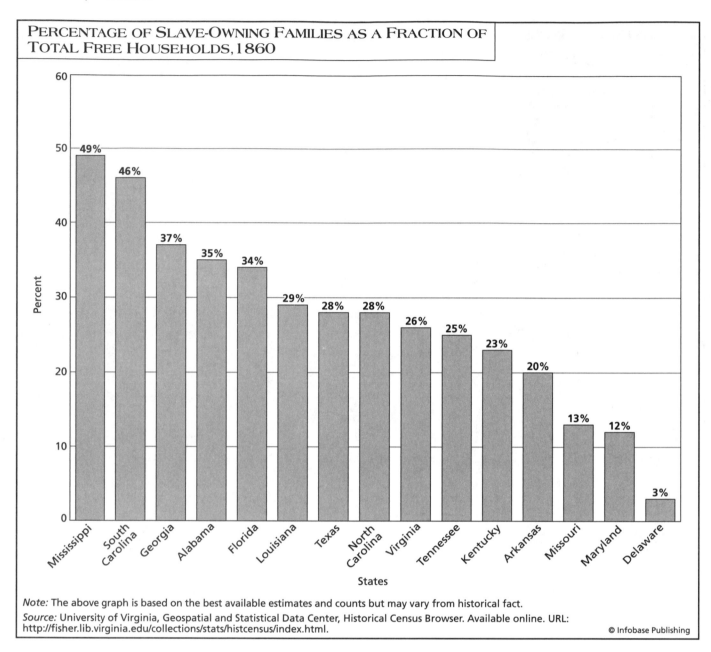

PERCENTAGE OF SLAVE-OWNING FAMILIES AS A FRACTION OF
TOTAL FREE HOUSEHOLDS, 1860

Note: The above graph is based on the best available estimates and counts but may vary from historical fact.

Source: University of Virginia, Geospatial and Statistical Data Center, Historical Census Browser. Available online. URL:
http://fisher.lib.virginia.edu/collections/stats/histcensus/index.html.

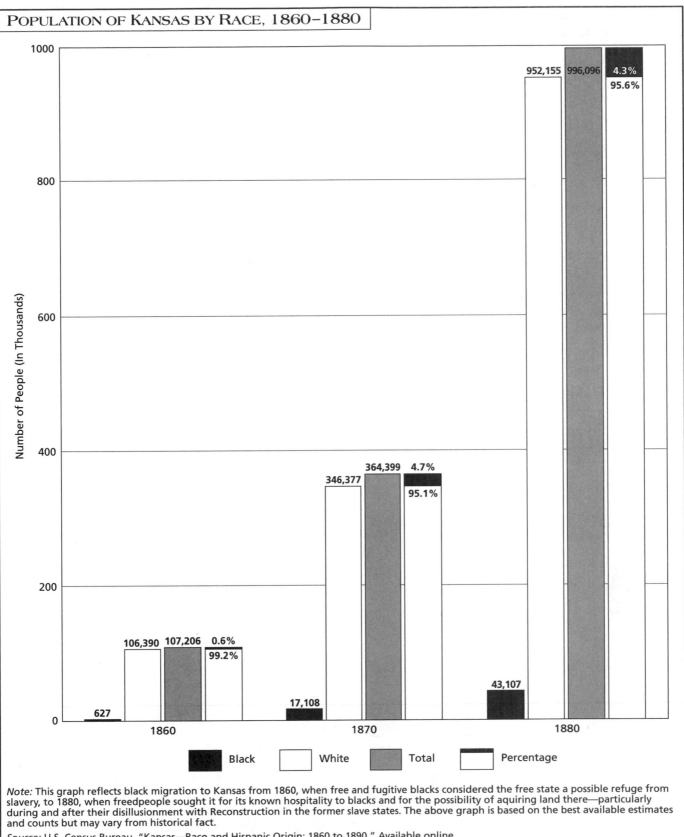

POPULATION OF KANSAS BY RACE, 1860–1880

Number of People (In Thousands)

1860
- 627
- 106,390
- 107,206
- 0.6%
- 99.2%

1870
- 17,108
- 346,377
- 364,399
- 4.7%
- 95.1%

1880
- 43,107
- 952,155
- 996,096
- 4.3%
- 95.6%

Black   **White**   **Total**   **Percentage**

Note: This graph reflects black migration to Kansas from 1860, when free and fugitive blacks considered the free state a possible refuge from slavery, to 1880, when freedpeople sought it for its known hospitality to blacks and for the possibility of aquiring land there—particularly during and after their disillusionment with Reconstruction in the former slave states. The above graph is based on the best available estimates and counts but may vary from historical fact.

Source: U.S. Census Bureau. "Kansas—Race and Hispanic Origin: 1860 to 1890." Available online.
URL: www.census.gov/population/documentation/twps0056/tab31.xls. Downloaded November 25, 2005.

© Infobase Publishing

PENSION APPLICATION SUCCESS: COMPARISON OF BLACK AND WHITE CIVIL WAR VETERANS AND THEIR SURVIVORS, 1861–1934

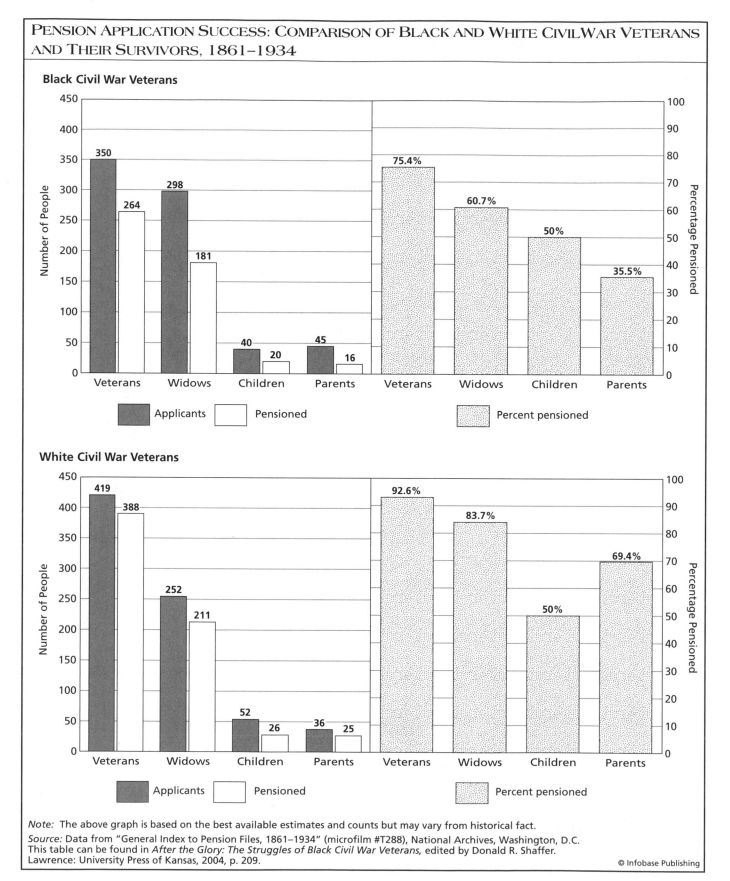

Black Civil War Veterans

White Civil War Veterans

Note: The above graph is based on the best available estimates and counts but may vary from historical fact.

Source: Data from "General Index to Pension Files, 1861–1934" (microfilm #T288), National Archives, Washington, D.C. This table can be found in *After the Glory: The Struggles of Black Civil War Veterans,* edited by Donald R. Shaffer. Lawrence: University Press of Kansas, 2004, p. 209.

© Infobase Publishing

BLACK OFFICEHOLDERS BY STATE AND VETERAN STATUS, 1667–1877

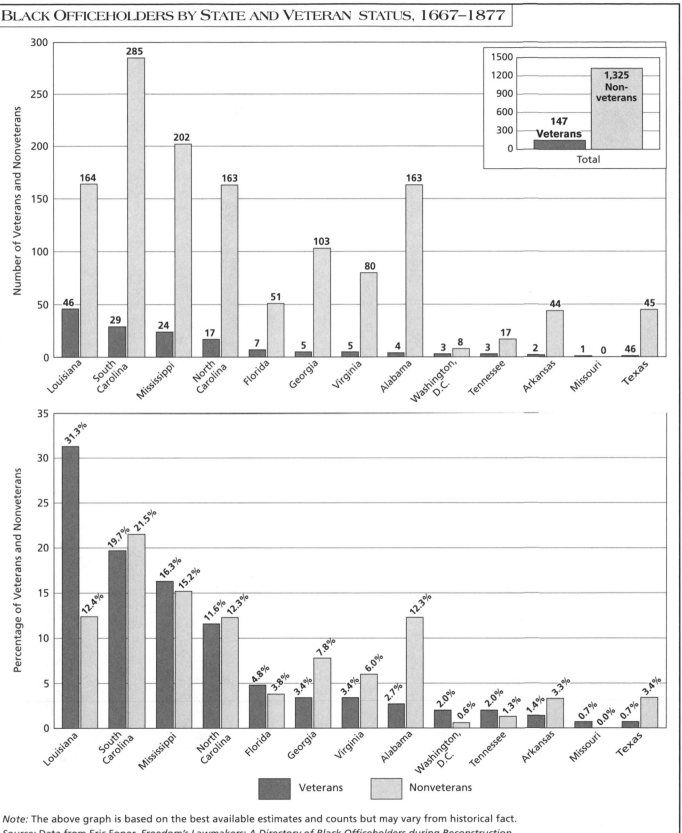

Note: The above graph is based on the best available estimates and counts but may vary from historical fact.

Source: Data from Eric Foner. *Freedom's Lawmakers: A Directory of Black Officeholders during Reconstruction.* Baton Rouge: Louisiana State University Press, 1999, p. XIV.

© Infobase Publishing

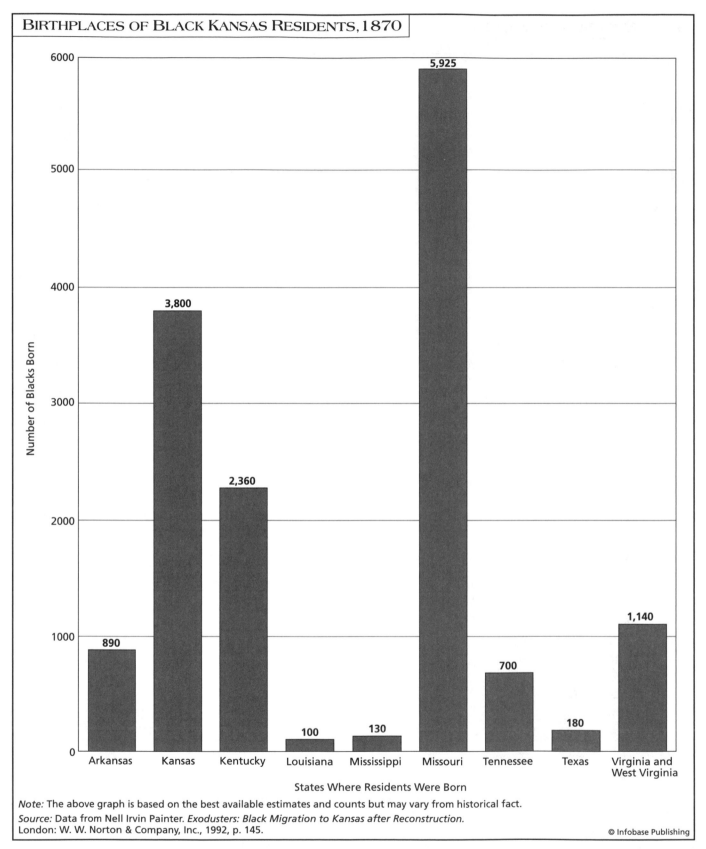

BIRTHPLACES OF BLACK KANSAS RESIDENTS, 1870

Note: The above graph is based on the best available estimates and counts but may vary from historical fact.

Source: Data from Nell Irvin Painter. *Exodusters: Black Migration to Kansas after Reconstruction.* London: W. W. Norton & Company, Inc., 1992, p. 145.

© Infobase Publishing

SURVIVAL RATES, BLACK AND WHITE UNION VETERANS, 1865

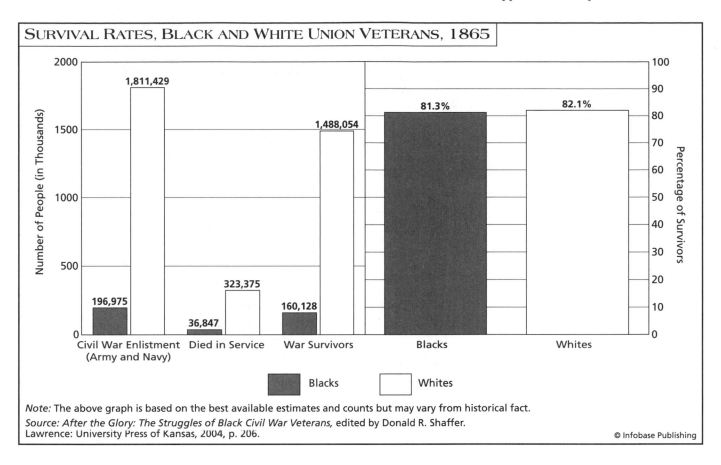

Blacks   Whites

Note: The above graph is based on the best available estimates and counts but may vary from historical fact.

Source: After the Glory: The Struggles of Black Civil War Veterans, edited by Donald R. Shaffer.
Lawrence: University Press of Kansas, 2004, p. 206.

© Infobase Publishing

Estimated Population of American Colonies, 1610–1780

Colony	1630	1640	1650	1660	1670	1680	1690	1700
White and Black								
Total	4,646	26,634	50,368	75,058	111,935	151,507	210,372	250,888
Maine		400	900	1,000				
New Hampshire	500	1,055	1,305	1,555	1,805	2,047	4,164	4,958
Vermont								
Plymouth	390	1,020	1,566	1,980	5,333	6,400	7,424	
Massachusetts	506	8,932	14,037	20,082	30,000	39,752	49,504	55,941
Rhode Island		300	785	1,539	2,155	3,017	4,224	5,894
Connecticut		1,472	4,139	7,980	12,603	17,246	21,645	25,970
New York	350	1,930	4,116	4,936	5,754	9,830	13,909	19,107
New Jersey					1,000	3,400	8,000	14,010
Pennsylvania						680	11,450	17,950
Delaware			185	540	700	1,005	1,482	2,470
Maryland		583	4,504	8,426	13,226	17,904	24,024	29,604
Virginia	2,500	10,442	18,731	27,020	35,309	43,596	53,046	58,560
N. Carolina					8,501,000	5,430	7,600	10,720
S. Carolina					200	1,200	3,900	5,704
Georgia								
Kentucky								
Tennessee								
Black								
Total	60	597	1,600	2,920	4,535	6,971	16,729	27,817
Maine								
New Hampshire		30	40	50	65	75	100	130
Vermont								
Massachusetts		150	295	422	160	170	400	800
Rhode Island			25	65	115	175	250	300
Connecticut		15	20	25	35	50	200	450
New York	10	232	500	600	690	1,200	1,670	2,256
New Jersey					60	200	450	840
Pennsylvania						25	270	430
Delaware			15	30	40	55	82	135
Maryland		20	300	758	1,190	1,611	2,162	3,227
Virginia	50	150	405	950	2,000	3,000	9,345	16,390
N. Carolina				20	150	210	300	415
S. Carolina					30	200	1,500	2,444
Georgia								
Kentucky								
Tennessee								

Colony	1710	1720	1730	1740	1750	1760	1770	1780
White and Black								
Total	331,711	466,185	629,445	905,563	1,170,760	1,593,625	2,148,076	2,780,369
Maine						20,000	31,257	49,133
New Hampshire	5,681	9,375	10,755	23,256	27,505	39,093	62,396	87,802
Vermont							10,000	47,620
Plymouth								
Massachusetts	62,390	91,008	114,116	151,613	188,000	202,600	235,308	268,627
Rhode Island	7,573	11,680	16,950	25,255	33,226	45,471	58,196	52,946
Connecticut	39,450	58,830	75,530	89,580	111,280	142,470	183,881	206,701
New York	21,625	36,919	48,594	63,665	76,696	117,138	162,920	210,541
New Jersey	19,872	29,818	37,510	51,373	71,393	93,813	117,431	139,627
Pennsylvania	24,450	30,962	51,707	85,637	119,666	183,703	240,057	327,305
Delaware	3,645	5,385	9,170	19,870	28,704	33,250	35,496	45,385
Maryland	42,741	66,133	91,113	116,093	141,073	162,267	202,599	245,474
Virginia	78,281	87,757	114,000	180,440	231,033	339,726	447,016	538,004
N. Carolina	15,120	21,270	30,000	51,760	72,984	110,442	197,200	270,133
S. Carolina	10,883	17,048	30,000	45,000	64,000	94,074	124,244	180,000
Georgia				2,021	5,200	9,578	23,375	56,071
Kentucky							15,700	45,000
Tennessee							1,000	10,000
Black								
Total	44,866	68,839	91,021	150,024	236,420	325,806	459,822	575,420
Maine						300	475	458
New Hampshire	150	170	200	500	550	600	654	541
Vermont							25	50
Massachusetts	1,310	2,150	2,780	3,035	4,075	4,566	4,754	4,822
Rhode Island	375	543	1,648	2,408	3,347	3,468	3,761	2,671
Connecticut	750	1,093	1,490	2,598	3,010	3,783	5,698	5,885
New York	2,811	5,740	6,956	8,996	11,014	16,340	19,112	21,054
New Jersey	1,332	2,385	3,008	4,366	5,354	6,567	8,220	10,460
Pennsylvania	1,575	2,000	1,241	2,055	2,872	4,409	5,761	7,855
Delaware	500	700	478	1,035	1,496	1,733	1,836	2,996
Maryland	7,945	12,499	17,220	24,031	43,450	49,004	63,818	80,515
Virginia	23,118	26,559	30,000	60,000	101,452	140,570	187,605	220,582
N. Carolina	900	3,000	6,000	11,000	19,800	33,554	69,600	91,000
S. Carolina	4,100	12,000	20,000	30,000	39,000	57,334	75,178	97,000
Georgia					1,000	3,578	10,625	20,831
Kentucky							2,500	7,200
Tennessee							200	1,500

Note: The above table is based on the best available estimates and counts but may vary from historical fact.
Source: U.S. Bureau of the Census, *Historical Statistics of the United States,* 2:1168.

Value of Slaves Imported into British North American Colonies, 1768–1772

Major Colonial Region	1768	1769	1770	1771	1772
New England	3	(Z)	—	(Z)	(Z)
Middle Colonies	1	(Z)	3	(Z)	1
Upper South	24	26	53	37	89
Lower South	50	205	45	141	300
Florida, The Bahamas, and Bermuda	5	8	7	4	1

(Z): Less than 500 pounds sterling
Note: The above table is based on the best available estimates and counts but may vary from historical fact.
Source: U.S. Bureau of the Census, *Historical Statistics of the United States* 2:1182.

Population by Sex, Race, Residence, and Median Age, 1790–1880
(in thousands)

Year	Male	Female	White	Black	Urban	Rural	Median Age
1790	NA	NA	3,172	757 (19.3%)	202	3,728	NA
1800	NA	NA	4,306	1,002 (18.9%)	322	4,986	NA
1810	NA	NA	5,862	1,378 (19%)	525	6,714	NA
1820	4,897	4,742	7,867	1,772 (18.4%)	693	8,945	16.7
1830	6,532	6,334	10,537	2,329 (18.1%)	1,127	11,739	17.2
1840	8,689	8,381	14,196	2,874 (16.8%)	1,845	15,224	17.8
1850	11,838	11,354	19,553	3,639 (15.7%)	3,544	19,648	18.9
1860	16,085	15,358	26,923	4,442 (14.1%)	6,217	25,227	19.4
1870	19,494	19,065	33,589	4,880 (12.7%)	9,902	28,656	20.2
1880	25,519	24,637	43,403	6,581 (13.1%)	14,130	36,026	20.9

NA = Not available.
Note: The above table is based on the best available estimates and counts but may vary from historical fact.
Source: Sloan, *Blacks in America 1492–1970: A Chronology and Fact Book,* p. 135. Washington, D.C.: Bureau of the Census, 1975.

Population of Regions of the United States by Sex and Race, 1790–1880
(in thousands)

Region and Year	Total Population	Male	Female	White	Black	Other
Northeast						
1880	14,507	7,161	7,347	14,274	229	4
1870	12,299	6,080	6,219	12,117	180	2
1860	10,594	5,266	5,329	10,438	156	(Z)
1850	8,627	4,339	4,287	8,477	150	—
1840	6,761	3,397	3,364	6,619	142	—
1830	5,542	2,784	2,751	5,417	125	—
1820	4,360	2,187	2,169	4,246	114	—
1810	3,487	1,714	1,670	3,384	102	—
1800	2,636	1,303	1,248	2,553	83	—
1790	1,968	961	940	1,901	67	—
North Central						
1880	17,364	9,016	8,348	16,961	386	17
1870	12,981	6,705	6,262	12,699	273	10
1860	9,097	4,743	4,354	8,900	184	13
1850	5,404	2,814	2,589	5,268	136	—
1840	3,352	1,758	1,594	3,262	89	—
1830	1,610	838	772	1,569	42	—
1820	859	453	406	841	18	—
1810	292	151	135	286	7	—
1800	51	27	23	50	1	—
South						
1880	16,517	8,272	8,244	10,555	5,954	7
1870	12,288	6,091	6,197	7,863	4,421	4
1860	11,133	5,655	5,478	7,034	4,097	2
1850	8,983	4,552	4,430	5,630	3,352	—
1840	6,951	3,528	3,423	4,309	2,642	—
1830	5,708	2,900	2,808	3,546	2,162	—
1820	4,419	2,255	2,163	2,776	1,644	—
1810	3,461	1,123	1,069	2,191	1,268	—
1800	2,622	874	830	1,704	918	—
1790	1,961	655	616	1,271	690	—
West						
1880	1,801	1,070	698	1,612	12	144
1870	991	609	381	910	6	74
1860	619	422	197	551	4	64
1850	179	132	47	178	1	—

Note: The above table is based on the best available estimates and counts but may vary from historical fact.
Source: U.S. Bureau of the Census, *Historical Statistics of the United States* 1:22.

Black Population, by Age, Sex, and Status as Free or Slave, 1820–1860

Free Males									
Year	Total	Under 10	10–19	20–29	30–39	40–49	50–59	60 and over	Unknown
1860	234,119	63,543	55,185	39,167	29,032	21,429	13,330	12,348	85
1850	208,724	59,125	46,456	35,782	26,153	18,199	11,771	11,088	150
Year	Total	Under 14	10–23	24–35	36–54		55 and over		
1840	186,481	56,284	52,805	35,321	28,274		13,797		—
1830	153,453	48,675	43,079	27,650	22,271		11,778		—
Year	Total	Under 14	14–25	26–44		45 and over			
1820	112,734	47,659	24,012	23,450		17,613			—
Free Females									
Year	Total	Under 10	10–19	20–29	30–39	40–49	50–59	60 and over	Unknown
1860	253,951	64,232	57,961	46,395	32,700	23,297	14,661	14,618	87
1850	225,771	59,748	49,646	41,765	29,072	19,741	12,582	13,081	136
Year	Total	Under 10	10–23	24–35	36–54		55 and over		
1840	199,822	55,062	56,592	41,682	30,371		16,115		—
1830	166,146	47,329	48,138	32,541	24,327		13,811		—
Year	Total	Under 14	14–25	26–44		45 and over			
1820	120,790	45,898	28,850	27,181		18,861			—
Slave Males									
Year	Total	Under 10	10–19	20–29	30–39	40–49	50–59	60 and over	Unknown
1860	1,982,625	609,455	497,293	355,018	218,346	140,791	79,776	68,267	13,679
1850	1,602,534	506,251	397,649	289,595	175,300	109,152	65,254	57,463	1,870
Year	Total	Under 10	10–23	24–35	36–54		55 and over		
1840	1,246,517	422,584	391,206	235,386	145,260		52,081		—
1830	1,012,823	353,498	312,567	185,585	118,880		42,293		—
Year	Total	Under 14	14–25	26–44		45 and over			
1820	788,028	343,852	203,088	163,723		77,365			—

| Slave Females | | | | | | | | | |
Year	Total	Under 10	10–19	20–29	30–39	40–49	50–59	60 and over	Unknown
1860	1,971,135	619,660	492,801	343,023	220,520	139,002	75,926	67,796	12,407
1850	1,601,779	513,331	395,825	282,615	178,355	110,780	61,762	57,289	1,822
Year	Total	Under 10	10–23	24–35	36–54		55 and over		
1840	1,240,938	421,465	390,117	239,825	139,204		50,327		—
1830	996,220	347,665	308,770	185,786	111,887		42,112		—
Year	Total	Under 14	14–25	26–44			45 and over		
1820	750,010	324,344	202,336	152,693			70,637		—

Note: The above table is based on the best available estimates and counts but may vary from historical fact.
Source: U.S. Bureau of the Census, *Historical Statistics of the United States* 1:18.

School Enrollment Rates per 100 Population by Sex and Race, 1850–1880

Year	Total	White	Black and Other Races	Total	White	Black and Other Races	Total	White	Black and Other Races
		Both Sexes			Male			Female	
1880	57.8	62.0	33.8	59.2	63.5	34.1	56.5	60.5	33.5
1870	48.4	54.4	9.9	49.8	56.0	9.6	46.9	52.7	10.0
1860	50.6	59.6	1.9	52.6	62.0	1.9	48.5	57.2	1.8
1850	47.2	56.2	1.8	49.6	59.0	2.0	44.8	53.3	1.8

Note: The above table is based on the best available estimates and counts but may vary from historical fact.
Source: U.S. Bureau of the Census, *Historical Statistics of the United States* 1:370.

Casualties in Ferrero's Division at the Battle of the Mine, July 30, 1864

Regiment	Killed	Wounded	Missing	Total
23rd U.S. Colored Infantry	74	115	121	310
29th U.S. Colored Infantry	21	56	47	124
31st U.S. Colored Infantry	27	56	47	135
43rd U.S. Colored Infantry	14	86	23	123
30th U.S. Colored Infantry	18	104	78	200
39th U.S. Colored Infantry	13	97	47	157
28th U.S. Colored Infantry	11	64	13	88
27th U.S. Colored Infantry	9	46	90	75
19th U.S. Colored Infantry	22	87	6	115
Total	209	697	421	1,327

Note: This table offers a sample of the losses incurred by black troops in the Civil War. Almost 40,000 black soldiers died during the war, 30,000 of illnesses, according to the National Archives. The table is based on the best available estimates and counts but may vary from historical fact.
Source: Shotgun's Home of the American Civil War. Information drawn from *Fox's Regimental Losses* (1889), 6. Available online. URL: http://www.civilwarhome.com/chapt6.htm.

Illiteracy in Persons 14 Years Old and Over, by Race and Nativity, 1870 and 1880

Year	Total	White			Black and Other
		Total	Native	Foreign-born	
1870	20.0	11.5	—	—	79.9
1880	17.0	9.4	8.7	12.0	70.0

Note: The above table is a representation of persons 14 years old and over who cannot read or write in any language. It is based on the best available estimates and counts but may vary from historical fact.
Source: National Center for Education Statistics. Available online. URL: http://nces.ed.gov/naal/historical-data/illiteracy.asp. Downloaded on November 21, 2005.

Glossary

asiento The privilege to supply slaves to Spain's American colonies.

barracoon An enclosure in which slaves were temporarily detained in Africa.

black belt Regions of the South, particularly in Georgia, Mississippi, the Carolinas, and Louisiana, characterized before the Civil War by plantation life and enslaved blacks and in the postbellum period populated partly by sharecroppers.

black trade Trade in Africa with the native people rather than with the European factors.

bound person One who is indentured.

buffalo soldier Loosely, a name given black troops in the U.S. army serving on the Western Frontier after the Civil War. The term originated among Indians, perhaps for the ferocity with which these soldiers fought.

carpetbaggers Northerners, black or white, who moved to the South after the Civil War, usually before 1867, and usually hoping for personal advancement in what they regarded as a promising area for economic development in a free-labor system. Although seldom accepted by southerners and therefore much maligned, most were well educated and middle class, and many had been prominent in their northern communities; most were Union veterans.

cat Cat-o'-nine-tails—a whip made of nine knotted cords attached to a handle.

coffle, or kaffle A train of slaves driven along together.

colonization Settling liberated slaves and other free blacks in communities, usually in places remote from their former American homes.

color line The separation of the races in public and private life.

comey, or coomey Duty paid to an African king for the privilege of trading.

commission merchant Agent who disposed of a planter's crop and bought supplies not available near home. He sometimes also bought or sold slaves for the planter.

contraband A slave who sought refuge with or was impressed by the Union forces. The term came into use because the Union argued that in wartime it had a right to free or enroll the property of its enemies.

dash Present or bribe given to African authorities for their cooperation in slave trading.

donatio causa mortis A gift made in contemplation of death, which the donor may revoke if he does not die as he expects.

driver *Slave driver* was used variously for a slave trader, a white overseer, or a black supervisor of field labor. A slave who supervised or policed field hands was also called by such terms as *foreman, overlooker, leading man, headman, boss, whipping boss, crew leader, overdriver, underdriver,* and *straw boss.*

factor Commission agent.

fancy girls Slave women, usually light skinned, used as concubines or prostitutes.

First Mississippi Plan A strategy instituted in 1875–76 to control black voting by violence, attacks on black political rallies, and the assassination of Republican leaders.

free black A person freed before the Civil War.

freedman A male freed in the course of the Civil War or soon thereafter.

freedperson A person freed in the course of the Civil War or soon thereafter.

freedwoman   A woman freed in the course of the Civil War or soon thereafter.

free produce movement   An effort to avoid the use of the products of slave labor.

gag rule   A congressional rule of 1836 that prevented abolitionist petitions from being introduced, read, or discussed in Congress.

griffe   Offspring of a black person and a mulatto. *Griffe* was used especially in the Deep South, where the term *mulatto* was sometimes limited to the offspring of one white and one black person.

hiring out   The practice by which a master either permitted his slave to work for someone else for a set sum of money or allowed a slave to negotiate an agreement to work for pay for someone else. In the latter case, far more common in cities than in the countryside, the slave usually paid the master a fixed sum each week and assumed responsibility for his or her own support.

hushharbor   Secret slave church in the woods, the sounds from which were muffled by walls made of trees, brush, and wet blankets hung from branches.

indenture   Contract by which an apprentice is bound to a master for a limited time period, sometimes with the promise of payment at the end of the term. Many Europeans indentured themselves for passage money to North America. Although they suffered some of the disadvantages of slaves, the law protected them against the worst abuses of slavery.

insurrection   A rising up against established authority; an incipient or limited rebellion.

intelligence   Often used, especially in defenses of slavery, to denote not inborn ability to learn and think but that ability as improved by education: Thus whites were said to have superior intelligence because they had the leisure and the means to acquire education.

intendant   A foreign official who supervises a certain district.

Ironclad Oath   Swearing that one had never voluntarily aided the Confederacy.

jackson whites   Term for a racially mixed (black, white, and Indian) group along the New Jersey–New York state line, possibly descended from Algonquin Indians, Dutch and British settlers, and free blacks. *Jacks* was an 18th-century term for freed slaves.

Jim Crow   Originally a figure in a minstrel show song of 1828, Jim Crow became a stock comedy character, and later a term applied to the laws and practices of racial oppression between 1865 and 1967, though some scholars date the Jim Crow era only from the 1890s. The term also was used as a racial slur against blacks and as a synonym for "segregated," as in "Jim Crow railroad car."

jump the broomstick   The most common irregular slave marriage ritual, in which the couple joined hands and stepped or jumped over a broomstick. Another such ritual was *marriage by the blanket,* in which the woman laid her blanket alongside the man's.

Knights of the White Camellia   A white supremacist secret organization founded in May 1867 to resist carpetbaggers and restore white control of government. Its members denied connection with the Ku Klux Klan and used less violent but equally effective measures. The organization functioned mostly in the lower South and effectively ceased to exist by 1870.

Ku Klux Klan   The most long-lived and largest white supremacist organization, whose members included both recognized ruffians and respectable men. Founded in Pulaski, Tennessee, in 1865, it survives even into the 21st century. During Reconstruction, it terrorized blacks, carpetbaggers, scalawags, and other Republicans. It required its members to take oaths that obligated them to put the organization and loyalty to other members before government, even to the extent of committing perjury.

manumission   An exercise of the property holder's right to renounce ownership of his property—thus, a slaveholder's freeing of his slave.

maroon   An escaped slave who joined with others to establish a colony where they defended themselves and sometimes preyed upon the surrounding countryside; or the colony itself. Synonymous with *outlyer.* Authorities variously ascribe the term as coming from a mountaintop, runaway slave, and hog hunter.

mestizo   A person of mixed parentage, especially, in the western United States, the offspring of a Spanish or Portuguese person and an American Indian.

minstrel show   A form of entertainment presented by whites, in which some of them wore blackface and caricatured the conduct and speech of blacks. Seated in a semicircle, the various entertainers rose to sing, dance, and engage in banter. These shows began in the 1830s, became widely popular by the Civil War, and lasted into the 1930s.

mulatto Any person of mixed black and white ancestry.

mustee Any person of mixed black and American Indian blood.

negro seamen laws Laws enacted in several southern states providing that black crew members of any ship coming into port must be arrested and held in jail until their vessel left. The constitutionality of these laws was much debated.

nullification An extremist doctrine of states rights holding that a state could declare null and void any federal law it deemed unconstitutional.

outlyer See **maroon.**

outside children Children born outside of wedlock; also *stolen children* or *children by the way.*

patting or clapping juba A slave creation, complex clapping patterns such as striking the hands on the knees, then striking the hands together, then striking the right shoulder with one hand, the left with the other, while keeping time with the feet and singing.

pani (pawnee) So many members of the Pawnee Indian tribe were enslaved that *pani* became a term for "Indian slave."

peonage A system by which debtors must labor for their creditors.

perpetuanas Coarse wool serges for trade with Africa.

personal liberty laws Laws enacted by many northern states to prevent kidnapping, in an effort to strike a balance between the rights of slaveholders and the rights of free blacks threatened by the fugitive slave laws.

popular sovereignty See **squatter sovereignty.**

preemption The act or right of buying land, etc., before, or in preference to, others; especially such a right granted to a settler on public land.

Redeemer A name adopted during Reconstruction by white southern Democrats determined to restore white supremacy.

Redemption A term applied by its advocates to a Reconstruction effort to restore white supremacy in the South.

Red Shirts Southern white terrorist groups that aimed to maintain white supremacy.

refugeeing Taking slaves to Texas to keep them out of the way of the advancing Union forces. The practice became common in late 1862 and continued through much of 1864.

rifle clubs Ku Klux Klan terrorist groups.

scalawag A southern white who supported the Republicans during Reconstruction. The term, used at the time by other southern whites as condemnatory for political reasons, has now broadened to designate a reprobate.

secret six This group of respectable citizens—philanthropist Gerrit Smith; teacher of the blind Dr. Samuel Gridley Howe; wealthy manufacturer George L. Stearns; liberal clergyman and commanding officer of a Civil War black regiment Rev. Thomas Wentworth Higginson; secretary of the Massachusetts Kansas Committee Franklin B. Sanborn; and Unitarian clergyman Rev. Theodore Parker, reputedly the most learned man of his time—helped finance John Brown's insurrection, for that purpose diverting money and arms contributed to the Massachusetts-Kansas Aid Committee for peaceable purposes. Brown left behind at his Maryland farmhouse papers implicating many people, causing all of the secret six but Higginson to panic; some fled.

sell a slave running Sell a slave who has run away, usually for a low price, the buyer speculating that he may be able to capture the slave and make a profit.

serf A person tied to land who owed labor service to a lord of that estate. Unlike a slave, a serf had rights to marry, establish a household, and hold property; the lord could not kill the serf with impunity.

shake the lion's paw Enter British territory; thus, for a slave, be freed.

sharecropping A system by which a farmer rents land for which he pays by a share of his crop, often enmeshing himself in endless debt.

shout A subdued form of dance, sometimes incorporated into worship; also called *dancing before the Lord.*

soul driver Slave trader.

Southampton Insurrection Nat Turner's rebellion of 1831.

squatter sovereignty   The idea, first proposed in 1847, that the settlers of a territory, not the federal government, should decide whether a new state should be slave or free. Also known as *popular sovereignty*.

Stalwart Republican   A pragmatic politician who focused not on ideology or reform so much as on winning office and mediating conflicts among economic and ethnic groups.

statu liberi   A legal term used in Louisiana, applying to slaves legally promised freedom in the future.

supercargo   Ship's officer in charge of cargo.

ten percent men   Private English traders in Africa obliged to pay that duty to maintain the trading forts.

Union Leagues   Groups of black, white, or black and white voters that originated in the North during the Civil War as a white man's patriotic organization but were most active in the South during Reconstruction. Their members pledged to support the Republican Party, the principle of equal rights, and one another. They emphasized political education, but they also encouraged the building of black schools and churches, collected funds to care for the sick, drafted petitions to gain and protect their rights, served freedmen's and southern hill-country whites' economic interests, and developed black political leaders. Frequently, informal self-defense organizations developed around the leagues.

Unionist   A resident in the Confederacy who remained loyal to the United States, often at great personal cost.

White League   A paramilitary group intent on securing white rule in Louisiana; its members disguised themselves. On April 13, 1873, in Colfax, Louisiana, the League's clash with the mostly black state militia killed some 100 black men, nearly half of whom were murdered after surrendering.

Notes

1. The West Coast of Africa: 1441–1866

1. 1854, quoted in Reynolds, *African Slavery*, 9.
2. Klein and Lovejoy, "Slavery in West Africa," 207.
3. Miller, *Way of Death*, 39–51.
4. Bontemps, ed., *Great Slave Narratives*, 12.
5. Miller, *Way of Death*, 94.
6. "As Jean Bazin has argued, a large percentage of those moved into trade at any time were probably already in slavery, that is to say, they were simply being reinslaved." Klein and Lovejoy, "Slavery in West Africa," 210.
7. *New York Times*, Connecticut section, September 20, 1998. See also the introduction in Reynolds, *Stand the Storm*.
8. Buckmaster, *Let My People Go*, 3.
9. Coughtry, *Notorious Triangle*, 18.
10. See, for instance, slave trader Capt. William Snelgrave, *A New Account of Some Parts of Guinea and the Slave Trade* (1734), in Dow, *Slave Ships*, xix–xxi.
11. Quoted in Dow, *Slave Ships*, 136–37.
12. Rice, *Radical Narratives*, 50.
13. Snelgrave, *New Account*, 9.
14. Donnan, ed., *Slave Trade Documents* 1:284–85.
15. Pope-Hennessy, *Sins of the Fathers*, 264.
16. Agent at Cape Coast, ca. 1700, in Davies, *Royal African Company*, 239.
17. 1704, quoted in Pope-Hennessy, *Sins of the Fathers*, 77.
18. Davies, *Royal African Company*, 217–18.
19. Pope-Hennessy, *Sins of the Fathers*, 234.
20. South Carolina Gazette, July 7, 1759, in Wax, "Negro Resistance," 5.
21. Donnan, ed., *Slave Trade Documents* 2:213.
22. Coughtry, *Notorious Triangle*, 116.
23. A State of the Trade to Africa presented to the House of Commons by the Council of Trade, 1709, in Donnan, ed., *Slave Trade Documents* 2:57.
24. Quoted in Wax, "Negro Resistance," 4.
25. Quoted in Rawley, *Transatlantic Slave Trade*, 294.
26. Miller, *Way of Death*, 661.
27. Quoted in Pope-Hennessy, *Sins of the Fathers*, 45.
28. Rawley, *Transatlantic Slave Trade*, 261.
29. *Revelations of a Slave Smuggler*, 1860, in Dow, *Slave Ships*, 212.
30. Howard, *American Slavers*, Appendix B, 224.
31. Introduction to Canot, *African Slaver*, ix–x.
32. Pope-Hennessy, *Sins of the Fathers*, 274.
33. Reynolds, *African Slavery*, 57; and Rawley, *Transatlantic Slave Trade*, 18.

2. The Middle Passage: 1500–1866

1. Donnan, eds., *Slave Trade Documents* 1:141–42.
2. Quoted in Anstey, *Atlantic Slave Trade*, 13.
3. Rawley, *Transatlantic Slave Trade*, 293.
4. Bontemps, ed., *Great Slave Narratives*, 28–29.
5. Donnan, ed., *Slave Trade Documents* 1:459.
6. Fabre, "The Slave Ship Dance," in Diedrich et al., eds., *Black Imagination and the Middle Passage*, 34–38 passim.
7. Bontemps, ed., *Great Slave Narratives*, 27.
8. Quoted in Dow, *Slave Ships*, 144.
9. Quoted in Reynolds, *African Slavery*, 50–51.
10. Miller, *Way of Death*, 438.
11. Quoted in Dow, *Slave Ships*, 148.
12. John Weskett, *A Complete Digest of the Laws, Theory and Practice of Insurance* (1781), quoted in Reynolds, *African Slavery*, 50.
13. William Vernon to Capt. Grey, August 27, 1786, in Coughtry, *Notorious Triangle*, 147.
14. Diedrich et al., eds., *Black Imagination and the Middle Passage*.
15. Harding, *River*, 22–23.
16. Quoted in Donnan, *Slave Trade Documents* 2:281–82.
17. Miller, *Way of Death*, 409–10.
18. Harding, *River*, 12.
19. Ibid., 20.

20. Wax, "Negro Resistance," 7.
21. Harding, *River*, 14.
22. Ibid., 20.
23. Donnan, ed., *Slave Trade Documents* 1:406–10.
24. Blassingame, *Slave Community*, 8; and *Hartford Courant*, September 21, 1998.
25. Donnan, eds., *Slave Trade Documents* 1:206–8.
26. Miller, *Way of Death*, 437–38.
27. Rawley, *Transatlantic Slave Trade*, 300–31.
28. Donnan, eds., *Slave Trade Documents* 1:141–45 passim.
29. Quoted in Miller, *Way of Death*, 426.
30. Donnan, ed., *Slave Trade Documents* 1:459.
31. Coughtry, *Notorious Triangle*, 98–99.
32. Rawley, *Transatlantic Slave Trade*, 294.
33. *Hartford Courant*, September 21, 1998.

3. Americans in the Slave Trade: 1526–1865

1. Higginbotham, *In the Matter of Color*, 20f.; and Buckmaster, *Let My People Go*, 3.
2. Owens, *Property*, 7–9.
3. Bancroft, *Slave Trading*, 2; and Owens, *Property*, 7–9.
4. Alford, *Prince among Slaves*, 131.
5. Quoted in Wax, "Preferences for Slaves," 377.
6. Coffin, *Reminiscences*, x–xi.
7. Mannix, *Black Cargoes*, 202, 203.
8. Oakes, *Ruling Race*, 230f.
9. Diedrich et al., eds., *Black Imagination and the Middle Passage*, 28.
10. Littlefield, *Rice and Slaves*, 65.
11. Higginbotham, *In the Matter of Color*, 5, 45, 120–21.
12. Quoted in Bancroft, *Slave Trading*, 69.
13. Quoted in Catterell, *Judicial Cases* 1:215.
14. Quoted in Rawick, *The American Slave* 1:173.
15. Quoted in Bancroft, *Slave Trading*, 81n36.
16. Quoted in Oakes, *Ruling Race*, 61–62.
17. Olmsted, *Cotton Kingdom*, 14.
18. Quoted in Tadman, *Speculators and Slaves*, 106.
19. Quoted in Bancroft, *Slave Trading*, 363–64.
20. Quoted in Tadman, *Speculators and Slaves*, 85.
21. Ibid., 88.
22. Higginbotham, *In the Matter of Color*, 53.
23. Ibid., 211–12.
24. Grimké, *Appeal to the Christian Women of the South* (1836), in Dumond, *Antislavery*, 192.
25. Higginbotham, *In the Matter of Color*, 113–17 passim.
26. Quoted in Tadman, *Speculators and Slaves*, 75.
27. Quoted in Blassingame, ed., *Slave Testimony*, 704–6.
28. Bancroft, *Slave Trading*, 204.
29. Phillips, *American Negro Slavery*, 189, 191.
30. Quoted in Goodell, *Slave Code*, 54.
31. Phillips, *American Negro Slavery*, 381–82.
32. Quoted in Bracey, *American Slavery*, 17.
33. Blassingame, ed., *Slave Testimony*, 403.
34. Murray, *Proud Shoes*, 97.
35. Quoted in Bancroft, *Slave Trading*, 322.
36. Ibid., 217.
37. Tadman, *Speculators and Slaves*, 101.
38. Ibid., 167.
39. Kay and Cary, *Slavery in North Carolina*, 204.
40. Botkin, ed., *Lay My Burden Down*, 184–85.
41. Aptheker, *Documentary History of the Negro People in the United States*, 126.
42. Oakes, *Ruling Race*, 118.
43. Torrey, *American Slave Trade*, 43–44n.
44. Wheeler, *Law of Slavery*, 385–86, 306.
45. Crowe, *With Thackeray in America*, 105.
46. Clinton, *Plantation Mistress*, 213.
47. Fehrenbacher, *Dred Scott Case*, 30.
48. Ibid., 31.

4. Slave Life: 1619–1865

1. Calhoun, "Remarks on the States Rights Resolutions in Regard to Abolition," U.S. Senate, January 10, 1838. Available online. URL: http://www.founding.com/library/lbody.cfm?id=338&parent=65.
2. Owens, *Property*, 7–9.
3. Tadman, *Speculators and Slaves*, 159; and Fox-Genovese, *Plantation Mistress*, 295.
4. Thomas, *Secret Eye*, 3n6.
5. Douglass, *Narrative*, 50.
6. Olmsted, *Cotton Kingdom*, 480.
7. Ibid., 80–81.
8. White, *Ar'n't I a Woman?* 83, 84.
9. Kemble, *Journal*, 67–68.
10. Olmsted, *Cotton Kingdom*, 95.
11. Bell, *Major Butler's Legacy*, 156.
12. Allen Brown, letter of December 7, 1834, in Owens, *Property*, 46.
13. Mattie Fannen, in Fox-Genovese, *Plantation Household*, 147.
14. Truth, *Narrative*, 13.
15. Dumond, *Antislavery*, 347–48.
16. Gutman, *Black Family*, 275, 276.
17. Ibid., 137.
18. Johnson, *God Struck Me Dead*, 156–57.

19. Kemble, *Journal*, 247–48.
20. Ibid., 245–46.
21. Gutman, *Black Family*, 66–73 passim.
22. Phillips, *American Negro Slavery*, 264–65.
23. Fox-Genovese, *Plantation Households*, 324.
24. Kemble, *Journal*, 240–41.
25. Grimké, in Goodell, *Slave Code*, 117.
26. Blassingame, ed., *Slave Testimony*, 594.
27. White, *Ar'n't I a Woman?* 89.
28. Colonies began to pass laws against such relationships in the late 17th century. As slavery spread and institutionalized, these laws multiplied and became more severe. For information on white-black sexual relations, see particularly Hodes, *White Women, Black Men*, passim.
29. Blane, *Excursion*, 204.
30. Fox-Genovese, *Plantation Household*, 9.
31. Kemble, *Journal*, 10–11.
32. Olmsted, *Cotton Kingdom*, 475n1.
33. Hodes, *White Women, Black Men*, 34.
34. Johnston, *Race Relations*, 255.
35. Early on, the children of white mothers by slave fathers had been held to be slaves, but this principle changed as colonies and then states tried to establish slavery on the basis of race alone. Hodes, *White Women, Black Men*, 29–30.
36. Ibid., 42.
37. Ibid., 27.
38. Ibid., 2.
39. Rachleff, "Lynching and Racial Violence," available online, URL: www.nathanielturner.com/lynchingandracialviolencepr.htm.
40. Olmsted, *Cotton Kingdom*, 329.
41. Williams, *History of the Negro Race*, 35–36.
42. Fox-Genovese, *Plantation Household*, 134.
43. Kemble, *Journal*, 159.
44. Johnston, *Race Relations*, 244–45.
45. Johnson and Roark, *Black Masters*, xiii, 33.
46. Ibid., 57.
47. Ibid., 63.
48. Fox-Genovese, *Plantation Household*, 315.
49. Berlin, *Freedom* Series 1, 3:7.
50. Kemble, *Journal*, 314.
51. Blassingame, *Slave Community*, 63.
52. DuBois, *Souls of Black Folk*, Chapter 10. Available online. URL: http://xroads.virginia.edu/~hyper/DUBOIS/ch10.html.
53. Early on, the Christian church in North America largely ignored blacks. Active missionary work among them began with the founding of the Society for the Propagation of the Gospel in Foreign Parts in 1701. The rapidly growing Methodist and Baptist denominations joined in.
54. Lambert, "I Saw the Book Talk," 195.
55. Johnson, *God Struck Me Dead*, ix.
56. Raboteau, *Slave Religion*, 8.
57. Ibid., 311–12.
58. Ibid., 67.
59. Botkin, ed., *Lay My Burden Down*, 36–37.
60. Owens, *Property*, 142.
61. Botkin, ed., *Lay My Burden Down*, 22–23.

5. Slave Work: 1619–1865

1. Fox-Genovese, *Plantation Household*, 165.
2. Rawick, *American Slave*, 1:14.
3. Kemble, *Journal*, 279.
4. Fox-Genovese, *Plantation Household*, 137.
5. Owens, *Property*, 118.
6. Ibid., 109.
7. DuBois, *The Negro*, 137.
8. Olmsted, *Cotton Kingdom*, 187.
9. Bell, *Major Butler's Legacy*, 116.
10. Owens, *Property*, 181.
11. Yancy, "The Stuart Double Plow," 48.
12. Kemble, *Journal*, 188.
13. Fox-Genovese, *Plantation Households*, 176.
14. Jordan, *Tumult and Silence*, 193.
15. Bell, *Major Butler's Legacy*, 146.
16. Olmsted, *Cotton Kingdom*, 192–94.
17. Bell, *Major Butler's Legacy*, 154.
18. Fogel and Engerman say that "only 30 percent of plantations with one hundred or more slaves employed white overseers." *Time on the Cross*, 211.
19. Blassingame, *Slave Community*, 173, 176.
20. Douglass, *Narrative*, 39–40.
21. Blassingame, *Slave Community*, 177.
22. Olmsted, *Cotton Kingdom*, 187, 188.
23. Fox-Genovese, *Plantation Households*, 186.
24. Gutman, *Black Family*, 77–78.
25. Murray, *Proud Shoes*, 39.
26. Campbell, *Empire*, 125.
27. Redpath, *Roving Editor*, 124–26.
28. Starobin, *Industrial Slavery*, 200–201.
29. Olmsted, *Cotton Kingdom*, 426–27.
30. Douglass, *Narrative*, 70.
31. Bontemps, ed., *Great Slave Narratives*, 208–9.
32. Owens, *Property*, 168.

33. Miller, *Dictionary of Afro-American Slavery*, 322.
34. Olmsted, *Cotton Kingdom*, 40.
35. Starobin, *Industrial Slavery*, 53.
36. Olmsted, *Cotton Kingdom*, 114–15.
37. Kay and Cary, *Slavery in North Carolina*, 49.
38. Wheeler, *Law of Slavery*, 447–48.
39. Olmsted, *Cotton Kingdom*, 75.
40. Trexler, *Slavery in Missouri*, 178.
41. Myers, ed., *Children of Pride*, 241.
42. Starobin, *Industrial Slavery*, 209–10.
43. Lewis, *Coal, Iron, and Slaves*, 227.
44. Bancroft, *Slave Trading*, 146.
45. Miller, *Dictionary of Afro-American Slavery*, 321, 323.
46. Easterby, *South Carolina Rice Plantation*, 350.
47. Fogel and Engerman, *Time on the Cross*, 149.
48. Bontemps, ed., *Four Fugitive Slave Narratives*, 62.

6. Runaways: 1619–1865

1. Botkin, ed., *Lay My Burden Down*, 179–80.
2. DuBois, ed., *Economic Co-operation*, 25–26.
3. Ibid., 27.
4. Ibid.
5. Redpath, *Roving Editor*, 40–41.
6. Letter, Anne Winchester Penniman collection.
7. Phillips, *American Negro Slavery*, 286.
8. Kemble, *Journal*, 344.
9. Siebert, *Underground Railroad*, 237, 340–42.
10. Gutman, *Black Family*, 267.
11. Siebert, *Underground Railroad*, 161–62.
12. Bontemps, ed., *Four Fugitive Slave Narratives*, 190.
13. Quoted in DuBois, ed., *Economic Co-operation*, 26–27.
14. Botkin, ed., *Lay My Burden Down*, 186–89.
15. Haviland, *A Woman's Life*, 65.
16. Hadden, *Slave Patrols*, chap. 5 passim.
17. Siebert, *Underground Railroad*, 90.
18. Ibid., 105–6.
19. *Troy Whig*, April 28, 1859, quoted in Bradford, *Harriet*, 143–49.

7. Canada, Other Refuges, and the Colonization/Emigration Movement: 1501–1877

1. Winks, *Blacks in Canada*, 9, 10. Professor Winks's excellent and readable book is the standard work on the subject; it is used for the figures cited herein.
2. Walker, *Black Loyalists*, 18ff.
3. Winks, *Blacks in Canada*, 33.
4. Ibid., 70.
5. Grant, "Black Immigrants into Nova Scotia," 255.
6. Winks, *Blacks in Canada*, 115.
7. *The Refugee*, quoted in DuBois, ed., *Economic Co-operation*, 97.
8. Moore, "We Feel the Want of Protection': The Politics of Law and Race in California, 1848–1878," in Burns and Orsi, eds., *Taming the Elephant*, 109.
9. Howe, *Refugee*, 69–70.
10. No reliable estimate of the total number of blacks who emigrated to Canada exists or can be made. Dumond, in *Anti-Slavery*, 336, surveys a number of estimates: The American Anti-Slavery Society investigation of 1837 showed 10,000 blacks in Upper Canada. Missionaries Isaac Rice and Hiram Wilson placed the number in Upper Canada (essentially Ontario, so-called until 1841) in 1850 at 20,000. Samuel J. May agreed, but William Wells Brown claimed 25,000. Rev. William Mitchell, a Canadian black missionary, estimated that at least 1,200 fugitives reached Toronto and its area every year. Levi Coffin estimated 40,000 in the whole of Canada in 1844. Within three months after the Fugitive Slave Act of 1850 passed, at least 3,000 reached Canada. By 1860 there were 60,000 blacks in Upper Canada alone, of whom 45,000 were fugitive slaves. Winks, *Blacks in Canada*, 176, 240.
11. Blassingame, eds., *Slave Testimony*, 164.
12. Woodson, "The Negroes of Cincinnati prior to the Civil War," 2–3, 4, available online, URL: www.gutenberg.org/catalog/world/readfile?pageno2&flk_files=99948.
13. Duncan "Tunis Campbell," available online. URL: http:www.geogiaencyclopedia.org/nge/Article.jsp?path=Religion/HistoricalFigures . . . id-h-2903.
14. DuBois, ed., *Economic Co-operation*, 32.
15. Delany, *Condition*, 178, 181.
16. Houzeau, *My Passage at the New Orleans* Tribune, *109*.
17. Of its first 18 expeditions after its start in 1820, the American Colonization Society reported in 1832 that it transported 1,487 emigrants, of whom 230 died. For the year 1853 it reported 782. Fox, *American Colonization Society*, 56; and Williams, *History of the Negro Race*, 98.

8. Rebels: 1526–1865

1. Carroll, *Slave Insurrections*, 103–4.
2. Campbell, *Empire*, 225–26.

3. Roger B. Taney, quoted in Desmond, *Antislavery*, 144.

4. Wheeler, *Law of Slavery*, 212–13.

5. Finkelman, *Law of Freedom*, 200.

6. White, *Ar'n't I a Woman?* 152.

7. Finkelman, *Law of Freedom*, 195.

8. Ibid., 199.

9. Ibid., 261.

10. Charlotte Foster, in Fox-Genovese, *Plantation Households*, 329.

11. Bracey, *American Slavery*, 55.

12. Douglass, *Narrative*, 81–83.

13. Mullin, *Flight and Rebellion*, 58–59.

14. Harding, *River*, 198–99.

15. Fox-Genovese, *Plantation Households*, 314.

16. Johnston, *Race Relations*, 21–22.

17. McLaurin, *Celia*, 86.

18. Owens, *Property*, 5.

19. Hine, ed., *Black Women in American History* 3:989.

20. Coffin, *Reminiscences*, 95.

21. Isaacson, *Benjamin Franklin*, 315.

22. Faust, *Mothers of Invention*, 59–60.

23. Kemble, *Journal*, 39.

24. Tise, *Proslavery*, 319–20.

25. Williams, *History of the Negro Race*, 227.

26. Fox-Genovese, *Plantation Households*, 303.

27. Newspaper account quoted in Aptheker, *One Continual Cry*, 86–87.

28. Starobin, *Industrial Slavery*, 90.

29. Porter, *Negro on the American Frontier*, 381.

30. Carroll, *Slave Insurrections*, 90.

31. Wade, "The Vesey Plot: A Reconsideration," in Bracey, *American Slavery*, 131.

32. Nat Turner's statement while a prisoner, in Aptheker, ed., *A Documentary History of the Negro People in the United States*, 120, 123–24.

33. Starobin, *Industrial Slavery*, 115.

34. Aptheker, *American Negro Slave Revolts*, 163.

35. Aptheker, "Additional Data on American Maroons," 452.

36. Dumond, *Antislavery*, 368.

9. Indians as Slaves, as Friends and Enemies of Black Slaves, and as Slaveholders: 1529–1877

1. Lauber, *Indian Slavery*, 311.

2. Olexer, *Enslavement of the American Indian*, 172.

3. Morris, *Southern Slavery*, 19.

4. Catterall, *Judicial Cases concerning Slavery* 4:455.

5. Phillips, *American Negro Slavery*, 102.

6. Gallay, *Indian Slave Trade*, 49.

7. Olexer, *Enslavement of the American Indian*, 199–200.

8. Cruz and Berson, "On Teaching the American Melting Pot?" available online, URL: http://www.oah.org/pubs/magazine/family/cruz-berson.html.

9. Morgan, *American Slavery, American Freedom*, 328–29.

10. Olexer, *Enslavement of the American Indian*, 116.

11. Lauber, *Indian Slavery*, 121.

12. Olexer, *Enslavement of the American Indian*, 109.

13. Ibid., 195–96.

14. Gallay, *Indian Slave Trade*, 295.

15. Blassingame, ed., *Slave Testimony*, 698.

16. Ibid., 238.

17. Webre, "The Problem of Indian Slavery," 119.

18. Katz, *Black Indians*, 133.

19. Porter, *Negro on the American Frontier*, 13.

20. Kalm, *Travels*, quoted in Porter, *Negro on the American Frontier*, 13.

21. Porter, *Negro on the American Frontier*, 34–35.

22. Johnston, *Race Relations*, 285.

23. Porter, *Negro on the American Frontier*, 70–71.

24. Strother, *Underground Railroad in Connecticut*, 19.

25. Porter, *Negro on the American Frontier*, 377–78.

26. Blassingame, ed., *Slave Testimony*, 321–23.

27. Porter, *Negro on the American Frontier*, 172.

28. Ibid., 105.

29. Miller, *Dictionary of Afro-American Slavery* 1:435.

30. Perdue, *Slavery and Cherokee Society*, 40.

31. Ibid., 78.

32. Katz, *Black Indians*, 138–39.

33. Quoted in Abel, *Slaveholding Indian as Secessionist*, 41–42. By 1859, Cooper was relieved that these missionaries had become advocates of slavery.

34. Perdue, "'Mixed Blood' Indians," 7.

35. Oakes, *Ruling Race*, 45ff.

36. Genovese, *From Rebellion to Revolution*, 74.

37. Wickett, *Contested Territory*, 7.

38 Katz, *Black Indians*, 139–40.

39. Botkin, ed., *Lay My Burden Down*, 130.

40. Perdue, *Slavery and Cherokee Society*, 81.

41. Porter, *Negro on the American Frontier*, 117.

42. Abel, *Slaveholding Indians* 3:14. Among the Cherokee, for instance, even black tribal members held slaves. King, *Great South*, available online, URL: http://docsouth.unc.edu/nc/king/king.html.

43. Ibid. 3:94.

44. Botkin, ed., *Lay My Burden Down*, 130–35 passim.

45. Abel, *American Indian under Reconstruction*, 192.
46. Abel, *Slaveholding Indians* 3:282–83n528.
47. Ibid. 3:323, 332.
48. Wickett, *Contested Territory*, 11. By the time black rights were ensured, the Cherokee were becoming extinct.
49. Information about Cow Tom is drawn from Walton-Raji, "Cow Tom," available online, URL:http://www.african-nativeamerican.com/cow/ton.htm.

10. The Argument over Slavery: 1637–1877

1. Levy, *First Emancipator*, passim; Simeone, "Robert Carter III" available online, URL: http://www.npr.org/programs/wate/features/2001/antijefferson/010901.antijefferson.html.
2. Coffin, *Reminiscences*, xi.
3. *New Travels in the United States of America*, quoted in Kates, "Abolition, Deportation, Integration," 38.
4. de Tocqueville, *Democracy in America*, 360.
5. Fisher, *Philadelphia Perspective*, 210–11.
6. Owens, *Property*, 3.
7. Bancroft, *Slave Trading*, 7.
8. Campbell, *Empire*, 3.
9. Buckmaster, *Let My People Go*, 64.
10. Oakes, *Ruling Race*, 134.
11. Bontemps, ed., *Great Slave Narratives*, 323.
12. Locke, *Anti-Slavery*, 59–60.
13. Ibid., 172–73.
14. Redpath, *Roving Editor*, 96–97.
15. Williams, *History of the Negro Race*, 1:211–12.
16. Letter in the Anne Winchester Penniman collection.
17. Berwanger, *Frontier against Slavery*, 125–26.
18. Kraditor, *American Abolitionism*, 197.
19. Harding, *River*, 127.
20. Ibid., 139.
21. Ibid., 203.
22. Ibid., 152.
23. Quarles, *Negro in the American Revolution*, 38.
24. Ibid., 44.
25. Fisher, *Philadelphia Perspective*, 306–7.
26. Dumond, *Antislavery*, 206.
27. Williams, *History of the Negro Race* 1:432.
28. Blake, *Slavery and the Slave Trade*, 526.
29. Kraditor, *American Abolitionism*, 233n91.
30. Ibid., 233n95.
31. Blake, *Slavery and the Slave Trade*, 669.
32. Ibid., 678.
33. Ira Berlin, New Forum chat room, April 1999.

11. Black Soldiers in America's Wars: 1635–1877

1. Kay and Cary, *Slavery in North Carolina*, 60.
2. Wilson, *Black Phalanx*, 26; Williams, *History* 1:194–95.
3. Quarles, *Negro in the American Revolution*, 8.
4. Higginbotham, *In the Matter of Color*, 222.
5. Porter, *Negro on the American Frontier*, 158.
6. Quarles, *Negro in the American Revolution*, 12.
7. Ibid., 9.
8. Dumond, *Antislavery*, 111; and Quarles, *Negro in the American Revolution*, 52.
9. Quarles, *Negro in the American Revolution*, 86–88. See also Aptheker, "Negro in the Union Navy," 170. On the creation of American navies, see Richard Buel Jr., *In Irons*, chap. 4.
10. Quarles, *Negro in the American Revolution*, 95.
11. Ibid., 27–29.
12. Ball, *Slaves in the Family*, 229–30.
13. Walker, *Black Loyalists*, 8.
14. Ibid., 3–4.
15. *Revolution Remembered*, 26. Ironically, Grant's master was a Tory.
16. Wesley, *In Freedom's Footsteps*, 146.
17. Wilson, *Black Phalanx*, 80.
18. Ibid., 83.
19. Williams, *History* 2:23; and Wesley, *In Freedom's Footsteps*, 148.
20. Aptheker, "The Negro in the Union Navy," 171.
21. Wesley, *In Freedom's Footsteps*, 149–50.
22. Walker, *Black Loyalists*, 389.
23. Porter, *Negro on the American Frontier*, 223–62.
24. Wilson, *Black Phalanx*, 104.
25. Ibid., 112.
26. Herbert Aptheker estimates that some 500,000 slaves escaped or came into the Union lines during the war. McPherson, *Negro's Civil War*, 56.
27. Porter, *The Negro on the American Frontier*, 467; Cornish, *Sable Arm*, chap. 4.
28. Cornish, *Sable Arm*, 92.
29. Hollandsworth, *Louisiana Native Guards*, 13–14.
30. No one knows how many of these early black soldiers were contrabands. General Butler's claim that his black troops were all free avoided political problems, but Wilson, in *Black Phalanx*, 95, estimates that more than half were fugitives. In other cases a policy of "don't ask, don't tell" obscures the record. Cornish, *Sable Arm*, 66.
31. Quarles, *Negro in the Civil War*, 184–85.

32. Ibid., 186–88.

33. Ibid., 191.

34. Winks, *Blacks in Canada*, 152.

35. Harding, *River*, 249–50.

36. Quarles, *Negro in the Civil War*, 199.

37. We relied for these figures on the Web site of the Louisiana Endowment for the Humanities, which gives the total number of black officers as 111. Weidman, in "Preserving the Legacy of the United States Colored Troops," finds "at least 87." The PBS program "The Civil War and Emancipation" estimates 100.

38. Keith Wilson, *Campfires of Freedom*, passim.

39. McPherson, *Negro's Civil War*, 205.

40. Ibid., 335–36n7; and Cornish, *Sable Arm*, chap. 9.

41. See Urwin, *Black Flag over Dixie*, passim, and correspondence between Union and Confederate officers about the Fort Pillow Case, available online, URL: www.civilwarhome.com/forrestcorrespondence.htm.

42. Roca, "Presence and Precedents," 94–95, 105–7.

43. McPherson, *Negro's Civil War*, 160.

44. Quarles, *Negro in the Civil War*, 230–32.

45. Aptheker, "The Negro in the Union Navy," 188.

46. Berlin, *Freedom* 1:675.

47. Steve Fry, article on blacks in the Confederate army in the *Topeka Capital Journal*, September 27, 2001. Available online at URL: http://www.scvcamp-469-nbf.com/theblackconfederatesoldier.htm.

48. For information on the Louisiana Native Guards, see their Web site at http://www2.netdoor.com/~jgh/officers.html, and Quarles, *Negro in the Civil War*, 38.

49. Nelson, "Confederate Slave Impressment," 392–410.

50. Berlin, *Freedom* 1:664.

51. Quoted in Blackett, ed., *Thomas Morris Chester*, 249–50.

52. Berlin, *Freedom* 1:679.

53. A roster of African-American Medal of Honor recipients is available online at the Americans.net Web site, www.medalofhonor.com/AfricanAmericanCivilWar.htm. Christian A. Fleetwood, who won that medal, became disillusioned by the army's mistreatment of black soldiers and changed his mind about pursuing a military career. See Fleetwood, letter to former employer, June 8, 1865, available online, URL: http://www.historynet.com/cwti/bl_drones.

54. Shaffer, *After the Glory*, 21.

55. Foner, *Reconstruction*, 9.

56. Shaffer, *After the Glory*, 120, 122.

57. George Armstrong Custer, for instance, refused a lieutenant colonelcy in a black regiment. "The Buffalo Soldiers on the Western Frontier." The International Museum of the Horse. Available online. URL: http://www.imh.org/imh/buf/buf2.html.

58. Leckie and Leckie, *Buffalo Soldiers*, 18

59. The origin of the term *buffalo soldier* is obscure. It may have originated in the fierceness with which black soldiers fought, or possibly as a reference to a similarity Indians perceived between the black soldiers' hair and buffalo coats. Wickett, *Contested Territory*, 134.

60. Williams, "Seminole Indian Scouts," 1.

12. The End of Slavery: 1861–1877

1. Faust, *Mothers of Invention*, 30.

2. Quoted in Harding, *River*, 225.

3. Botkin, ed., *Lay My Burden Down*, 124.

4. Lincoln, *Collected Works*, 5:144–146.

5. Franklin, *Emancipation Proclamation*, 82.

6. Berlin, *Free at Last*, 349.

7. Livermore, *My Story of the War*, 350.

8. Johnson, *God Struck Me Dead*, 117.

9. Brown, *American Rebellion*, 144–45.

10. Coffin, *Reminiscences*, 355.

11. Ibid., 356–57.

12. Berlin, *Free at Last*, 189.

13. Raboteau, *Slave Religion*, 320.

14. Taylor, *Civil War Memoirs*, 52.

15. Haviland, *A Woman's Life-Work*, 360–61.

16. DuBois, "The Freedmen's Bureau," 356.

17. Messer-Kruse, Course Outline, History 101, University of Wisconsin–Madison, Week 15, available online. URL: http:www.freeuniv.com/mirror/h1o1w15.htm.

18. Grant, *Personal Memoirs*, 426.

19. "Letter from Chaplain James," *The Congregationalist* 15 (September 18, 1863): 149. Click, "History of the Roanoke Island Freedmen's Colony, available online, URL: http:www.coankoefreedmenscolony.com/jameslet.html.

20. DuBois, ed., *Economic Co-operation*, 35–36.

21. Townsell, "Slaves Found Refuge at Freedman's Village," available online, URL: http://www.demilitary.com/army/pentagram/archives/feb6/pt_e2698.html. Also National Park Service, "Emancipation at Arlington: Freedmen's Village, 1863," available online, URL: http://www/nps.gov/arho/tour/history/arlingtoninbetween3.html.

22. DuBois, ed., *Economic Co-operation*, 73.

23. Sherman, Field Order 15.

24. Russell Duncan, "Tunis Campbell," *New Georgia Encyclopedia*. Available online. URL: http://www.georgiaencyclopedia.org/nge/Article/jsp?path=/Religion/HistoricalFigures &id=h-2903.

25. Faust, *Mothers of Invention*, 32.

26. Myers, ed., *Children of Pride*, 939–40.

27. Jordan, *Tumult and Silence*, Document K, 324.

28. Information on black spies is drawn mainly from Rose, "The Civil War: Black American Contributions to Union Intelligence," available online, URL: http://www.cia.gov/cia/publications/dispatches/dispatch/html.

29. Garrone, "Civil War Spies: Good Intelligence Knows No Gender," American Forces Information News Articles, U.S. Department of Defense Web site, March 23, 2005. Available online. URL: http:www.defenselink.mil/news/Feb2001/n02272001_200102274.html.

30. Markle, *Spies and Spymasters*, 62.

31. Ibid., 60.

32. Botkin, ed., *Lay My Burden Down*, 238–39.

33. Ibid., 218.

34. Campbell, *Empire*, 238.

35. Confederate president Jefferson Davis, November 7, 1864, message to the Confederate Congress, quoted in Durden, *Gray and the Black*, 102–3.

36. Faust, *Mothers of Invention*, 73–74.

37. Ibid., 58.

38. Myers, ed., *Children of Pride*, 1267.

13. Reconstruction: 1865–1877

1. Naragon, "From Chattel to Citizen," in Temperley, ed., *After Slavery*, 96–97.

2. Schurz, *Report on the Condition of the South*, 1865, available online, URL: http://www.gutemberg.org/dirsletext05/cnsth10.txt.

3. Ibid.

4. In North Carolina, the Goldsboro *State* commented, "It is a sad fact for this worn-out and famished State, that of the thousands of men who came hither, invested their means, and attempted to make homes under Republican rule, to-day but few remain. At the loss of their all they have wandered away to seek a home where they can speak their sentiments and vote as they deem best, without subjection to insult, abuse and vilification. . . ." Quoted in Green, *Recollections of the Inhabitants*, 145, available online, URL: http://docsouth.unc.edu/southlit/green/green.html.

5. See Tunnell, *Edge of the Sword*, passim.

6. Morgan, *Yazoo; or, On the Picket Line of Freedom in the South*, 344.

7. Schurz, *Report on the Condition of the South*.

8. As Painter comments in *Exodusters*, 9, "In the very same way that whites interpreted Black hopes for land as insurrectionary, they misunderstood Black solidarity . . . as antiwhite militance."

9. Houzeau, *My Passage at the New Orleans* Tribune, 144–45.

10. Historian James Horton, quoted in Tolson, "The Complex Story of Slavery," 67. Ex-governor Zebulon Vance of North Carolina estimated the South's total losses at $5 billion. "The Duties of Defeat," 1866, available online, URL: http://docsouth.unc.ed/nc/vance/menu.html.

11. Schurz, *Report on the Condition of the South*.

12. Foner, *Reconstruction*, 177, 181. On July 18, 1865, the Philadelphia *Press* reported that President Johnson had told a black delegation, "The colored man and his master combined kept [the poor white] in slavery by depriving him of a fair participation in the labor and productions of the rich land of the country." Quoted in Foner, *Reconstruction*, 181.

13. Sherman, Field Order 15.

14. Schurz, *Report on the Condition of the South*.

15. African-American History, "The Black Codes of 1865," available online, URL: http://astroamhistory.about.com/library/weekly/aa121900.htm.

16. Ibid.

17. Foner, *Reconstruction*, 200.

18. Schurz, *Report on the Condition of the South*.

19. Foner, *Reconstruction*, 283ff.

20. Ibid., 355.

21. Ibid., 528.

22. Danielle Alexander, "Forty Acres and a Mule." Available online. URL: http://www.neh.gov/news/humanities/2004-01/reconstruction.html.

23. His efforts to annex Santo Domingo in the early 1870s reflected his hope for colonization of blacks there.

24. Richardson, *Christian Reconstruction*, 252–53.

25. Foner, *Reconstruction*, 567–69.

26. DuBois, *Black Reconstruction in America*, 30.

27. DuBois, "The Freedmen's Bureau," 7, available online, URL: eserver.org/history/freedmans-bureau.txt.

28. Miller, "The Freedmen's Bureau and Reconstruction," in Cimbala and Miller, eds., *The Freedmen's Bureau and Reconstruction*, xxi, xxix.

29. Quoted in DuBois, ed., *Economic Co-operation*, 40. The bureau's educational and bounty departments were

to continue to function until 1872. The nation repaid General Howard's long and devoted labors by court-martialing him in 1874, though in the end he was exonerated and his work commended.

30. DuBois, "The Freedmen's Bureau," passim.

31. Ibid., 9. See also Shaffer, *After the Glory*, passim.

32. Schurz, *Report on the Condition of the South.*

33. DuBois, "The Freedmen's Bureau," 9–10.

34. Houzeau, *My Passage at the New Orleans* Tribune, 104.

35. Cohen, *At Freedom's Edge*, 19.

36. Ibid., 16.

37. For a study of bureau problems with Virginia freed-women, see Farmer, "Because They Are Women," in Cimbala and Miller, eds., *The Freedmen's Bureau and Reconstruction*, 161–92.

38. Zipf, "Reconstructing 'Free Woman,'" *Journal of Women's History* 12, no. 1 (March 2000): 7, 8, available online, URL: http:iupjournals.org/jwh/jwh12-1.html.

39. Ibid., 2.

40. Ibid., 11–15.

41. Public Broadcasting System, "The American Experience: Reconstruction, the Second Civil War," available online, URL: http://www.pbs.org/wgbh/annex/reconstruction.

42. Foner, *Reconstruction*, 173.

43. Ibid., 408.

44. Washington, "The Freedmen's Savings and Trust Company," 2, available online. URL: http://www.archives.gov/publications/prologue/1997/summer/freedmens-savings-and.trust.html.

45. DuBois, *Black Reconstruction*, 599–600; James, "Blacks in Roosevelt, Long Island," available online, URL: http:rooseveltlongisland.org. "Guide to Tallahassee's African-American History," available online, URL: http://www.rileymuseum.org/tallyguide.htm.

46. Reginald Washington, "The Freedman's Savings and Trust Company."

47. Foner, *Reconstruction*, 531–32.

48. Washington, *Frederick Douglass*, 277, available online, URL: http://docsouth.unc.edu/nch/dong1906/dong1906.html.

49. Behrend, "Lily Ann Granderson," available online, URL: http://www.slaveryinamerica.org/narratives/bio_lily_ann_granderson.htm.

50. DuBois, *Black Reconstruction*, 638, 644. A clandestine school for free blacks was founded in Savannah, Georgia, in 1818 or 1819 by black Frenchman Julien Froumontaine.

51. Foner, *Reconstruction*, 97.

52. Butchart, "Freedmen's Education during Reconstruction," *New Georgia Encyclopedia*, available online, URL: http://www.georgiaencyclopedia.org/nge/Article.jsp?id=h-634.

53. DuBois, *Black Reconstruction*, 638.

54. Butchart and Rolleri, "Urban Schools for Rural Learners: Bringing the Northern Urban School to the Rural Black South," available online, URL: http://www.inrp.fr/she/ische/abstracts.2001/ButchertA.rtf.

55. Letter attached to Schurz, *Report on the Condition of the South.*

56. Miller, "The Freedmen's Bureau and Reconstruction," xxviii.

57. Butchart, "Freedmen's Education during Reconstruction," *New Georgia Encyclopedia.*

58. Foner, *Reconstruction*, 145.

59. "History of Atlanta Public Schools," available online, URL: http://www.atlanta.k12.gains/inside_aps/archives/apsmuseum/apshistory.

60. "Prudence Crandall," in *The Reader's Companion to American History*, available online. URL: http:college.hmco.com/history/readerscomp/rcah/html/ah_021600_crandallprud.htm.

61. James W. Hood, later North Carolina's assistant superintendent of education, quoted in Foner, *Reconstruction*, 322.

62. DuBois, ed., *Economic Co-operation*, 80, available online, URL: http://docsouth.unc.edu/church/dubois07/dubois.html.

63. Foner, *Reconstruction*, 367, 368.

64. DuBois, ed., *Economic Co-operation*, 79.

65. Foner, *Reconstruction*, 421–22.

66. Ibid., 366. The National Center for Educational Statistics shows that between 1870 and 1880 black illiteracy dropped from 79.9 to 70 percent.

67. DuBois, *Black Reconstruction*, 665.

68. Painter, *Exodusters*, 11.

69. Public Broadcasting System, "Africans in America: The First African Baptist Church in Savannah," available online, URL: http://www.pbs.org/wghb/aia/part2/2p30.html. Also entry for George Liele in Logan and Winston, eds., *Dictionary of American Negro Biography.*

70. "The African Methodist Episcopal Church: An Historical Note," available, URL: http://www.ame-church.org/amehist.html.

71. DuBois, ed., *Economic Co-operation*, 57.

72. Ibid., 25–26.

73. Ibid., 93, 98.

74. Ibid., 150.

75. Katz, *Eyewitness: The Negro in American History,* 293–94.

76. Foner, *Reconstruction,* 27–28.

77. "In occupied Virginia and North Carolina, a few freedmen were settled on abandoned land, and several hundred managed to lease farms in the Mississippi Valley. Often, however, these were merely tiny garden plots . . . , to which blacks' legal title would prove anything but secure." Ibid., 38.

78. For a study of Davis Bend, see Hermann, *The Pursuit of a Dream.* Jefferson Davis, who became president of the Confederacy, owned adjacent land, which Joseph Davis frequently managed.

79. Wormser, "Isaiah Montgomery," in "Jim Crow Stories," Educational Broadcasting Corporation Web site, available online, URL: http://www.pbs.org/wnet/jimcrow/stories_people_mont/html.

80. Cohen, *At Freedom's Edge,* 44.

81. Ibid., 91.

82. Painter, *Exodusters,* 83.

83. Statement by the Kansas Freedman's Association quoted in National Park Service, "Nicodemus," available online, URL: http//www.nps.gov/nico/.

84. Fleming, "'Pap' Singleton, The Moses of the Colored Exodus," *American Journal of Sociology* 15:61–82, available online, URL: http://docsouth.unc.edu/nch/fleming/menu.html. See also DuBois, ed., *Economic Co-operation,* 49. Eventually Pap Singleton, disillusioned by racial prejudice in Kansas, formed the United Transatlantic Society to encourage the founding of a separate black nation. "Black Towns: Kansas," available online, URL: http://www.soulofamerica.com/towns/Kstowns.html.

85. Painter, *Exodusters,* 148–49.

86. Cohen, *At Freedom's Edge,* 175.

87. DuBois, ed., *Economic Co-operation,* 54.

88. Ibid., 25–26.

Bibliography

Abel, Annie Heloise. *The American Indian as Slaveholder and Secessionist.* Lincoln: University of Nebraska Press, 1992 [1915].

————. *The Slaveholding Indians.* 3 vols. Cleveland, Ohio: A. H. Clark, 1915–25.

Achates. *Reflections Occasioned by the Late Disturbances in Charleston.* 1822. In *Slave Insurrections: Selected Documents,* 5–29. Westport, Conn.: Negro Universities Press, 1970 [1822, 1860].

Adams, John Quincy. *Memoirs.* Edited by Charles Francis Adams. 12 vols. Freeport, N.Y.: Books for Libraries Press, 1959 [1874–77].

Adelke, Tunde. *Without Regard to Race: The Other Martin Roblison Delany.* Jackson: University Press of Mississippi, 2003.

Affonso, King of Congo, to King of Portugal João III, October 18, 1526. Available online. URL: http://www.bbc.co.uk/worldservice/africa/features/storyofafrica/index_section9.shtml. Downloaded on September 25, 2004.

"The African Methodist Episcopal Church: An Historical Note," African Methodist Episcopal Church Web site. Available online. URL: http://www.ame-church.org/amehist.html. Downloaded on March 16, 2005.

African-American citizens of Calhoun, Georgia. Letter requesting protection from federal troops of the Third Military District. "Reconstruction: The Second Civil War," The American Experience, Public Broadcasting System Online. Available online. URL: http://www.pbs.org/wgbh/amex/reconstruction/activism/ps_calhoun.html. Downloaded on August 13, 2004.

African-American History. "The Black Codes of 1865." Available online. URL: http://afroamhistory.about.com/library/weekly/aa121900a.htm. Downloaded on February 22, 2005.

"Africans in America: The First African Baptist Church in Savannah." Public Broadcasting System. Available online. URL: http://www.pbs.org/wgbh/aia/part2/2p30.html. Downloaded on March 24, 2005.

Albert, Mrs. Victoria V. Rogers. *The House of Bondage; or, Charlotte Brooks and Other Slaves Original and Life-like, as They Appeared in Their Old Plantation and City Slave Life; Together with Pen-Pictures of the Peculiar Institution, with Sights and Insights into Their New Relations as Freedmen, Freemen, and Citizens.* New York: Hunt & Eaton, 1890. Available online. URL: http://docsouth.unc.edu/neh/albert/albert.html#albert119. Downloaded on August 31, 2004.

Alexander, Danielle. "Forty Acres and a Mule." Available online. URL: http://www.neh.gov/news/humanities/2004-01/reconstruction.html. Downloaded on March 15, 2006.

————. "The Negro in the Union Navy." *Journal of Negro History* 32 (1947): 171ff.

————. *"One Continual Cry": David Walker's Appeal to the Colored Citizens of the World (1829–1830).* New York: Humanities Press, 1965.

————, ed. *A Documentary History of the Negro People in the United States.* 2 vols. New York: Citadel, 1990 [1951].

Alford, Terry. *Prince among Slaves.* New York: Harcourt Brace Jovanovich, 1977.

"The American Experience: Jubilee Singers, Sacrifice and Glory." Available online. URL: http://www.pbs.organization. Downloaded on August 15, 2004.

"The American Experience: Reconstruction, the Second Civil War." Public Broadcasting System Online. Available online. URL: http://www.pbs.org/wgbh/amex/reconstruction/. Downloaded on August 13, 2004.

"The American Experience: Slavery and the Making of America." Public Broadcasting System Online. Available online. URL: http://www.pbs.org/wnet/slavery. Downloaded on February 17, 2005.

American Freedmen's Inquiry Commission. "Final Report to the Secretary of War." May 15, 1864. Available online. URL: http://www.civilwarhome.com/commissionreport.htm. Downloaded on July 30, 2004.

Ames, Mary. *From a New England Woman's Diary in Dixie in 1865.* Norwood, Mass.: Plimpton Press, 1906.

Andrews, Ethan Allen. *Slavery and the Domestic Slave Trade in the United States.* Freeport, N.Y.: Books for Libraries Press, 1971 [1836].

Andrews, William L., ed. *Sisters of the Spirit: Three Black Women's Autobiographies of the Nineteenth Century.* Bloomington: Indiana University Press, 1986.

Anstey, Roger T. *The Atlantic Slave Trade and British Abolition, 1760–1810.* Atlantic Highlands, N.J.: Humanities Press, 1975.

Aptheker, Herbert. "Additional Data on American Maroons." *Journal of Negro History* 32 (1947): 452–60.

———. *American Negro Slave Revolts.* New York: International, 1943.

———. "Maroons within the Present Limits of the United States." *American Journal of Negro History* 24 (1939): 167–84.

Bacon, Thomas. *Sermons Addressed to Masters and Servants, Published in the Year 1734.* Winchester, Va., 1813.

Bailey, Anne C. *African Voices of the Atlantic Slave Trade: Beyond the Silence and the Shame.* Boston: Beacon, 2004.

Baily, Marilyn. "From Cincinnati, Ohio to Wilberforce, Canada: A Note on Antebellum Colonization." *Journal of Negro History* 58, no. 4 (1973): 427–40.

Ball, Edward. *Slaves in the Family.* New York: Farrar, Straus & Giroux, 1998.

Ballenger, Seale. *Hell's Bells: A Tribute to the Spitfires, Bad Seeds, & Steel Magnolias of the New and Old South.* Berkeley, Calif.: Conari, 1997.

Bancroft, Frederic. *Slave Trading in the Old South.* New York: Frederick Ungar, 1931.

Baptist, Edward E., and Stephanie M. H. Camp, eds. *New Studies in the History of American Slavery.* Athens: University of Georgia Press, 2006.

Baquaqua, Mahommah Gardo, and Samuel Moore. *Biography of Mahommah G. Baquaqua, a Native of Zoogoo, in the Interior of Africa. (A Convert to Christianity,) With a Description of That Part of the World; Including the Manners and Customs of the Inhabitants. . . .* Printed for the author, Mahommah Gardo Baquaqua, by Geo. E. Pomeroy & Co., Tribune Office, (January 1, 1854). Available online. URL: http://docsouth.unc.edu/neh/baquaqua/baquaqua.html. Downloaded on January 10, 2005.

Bardolph, Richard. *The Civil Rights Record: Black Americans and the Law, 1849–1970.* New York: Thomas Y. Crow, 1970.

Bauer, Raymond A., and Alice H. Bauer. "Day to Day Resistance to Slavery." *Journal of Negro History* 27 (1942): 388–419.

Beale, Jane Howison. *The Journal of Jane Howison Beale of Fredericksburg, Virginia, 1850–1862.* Fredericksburg, Va.: Historic Fredericksburg Foundation, 1979.

Behrend, Justin. "Lily Ann Granderson." Slavery in America Web site. Available online. URL: http://www.slaveryinamerica.org/narratives/bio_lily_ann_granderson.htm. Downloaded on May 13, 2005.

Bell, Howard H. "Negro Nationalism: A Factor in Emigration Projects, 1858–1861." *Journal of Negro History* 28 (1962): 42–53.

Bell, Malcolm, Jr. *Major Butler's Legacy: Five Generations of a Slaveholding Family.* Athens: University of Georgia Press, 1987.

Bellamy, Donnie D. "The Legal Status of Black Georgians during the Colonial and Revolutionary Eras." *Journal of Negro History* 74 (1989): 1–4.

Berlin, Ira. "After Nat Turner: A Letter from the North." *Journal of Negro History* 55 (1970): 144–50.

———. "American Slavery in History and Memory and the Search for Social Justice." *Journal of American History* (March 2004): 1251ff.

———. *Generations of Captivity: A History of African-American Slaves.* Cambridge, Mass.: Belknap Press of Harvard University Press, 2003.

———. *Many Thousands Gone: The First Two Centuries of Slavery in North America.* Cambridge, Mass.: Harvard University Press, 1998.

———. *Slaves without Masters: The Free Negro in the Antebellum South.* New York: Random House, 1974.

Berlin, Ira, et al., eds. *Free at Last: A Documentary History of Slavery, Freedom, and the Civil War.* New York: New Press, 1992.

———, eds. *Freedom: A Documentary History of Emancipation, 1861–67,* Series 1 and 2. New York: Cambridge University Press, 1985.

Berlin, Ira, Joseph P. Reidy, and Leslie S. Rowland, eds. *The Black Military Experience.* New York: Cambridge University Press, 1983.

Berwanger, Eugene. *The Frontier against Slavery: Western Anti-Negro Prejudice and the Slavery Extension Controversy.* Urbana: University of Illinois Press, 1967.

Betts, Robert B. *In Search of York: The Slave Who Went to the Pacific with Lewis and Clark.* Boulder: Colorado Associated University Press, 1985.

Beverly, Robert. *The History of Virginia in Four Parts.* 2nd ed. London: Printed for B. and S. Tooke, 1722.

Bibb, Henry. *Narrative of the Life and Adventures of Henry Bibb.* In *Puttin' on Ole Massa,* edited by Gilbert Osofsky, 106–203. New York: Harper & Row, 1969.

Billington, Monroe Lee, and Roger D. Hardaway. *African Americans on the Western Frontier.* Boulder: University Press of Colorado, 1998.

Black, Frederick R. "Benjamin Drew's Refugee and the Black Family." *Journal of Negro History* 57 (1972): 284–89.

Blackett, R. J. M. *Building an Antislavery Wall: Black Americans in the Atlantic Abolitionist Movement, 1830–1860.* Baton Rouge: Louisiana State University Press, 1983.

———, ed. *Thomas Morris Chester, Black Civil War Correspondent.* Baton Rouge, La.: Da Capo, 1989.

"Black Towns: Kansas." Soul of America Web site. Available online. URL: http://www.soulofamerica.com/towns/kstowns.html. Downloaded on September 23, 2004.

Blair, Norvel. *Book for the People! To Be Read by All Voters, Black and White, with Thrilling Events of the Life of Norvel Blair, of Grundy County, State of Illinois. Written and Published by Him, and with the Money He Earned by His Own Labor, and Is Sent Out with the Sincere Hope That If Carefully Read, It Will Tend to Put a Stop to Northern Bull-Dozing and Will Give to All a Free Ballot, without Fear, Favor or Affection and Respect.* Joliet,

Ill.: Joliet Daily Record, 1880. Available online. URL: http://docsouth.unc.edu/neh/blair/blair.html. Downloaded on August 25, 2004.

Blake, W. O. *The History of Slavery and the Slave Trade.* Columbus, Ohio: J. H. Miller, 1858.

Blane, William N. *An Excursion through the United States and Canada during the Years 1822–1823.* New York: Negro University Press, 1969 [1824].

Blassingame, John W. "The Planter on the Couch: Earle Thorpe and the Psychodynamics of Slavery." *Journal of Negro History* 60 (1975), 320–31.

———. *The Slave Community: Plantation Life in the Antebellum South.* New York: Oxford University Press, 1972.

———, ed. *Slave Testimony: Two Centuries of Letters, Speeches, Interviews, and Autobiographies.* Baton Rouge: Louisiana State University Press, 1977.

Blight, David W. "America: Made and Unmade by Slavery," *The Chronicle of Higher Education,* February 4, 2005, B15–16.

———. *Race and Reunion: The Civil War in American Memory.* Cambridge, Mass.: Harvard University Press, 2001.

Blue, Frederick J. *No Taint of Compromise: Crusaders in Antislavery Politics.* Baton Rouge: Louisiana State University Press, 2005.

Bogin, Ruth. "Sarah Parker Remond: Black Abolitionist from Salem." In *Black Women in American History,* edited by Darlene Clark Hine. Vol. 1, 135–66. Brooklyn, N.Y.: Carlson, 1990.

Bontemps, Arna. *Five Black Lives.* Middletown, Conn.: Wesleyan University Press, 1971.

———. *Great Slave Narratives.* Boston: Beacon, 1969.

Botkin, B. A., ed. *Lay My Burden Down: A Folk History of Slavery.* Chicago: University of Chicago Press, 1945.

Boxer, Charles R. *The Golden Age of Brazil, 1695–1750.* Berkeley: University of California Press, 1962.

———. *The Portuguese Seaborne Empire, 1415–1825.* New York: Knopf, 1969.

Bracey, John, August Meirer, and Elliott Rudwick, eds. *American Slavery: The Question of Resistance.* Belmont, Calif.: Wadsworth, 1971.

Bradford, Sarah H. *Harriet Tubman: The Moses of Her People,* 2nd ed. New York: Corinth, 1994 [1886].

Britannica Online Editors. "Griffing, Josephine Sophia White." Women in American History. *Encyclopedia Britannica.* Available online. URL: http://search.eb.com/women/articles/Griffing_Josephine_Sophia_White.html. Downloaded on October 6, 2004.

Brown, William Wells. *Narrative of William W. Brown, A Fugitive Slave.* In *Four Fugitive Slave Narratives,* edited by Robin W. Winks et al. Reading, Mass.: Addison Wesley, 1969.

———. *The Negro in the American Rebellion: His Heroism and His Fidelity.* New York: Citadel, 1971 [1867].

Bruce, Dickson D., Jr. *Archibald Grimke: Portrait of a Black Independent.* Baton Rouge: Louisiana State University Press, 1993.

Bruce, H. C. *The New Man: Twenty-Nine Years a Slave; Twenty-Nine Years a Free Man: Recollections of H. C. Bruce.* York, Penn.: P. Anstadt, 1895. Available online. URL: http://docsouth.unc.edu/bruce/bruce.html. Downloaded on August 21, 2004.

Bryan, Mary Norcott. *A Grandmother's Recollections of Dixie.* New Bern, N.C.: Owen G. Dunn, 1912. Available online. URL: http://docsouth.unc.edu/bryan/menu.html. Downloaded on August 20, 2004.

Buchanan, Thomas C. *Black Life on the Mississippi: Slaves, Free Blacks, and the Western Steamboat World.* Chapel Hill: University of North Carolina Press, 2004.

Buckingham, J. S. *The Slave States of America.* 2 vols. New York, 1968 [1842].

Buckmaster, Henrietta. *Let My People Go: The Story of the Underground Railroad and the Growth of the Abolition Movement.* Columbia: University of South Carolina Press, 1992 [1941].

Buel, Richard. *In Irons: Britain's Naval Supremacy and the American Revolutionary Economy.* New Haven, Conn.: Yale University Press, 1998.

Burchard, Peter. *One Gallant Rush: Robert Gould Shaw and His Brave Black Regiment.* New York: St. Martin's, 1965.

Burin, Eric. *Slavery and the Peculiar Solution: A History of the American Colonization Society.* Gainesville: University Press of Florida, 2005.

Butchart, Ronald E. "Freedmen's Education during Reconstruction," *New Georgia Encyclopedia.* Available online. URL: http://www.georgiaencyclopedia.org/nge/Article.jsp?id=h-634. Downloaded on January 27, 2005.

Butchart, Ronald E., and Amy Rolleri. "Urban Schools for Rural Learners: Bringing the Northern Urban School to the Rural Black South." Abstract. 2001 International Standing Conference for the History of Education. Available online. URL: http://www.inrp.fr/she/ische/abstracts2001/ButchartA.rtf. Downloaded on January 27, 2005.

Calhoun, John C. "Remarks on the States Rights Resolutions in Regard to Abolition," U.S. Senate, January 10, 1838. Available online. URL: http://www.founding.com/library/lbody.cfm?id=338&parent=65. Downloaded on March 15, 2006.

Camp, Stephanie M. H. *Closer to Freedom: Enslaved Women and Everyday Resistance in the Plantation South.* Durham: University of North Carolina Press, 2004.

Campbell, Randolph B. *An Empire for Slavery: The Peculiar Institution in Texas, 1821–1865.* Baton Rouge: Louisiana State University Press, 1989.

Campbell, Stanley W. *The Slave Catchers: Enforcement of the Fugitive Slave Law, 1850–1860.* New York: W. W. Norton, 1972 [1968].

Canot, Theodore. *Adventures of an African Slaver.* New York: Dover, 1969 [1854].

Carretta, Vincent. *Equiano, the African: Biography of a Self-Made Man.* Athens: University of Georgia Press, 2005.

Carroll, John M., ed. *The Black Military Experience in the American Midwest.* New York: Liveright, 1971.

Carroll, Joseph Cephas. *Slave Insurrections in the United States, 1800–1865.* New York: New American Library, 1938.

Cassell, Frank A. "Slaves of the Chesapeake Bay Area and the War of 1812." *Journal of Negro History* 57 (1972): 144–55.

Castel, Albert. "Civil War Kansas and the Negro." *Journal of Negro History* 51 (1966): 125–38.

———. *The Presidency of Andrew Johnson.* Lawrence: University Press of Kansas, 1979.

Caswall, Henry. "The Western World Revisited, 1854." *Journal of Negro History* 2 (1917): 184–85.

Catterall, Helen T., ed. *Judicial Cases concerning American Slavery and the Negro.* 5 vols. New York: Octagon, 1968.

Ceasar, Samson. *Letters to David S. Haselden and Henry F. Westfal, 1834–35.* University of Virginia Library Special Collections, Accession #10595. Available online. URL: http://etext.lib.virginia.edu/subjects/liberia/samson.html. Downloaded on August 27, 2004.

Chesnut, Mary. *Mary Chesnut's Civil War.* Edited by C. Vann Woodward. New Haven, Conn.: Yale University Press, 1981.

———. *The Private Mary Chesnut: The Unpublished Civil War Diaries.* Edited by C. Vann Woodward and Elisabeth Muhlenfeld. New York: Oxford University Press, 1984.

Chicago Tribune, early 1870s, quoted on Public Broadcasting System, "The American Experience: Reconstruction." Available online. URL: http://www.pbs. orgwgbh/amex/reconstruction/players/vb_nast_tr_rm.html. Downloaded on August 16, 2004.

Child, Lydia Maria. *An Appeal in Favor of That Class of Americans Called Africans.* New York: Arno and the *New York Times,* 1968 [1836].

———. *The Freedmen's Book.* New York: Arno and the *New York Times,* 1968 [1865].

Cimbala, Paul A. *The Freedmen's Bureau: Reconstructing the American South after the Civil War.* Melbourne, Fla.: Krieger, 2005.

———. *Under the Guardianship of the Nation: The Freedmen's Bureau and the Reconstruction of Georgia, 1865–1870.* Athens: University of Georgia Press, 1997.

Cimbala, Paul A., and Randall M. Miller, eds. *The Freedmen's Bureau and Reconstruction.* New York: Fordham University Press, 1999.

"The Civil War and Emancipation." Part 4 of "Africans in America." Public Broadcasting System program. Available online. URL: http://www.pbs.org/wgbh/aia/part4/4p2967.html. Downloaded on May 27, 2005.

Clayton, Ralph. *Cash for Blood: The Baltimore to New Orleans Domestic Slave Trade.* New York: Heritage, 2002.

Click, Patricia C. "History of The Roanoke Island Freedmen's Colony." Available online. URL: http://www.roanokefreedmenscolony.com/jameslet.html. Downloaded on March 17, 2005.

Clinton, Catherine. "Caught in the Web of the Big House: Women and Slavery." In *The Web of Southern Relations: Women, Family and Education,* edited by Walter J. Fraser Jr., R. Frank Saunders Jr., and Jon L. Wakelyn, 19–34. Athens: University of Georgia Press, 1985.

———. *Harriet Tubman: The Road to Freedom.* New York: Little, Brown, 2004.

———. *The Plantation Mistress: Woman's World in the Old South.* New York: Pantheon, 1982.

Cobb, Thomas R. R. *An Inquiry into the Law of Negro Slavery in the United States of America to Which Is Prefixed an Historical Sketch of Slavery.* New York: Negro University Press, 1968 [1858].

Cockrell, Thomas D., and Michael B. Ballard. *Chickasaw, A Mississippi Scout for the Union: The Civil War Memoir of Levi B. Narron.* Baton Rouge: Louisiana State University Press, 2005.

Coffin, Joshua. "An Account of Some of the Principal Slave Insurrections . . . during the Last Two Centuries." In *Slave Insurrections, Selected Documents,* 3–25. Westport, Conn.: Negro Universities Press, 1970 [1822, 1860].

Coffin, Levi. *Reminiscences of Levi Coffin: The Reputed President of the Underground Railroad.* Edited by Ben Richmond. Richmond, Ind.: Friends United Press, 1991 [1876].

Cohen, William. *At Freedom's Edge: Black Mobility and the Southern White Quest for Racial Control, 1861–1915.* Baton Rouge: Lousiana State University Press, 1991.

Cole, Johnetta. "Militant Black Women in Early United States History." In *Black Women in American History*, edited by Darlene Clark Hine. Vol. 1, 261–67. Brooklyn, N.Y.: Carlson, 1990.

"Complicity: How Connecticut Chained Itself to Slavery." Special issue of *Northeast Magazine, Hartford Courant*, September 4, 2005.

Connor, Sam. "Cleburne and the Unthinkable." *Civil War Times* (February 1998): 45–47.

Conway, Moncure D. *Autobiography: Memories and Experiences.* 2 vols. Boston: Houghton, Mifflin, 1904.

Cornish, Dudley T. *The Sable Arm: Black Troops in the Union Army, 1861–1865.* Lawrence: University Press of Kansas, 1987.

Correspondence between Union and Confederate officers about the Fort Pillow Case. Shotgun's Home of the American Civil War. Available online. URL: http://www.civilwarhome.com/forrestcorrespondence.htm. Downloaded on January 18, 2005.

Cott, Nancy F., ed. *Roots of Bitterness: Documents of the Social History of American Women.* New York: Dutton, 1972.

Coughtry, Jay. *The Notorious Triangle: Rhode Island and the African Slave Trade, 1700–1807.* Philadelphia: Temple University Press, 1981.

Cox, Jacob D. *Sherman's Hood's Tennessee Campaign and the March to the Sea. Carolina Campaigns of 1865.* New York: DaCapo, 1994 (1882).

Craft, William, and Ellen Craft. *Running a Thousand Miles for Freedom; or, The Escape of William and Ellen Craft from Slavery, 1860.* In *Great Slave Narratives*, edited by Arna Bontemps, 269ff. Boston: Beacon, 1969.

Crow, Jeffrey J., and Larry E. Tise, eds. *The Southern Experience in the American Revolution.* Chapel Hill: University of North Carolina Press, 1978.

Crowe, Eyre. *With Thackeray in America.* New York: Scribner, 1893.

Cruz, Barbara C., and Michael J. Berson. "On Teaching the American Melting Pot? Miscegenation Laws in the United States," *OAH Magazine of History* 15, no. 4 (Summer 2001). Available online. URL: http://www.oah.org/pubs/magazine/family/cruz-berson.html. Downloaded on April 5, 2005.

Culpepper, Marilyn M. *Trials and Triumphs: Women of the American Civil War.* East Lansing: Michigan State University Press, 1991.

Cunningham, Constance A. "Sin of Omission: Black Women in 19th Century American History." In *Black Women in American History*, edited by Darlene Clark Hine, Vol. 1. 275–86. Brooklyn, N.Y.: Carlson, 1990.

Curtin, Phillip. *The Atlantic Slave Trade: A Census.* Madison: University of Wisconsin Press, 1969.

———, ed. *Africa Remembered: Narratives by West Africans from the Era of the Slave Trade.* Madison: University of Wisconsin Press, 1967.

Dann, John C., ed. *The Revolution Remembered: Eyewitness Accounts of the War for Independence.* Chicago: University of Chicago Press, 1980.

Davidson, Basil. *The African Slave Trade: Precolonial.* Boston: Little, Brown, 1961.

Davies, K. G. *The Royal African Company.* New York: Octagon, 1975.

Davis, Charles T., and Henry Louis Gates Jr., eds. *The Slave's Narrative*. New York: Oxford University Press, 1985.

Davis, Edwin Adams. *Plantation Life in the Florida Parishes of Louisiana, 1836–1846, as Reflected in the Diary of Bennet H. Barrow*. New York: Columbia University Press, 1943.

Davis, Ronald L. F. "Creating Jim Crow." On The History of Jim Crow Web site. Available online. URL: http://www.jimcrowhistory.org/history/creating.htm. Downloaded on July 13, 2004.

———. "Racial Etiquette: The Racial Customs and Rules of Racial Behavior in Jim Crow America." On The History of Jim Crow Web site. Available online. URL: http://www.jimcrowhistory.org/history/resisting2.htm. Downloaded on July 13, 2004.

———. "Resisting Jim Crow." On The History of Jim Crow Web site. Available online. URL: http://www.jimcrowhistory.org/history/resisting2.htm. Downloaded on July 13, 2004.

———. "Surviving Jim Crow." On The History of Jim Crow Web site. Available online. URL: http://www.jimcrowhistory.org/history/resisting2.htm. Downloaded on July 13, 2004.

Davis, Stanford L. "Seminole-Negro Indian Scouts." Buffalo Soldier Network. Available online. URL: http://www.buffalosoldier.net/SeminoleNegroIndianScouts.htm. Downloaded on May 18, 2005.

Davis, Thomas J. "The New York Slave Conspiracy of 1741 as Black Protest." *Journal of Negro History* 56 (1971): 17–30.

Dean, Eddie. "The Black and the Gray," *Washington City Paper*, July 17, 1998. Available online. URL: http://www.37thtexas.org/html/Wshcitypaper.html. Downloaded on May 5, 2005.

de Crevecoeur, J. Hector St. John. *Letters from an American Farmer and Sketches of Eighteenth-Century America*. Edited by Albert E. Stone. New York: Penguin, 1981.

de Graef, Lawrence B. "Race, Sex, and Region: Black Women in the American West, 1850–1920." In *Black Women in American History*, edited by Darlene Clark Hine. Vol. 1. 303–13. Brooklyn, N.Y.: Carlson, 1990.

Delany, Martin. "A Model Contract." *Reconstruction: The Second Civil War*, American Experience, Public Broadcasting System Online. Available online. URL: http://www.pbs.org/wgbh/amex/reconstruction/sharecrop/ps_delany2.html. Downloaded on August 16, 2004.

De Miranda, Francisco. *The New Democracy in America: Travels of Francisco de Miranda in the United States, 1783–84*. Translated by Judson P. Wood. Edited by John S. Ezell. Norman: University of Oklahoma Press, 1963.

Dessens, Nathalie. *Myths of the Plantation Society: Slavery in the American South and the West Indies*. Gainesville: University Press of Florida, 2003.

Deutrich, Mabel E., and Virginia C. Purdy, eds. *Clio Was a Woman: Studies in the History of American Women*. Washington, D.C.: Howard University Press, 1980.

Diedrich, Maria, Henry Louis Gates Jr., and Carl Pedersen, eds. *Black Imagination and the Middle Passage*. New York: Oxford University Press, 1999.

Diene, Doudou, ed. *From Chains to Bonds: The Slave Trade Revisited*. New York: Berghahn Books, 2001.

Diouf, Sylviane A., ed. *Fighting the Slave Trade: West African Strategies*. Athens: Ohio University Press, 2003.

Donnan, Elizabeth, ed. *Documents Illustrative of the History of the Slave Trade to America.* 2 vols. New York: Octagon, 1965 [1930].

Douglass, Frederick. *Narrative of the Life of Frederick Douglass, an American Slave.* New York: Signet, 1968 [1845].

———. "Reconstruction," *The Atlantic Monthly* 18, no. 100 (December 1866): 761–65. Available online. URL: http://afroamhistory.about.com/library/bldouglass_reconstruction.htm. Downloaded on July 23, 2004.

Dow, George Francis. *Slave Ships and Slaving.* Salem, Mass.: Marine Research Society, 1927.

Drake, Frederick C., ed. "Secret History of the Slave Trade to Cuba Written by an American Naval Officer, Robert Wilson Schufeldt." *Journal of American History* 55 (1970): 220–30.

Drew, Benjamin, ed. *A North-Side View of Slavery: The Refugee; or, the Narratives of Fugitive Slaves in Canada.* Boston: John P. Jewett, 1856.

DuBois, W. E. B. *Black Reconstruction in America, 1860–1880.* New York: Free Press, 1992 [1935].

———. "The Freedmen's Bureau," *The Atlantic Monthly* 87, no. 521 (March 1901): 354–65. Available online. URL: http://eserver.org/history/freedmens-bureau.txt. Downloaded on July 23, 2004.

———. *The Negro.* 1915. Available online. URL: http://www.sacred-texts.com/afr/dbn/. Downloaded on December 12, 2005.

———. *The Souls of Black Folk.* Available online. URL: http://xroads.virginia.edu/~hyper/DUBOIS/ch10.html. Downloaded on March 15, 2006.

———, ed. *Economic Co-operation among Negro Americans. Report of a Study Made by Atlanta University, . . . , Together with the Proceedings of the 12th Conference for the Study of the Negro Problems, Held at Atlanta University, on Tuesday, May the 28th, 1907.* Atlanta, Ga.: Atlanta University Press, 1907. Available online. URL: http://docsouth.unc.edu/church/dubois07/dubois.html. Downloaded on August 23, 2004.

———. *The Negro Common School; Report of a Social Study Made under the Direction of Atlanta University.* . . . Atlanta, Ga.: Atlanta University Press, 1901.

Dumond, Dwight Lowell. *Antislavery: The Crusade for Freedom to America.* New York: W. W. Norton, 1966 [1961].

Duncan, Russell. *Freedom's Shore: Tunis Campbell and the Georgia Freedmen.* Athens: University of Georgia Press, 1986.

———. "Tunis Campbell," *New Georgia Encyclopedia.* Available online. URL: http://www.georgiaencyclopedia.org/nge/Arti cle.jsp?path=/Religion/HistoricalFigures&id=h-2903. Downloaded on January 28, 2005.

Durden, Robert F. *The Gray and the Black: The Confederate Debate on Emancipation.* Baton Rouge: Louisiana State University Press, 1972.

Easterby, J. H., ed. *The South Carolina Rice Plantation as Revealed in the Papers of Robert F. W. Allston.* Chicago: University of Chicago Press, 1945.

Eastman, H. A. "List of Murders in Counties of Maury and Marshall, Tenn., from July 1, 1867, to July 1, 1868." Freedmen's Bureau Online. Available online. URL: http://www.freedmensbureau.com/tennessee/outrages/columbia.htm. Downloaded on July 30, 2004.

Eaton, John. *Report of the General Superintendent of Freedmen, Department of the Tennessee and State of Arkansas for 1864.* Memphis, Tenn., 1865.

Edelstein, Tilden G. *Strange Enthusiasm: A Life of Thomas Wentworth Higginson.* New Haven, Conn.: Yale University Press, 1968.

Edmonia Lewis biography. Women in History. Lakewood Public Library. Available online. URL: http://www.lkwdpl.org/wihohio/lewi-edm.htm. Downloaded on January 19, 2005.

Egypt, Ophelia S., J. Masuoka, and Charles S. Johnson, eds. *The Unwritten History of Slavery: Autobiographical Accounts of Negro Ex-Slaves.* Nashville, Tenn.: Fisk University Press, 1945.

Ehrlich, Walter. "The Origins of the Dred Scott Case." *Journal of Negro History* 59 (1974): 132–42.

Elkins, Stanley M. *Slavery: A Problem in American Institutional and Intellectual Life.* 2nd ed. Chicago: University of Chicago Press, 1968 [1959].

Elliott, E. N., ed. *Cotton Is King and Pro-slavery Arguments.* New York: Johnson Reprint, 1968 [1860].

Eltis, David, David Richardson, and Stephen D. Behrendt. "Patterns in the Transatlantic Slave Trade, 1662–1867." In *Black Imagination and the Middle Passage,* edited by Maria Diedrich, Henry Louis Gates Jr., and Carl Pedersen, 21–32. New York: Oxford University Press, 1999.

"Emancipation at Arlington: Freedmen's Village, 1863." National Park Service. Available online. URL: http://www.nps.gov/arho/tour/history/arlingtoninbetween3.html. Downloaded on February 22, 2005.

Encyclopedia of North American Indians: Native American History, Culture, and Life from Paleo-Indians to the Present, ed. Frederick E. Hoxie. New York: Houghton Mifflin, 1986.

Eppes, Susan Bradford. *The Negro of the Old South: A Bit of Period History.* Macon, Ga.: J. W. Burke, 1941.

Fabre, Genevieve. "The Slave Ship Dance." In *Black Imagination and the Middle Passage,* edited by Maria Diedrich, Henry Louis Gates Jr., and Carl Pedersen, 33–46. New York: Oxford University Press, 1999.

Falck, Susan. "Jim Crow Legislation Overview." On The History of Jim Crow Web site. Available online. URL: http://www.jimcrowhistory.org/history/resisting2.htm. Downloaded on July 13, 2004.

Farmer, Mary J. "'Because They Are Women': Gender and the Virginia Freedmen's Bureau's 'War on Dependency.'" In *The Freedmen's Bureau and Reconstruction,* edited by Paul A. Cimbala and Randall M. Miller, 161–92. New York: Fordham University Press, 1999.

Farr, James. "A Slow Boat to Nowhere: The Multi-racial Crews of the American Whaling Industry." *Journal of Negro History* 68 (1983): 159–70.

Faust, Drew Gilpin. *Mothers of Invention: Women of the Slaveholding South in the American Civil War.* Chapel Hill: University of North Carolina Press, 1996.

———, ed. *Ideology of Slavery: Proslavery Thought in the Antebellum South, 1830–1860.* Baton Rouge: University of Louisiana Press, 1981.

Fehrenbacher, Don E. *Slavery, Law, and Politics: The Dred Scott Case in Historical Perspective.* New York: Oxford University Press, 1981.

"Final Report to the South Carolina House, 1874," *Journal of the House of Representatives of the State of South Carolina, for the Regular Session of 1874–1874* (Columbia, 1874): 549–53. Available online. URL: http://www.pbs.org/wgbh/amex/reconstruction/schools/ps_report.html. Downloaded on August 12, 2004.

Finkelman, Paul. *Emancipation and Reconstruction.* Vol. 3. New York: Garland, 1992.

———. *The Law of Freedom and Bondage: A Casebook.* New York: Oceana, 1986.

———. *Slavery and the Law.* New York: Madison House, 1997.

————. *Slavery in the Courtroom: An Annotated Bibliography of American Cases.* Washington, D.C.: Library of Congress, 1985.

————, ed. *African Americans and the Law.* New York: Garland, 1992.

Fishel, L. H., and Benjamin Quarles, eds. *The Negro American: A Documentary History.* Glenview, Ill.: Scott, Foresman, 1967.

Fisher, Miles Mark. "Lott Cary, the Colonizing Missionary." *Journal of Negro History* 7, no. 4 (October 1922), 380–418. Available online. URL: http://docsouth. unc.edu/church/fisher/menu.html. Downloaded on July 21, 2004.

Fisher, Sidney George. *A Philadelphia Perspective: The Diary of Sidney George Fisher Covering the Years 1834–1871.* Edited by Nicholas B. Wainwright. Philadelphia: Historical Society of Pennsylvania, 1967.

Fitzgerald, Michael W. "Emancipation and Military Pacification: The Freedmen's Bureau and Social Control in Alabama." In *The Freedmen's Bureau and Reconstruction,* edited by Paul A. Cimbala and Randall M. Miller, 46–66. New York: Fordham University Press, 1999.

Fitzhugh, George. *Cannibals All! Or, Slaves without Masters.* Cambridge, Mass.: Harvard University Press, 1960 [1857].

Fleetwood, Christian A. Letter to former employer, June 8, 1865. *Civil War Times Illustrated* (December 1995). Available online. URL: http://www.historynet. com/cwti/bl_drones/. Downloaded on March 23, 2005.

Fleming, Walter L. "'Pap' Singleton, The Moses of the Colored Exodus." *American Journal of Sociology* 15 (July 1909): 61–82. Available online. URL: http://docsouth.unc.edu/neh/fleming/mcnu.html. Downloaded on February 21, 2005.

Fogel, Robert William. *Without Consent or Contract.* New York: W. W. Norton, 1989.

Fogel, Robert William, and Stanley L. Engerman. *Time on the Cross: The Economics of American Negro Slavery.* Boston: Little, Brown, 1974.

Follett, Richard. *The Sugar Masters: Planters and Slaves in Louisiana's Cane World, 1820–1860.* Baton Rouge: Louisiana State University, 1997.

Foner, Eric. *Forever Free: The Story of Emancipation and Reconstruction.* New York: Knopf, 2005.

————. *Freedom's Lawmakers: A Directory of Black Officeholders during Reconstruction.* New York: Oxford University Press, 1993.

————. "Impeachment 1868/1999." History Matters: The U.S. Survey Course on the Web, American Social History Project/Center for Media & Learning, CUNY, and the Center for History and New Media, George Mason University. Available online. URL: http://historymatters.gmu.edu/d/176. Downloaded on July 28, 2004.

————. *Reconstruction: America's Unfinished Revolution, 1863–1877.* New York: Harper & Row, 1989 [1988].

Foner, Philip S. *Business and Slavery: The New York Merchants and the Irrepressible Conflict.* Chapel Hill: University of North Carolina Press, 1941.

————, ed. *The Life and Writings of Frederick Douglass.* 5 vols. New York: International Publishers, 1950–75.

Forbes, Jack D. *Africans and Native Americans: The Language of Race and the Evolution of Red-Black Peoples.* 2nd ed. Urbana: University of Illinois Press, 1993.

Forret, Jeff. *Race Relations at the Margins: Slaves and Poor Whites in the Antebellum Southern Countryside.* Baton Rouge: Louisiana State University Press, 2006.

Forten, Charlotte. *The Journal of Charlotte Forten.* Edited by Ray A. Billington. New York: W. W. Norton, 1981 [1953].

————. "Life on the Sea Islands." *Atlantic Monthly* 13 (1864): 589–94.

Four Fugitive Slave Narratives. With an introduction by Robin W. Winks. Reading, Mass.: Addison-Wesley, 1969.

Fox, Early Lee. *The American Colonization Society, 1817–1840*. Baltimore: Johns Hopkins University Press, 1919.

Fox, Wells B. *What I Remember of the Great Rebellion*. Lansing, Mich.: Darius D. Thorp, 1892.

Fox-Genovese, Elizabeth. "Strategies and Forms of Resistance: Focus on Slave Women in the United States." In *Black Women in American History*, edited by Darlene Clark Hine. Vol. 2. 409–31. Brooklyn, N.Y.: Carlson, 1990.

————. *Within the Plantation Household: Black and White Women of the Old South*. Chapel Hill: University of North Carolina Press, 1988.

Fox-Genovese, Elizabeth, and Eugene D. Genovese. *The Mind of the Master Class: History and Faith in the Southern Slaveholders' Worldview*. New York: Cambridge University Press, 2005.

Franklin, John Hope. *The Emancipation Proclamation*. Garden City, N.Y.: Doubleday, 1963.

————. "The Enslavement of Free Negroes in North Carolina." *Journal of Negro History* 29 (1944): 401–28.

————. *From Slavery to Freedom: A History of American Negroes*. New York: Knopf, 1994 [1956].

————. *George Washington Williams: A Biography*. Durham, N.C.: Duke University Press, 1998 [1985].

Franklin, John Hope, and Loren Schweninger. *In Search of the Promised Land: A Black Family and the Old South*. New York: Oxford University Press, 2005.

Fraser, Walter J., Jr., R. Frank Saunders Jr., and Jon L. Wakelyn, eds. *The Web of Southern Social Relations: Women, Family, & Education*. Athens: University of Georgia Press, 1985.

Freedom: A Documentary History of Emancipation. Freedom and Southern Society Project, University of Maryland. Available online. URL: http://www.history.umd.edu/Freedmen/home.html. Downloaded on July 29, 2004.

Freeman, Gerene L. "What about My 40 Acres & a Mule?" Yale-New Haven Teachers Institute Curriculum Unit 94.04.01. Available online. URL: http://www.yale.edu/ynhti/curriculum/units/1994/4/944.04.01.x.html#c. Downloaded on February 22, 2005.

Fry, Steve. Untitled article on black Confederate soldiers. *Topeka Capital Journal*, September 27, 2001. Available online. URL: http://www.scvcamp469-nbf-com/theblackconfederatesoldier.htm. Downloaded on March 19, 2006.

Gallay, Alan. *The Indian Slave Trade: The Rise of the English Empire in the American South, 1670–1717*. New Haven, Conn.: Yale University Press, 2002.

Garamone, Jim. "Civil War Spies: Good Intell Knows No Gender." American Forces Information News Articles U.S. Department of Defense Web site. March 23, 2005. Available online. URL: http://www.defenselink.mil/news/Feb2001/n02272001_200102274.html. Downloaded on March 23, 2005.

Garrett, Raneo B. *Famous First Facts about Negroes*. New York: Arno, 1972.

Garrison, William Lloyd. *The Letters of William Lloyd Garrison*. 6 vols. Edited by Walter M. Merrill and Louis Ruchames. Cambridge, Mass.: Harvard University Press, 1971–81.

Gemery, Henry A., and Jan S. Hogendorn, eds. *The Uncommon Market: Essays in the Economic History of the Atlantic Slave Trade.* New York: Academic Press, 1979.

Genovese, Eugene D. *From Rebellion to Revolution: Afro-American Slave Revolts in the Making of the Modern World.* Baton Rouge: Louisiana State University Press, 1979.

———. *Roll, Jordan, Roll: The World the Slaves Made.* New York: Vintage Books, 1974.

Gerteis, Louis S. *From Contraband to Freedman: Federal Policy toward Southern Blacks.* Westport, Conn.: Greenwood, 1973.

Gilbert, Olive. *Narrative of Sojourner Truth, A Northern Slave, Emancipated from Bodily Servitude by the State of New York in 1828, Including a Book of Life.* Edited by Frances Titus. Salem, N.H.: Ayer, 1987 [1878].

Gilder Lehrman Center for the Study of Slavery, Resistance, and Abolition. Bibliography of Online Documents. Available online. URL: http://www.yale.edu/glc/archive/. Downloaded on March 22, 2005.

Glaeser, Edward L. "The Political Economy of Hatred," Discussion Paper #170, Harvard Institute of Economic Research, Working Paper, August 16, 2002. Available online. URL: http://papers.nber.org/papers/w9171. Downloaded on October 5, 2004.

Glatthaar, Joseph T. *Forged in Battle: The Civil War Alliance of Black Soldiers and White Officers.* New York: Free Press, 1990.

Godson, Martha Graham. "Medical-Botanical Contribution of African Slave Women to American Medicine." In *Black Women in American History,* edited by Darlene Clark Hine. Vol. 2. 473–84. Brooklyn, N.Y.: Carlson, 1990.

Goodell, William. *The American Slave Code in Theory and Practice.* New York: Negro Universities Press, 1968 [1853].

Goodman, Paul. *Of One Blood: Abolitionism and the Origins of Racial Equality.* Berkeley: University of California Press, 1998.

Gould, Virginia Meacham. *Chained to the Rock of Adversity: To Be Free, Black, and Female in the Old South.* Athens: University of Georgia Press, 1998.

Grant, Anne. *Memoirs of an American Lady, with Sketches of the Manners and Customs in America as They Existed Previous to the Revolution.* London: Printed for Longman, Hurst, Rees, and Orme, 1808.

Grant, John N. "Black Immigrants into Nova Scotia, 1776–1815." *Journal of Negro History* 58 (1973): 253–70.

Grant, Ulysses S. *Personal Memoirs of U.S. Grant.* 2 vols. New York: C. L. Webster, 1885–86.

Greeley, Horace. Letter to Josephine Griffing, September 7, 1870. Women and Social Movements in the United States, 1600–2000, Center for the Historical Study of Women and Gender, Binghamton University. Available online. URL: http://womhist.binghamton.edu/teacher/DBQaid6.htm. Downloaded on October 6, 2004.

Green, John Patterson. *Recollections of the Inhabitants, Localities, Superstitions, and KuKlux Outrages of the Carolinas by a "Carpet-Bagger" Who Was Born and Lived There,* 1880. Available online. URL: http://docsouth.unc.edu/southlit/green/green.html. Downloaded on August 26, 2004.

Greenberg, Kenneth S., ed. *Nat Turner: A Slave Rebellion in History and Memory.* New York: Oxford University Press, 2003.

Gregory, Chester W. "Black Women in Pre-Federal America." In *Clio Was a Woman: Studies in the History of American Women,* edited by Mabel E. Deutrich and Virginia C. Purdy, 57–72. Washington, D.C.: Howard University Press, 1980.

Grimes, William. *Life of William Grimes, the Runaway Slave.* 1855. In *Five Black Lives,* edited by Arna Bontemps. 59–128. Middletown, Conn.: Wesleyan University Press, 1971.

Grimké, Angelina. "An Appeal to the Christian Women of the South." 1836. In *The Feminist Papers,* edited by Alice S. Rossi, 296–304. Boston: Northeastern University Press, 1988.

"Guide to Tallahassee's African American Heritage," John Gilmore Riley Center/ Museum of African-American History & Culture Web site. Available online. URL: http://www.rileymuseum.org/tallyguide.htm. Downloaded on May 13, 2005.

Gutman, Herbert. *The Black Family in Slavery and Freedom, 1750–1925.* New York: Vintage Books, 1976.

Gwaltney, William. "Footprints along the Border: Story of the Seminole-Negro Indian Scouts." Available online. URL: http://www.coax.net/people/lwf/FT-PRINTS.HTM. Downloaded on May 23, 2005.

Hadden, Sally E. *Slave Patrols: Law and Violence in Virginia and the Carolinas.* Cambridge, Mass.: Harvard University Press, 2001.

Hahn, Steven. *A Nation under Our Feet: Black Political Struggles in the Rural South from Slavery to the Great Migration.* Cambridge, Mass.: Harvard University Press, 2003.

Hakluyt, Richard. *Hakluyt's Voyages; Principal Navigations, Voyages, Traffiques, and Discoveries of the English Nation.* New York: Viking, 1965 [1903–5].

Halliburton, R., Jr. *Red over Black: Black Slavery among the Cherokee Indians.* Westport, Conn.: Greenwood, 1977.

Hamilton, Cynthia S. "Dislocation, Violence, and the Language of Sentiment." In *Black Imagination and the Middle Passage,* edited by Maria Diedrich, Henry Louis Gates Jr., and Carl Pedersen. New York: Oxford University Press, 1999.

Hamilton, J. "An Account of the Late Intended Insurrection among a Portion of the Blacks of This City, Charleston, S.C." In *Slave Insurrections: Selected Documents,* 103–16. Westport, Conn.: Negro Universities Press, 1970 [1822, 1860].

Hamilton, Jeff. *My Master: The Inside Story of Sam Houston and His Times.* Edited by Lenoir Hunt. Dallas, Tex.: State House Press, 1992 [1940].

Harding, Vincent. *There Is a River: The Black Struggle for Freedom in America.* New York: Harcourt Brace, 1981.

Harper, Cecil, Jr. "Freedmen's Bureau." *The Handbook of Texas Online.* Available online. URL: http://www.tsha.utexas.edu/handbook/online. Downloaded on July 29, 2004.

Harper, Ida Husted. *The Life and Works of Susan B. Anthony.* 3 vols. Indianapolis: Hollenbeck, 1898.

Harper, William. "Harper on Slavery." In *Cotton Is King and Pro-slavery Arguments,* edited by E. N. Elliot. New York: Johnson Reprint, 1968 [1860].

Harris, Sheldon H. "An American's Impressions of Sierra Leone in 1811." *Journal of Negro History* 47 (1962): 35–41.

Hartgrove, W. B. "The Story of Maria Louise Moore and Fannie M. Richards." *Journal of Negro History* 1 (1916): 23–33.

Haven, R. "John Brown and Heman Humphrey: An Unpublished Letter." *Journal of Negro History* 52 (1967): 220–24.

Haviland, Laura S. *A Woman's Life-Work: Labors and Experiences of Laura S. Haviland.* New York: Arno, 1969 [1889].

Hawks, Esther Hill. *A Woman Doctor's Civil War: Esther Hill Hawks' Diary.* Edited by Gerald Schwartz. Columbia: University of South Carolina Press, 1984.

Haygood, Atticus G. *Our Brother in Black: His Freedom and His Future.* New York: Phillips & Hunt, 1881. Available online. URL: http://docsouth.unc.edu/church/haygood/menu.html. Downloaded on August 31, 2004.

Henson, Josiah. *Life of Josiah Henson, Formerly a Slave, Now an Inhabitant of Canada, as Narrated by Himself.* In *Four Fugitive Slave Narratives,* 3–75. Reading, Mass.: Addison-Wesley, 1969 [1849].

Hermann, Janet Sharp. *Pursuit of a Dream.* New York: Vintage, 1983 [1981].

Higginbotham, A. Leon, Jr. *In the Matter of Color: Race and the American Legal Process: The Colonial Period.* New York: Oxford University Press, 1978.

Higginson, Thomas Wentworth. *Army Life in a Black Regiment.* Williamstown, Mass.: Corner House, 1971 [1870].

Highgate, Edmonia. Letter to M. E. Strieby, December 17, 1866. Papers of the American Missionary Association, Box 58, American Missionary Association Archives, Amistad Research Center, Tulane University, New Orleans, Louisiana.

Hine, Darlene Clark, ed. *Black Women in American History.* 4 vols. Brooklyn, N.Y.: Carlson, 1990.

Hine, Darlene Clark, and Kathleen Thompson. *A Shining Thread of Hope: The History of Black Women in America.* New York: Broadway Books, 1997.

"History of Atlanta Public Schools." Atlanta Public Schools Archives & Museum. Available online. URL: http://www.atlanta.k12.ga.us/inside_aps/archives/apsmuseum/apshistory/. Downloaded on August 24, 2004.

The History of Jim Crow. Available online. URL: http://www.jimcrowhistory.org/history/resisting2.htm. Downloaded on July 13, 2004.

Hodes, Martha. "Miscegenation." Reader's Companion to Women's History. Houghton-Mifflin College Division Web site. Available online. URL: http://college.hmco.com/history/readerscomp/women/html/wh_023000_miscegenatio.htm. Downloaded on April 7, 2006.

———. *White Women, Black Men: Illicit Sex in the Nineteenth-Century South.* New Haven, Conn.: Yale University Press, 1997.

———, ed. *Sex, Love, Race: Crossing Boundaries in North American History.* New York: New York University Press, 1999.

Holden, W. W. *Memoirs of W. W. Holden.* The John Lawson Monographs of the Trinity College Historical Society, Durham, N.C., vol. 11. Durham, N.C.: Seeman Printery, 1911. Available online. URL: http://docsouth.unc.edu/holden/holden.html. Downloaded on August 26, 2004.

Holley, Sallie. *A Life for Liberty: Anti-Slavery and Other Letters of Sallie Holley.* Edited by John White Chadwick. New York: G. P. Putnam's Sons, 1899.

Holmes, Jack D. L. "The Abortive Slave Revolt at Pointe Coupe, Louisiana, 1795." *Louisiana History* 11 (1970): 341–62.

Horton, James Oliver, and Lois E. Horton. *Slavery and the Making of America.* New York: Oxford University Press, 2004.

Horton, Paul. "Submitting to the 'Shadow of Slavery': The Secession Crisis and Civil War in Alabama's Lawrence County." *Civil War History* 44 (1988): 130ff.

Houghton, W. R., and M. B. Houghton. *Two Boys in the Civil War and After.* Montgomery, Ala.: Paragon Press, 1912. Available online. URL: http://docsouth.unc.edu/houghton/houghton.html. Downloaded on August 19, 2004.

Houzeau, Jean-Charles. *My Passage at the* New Orleans Tribune: *A Memoir of the Civil War Era.* Edited by David C. Rankin. Translated by Gerard F. Denault. Baton Rouge: Lousiana State University Press, 2001.

Howard, Jennifer. "Unraveling the Narrative." *Chronicle of Higher Education,* September 9, 2005, A11ff.

Howe, M. A. De Wolfe, ed. *Home Letters of General Sherman.* New York: C. Scribner's Sons, 1909.

Howe, Samuel Gridley. *Report to the Freedmen's Inquiry Committee: The Refugees from Slavery in Canada West.* New York: Arno, 1969 [1864].

Hudson, Charles M., ed. *Red, White, and Black: Symposium on Indians in the Old South.* Athens: University of Georgia Press, 1971.

Hunter, Tera W. *To 'Joy My Freedom: Southern Black Women's Lives and Labors after the Civil War.* Cambridge, Mass.: Harvard University Press, 1997.

Hymowitz, Carol, and Michaele Weissman. *A History of Women in America.* New York: Bantam, 1978.

Isaacson, Walter. *Benjamin Franklin: An American Life.* New York: Simon & Schuster, 2003.

Jackson, Mattie J. *The Story of Mattie J. Jackson; Her Parentage—Experience of Eighteen Years in Slavery—Incidents during the War—Her Escape from Slavery. A True Story, Written and Arranged by Dr. L. S. Thompson, as Given by Mattie.* Lawrence, Kans.: Sentinel Office, 1866. Available online. URL: http://docsouth.unc.edu/jacksonm/jackson.html. Downloaded on August 31, 2004.

Jacobs, Harriet. *Incidents in the Life of a Slave Girl.* Edited by Lydia Maria Child. Introduction by Valerie Smith. New York: Oxford University Press, 1988 [1861].

James, Horace. "Letter to the Public," June 27, 1863, Letters Received, Department of North Carolina, Record Group 393, Pt. 1, Series 3238, Box 2, National Archives. Available online. URL: http://www.roanokefreedmenscolony.com/james27.pdf. Downloaded on July 31, 2004.

James, Marquita L. "Blacks in Roosevelt, Long Island," African American Media Network Web site. Available online. URL: RooseveltLongIsland.org. Downloaded on May 13, 2005.

Jefferson, Thomas. *The Portable Thomas Jefferson.* Edited by Merrill D. Peterson. New York: Penguin, 1975.

Johnson, Charles S., ed. *God Struck Me Dead: Religious Conversion Experiences and Autobiographies of Negro Ex-Slaves.* Philadelphia: United Church Press, 1969 [1945].

Johnson, Michael P. "Runaway Slaves and the Slave Communities in South Carolina, 1799 to 1830." *William and Mary Quarterly* 38 (1981): 418–41.

———. "Smothered Slave Infants: Were Slave Mothers at Fault?" *Journal of Southern History* 47 (1981): 493–520.

Johnson, Michael P., and James L. Roark. *Black Masters: A Free Family of Color in the Old South.* New York: W. W. Norton, 1984.

Johnson, Walter. *Soul by Soul: Life Inside the Antebellum Slave Market.* Cambridge, Mass.: Harvard University Press, 1999.

Johnston, James H. *Race Relations in Virginia and Miscegenation in the South, 1776–1860.* Amherst: University of Massachusetts Press, 1970.

Jones, Charles C. *A Catechism of Scripture, Doctrine and Practice for Families and Sabbath Schools. Designed Also for the Oral Instruction of Colored Persons.* 3rd ed. Savannah, Ga.: Thomas Purse, 1844 [1837].

———. *The Religious Instruction of the Negroes in the United States.* Savannah, Ga.: Thomas Purse, 1842.

Jones, George Fenwick. "The Black Hessians: Negroes Recruited by the Hessians in South Carolina and Other Colonies." *South Carolina Historical Magazine* 83 (1982).

Jones, Howard. *Mutiny on the Amistad.* New York: Oxford University Press, 1987.

Jones, Jacqueline. *Labor of Love, Labor of Sorrow: Black Women, Work, and the Family from Slavery to the Present.* New York: Basic Books, 1985.

Jones, Thomas. *The Experience of Thomas Jones, Who Was a Slave for Forty-Three Years.* Boston: H. B. Skinner, 1850.

Jordan, Erwin L., Jr. *Black Confederates and Afro-Yankees in Civil War Virginia.* Charlottesville: University Press of Virginia, 1995.

Jordan, Winthrop D. *Tumult and Silence at Second Creek: An Inquiry into a Civil War Slave Conspiracy.* Baton Rouge: Louisiana State University Press, 1993.

———. *White over Black: American Attitudes toward the Negro, 1550–1812.* Chapel Hill: University of North Carolina Press, 1968.

Josephy, Alvin M. *The Civil War in the American West.* New York: Vintage Books, 1993.

Karcher, Carolyn K. *The First Woman in the Republic.* Durham, N.C.: Duke University Press, 1994.

Kates, Don B., Jr. "Abolition, Deportation, Integration: Attitudes toward Slavery in the Early Republic." *Journal of Negro History* 53 (1968): 33–47.

Katz, William Loren. *Black Indians.* New York: Atheneum, 1986.

———. *Eyewitness: The Negro in American History.* New York: Pitman, 1971.

Kay, Marvin L. Michael, and Lorin Lee Cary. *Slavery in North Carolina, 1748–1775.* Chapel Hill: University of North Carolina Press, 1995.

Keckley, Elizabeth. *Behind the Scenes: Thirty Years a Slave, and Four Years in the White House.* New York: Beaufort Books, 1968 [1868].

Kemble, Frances Anne. *Further Records.* New York: Henry Holt, 1891.

———. *Journal of a Residence on a Georgian Plantation in 1838–1839.* Edited by John A. Scott. New York: Alfred A. Knopf, 1961.

King, Edward. *The Great South: A Record of Journeys in Louisiana, Texas, the Indian Territory, Missouri, Arkansas, Mississippi, Alabama, Georgia, Florida, South Carolina, North Carolina, Kentucky, Tennessee, Virginia, West Virginia, and Maryland.* Hartford, Conn.: American Publishing Company, 1875. Available online. URL: http://docsouth.unc.edu/nc/king/king.html. Downloaded on August 25, 2004.

Klein, Herbert S. *The Middle Passage: Comparative Studies in the Atlantic Slave Trade.* Princeton, N.J.: Princeton University Press, 1978.

Klein, Martin, and Paul E. Lovejoy. "Slavery in West Africa." In *The Uncommon Market: Essays in the Economic History of the Atlantic Slave Trade,* edited by Henry A. Gemery and Jan S. Hogendorn, 181–212. New York: Academic Press, 1979.

"Knights of the White Camellia." The Handbook of Texas Online, Texas State Historical Association, University of Texas at Austin. Available online. URL: http://www.tsha.utexas.edu/handbook/online/articles/view/KK/vek1.html. Downloaded on August 23, 2004.

Koger, Larry. *Black Slaveowners: Free Black Slave Masters in South Carolina, 1790–1860.* Columbia: University of South Carolina Press, 1994.

Kraditor, Aileen S. *Means and Ends in American Abolitionism: Garrison and His Critics on Strategy and Tactics, 1834–1850.* Chicago: Elephant Paperbacks, 1989 [1967].

Lakewood Public Library. Edmonia Lewis biography, Women in History. Available online. URL: http://www.lkwdpl.org/wihohio/lewi-edm.htm. Downloaded on January 19, 2005.

Lambert, Frank. "'I Saw the Book Talk': Slave Readings of the First Great Awakening." *Journal of Negro History* 77 (1992): 184–98.

Landon, Fred. "The Negro Migration to Canada after the Passing of the Fugitive Slave Act." *Journal of Negro History* 5 (1920): 22.

Lane, Lunsford. *Narrative of Lunsford Lane, Formerly of Raleigh, N.C., Embracing an Account of His Early Life, the Redemption by Purchase of Himself and Family from Slavery, and His Banishment from the Place of His Birth for the Crime of Wearing a Colored Skin. Published by Himself.* Boston: J. G. Torrey, Printer, 1842. Available online. URL: http://docsouth.unc.edu/lanelunsford/menu.html. Downloaded on March 21, 2006.

Langley, Harold D. "The Negro in the Navy and Merchant Service 1798–1860." *Journal of Negro History* 52 (1967): 273–86.

Lanning, Michael L. *The African-American Soldier.* Secaucus, N.J.: Carol, 1997.

Lanza, Michael L. "'One of the Most Appreciated Labors of the Bureau': The Freedmen's Bureau and the Southern Homestead Act." In *The Freedmen's Bureau and Reconstruction,* edited by Paul A. Cimbala and Randall M. Miller, 67–93. New York: Fordham University Press, 1999.

Lapasansky-Werner, Emma J., and Margaret Hope Bacon, eds. *Back to Africa: Benjamin Coates and the Colonization Movement in America, 1848–1880.* University Park: Penn State University Press, 2005.

Lapp, Rudolph M. "The Negro in Gold Rush California." *Journal of Negro History* 49 (1964): 81–98.

Lauber, Almon Wheeler. *Indian Slavery in Colonial Times within the Present Limits of the United States.* New York: Columbia University Press, 1913.

Leckie, William H., and Shirley Leckie. *The Buffalo Soldiers: A Narrative of the Black Cavalry in the West.* Rev. ed. Norman: University of Oklahoma Press, 2003.

Lede, Naomi. "The Stride toward Freedom: Juneteenth," *The Huntsville Item,* July 23, 2004, 1. Available online. URL: http://www.itemonline.com/articles/2004/06/30/opinion/opinion14.txt. Downloaded on July 23, 2004.

Leigh, Frances Butler. *Ten Years on a Georgia Plantation since the War.* New York: Negro Universities Press, 1969 [1883]. Available online. URL: http://docsouth.unc.edu/leigh/leigh.html. Downloaded on May 5, 2005.

Lepore, Jill. *The Name of War: King Philip's War and the Origins of American Identity.* New York: Knopf, 1998.

———. *New York Burning: Liberty, Slavery, and Conspiracy in Eighteenth-Century Manhattan.* New York: Knopf, 2005.

Lerner, Gerda. *The Grimké Sisters from South Carolina: Pioneers for Women's Rights and Abolition.* New York: Schocken, 1967.

———, ed. *Black Women in White America: A Documentary History.* New York: Vintage, 1973.

"Letters Largely Personal or Private." *Journal of Negro History* 11 (1926): 63–64.

Letters of Theodore Dwight Weld, Angelina Grimke Weld and Sarah Grimke, 1822–1844. Gloucester, Mass.: Peter Smith/American Historical Association, 1965.

Levine, Bruce. *Confederate Emancipation: Southern Plans to Free and Arm Slaves during the Civil War.* New York: Oxford University Press, 2005.

Levy, Andrew. *The First Emancipator: The Forgotten Story of Robert Carter, the Founding Father Who Freed His Slaves.* New York: Random House, 2005.

Lewis, Ronald L. *Coal, Iron, and Slaves: Industrial Slavery in Maryland and Virginia, 1715–1865.* Westport, Conn.: Greenwood, 1979.

———. "Slavery on Chesapeake Iron Plantations before the American Revolution." *Journal of Negro History* 59 (1974): 242–54.

Libby David J. *Slavery and Frontier Mississippi, 1720–1835.* Jackson: University Press of Mississippi, 2004.

Lincoln, Abraham. *The Collected Works of Abraham Lincoln,* edited by Roy P. Marion Dolores Pratt and Lloyd A. Dunlap. 9 vols. New Brunswick: Rutgers University Press, 1953–55.

Lind, Michael. *What Lincoln Believed: The Values and Convictions of America's Greatest President.* New York: Doubleday, 2005.

Littlefield, Daniel F. *Africans and Seminoles: From Removal to Emancipation.* Westport, Conn.: Greenwood, 1977.

———. *Rice and Slaves: Ethnicity and the Slave Trade in Colonial South Carolina.* Baton Rouge: Louisiana State University Press, 1981.

Litwak, Leon F. *Been in the Storm So Long: The Aftermath of Slavery.* New York: Knopf, 1979.

Livermore, Mary Ashton Rice. *My Story of the War: A Woman's Narrative of Four Years Personal Experience as Nurse in the Union Army, and in Relief Work at Home, in Hospitals, Camps, and at the Front during the War of Rebellion.* New York: DaCapo, 1995 [1887].

Locke, Mary S. *Anti-slavery in America, from the Introduction of African Slaves to the Prohibition of the Slave Trade.* New York: Johnson Reprints, 1968 [1901].

Logan, Raymond W., and Michael R. Winston, eds. *Dictionary of American Negro Biography.* New York: W. W. Norton, 1982.

Louisiana Negro Convention, 1879 (Selections). In *A Documentary History of the Negro People in the United States,* edited by Herbert Aptheker, 714. New York: Citadel, 1951. Available online. URL: http://www.yale.edu/glc/archive/1128.htm. Downloaded on July 13, 2004.

Lovejoy, Paul E. *Transformations in Slavery: A History of Slavery in Africa.* 2nd ed. New York: Cambridge University Press, 2000 (1983).

———, ed. *The Ideology of Slavery in Africa.* Beverly Hills, Calif.: Sage, 1981.

Lovejoy, Paul E., and Jan S. Hogendorn. "Slave Marketing in West Africa." In *The Uncommon Market: Essays in the Economic History of the Atlantic Slave Trade,* edited by Henry A. Gemery and Jan S. Hogendorn, 213–35. New York: Academic Press, 1979.

Lovett, Laura. "African and Cherokee by Choice." *American Indian Quarterly* 22 (Winter/Spring 1988): 205.

Lowe, William C. "Big Gun Bombardment of Port Royal." *America's Civil War* (January 2001). Available online. URL: http://www.thehistorynet.com/acw/blportroyal/index3.html. Downloaded on January 22, 2005.

Lundy, Benjamin. *The Life, Travels and Opinions of Benjamin Lundy.* Edited by Thomas Earle. New York: Negro Universities Press, 1969 [1847].

Maginnes, David R. "The Case of the Court House Rioters in the Rendition of the Fugitive Slave Anthony Burns, 1854." *Journal of Negro History* 56 (1971): 31–43.

Malcolmson, Scott. "The Great Democrat," *New York Times Book Review,* May 22, 2005, 22.

Mannix, Daniel Pratt. *Black Cargoes: A History of the Atlantic Slave Trade, 1518–1865*. New York: Viking, 1962.

Markle, Donald E. *Spies and Spymasters of the Civil War*. Rev. ed. New York: Hippocrene, 2004.

Mars, James. *Life of James Mars, a Slave, Born and Sold in Connecticut, Written by Himself*. Hartford, Conn.: Case, Lockwood, 1866.

Marston, B. W. Testimony in Coushatta, Louisiana, June 7, 1876. *Reconstruction: The Second Civil War*, Public Broadcasting System Online. Available online. URL: http://www.pbs.org/wgbh/amex/reconstruction/players/p2_09_tr_qry.html. Downloaded on August 16, 2004.

Martin, Jonathan D. *Divided Mastery: Slave Hiring in the American South*. Cambridge, Mass.: Harvard University Press, 2004.

Martin, W. "Report of the Franklin, Tennessee, Riot on July 6, 1867." *Records of the Assistant Commissioner of the State of Tennessee*. Freedmen's Bureau Online. Available online. URL: http://www.freedmensbureau.com/tennessee/outrages/franklinriot.htm. Downloaded on July 30, 2004.

[Martineau, Harriet.] *The Martyr Age of the United States of America*. New York: Arno, 1969 [1839].

———. *Society in America*. 3 vols. London: Saunders & Otley, 1837.

Massey, Mary E. *Refugee Life in the Confederacy*. Baton Rouge: Louisiana State University Press, 1964.

Maury, Ann. *Memoirs of a Huguenot Family*. New York: G. P. Putnam, 1907 [1872].

May, Samuel. *Some Recollections of Our Anti-slavery Conflict*. New York: Arno, 1968 [1869].

McCord, Louisa Susannah. "Uncle Tom's Cabin." *Southern Quarterly Review* 23 (1853): 81–120.

McCrady, Edward. *The History of South Carolina under the Proprietary Government, 1670–1719*. New York: Macmillan, 1897.

McCurry, Stephanie. *Masters of Small Worlds: Yeoman Households, Gender Relations, and the Political Culture in the Antebellum South Carolina Low Country*. New York: Oxford University Press, 1995.

McDonogh, John. "A Letter of John McDonogh on African Colonization." *African Repository* (February 19, 1843): 48–62.

McFeely, William S. *Frederick Douglass*. New York: W. W. Norton, 1991.

McLaurin, Melton A. *Celia: A Slave*. Athens: University of Georgia Press, 1991.

McLoughlin, William G. *The Cherokee Ghost Dance: Essays on the Southeastern Indians, 1789–1861*. Macon, Ga.: Mercer University Press, 1994.

———. *Tongue of Flame: The Life of Lydia Maria Child*. New York: Thomas Y. Crowell, 1965.

McPherson, James M. "Days of Wrath," *New York Times Book Review*, May 12, 2005, 14–17.

———. *For Cause and Comrades: Why Men Fought in the Civil War*. New York: Oxford University Press, 1997.

———. *Marching toward Freedom: Blacks in the Civil War*. New York: Facts On File, 1991.

———. *The Negro's Civil War: How American Blacks Felt and Acted during the War for the Union*. New York: Ballantine, 1991.

Merrell, James H. "'Our Bond of Peace': Patterns of Intercultural Exchange in the Carolina Piedmont, 1650–1750." In *Powhatan's Mantle: Indians in the Colonial*

Southwest, edited by Peter H. Wood, Gregory A. Wasselkov, and M. Thomas Hatley, 196–222. Lincoln: University of Nebraska Press, 1989.

Messer-Kruse, Timothy. Course Outline, History 101, University of Wisconsin–Madison, Week 15. Available online. URL: http://www.freeuniv.com/mirror/h101w15.htm. Downloaded on March 13, 2005.

Miles, Tiya. *Ties That Bind: The Story of an Afro-Cherokee Family in Slavery and Freedom.* Berkeley: University of California Press, 2005.

Miller, Edward A., Jr. *The Black Civil War Soldiers of Illinois: The Story of the Twenty-ninth U.S. Colored Infantry.* Columbia: University of South Carolina Press, 1998.

Miller, Joseph C. "Some Aspects of the Commercial Organization of Slaving at Luanda, Angola—1760–1830." In *The Uncommon Market: Essays in the Economic History of the Atlantic Slave Trade,* edited by Henry A. Gemery and Jan S. Hagedorn, 77–106. New York: Academic Press, 1979.

———. *Way of Death: Merchant Capitalism and the Angolan Slave Trade, 1730–1830.* Madison: University of Wisconsin Press, 1988.

Miller, Randall M. "The Freedmen's Bureau and Reconstruction: An Overview." In *The Freedmen's Bureau and Reconstruction,* edited by Paul A. Cimbala and Randall M. Miller, xiii–xxxiii. New York: Fordham University Press, 1999.

Miller, Randall M., and John David Smith, eds. *Dictionary of Afro-American Slavery.* Westport, Conn.: Greenwood, 1997.

Miller, William Lee. *Arguing about Slavery: John Quincy Adams and the Great Battle in the United States Congress.* New York: Vintage Books, 1998.

Mills, Cynthia, and Pamela H. Simpson. *Monuments to the Lost Cause.* Knoxville: University of Tennessee Press, 2003.

Minges, Patrick, ed. *Black Indian Slave Narratives.* Winston-Salem, N.C.: J. F. Blair, 2004.

Minutes of the Freedmen's Convention Held in the City of Raleigh on the 2nd, 3rd, 4th, and 5th of October, 1866. Raleigh, N.C.: Standard Book and Job Office, 1866.

Montgomery, Frank A. *Reminiscences of a Mississippian in Peace and War.* Cincinnati, Ohio: Robert Clarke, 1901. Available online. URL: http://docsouth.unc.edu/montgomery/montgom.html. Downloaded on August 18, 2004.

Moore, George H. *Notes on the History of Slavery in Massachusetts.* New York: Negro Universities Press, 1968.

Moore, Shirley Ann Wilson. "'We Feel the Want of Protection': The Politics of Law and Race in California, 1848–1878." In *Taming the Elephant: Politics, Government, and Law in Pioneer California,* edited by John F. Burns and Richard J. Orsi, 96–125. Berkeley: University of California Press, 2003.

Morgan, Albert T. *Yazoo; or, On the Picket Line of Freedom in the South.* Columbia: University of South Carolina Press, 2000 [1884].

Morgan, Edmund S. *American Slavery, American Freedom: The Ordeal of Colonial Virginia.* New York: W. W. Norton, 1975.

Morgan, Philip D. *Slave Counterpoint: Black Culture in the Eighteenth-Century Chesapeake and Lowcountry.* Chapel Hill: University of North Carolina Press, 1998.

Morgan, Sarah. *The Civil War Diary of Sarah Morgan.* Edited by Charles East. Athens: University of Georgia Press, 1991.

Morris, Thomas D. *Southern Slavery and the Law, 1619–1860.* Chapel Hill: University of North Carolina Press, 1996.

Morrison, Michael A. *Slavery and the American West: The Eclipse of Manifest Destiny and the Coming of the Civil War.* Chapel Hill: University of North Carolina Press, 1997.

Morrone, Francis E. "The Buffalo Soldiers." Leavey Foundation for Historic Preservation Web site. Available online. URL: http://www.ushist.com/buffalo-soldiers.htm. Downloaded on May 17, 2005.

Morse, Jedidiah. *A Report to the Secretary of War on Indian Affairs.* New Haven, Conn.: S. Converse, 1822.

Motley, Constance Baker. *Equal Justice under Law.* New York: Farrar, Straus & Giroux, 1998.

Mullin, Gerald W. *Flight and Rebellion: Slave Resistance in Eighteenth-Century Virginia.* New York: Oxford University Press, 1972.

Munford, Clarence J., and Michael Zeuske. "Black Slavery, Class Struggle, Fear and Revolution in St. Domingue and Cuba, 1785–1795." *Journal of Negro History* 73 (1988): 12–32.

Murray, Pauli. *Proud Shoes.* New York: Harper & Row, 1978.

Muskat, Beth Taylor. "Mobile's Black Militia: Major R. R. Mims and Gilmer's Rifles." *Alabama Review* (July 2004). Available online. URL: http://www.find-articles.com/p/articles/mi_qa3880/is_200407/ai_n9439245#. Downloaded on May 20, 2005.

Myers, Robert Manson, ed. *The Children of Pride: A True Story of Georgia and the Civil War.* New Haven, Conn.: Yale University Press, 1972.

Naragon, Michael. "From Chattel to Citizen." In *After Slavery: Emancipation and Its Discontents,* edited by Howard Temperley, 93–116. Portland, Ore.: Frank Cass, 2000.

Nash, Gary B., and Jean R. Soderlund. *Freedom by Degrees: Emancipation in Pennsylvania and Its Aftermath.* New York: Oxford University Press, 1991.

National Center for Education Statistics. "Percentage of Persons 14 Years Old and Over Illiterate (Unable to Read or Write in Any Language), by Race and Nativity." Available online. URL: http://nces.ed.gov/naal/historicaldata/illiteracy.asp. Downloaded on November 21, 2005.

"The Nation's Highest Military Award, the Medal of Honor." Americans.net Web site. Available online. URL: http://www.medalofhonor.com/AfricanAmericanCivilWar.htm. Downloaded on May 27, 2005.

"The Native Guards' Black Officers." Web site of the Louisiana Native Guards. Available online. URL: http://www2.netdoor.com/~jgh/officers.html. Downloaded on May 27, 2005.

Nelson, Bernard H. "Confederate Slave Impressment Legislation, 1861–1865." *Journal of Negro History* 31 (1946): 392–410.

Newman, Debra L. "Black Women in the Era of the American Revolution in Pennsylvania." *Journal of Negro History* 61 (1976): 276–89.

Nichols, Roger L. *Indians in the United States and Canada: A Comparative History.* Lincoln: University of Nebraska Press, 1998.

"Nicodemus." Available online. URL: http://www.nps.gov/nico/. Downloaded on February 21, 2005.

"Nicodemus, Kansas, A Black Pioneer Town." Legends of America Web site. Available online. URL: http://www.legendsofamerica.com/OZ-Nicodemus.html. Downloaded on July 13, 2004.

Noble, Jeanne. *Beautiful, Also, Are the Souls of My Black Sisters: A History of the Black Woman in America.* Englewood Cliffs, N.J.: Prentice Hall, 1978.

Noon, John A. *Law and Government of the Grand River Iroquois.* New York: Viking Fund, 1949.

North Carolina Black Soldiers to the Freedmen's Bureau Commissioner, May or June 1865. Freedom and Southern Society Project, *Freedom*. Available online. URL: http://www.history.umd.edu/Freedmen/roanoke.htm. Downloaded on July 29, 2004.

Oakes, James. *The Ruling Race: A History of American Slaveholders*. New York: Knopf, 1982.

Oates, Stephen B. *The Approaching Fury: Voices of the Storm, 1820–1861*. New York: HarperCollins, 1997.

———. *The Fires of Jubilee: Nat Turner's Fierce Rebellion*. New York: HarperCollins, 1975.

———. *To Purge This Land with Blood: A Biography of John Brown*. Amherst: University of Massachusetts Press, 1984.

Obitko, Mary Ellen. "Custodians of a House of Resistance: Black Women Respond to Slavery." In *Black Women in American History*, edited by Darlene Clark Hine. Vol. 3. 985–98. Brooklyn, N.Y.: Carlson, 1990.

O'Brien, Robert W., and Bernard E. Squires. "The Negro in the Northwest before the Civil War," *NHB* (June 1942): 195–97.

Official Records of the Union and Confederate Armies. Washington, D.C., 1880–1901.

Official Records of the Union and Confederate Navies. Washington, D.C., 1894–1927.

Olexer, Barbara. *The Enslavement of the American Indian*. Monroe, N.Y.: Library Research Associates, 1982.

Olmsted, Frederick Law. *The Cotton Kingdom: A Traveller's Observations on Cotton and Slavery in the American Slave States*. Edited by Arthur M. Schlesinger. New York: Alfred A. Knopf, 1966.

Osofsky, Gilbert, ed. *Puttin' on Ole Massa*. New York: Harper & Row, 1969.

Owens, Leslie Howard. *This Species of Property: Slave Life and Culture in the Old South*. New York: Oxford University Press, 1976.

Painter, Nell Irvin. *Exodusters: Black Migration to Kansas after Reconstruction*. New York: Alfred A. Knopf, 1977.

Parker, William. "The Freedman's Story, in Two Parts," *Atlantic Monthly* February 1866, 152–66; March 1866, 276–95. Available online. URL: http://docsouth.unc.edu/parker/menu.html. Downloaded on August 31, 2004.

Parkhurst, Jessie W. "The Role of the Black Mammy in the Plantation Household." *Journal of Negro History* 23 (1938): 349–69.

Parrish, Lydia. *Slave Songs of the Georgia Sea Islands*. Athens: University of Georgia Press, 1942.

Patrick, Jeffrey L., and Robert J. Willey, eds. *Fighting for Liberty and Right: The Civil War Diary of William Bluffton Miller, 1st Sergeant, Company K, 75th Indiana Volunteer Infantry*. Nashville: University of Tennessee Press, 2005.

Pearson, Henry G. *James S. Wadsworth of Genesco*. New York: Charles Scribner's Sons, 1913.

Pease, Jane H., and William H. Pease. *The Fugitive Slave Law and Anthony Burns: A Problem in Law Enforcement*. Philadelphia: J. B. Lippincott, 1975.

———. "Organized Negro Communities: A North American Experiment." *Journal of Negro History* 47 (1962): 19–34.

———. "Walker's Appeal Comes to Charleston: A Note and Documents." *Journal of Negro History* 59 (1965): 287–92.

Pennington, James W. C. *The Fugitive Blacksmith: or, Events in the History of James W. C. Pennington, Pastor of a Presbyterian Church, New York, Formerly a Slave in the State of Maryland.* 1849. In *Great Slave Narratives*, edited by Arna Bontemps, 193–268. Boston: Beacon, 1969.

"Percentage of Slave-Owning Families as a Fraction of Total Free Households." University of Virginia, Geospatial and Statistical Data Center, Historical Census Browser. Available online. URL: http://fisher.lib.virginia.edu/collections/ stats/histcensus/index.html. Downloaded on February 1, 2005.

Perdue, Theda. *"Mixed Blood" Indians: Racial Construction in the Early South.* Athens: University of Georgia Press, 2003.

———. "Slavery." *Encyclopedia of North American Indians: Native American History, Culture, and Life from Paleo-Indians to the Present,* edited by Frederick E. Hoxie, 596–98. New York: Houghton Mifflin, 1986.

———. "Slavery." *Encyclopedia of North American Indians.* Available online. URL: http://college.hmco.com/history/readerscomp/naind/html/na_036400_ slavery.htm. Downloaded on November 15, 2004.

———. *Slavery and the Evolution of Cherokee Society, 1540–1866.* Knoxville: University of Tennessee Press, 1979.

Peterson, Merrill D. *John Brown: The Legend Revisited.* Charlottesville: University of Virginia Press, 2005.

Pettit, Eber M. *Sketches in the History of the Underground Railroad.* Freeport, N.Y.: Books for Libraries Press, 1971 [1879].

Phillips, Ulrich B. *American Negro Slavery: A Survey of the Supply, Employment and Control of Negro Labor as Determined by the Plantation Regime.* Baton Rouge: Louisiana State University Press, 1969 [1918].

———. *Plantation and Frontier Documents, 1649–1863.* 2 vols. Cleveland, Ohio: Arthur H. Clarke, 1909.

Pickard, Kate E. R. *The Kidnapped and the Ransomed, Being the Personal Recollections of Peter Still and His Wife "Vina," after Forty Years of Slavery.* New York: Negro Universities Press, 1968 [1856].

Pierce, Edward L. "The Contrabands at Fortress Monroe," *Atlantic Monthly* November 1861, 626. Available online. URL: http://www.millikensbend.org/articles-docs/atlantic-monthly/contrabands/contrabands2.html. Downloaded on January 22, 2005.

———. "The Freedmen at Port Royal," *Atlantic Monthly* 12 (1863): 291–315. Available online. URL: http://cdl.library.cornell.edu/moa/browse.journals/atla. html. Downloaded on January 22, 2005.

———. *Memoir and Letters of Charles Sumner.* 2 vols. Boston: Roberts Brothers, 1877.

Pinckney, Thomas. "Reflections, Occasioned by the Late Disturbances in Charleston." In *Slave Insurrections: Selected Documents.* Westport, Conn.: Negro Universities Press, 1970 [1822, 1860].

Pope-Hennessy, James. *Sins of the Fathers: A Study of the Atlantic Slave Traders, 1441– 1807.* New York: Capricorn, 1969.

Porter, Dorothy B. "Sarah Parker Remond, Abolitionist and Physician." In *Black Women in American History,* edited by Darlene Clark Hine. Vol. 4. 1125–31. Brooklyn, N.Y.: Carlson, 1990.

Porter, Kenneth Wiggins. *The Negro on the American Frontier.* New York: Arno, 1971.

———. "Relations between Negroes and Indians within the Present Limits of the United States." *Journal of Negro History* 17 (1932): 287–367.

Price, Richard. *Maroon Societies: Rebel Slave Communities in the Americas.* New York: Anchor/Doubleday, 1973.

Putney, Martha S. "Black Merchant Seamen of Newport, 1803–1865: A Case Study in Foreign Commerce." *Journal of Negro History* 57 (1972): 156–68.

Quarles, Benjamin. *Black Abolitionists.* New York: DaCapo, 1991 [1969].

———. "Harriet Tubman's Unlikely Leadership." In *Black Women in American History,* edited by Darlene Clark Hine. Vol. 4. 1133–47. Brooklyn, N.Y.: Carlson, 1990.

———. *The Negro in the American Revolution.* New York: W. W. Norton, 1973.

———. *The Negro in the Civil War.* Boston: Little, Brown, 1969.

Rabinowitz, Howard N. *Race Relations in the Urban South, 1865–1890.* Urbana: University of Illinois Press, 1980.

Raboteau, Albert J. *Slave Religion: The "Invisible Institution" in the Antebellum South.* New York: Oxford University Press, 1978.

Rachleff, Peter. "Lynching and Racial Violence: Histories & Legacies: Report from a Conference." *ChickenBones: A Journal for Literary & Artistic African-American Themes.* Available online. URL: http://www.nathanielturner.com/lynchingandracialviolencepr.htm. Downloaded on April 26, 2005.

Rankin, John. *Letters on American Slavery.* New York: Arno, 1969 [1838].

Rawick, George. *The American Slave: A Composite Autobiography.* 19 vols. and supplements. Westport, Conn.: Greenwood, 1972.

Rawley, James A. *The Transatlantic Slave Trade: A History.* New York: W. W. Norton, 1981.

The Reader's Companion to American History. Available online. URL: http://college.hmco.com/history/readerscomp/rcah/html/ah_021600_crandallprud.htm. Downloaded on March 18, 2006.

Redford, Dorothy Spruill, with Michael D'Orso. *Somerset Homecoming: Recovering a Lost Heritage.* New York: Doubleday, 1988.

Redkey, Edwin S., ed. *A Grand Army of Black Men: Letters from African-American Soldiers in the Union Army, 1861–1865.* New York: Cambridge University Press, 1992.

Redpath, James. *The Roving Editor; or, Talks with Slaves in Southern States.* Edited by John R. McKivigan. University Park: Pennsylvania State University Press, 1996 [1859].

Reid, Whitelaw. *After the War: A Southern Tour, May 1, 1865–May 1, 1866.* London, England: Sampson Low, Son, & Marston, 1866. Available online. URL: http://www.hti.umich.edu/cgi/t/text/text-idx?c=moa;idno=AFJ8942.0001.001. Downloaded on March 15, 2006.

Reynolds, David S. *John Brown, Abolitionist: The Man Who Killed Slavery, Sparked the Civil War, and Seeded Civil Rights.* New York: Knopf, 2005.

Reynolds, Edward. *Stand the Storm: A History of the Atlantic Slave Trade.* New York: Allison & Busby, 1985.

Rice, Allan J. *Radical Narratives of the Black Atlantic.* New York: Continuum, 2003.

Richardson, Joe M. *Christian Reconstruction: The American Missionary Association and Southern Blacks, 1861–1890.* Athens: University of Georgia Press, 1986.

Ripley, C. Peter, ed. *The Black Abolitionist Papers.* 5 vols. Chapel Hill: University of North Carolina Press, 1987–1992.

"Robert Carter III of Nomini," *Marietta Times*, July 29, 1991. Available online. URL: http://www.coax.net/people/lwf/hb_rc.htm. Downloaded on May 10, 2005.

Robinson, Armstead. "Day of Jubilo: Civil War and the Demise of Slavery in the Mississippi Valley, 1861–1865." Ph.D. diss. University of Rochester, 1976.

Roca, Steven Louis. "Presence and Precedents: The USS *Red Rover* during the American Civil War, 1861–1865." *Civil War History* 44 (1998): 91–110.

Roethler, Michael Donald. *Negro Slavery among the Cherokee Indians, 1540–1866.* New York: Fordham University Press, 1964.

Rollin, Richard, ed. *Black Southerners in Gray: Essays on Afro-Americans in Confederate Armies.* Redondo Beach, Calif.: Rank & File, 1994.

Ronnick, Michele Valerie. *The Autobiography of William Sanders Scarborough.* Detroit, Mich.: Wayne State University Press, 2005.

Rose, P. K. "The Civil War: Black American Contributions to Union Intelligence." U.S. Central Intelligence Agency Web site. Available online. URL: http://www.cia.gov/cia/publications/dispatches/dispatch.html. Downloaded on March 23, 2005.

Rose, William Lee. *Rehearsal for Reconstruction: The Port Royal Experiment.* New York: Oxford University Press, 1976.

Rosengarten, Theodore. *Tombee: Portrait of a Cotton Planter, with the Plantation Journal of Thomas B. Chaplin (1822–1890).* New York: William Morrow, 1986.

Ross, Alexander Milton. *Recollections and Experiences of an Abolitionist from 1855 to 1865.* Northbrook, Ill.: Metro Books, 1972 [1876].

Rossi, Alice, ed. *The Feminist Papers: From Adams to de Beauvoir.* New York: Columbia University Press, 1973.

Rubin, Richard. "The Colfax Riot," *The Atlantic Monthly*, July–August 2003. Available online. URL: http://www.theatlantic.com/issues/2003/07/rubin.htm. Downloaded on July 9, 2004.

Russo, Peggy, and Paul Finkelman, eds. *Terrible Swift Sword: The Legacy of John Brown.* Athens: Ohio University Press, 2005.

Salerno, Beth A. *Sister Societies: Women's Antislavery Organizations in Antebellum America.* Princeton, N.J.: Princeton University Press, 2005.

Saunt, Claudio. *Black, White, and Indian: Race and the Unmaking of an American Family.* New York: Oxford University Press, 2005.

Savage, W. Sherman. "The Negro in the History of the Pacific Northwest." *Journal of Negro History* 13 (1928): 255–64.

———. "The Negro in the Westward Movement." *Journal of Negro History* 25 (1940): 533–34.

Scarborough, W. S. *The Autobiography of William Sanders Scarborough.* Edited by Michele Valerie Ronnick. Detroit, Mich.: Wayne State University Press, 2004.

Scarborough, William K. *The Overseer: Plantation Management in the Old South.* Baton Rouge: Louisiana State University Press, 1988.

Schultz, Jane E. "Between Scylla and Charybdis: Clara Barton's Wartime Odyssey." *Minerva: Quarterly Report on Women and the Military* 14 (1996): 45–68.

———. "Women at the Front: Gender and Genre in Literature of the American Civil War." Ph.D. diss., University of Michigan, 1988.

Schurz, Carl. *Report on the Condition of the South.* 1865. Project Gutenberg. Available online. URL: http://www.gutenberg.org/dirs/etext05/cnsth10.txt. Downloaded on September 30, 2004.

Seybert, Tony. "The Historic Black Press." *The History of Jim Crow.* Available online. URL: http://www.jimcrowhistory.org/history/resisting2.htm. Downloaded on July 13, 2004.

Shaffer, Donald R. *After the Glory: The Struggles of Black Civil War Veterans.* Lawrence: University of Kansas Press, 2004.

Sherman, William T. Field Order 15, Savannah, Georgia, January 16, 1865.

———. *Memoirs.* 2 vols. New York: DaCapo, 1984 [1875].

Shotgun's Home of the American Civil War. Information drawn from Fox's Regimental Losses (1889), ch. 6. Available online. URL: http://www.civilwarhome.com/chapt6.htm. Downloaded on November 26, 2005.

Siddali, Silvana R. *From Property to Person: Slavery and the Confiscation Acts, 1861–1862.* Baton Rouge: Louisiana State University Press, 2005.

Siebert, Wilbur H. *The Underground Railroad from Slavery to Freedom.* New York: Macmillan, 1898.

Simeone, Lisa. Interview with Andrew Levy, reported in "Robert Carter III: The Abolitionist That Time Forgot." National Public Radio's Weekend *All Things Considered.* Available online. URL: http://www.npr.org/programs/watc/features/2001/antijefferson/010901.antijefferson.html. Downloaded on May 10, 2005.

Simpson, Brooks D. "Ulysses S. Grant and the Freedmen's Bureau." In *The Freedmen's Bureau and Reconstruction,* edited by Paul A. Cimbala and Randall M. Miller, 1–28. New York: Fordham University Press, 1999.

Singleton, William Henry. *Recollections of My Slavery Days.* Raleigh: Division of Archives and History, North Carolina Department of Cultural Resources, 1999.

Six Women's Slave Narratives. New York: Oxford University Press, 1988.

Slave Insurrections: Selected Documents. Westport, Conn.: Negro Universities Press, 1970 [1822, 1860].

Sloan, Irving J., comp. and ed. *Blacks in America 1492–1970: A Chronology and Fact Book.* Dobbs Ferry, N.Y.: Oceana, 1921.

Smedley, R. C. *History of the Underground Railroad in Chester and the Neighboring Counties of Pennsylvania.* Lancaster, Penn.: Office of the Journal, 1883.

Smith, Abbott E. *Colonists in Bondage.* Chapel Hill: University of North Carolina Press, 1947.

Smith, Amanda. *An Autobiography: The Story of the Lord's Dealings with Mrs. Amanda Smith, the Colored Evangelist.* New York: Oxford University Press, 1988 [1893].

Smith, Gerrit. *Sermons and Speeches of Gerrit Smith.* New York: Orno, 1969 [1861].

Smith, James L. *Autobiography of James L. Smith.* In *Five Black Lives,* edited by Arna Bontemps. Middletown, Conn.: Wesleyan University Press, 1971 [1881]. Also available online at URL: http://docsouth.unc.edu/neh/smithj/smithj.html. Downloaded on August 27, 2004.

Smith, John David. *Black Soldiers in Blue: African American Troops in the Civil War Era.* Chapel Hill: University of North Carolina Press, 2002.

Smith, Venture. *A Narrative of the Life and Adventures of Venture, a Native of Africa.* New London, Conn.: Printed by C. Holt, 1798.

Smith, William A. *Lectures on the Philosophy and Practice of Slavery, as Exhibited in the Institution of Domestic Slavery in the United States, with the Duties of Masters to Slaves.* Nashville, Tenn.: Stevenson & Evans, 1856.

The South Vindicated from the Treason and Fanaticism of the Northern Abolitionists. New York: Negro Universities Press, 1969 [1836].

Spector, Robert M. "The Quock Walker Cases (1781–83): The Abolition of Slavery and Negro Citizenship in Early Massachusetts." *Journal of Negro History* 53 (1968): 12–32.

Stampp, Kenneth M. *The Peculiar Institution: Slavery in the Ante-bellum South.* New York: Vintage Books, 1956.

Stanton, Elizabeth Cady. *Eighty Years and More: Reminiscences, 1815–1897.* New York: Schocken, 1971 [1898].

Stanton, Theodore, and Harriot Stanton Blatch, eds. *Elizabeth Cady Stanton: As Revealed in Her Letters, Diary and Reminiscences.* 2 vols. New York: Arno and the *New York Times,* 1969 [1922].

Staples, Brent. "The Shifting Meanings of Black and White." Editorial, *New York Times,* November 15, 1998, sec. 4, p. 14.

Starobin, Robert. "Disciplining Industrial Slaves in the Old South." *Journal of Negro History* 53 (1968): 111–28.

———. *Industrial Slavery in the Old South.* New York: Oxford University Press, 1970.

———, ed. *Blacks in Bondage: Letters from American Slaves.* Princeton, N.J.: Markus Wiener, 1974.

Stavisky, Leonard. "Negro Craftsmanship in Colonial America." *Journal of Negro History* 32 (1947): 421.

Stealey, John Edmund, III. "Slavery and the West Virginia Salt Industry." *Journal of Negro History* 59 (1974): 105–31.

Stepto, Robert B. *From behind the Veil: A Study of Afro-American Narrative.* Urbana: University of Illinois Press, 1979.

———. *The Making of an Afro-American: Martin Robison Delany, 1812–1885.* Garden City, N.Y.: Doubleday, 1971.

Sterling, Ada. *A Belle of the Fifties: Memoirs of Mrs. Clay, of Alabama, Covering Social and Political Life in Washington and the South, 1853–66.* New York: Doubleday, Page, 1905. Available online. URL: http://docsouth.unc.edu/clay/clay.html. Downloaded on September 1, 2004.

Sterling, Dorothy. *Captain of the* Planter: *The Story of Robert Smalls.* Garden City, N.Y.: Doubleday, 1958.

———, ed. *We Are Your Sisters: Black Women in the Nineteenth Century.* New York: W. W. Norton, 1984.

———, ed. *The Trouble They Seen, the Story of Reconstruction in the Words of African-Americans.* Garden City, N.Y.: Doubleday, 1976.

Steward, Austin. *Twenty-two Years a Slave and Forty Years a Freeman.* 1857. In *Four Fugitive Slave Narratives,* with introductions by Robin W. Winks et al. Reading, Mass.: Addison-Wesley, 1969.

Steward, Theophilus Gould. *From 1864 to 1914: Fifty Years in the Gospel Ministry.* Philadelphia, Penn.: A.M.E. Book Concern, ca. 1921. Available online. URL: http://docsouth.unc.edu/church/steward/steward.html. Downloaded on August 27, 2004.

[Stewart, Maria W.] *Maria W. Stewart: America's First Black Woman Political Writer, Essays and Speeches.* Edited by Marilyn Richardson. Bloomington: Indiana University Press, 1987.

Still, Peter, and Vina Still. *The Kidnapped and the Ransomed.* New York: Negro Universities Press, 1968 [1856].

Still, William. *The Underground Railroad: A Record of Facts, Authentic Narratives, Letters, etc.* Philadelphia: Porter & Coates, 1872.

[Stone, Kate.] *Brokenburn: The Journal of Kate Stone, 1861–1868.* Edited by John Q. Anderson. Baton Rouge: Louisiana State University Press, 1955.

Storey, Margaret M. *Loyalty and Loss: Alabama's Unionists in the Civil War and Reconstruction.* Baton Rouge: Louisiana State University Press, 2004.

"The Story of Nicodemus." National Park Service. Available online. URL: http://www.nps.gov/features/nicodemus/nonflash.htm. Downloaded on July 13, 2004.

Straubing, Harold Elk, comp. *In Hospital and Camp, the Civil War through the Eyes of Its Doctors and Nurses.* Harrisburg, Penn.: Stackpole Books, 1993.

Strother, Horatio T. *The Underground Railroad in Connecticut.* Middletown, Conn.: Wesleyan University Press, 1962.

Styron, William. *The Confessions of Nat Turner.* New York: Random House, 1967.

Tadman, Michael. *Speculators and Slaves: Masters, Traders, and Slaves in the Old South.* Madison: University of Wisconsin Press, 1989.

Takaki, Ronald T. *A Pro-slavery Crusade: The Agitation to Reopen the African Slave Trade.* New York: Free Press, 1971.

Taylor, Frances Cloud. *The Trackless Trail Leads On.* Kennett Square, Pa.: KNA, 1995.

Taylor, Richard. *Destruction and Reconstruction: Personal Experiences of the Late War.* New York: D. Appleton, 1879. Available online. URL: http://docsouth.unc.edu/taylor/menu.html. Downloaded on August 17, 2004.

Taylor, Susie King. *A Black Woman's Civil War Memoirs.* Edited by Patricia W. Romero and Willie Lee Rose. Princeton, N.J.: Markus Wiener, 1997.

Temperley, Howard, ed. *After Slavery: Emancipation and Its Discontents.* Portland, Ore.: Frank Cass, 2000.

Thomas, Edward J. *Memoirs of a Southerner, 1840–1923.* Savannah, Georgia: n.p., 1923. Available online. URL: http://docsouth.unc.edu/thomas/thomas.html. Downloaded on August 24, 2004.

[Thomas, Ella Gertrude Clanton.] *The Secret Eye: The Journal of Ella Gertrude Clanton Thomas, 1848–1889.* Edited by Virginia Ingraham Burr. Chapel Hill: University of North Carolina Press, 1990.

Thomas, William Hannibal. *The American Negro: What He Was, What He Is, and What He May Become: A Critical and Practical Discussion.* New York: Macmillan, 1901. Available online. URL: http://docsouth.unc.edu/church/thomas/thomas.html. Downloaded on August 26, 2004.

Thompson, Elizabeth Lee. *The Reconstruction of Southern Debtors: Bankruptcy after the Civil War.* Athens: University of Georgia Press, 2004.

Three Negro Classics. With an introduction by John Hope Franklin. New York: Avon, 1965.

Tise, Larry E. *Proslavery: A History of the Defense of Slavery in America, 1701–1840.* Athens: University of Georgia Press, 1987.

de Tocqueville, Alexis. *Democracy in America.* Translated by George Lawrence. Edited by J. P. Mayer. Garden City, N.Y.: Anchor, 1969.

Tolson, Jay. "The Complex Story of Slavery," *U.S. News & World Report*, February 14, 2005, 66–67.

Torrey, Jesse. *American Slave Trade.* New York: Negro Universities Press, 1971 [1822].

[Towne, Laura M.] *Letters and Diary of Laura M. Towne Written from the Sea Islands of South Carolina, 1862–1884.* Edited by Rupert Sargent Holland. New York: Negro Universities Press, 1969 [1912].

Townsell, Tonya K. "Slaves Found Refuge at Freedman's Village," Pentagram, DC Military.com. February 6, 1998. Available online. URL: http://www.dcmilitary.com/army/pentagram/archives/feb6/pt_e2698.html. Downloaded on February 22, 2005.

Trefousse, Hans L. "Andrew Johnson and the Freedmen's Bureau." In *The Freedmen's Bureau and Reconstruction*, edited by Paul A. Cimbala and Randall M. Miller, 29–45. New York: Fordham University Press, 1999.

Trexler, Harrison Anthony. *Slavery in Missouri, 1804–1865.* Baltimore: Johns Hopkins University Press, 1914.

[Truth, Sojourner.] *Narrative of Sojourner Truth.* Edited by Margaret Washington. New York: Vintage, 1993 [1850].

Tunnell, Ted. *Edge of the Sword: The Ordeal of Carpetbagger Marshall H. Twitchell in the Civil War and Reconstruction.* Baton Rouge: Louisiana State University Press, 2001.

Tushnet, Mark V. *The American Law of Slavery, 1810–1860: Considerations of Humanity and Interest.* Princeton, N.J.: Princeton University Press, 1981.

[Twitchell, Marshall Harvey.] *Carpetbagger from Vermont: The Autobiography of Marshall Harvey Twitchell.* Baton Rouge: Louisiana State University Press, 1989. Excerpt available online. URL: http://www.pbs.org/wgbh/amex/reconstruction/. Downloaded on August 13, 2004.

Tyler, Ronnie C. "Fugitive Slaves in Mexico." *Journal of Negro History* 57 (1972): 1–12.

Tyler-McGraw, Marie. "The Hues and Uses of Liberia." In *Black Imagination and the Middle Passage*, edited by Maria Diedrich, Henry Louis Gates, Jr., and Carl Pedersen, 191–202. New York: Oxford University Press, 1999.

University of Virginia, Geospatial and Statistical Data Center, Historical Census Browser. "Percentage of Slave-Owning Families as a Fraction of Total Free Households." Available online. URL: http://fisher.lib.virginia.edu/collections/stats/histcensus/index.html. Downloaded on February 1, 2005.

[Upson, Theodore F.] *With Sherman to the Sea: The Civil War Letters, Diaries, & Reminiscences of Theodore F. Upson.* Edited by Oscar Osburn Winther. Bloomington: Indiana University Press. Available online. URL: http://www. Press, 1958.

Urwin, Gregory J. W. *Black Flag over Dixie: Racial Atrocities and Reprisals in the Civil War.* Carbondale: Southern Illinois University Press, 2003.

U.S. Bureau of the Census. *Historical Statistics of the United States: Colonial Times to 1957.* Washington, D.C.: U.S. Bureau of the Census, 1960.

———. *Historical Statistics of the United States: Colonial Times to 1970.* 2 vols. Washington, D.C.: U.S. Bureau of the Census, 1975.

———. "Kansas—Race and Hispanic Origin: 1860 to 1890." Available online. URL: http://www.census.gov/population/documentation/twps0056/tab31.xls. Downloaded on November 25, 2005.

————. *Statistical Atlas of the United States.* Edited by Charles S. Sloan. Washington, D.C.: Government Printing Office, 1914.

U.S. National Park Service. "Emancipation at Arlington: Freedmen's Village, 1863." Available online. URL: http://www.nps.gov/arho/tour/history/arlingtonin-between3.html. Downloaded on February 22, 2005.

U.S. War Department. *The War of the Rebellion: A Compilation of the Official Records of the Union and Confederate Armies.* 128 volumes. Washington, D.C.: Government Printing Office, 1880–1901. Available online. URL: http://www.bjmr.com/contraband/contrabands3.htm. Downloaded on July 17, 2004.

Usner, Daniel H., Jr. "American Indians in Colonial New Orleans." In *Powhatan's Mantle: Indians in the Colonial Southwest.* Edited by Peter H. Wood, Gregory A. Waselkov, and M. Thomas Hatley, 104–27. Lincoln: University of Nebraska Press, 1989.

Vance, Zebulon Baird. "The Duties of Defeat. An Address Delivered before the Two Literary Societies of the University of North Carolina, June 7, 1866." Raleigh, N.C.: William B. Smith, 1866. Available online. URL: http://docsouth.unc.edu/nc/vance/menu.html. Downloaded on August 17, 2004.

Van Deburg, William L. *The Slave Drivers: Black Agricultural Labor Supervisors in the Antebellum South.* Westport, Conn.: Greenwood Press, 1979.

Vassa, Gustavus. *The Life of Olaudah Equiano, or Gustavus Vassa, The African.* 1794. In *Great Slave Narratives,* edited by Arna Bontemps, 1–192. Boston: Beacon, 1969.

Venture. *A Narrative of the Life and Adventures of Venture.* In *Five Black Lives,* introduced by Arna Bontemps, 3–34. Middletown, Conn.: Wesleyan University Press, 1971.

Vorenberg, Michael. *Final Freedom: The Civil War, the Abolition of Slavery, and the Thirteenth Amendment.* New York: Cambridge University Press, 2001.

Wakeman, Sarah Rosetta. *An Uncommon Soldier: The Civil War Letters of Sarah Rosetta Wakeman, alias Private Lyons Wakeman.* Edited by Lauren Cook Burgess. Pasadena, Md.: Minerva Center, 1994.

Walker, David. *Walker's Appeal, . . . to the Coloured Citizens of the World, But in Particular and Very Expressly, to Those of the United States of America.* Boston: David Walker, 1830.

Walker, James W. St. G. *The Black Loyalists: The Search for a Promised Land in Nova Scotia and Sierra Leone, 1783–1870.* Toronto: University of Toronto Press, 1992 (1976).

Walker, Juliet E. K. "Pioneer Slave Entrepreneurship—Patterns, Processes, and Perspectives: The Case of the Slave Free Frank on the Kentucky Pennyroyal, 1795–1819." *Journal of Negro History* 68 (1983): 289–308.

Walton-Raji, Angela Y. "Cow Tom." The African- and Native-American Genealogy and Web Page. Available online. URL: http://www.african-nativeameri-can.com/cow_tom.htm. Downloaded on March 13, 2005.

Ward, Derrick. "Urban Race Riots in the Jim Crow Era." *The History of Jim Crow.* Available online. URL: http://www.jimcrowhistory.org/history/resisting2.htm. Downloaded on July 13, 2004.

Washburn, Cadwallader C., Major General. Reports March 16–April 14, 1864. Forrest Correspondence. Shotgun's Home of the Civil War. Available online. URL: http://www.civilwarhome.com/forrestcorrespondence.htm. Downloaded on May 27, 2005.

Washington, Booker T. *Frederick Douglass.* London: Hodder & Stoughton, 1906. Available online. URL: http://docsouth.unc.edu/neh/doug1906/doug1906. html. Downloaded on August 20, 2004.

————. *Up From Slavery.* In *Three Negro Classics,* with an introduction by John Hope Franklin, 23–206. New York: Avon, 1965 [1901].

Washington, Reginald. "The Freedmen's Savings and Trust Company and African American Genealogical Research." *Federal Records and African American History* 29, no. 2 (Summer 1997). Available online. URL: http://www.archives. gov/publications/prologue/1997/summer/freedmans-savings-and-trust.html. Downloaded on May 13, 2005.

Wax, Donald D. "'The Great Risque We Run': The Aftermath of Slave Rebellion at Stono, South Carolina, 1739–1745." *Journal of Negro History* 67 (1982): 136–47.

————. "Negro Resistance to the Early American Slave Trade." *Journal of Negro History* 51 (1966): 1–15.

————. "Preferences for Slaves in Colonial America." *Journal of Negro History* 58 (1973): 371–401.

Webber, Thomas L. *Deep like the Rivers: Education in the Slave Quarter Community, 1831–1865.* New York: W. W. Norton, 1978.

Webre, Stephen. "The Problem of Indian Slavery in Spanish Louisiana, 1769–1803." *Louisiana History* 25 (1984): 117–35.

Weidman, Budge. "Preserving the Legacy of the United States Colored Troops." National Archives publication. Available online. URL: http://www.archives. gov/education/lessons/blacks-civil-war/article.html. Downloaded on May 5, 2005.

Weiner, Marli Frances. *Mistresses and Slaves: Plantation Women in South Carolina, 1830–80.* Urbana: University of Illinois Press, 1997.

————. "Plantation Mistress and Female Slaves: Gender, Race, and South Carolina Women, 1830–1880." Ph.D. diss., University of Rochester, 1985.

Weisenberger, Steven. *Modern Medea: A Family Story of Slavery and Child-Murder from the Old South.* New York: Hill & Wang, 1998.

Weld, Theodore Dwight. *American Slavery as It Is: The Testimony of a Thousand Witnesses.* New York: Arno, 1968 [1839].

Wells, Tom Henderson. "Charles Augustus Lafayette Lamar: Gentleman Slave Trader." *Georgia Historical Quarterly* 47 (1963).

Wesley, Charles H. *In Freedom's Footsteps: From the African Background to the Civil War.* Cornwells Heights, Pa.: Publishers Company, 1978.

West, Emily. *Chains of Love: Slave Couples in Antebellum South Carolina.* Urbana: University of Illinois Press, 2004.

Weston, G. M. *The Progress of Slavery in the United States.* Washington, D.C.: Negro Universities Press, 1969 [1858].

Westwood, Howard. "Mr. Smalls: A Slave No More," *Civil War Times Illustrated* (May 1986). Available online. URL: http://www.thehistorynet.com/cwti/blmrs-malls/index2.html. Downloaded on January 22, 2005.

Wheeler, Jacob D. *A Practical Treatise on the Law of Slavery.* New York: Negro Universities Press, 1968 [1837].

Wheeler, Leslie, ed. *Loving Warriors: Selected Letters of Lucy Stone and Henry B. Blackwell, 1853 to 1893.* New York: Dial, 1981.

White, Deborah Gray. *Ar'n't I a Woman? Female Slaves in the Plantation South.* New York: W. W. Norton, 1985.

Whitten, David O. *Andrew Durnford: A Black Sugar Planter in Antebellum Louisiana.* Natchitoches, La.: Northwestern State University Press, 1981.

Wickett, Murray R. *Contested Territory: Whites, Native Americans, and African Americans in Oklahoma.* Baton Rouge: Louisiana State University Press, 2000.

"Wildfire Edmonia Lewis." Available online. URL: http://www.haven.net/people/annie/EDMUNIA/edmonia.htm. Downloaded on January 18, 2005.

Williams, George W. *A History of the Negro Race in America from 1619 to 1880.* 2 vols. New York: Bergman, 1968 [1883].

———. *History of the Negro Troops in the War of the Rebellion.* New York: Harper, 1888.

Williams, Heather Andrea. *Self-Taught: African American Education in Slavery and Freedom.* Durham: University of North Carolina Press, 2005.

Williams, Mary L. "Seminole-Negro Indian Scouts." Posted by Permission of the Superintendent, Fort Davis National Historic Site, National Park Service. Available online. URL: http://www.coax.net/people/lsf/scouts.htm. Downloaded on August 23, 2004.

Williamson, Hugh P. "Document: The State of Missouri against Celia, a Slave." *Midwest Journal* 8 (1956): 408–20.

Williamson, Joel. *The Crucible of Race: Black-White Relations in the American South since Emancipation.* New York: Oxford University Press, 1986.

———. *New People: Miscegenation and Mulattoes in the United States.* New York: Free Press, 1980.

Wilson, Joseph T. *The Black Phalanx: African-American Soldiers in the War of Independence, the War of 1812, and the Civil War.* New York: DaCapo, 1994 [1887].

Wilson, Keith P. *Campfires of Freedom: The Camp Life of Black Soldiers during the Civil War.* Kent, Ohio: Kent State University Press, 2002.

Winks, Robin W. *The Blacks in Canada: A History.* Montreal: McGill-Queen's University Press, 1971.

Winston, Sanford. "Indian Slavery in the Carolina Region." *Journal of Negro History* 19 (1934): 431–38.

Winther, Oscar Osburn, ed. *Theodore Upson: With Sherman to the Sea.* Baton Rouge: University of Louisiana Press, 1943.

Wish, Harvey. "American Slave Insurrections before 1861." *Journal of Negro History* 22 (1937): 299–320.

Wittenmyer, Annie Turner. *Under the Guns: A Woman's Reminiscences of the Civil War.* Boston: E. B. Stillings, 1895.

"Women and Social Movements in the United States, 1600–2000." Web site of the State University of New York at Binghamton. Available online. URL: http://womhist.binghamton.edu. Downloaded on March 26, 2005.

Wood, Betty. *The Origins of American Slavery.* New York: Hill & Wang, 1997.

Wood, J. Taylor. "Capture of a Slave," *The Atlantic Monthly* October 1900, 451–63. Available online. URL: http://www.niggerati.net/node/185. Downloaded on February 28, 2006.

Wood, Kirsten E. *Masterful Women: Slaveholding Widows from the American Revolution through the Civil War.* Durham: University of North Carolina Press, 2004.

Wood, Peter H. *Black Majority: Negroes in Colonial South Carolina from 1670 through the Stono Rebellion.* New York: Knopf, 1974.

Wood, Peter H., Gregory A. Wasselkov, and M. Thomas Hatley, eds. *Powhatan's Mantle: Indians in the Colonial Southwest.* Lincoln: University of Nebraska Press, 1989.

Woodson, Carter G. "The Negroes of Cincinnati prior to the Civil War." *Journal of Negro History* 1 (January 1916): 2. Available online. URL: http://www.gutenberg.org/catalog/wor ld/readfile?pageno=2&fk_files=99848. Downloaded on January 18, 2005.

Woodward, C. Vann. *The Burden of Southern History.* Baton Rouge: Louisiana State University Press, 1960.

Worger, William H., Nancy L. Clark, and Edward A. Alpers. *Africa and the West: A Documentary History from the Slave Trade to Independence.* Phoenix, Ariz.: Oryx Press, 2001.

Wormser, Richard. "Isaiah Montgomery." "Jim Crow Stories," Educational Broadcasting Corporation Web site. Available online. URL: http://www.pbs.org/wnet/jimcrow/stories_people_mont.html. Downloaded on August 11, 2004.

Yancy, Dorothy Cowser. "The Stuart Double Plow and Double Scraper: The Invention of a Slave." *Journal of Negro History* 69 (1984): 48–52.

Yellin, Jean Fagan. *Harriet Jacobs: A Life.* New York: Civitas/Basic Books, 2004.

———. "The Text and Contexts of Harriet Jacobs' *Incidents in the Life of a Slave Girl: Written by Herself.*" In *The Slave's Narrative,* edited by Charles T. Davis and Henry Louis Gates, Jr., Oxford: Oxford University Press, 1985.

———, and John C. Van Horne, eds. *The Abolitionist Sisterhood: Women's Political Culture in Antebellum America.* Ithaca, N.Y.: Cornell University Press, 1994.

Yetman, Norman R., ed. *Life under the "Peculiar Institution": Selections from the Slave Narrative Collection.* New York: Holt, Rinehart, & Winston, 1970.

Zipf, Karin L. "Reconstructing 'Free Woman': African-American Women, Apprenticeship, and Custody Rights during Reconstruction." *Journal of Women's History* 12, no. 1. Available online. URL: http://iupjournals.org/jwh/jwh12-1.html. Downloaded on April 5, 2005.

Index

Locators in *italics* indicate illustrations. Locators in **boldface** indicate main entries. Locators followed by *m* indicate maps. Locators followed by *t* indicate graphs and tables. Locators followed by *g* indicate glossary entries. Locators followed by *c* indicate chronology entries.